Adapting Early Childhood Curricula for Children in Inclusive Settings

FIFTH EDITION

Adapting Early Childhood Curricula for Children in Inclusive Settings

Ruth E. Cook
Santa Clara University

Annette Tessier
Professor Emerita,
California State University—Los Angeles

M. Diane Klein
California State University—Los Angeles

Merrill,
an imprint of Prentice Hall
Englewood Cliffs, New Jersey   Columbus, Ohio

Library of Congress Cataloging-in-Publication Data

Cook, Ruth E.

   Adapting early childhood curricula for children in inclusive settings/Ruth E. Cook, Annette Tessier, M. Diane Klein, —5th ed.

      p.   cm.

   Includes bibliographical references and index.

   ISBN 0-13-083201-4

   1. Handicapped children—Education (Preschool) 2. Handicapped children—Education (Preschool)—Curricula. 3. Mainstreaming in education. I. Tessier, Annette. II. Klein, M. Diane. III. Cook, Ruth E. Adapting early childhood curricula for children with special needs. IV. Title.

LC4019.2.C66 2000

371.9'0472—dc21

99-15564
CIP

Cover photo: UniPhoto
Editor: Ann Castel Davis
Production Editor: Sheryl Glicker Langner
Cover Designer: Dan Eckel
Production Manager: Laura Messerly
Editorial Assistant: Pat Grogg
Director of Marketing: Kevin Flanagan
Marketing Manager: Meghan Shepherd
Marketing Coordinator: Krista Groshong

This book was set in Garamond by Carlisle Communications, Ltd. and was printed and bound by R. R. Donnelly & Sons Company. The cover was printed by Phoenix Color Corp.

© 2000, 1996 by Prentice-Hall, Inc.
Pearson Education
Upper Saddle River, New Jersey 07458

Earlier editions, entitled *Adapting Early Childhood Curricula for Children with Special Needs*, © 1992 by Macmillan Publishing Company, a division of Macmillan, Inc., and © 1987, 1983 by Merrill Publishing Company.

Photo Credits: Anne Vega/Merrill, pp. 2, 5, 31, 98, 137, 196, 290, 306, and 403; Scott Cunningham/Merrill, pp. 14, 134, and 390; Dan Floss/Merrill, pp. 76 and 377; Anthony Magnacca/Merrill, pp. 90 and 106; Julie Tober/Merrill, pp. 340. All other photos supplied by authors.

Printed in the United States of America

10 9 8 7 6 5 4 3 2 1

ISBN: 0-13-083201-4

Prentice-Hall International (UK) Limited, *London*
Prentice-Hall of Australia Pty. Limited, *Sydney*
Prentice-Hall of Canada, Inc., *Toronto*
Prentice-Hall Hispanoamericana, S.A., *Mexico*
Prentice-Hall of India Private Limited, *New Delhi*
Prentice-Hall of Japan, Inc., *Tokyo*
Prentice-Hall (Singapore) Pte. Ltd., *Singapore*
Editora Prentice-Hall do Brasil, Ltda., *Rio de Janeiro*

We dedicate this edition to the following friends and colleagues, who have significantly touched the lives of young children with special needs and their families:

Virginia B. Armbruster, M.A., CCC-Sp
LaVonne Bergstrom, M.D.
Margaret H. Jones, M.D.
Janice M. Kyne, M.A.
Jeanne Mendoza, M.F.C.C., Ph.D.
M. Patricia Simmons, Ph.D.

Foreword

❈ ❈ ❈ ❈ ❈

The first edition of this book was published in 1982. At that time there were relatively few publications that specifically addressed early childhood special education and, indeed, relatively few comprehensive programs that served infants and young children with disabilities and their families. Thus the first edition met a real need, a need that has continued to grow over the almost twenty years between the first and this fifth edition. Increasing numbers of infants and young children with disabilities are now identified and many services are mandated. Major strides in understanding and in services are evident, and I am pleased to say that these changes are evident in this edition. Two themes are especially salient: The importance of families in interventions, and the impact of the inclusion movement on children with special needs.

Perhaps the most notable change in the field as a whole is the realization that services cannot be directed exclusively at a child with problems. Rather, it is clear that intervention planning and intervention services must take into account the child in context. For young special needs children, context primarily means family and, therefore, services must be family based. This concept is formalized in the Individual Family Service Plan (IFSP) that expanded the Individual Education Plan (IEP), the latter often being exclusively child focused. On the surface the idea of family involvement is a straightforward one, reflecting both common sense and political rhetoric. The implementation of family-based programs is more complex, however, because families as well as children have particular characteristics and unique needs. Thus one size does not fit all. Adaptations must fit the individual child and the individual family. In earlier editions of this book, the authors were sensitive to family needs and to the importance of family involvement in interventions for their chil-

dren. The implications of family involvement are more fully developed in the present work.

A second major theme in this edition is how to make adaptations for young children with special needs in inclusive or regular program settings. There is widespread support for the notion that children with special needs should be served in regular programs whenever possible. This is a given, and has many benefits. What is less clear, however, is how to make the necessary adaptations to ensure that the program content and methods meet the needs of children with limitations. Mere presence in a regular program is not enough. The important question is how to adapt program content and instructional methods to fit the individual needs of all children, including those with problems. The authors have done an excellent job in identifying and emphasizing the kinds of adaptations that are necessary when working with young children with special needs. Clinicians and educators will find these adaptations especially relevant when implementing services in inclusive settings.

Overall this edition follows the general format of earlier editions, but updates information about identification and assessment, planning intervention strategies, and adaptations in areas of cognition, motor skills, communication, and social and emotional development. These, of course, are domains in which young children may have special limitations and needs. They are also areas in which both interventionists and parents have important roles to play. The current edition contains useful updates of legislation and relevant research, but always against the template of the needs of children and their families.

I have known the authors of this book for many years, and admire their understanding of the substantive problems and special needs of children with developmental problems. The insights and the practical suggestions found in this book should be useful to all those who work with infants and young children with special needs.

Barbara K. Keogh, Ph.D.
Professor Emerita
University of California at Los Angeles

Preface

⌘ ⌘ ⌘ ⌘ ⌘

This book is written with you, the student of either early childhood or special education, in mind. Whether you are studying to become a teacher of young children with special needs or are an early interventionist with a related background who wishes to develop greater versatility in your chosen field, we have designed this to be an easy-to-read, interesting, and comprehensive resource for you. It provides extensive use of examples, dialogues, practical illustrations, checksheets, and a focus on the best practices in the field.

When this text was originally published in 1983, intervention with young children with special needs was in its formative years. Since that time the field has expanded, and this book has successfully grown with it. Young children with special needs are now enrolled in a variety of settings and are served by professionals and paraprofessionals with diverse backgrounds. Our objective now, as it was in the first four editions, is to present a text that will play a major role in the development of all of these professionals. The focus is on the skills necessary to assist infants, young children, and their families to meet their special challenges and develop to their fullest potential.

Distinguishing Features

This book has four main strengths that make it a compelling self-teaching resource:

1. It emphasizes the importance of understanding the natures of all young children and how they learn. Adapting curricula and intervention approaches for children with special needs works effectively only when professionals build on a strong foundation of understanding of what is common to all young children. On the basis of this necessary foundation, students can begin to consider strategies for meeting the developmental and educational needs of infants and young children who have disabilities or who experience circumstances and conditions that potentially interfere with optimal growth and adjustment.

2. The approach taken in this text also stresses the absolute necessity of understanding young children within the context of the family. Every family is unique and complex, reflecting the many influences of history, culture or ethnicity, economics, and family dynamics. Early interventionists must focus not on the detailed analysis of these many factors, but on ways of supporting families that will maximize their day-to-day fulfillment as caregivers of their young. As explained in the text, your job, in part, is to help parents develop a sense of competence in their own abilities to nurture their children regardless of family circumstances. Appreciation of families, roles in the development of children and respect for families, concerns and priorities are critical to effective curriculum design and program development.

3. A significant portion of the text is organized according to traditional developmental domains: social-emotional, motor, communication, and cognitive skills. As an early childhood special education professional, these are the growth areas you will seek to develop in the children entrusted to you. Thus, you must develop a thorough understanding of each of these complex domains.

4. Finally, you must ultimately understand that all of the growth areas and individual and family background factors must be synthesized into a view of the whole child. As in any other form of synergy, the whole child is much greater than the sum of his or her parts. This holistic view relates directly to the book's emphasis on activity-based and play-based approaches to intervention. You will learn how to integrate goals and objectives for all domains into developmentally

appropriate and motivating activities. Throughout, best practices are explained for home, center, or classroom application.

What is new about this fifth edition? The four points just mentioned suggest the framework and approach that have consistently made this book appealing to readers of four earlier editions. They have been time tested and consistently found to be helpful. However, changes have been made in substance.

The fifth edition includes important updates in several areas:

- Information related to the implementation of Part H, including descriptions of the provisions of Public Law 102-119 and the components required in designing service coordination and individualized family service plans.

- Updates in Chapter 2 on issues related to the application of developmentally appropriate practices for young children with disabilities.

- Expansion of Chapter 3 to include material related to cultural influences on childrearing attitudes and practices.

- Restructuring of Chapter 4 to consider current issues and trends in the area of assessment such as authentic and play-based assessment.

- A review of recent research on the effects of prenatal exposure to drugs in Chapter 7.

- Expansion in Chapter 8 on specific techniques for encouraging the development of self-help skills.

- Inclusion in Chapter 9 of strategies for developing an augmetative communication system for young children who do not produce speech.

- Expansion of the section on emergent literacy in Chapter 10.

- Updated, student-friendly annotated bibliographies, lesson plans, a glossary, developmental charts, and a list of early intervention competencies.

Organization

The text opens with a presentation of our philosophy for working with children who have special needs. It recognizes human likenesses and value differences and discusses our belief in the importance of providing services in the most normalized settings possible. Chapter 1 offers specific inclusion strategies in support of this belief. Chapter 2 highlights the historical contributions of the fields of early childhood education and special education. Important features and implications of Public Laws 94-142; 99-457; 101-476; 101-336; 102-119, and 105-17 are summarized, along with alternative approaches to service delivery.

Chapter 3 presents techniques to involve families in a collaborative partnership with the variety of professionals with whom they must interface. In developing a family-focused approach, students are encouraged to view families from a systems perspective. Special attention is given to the various methods of parent involvement that can accommodate cultural diversity, language differences, and unique family situations.

Issues and methods of infant and child assessment, including both formal and informal methods, are presented in Chapter 4. Students are introduced to team approaches and the importance of ecologically valid assessments. Chapter 5 defines the components of individualized education programs and individualized family service plans. Strategies for collaborative program and transition planning are outlined. Chapter 6 focuses on curriculum development within a framework of generic instructional strategies. Specific adaptations for young children with special needs provide a point of departure for facilitating inclusion.

Chapter 7 begins by describing the stages of psychosocial development as a precursor to understanding how to facilitate social skills through the medium of play. Considerable attention is given to helping children who experience particular emotional and behavioral challenges and working with those who have been maltreated and/or exposed prenatally to drugs. After describing typical development of motor skills, Chapter 8 examines atypical motor development. Practical intervention strategies are offered, including handling and positioning guidelines.

Chapters 9 and 10 focus on the development of communication and cognition. The importance of caregiver-child interactions and the role of play in optimal development is recognized throughout. Special attention is devoted to specific strategies for enhancing communication skills in children with severe disabilities, visual impairments, and hearing impairments, as well as children from non-English-speaking families. Unique is the section devoted to understanding the social and linguistic factors related to children's emergent literacy skills and strategies for encouraging these skills. An expanded section on facilitation of phonological and phonemic awareness has been added to this section.

The final chapter prepares early childhood educators to work effectively with paraprofessionals. The potential for paraprofessionals is increasingly being recognized in light of the shortage of trained early intervention specialists. The format and tone of this chapter are somewhat different because we believe that students must learn to be managers of the human resources available to them. If they do not, precious time and skills will be wasted.

Finally, the appendices offer a wealth of practical information, including developmental guidelines, recommended materials, periodicals, website addresses, and a list of competencies that we hope will be developed by each and every reader.

Acknowledgments

We present this book with gratitude to the hundreds of children and parents who have been our teachers. From them we have learned to value and nurture the uniqueness of each child regardless of background, skills, or abilities. We believe we have found a way to meet children's unique needs in whatever setting they appear. It has been our purpose to convey the essence of this process to anyone interested in working with young children.

We wish to thank sincerely the many colleagues and friends who assisted and supported us throughout the many years since the original edition of this book. We are especially grateful for the conscientious efforts of those who so kindly read and commented on the prospectus and rough drafts of the present edition: Elizabeth Brennan, San Francisco State University; Barbara Lowenthal, Northeastern Illinois University; Maureen R. Norris, Bellarmine College (KY); and Helmi C. Owens, Pacific Lutheran University.

There are many people who enrich and enhance one's personal and professional life along the way. We are grateful to be blessed with such a wonderful mentor and friend in the person of Dr. Barbara Keogh, who watched over us in our studies at the University of California at Los Angeles. We are honored to once again include a foreword by Dr. Keogh, and we wish her well in her richly deserved retirement.

Personal appreciation is extended by Annette to some other very special people, including her large extended family, Ruth Westphal of Concept Media and Linda Laisure (H.O.M.E.), for their continuous support and encouragement. Diane expresses her gratitude to Bridgitte Ammons, Anne Marie Richardson-Gibbs, and all the California State University at Los Angeles students for helping her learn what good teachers need to know. Ruth extends appreciation to Shirley Sparks from Santa Clara University and Peggy and Ray Ellis for their generous support and encouragement.

Throughout this project, the personal support of those with whom we live and work has been invaluable. After all, it was the close working relationship between Ruth Cook and the late Virginia Armbruster that brought the first edition to fruition. Virginia's deep love of children and thoughtful wisdom continue to permeate the pages of the text.

Deep appreciation is extended to the parents, children, and outstanding staff of Centro de Niños y Padres, at California State University at Los Angeles, the Southern Illinois University Early Childhood Center, and the Mount Saint Mary College at Los Angeles Child Development Center, whose inspiration is a source of strength.

Very special thanks go to Erin Klein and Christopher and Kimberly Cook, without whose own being our understandings of child growth, and development would have been superficial, at best. Sincere gratitude goes to Curtis Cook, whose patience, tolerance, and editorial skills over the years made this project possible.

The editors and staff at Merrill, an imprint of Prentice Hall, have been most pleasant to work with and have managed to keep us on target. Particular praise and gratitude go to our editor, Ann Castel Davis and her assistant, Pat Grogg; their patience and caring have been invaluable throughout the acquisition and development of this manuscript. Finally, we offer our thanks to Mary Jo Graham for her conscientious efforts and expertise throughout production.

Ruth E. Cook
Annette Tessier
M. Diane Klein

Contents

Chapter 1

Introduction

Key Concepts

- The goal of early intervention is to optimize each child's learning potential and daily well-being, as well as to increase opportunities for the child to function effectively in the community.

- The current focus in early childhood special education is not *whether* young children with special needs can be served in inclusive environments, but *how* inclusive programs can be designed most effectively.

- Programs for infants and toddlers with special needs must be based on the same developmentally appropriate strategies that are considered best practices for *all* young children.

- The effective early childhood special educator must first understand how children learn within a responsive environment.

- To successfully include young children with special needs, educators must make careful curricular adaptations.

- Success is dependent on systematic planning, consideration of individual needs, parent-professional partnerships, respect for cultural diversity, and collaboration among families, professionals, and community agencies.

- The early years are optimal for inclusion of children with disabilities.

- Labels must be used with caution.

- All early intervention goals are dependent on the positive attitudes of well-trained early intervention specialists.

◆ ◆ ◆

From the mother of a 5-year-old child with special needs:

I have come to accept that my daughter will not be quite like everybody else when she grows up, but then who of us is? We are all unique individuals, and we should appreciate our differences rather than scorn them. We all have our strengths and weaknesses, and how many of us, even without disabilities, ever realize our full human potential?

Lora Jerugim

Helping children to realize their full human potential: This is our challenge. By recognizing the human similarities in each of us and by positively valuing differences, parents and educators together can provide each child with the opportunity to develop his or her unique strengths. For children who appear to have developmental disabilities or characteristics that interfere with normal growth and learning, the stage must be prepared more thoughtfully. It is expected that parents, educators, and other community members will work together to create a nurturing environment sensitive to, but not solicitous of, children's special needs.

Many aspects of mental and physical development seem to "just happen" to most children. They are, however, the result of interaction between innate capacities and appropriate environmental experiences. With most children, comparatively little deliberate effort has to be made to synchronize capacities and experiences. Most have a repertoire of skills and interests that motivates them to explore, experiment, and therefore learn. However, children with special needs may not be able to learn spontaneously from the play experiences they naturally encounter.

Educators must carefully adapt materials, equipment, space, instructions, and expectations to provide environmental experiences conducive to learning.

The intent of this text is to identify ways and means to make it possible for children with special needs to be educated appropriately in regular early childhood programs with "typical" peers. Indeed, Part C of the Individuals with Disabilities Education Act of 1997 states that (1) "To the maximum extent appropriate, early intervention services are provided in natural environments; and (2) the provision of early intervention services occurs in a setting other than a natural environment only when early intervention cannot be achieved satisfactorily for the infant or toddler in a natural environment" [Section 635(a)(16)]. Part B addresses the needs of preschoolers by stating that "To the maximum extent appropriate, children with disabilities are educated with children who are not disabled." This part also goes on to state in Section 612 that preschoolers are not to be removed from the regular educational environment unless "education in regular classes with the use of supplementary aids and services cannot be achieved satisfactorily."

PHILOSOPHY OF THIS TEXT

The philosophy of this text emphasizes that the goal of early intervention is to optimize each child's learning potential and daily well-being, as well as to increase opportunities for the child to function effectively in the community. We believe this is best accomplished by facilitating the child's underlying developmental processes by encouraging the child's active and dynamic interactions with the world around him or her, particularly the social world. Perhaps the term that best reflects this orientation is **transactional.** It is through the child's active and successful transactions with the environment that optimal growth and development can best be achieved.

To achieve this end, early interventionists must first have a thorough understanding of how children learn. Programs for infants and young children with special needs must be based on **developmentally appropriate** practices that are effective for *all* children.

In addition, **systematic planning** to meet the **individualized needs** of each child is critical to the success of early childhood programs that include children with special challenges and disabilities. This cannot be accomplished without establishing mutually respectful **partnerships** between early childhood professionals and families. Successful assessment and intervention require a thorough understanding of the child within the context of the family **system** and a **respect for the diverse cultural backgrounds** represented by families in early childhood centers.

The importance of **collaboration** among families, professionals, and community agencies is acknowledged throughout the text. Understanding the roles of various disciplines and specialists and the importance of assisting families in accessing community agencies and resources are also critical elements in the success of early intervention.

Many tools and strategies are available to assist the early interventionist. This text describes the basic principles of how children learn, as well as specific teaching strategies. It also demonstrates applications of these principles and strategies to meet the needs of a wide range of children within inclusive environments.

As we strive toward successful inclusion of young children with special needs, it is interesting to note that we continue to face the basic issue put forth by Guralnick (1990) a decade ago:

Perhaps the single most significant achievement in the field of early childhood education in the decade of the 1980s was the repeated demonstration that mainstreamed programs can be implemented effectively. ...The contemporary issue is clearly not whether early childhood mainstreaming is feasible and should be encouraged, but rather how one can design programs to maximize its effectiveness. (p. 3)

The Optimal Early Years

There are many reasons why the early years are optimal ones for including children with disabilities. First, most early education programs expect children to mature at varying rates during these years of enhanced growth and development. Differences in skills are expected and accommodated within the curriculum. The range of so-called "normalcy" in early education is much broader than that usually found in elementary school classrooms.

Early childhood educators also tend to focus on the *process* more than the product of learning. They are busy setting up centers to allow for sensory exploration rather than grading spelling papers or preparing the next day's language test. In addition, the methods and materials usually found in early education centers are conducive to the development of all young children. Exploration, manipulation, expression, sharing, and active involvement provide easy opportunities for educators to structure and reinforce meaningful interaction between children with disabilities and those without.

Anyone who has worked with young children is readily aware of their natural abilities to accept and even appreciate individual differences. Children respond to one another without making judgments and comparisons. Spontaneous friendships abound, with little in the way of ongoing expectations. When dif-ferences are observed, questions reflect a natural curiosity. If answered in genuine, thoughtful ways, children tend to accommodate and accept those who are different.

Researchers appear to agree that simply placing children with disabilities in the same educational settings with nondisabled children does not accomplish all the goals of inclusion (McLean & Hanline, 1990; Jones and Rapport, 1997). Recognizing this fact, the purpose of this book is to provide information and strategies that will assist early childhood professionals in successfully including children with special needs.

The Hazards of Labels

Children with presumed developmental delays or differences traditionally have been given labels such as mentally retarded, emotionally disturbed, learning disabled, or at risk for academic failure. Advocates argue that labels lead to efficiency of "treatment" and are often required for financial reimbursement for services.

But most who make recommendations for young children try to avoid attaching labels. They realize how tenuous the diagnostic results for children are prior to school age and they strive to use assessment information to derive sound intervention. As Greenspan and Meisels (1996) stated,

Under pressure to produce quick formulations, or 'scores, professionals have often called on their experiences with procedures and instruments developed for assessing selected competencies and skills in older children. These procedures and instruments can often yield misleading information (p. 15). Previous practice was to use test information to label children; now, we have come to understand that this information is best used for hypothesis formation in order to devise potential interventions. We have moved from a firm policy of assessment in the absence of intervention to the development of methods of assessment that simply cannot exist apart from intervention. (Meisels, 1996, p. 49).

Yes, educators do question techniques of early assessment and labeling of young children. Services

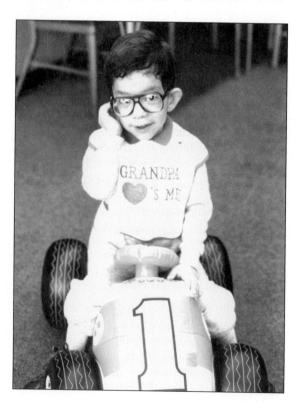

must be based on the obvious and changing individual needs of children, not on static and narrowly defined labels. There is a valid and longstanding concern that labels may bias the behavior of others toward those who are labeled, negatively affecting self-esteem. In fact, reauthorization of federal legislation has made it permissible for states to change old disability labels to a non-categorical one of developmental delay in order to avoid labels that may be perceived as overly negative.

Because of the obvious dangers involved in labeling, the format of this book has avoided the traditional categorical approach. Although several terms are used throughout the book (for example, *special needs, developmental delays,* and *deaf and hard of hearing*), their use does not suggest that labeling should occur. These terms are used for clarity of communication, not as diagnostic labels.

EARLY INTERVENTION SPECIALISTS: THEIR ROLE IN THE INCLUSION OF CHILDREN WITH SPECIAL NEEDS

It has long been recognized that professionals who specialize in early childhood education (ECE) and early childhood special education (ECSE) will play the most extensive role in the inclusion of young children with special needs. "The research on inclusion consistently emphasizes the teacher's role in supporting positive inclusive experiences in children" (Jones and Rapport, 1997, p. 57). It is the teacher who must structure the environment, adapt the materials, determine the child's most profitable mode of learning, initiate the desired responses, and reinforce those that should be encouraged. Research to date suggests that systematic intervention efforts guided by the teacher are necessary in order to promote successful inclusion (Rose & Smith, 1993; Bricker, 1995).

To fulfill such a multifaceted role, teachers are expected to develop competencies characteristic of both the early childhood educator and the special educator. Fortunately, the skills needed include the same skills that are necessary to work with *all* young children. However, successful inclusion of children with disabilities requires additional skills and expertise. These are discussed below.

Skills and Strategies for Successful Inclusion

As mentioned earlier there are many characteristics unique to early childhood education that support the inclusion of children with disabilities in community-based settings and regular preschools. Nevertheless, there are also significant challenges. These challenges are even greater when the infant or preschool child has severe or multiple disabilities. It is our belief that appropriate and adequate support must be provided for each child if inclusion is to be more than a placement. Mere proximity to non-disabled peers does not ensure optimal learning and development of skills for all children with disabilities. It is the responsibility of early educators to provide the adaptations and supports necessary to make placement in the least restrictive environment successful. Bricker (1995) has stated that the success of inclusion is dependent upon the program's access to well-trained specialists..

Various models have been developed for providing support for young children in inclusive settings. The two most common are **inclusion support consultant** models and **co-teaching** models. In consultant models, the inclusion support person works as an itinerant who visits the inclusive site. The frequency of these visits varies, depending on the policy of the program or agency and on the needs of the child. Also, the types of services provided by the inclusion consultant are highly variable. The list provided in Figure 1–1 includes examples of inclusion support services and activities.

Models of Inclusion Support. Consultant models range from traditional "expert consultant" models where the consultant is viewed as the expert who can provide specific information and problem solving, to "collaborative consultation" models in which partnerships are established among the key players (i.e., the consultant, parents, early education staff, administrators, etc.). In this model the consul-

tant does assume some coordinating responsibility but relationships are more reciprocal than in the expert model.

Co-teaching models include both an early childhood teacher and an early childhood special educator, or early interventionist, as team members on the same site. In co-teaching models, the special educator may either assume part of the teaching responsibilities for the entire group, or may serve primarily as a

---

Inclusion Support Activities and Services

- Provide inservice and information to staff members regarding the characteristics of the child's specific disability (e.g., autism, Down syndrome, sensory impairment).
- Provide demonstration of specific intervention and teaching strategies.
- Conduct ongoing observation and assessment of the child within the inclusive setting.
- Provide ongoing discussion and feedback to ECE staff regarding child's development and performance across program objectives and developmental domains.
- Meet regularly with families to obtain input regarding their perceptions and concerns regarding child's adjustment and progress in the inclusive setting.
- Provide direct instruction to child as necessary to encourage achievement of specific outcomes and to demonstrate strategies to staff (e.g., participation in group activities, behavior management, development of communication skills or systems).
- Use videotape or data recording to provide feedback to staff regarding specific behaviors and to assist with problem-solving processes.
- Develop effective and efficient mechanisms for ongoing communication with ECE staff.
- Participate in team meetings, including regular site staff meetings and IEP/IFSP meetings.
- Engage in problem-solving and conflict-resolution processes.

Figure 1–1

support assistant for the children with special needs. It is the special educator's responsibility to maximize each child's participation and to track achievement related to individual program objectives and/or outcomes.

Inclusion   Support   Competencies. Project Support, a model for training early intervention inclusion support consultants (Klein, Richardson-Gibbs, and Kilpatrick, 1997) has identified the following competency areas for inclusion support personnel working in community based settings:

A. Knowledge of typical child development and developmentally appropriate practice in early childhood education.
B. Knowledge of characteristics and challenges of specific disabilities during the early childhood years.
C. Knowledge of "preferred practices" in early intervention and early childhood special education (ECSE).
D. Knowledge of specific strategies and methods for supporting inclusion of children with disabilities.
E. Knowledge of effective techniques for collaborative consultation, team building, and conflict resolution.

Although the first four of these competency areas typically are included in preservice training in early childhood special education, in-depth training related to collaborative consultation and conflict resolution is rare. The need for collaborative consultation skills to ensure school-age children's success in inclusive classrooms has been well-documented (Heron & Harris, 1993). The kinds of challenges related to successful inclusion of children in the birth-to-five age range are somewhat different from those encountered in educational inclusion in K-12. Gallagher (1997) discusses the changing roles of ECSE professionals as they move from teachers to

consultants. After 3 years of work providing inclusion support, Richardson-Gibbs (1998) reports the following specific challenges:

1. With a well-documented shortage of quality day care for typically developing children, how can families of children with disabilities be assured of quality, developmentally appropriate community options?
2. How can low-wage, minimally trained child care staff be adequately supported to meet the intense needs of those children whose challenges and disabilities are complex?
3. Who will provide the problem solving necessary to address the sometimes divergent needs and philosophies of the community setting, the parents, and the child?
4. How will an adequate supply of early intervention and ECSE professionals be trained to offer effective supports across a wide range of settings in which only one or two children with disabilities are placed?

These and many other questions will need to be addressed in the immediate future to ensure the success of inclusion efforts in early childhood programs. Figure 1-2 offers an outline of a specific approach to collaborative consultation in early childhood settings. Successful inclusion of young children in community-based settings is an important challenge. It requires not only a thorough understanding and skills related to the learning needs of children with disabilities, but it also requires an additional skill base related to working collaboratively with agencies, parents and professionals, across a wide range of settings.

The next chapter will review the history of early intervention and discuss models for accommodating unique needs. It will also discuss the impact of legislation on the field and will introduce the key features of influential public laws. Finally, it will discuss current trends and best practices for delivery of early intervention services.

Sample Inclusion Support Procedures
(Adapted from Bridges and Richardson-Gibbs, 1998)

I. Getting Started

    A. Gather information from referral source.

        Include IFSP/IEP, progress notes, and assessment data.

    B. Meet with family.

        Discuss family's concerns, priorities, and resources. *Remember, parents know their child better than anyone and will have very accurate perceptions of both the challenges and the potential benefits derived from the inclusive setting.*

    C. Determine who the contact person is at the site (e.g., administrator, teacher) and make an initial phone call.

    D. Contact any other support providers, e.g., therapists, behavior specialist, disability specialist, etc.

    E. Explain the kinds of services you can provide to all parties involved; determine their expectations and needs. (*NOTE: For many communities, inclusion support may be a relatively new and unfamiliar service. Families may not understand your role, and ECE staff may believe you will be critically evaluating them in some way. It is extremely important to clarify these issues before beginning your visits to the site.*)

    F. Work out specific details of how you will provide service, including:

        Frequency of visits and written reports

        Strategies and times for providing feedback

        Opportunities for suggestions and questions from parents and ECE staff.

II. The First Visit

    A. It is important that the initial contacts above be made *before* you observe the child at the site.

    B. Set up a time for initial visit.

        Be sure to touch base with the site administrator.

        Ask him or her to show you to the classroom and introduce you to the staff

    C. If the initial contact described above was not with the classroom teacher, you will need to briefly explain your role.

    D. If possible, provide written material describing the possible services and activities you can offer. (*Keep in mind that you may be the first person the teacher has had contact with who has expertise and knowledge related to the nature of the child's disability. Be prepared to answer questions and be willing (if necessary) to obtain additional information to share with staff.*)

    E. During the first visit or two it may be best to just observe the child, take careful notes, and (without being intrusive) chat with the teacher. *This is a critical time for building trust. The inclusion consultant must be very aware of two important issues at this point:*

        1. *ECE staff are extremely busy and often shorthanded.*

        2. *They are unsure of your role. (Common misperceptions of your role can range from believing you are there to directly teach the child or do therapy, to suspicions that you are there to evaluate their setting and their teaching skills.)*

(*continued*)

Figure 1–2

F. Document each visit. Develop a functional Inclusion Support Summary Form on NCR paper so that both you and the ECE teacher have a record of your visit. These can also be provided to parents, if they so desire.

This form can include:

- Date and time of visit
- Your observations of the child's progress (Be as positive as possible, giving credit to ECE staff for supporting child's adjustment, using adaptations, etc.)
- Specific suggestions to address problems identified by staff or parents
- A statement of what you will do (e.g., make communication board, help with behavior analysis, make referral, discuss something with parents, etc.)
- Date and time of next visit
- Your name and phone numbers

G. During initial visits try to learn other children's names. Developing relationships with several children in the class can be a helpful strategy for encouraging peer interactions. (*NOTE: It is important that the children in the class become comfortable with you. Also, try not to highlight the fact that you are there to help a particular child—although children will eventually figure this out anyway.*

III. Ongoing Visits

A. *Individualize* your inclusion support activities.

- Determine the child's needs
- Determine what is most comfortable for the ECE staff. Remember it may take time to feel comfortable in the setting. You will react differently to different sites because of personality factors, program philosophy, location and physical characteristics of the site, etc.

B. Adjust the frequency of visits as needed, in consultation with parents, staff, and funding agencies.

C. Learn to *balance* the needs and expectations of the family and the ECE staff.

One of the most difficult challenges for many inclusion consultants is the need to balance the needs of the family, the ECE program staff, and the child when these appear to be in conflict with one another. The inclusion consultant must prioritize family preferences and must work within the existing format of the inclusive setting. Sometimes it will be necessary for the inclusion support person to set aside his or her own biases about what is best for the child and the desire to change the practices or the philosophy of the community setting.

D. When conflicts arise that are not easily solved, use conflict resolution strategies.

E. At least quarterly, write a detailed report documenting the child's progress, current needs, and agreed-upon next steps and short-term goals.

F. At transition ages, or as the need or desire arises for the family to consider a new placement, assist the family in this often difficult decision-making process.

Figure 1–2 (*continued*)

Summary

Young children with developmental lags or special needs require individualized educational experiences to promote attainment of their unique potential. Within early education programs, this involves sensitive adaptation of curriculum, materials, space, instruction, and adult expectations to stimulate a nurturing environment.

The question of how to provide learning opportunities best for young children with special needs has sparked controversy and differing philosophies among educators for generations. Currently the scales are tipped in favor of including young children with special needs with normally developing children within regular community programs. There are educational advantages that make inclusion especially workable for most young children with special needs.

During the early years, the educational focus is more on the processes of exploration, manipulation, expression, sharing, and active involvement than on the content or products of learning. Such processes, when modified for the child with special needs, enhance growth and development within the context of the regular early education experience.

The early inclusion of children with special needs in the educational mainstream carries certain cautions and challenges that are not commonly encountered in early education programs without children with disabilities. Diagnostic labels, which categorize the type of disability, may accentuate the effects of the disability (leading to self-fulfilling prophecies) rather than help the search for appropriate intervention strategies.

The ability and attitude of the educator are key factors in successful inclusion. Knowledge of how to individualize instruction within a regular curriculum becomes a requisite skill. The ability to individualize instruction is built on a series of skills beginning with an understanding of normal and atypical stages of child development. These skills range from recording observed behaviors to preparing appropriate developmental goals and objectives; to task analyzing and sequencing lessons; to working directly with families, paraprofessionals, specialists, and community agencies.

The value of early inclusion of children with special needs within programs designed for typically developing children achieved national importance with the passage of Public Law 94–142 over 2 decades ago. This law mandated that children with special needs be placed in the *least restrictive environment* appropriate to their needs. We are still struggling to fulfill this mandate. If inclusion is to be successful, it is critical that appropriate and adequate support be provided to regular early childhood staff.

References

Bricker, D. (1995). The challenge of inclusion. *Journal of Early Intervention, 19*(3), 179–194.

Bridges, V., & Richardson-Gibbs, A. M. (1998). *Centro de Ninos y padres inclusion consulting handbook.* Unpublished document. Los Angeles, CA: California State University, Los Angeles.

Gallagher, P. A. (1997). Teachers and inclusion: Perspectives on changing roles. *Topics in Early Childhood Special Education, 17*(3), 363–386.

Greenspan, S. I., & Meisels, S. J. (1996). Toward a new vision for the developmental assessment of infants and young children. In S. J. Meisels & E. Fenichel (Eds.), *New vi-sions for the developmental assessment of infants and young children* (pp. 11–26). Washington, D.C.: National Center for Infants, Toddlers, and Families.

Guralnick, M. J. (1990). Early childhood mainstreaming. *Topics in Early Childhood Special Education, 10*(2), 1–17.

Heron, T. E., & Harris, K. C. (1993). *The educational consultant.* Austin, TX: Pro-Ed.

Jerugim, L. (1998). A personal perspective on raising a child with developmental problems. (Unpublished paper).

Jones, H. A., & Rapport, M. J. K. (1997). Research-to-practice in inclusive early childhood education. *Teaching Exceptional Children,* 57–61.

Klein, M. D., Richardson-Gibbs, A. M. & Kilpatrick, S., (November, 1997). Project Support: Training early childhood inclusion consultants. Paper presented at the national conference of the Division for Early Childhood. New Orleans, LA.

McLean, M., & Hanline, M. F. (1990). Providing early intervention services in integrated environments: Challenges and opportunities for the future. *Topics in Early Childhood Special Education, 10* (2), 62-77.

Meisels, S. J. (1996). Charting the continuum of assessment and intervention. In S. J. Meisels & E. Fenichel (Eds.), *New visions for the developmental assessment of infants and young children* (pp. 27-52). Washington, D.C.: National Center for Infants, Toddler, and Families.

Richardson-Gibbs, A. M. (1998). Natural environments: What do we do next? *California Infant Development Association (IDA) Newsletter,* 25(3), 2-3.

Rose, D. F., & Smith, B. J. (1993). Preschool mainstreaming: Attitude barriers and strategies for addressing them. *Young Children, 48* (4), 59-62.

Strain, P. S. (1995). The challenge of inclusion: Points well-taken and related challenges. *Journal of Early Intervention, 19*(3), 195-196.

Chapter 2

Providing for Special Needs in Early Education: The Challenge

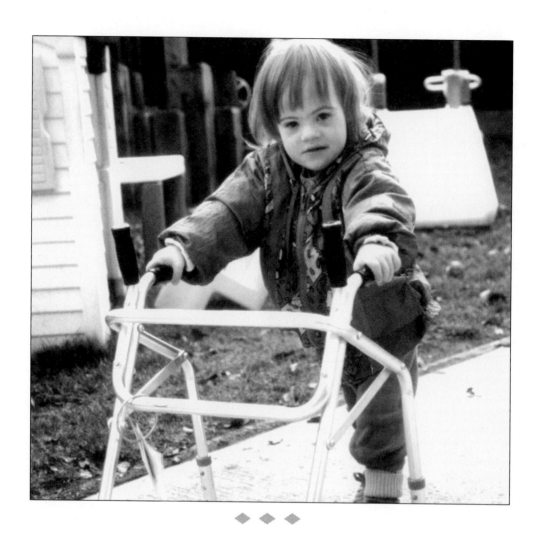

Key Concepts

- The history of early childhood special education reflects influences from both the field of early childhood education and the field of special education.

- Increasingly, attention is being focused on the impact of caregiver-child relationships.

- Public pressure has resulted in federal legislation that has provided an important impetus to the development of programs for infants and young children with special needs.

- Evolving trends in the field include:

- Relationship-focused interventions

- Focus on families

- Community-based inclusive settings

- Increased cultural competence

- Coordinated, comprehensive services

- Developmentally appropriate activities in natural settings

- Functional-ecological and social-transactional approaches to curriculum development

- Recommended practices in early childhood special education include those identified by the Council for Exceptional Children, Division for Early Childhood Education (DEC) and the National Association for the Education of Young Children (NAEYC). These organizations have provided guidelines offering practical suggestions on how to develop programs based on the individual needs of each child while recognizing that best medium through which to meet these needs is children's play guided by skilled early educators.

- A child with special needs must be viewed as a child first; the special need or disability is secondary. All children are best understood within the context of their families, rather than within the context of their disabilities.

- Children's needs can be met through a variety of service delivery models within various settings that include both home and group-based programs.

Attitudes toward young children with disabilities have changed dramatically in the last 100 years. In the 19th century children were required to work on farms and in factories at a very early age. In the initial part of the 20th century, large numbers of children under age 10 worked 12 hours a day, 6 days a week, for a total wage of 75 cents a week! Going to school at all was a luxury. Children were "to be seen and not heard." In an environment that encouraged child labor, the weak, the infirm, and those with disabilities presented an intolerable burden to all but the wealthiest of families.

Imagine you are the parent of a child with a disability about 100 years ago.

You've just become a parent. You are so excited, but you look at John and he doesn't look right. Your child grows, but he is different. He doesn't walk as early as your other children or as early as your neighbor's child. He falls a lot. His speech is very difficult to understand. It is 1880. There is little you can do to help John. No one seems to care about him. As time goes on, you will be able to send him away to an institution and you will be advised to forget him.

Continue to imagine. Times have changed. You are parents halfway through the 20th century. It is 1945. People do care. Your child, Jimmy, will be tested, labeled, and put into a special program. That special program will be in a separate school. It may be far from your home. He will not bother anyone. He certainly won't get in the way of the "normal" children. You are encouraged to accept him and to take advantage of the special facilities provided. If you have means, you have the option of sending him away to a private school.

Imagine again. Now it is 1978. Experts are eager to identify your child, Mary, as soon as possible. They want to help both of you. In fact, you are even being told that she will receive part of her education in the classroom with typical children. They are going to do something for her called "mainstreaming." You will be asked to help decide what education will be the most appropriate for Mary. You have some choices, because a range of special services is available. You are excited but somewhat apprehensive.

And now we are into the 2000s. Not only are professionals and parents around the nation collaborating to find and offer services that will help Jose function well in natural environments, but they wish to make it easier for your family to cope with the demands of parenting a child with special needs.

Being the parent of a child with special needs, one who is different, has never been easy. It is not easy today, either. But times are changing, and help is more readily available than before. Parents are able to choose from a variety of placement alternatives. Specialists work with parents in choosing the placement and array of special services that are most *appropriate*. In fact, legislation passed in the form of Public Law 102–119, the Individuals with Disabilities Education Act (formerly known as the Education for All Handicapped Children Act of 1975), and Public Law 99–457, the Education of the Handicapped

Amendments of 1986, require children to be educated in *natural environments* or *in the least restrictive settings* possible. When developing individualized program plans, schools serving young children with special needs are required to include a statement indicating the extent to which the child will be participating in the regular education environment. Such a mandate presents a continuing challenge, both legally and professionally: how best to adapt early childhood curricula for children with special needs? To meet this challenge, educators from early childhood education and special education have combined forces in creating the emerging field of early childhood special education.

EARLY CHILDHOOD SPECIAL EDUCATION: AN EVOLVING FIELD

While the 1980s opened with concern for the rights of individuals with disabilities, the 1990s recognized the rights and needs of the *families* of those with special needs. Children are no longer viewed in isolation. Attention is focused on understanding the needs of the child within the context of his or her family. Early intervention services gained new momentum as the nation recognized its responsibility to provide services from the moment of birth.

The actual field of early childhood special education is relatively new. So new, in fact, that a number of states have not fully developed certification programs. Despite this, however, there are historical roots, not only in regular early childhood education, compensatory education, and school-age special education, but also in allied fields such as psychology, human development, nursing, and sociology. A few of the major historical forces shaping the expanding field of early childhood special education are outlined in this section.

Pioneering Influences

Jean-Marc Itard undertook one of the first documented efforts to provide intervention services to a child with special needs. In 1799, a child approxi-

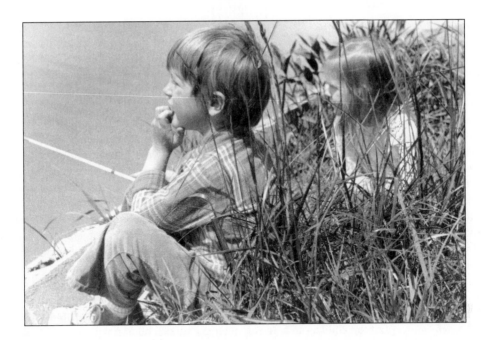

mately 12 years old was found living in the forest near Aveyron, France. The boy, named Victor, was thought to have been raised by animals and was described as "an incurable idiot." Itard refused to accept the idea that Victor's condition was incurable and irreversible. Itard believed in what later became known as an "interactionist viewpoint" (Bijou, 1977). That is, Victor's learning potential could be enhanced through intervention that changed the stimulation in his environment. Therefore, Itard undertook to humanize Victor through a series of carefully planned lessons stimulating the senses.

Itard (1962) recounted his feelings of optimism, frustration, anger, hope, and despair in *The Wild Boy of Aveyron*. Teachers today who work with children who have extreme disabilities may easily recognize these feelings. Although Itard did not achieve the success he visualized, his efforts had a significant impact on the future of special education. Itard was one of the first to demonstrate and record an attempt to understand empathically the needs of a child with disabilities.

Casa dei Bambini.   About a century later, another physician, Maria Montessori, was busy in Italy creating a nursery school, Casa dei Bambini, that revolutionized the notion of early education. Because of her training, early interests, and the nature of the school she was asked to develop, Montessori stressed cleanliness, order, and housekeeping skills as well as reading, writing, and arithmetic. Aspects of both the discovery approach to learning and programmed instruction can be found in the techniques developed by Montessori. She suggested that teachers observe the natural, spontaneous behavior of children and then arrange learning experiences to encourage their development.

Like Itard, Montessori believed in developing the child's natural curiosity through systematic training of the senses. Both proceeded with optimism and determination to train those whom some might believe to be beyond hope. Today, Montessori's "sensorial" materials are advocated for use with children with disabilities because they are manipulable, three-dimensional, and concrete. Advocates cite the emphasis on task analysis, sequencing, and individualization evident in the Montessori approach as worthy for use with children who have limited abilities as well as those who are gifted.

Piaget's Spontaneous Cognition. Until his death in 1980 at the age of 84, Jean Piaget continued to influence our understanding of cognitive development. Piaget proposed an inborn tendency toward adaptation that, in its encounter with the environment, results in categories of knowledge that are remarkably similar among all human beings. Piaget's concept of child development and his stages of cognitive development will be considered again in Chapter 10. His prolific writings and those of followers continue to remind us of the need to be aware of the unfolding internal mental capacities of children.

According to Piaget, the purpose of education is to provide opportunities that allow a child to combine experiences into coherent systems (schemes) that constitute the child's knowledge. "Knowledge" then is constructed from within rather than acquired from without (Furth, 1970). Therefore, each child's capacity to learn is thought to be uniquely experientially based. Piaget's concept of the child as an active learner stimulated by inborn curiosity has prompted the development of preschool programs designed to allow the child to become an active initiator of learning experiences. From a developmental point of view, a child's strengths, rather than deficits, receive emphasis. Most notable of the Piagetian-based programs is the Perry Preschool Project developed in the late 1950s in Ypsilanti, Michigan. An extension known as the High/Scope First Chance Preschool serves as a model program for those desiring to integrate preschoolers with disabilities into programs with nondisabled preschoolers (Banet, 1979).

The Beginnings of Early Intervention

One of the earliest attempts to demonstrate the close relationship among nurturing, environmental stimulation, and mental growth processes grew out of the Iowa growth studies in the late 1930s. Skeels and Dye (1939) transferred 12 children under 3 years of age from an orphanage to an institution for individuals with mental retardation. In the institution the children were cared for with great affection by adolescent girls who were considered to have retardation. A comparison group of children remained in the orphanage, where they received no specialized attention. Follow-up testing demonstrated that those placed in the stimulating environment increased their intelligence test scores while those who remained in the orphanage decreased their intelligence test scores (Skeels, 1942). Twenty-one years later, Skeels (1966) found dramatic differences between those who had been placed in the enriching environment and those who had not. The 12 children in the experimental group were found to be self-supporting. Of the comparison group, four had been institutionalized and 1 had died. Educationally speaking, four of those who had been in the enriching environment completed college, and the others had a median high school education. On the other hand, the median education for the comparison group was only at the third-grade level.

Samuel Kirk (1958) also conducted experiments on the influence of early education on the development of young children with mental disabilities. In his textbook, Kirk's suggestion that an inadequate cultural environment might be a cause of mental retardation helped to convince politicians of the need for compensatory educational programs for young children. Perhaps more convincing was the conclusion reached by Benjamin Bloom (1964) that claimed that about "50% of the [intellectual] development takes place between conception and age 4, and about 30% between ages 4 and 8, and 20% between ages 8 and 17" (p. 88).

Bloom's argument was built on J. McVicker Hunt's popular book *Intelligence and Experience* (1961), which argued eloquently against the notion of fixed intelligence. Attempting to lay to rest the heredity versus environment controversy, Hunt supported well his contention that heredity sets the limits, whereas environment determines the extent to which the limits will be achieved. And so, under the belief that children's intelligence develops early and rapidly and that enrichment early in life can have profound influences on the child's development, federal funding for Project Head Start was provided in 1965.

Project Head Start: A Breakthrough. The primary purpose in passing the Economic Opportunity

Act of 1964 was to break the cycle of poverty by providing educational and social opportunities for children from low-income families. The result was the implementation of Head Start during the summer of 1965 with approximately 550,000 children in 2,500 child development centers. Parent involvement both within the Head Start classroom and on policy committees set a precedent. This has, no doubt, influenced legislators to require parent involvement in current decisions involving children with disabilities.

The Head Start program had a significant impact on the development of early childhood special education. It was the first major public exposure to the importance of early educational experiences. As Caldwell (1973) pointed out, "the implicit strategy of early Head Start was to devise a program that fits the children as they are found and that institutes remedial procedures to correct whatever deficiencies they have, whether they are nutritional, experiential, or medical" (p. 5).

Legislation enacted in 1972 required Head Start programs to include children with disabilities to the extent of at least 10% of their enrollment. Including children with disabilities in classrooms with typical children has become a major activity of Head Start. In fact, even in 1985 Head Start enrollment of preschoolers with disabilities exceeded 60,000.

Doubts. After the extreme optimism that accompanied the establishment of Head Start, it came as a shock to those who worked daily with the children and their parents that the program failed to produce documented gains. The Westinghouse report of 1969 cited data suggesting that measured gains made by Head Starters faded rapidly. By the end of the first grade, there often were no significant differences between the overall academic performance of children who had attended Head Start programs and those from the same kinds of homes who had not. Doubting the validity of this investigation, influential people fought for a stay of execution (Gotts, 1973). Among them was Edward Zigler, a member of the original planning committee that conceptualized Head Start and later director of the Office of Child Development. Zigler (1978) retorted, "I ask my colleagues in the re-

search community to forego the temptation of delivering definitive pronouncements concerning the fade-out issue and await instead the collection and analyses of more data" (p. 73).

Impact of Early Intervention

Indeed, Zigler was to be rewarded for his faith. Both the quantity and quality of research on the effectiveness of early intervention programs has been improving (Farran, 1990; Shonkoff, Hauser-Cram, Krauss, & Upshur, 1992). Perhaps the research that received the most attention was that of Lazar and Darlington (1979, 1982) and The Consortium on Developmental Continuity. These researchers conducted longitudinal investigations into the persistence of the effects of early intervention programs throughout the United States. The evidence from the projects clearly indicated that there were long-lasting positive effects from early intervention programs. Tracing children who had been involved in preschool programs into their teens or early 20s, Lazar found that children with some form of early education were far less likely to require special education or to be held back a grade.

A powerful case for federal support of early intervention programs appears in the report of a well-designed 19-year longitudinal study of the effects of the Perry Preschool Project (Schweinhart & Weikart, 1988). Exhibit 2–1 lists some of the gains attributed to early intervention with children who are primarily at risk and disadvantaged. While children in these programs did not have disabilities, they were considered to be at risk. The progress of these children definitely helped to promote financial and social support of programs providing early intervention.

Early Intervention with Children with Disabilities. Responding to the need to understand the effects of early intervention on children with disabilities, the Utah State Early Intervention Research Institute has analyzed the most comprehensive collection of early intervention research studies available. After considering the research design difficulties inherent in research with young children with special

---

EXHIBIT 2–1

Effects of Early Education/Intervention

Children who have participated in early education programs:

1. Are less likely to be assigned to special education classes or to be held back a grade.
2. Have more positive attitudes toward high school and are more likely to graduate.
3. Are less likely to be arrested as youth and young adults.
4. Are less likely to experience teen pregnancy.
5. Are more likely to secure gainful employment after leaving school.

---

needs, these researchers have offered some tentative conclusions (personal communication, S. Barnett, July 1990; Guralnick, M., 1997). It appears that (a) early intervention does produce immediate and short-run positive effects on cognitive and motor development; (b) these effects do persist at least to school entry; and (c) larger effects are produced if early intervention is begun before age 2 than if it is begun between ages 2 and 4. Too little information is available to draw conclusions regarding duration and intensity of programs. However, it appears that programs for children with special needs that include parents are more effective than those that do not.

In interpreting the findings of early intervention research, it is important to keep in mind the diversity with which this field deals. When policymakers ask, "What are the benefits of early intervention?" the response will inevitably be, "It depends." This is not because researchers cannot agree or because of the limitations of research methods, but because of the great diversity among children and families and the circumstances in which they live. There is no one best intervention for everyone all of the time. There is

not even one best intervention for a very narrowly defined group such as infants with Down syndrome and their families. Even infants with Down syndrome differ so much from one another that any specific intervention for a group of these infants probably would not be very successful. Research does provide some pieces of this complex, highly individualized puzzle indicating that early intervention can yield important benefits. Because of the complexities involved in documenting positive effects of early intervention, professionals in the field do not know enough to put the complete picture together to produce reliable generalizations.

Relationship-focused Models of Early Intervention. Considerable attention is being given to the role of caregiver-child interaction in early intervention. (See Greenspan and Wieder, 1998). Mahoney, Boyce, Fewell, Spiker, and Wheeden (1998) examined the developmental outcomes achieved in four independent intervention research studies. These included the Infant Health and Development Program (1990), the Longitudinal Studies of the Effects and Costs of Alternative Types of Early Intervention (Casto & White, 1993), the Play and Learning Strategies program (Fewell & Wheeden, 1998), and the Family-Centered Outcomes study (Mahoney & Bella, 1999). Findings provide support for assumptions underlying the relationship-focused intervention model. That is, intervention effectiveness is dependent on parent-child interaction. In fact, intervention effects on child development did not appear to occur unless mothers changed their style of interaction with their child. The factor that was significantly associated with positive child development was maternal responsiveness. In addition, Achenbach, Howell, Aoki, & Rauh (1993) reported long-term positive effects on child development when early intervention focused significantly on maternal involvement.

Given the results of these and other projects, the mechanism that maintains child change over time may be obvious. The parent/caregiver appears to be the factor that assists the child in maintaining the advantage stimulated by the early intervention. Even though a great deal of research is needed to explore how specific interventions can influence parent-child relationships, research results to date suggest a cumulative-transactional model of development (Foley & Hochman, 1998). Early on, Part H of P.L. 99–457 recognized the impact of the interaction between a child and his or her environment by viewing the family as a system embedded within a larger ecological network. The requirement of an Individualized Family Service Plan, to be discussed in Chapter 5, attests to this realization.

If, as speculation suggests, the mechanism that facilitates and maintains the impact of early intervention services is the caregiver, current programs will need to consider focusing more of their efforts on the caregiving environment than on the infant or child. Changes in the child may enhance parental attitudes as well as improve the interactional nature of the parent-child relationship. Conversely, changes in parent responses can reinforce and build desired responses in the child. Thus, a mutually reinforcing cycle of parent-child interactions will help to maintain the impact of early intervention services. As Meisels stated as early as 1985, "the primary intervention target should not be the child, but the child within the context of the family" (p. 8).

This recommendation is underscored by Krauss (1997) in a review of research:

. . . . empirical studies have shown that interventions designed to enhance the ability of mothers to interact in more developmentally appropriate ways with their infants and toddlers have salutary and lasting positive effects on both the mother and the child's subsequent development (p. 615).

PROBABLE DIMENSIONS OF EFFECTIVE EARLY INTERVENTION PROGRAMS

Even though evaluation studies have failed to determine that any one model of early childhood education is the most effective, the Division for Early Childhood (DEC, 1993) recommended some probable dimensions of effective programs. In brief, interventionists are urged to consider the following elements as basic quality indicators when initiating or evaluating a program:

1. Programs practice a cross-disciplinary approach to assessment and service delivery utilizing a team of professionals from different disciplines. Such an approach requires extensive and cooperative team planning and interagency coordination.
2. A well-defined program model that respects the values and opinions of family members and promotes a high level of family involvement and support through family-professional collaboration.
3. Responsive adults respond sensitively to cultural differences and values in daily activities and during ongoing communication.
4. Incorporation of "best practices" as they are continually determined through practice and research in the field.
5. Children's activities are chronologically age appropriate as well as developmentally appropriate.
6. Interventions should be based on the least intrusive and most normal strategies possible.
7. Facilitation of functional skills to enable children to cope with environmental expectations as determined through individualized program and service planning.
8. The effects of program elements should be regularly monitored and adjusted as appropriate.
9. Early childhood professionals should actively engage families in systematic planning and preparation for transitions to new learning environments.

CHANGING POLICIES: THE IMPACT OF PUBLIC PRESSURE AND LEGISLATION

Concerned citizens and active parent and professional associations have played a vital role in changing public policy toward children with special needs.

Development of Professional Groups

It has been said that Alexander Graham Bell, inventor of the telephone and a strong advocate of oral education of the deaf, should be given credit for organizing professional advocates of special education.

He petitioned the National Education Association (NEA) to establish a division to be concerned about the needs of people with disabilities. In 1897, the NEA established such a division and named it the Department of Education of the Deaf, Blind, and the Feeble-minded. As attitudes toward and knowledge of this population changed, this name was later changed to the Department of Special Education.

The formation of The International Council for Exceptional Children in 1922 provided the impetus for what some believe to be the most influential advocacy group continuing to provide national leadership on behalf of children with special needs. The 1930 White House Conference on Child Health and Protection was a milestone in marking the first time that special education had received national recognition. Today, over 7,000 educators turn to the Division for Early Childhood (DEC) of The Council for Exceptional Children as a continuing source of advocacy for young children with disabilities.

The Power of Private Citizens

Several factors came together after World War II to give rise to the development of strong parent organizations in the late 1940s. Professional knowledge was expanding, the country felt responsible for aiding its wounded, and prominent people such as Pearl Buck, Roy Rogers and Dale Evans, and the Kennedy family were visibly calling for better education of individuals with special needs. Parents no longer felt the need to hide their children with disabilities. Pressure groups such as the United Cerebral Palsy Association, the National Association for Retarded Citizens, and the American Foundation for the Blind began to demand alternatives other than institutionalization for the education of their children with disabilities.

Professional groups joined parent groups in capitalizing on the historic Supreme Court decision in *Brown v. Board of Education of Topeka* (1954). Although primarily a racial integration initiative, the Court ruled that state laws that permitted segregated public schools were in violation of the Fourteenth Amendment's "equal protection under the law" clause. Realizing that decisions applicable to one mi-

nority group must be applicable to another, pressure groups sought to secure legislation that would create significant educational changes on behalf of children with special needs. However, little actually occurred until after the publication of an article by Dunn (1968) that provided a blueprint for changes recognizing the rights of students with disabilities.

The First Chance (HCEEP) Program

In 1968, Congress recognized the need for seed money to develop model programs to spur the development of services for children with disabilities from birth through age 8. Legislation in the form of P.L. 90–538 was enacted to establish the Handicapped Children's Early Education Program (HCEEP), better known as the First Chance program. These projects were required to include parents in their activities, run inservice training, evaluate the progress of both the children and the program, coordinate activities with public schools, and disseminate information on the project to professionals and the public. In 1980, the total number of funded projects was 177, with 111 including infants in their population (Swan, 1981). These projects served two basic purposes: (1) to provide models of exemplary services that can be replicated for young children with disabilities and (2) to disseminate information that will encourage this replication.

Model Delivery Systems. The concept of delivery systems applies to how, when, and where services are delivered to children and their families. Karnes and Zehrbach (1977) summarized the unique approaches of 120 HCEEP programs. The majority of these fell under the following delivery system headings: (a) home, (b) home followed by center, (c) home and center, (d) center, and (e) technical assistance and consultative services.

Most projects that delivered only home-based services viewed the parents as the primary teachers of their children. Beller (1979) described these as "parent-oriented" programs. Such programs are especially useful in rural areas or where parents are reluctant to have their children leave home. For example, the Portage Project (Shearer & Shearer, 1976) developed a home-based program to meet the needs of children where geography prevented transportation. Such home- based programs had the advantage of allowing intervention within the natural setting of the home. However, these programs put added stress on the parents, who have little respite from their children and must take on more teaching responsibilities.

Many of the children originally served only at home often entered a center program around the age of 18 months. Some received services in both a center and at home. Staff members modeled appropriate teaching techniques in the child's home. A number of the center-based programs not only were cross categorical but also included children who had no disabilities. According to Beller (1979), center-based programs tended to be child oriented, emphasizing direct intervention with the child. Finally, those centers that used technical assistance did so for help with diagnosis and inservice training.

The HCEEP seed money was well spent. Hebbeler, Smith, and Black (1991) reported that of the demonstration projects funded, 80% were able to locate funding to continue to operate beyond the funding period. After 10 years, the 140 outreach projects resulted in 1,991 known replications of the models. These replications served nearly 108,000 children.

Public Law 94–142—The Education for All Handicapped Children Act of 1975 (EHA)

In 1975, with the passage of P.L. 94–142, the right to a free, appropriate public education was mandated for all children of school age. This law was limited in that it did not require states to offer services to young children with disabilities, but it did provide financial incentives for states to provide services to children with special needs as young as 3 years of age.

Purpose. The purpose of P.L. 94–142 is to insure that all handicapped children have available to them . . . a free, appropriate public education which includes special education and related services de-

signed to meet their unique needs, to insure that the rights of handicapped children and their parents or guardians are protected, to assist States and localities to provide for the education of all handicapped children and to assess and insure the effectiveness of efforts to educate handicapped children. (Sec. 601 [c])

In addition, the National Center for Clinical Infant Programs (NCCIP) was founded in 1977 to recognize and support the needs of very young children and their families.

Free Appropriate Public Education (FAPE). The law requires that a qualified school representative, teacher, the parents or guardian, and whenever possible the child join together in the development of an individualized education program (IEP). This written statement must include (a) a statement of the child's present level of academic functioning; (b) a declaration of annual goals complete with appropriate short-term instructional objectives; (c) a description of specific educational services to be provided to the child and the degree to which the child will participate in regular educational programs; (d) the proposed date for initiation and estimation of the required length of services; and (e) annual evaluation procedures specifying objective criteria designed to determine whether or not the short-term instructional objectives have been met (Sec. 602, 19).

Procedural Safeguards. The law requires that children with disabilities be served in the **least restrictive environment** appropriate to their educational needs. Children can be placed in separate classes or schools only when their disabilities are so severe that regular school placement is considered inappropriate. The act also requires nondiscriminatory testing and the use of multiple criteria in the determination of placement (Sec. 612, 5, C). This requirement implies the need for all teachers to become skilled in the education of children who exhibit a variety of educational needs.

P.L. 94–142 provided for the right of parents or guardians to examine all records, obtain independent evaluation, and require written notification in their native language when there are plans to change a

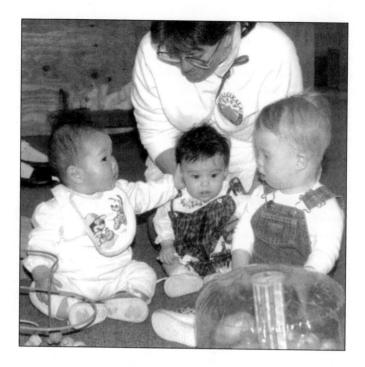

child's educational program. The intent is to ensure that the child's rights are legally protected. Parents or guardians are entitled to a hearing before termination, exclusion, or classification of a student into a special program.

Public Law 99–457—The Education of the Handicapped Act Amendments of 1986

P.L. 99-457 is thought by some to be the law that has legitimized the field of early childhood special education (Bricker, 1988). At the very least, it has created a national agenda that has federal, state, and local planners collaborating with parents in unprecedented efforts to develop new and expanded services for infants and young children who have disabilities or are at risk and their families. Part B of the law required all states to extend all of the provisions of P.L. 94-142 to children 3 to 5 years old by the 1990-1991 school year. States that did not comply were to lose federal monies they had been receiving for other preschool services.

School districts throughout the country have already developed early intervention services for preschool-aged children with severe disabilities. Amendments to P.L. 94-142 required school districts to provide services to those with mild disabilities just as they do for older children with less-intensive needs. Major features of the most influential P.L. 99-457 are listed in Exhibit 2-2.

Part H. Part H of P.L. 99-457 established a discretionary program for states to facilitate the design and implementation of comprehensive systems of early intervention services for infants and toddlers with developmental delays or disabilities. As defined by the law, early intervention services "are designed to meet a handicapped infant's or toddler's developmental needs in any one or more of the following areas: physical development; cognitive development; language and speech development; psychosocial development; or self-help skills" (Sec. 672).

Part H defined the **eligible** population as all children from birth through age 2 (up to the 3rd birth-

◆ ◆ ◆

EXHIBIT 2–2

Major Features of P.L. 99–457

- Establishes state-level interagency councils on early intervention.
- Institutes individualized family service plans.
- Provides case management services to families.
- Maintains a public awareness program that includes a comprehensive child find system and a central early intervention resource directory.
- Establishes a single line of responsibility for general supervision and monitoring of services.
- Requires the development of a multidisciplinary, coordinated interagency model of service delivery.
- Establishes procedural safeguards.
- Acknowledges the family to be the central focus of service.
- Provides for smooth transitions as a family moves from one service or system to another.
- Facilitates development of a comprehensive system of personnel development.

day) who have developmental delays, have conditions that typically result in delay, or are at risk for significant developmental delay. States have had to make independent decisions about the definition of developmental delay and "at risk" as well as the criteria used to make these determinations. Therefore, the populations of children eligible for services varies from state to state. In order to design "a statewide, comprehensive, coordinated, multidisciplinary, interagency program of early intervention services for all handicapped infants and their families" (Sec. 671), each governor appointed a **lead agency** and established an **interagency coordinating council.** States continue to struggle through the conceptual

morass and face the political challenges that will determine the nature of early intervention services into the year 2000 and beyond.

Public Law 101–476—The Education of the Handicapped Act Amendments of 1990

P.L. 101-476, an amendment to P.L. 99-457, changed the title of EHA to the Individuals with Disabilities Education Act (IDEA). By dropping the phrase "handicapped children" and replacing it with "individuals with disabilities," Congress intended that children with special needs be recognized as children first and, if necessary, as children with disabilities second. Throughout the law, all phrases putting the term *handicapped* before children or youth were deleted. This law became known as "person-first" language. It also reauthorized and expanded the discretionary programs and mandated transition services and the inclusion of assistive technology services.

Public Law 102–119—The Individuals with Disabilities Education Act Amendments of 1991

IDEA was amended again in 1991 in the form of P.L. 102-119. There were two sections of the amended IDEA that contributed to the expansion and improvement of the mandate for services to infants, toddlers, and preschoolers with disabilities and their families. The first is Part H, initially included in the 1986 amendments as discussed earlier. Recall that it created a new, discretionary program designed to provide the incentive to states to develop and implement a statewide system of comprehensive, coordinated, multidisciplinary, interagency services for all children from birth to age 3 with disabilities and their families.

The second section of direct interest is Part B-Section 619, also included in the 1986 amendments, which extended the mandate to full provision of a free, appropriate public education (FAPE) to 3- to 5-year-olds and increased funding through the Preschool Grant Program. IDEA places special emphasis on the provision of services designed to facilitate a smooth transition from services required through Part H to services provided through Part B.

Public Law 105–17—The Individuals with Disabilities Education Act Amendments of 1997

Amendments were made to IDEA again in 1997 that became effective in 1998. These amendments repealed the old Part H and reauthorized the early intervention program under a revised Part C. The new Part C allows states greater flexibility to serve at-risk infants and toddlers. It also requires Individualized Family Service Plans (IFSPs) to contain statements about the natural environments in which early intervention services will be provided. The IFSP must include a statement of justification when services are not provided in the natural environment. States were also encouraged to employ appropriately trained paraprofessionals to help provide early intervention services. Part B now requires that school districts must participate in transition planning when children move from early intervention into preschool special education services. It also allows states to use the term *developmental delay* for children aged 3 to 9 instead of more detrimental labels such as *mental retardation.* In addition, Part B funds can be used for special education and related services as required on Individualized Education Programs (IEPs) even if children without disabilities benefit from these services.

Public Law 101-336—The Americans with Disabilities Act of 1990

The Americans with Disabilities Act (ADA) is the most significant federal law ensuring the full civil rights of individuals with disabilities. While the laws described previously focused primarily on education and related services, this law is broad-reaching in guaranteeing equal opportunity in employment, public accommodation, transportation, state and local government services, and telecommunications. Of particular significance is the fact that child-care centers and family day-care homes are included in the law's definition of public accommodations.

According to the ADA, child-care centers must make reasonable modifications in their policies and procedures to accommodate children and adults with disabilities. This may mean that centers who do not normally accept children who are not yet toilet trained may have to make accommodations to do so if a disability is an obstacle to the toilet training. A center must also provide auxiliary aids and services when they are necessary to ensure communication with children or parents with hearing, vision, or speech disabilities. Physical access to the center is also required. Although this law creates many questions to clarify its full impact, the intent is, nevertheless, clear. Society is expected to move toward full inclusion of individuals with disabilities in all aspects of daily living. The most significant legislation is summarized in Exhibit 2–3.

EVOLVING TRENDS IN EARLY CHILDHOOD SPECIAL EDUCATION

After reviewing the major public policy changes influencing the field of Early Childhood Special Education, it is important to note the trends that continue to evolve as this policy is being implemented. Figure 2–1 (Lynch, 1990) reflects major philosophical changes that were recognized in early 1990 and continue to influence the development of program "best practices" now and beyond the year 2000.

Family-Centered Services

The original framers of P.L. 99-457 recognized the family as the constant in the life of the child as evidenced in their mandate for a family-centered approach to implementation of the law. Rather than the traditional focus on the child, a family-centered approach views the child's development within the context of the family system. Increasingly, it is recognized that effective service delivery is guided by a thorough understanding of family systems, including

EXHIBIT 2–3

Significant Legislation

Public Law 90–538 (1968)
Handicapped Children's Early Education Assistance Act

Significant to the education of preschool children with disabilities; established experimental early education programs throughout the country, through the Handicapped Children's Early Education Program (HCEEP).

Public Law 92–424 (1972)
Economic Opportunity Act Amendments

Established a preschool mandate that required that not less than 10% of the total number of Head Start placements be reserved for children with disabilities.

Public Law 93–380 (1974)
Education Amendments

Preceded P.L. 94–142 and established a total federal commitment to the education of children with disabilities; concerns included education within the least restrictive environment, nondiscriminatory testing, and privacy rights (Title V., "Buckley Amendment").

Public Law 94–142 (1975)
Education for All Handicapped Children Act

Revised and expanded P.L. 93–380; provided a free, appropriate public education with related services to all children with disabilities between ages 3 and 21.

Public Law 98–199 (1983)
The Education of the Handicapped Act Amendments of 1983

Provided financial incentives for states to extend service levels down to birth.

Public Law 99–457 (1986)
The Education of the Handicapped Act Amendments of 1986

Extended P.L. 94–142 to include 3- to 5-year-olds; added a new grant program to assist states in establishing a comprehensive system of early intervention services for infants and toddlers with disabilities and their families.

Public Law 101–476 (1990)
Individuals with Disabilities Education Act (IDEA)

Reauthorization of P.L. 94–142 to reflect a change in philosophy away from labeling children as "handicapped children" to referring to them as *individuals* first, with "disabilities" following as a secondary description.

Public Law 102–119 (1991)
The Individuals with Disabilities Education Act Amendments of 1991

Reauthorization of P.L. 101–476 ensuring comprehensive early intervention services to young children and their families.

Public Law 105–17 (1997)
The Individuals with Disabilities Education Act Amendments of 1997

Reauthorization of P.L. 102–119 authorizing comprehensive services for infants and toddlers under Part C and for preschoolers under Part B.

Public Law 101–336 (1990)
The Americans with Disabilities Act (ADA)

Assures full civil rights of all individuals with disabilities including reasonable accommodations in preschools and child-care centers.

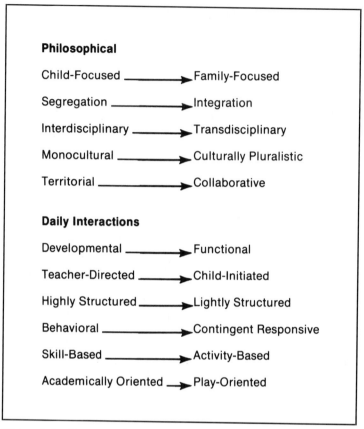

Figure 2–1   Best practice continua for children who have disabilities or are at risk and their families. (Source: Eleanor Lynch, April 1990.)

family stresses, factors influencing family functioning, and the family's ability to cope with the challenges of raising a child with special needs. Professionals are being urged to reexamine traditional agency roles and practices as they promote the collaborative family-directed partnerships essential to success in planning processes such as assessment, prioritizing goals, and designing and implementing intervention plans.

Community-Based Inclusive Settings

One of the basic premises of the Individuals with Disabilities Education Act is the inclusion of young children with special needs in the least restrictive en-vironment (LRE). Indeed, Part C states that early intervention services for children from birth to age 3 are to be provided in "…natural environments, including the home, and community settings in which children without disabilities participate" (P.L. 105-17, 1997). Each child's individual plan must state the degree to which the child will receive services in "natural environments." **Natural environments** may include the child's home, neighborhood play group, child development center, Head Start programs, or any other setting designed for children without disabilities.

The practice of fully including children with special needs in programs and settings primarily designed for nondisabled children received a boost through the 1990 passage of the Americans with Disabilities Act.

The challenge of providing services sufficient to enable all young children to function as optimally as possible within normal environments appears to be the challenge of the new millennium. At the very least, early childhood special educators are being asked to move outside the walls of a self-contained classroom and to become integrated into early education programs within the community.

Interdisciplinary Collaboration

In addition to the mandate of delivering coordinated multiagency services, the field of early childhood special education is confronted with the need to avoid the difficulties inherent in a strict categorical response to the needs of young children and their families. Part C mandates service coordination designed to provide the critical mechanism for coordinating among complex and diverse human service personnel. Deliberate service coordination reduces duplication of intake procedures, assessment of child and family needs, and direct service delivery.

This focus on interagency and interdisciplinary collaboration facilitates the learning of skills necessary to work in teams comprising various disciplines, sometimes from several agencies. As discussed further in Chapter 4, the **transdisciplinary** approach allows the child and family to benefit from the expertise of several disciplines without, necessarily, having to be handled or meet face-to-face with a myriad of professionals. Professionals from various disciplines work together cooperatively to educate one another so that one professional can provide a broader range of essential services. For example, a teacher or caregiver may, on the advice of a speech-language pathologist, redirect an informal playground activity to facilitate language development.

Cultural Competence

Naturally, the families of young children with disabilities reflect the diversity of families in the general population. The last two decades have brought dramatic changes in the concept and reality of the family. Increasingly, definitions of the family conceptualize it as any unit that defines itself as a family. A family includes any persons who are related by blood or marriage as well as those who have made a commitment to share their lives (Lynch & Hanson, 1998). Family characteristics will continue to become more diverse and complex. Early intervention service delivery models are and will continue to undergo reconceptualization in order to serve effectively the families of the 1990s and beyond.

Given the great diversity found among families, moving from a child-oriented view to a child and family service orientation creates a continuing challenge for change. Viewing the family as the primary mediator of child development necessitates a reconsideration of service goals. Part C recognizes this need by requiring parents to be the primary decision makers when outcomes or goals are targeted in the service plan. A culturally pluralistic orientation is essential to service delivery mechanisms that can respond to constantly changing family characteristics.

Coordinated, Comprehensive Services

Collaboration between parents and professionals and among agency professionals is essential to the provision of coordinated, comprehensive services as required by the law. Buysse and Wesley (1993) point out the challenges created by significant shifts in role emphasis as professionals develop partnerships not only with families but also with an increasing array of community service providers. The literature increasingly discusses the shift away from stimulation and/or remediation programs to a new paradigm reflecting the ecological view of the child and family embedded within the larger community (Crnic & Stormshak, 1997). To meet the demands of this paradigm shift, training programs have moved away from curricula that follow traditional disciplinary boundaries toward curricula that foster multiagency and multidisciplinary collaboration. Such programs enable professionals from several disciplines to work together with families through a variety of approaches, integrating the best of the consultant, transdisciplinary, and multidisciplinary models with the best practices from special and "regular" early childhood education.

BUILDING ON BEST PRACTICES

During the last decade, the two major professional groups that relate to early intervention services have issued definite statements of "best practices" for developmentally appropriate procedures to guide program development and evaluation. Building on the position statements offered by the National Association for the Education of Young Children (NAEYC, 1986, 1987), the Division for Early Childhood of the Council for Exceptional Children issued "DEC Recommended Practices: Indicators of Quality in Programs for Infants and Young Children with Special Needs and Their Families" (DEC, 1993).

Several key recommendations emerge within the NAEYC framework related to curriculum, adult-child interactions, family involvement, and evaluation that are essential to high-quality early intervention programs. These are summarized below. However, it will become apparent throughout the remainder of this text that early interventionists must move beyond the criteria of NAEYC's best practices to ensure specific instructional techniques necessary to meet the unique needs of young children with disabilities and their families. The field of early childhood special education is built on best practices from the fields of both early childhood and special education. Reference to these practices is incorporated throughout this text.

Curriculum

- Educational goals are incorporated into all daily activities. Objectives are not taught in isolation, but are integrated into meaningful activities and events.

- Curriculum planning and intervention are based on the teacher's specific observations of each child in natural contexts.

- Learning is an *interactive* process. Children's interactions with adults, peers, and the physical environment are all important.

- Learning activities and materials must be concrete and *relevant* to children's lives. Teachers should make use of real-life objects and activities

(e.g., make a trip to the fire station, not just read a story about fire engines).

- Programs must be able to meet a wide range of interests and abilities. Teachers are expected to *individualize* instructional programs.

- Teachers must increase the difficulty and challenge of activities gradually and skillfully.

- Teachers must be able to facilitate *engagement* of each child by offering choices, making suggestions, asking questions, and describing events in ways that are meaningful and interesting to the child.

- Children should be given opportunities for *self-initiation, self-direction,* and *repeated practice.*

- Teachers must accept and appreciate cultural differences in children and families and avoid ethnic and gender stereotypes.

- Programs must provide a balance between rest and activity and should include outdoor activities each day.

- Outdoor activities should be *planned,* not simply opportunities to release pent-up energy.

- Programs must create careful *transitions* from one activity to the next. Children should not be rushed, and schedules should be flexible enough to take advantage of impromptu experiences.

Adult-Child Interaction

- Adults should respond quickly and directly to children's needs and attempts to communicate. Whenever possible, adults should be at eye level with children.

- Children must be provided with a variety of opportunities to communicate. Interaction is best facilitated on a one-to-one basis, or in groups of two to three children. Large-group instruction is less effective in facilitating communication.

- Professionals must be alert to signs of stress and provide sensitive, appropriate assistance to children.

- Adults must facilitate the development of self-esteem by "expressing respect, acceptance, and comfort for children, regardless of the child's behavior" (NAEYC, 1986, p. 14).

- Adults must use disciplinary techniques that enhance the development of self-control. These include setting clear, consistent limits; redirecting inappropriate behavior; valuing mistakes; listening to children's concerns and frustrations; helping children solve conflicts; and patiently reminding children of rules as needed.

- Adults must be responsible for all children at all times. Health and safety issues must be addressed constantly.

- Adults must plan for gradually increasing children's independence.

Family Involvement

- Families have the right and the responsibility to share in decision making regarding their children's care and education. Professionals must maintain frequent contact, and families should be encouraged to participate.

- Professionals must regularly share information and resources with parents, including information regarding stages of child development. They must also obtain and respect caregivers' views of individual children's behavior and development.

Evaluation

- Child evaluations should not rely on a single instrument.

- Evaluations should identify children with special needs and provide information that will lead to meaningful early interventions.

- Evaluations must be culturally appropriate.

Developmentally Appropriate Activities in Natural Settings

Program practices emphasize teaching children within the context of play and developmentally appropriate activities. Greater value is placed on children's initiation. Program goals are functional and relevant to children's and families' lives. Highly structured approaches utilizing strategies of behavior analysis and behavior modification are seen as useful tools for refinement of specific behaviors rather than as predominant teaching methodologies.

Functional-Ecological and Social-Transactional Approaches to Curriculum Development. Two established trends in curriculum development are the functional-ecological approach and the social-transactional approach. Guess and Noonan (1982) argued that educational goals should be selected on the basis of their functional utility for the child in his or her immediate or next environment. Emphasis is on the importance of identifying goals that have meaning and relevance within the child's real-life environment of home and community (Udell, Peters, & Templeman, 1998). These ideas form the basis of the **functional-ecological approach** to early intervention.

The **social-transactional approach** emphasizes the role of social and communicative interactions in children's development. Research and theoretical discussions forming the basis of this approach are abundant (Sameroff & Fiese, 1990). According to Mahoney and Powell (1988), this approach suggests that the main goal of intervention is to maximize children's intrinsic motivation through effective interactions. The focus of interventions is on the *quality* of interactions between children and their caregivers. The major strategy is to provide opportunities that encourage children to increase the frequency of interactive experiences that seem appropriate to the promotion of their development. The role of the interventionist is to assist parents and other primary caregivers to function more effectively as children's partners.

DAP and Children with Disabilities

The NAEYC best-practice guidelines just described are referred to as principles of "developmentally appropriate practice," or DAP. There continues to be discussion within the field as to whether or not DAP guidelines and strategies are sufficient to meet the needs of all children with disabilities (Carta, Atwater, Schwartz, & McConnell, 1993; Bruder, 1997).

Although there is substantial overlap between the "best practices" from early childhood education (ECE) and the "recommended practices" from early childhood special education (ECSE), there are certain differences. The roots of some of these differences are historical. The NAEYC guidelines for developmentally

appropriate practice were generated by ECE professionals who were dismayed at the growing emphasis on academic performance and structure in preschool and kindergarten classrooms (Bredekamp, 1993; Johnson & Johnson, 1992). Thus, the major focus of the NAEYC (1986/87) guidelines was upon expectations and learning environments that were appropriate for the developmental levels of young children. There was also a negative reaction to strongly teacher-directed approaches and to the teaching and tracking of specific skills. DAP practices valued the *process* rather than the *products* of learning. However, Bredekamp (1993) reasserted the value of the educator's role in guiding learning in her discussion of the relationship between early childhood education and early childhood special education.

ECSE, on the other hand, has been strongly influenced by the values and tenets of special education and Public Law 94–142. There is a strong emphasis on the identification of specific expected outcomes, accountability of professionals for ensuring steady progress toward these outcomes, the importance of direct instruction and a strong commitment to individualized instruction.

In addition to these historical differences, the field of ECSE also places relatively stronger emphasis than does ECE upon the following:

1. Parent-professional collaboration and family empowerment.
2. Transition planning and training for the next environment.
3. Interdisciplinary and interagency collaboration.

The early childhood special education literature has contained lively discussion of the extent to which DAP principles of early childhood education and the traditional recommended practices of ECSE are incompatible. Today there is an exciting trend toward a mutual incorporation of the best practices and philosophies of both fields. Bredekamp (1993) suggested that ECE has recognized the importance of the following ECSE practices:

1. A stronger emphasis upon collaboration with families and other professionals.
2. Greater emphasis upon supporting the specific needs of individual children.

3. Greater emphasis upon the birth-to-3 age range.
4. Viewing teacher-centered versus child-centered not as a dichotomy but as a continuum; understanding that child-centered approaches do not exclude the use of teacher-directed strategies in certain situations.
5. Greater emphasis upon transition planning.

Similarly, the field of ECSE recognized the importance of several key best practices of DAP (Carta, Atwater, Schwartz, & McConnell, 1993; Wolery, & Wilbers, 1994). These include:

1. Training in natural environments, particularly within the context of play.
2. Importance of child-initiated activities.
3. Deemphasis of standardized assessment and integration of assessment and curriculum.
4. Importance of active child engagement throughout the day in naturally occurring routines and activities.
5. Emphasis on social interaction.
6. The importance of cultural sensitivity and competence.

The following quote clarifies one of the issues of controversy related to the degree of direct instruction that is appropriate in working with young children:

Teachers following DAP ideally aspire toward precision contingency teaching, thus becoming as directive as needed under specific circumstances. Contingency teaching entails reading cues from the child in the task context and seeking the optimal degree of structure and direction. (Johnson & Johnson, 1992, p. 444)

The goal of many professionals in the fields of ECE and ECSE is that there be no division between the two. Especially in light of the growing diversity and special needs of children from multirisk families and communities, all early childhood professionals need the range of skills which currently characterize professional development within each field. The most recent revision of DAP (Bredekamp & Copple, 1997) suggest continuing convergence of philosophies as noted in greater emphasis on forming partnerships with parents and the importance of social and cultural contexts when considering appropriateness of practices.

A Cautionary Note

Students of early childhood special must realize that, as is the case with any new field, early childhood special education is constantly evolving. The ideas and notions that comprise today's "best or recommended practices" may be very different from those that evolve a decade from now. Early intervention professionals must have a thirst for knowledge and a genuine desire to better understand how to meet the needs of young children with disabilities. They must also have considerable tolerance for ambiguity as the field continues to define itself and its methodologies. Finally, early interventionists must have an understanding of the potential contribution of research. Practitioners must be responsible for maintaining an important two-way dialogue with the field's researchers. They must help identify important research questions, insist on the use of research methods that are appropriate to answer those questions, and then apply the findings of that research to their own practice.

VIEWING THE CHILD WITH SPECIAL NEEDS AS A CHILD FIRST

It is impossible to overstate the point that children with special needs are children first—children who have the same characteristics and needs as so-called "typical" children. The beauty of being young and "new" is the potential for growth and change. All infants and young children, no matter how significantly challenged or disabled, will benefit from those best practices that create supportive and nurturing environments for all young children. This belief must be the foundation of early childhood special education.

For some children, additional strategies, techniques, and adaptations will be required to maximize their opportunities to experience, enjoy, and learn from the world around them. Thus, students of early childhood special education must master two sets of skills: one related to facilitating learning and healthy growth and development in all children, and another related to the very specific and special needs of children with disabilities. Appendix D provides a sample list of important competencies for professionals in early childhood special education to master.

SERVICE DELIVERY SYSTEMS

The placement options available for young children with special needs are, of course, dependent on the service delivery systems within their communities. The term *service delivery system* in early intervention refers to several components that, together, describe and define the parameters of any early intervention program. According to Peterson (1987), these include the following components:

1. *Who:* The target of service (e.g., child, mother, family).
2. *When:* The beginning point of service (e.g., birth, infancy, preschool).
3. *What:* The services that are provided (e.g., screening, diagnostic assessment, education programs, therapeutic services, family counseling, medical services, transportation, etc.).
4. *Where:* The setting of the services (e.g., home-based, center-based day care or preschool, clinic, etc.).
5. *By Whom:* The primary intervention agent (e.g., parent, teacher, paraprofessional, transdisciplinary team, etc.).
6. *With Whom:* The social context of services (e.g., individual program, integrated program, segregated program).
7. *Through Whom:* The agencies providing the services (e.g., public schools, private programs, government agencies, etc.).

Several of these parameters are of special interest today as professionals plan and families select service delivery alternatives. Of particular concern to parents may be the issues of who is the focus of service, where the service will be offered, who will provide the service, and to what extent their child will be provided service alongside normal peers. Professionals are required to offer the service delivery option that is most appropriate for each child. While the term *ap-*propriate is not well defined, the law does, at least, require each placement team to specify the extent to which preschool children will participate in regular educational programs.

The following section summarizes some of the major points related to the determination of individually appropriate placement options and services to be delivered.

Infants and Toddlers

As stated earlier, Part C states that early intervention services are to be provided in natural environments, including the child's home and a variety of community settings. To provide the most appropriate option for each child and family, communities are increasingly developing what is sometimes referred to as a "menu of services." For infants and children with severe disabilities, home-based services often are considered to be the least restrictive because they are in the most "normal" environment. Sometimes home-based services are offered in the home of a relative or child-care provider.

Home-based programs are determined by the individual needs of each child and family. Providers are able to assess the family's priorities and resources. Such assessment can be sensitive to the functional demands of the child's environment. Home visitors include a wide variety of professionals from various community agencies. For young infants, early intervention services may be provided by a public health nurse who focuses on health care issues. A nutritionist may work with the family in serving a child with unique nutritional needs. The visits may center around sensory stimulation activities modeled by an infant educator or provided by an occupational or physical therapist.

It is "normal" for toddlers to attend center-based day-care and preschool programs. These center-based programs are typically somewhat structured group settings to which families bring their children. As with home-based programs, the frequency varies. However, there is typically more frequent contact, ranging from 1 to 5 times weekly. Some service delivery models combine home- and center-based services. Children may be enrolled in a center 2 or 3 days per week while home visits continue ranging from monthly to quarterly.

Other center or group settings may include public and private child-care settings in natural environments. Some children may experience dual enrollment by attending an agency-sponsored segregated center-based program for children with disabilities for part of the day and participate in a normalized child-care setting for the remainder of the day. As P.L. 101–336, The Americans with Disabilities Act (ADA), increases in influence, a greater number of infants and toddlers will be served in normalized child-care settings.

Special Considerations for Infant/Toddler Group Care

Any group care programs for children from birth to 3 years of age must be designed to create and sustain *intimacy.* Lally, Torres, and Phelps (1994) discuss six key components of group care for young children in this age range.

1. *Group Size.* The adult-child ratio in programs serving young children under age 3 should be no greater than 1:3. However, the issue of group size is not simply the need to maintain a low adult-child ratio. Total group size is at least as important as ratio. As group size increases, so does the level of stimulation. This creates a stressful environment for both infants and staff. A noisy, chaotic environment makes it difficult for staff to be sensitive and responsive to child cues and decreases the opportunity for quiet, intimate interactions.

2. *Physical Environment.* Arrangement of physical environment can either facilitate or interfere with flexible, individualized, responsive care. For example, easy and frequent access to food and to outdoor space allows greater individualization. Furniture that is comfortable for adults, such as rocking chairs and couches, encourages holding and reading to infants. Reduction of off-limits items and areas minimizes discipline problems and negative adult-child interactions. Small, well-

defined areas for certain types of play help control overstimulation and help young children focus.

3. *Assignment of Primary Caregiver.* An extremely important factor in center-based care for young children is the assignment of a primary caregiver to each child. This facilitates the development of trust and intimacy. This does not mean that the child interacts *exclusively* with only one adult; rather, that on most days there will be a very familiar and "special" person on whom the child can rely. The assignment of a primary caregiver also increases the likelihood that at least one staff person knows each child well. This knowledge of temperament, communication cues, likes, dislikes, and fears can be shared with other staff members. This in turn increases the opportunity for responsive and appropriate interactions with the infant.

4. *Continuity of Care.* Related to the issue of primary caregiver, Lally and associates (1994) also stress the importance of continuity of care:

When a very young child loses a caregiver, he really loses part of his sense of himself and the way the world operates: The things that the child knows how to do, and the ways that he knows to be simply don't work anymore. Too many changes in caregiver can lead to a child's reluctance to form new relationships (Lally, Torres, & Phelps., 1994, p. 6).

Changing caregivers every 6 to 9 months can have a very negative effect upon infants and young children. Changing the caregiver (or teacher, in an early intervention program) is also difficult for the child's parents. This requires the reestablishment of trust and communication patterns.

5. *Cultural and Familial Continuity.* Ideally, programs should employ staff whose cultural backgrounds match the families they serve. Children and parents are sensitive to significant mismatches in the childrearing values and practices of family and staff. (See Chapter 3 for discussion of this issue.)

It is imperative that individuals working with young children from cultures different than their own carefully examine the roots of their own biases and values. They must also be knowledgeable of the values and attitudes of the cultural groups in their local community and work to avoid being judgmental when there are significant differences.

Preschoolers

Part B of IDEA also requires that children be placed in the least restrictive environment (LRE). The LRE for 3- to 5-year-olds with severe disabilities may continue to be in a home or family setting. Preschoolers with less severe disabilities may attend segregated preschool classes for children with disabilities, usually provided by the public school system. These are usually self-contained special education classrooms on public school sites. Children are most often grouped heterogeneously in noncategorical classes.

Special education preschool classrooms are staffed by teachers with special education credentials. Some states have specific Early Childhood Special Education certification. The staff-to-child ratios are smaller than in standard child-care settings. At least one teacher's aide is available to assist. While parents are usually encouraged to be present, they may be less involved than the parents of infants and toddlers, where attendance is sometimes required.

In all center-based programs designed to serve young children with special needs, a transdisciplinary team of therapists is essential to the progress of children. Throughout the text, the roles of these related service personnel will be illustrated.

Inclusive Settings

Probably the most well-known inclusive preschool service delivery option is Head Start, where at least 10% of the children enrolled must have disabilities. Head Start is a federally sponsored preschool program for economically disadvantaged children. It is designed to provide the enrichment necessary to prepare children to succeed in the public schools. Federal and community resources have made it possible for Head Start programs to offer a rich variety of services to both children and parents. Such programs are keenly sensitive to the needs of a culturally diverse clientele and have staff well trained to address individual needs.

Integral to this textbook is the belief that any well-developed preschool program is potentially an inclusive setting if staff are trained and resources are available to accommodate special needs. Early intervention specialists are increasingly being trained to function as resource specialists who consult with staff of any normalized preschool program (Gallagher, 1997). The collaboration between the National Association for the Education of Young Children and the Council for Exceptional Children will serve to facilitate increased collaborative interaction between regular and special early childhood educators.

CENTER- VS. HOME-BASED SETTINGS

Setting alone does not determine the effectiveness of an early intervention program. Because there is much variability across program types (e.g., frequency, degree of parent involvement, strategies used, etc.), it is difficult to compare the relative effectiveness of home-based versus center-based programs. While there have been few carefully conducted studies comparing the two types of approaches, Bailey and Simeonsson (1988) suggested the following possible advantages and disadvantages of each:

1. Center-based programs may be more effective in preparing children for school environments by emphasizing skills such as focusing attention, following directions and schedules, completing tasks, and so on.
2. Home-based programs may offer more intensive one-on-one intervention, and children may spend less time waiting their turn to participate in activities.
3. Home-based programs may have a greater effect on parent-child interactions, since this is often more of an emphasis in home-based than in center-based programs. On the other hand, home-based programs that emphasize the parent's role as teacher may place stress on parents that interferes with their spontaneity and their interactions as parents and nurturers.
4. Center-based programs can provide relief from the often overwhelming caregiving responsibilities of parents of children with special needs.
5. Infectious diseases such as otitis media and diarrhea occur at higher rates among children who attend center-based programs than those who do not. However, for children from impoverished environments, center-based programs may offer opportunities to obtain nutritious meals.
6. Some studies have suggested that parents in home-based programs have more positive attitudes toward their children than parents of children in center-based programs.
7. Parents participating in center-based programs are more likely to develop social networks and gain support from other parents.

It should be clear that no one setting is definitely the best for all children and families. Settings must be selected by families with assistance from professionals according to the specific needs of each child and his or her family. When determining which setting is most appropriate, primary attention must focus on whether or not the services available will increase the chances that the child will be able to function more independently as he or she grows older. The setting selected will have to be culturally compatible with the values and child-rearing practices of the child's family if the child is to be in an environment that is most normal for him or her.

Child-Focused and Family-Focused Programs

Another parameter of service delivery of particular interest today is the target of intervention, that is, whether intervention is directed primarily toward the child or the caregiver. In both instances, with the passage of P.L. 99–457, the family must be the primary focal point and context within which the child is viewed. However, even within this family-centered framework, intervention may be focused more on the child or on the caregiver.

Child-Focused Approaches. Bricker and Veltman (1990) defined child-focused programs as those that have as their primary focus the enhancement of the child's development. They stated that such programs are based on two theoretical assumptions: (1) that biological problems can be overcome or ameliorated and (2) that early experience is important. Related to the latter assumption is a third assumption: that the potential to have a positive impact on children's development is greater when intervention occurs at younger ages.

Traditionally, under the influence of behavioral theories and the field of special education, child-focused programs have been more teacher directed than child directed. Such approaches have been characterized by carefully planned and highly structured programs that were controlled primarily by a teacher using behavioral analysis techniques.

Currently, child-focused programs are becoming more child directed. Child-directed programs assume that the child's development can best be facilitated through opportunities for self-initiation and exploration that are carefully mediated by responsive adults.

Child-focused programs do not ignore family needs. Family involvement is primarily in the context of enabling family members to meet the child's needs while at the same time having some of their own needs met. Parents are included as partners with professionals and as members of the child's intervention team.

Caregiver-Focused Approaches. Caregiver-focused approaches are those that concentrate primarily on the delivery of services to parents. Within this category there are two fairly distinct kinds of programs. The first seeks to establish a clinical therapeutic relationship with the parents, usually the mother, in an effort to bring about some psychodynamic change. For example, this may include changes in the caregiver's view of herself and how she perceives and experiences her infant. In this approach, it is assumed that once these psychoemotional changes are brought

about, the mother's interactions and relationship with her child will automatically be positive and facilitative. Other approaches may be less focused on a therapeutic relationship, but they continue to assume that providing emotional support and guidance for the caregiver will have positive effects on the infant (Krauss, 1997).

A second major category of caregiver-focused intervention programs are those that concentrate specifically on the training of caregiver-infant interaction strategies, often focusing particularly on communicative interaction. These approaches attempt to change or enhance caregivers' behaviors as they care for their infants or young children within the context of daily routines. This approach does not ask parents to be trainers, but rather to be responsive in particular ways to their infant's naturally occurring cues. (See Chapter 9 for a fuller discussion of the bases of these programs.)

It is readily apparent that selection of systems in which to deliver or receive services is a complex process requiring careful collaboration between parents and professionals. The more in tune professionals are with child and family needs, the more likely it is that appropriate recommendations will be made. One of the points emphasized in this review of the best practices for early intervention services is that interventionists must view all children within the context of their families and communities. The next chapter discusses the family-focused skills that enable the development of family-professional partnerships. It also discusses how families affect and are affected by children with special needs, and it offers a variety of involvement options for families.

Summary

This chapter offers historical perspectives on the evolving field of early childhood special education historically and theoretically. Over the past 100 years, the lot of children with special needs has shifted from "hide and forget" to "identify and help." Jean-Marc Itard, Maria Montessori, and Jean Piaget were a few of the most notable pioneers in this new field. Their contributions paved the way for the development of curricular adaptations to accommodate young children with special needs in a variety of settings.

Results of several research studies led to greater acceptance by the mid-1960s of the belief that intelligence develops rapidly in the primary years of life and that early stimulation can influence this development. Head Start began as a federally funded project in 1965 to provide enrichment opportunities for young children in impoverished families and was subsequently extended to include at least 10% of children with disabilities. Initial research indicated that the immediate educational gains for Head Start children quickly faded, but longitudinal studies have substantiated long-term persistence of this early intervention. Children between birth and 8 years of age who have disabilities were given a boost in 1968 through legislation that created the Handicapped Children's Early Education Program. The resulting model programs emphasized inclusion of parents in their child's educational activities.

P.L. 94–142 mandated that appropriate public education be made available to all children with disabilities as early as possible. One significant provision of this law is that each child should have a written IEP. Children with disabilities also are to be served in the least restrictive environment that meets their needs. The law mandates inclusion in a regular classroom unless the child's disabilities are too severe. In effect, the thrust is to fit the schooling to the child rather than fit the child to the school. Such an aim provides the major impetus of this book. This aim is pursued through informed selection of intervention strategies, with preparation of the interventionist as the critical foundation.

P.L. 99–457 initiated legitimization of the field of early childhood special education. Federal, state, and local planners are collaborating with parents in unprecedented efforts to develop new and expanded services for infants and young children who have disabilities or are at risk and their families. Part H provides incentives for states to provide comprehensive, coordinated family-focused interagency programs for children from birth through age 2. Unique to this law and following amendments are the requirements for collaborative service coordination designed to implement individualized family service plans (IFSPs).

Strategies for inclusion of children with special needs in the early education curriculum have had several theoretical origins. Current approaches to early childhood special education continue to combine influences from both the early education and special education fields. The child development and early education literature emphasizes the importance of child-directed methods that are developmentally appropriate and utilize play and social interaction as primary vehicles for teaching and learning. Special education legislation has mandated a focus on family involvement and education within integrated, community-based settings. Researchers have pointed out the importance of functional, ecologically relevant goals appropriate to both child and family priorities and needs.

Although they are by no means clearly defined, two major curricular approaches have emerged: a social-transactional approach and a functional-ecological approach. Fortunately, these two emphases are complementary. They are effectively combined in the operation of many programs. It will become evident that both approaches are also highly compatible with the philosophy of this textbook.

Finally, the field of early childhood special education is fortunate to be able to combine what researchers and practitioners have found to be the best practices of the two dynamic disciplines of early childhood education and special education. The evolving delivery systems offer a variety of opportunities to meet the unique needs of each child and his or her family.

Discussion Topics and Activities

1. Characterize the impact on an interventionist's behavior of the belief that a child's growth is determined primarily by heredity-nature or the belief that growth is determined primarily by the environment. What is your belief? How do or how will your beliefs influence your behavior as a teacher?

2. Choose at least six articles about childrearing or education that have appeared in leading popular magazines during the past year. Discuss these in light of the beliefs espoused. How can these beliefs influence behavior of parents and early interventionists? Do you see any relationship between these beliefs and historical developments? In what way might these be setting precedents?

3. Read the summary or complete report from Lazar and Darlington (1982). Discuss the full implications of the research results with class members. What aspects should be translated into classroom or center practice or program development and how?

4. Research one of the First Chance programs or any program funded through the Handicapped Children's Early Education Program. Send for liter-ature or visit a program, if possible. Share what you have learned with classmates.

5. Discuss specific criteria an evaluator might use to determine whether or not a program encompasses the best practices of effective intervention programs listed in this chapter.

6. Obtain and study copies of guidelines explaining state and local legislation.

7. Compare and contrast NAEYC best practices with the recommended practices of the Division for Early Childhood Education (DEC).

8. Become informed of the service delivery options available in your area. Role play a transdisciplinary team meeting to determine which would be the most appropriate options for children and families with differing needs.

Annotated Bibliography

Historical Perspectives on Early Childhood Special Education

Berrueta-Clement, J. R., Schweinhart, L. J., Barnett, W. S., Epstein, A. S., & Weikart, D. P. (1984). *Changed lives: The effects of the Perry Preschool Program on youths through age 19.* Ypsilanti, MI: High/Scope Press.

This most influential book details the results of 20 years of study of children who attended the Perry Preschool Project in the 1960s. The positive findings should be helpful in convincing legislators, school board members, and other concerned citizens of the societal benefits derived from high-quality early educational experiences.

Bowe, F. (1995). *Birth to five: Early childhood special education.* Albany, NY: Delmar Publishers.

Part I of this text introduces early childhood special education and discusses how it is different from the broader field of early childhood education. In doing so, it gives the historical and philosophical roots of early childhood special education. Part IV reviews the federal laws that authorize and fund programs for young children with special needs.

Gray, S. W., Klaus, R. A., & Ramsey, B. K. (1982). *From three to twenty: The early training project.* Baltimore: University Park Press.

Here is the summary of a unique longitudinal study of an early intervention project initiated prior to Head Start. This book is nicely organized and well written. It is based on a study with an excellent research design. The findings of this research are suggestive of the long-range motivational impact of early intervention.

Guralnick, M. J. (Ed.) (1997). *The effectiveness of early intervention.* Baltimore: Paul H. Brookes Publishing Co.

This beautifully edited book presents reviews that bring us up-to-date on what research has to say about the effectiveness of early intervention and shows us how far the field of intervention has progressed since the beginning of intervention efforts in the 1960s. While it focuses on what can be learned from the first generation of research conducted prior to the passe of PL 99–457 in 1986, it provides the context for the second generation of research. It establishes and agenda for scholars to focus on what interventions work best, for whom, under what conditions and for what purposes.

Jordan, J. B., Hayden, A. H., Karnes, M. B., & Wood, M. M. (Eds.). (1977). *Early childhood education for exceptional children.* Reston, VA: The Council for Exceptional Children.

This book focuses on the First Chance programs and presents exemplary practices in areas such as identification, recordkeeping, curriculum, physical environments, parent involvement, staffing patterns, and evaluation. Included is a directory of the BEH First Chance programs along with a list of standardized tests used by these programs. This is a valuable resource because it offers insight into the legislation that established the First Chance programs as well as providing an excellent overview of the contributions of these programs.

Lazar, I., & Darlington, R. (1982). Lasting effects of education: A report from the Consortium for Longitudinal Studies. *Monographs of the Society for Research in Child Development, 47* (Serial No. 195).

This report is the result of a collaborative effort of 12 research groups conducting longitudinal studies of low-income children who participated in experimental infant and preschool programs initiated in the 1960s. It is essential reading for anyone who doubts or wishes to secure evidence for the value of early childhood education.

Weber, E. (1984). *Ideas influencing early childhood education: A theoretical analysis.* New York: Teachers College Press.

This volume examines the ideas that have shaped the behavior of several generations of early childhood educators. Advanced students interested in the diversity, even turbulence, existing in the theory and practice of early childhood education will appreciate this book.

Intervention Programs and Strategies for the Inclusion of Young Children with Special Needs

Allen, K. E., & Schwartz, I. S. (1996). *The exceptional child: Inclusion in early childhood education.* Albany, NY: Delmar Publishers.

Here is a book that includes both the philosophy of inclusion and practical strategies about how to implement inclusive practices. It emphasizes the importance of facilitating good communication with families and utilizing developmentally appropriate practices.

Bredekamp, S. (Ed.). (1986). *Developmentally appropriate practice.* Washington, DC: National Association for the Education of Young Children.

This book contains clear statements describing what NAEYC considers to be developmentally appropriate practices or "best practices" in early childhood programs serving children from birth through age 8. The book can be obtained from NAEYC and is a "must" for any caregiver or teacher of young children.

Bredekamp, S., & Copple, C. (Eds.) (1997). *Developmentally appropriate practice in early childhood programs.* Washington DC: National Association for the Education of Young Children.

This book revises the 1987 edition of the NAEYC Developmentally Appropriate Practice. It explains more fully the principles underlying developmentally appropriate practice, the teacher's role, and guidelines for decision making. An overview of each stage of development in young children is given with extensive examples of appropriate and inappropriate practices for each age group.

Chandler, P. (1994). *A place for me: Including children with special needs in early care and education settings.* Washington, D.C.: National Association for the Education of Young Children.

This book gives teachers and caregivers sensible help designed to meet the challenges involved in making inclusion work. Content includes dealing with one's own feelings, preparing oneself and the physical environment, adaptation of regular activities, strategies for encouraging independence, working with parents and with other agencies.

Hanson, M. J., & Lynch, E. W. (1995). *Early intervention: Implementing child and family services for infants and toddlers who are at-risk or disabled.* Austin, TX: PRO-ED.

A reader-friendly text with a best/recommended practices approach to early intervention. Underlying the authors' recommendations for services is the philosophy of (a) a transactional model of child development; (b) a family-focused model; (c) a collaborative, community-based, transdisciplinary approach; (d) a continuum of services; and (e) an approach that is systematically planned and structured around achievement of specific goals.

Johnson, L. J., Gallagher, R. J., LaMontagne, M. J., Jordan, J, Gallagher, J. J., Hutinger, P. L., & Karnes, M. (Eds.). (1994). *Meeting early intervention challenges: Issues from birth to three.* Reston, VA: The Council for Exceptional Children.

Critical new approaches to service delivery and concrete strategies for policy application are detailed. This revised edition reveals how states have resolved questions concerning collaboration, competency issues, eligibility, evaluation, programmatic practices, parental involvement, and public policy.

Johnson, L. J., LaMontagne, M. J., Elgas, P. M., & Bauer, A. M. (1998). Early childhood education: Blending, theory, blending practice. Baltimore: Paul H. Brookes.

These authors describe how blending practices from early childhood education and early childhood special education can effectively create collaborative environments in which all young children thrive. Curriculum strategies are offered that will enhance children's participation by implementing developmentally and individually appropriate practices.

Meisels, S. J., & Shonkoff, J. P. (Eds.). (1990). *Handbook of early childhood intervention.* New York: Cambridge University Press.

Here is a handbook designed to integrate the theory, research, and practical knowledge that guide current practice in the field of early intervention. It summarizes and synthesizes the vast knowledge base arising across the many disciplines involved in early intervention services. This is an excellent resource for serious students who wish to become familiar with the substantial literature underpinning this new field of study.

Noonan, M. J., & McCormick, L. (1993). *Early intervention in natural environments.* Pacific Grove, CA: Brooks/Cole.

This is a practical book organized according to key concepts and functions. It offers guidelines for implementation of a naturalistic curriculum and describes numerous specialized methods. Students will find it to be an important addition to a text organized by traditional developmental domains.

Odom, S. L., & McLean, M. E. (Eds.) (1996). *Early intervention/ early childhood special education: Recommended Practices.* Austin, TX: PRO-ED.

The purpose of this book is to elaborate the recommended practices identified by the Division for Early Childhood (DEC) of the Council for Exceptional Children. It also describes support for these practices from the literature.

Peters, D., Neisworth, J. T., & Yawkey, T. D. (1985). *Early childhood education—From theory to practice.* Monterey, CA: Brooks/Cole.

This readable text places early childhood education within a historical and cultural context. It also provides an extensive presentation of operant behavior theory and cognitive-developmental theory, with classroom applications included for each model. This book is highly recommended for those who wish to understand just how to apply theory to daily practice.

Project Head Start. (1978). *Head Start, mainstreaming preschoolers series.* Washington, DC: U.S. Department of Health and Human Services, OHD—OCD.

This series of eight guides may be out of print, but it can be found in libraries and at Head Start centers. These are excellent resource guides. Looking for them is worth the effort. There is one for each traditional category of exceptionality. Although originally intended for teachers, parents, and volunteers who work in the Head Start program, anyone working with young children with disabilities will find this series to be extremely practical, well organized, and easy to understand.

Safford, P. L. (1989). *Integrated teaching in early childhood.* White Plains, NY: Longman.

The purpose of this text is to demonstrate a teaching philosophy that enables all teachers in public schools and preschools to respond effectively to the special needs of all children. It focuses on individualization, social interaction,

working with parents, and use of resources. Also included is a section on integrating young gifted children.

Shonkoff, J. P., Hauser-Cram, P., Krauss, M. W., & Upshur, C. C., (1992). Development of infants with disabilities and their families. *Monographs of the Society for Research in Child Development, 57* (6), Serial No. 230, 1–151.

This monograph reports the results of a prospective study of 190 infants with developmental disabilities or delays and their families. The study examined a number of child and family variables during the first year in which the family received early intervention services. The report described the tremendous complexity and variation in the nature of early intervention services, in the effects of various service components, and the interactions among outcome variables and family and child characteristics.

Thurman, S. K., & Widerstrom, A. H. (1990). *Infants and young children with special needs: A developmental and ecological approach.* Baltimore, MD: Paul H. Brookes.

Chapter 13 of this text discusses the models of early education based on delivery systems as well as the models based on philosophy. A fine array of example programs is described in sufficient detail. Readers can see how different approaches can provide necessary early educational experiences.

Udell, T., Peters, J. & Templeman, T. P. (1998). From philosophy to practice in inclusive early childhood programs. *Teaching exceptional children, 30*(3), 44–53.

This article seeks to look at both recommended practices from early childhood special education and best practices from early childhood education to find points of congruence. It offers practical suggestions on how to understand both sets of practices in order to merge practices into programs truly appropriate for all children being served.

Widerstrom, A. H., Mowder, B. A., & Sandall, S. R. (1991). *At-risk and handicapped newborns and infants.* Englewood Cliffs, NJ: Prentice Hall.

This book addresses the major issues and trends confronting early interventionists working with very young children and their families. Especially valuable is the chapter that outlines the determinants of risk in infancy.

Wolery, M. (1993). Relationship between general and special early childhood education. *Topics in Early Childhood Special Education. 13* (3), 1–393 (entire issue).

This journal issue includes several articles that consider differences and similarities in regular early childhood and early childhood special education philosophies and best practices, as well as considerations for combining the two fields in university personnel preparation programs. Also included are articles that describe successful programs and strategies for including children with disabilities in early childhood settings.

Societal Pressures: The Impact of Public Pressure and Legislation

Brown, W. (1994). *Early intervention regulation: Annotation and analysis.* Horsham, PA: LRP Publications.

This comprehensive reference book contains complete statutes, legislative history and regulations, with analysis, for Part H of the Individuals with Disabilities Education Act. It contains the reauthorization of Part H, sections on preschool and Head Start services, and discussion of new issues, including eligibility, natural environments, and assistive technology.

Division for Early Childhood. (1994). *New opportunities for collaboration: A policy and implementation resource training manual for the Head Start regulations for children with disabilities.* Reston, VA: The Council for Exceptional Children.

This is a technical assistance manual designed to assist local communities in the adoption of policies for promoting collaboration between Head Start and the public school programs for 3- to 5-year-olds. It includes transparency masters with highlights of the new Head Start regulations, a side-by-side analysis of the Head Start regulations and Part B regulations along with a listing of relevant resources.

Gallagher, J. J., Trohanis, P. L., & Clifford, R. M. (Eds.) (1989). *Policy Implementation and PL 99-457.* Baltimore, MD: Paul H. Brookes.

This resource text offers guidelines and action plans for assisting policy makers to move toward full compliance with P.L. 99-457. It is a helpful reference for those who wish to more fully understand lessons learned from P.L. 94-142 and the issues currently being considered as states move toward full implementation of P.L. 99-457.

Turnbull, H. R. & Turnbull, A. P. (1998). *Free appropriate public education.* Denver, CO: Love Publishing Co.

This extremely valuable resource covers the six principles of the Individuals with Disabilities Education Act as most recently enacted in 1997. These six principles include zero reject, nondiscriminatory evaluation, least restrictive environment, due process, appropriate education, and parent participation. It also discusses the early provisions of IDEA, providing an insight into historical developments.

References

Achenbach, T. M., Howell, C. T., Aoki, M. F., & Rauch, V. A. (1993). Nine-year outcome of the Vermont intervention program for low birth weight infants. *Pediatrics, 91,* 45-55.

Bailey, D., & Simeonsson, R. (1988). Home-based early intervention. In S. Odom & M. Karnes (Eds.), *Early intervention for infants and children with handicaps: An empirical base* (pp. 199-215). Baltimore: Paul H. Brookes.

Banet, B. A. (1979). A developmental approach for preschool children with special needs. In S. J. Meisels (Ed.), *Special education and development.* Baltimore: University Park Press.

Beller, E. K. (1979). Early intervention programs. In J.D. Osofsky (Ed.), *Handbook of infancy research.* New York: Wiley.

Bijou, S. W. (1977). Practical implications of an interactional model of child development. *Exceptional Children, 44,* 6-14.

Bloom, B. S. (1964). *Stability and change in human characteristics.* New York: Wiley.

Bredekamp, S. (1993). The relationship between early childhood education and early childhood special education: Healthy marriage or family feud? *Topics in Early Childhood Special Education 13*(3), 258-273.

Bredekamp, S., & Copple, C. (Eds.) (1997). *Developmentally appropriate practice in early childhood programs.* Washington, DC: National Association for the Education of Young Children.

Bricker, D. D. (1988). Commentary: The future of early childhood/special education. *Journal of the Division of Early Childhood, 12,* 276-278.

Bricker, D., & Veltman, M. (1990). Early intervention programs: Child-focused approaches. In S. Meisels & J. Shonkoff (Eds.), *Handbook of early childhood intervention* (pp. 373-399). New York: Cambridge University Press.

Brown v. Board of Education. 347 U.S. 483, 1954.

Bruder, M. B. (1997). The effectiveness of specific educational/developmental curricula for children with established disabilities. In M. J. Guralnick (Ed.), *The effectiveness of early intervention.* (pp. 523-548). Baltimore: Paul H. Brookes.

Buysse, V., & Wesley, P. W. (1993). The identity crisis in early childhood special education: A call for professional role clarification. *Topics in Early Childhood Special Education, 13,* 418-429.

Caldwell, B. M. (1973). The importance of beginning early. In J. B. Jordan & R. F. Dailey (Eds.), *Not all little wagons are red: The exceptional child's early years.* Reston, VA: The Council for Exceptional Children.

Carta, J. J., Atwater, J. B., Schwartz, I. S., & McConnell, S. R. (1993). A reaction to Johnson and McChesney Johnson. *Topics in Early Childhood Special Education, 13,* 243-254.

Casto, G., & White, K. R. (1993). Longitudinal studies of alternative types of early intervention: Rationale and design. *Early Education and Development, 4,* 224-237.

Crnic, K., & Stormshak, E. (1997). The effectiveness of providing social support for families of children at risk. In M. J. Guralnick (Ed). *The effectiveness of early intervention* (pp. 209-226). Baltimore: Paul H. Brookes.

DEC Task force on Recommended Practices. (1993). *DEC Recommended Practices: Indicators of quality in programs for infants and young children with special needs and their families.* Reston, VA: The Council for Exceptional Children.

Dunn, L. M. (1968). Special education for the mildly retarded—Is much of it justifiable? *Exceptional Children, 35,* 5-22.

Farran, D. C. (1990). Effects of intervention with disadvantaged and disabled children: A decade review. In S. J. Meisels & J. P. Shonkoff (Eds.), *Handbook of early childhood intervention* (pp. 501-539). New York: Cambridge University Press.

Fewell, R., & Wheeden, C. A. (1998). A pilot study of intervention with adolescent mothers and their children: A preliminary examination of child outcomes. *Topics in Early Childhood Special Education, 18*(1), 18-25.

Foley, G. M. & Hochman, J. D. (1997/98). Programs, parents and practitioners: Perspectives on integrating early intervention and mental health. *Zero to Three, 18* (3), 13-18.

Furth, H. (1970). *Piaget for teachers.* Englewood Cliffs, NJ: Prentice-Hall.

Gotts, E. E. (1973). Headstart research, development and evaluation. In J. L. Frost (Ed.), *Revisiting early childhood education.* New York: Holt, Rinehart & Winston.

Greenspan, S. I., & Weider, S. (1998) *The child with special needs: Encouraging intellectual and emotional growth.* Reading, MA: Addison-Wesley.

Guess, D., & Noonan, M. J. (1982). Curricula and instructional procedures for severely handicapped students. *Focus on Exceptional Children, 14,* 1-12.

Guralnick, M. J. (1997). *The effectiveness of early intervention.* Baltimore: Paul H. Brookes.

Hebbeler, K. M., Smith, B. J., & Black, T. L. (1991). Federal early childhood special education policy: A model for the improvement of services for children with disabilities. *Exceptional Children, 58,* 104-111.

Hunt, J. M. (1961). *Intelligence and experience.* New York: Ronald.

The Infant Health and Development Program. (1990). Enhancing the outcomes of low-birth-weight, premature infants. *Journal of the American Medical Association, 263*(22), 3035-3042.

Itard, J. M. G. (1962). *The wild boy of Aveyron.* New York: Appleton-Century-Crofts.

Johnson, J. E., & Johnson, K. M. (1992). Clarifying the developmental perspective in response to Carta, Schwartz, Atwater, & McConnell. *Topics in Early Childhood Special Education, 12,* 439-457.

Karnes, M. B., & Zehrbach, R. R. (1977). Alternative models for delivering services to young handicapped children. In J. B. Jordan, A. H. Hayden, M. B. Karnes & M. M. Wood, (Eds.), *Early childhood education for exceptional children.* Reston, VA: The Council for Exceptional Children.

Kirk, S. (1958). *Early education of the mentally retarded.* Urbana, IL: University of Illinois Press.

Krauss, M. W. (1997). Two generations of family research in early intervention. In M. J. Guralnick (Ed.) *The effectiveness of early intervention* (pp. 611-624). Baltimore: Paul H. Brookes.

Lally, J. R., Torres, Y. L., & Phelps, M. C. (1994). Caring for infants and toddlers in groups: Necessary considerations for emotional, social, and cognitive development. *Zero to Three, 14,* 1-8.

Lazar, I., & Darlington, R. (1979). *Lasting effects after preschool.* (OHDS 79-30179). Washington, DC: Administration for Children, Youth and Families, Office of Human Development Services.

Lazar, I., & Darlington, R. (1982). Lasting effects of early education: A report from the Consortium for Longitudinal Studies. *Monographs of the Society for Research in Child Development, 47* (Serial No. 195).

Lynch, E. (1990, April 16). *Best practice continua for children who are at-risk or disabled and their families.* Paper presented at San Jose State University.

Lynch, E. W., & Hanson, M. (1998). *Developing cross-cultural competence.* Baltimore: Paul H. Brookes..

Mahoney, G., Boyce, G., Fewell, R. R., Spiker, D., & Wheeden, C. A. (1998). The relationship of parent-child interaction to the effectiveness of early intervention services for at-risk children and children with disabilities. *Topics in Early Childhood Special Education, 18*(1), 5-17.

Mahoney, G., & Bella, J. (in press). Family-centered outcomes: A field based study. *Topics in Early Childhood Special Education.*

Mahoney, G., & Powell, A. (1988). Modifying parent-child interaction: Enhancing the development of handicapped children. *Journal of Special Education, 22* (1), 82-96.

Meisels, S. J. (1985). The efficacy of early intervention: Why are we still asking the question? *Topics in Early Childhood Special Education, 5*(2), 1-11.

National Association for the Education of Young Children (NAEYC). (1986). Position statements on developmentally appropriate practice in early childhood programs. *Young Children, 41*, 3-29.

Peterson, N. (1987). *Early intervention for handicapped and at-risk children.* Denver, CO: Love..

Public Laws 85-926, 88-164, 90-538, 92-424, 93-380, 94-142, 95-568, 98-199, 99-457, 101-336, 101-476, 102-119, 105-17. Washington, DC: U.S. Government Printing Office.

Safford, P. L. (1989). *Integrated teaching in early childhood.* New York: Longman Inc.

Sameroff, A. J. & Fiese, B. H. (1990). Transactional regulation and early intervention. In S. J. Meisels & J. P. Shonkoff (Eds.), *Handbook of early childhood intervention* (pp. 119-145). New York: Cambright University Press.

Schweinhart, L. J., & Weikart, D. P. (1988). The High/Scope Perry Preschool Program. In R. H. Price, E. L. Cowen, R. P. Lorion, & J. R. Mc-Kay, (Eds.), *14 ounces of prevention* (pp. 53-65). Washington, DC: American Psychological Association.

Shearer, D. E., & Shearer, M. S. (1976). The Portage Project: A model for early childhood intervention. In T. D. Tjossem (Ed.), *Intervention strategies for high risk infants and young children.* Baltimore: University Park Press.

Shonkoff, J. P., Hauser-Cram, P., Krauss, M. W., & Upshur, C. C. (1988). Early intervention efficacy research: What have we learned and where do we go from here? *Topics in Early Childhood Special Education, 8*(1), 81-93.

Skeels, H. (1942). A study of the effects of differential stimulation on mentally retarded children: A follow-up study. *American Journal of Mental Deficiency, 46*, 340-350.

Skeels, H. (1966). Adult status of children with contrasting early life experiences. *Monographs of the Society for Research in Child Development, 32*(2).

Skeels, H., & Dye, H. A. (1939). A study of the effects of differential stimulation on mentally retarded children. *Proceedings of the American Association on Mental Deficiency, 44*, 114-136.

Swan, W. (1981). Programs for handicapped infants and their families supported by the office of special education. *The Communicator, 7*(2), 1-15.

Udell, T., Peters, J., & Templeman, T. P. (1998). From philosophy to practice in inclusive early childhood programs. *Teaching exceptional children, 30*(3), 44-49.

Westinghouse Learning Corporation, Ohio University. (1969). *The impact of Head Start: An evaluation of the Head Start experience on children's cognitive and affective development.* Washington, DC: Department of Health and Human Services.

Wolery, M., & Wilbers, J. S. (Eds.). (1994). Including children with special needs in early childhood programs. Washington, D.C.: National Association for the Education of Young Children.

Zigler, E. (1978). The effectiveness of Head Start: Another look. *Educational Psychologist, 13*, 71-77.

Chapter 3

In Partnership with Families

Key Concepts

- Early intervention specialists must learn effective ways of recognizing and helping to provide for the basic needs of families who exhibit individual styles of coping with disability.

- A child with special needs can only be understood within the context of his or her family.

- Families are best understood as dynamic social systems. Each comprises its own values, roles and functions, and life cycle.

- Successful intervention for children with special needs is dependent on the formation of true partnerships with those who serve as the child's caregivers.

- Early intervention professionals must be able to use a variety of communication and involvement strategies to meet the needs of individual families.

- Understanding the range of possible cultural differences among families and respecting those differences is essential to successful early intervention. Cultural stereotyping must be avoided.

- ECSE professionals must acquire strategies for working with special populations of parents, such as those who have developmental disabilities or who are teen or foster parents.

Helping parents to understand that parent-child interaction may be the single best predictor of child outcome is clearly a responsibility of early intervention specialists. Collaboration with parents or other caregivers is essential to the development of families' awareness of the importance of their role in facilitating, guiding, and supporting their infants' development. With time and understanding, parents do become their child's best ally in interpreting his or her needs. The following parent perspective illustrates how time and professional concern helped to enable one parent to develop the coping skills needed to face the day-to-day realities of parenting a young child with special needs.

A Personal Perspective on Raising a Child with Developmental Problems*
by Lora Jerugim

My daughter Elisa is five years old. She is a developmentally delayed child whose delays range from mild to borderline and are of unknown etiology. I do not have any research findings to present. I have no statistics for you. But what I can share with you is something that I know a lot about—what it *feels* like to raise a child with developmental problems.

When Elisa was born, I was ecstatic. I had two sons, and I had dreamed about having a daughter. I had fantasies about who she would be and what we would share. Of course she would be completely articulate by the age of 2, and someday I would teach her to play the piano. And when she grew older we would recommend books to each other to read, and I had images of our whole family sitting at a table assembling a thousand-piece puzzle together. So much for the fantasy.

Elisa's birth was 5-6 weeks premature, but it was normal and no one suspected that there was anything wrong with her. So I took home what I thought was a perfectly normal baby. Elisa always seemed alert and responsive, but by the time she was 6 months old and was not able to roll over, I sensed that something was wrong. Like so many parents, I was encouraged to believe that Elisa would catch up, and I only wish that pediatricians could be as attuned to the signs of delay as parents are so that we would not lose so much precious time in getting help for our children. By the time Elisa was a year old, she couldn't sit up and was severely hypotonic. It was clear at that point that she was not developing normally, and we were finally referred to a developmental specialist. What was once like a dream come true had turned into a living nightmare. My first reaction was one of complete shock and disbelief. I would wake up in the morning and wonder if it was all just a bad dream. Certainly disabled children are born every day, but it couldn't be happening to me . . . not my child. I felt a sense of panic and helplessness as I waited for almost 2 months for the test results to come back. And when I learned that the results were negative, I felt relieved and yet confused. Elisa had no diagnosis and consequently no clear prognosis. I was told that she might have a brain dysfunction, but having a label to hold onto didn't seem to help much. We don't know what caused this dysfunction, and although I feel somehow responsible, I have nowhere to place my diffused sense of guilt. In a way I feel lucky that I do not know precisely what happened, because if I did I would probably run that moment over in my mind for the rest of my life wishing that I'd done something differently.

There are times when I feel such rage that this has happened to my child and to our whole family. I am angry with a world that is intolerant of people who are different—a society that is so focused on achievement that we often forget to look into a person's soul. I feel jealous and lonely as I listen to friends discuss whether their children are highly gifted or just gifted, while I'm praying that someday my daughter will be capable of leading an independent life. I feel so much pain as I watch Elisa at nursery school struggling to do things that younger children do with ease. I am exhausted because a special child requires twice the work to get half the distance. But most of all I live in fear of the unknown, because I don't know what limitations my daughter's handicap will impose on her, and I do not know how the world will respond to her being different.

Having a young child whose development is delayed but whose disability is not visible poses a number of special problems. These children seem to be caught somewhere between the normal world and the handicapped world. Normal toddler programs are not quite appropriate, and yet early intervention programs in the area are populated with children whose disabilities are more severe and/or visible. When Elisa entered her first intervention program at 20 months, I was traumatized. I wept on and off for weeks. I had never had any exposure to handicapped children and being in their presence was a painful reminder of life's incomprehensible injustices. I also realized that I wasn't just visiting the class. I was there because my daughter was handicapped and this was her school! But it was this same environment that fostered my denial of Elisa's problems. After all, Elisa looked so "normal" compared to most of the other children.

Attending parent groups often made me feel more depressed. I felt so guilty that I experienced such despair over Elisa's condition, when other parents envied me and thought my daughter seemed like a genius compared to their children. Furthermore, most of the children had been diagnosed at birth, and not only did a diagnosis help the parents face the reality of their situations, but they'd had so much more time to come to terms with their children's disabilities, while I felt as though I was just beginning. They also had special support groups and an abundance of literature to refer to dealing with their children's specific disabilities.

I also decided to place my daughter in a normal nursery school part time where she was the only handicapped child, and although my daughter, who is very competent socially, adjusted fairly well, I felt lonely, isolated, depressed, and at times embarrassed. During my daughter's first few weeks there, when I stayed with her to ease her separation, I had to leave the room on a few occasions when I began to cry. Being around all those normal 3-year-olds was a constant reminder of how verbal and adept little children are and how far behind Elisa was in her development.

Furthermore, when my sons were in nursery school, I became acquainted with the other parents primarily through my children playing after school with other children or being invited to birthday parties. Elisa is rarely invited to birthday parties, and she has been invited to play at another child's house twice in 2 years. I have made some attempts to invite children over, but I not only have to find an appropriate playmate, I also must determine if the parent is the type who would be receptive to having their child play with a child who is "slow."

There were times in the past when my feeling of isolation became so pervasive that I found myself wishing that somebody I knew, whether family or friend, would give birth to a disabled child just so that someone close to me would truly understand what I was experiencing and that I would no longer feel so alone. Then, of course, just the idea that I could entertain such a terrible thought made me feel the most unbearable guilt. For several years I felt as though I was riding a roller coaster in the dark. I could never see when the dips were coming, and when they did, I would be dropped into a depression that could last for weeks. Sometimes a stranger's question would be enough to do it, like the woman who asked me how old my daughter was and proceeded to ask me why she couldn't talk. If Elisa had been in a wheelchair, that woman would never have dared to ask me that question.

Parents of children with delays must endure many types of stress. We live with financial stress, and we worry about governmental budget cuts and changes in the laws protecting handicapped children. We are responsible for selecting schools and therapies, but when our children are receiving such a variety of services, how are we supposed to determine what's working and what's not? Often we do not know from one year to the next where our children will go to school, because we can't predict what their needs will be in a year, and we don't know what programs will be available. Even a class that is appropriate now may not be appropriate 6 months from now just because the population of children in the class may change so radically. We find ourselves battling with school districts and forever fighting against society's prejudicial attitudes towards the disabled. I've often wished that I could hire a full time advocate to deal with all these external stresses so that I could just focus my energies on raising my daughter.

There are constant family stresses as well, since one child requires more help and attention than the others. Resentments build up, and I find myself doing a perennial balancing act with my husband and children trying to make sure that everyone gets their fair share of me. All this is aggravated by the fact that when you have a delayed preschooler, what you really have on your hands is a child who seems to be stuck in the terrible two's. I'm sure any of you who have raised children will remember the nightmare of the terrible two's and how grateful you were that it only lasted a year. Try to imagine the shape our nerves are in after we've endured the terrible two's for 2 or 3 years and with no end in sight. Elisa is destructive without malintent and is forever testing us. She frequently spills her drinks, and the other day she tried to pour herself a bowl of cereal and poured cereal all over the floor. I sometimes wonder if she'll ever be fully toilet trained or if she will ever sleep through the night.

Testing is another source of stress for parents of delayed youngsters. Elisa's behavior and skills vary from day to day and often from one part of the day to another, so she is difficult to assess. Her most organized time of the day is usually the evening, and evaluations are generally done in the morning. Furthermore, her fine motor and language problems make assessment even more difficult. In one testing situation, she was asked to stack 1-inch cubes and was then scored in two areas: fine motor and cognitive. Her poor fine motor development prevented her from stacking more than a few blocks, so I asked the woman who was administering the test if she would try it again while steadying the tower for Elisa. Elisa then stacked all 10 blocks, and her cognitive score on that item jumped by 18 months! Sometimes Elisa can show where a puzzle piece should go but can't maneuver it into place. I often feel that the standard tests used are designed for normal children and, consequently, are inadequate for handicapped children. They certainly fail to pick up the qualitative changes that our children's abilities undergo over time. Professionals also need to be aware that the whole concept of testing triggers a special response in well-educated parents, because for us, perhaps on a subconscious level, poor performance is equated with failure.

Perhaps one of my areas of greatest frustration, anger and despair has been the area of diagnosis. How much more difficult it is to accept your child's handicap when you don't know what it is. I have received so many conflicting opinions about who Elisa is that I've stopped listening. I just don't care anymore about having a label for her, because the only appropriate label for my daughter is the one I gave her at birth: ELISA. One physician told me that I'd thoroughly confused Elisa's diagnosis by all the work I'd done with her. I remember thinking at the time that you can't teach a child anything they're not capable of learning. A psychologist labeled her mentally retarded, and 2 weeks later, I was told that according to test results from a research project, Elisa did *not* appear to be mentally retarded. I had another doctor tell me that Elisa would grow up and be able to feed herself and dress herself, while yet another doctor told me that we should have expectations of normalcy for Elisa and that she in turn would have those expectations for herself. He said that by working with disabled children for 30 years he knew by observing Elisa that she was not mentally retarded.

Looking at the child seemed more important to him in his assessment than simply looking at test scores. He also told me that she would grow up and be able to lead a normal life, that she would not be a Phi Beta Kappa, but that where she would fall in between no expert could ascertain. The level she would attain would depend on many variables that could not be measured, and that the most important of them would be her own motivation to succeed.

This particular doctor deserves special mention, because he is not only a skilled physician, he is a humanist as well. He still sees Elisa regularly, and I feel that the way he has related to us over the years could well serve as an example to everyone in the helping professions. He has treated us with sensitivity and respect and has valued our input, recognizing that we, as Elisa's parents, probably know her better than anyone else in the world. He has been honest with us and has freely admitted that he doesn't have all the answers. He has always looked at Elisa as a human being and not simply as a composite of her problems. He has made us aware of her strengths, and he has acknowledged our efforts in providing Elisa with the help that she needs. He always questions us about our whole family and reminds us of the importance of keeping our lives in balance. But the most important lesson to be learned from this man is that you must not take parents' hope away. Hope is what keeps us going, even if it's only the hope that things will be a little better than they are today. Without hope, we would stop fighting for our children and working so hard to provide the services they need. I believe that parents and professionals share the same goals for our disabled children. We want them to grow up to be independent, productive, and self-actualized human beings, so we must be sure that we are working together towards these goals, rather than in opposition.

A friend of mine shared a quote with me that says, "Thank you, God, for reminding me that thorns have roses," and with that thought in mind, I want to share with you the joy and growth I've experienced in raising Elisa, and not just the pain and frustration.

Elisa has taught me more about love and patience than anyone I have ever known, and she has drastically altered my perception of what matters in life. And as I have watched her development and lived with the uncertainty of not knowing when or even *if* she will acquire certain skills, I have come to appreciate my sons' normal growth in a way that I never could before. She has shown me that a "spoken word" and a simple "step" are among life's greatest gifts and that the miracle of normal development must never be taken for granted.

I have come to accept that my daughter will not be quite like everybody else when she grows up, but then who of us is? We are all unique individuals, and we should appreciate our differences rather than scorn them. We all have our strengths and weaknesses, and how many of us, even without disabilities, ever realize our full human potential?

I have struggled to redefine the meaning of joy in my life, and I have learned to live with sorrow and to move beyond it. I have discovered that life is very precious and that none of us has any guarantee of what the future will hold. Parenting Elisa has been a challenge for me, and I have found a strength within myself that I didn't know existed.

I've also become aware of the importance of seeing myself as a human being separate from mother and wife and of nurturing my own growth. And as I nourish myself, I find that I have just that much more to give. Elisa's education is in good hands, and I no longer want to be her teacher. I just want to be her mother and to teach her the things that I know about: appreciating life and being a caring human being. At the same time, she is teaching me, because Elisa has no prejudices and doesn't let her head get in the way of establishing human relationships. Instead, she seems to have a direct line to people's hearts.

I can honestly say that I love and accept my imperfectly perfect daughter for exactly who she is rather than for who she might have been. I hope that sharing my experiences will in some way help the professional community to be more sensitive to the needs of parents of delayed children and that we will be better able to work together to serve these children.

As this parent so clearly illustrates, all children do affect and are affected by their families. Conceptual contributions such as the transactional model of child development elaborated by Sameroff (1987) have played a significant role in helping early interventionists understand the continuous dynamic interactions of the child within the context of the family. When children with special needs began to receive early intervention services, parents were usually passive bystanders watching their children "receive" therapy or infant stimulation. Then, Public Law 94-142 formalized parents' participation in the educational planning process of school-age children. Parents were encouraged to become involved, but the nature of the involvement was not clearly delineated. Parents of young children with special needs often were trained to carry out therapeutic or instructional activities with their children. Although many found their role as "teachers" to be fulfilling, others became frustrated with these teaching expectations. Their lives were too demanding to cope with one more expectation.

Public Law 105-17 strengthen the recognition of families as integral partners in the early intervention process. The recognition of the family as a legitimate client in early intervention is spelled out in the formal requirements of family assessment, family outcomes, and family services within the regulations of P.L.105-17. Experiences provided for the child are not viewed as independent of the family. The family is seen as the essential component of the caregiving environment that influences and is influenced by the child over time, resulting in different outcomes for both the child and the family (Simeonsson & Bailey, 1990). To understand the reciprocal nature of the relationship between young children with special needs and their families, the family is viewed as a system with interacting subsystems. No family member is thought to function in isolation from other family members. Therefore, after reviewing some of the needs and emotions that appear to be characteristic of families with special needs, we will explore family dynamics from a **family systems perspective** (Turnbull & Turnbull, 1997).

EMOTIONAL NEEDS OF FAMILIES WITH CHILDREN WHO HAVE SPECIAL NEEDS

The majority of new parents start out with little or no preparation to meet the unique, ongoing challenges of caring for a newborn. Even experienced parents must readjust their style of living whenever another child is added to the family. The birth of any child brings adjustments within family systems. Parents of infants with special needs must deal not only with the usual adjustments of parenthood but also with additional stresses and concerns for which they are not likely to be prepared. Each change in their child's condition brings about new questions, concerns, and challenges.

Today there are many ways that parents can obtain help and emotional support. For example, they can join support and therapy groups composed of other parents of children with special needs. Participants offer support and encouragement to one another and exchange information about useful resources. Part C of Public Law 105–17 mandates that psychological and service coordination services be provided to families of children from birth to age 3 who may have developmental delays or be at risk for such delays. When emotionally supportive services are provided while children are very young, adjustments within family systems may be made more readily. However, it must be remembered that the emotional needs of families may be constantly changing, and the emotional and physical demands that accompany the advent of a child with special needs should never be underestimated. The following description of basic family needs and perceived emotional responses is offered to facilitate understanding of individual family reactions.

Indeed, the law requires professionals to specifically address the concerns and priorities of families through the Individualized Family Service Plans (discussed in Chapter 5). This requirement recognizes that it is difficult for families to have the time and energy necessary to address children's needs if the family's basic survival needs have not been met.

Basic Needs

Certain needs are basic to all parents who seek professional help. First, they want to be assured that they are receiving the best and most up-to-date information possible. They want to have confidence in those who profess to know how to help their child. Second, parents want to be recognized as caring, intelligent people. They need to be viewed as individuals capable of effective parenting, and they want to know that they are seen in this way. Third, they want and urgently need guidance in what to do in the immediate *now*. Although they want positive opinions about what the future holds, they need to have useful suggestions immediately.

Failure to Consider Basic Needs. Many of the emotional reactions attributed to families may be heightened by the failure of those to whom the families have turned for help to consider their basic needs. Professional mishandling of families' needs is a serious problem. Roos (1975) identified the following eight categories of mishandling that are still prevalent:

1. *Professional ignorance.* Professionals fail to recognize a disabling condition. They tend to predict either that the child will outgrow the problem or that the child's condition is hopeless.

2. *Professional hopelessness.* Professionals generate self-fulfilling and self-limiting prophecies. They convey defeatist or negative attitudes.

3. *Referral ad infinitum.* Perhaps because of a lack of expertise, some professionals refer parents from professional to professional. Although it is true that some parents shop around hoping for more-positive diagnoses, numerous occasions of unneeded referrals do occur.

4. *Veil of secrecy.* Despite the encouragement of federal legislation to include parents in making decisions involving their children, some medical and mental health professionals still attempt to withhold information necessary to effective decision making.

5. *Deaf ear syndrome.* Many parents still experience the frustration of having their requests ignored or their opinions seemingly unheard.

6. *Professional omniscience.* Whereas most parents can accept the honesty of a professional who readily admits that he or she does not have all of the answers, it is difficult for parents to cope with one who wishes to claim that he or she knows everything.

7. *Professional omnipotence.* Many parents still believe that only professionals have enough wisdom to determine what is best for a child. Adherence to existing legal requirements will ideally stop the practice of professionals informing parents *after* they have made important decisions about a child's educational program.

8. *Parents as patients.* As some professionals still continue to see the parents as having a problem (a child with disabilities); they have the tendency to confuse a need for information with a need for "therapy."

Even if early interventionists do not mishandle the needs of parents in any of these ways, they should realize that some parents may have experienced such treatment by someone. This realization will help interventionists to sustain the patience and understanding so necessary when working with parents who are anxious, angry, or troubled.

The Need for Emotional Support. Parents need emotional support. Assuming that parents are seen as partners by all of the professionals with whom they come into contact, parents' ability to cope effectively with their problems will influence what they do and how well they are able to do it.

Families continue to express the following six needs identified by Mori in 1983 as typical of families of young children with disabilities:

1. Need for self-esteem
2. Need to achieve self-confidence in parenting skills
3. Need to overcome feelings of isolation, depression, and ambivalence toward the child

4. Need to attend to their own needs and the needs of other family members
5. Need for the working mother to overcome guilt
6. Need to know what to expect from the child, the program of intervention, and the future. (pp. 211–213)

In order to assist parents in meeting these basic needs, professionals must learn to provide emotional support as well as educational programming or therapeutic intervention. Parents of young children with disabilities need to feel the warmth and caring support of people who understand.

PARENTAL REACTIONS

A number of writers, both parents and professionals, have described various phases of adjustment in parents' acceptance of their child and his or her disabling condition. Early on, Boyd (1950) discussed three levels of adaptation: the need to pull back and focus solely on one's own needs, a gradual turning toward the needs of one's immediate family, and a desire to aid others with similar problems. Writers later turned to the grieving process described by Kübler-Ross (1969; Zolko, 1991) for an understanding of the possible emotional reactions of some parents to the perceived "death" of a normal child. Anderegg, Vergason, and Smith (1992) involved 130 families in a study of the grief process. Their work produced a slightly different model that is in keeping with earlier work. This research suggests that family members pass through three phases of adjustment. These include (1) confrontation (denial, blame/guilt, shock); (2) adjustment (depression, anger, bargaining); and (3) adaptation (life-cycle changes, realistic planning, adjusting expectations).

Figure 3–1 illustrates a summary of the phases of emotional reactions that may be experienced by families with children who have special needs. It is important to remember, however, that parental reactions are unique. Some parents take issue with the whole concept of stages or phases of emotional adjustment (Blacher, 1984). Early interventionists

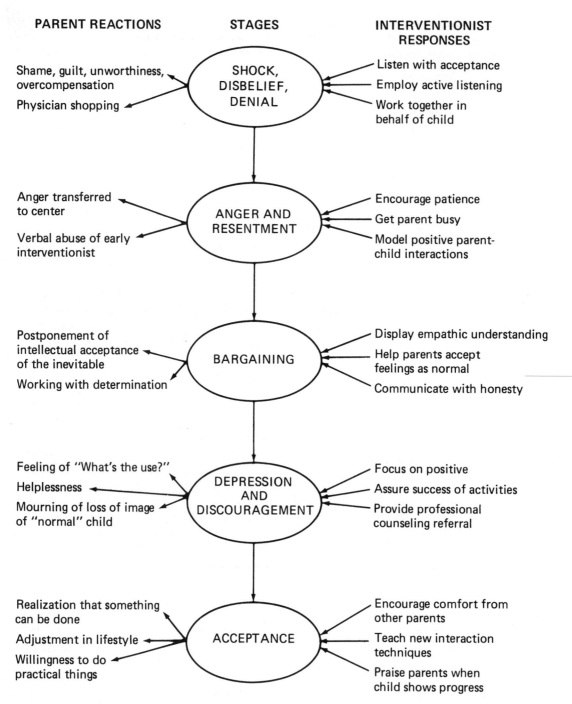

PARENT REACTIONS

Shame, guilt, unworthiness, overcompensation

Physician shopping

Anger transferred to center

Verbal abuse of early interventionist

Postponement of intellectual acceptance of the inevitable

Working with determination

Feeling of "What's the use?"

Helplessness

Mourning of loss of image of "normal" child

Realization that something can be done

Adjustment in lifestyle

Willingness to do practical things

STAGES

SHOCK, DISBELIEF, DENIAL

ANGER AND RESENTMENT

BARGAINING

DEPRESSION AND DISCOURAGEMENT

ACCEPTANCE

INTERVENTIONIST RESPONSES

Listen with acceptance

Employ active listening

Work together in behalf of child

Encourage patience

Get parent busy

Model positive parent-child interactions

Display empathic understanding

Help parents accept feelings as normal

Communicate with honesty

Focus on positive

Assure success of activities

Provide professional counseling referral

Encourage comfort from other parents

Teach new interaction techniques

Praise parents when child shows progress

Figure 3–1 Possible parental reactions.

must therefore apply the concept of stages cautiously, realizing that the sequence and completeness of each phase of adjustment may differ with each individual. Individual family members may differ from each other in developing an accepting attitude. Some may never fully accept their child and his or her condition. It is the professional's responsibility to assist families to cope with the demands of their reality.

Shock, Disbelief, and Denial

Parents and professionals alike describe the first stage of parental reaction as one of shock and disbelief upon learning of a child's disability or disfigurement. This shock and possible disbelief may be accompanied by feelings of shame, guilt, and unworthiness. As the reality of the child's condition is slowly assimilated, parents may try to deny the existing problems. Often, first attempts to find out what is wrong are really attempts to find someone who will say that nothing is wrong. For this reason, some parents go from doctor to doctor and from clinic to clinic seeking opinions. Some parents do this, however, because each professional recommends that they seek additional opinions. Diagnosis of problems in young children is far from an exact science. Rather, it is a piecing together of diverse observations, bits of information, and confusing evidence. Cause and effect interact to the point that it is difficult to decide which is which.

Some parents refuse to seek any guidance. They can be heard telling relatives and friends, "Oh, he's just like Uncle Joe. He didn't talk until he was 7," or "Aunt Susie never did learn how to do puzzles, and our Sally is just like her."

Moses (1987) summarized the role of denial in the parental grieving process as follows:

Denial buys the time needed to blunt the initial impact of the shattered dream, to discover the inner strengths needed to confront what has really happened, and to find the people and resources needed to deal with a crisis for which one could not be prepared. (p. 8)

Other parents may deprive the rest of their family while working diligently to prove diagnosticians wrong. They hope that intensive instruction will elim-

inate whatever developmental lag exists. But their nagging suspicions continue to grow. Unless parents can and will accept available guidance, precious time is lost. Fear that is allowed to grow undermines effective solutions to the simplest of problems.

Early Interventionists Can Help. The interventionist can help if he or she suspects that a parent is feeling fearful, guilty, or anxious while experiencing shock, disbelief, or denial. The parent needs help to understand that these feelings and experiences are appropriate. It is normal and acceptable for parents temporarily to blame, reject, or even hate the child or themselves. Professionals should listen with acceptance. Pushing parents to "face the child's limitations" will only create defensiveness. Professionals must learn to allow family members to grieve and feel their feelings. They must be allowed to remain in denial until they have the psychological resources to deal with reality. This is a time when families turn to professionals for support. Professionals must be nonjudgmental, active listeners while providing information and appropriate referral sources.

Interventionists must remember that anxiety creates problems, and that lack of knowing what to do creates anxiety. This is why parent-infant programs are needed. Initial fear and grief can be minimized if parents can be taught to do constructive things from the beginning. Energy is wasted by grief and anger. Energy used to play with children in positive ways minimizes grieving time. Professionals should take to heart the words of this parent: "Encourage me not to make every moment with my child a therapy session. She just needs loving and fun parenting sometimes" (Poyadue, 1998).

Anger and Resentment

When parents can no longer deny the existence of their child or his or her condition, they may feel anger, resentment, rage, or envy. Even though they may have accepted the child's problems intellectually, they may be so caught up in their emotions that they cannot focus on positive approaches to their concerns. They may even direct their anger at the very professionals who are trying to help the most. Suspicions about a professional's motives may explode in angry accusations. Other parents try to prove that the interventionist is "wrong." Verbal abuse is common. At this stage interventionists need to demonstrate true professionalism. They need to be understanding, compassionate, and gently caring.

Getting Parents Busy. The anger will pass, and it will pass more quickly if the parents are given appropriate activities to do with their children at which they absolutely cannot fail. This is not the time to try to make rapid progress with either children or their parents. Rather, the parents need to have constant reminders that they do indeed make a difference to their children. They must discover and rediscover that they have resources within themselves that they did not know were there. They must be provided with supports that match their individual needs. All of this must be done with a kindness that refuses to blame or to react to the unreasonable demands that accompany the grief of parents.

Bargaining

Some parents may try to resolve their anger and resentment by going through what Kübler-Ross (1969) described as a process of bargaining. It resembles an attempt to postpone complete intellectual and emotional acceptance of the inevitable. During this time, parents and other family members may work with great diligence and determination. It is as if they are saying "If I do everything you tell me to do, then surely this problem will go away." If progress is not as rapid or as great as they expect, bargaining is sometimes followed by the gray-black world of depression.

Empathy Is Essential. To be helpful, interventionists must display empathic understanding by accurately perceiving and accepting the natural feelings of the parents (Moses, 1992). Helping parents to realize that their feelings and states of mind are normal can convey an attitude of interest and caring. A simple statement reflecting active listening such as "It must be very frustrating and tiring to have to take your

child to so many medical appointments" shows an attempt to understand some of the stress being experienced by the family.

Depression and Discouragement

"What's the use?" and "Why bother?" can become the reaction of some parents to all suggestions. An oppressive weight of hopelessness can add new dimensions to the problems. It is very common for parents to feel totally powerless. For some, this very feeling of helplessness may make them more amenable to being helped. Because of feeling helpless, they may be more likely to ask for assistance. A parent of a child with disabilities, Poyadue (1998) described what she has learned about the need to grieve. "From personal experience, and from the hundreds of families I work with, I have learned that the grief is not so much, if at all, for the loss of the normal child, but rather for the loss of their plans, dreams and schemes for a normal family life, and for an old age free of child responsibilities" (p. 3).

Focus on the Positive. Professionals must focus on the positive and avoid adding to parents' depression by their own eagerness to get on with the task of teaching the child. During this time, activities must be planned for the parents in a way that ensures success. Interventionists must halt the growth of seeds of self-doubt about being a good parent. They should avoid all indirect and direct criticism. They must also avoid giving excessive, unwarranted praise, because parents interpret it as insincere. Instead, they must believe in the resilience of families and in their ability to solve problems. By doing so, they can help to empower families to handle the inevitable stresses they will face.

Parents who continue to suffer deep depression may need professional counseling. Interventionists should not hesitate to find some tactful way to suggest this. Often the simplest way is to listen carefully to the cry of "What's the use?" and then suggest that they may find help in many ways. Some parents will want and need the counsel of psychologists and psychiatrists. Others may find great comfort from other parents who have passed through depression and have moved on to practical solutions to their problems. An informal parent support group may help some parents find comfort from one another. Many might benefit from an opportunity to look through a carefully developed file of local resources, including churches, synagogues, mental health agencies, and parenting groups. All parents need to know someone cares.

Acceptance

Acceptance, the final stage in parents' emotional recognition of the need to modify their lives or their interactions with the child with disabilities, means parents have an increasing willingness to do practical, useful things. Acceptance means that today's needs are recognized, not denied. It means they have a willingness to learn and to apply new knowledge to meet day-to-day demands. It means they have a deep conviction that each human being is unique, special, and worthy of love and affection.

Acceptance should not mean that the disabling condition is accepted as unalterable. Rather parents accept the need to learn skillful ways to alter the negative effects of the condition. True acceptance includes the conviction that much needs to be done and that what is done will make a difference.

Consider this mother's definition of acceptance:

To me acceptance means finding whatever pleasure I can in caring for Benjamin day to day. It means looking at other children without always wishing that he were like them. It means looking at the situation not in terms of what Benjamin can do for me, but what I can do to enhance his potential. (Lepler, 1978, p. 33)

Encourage Patience. Interventionists must encourage patience when parents have begun to accept their children as they are, because most can achieve realistic expectations and give appropriate help. They will quickly and often eagerly learn new interaction techniques. There will be occasions, however, when they will feel stupid and confused. They must be helped to

understand that the disability they are dealing with is a new experience and they will need time to grow accustomed to it. Parents can be helped to learn to read their child's unique cues. Professionals must give the parents much praise for their child's progress and for the parents' participation. All parents feel better when they are able to see themselves as vital contributors to their child's progress. Parents who focus on positive interaction techniques will provide constructive options for mutually satisfying interactions.

A Father's Perspective

Commenting to a group of educators on his own experience as a father, Kirk (1979) stated,

If you help us to recognize the normality of our "abnormality," the appropriateness of our strange and sometimes frightening feelings, we will more quickly and smoothly graduate to acceptance. We need your nurturance and acceptance, your sharing of the commitment that has drawn you to this work. I believe that with you we can more fully realize that we can grow stronger and stand taller as a result of our pain and frustration—that we can mend our shattered egos and evolve into more sensitive, more tolerant and wiser parents. (p. 6).

Mending shattered egos may be particularly difficult for some fathers. "Fathers appear to be more affected by attributes that stigmatize the family's social and community image and are particularly affected by the birth of a handicapped son, often reacting in extremes of total involvement or total withdrawal" (Bristol & Gallagher, 1982, p. 146). Fathers (or mothers) whose daily life is oriented to the outside world may experience more stress when the child fails to conform to its norms. Such times as school entrance or soccer sign-up may create special crisis periods that can be extremely threatening to parental self-esteem.

Crisis Periods

Crisis periods can occur at any point from conception on through life. Parents often report that they "recycle" through the stages described earlier in this chapter. This is especially likely to occur at times of crisis. Some parents conceal these crises from professionals; others do not. Nevertheless, a supportive atmosphere that offers help and encourages adaptations can make a significant difference. Parents are comforted when they know someone understands their need to cry, yell, or scream.

Even though parents may have basically accepted their child and the disabling condition, adaptation may never be complete for some (Berry & Hardman, 1998). Parents report that tears come even as the child grows into adulthood. Sometimes a crisis brings out the incompleteness of a parent's adaptation. Interventionists can avoid judging or comparing parents' coping skills. The reassurance that someone who understands is available to listen may make the difference between a productive reaction to a crisis and a debilitating one. Professionals will remember that the emotional needs of families are as unique as the needs of the child. Reactions to the shattering of parental expectations and to the real concerns of daily care and worry about the future must be coped with adequately before parents can fully participate in whatever parent involvement opportunities are available.

THE FAMILY AS A SYSTEM

From a **family systems perspective,** the reciprocal nature of the relationship between young children with special needs and their families becomes clearer. No family member is seen to function in isolation from other family members. Any intervention with one family member is found to affect other members and interactions in the family (Hanson & Lynch, 1995). The needs of the child and of the parents or siblings are viewed within the context of the entire family as it functions within the larger societal system. Every family system is composed of subsystems. Turnbull and Turnbull (1997) described four such subsystems: The **marital subsystem** (parent-parent), the **parental subsystem** (parent-child), the **sibling subsystem** (child-child), and the **extrafamilial subsystem** (family-extrafamily). Of course, the actual makeup of families differs greatly. For example, single-parent families may have no marital subsystem.

However, a single-parent family may have more than one person exercising a parental role if extended family members are actively involved.

How a family member functions in one role in a subsystem is not predictive of how he or she will behave in another subsystem. Parents behave differently when interacting with one another than they do when interacting with their children. Whole families behave differently toward one another at home than they do when visiting with their neighbors. The advent of a child with disabilities has implications for all four subsystems. The special needs of the child may impose additional stress on the marital subsystem, while the extrafamilial subsystem is hardly affected. There may be no sibling subsystem if fear of giving birth to another child with special needs curtails future pregnancies. Alternatively, older siblings may be brought into the parental role to help alleviate the stress placed on either the marital or parental subsystem. Anything that happens in one subsystem has effects on all of the others.

The manner in which a child with special needs affects family members cannot be predicted or assumed, because families differ along many dimensions. Although it is not the role of early interventionists to intervene in family interactions, they can better understand and appreciate family dynamics by fostering an awareness of the entire family system. Professionals who look at each family in relation to its own interactional system and the manner in which these interactions are used as tools to fulfill the tasks of daily life will find it easier to provide services to meet the total needs of the family.

It is clear that the unique needs of families cannot be met by providing the same prescribed set of services for each family. When designing early intervention services, Turnbull, Summers, and Brotherson (1983) recommended adoption of the following four assumptions:

1. Each family is unique due to the infinite variations in membership characteristics, cultural and ideological styles.
2. The family is an interactional system whose component parts have constantly shifting boundaries and varying degrees of resistance to change.

3. Families have a variety of functions to fulfill for each member collectively and individually to aid their continued growth and development.

4. Families pass through developmental and nondevelopmental changes which produce varying amounts of stress affecting all members. (pp. 4–5)

Interventions planned from a family systems perspective will also carefully consider four major components described by Turnbull and Turnbull (1997). These include family resources, family interactions, family functions, and the family's life cycle. **Family resources** include the characteristics and strengths available to families to help them meet their needs. The effectiveness of early intervention may depend on the existence of productive interactions between the resources of professionals and the resources of families.

Family interactions are the processes families use to accomplish the "duties" of the family system. Families meet their needs through such processes as sharing affection, planning together, resolving conflicts, teaching new skills, and accomplishing daily tasks. **Family functions** are the outputs of the interactional system. These represent major areas of need such as economic, domestic/health care, recreation, socialization, self-identity, affection and educational/vocational (Turnbull & Turnbull, 1997). **Family life cycle** refers to the developmental and nondevelopmental changes that alter the family's structure and needs over time. Issues evolving at each stage in the family life cycle impact every member of the family. Barber, Turnbull, Behr, and Kerns (1988) offered possible issues encountered when the child with special needs is in the early childhood life cycle stage. These are illustrated in Table 3–1. Of course, it is not enough to support families during the early years. They must be helped to develop coping strategies that will help them avoid the burnout that can come from lifelong challenges.

SIBLING AND EXTENDED FAMILY NEEDS AND REACTIONS

As predicted from family systems theory, siblings and the extended family of the child also have needs and reactions. Grandparents grieve deeply, too. Theirs is often a double hurt because they not only experience pain for their grandchild, but they also grieve for their own children. Seeing a loved son or daughter try to cope with long-term problems is disheartening. One grandfather arrived at a diagnostic clinic with a blank check. "Just tell me what it costs," he said, "I'll find the money somehow."

Denial, blame, and anger may run rampant among grandparents. They may say "It's because she smoked while she was pregnant," or "His family never was any good," or "If only they hadn't. . . ." There is no doubt to whom the angry grandparents are referring.

Table 3–1 Possible issues encountered during the early childhood years

Life Cycle Stage	Parents	Siblings
Early childhood, ages 0–5	Obtaining an accurate diagnosis Informing siblings and relatives Locating services Seeking to find meaning in the exceptionality Clarifying a personal ideology to guide decision-making Addressing issues of stigma Identifying positive contributions of exceptionality	Less parental time and energy for sibling needs Feelings of jealousy over less attention Fears associated with misunderstandings of exceptionality

Source: Barber et al., p. 194.

Most grandparents and other close relatives, however, can be helped to provide needed moral, mental, and emotional support (Berry & Hardman, 1998). Often relatives are the major source of babysitting relief for parents. All of those who spend much time caring for a child with disabilities will find it helpful to be included in conferences and planning and teaching demonstrations. Often involved grandparents feel left out and deeply confused about what they should do. Professionals must be sensitive to this, and, with the parents' approval, include these extended family members.

Berry and Hardman (1998) discuss the changing needs of nondisabled siblings. For example, young children need to be reassured that they cannot catch their sibling's disability. School-age children need information to answer their own questions and those posed by peers about their sibling's disability. Teenagers and young adults need additional information about their sibling's future and the role they will play in that future. Bringing siblings "into the loop" through inclusion in meetings as valued members of the team benefits all members of the family.

Parents and professionals can help siblings cope with their needs. Another effective way is to provide siblings with opportunities to participate in working with their brother or sister with disabilities. Even very young children can learn to be effective teachers. In fact, young children who have just learned how to do something themselves may be superior teachers. It is imperative, however, that parents be sensitive in their requests of able-bodied siblings. In discussing sibling-related problems, Bowe (1995) warned that siblings who assume too much responsibility for the care of their sibling with disabilities can be forced prematurely into adult roles. Along these same lines, it is essential that parents refrain from expecting too much from siblings. Sometimes the siblings are expected to make up for what the son or daughter who has disabilities cannot do.

In his discussion of concerns and questions of siblings, Gargiulo (1985) cited the following list originally prepared by Cansler and Martin (1974):

1. Siblings wonder about the cause of their brother's or sister's handicap, and sometimes fear that something may be wrong with themselves.

2. Siblings sometimes feel that having to help take care of the handicapped child interferes with their own activities.
3. Siblings may want to talk with their parents about the handicapped child's problems but do not know how to bring up the subject.
4. Siblings may feel upset and angry when parents have to spend a lot of time with the handicapped child. Sometimes siblings try to get attention from the parents by acting like the handicapped child.
5. Some siblings feel that they have to work extra hard (in school, sports, etc.) to make up to the parent for the handicapped child's deficiencies.
6. Siblings worry about how to tell their friends that they have a retarded brother or sister and wonder if their friends will make fun of them or their family for being different.
7. Siblings wonder if they will be able to get married and have children.
8. Siblings may worry about whether they will have to take care of the handicapped child in the future; they may wonder if they will be able to take care of him or her if anything happened to their parents.
9. Siblings may want to know how they can get along better with their handicapped brother or sister—how to help him/her learn to do things, how to play with him/her, what to do when babysitting. (p. viii)

In reviewing the effects of children with disabilities on their siblings, Gallagher and Powell (1989) reported that able-bodied older siblings tended to be kinder when their younger siblings had disabilities than when younger siblings did not have special needs. Similarly, sibling interactions, in general, were rated as more positive when at least one child had disabilities.

One should never assume that parents are unaware of the impact of a disabled sibling on brothers and sisters. Professionals need to listen carefully and take the time to learn about the needs of the whole family; not just the child with special needs and his or her parents. Think about the words of a parent: "Let me talk about my child's siblings. They need time and attention and praise too. Especially when they are present, I like to and need to say nice things about them. Believe it or not, this helps them accept my delayed child. They get more involved with him that way, and that helps him" (Poyadue, 1998).

Regardless of the age or the relationship of the extended family members, the interventionist must be tactful, open, and honest. The parents' feelings and attitudes must always be given careful consideration and top priority. Everyone in the family interacts in some way with everyone else. Insofar as the interventionist can influence these interactions in positive ways, the children will gain. Having faith that one can be a positive help to a child with special needs buoys young siblings and mature grandparents. Specific tasks at which success is guaranteed are the place to begin. Then everyone benefits.

CAREGIVERS AS TEAM MEMBERS

Professionals have become more aware that caregivers play an important role not only in providing an emotional support system for the developing child but also as contributing team members in educating and instructing their child in classes and at home. However, some parents of young children with special needs feel that often too much emphasis is placed on the parent as teacher. To avoid creating additional stress, professionals should try not to overwhelm the parents as they become involved in their child's education.

In helping caregivers understand the intervention needs of their children, those who evaluate children's skills and developmental levels are expected to communicate the results of their testing to caregivers meaningfully. If caregivers are to become contributing team members, they first need to understand what the professionals are talking about. This means that information must not be given in professional jargon. Professionals can translate test results and implications into layman's language. For example, telling parents that their child may have a "visual perceptual problem" is meaningless to many of them. But parents can grasp their child's problem readily when the interventionist describes tasks using the eyes and the hands at the same time, such as buttoning, eating, doing puzzles, or stacking blocks. The caregiver's role in child assessment will be discussed further in Chapter 4.

P.L. 105–17 provides a legal mandate to ensure that in all stages of planning and implementation of services, caregivers are an integral part of the early intervention team.

Children with Disabilities and Children Without: More Alike Than Different

Success in working with children with special needs often depends on the realization that children with special needs and children without are more alike than different. Early interventionists can help parents understand that all children exhibit frustrations, misbehave, and refuse to cooperate at times. Parents of a child with a mild disability often interpret every childish antic as a symptom of some serious problem. Minor infractions of parental rules are seen as major catastrophes. All children, however, behave unpredictably. Most of them learn to manipulate their parents well before they are 2 years old. This comes as a genuine surprise to many parents. Even in the presence of overwhelming evidence, it is difficult for some adults to believe that such little ones are astute observers and efficient managers of parents.

Normally developing children experience many traumas, fears, and aggravations as they learn and grow. Alert parents and professionals seek to allow reasonable challenges. They try to prevent overwhelming demands on young children whenever possible. One "exceptional" parent summed up the need to accept the challenges presented by a developing child as follows:

A handicapped child takes just the same knowledge and love that a normal child takes, but you have to learn to accept that child for what he is. And if he can't walk, then he can't walk (Hodel, 1981).

OPTIONS FOR FAMILY PARTICIPATION

Just as children with special needs and nondisabled children are more alike than different, so are parents of children with special needs and parents of nondis-abled children more alike than different. They have needs, frustrations, hopes, fears, and dreams similar to those of any other parent, although they also have feelings that may be unique to parents of children with special needs. Even so, interventionists cannot expect to use the same method of working with all families, just as they cannot expect to use the same method of working with all children. According to Powell (1986), research indicates that "there is no convincing evidence that one particular program [of parent participation] is more effective than another" (p. 49). Powell went on to enumerate some of the reasons why an unstructured discussion group can be as effective as a highly structured behavioral group or why parent support groups can be as effective as parent education groups. As stated earlier, parents may be coming from different developmental stages and different circumstances. Parents' personality factors tend to influence participation. Some parents relate more readily to staff members, while others prefer to relate to other parents. Socioeconomic and ethnic background may determine response to differing program contents (Wayman, Lynch, & Hanson, 1991). Therefore, attempts must be made to match total family needs with available parent involvement opportunities (Shea & Bauer, 1991).

It is extremely important to remember that families should clearly feel that participation is, indeed, an *option*. Professionals must help families understand the continuum of services and opportunities from which they may make choices. Procedures for helping families identify their resources and needs, as well as appropriate participation, will be discussed in Chapter 5.

A Continuum

Even though P.L. 105–17 sets the stage for **family-focused or family-centered early intervention,** in reality family involvement will fall along a continuum. Some families may elect not to be involved in early intervention services, while others will seek the fullest possible involvement. Simeonsson and Bailey (1990) have outlined hierarchical levels of involvement ranging from electing not to be involved to ac-

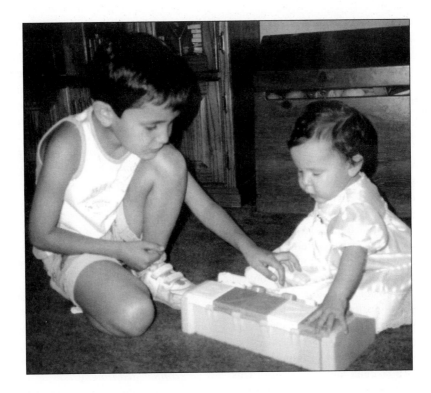

tive participation in decision making, program implementation, and advocacy activities. Each successive level illustrates an increase in the comprehensiveness of services and the family's desire for these services. Each higher level includes and extends services from the lower levels. Family needs, values, and lifestyles, as well as program characteristics, are likely to determine the level of family involvement. Early interventionists may be directly involved as therapists or teachers or they may only provide referral information. It is the intent of the individualized family service plan to clearly delineate the level of both family and professional involvement. *It is important for professionals to avoid implying that the degree of parent involvement is synonymous with parent concern. Parent involvement is certainly not a measure of parent concern.*

Individual needs and capabilities must be balanced with the goals of parent involvement. Some parents will have a greater need and capacity for cognitive information delivered through lectures, panel discussions, and films. Other parents may most desire and need one-to-one conversations with the professional when privacy is assured and they can feel comfortably accepted. Still other parents will thrive on being shown how to teach their child.

The remainder of this chapter focuses on the primary considerations to be thought through carefully in making each type of involvement effective. Unique needs are also discussed, along with helpful hints for the professionals who must work with these unique needs.

Home-Based Intervention Programs

Home-based intervention programs offer many advantages. Young children and parents are most natural at home. At home they do not have to develop the feeling of comfortable belonging; they do not have to be transported either by the parents or a school bus. Interventionists can take the home life into consideration when planning for the child.

Generally a teacher, nurse, therapist, or trained paraprofessional makes regularly scheduled visits (weekly or monthly) to offer educational services and sometimes social and health services. Parents are encouraged and taught how to interact with their own children using household objects or materials. Integrating intervention activities into daily living obviates the necessity for planning special times for "lessons." For instance, the parent of a young child with cerebral palsy might integrate stretching exercises into diapering time or language activities during feeding.

At first some parents may feel uncomfortable having a professional in their homes. Tact, courtesy, and sensitivity can overcome this initial discomfort very quickly. The professional or trained paraprofessional becomes an anticipated visitor. Toys to share, ideas that work, and a sympathetic ear usually endear the home visitor to both parents and children.

The success of these visitations is highly dependent on the visitor's training and preparation. This section offers practical suggestions for effective home intervention and discusses important considerations when making home visits. Because only the most critical points are covered, readers are urged to consult the references for more in-depth consideration of home-based programs and resources available. Practical suggestions for the home visitation follow:

1. *Clearly communicate the purpose of your visit.*
2. *Take time to gain information on family life and daily schedules.* This knowledge gives insight into optimal times for home visits and functional activities.
3. *Be informal, but not too casual.* You are functioning as a professional.
4. *Be prepared.* Have materials, activity plans, and backup ideas ready. To interact more freely, try to avoid filling out forms. If writing is necessary, explain what you are doing and why.
5. *Be flexible.* If what was planned is inappropriate for any reason, change it at once. Also encourage parents to vary the activities to meet their needs, as well as the child's needs. Do not

plan too much for the parents to do. They have other responsibilities.

6. *Carry materials in a colorful container.* Briefcases look too much like a doctor's medical bag. Be sure to include an appealing game to play and a surprise that the child may keep. You might include a toy or game for siblings to use during the visit.
7. *Be ready to admire pet frogs, favorite toys, and other family treasures.* Take the time to know what the children and their parents are proud of and what they value most. Compliment the home in some way.
8. *Encourage parents to show or demonstrate how they interact with their child.* Show that their ideas are worthwhile. Express approval and admiration. Avoid direct criticism. Rather, suggest changes by saying something such as "Some of the time you will want to try _____," or "At school we notice that children seem to progress faster when _____."
9. *Be aware of family rituals and customs, for example, "tea time."*
10. *Avoid confrontations.* Even if parents insist that what has been suggested won't work or is not something they can or will do, the visitor must not argue or insist that parents should conform.
11. *Begin and end your visit on time.*
12. *Before you leave, schedule and discuss the next visit.* Review with the parents what you did today and what you will do during the next visit. Write out any suggestions for activities for parents to follow. Schedule the next visit and write the date and time on the activity plan form left with the parents. Assure them that they can reach you by telephone if they should have any questions or comments.
13. *Maintain confidentiality.* At all times remember that you are a professional. Whatever you observe in the parents' home and any judgments you make are not to be discussed in public. Families have a right to their privacy and their choice of living style. The effectiveness of visits may depend on your ability to be mature, objective, and professional.

EXHIBIT 3–1

Don't Let It Happen to You: Safety Tips for Home Visitors

Be Alert to High-Risk Situations

- Isolated areas, no telephone, dirt roads
- Different people in the home each week
- People loitering outside
- Dangerous dogs
- Families who often will not let you into the house or ask you to wait outside for a while before letting you in
- Individuals in the home appear to be under the influence of drugs
- Drug paraphernalia in the home
- Indications of drug traffic in the home
- Your instincts tell you "This is a high-risk situation"

Precautions to Prevent Problems

- Before going on a high-risk visit, let someone else know where you are going, when you are leaving, and when you expect to return (put this information in writing)
- Visit in pairs
- Make early morning appointments
- Avoid visits on days when welfare checks arrive
- Plan your route in advance
- Do not circle the block looking for the home (someone may think you are looking for drugs)
- Meet in a well-peopled place such as a popular restaurant
- Keep a cell phone within easy reach
- Do not carry a purse, wear jewelry, or take valuables with you
- Ask to be introduced to all people in the house
- Introduce yourself to apartment complex managers
- Research the area ahead of time—learn the gang colors of any existing gangs and do not wear them
- Do use cars marked as county or state vehicles
- Carry identification on your person
- Ask families about the safety of their neighborhoods
- Park in front of the home if at all possible
- Keep car doors locked and windows rolled up
- Do not hide an extra key anywhere in or on your car
- Be aware of avenues of escape
- Always stand to the side of the door when knocking
- ASSESS the situation before entering—give preliminary information outside—ask permission to enter—ASK WHO IS HOME (watch body language)
- Do not walk in when someone yells "come in"
- Make other plans to visit if anyone in the household appears to be under the influence of alcohol or drugs
- Position yourself where no one can come in behind you
- Avoid isolating yourself in a room without a second exit
- Project an air of authority—keep your eyes direct and scan the environment with your head up. Wear pants and flat shoes
- If there is an altercation outside—leave when you assess it is safe and ask someone from the house to accompany you

Important Considerations When Making Home Visits.   In addition to the preceding points, home interventionists should remember the following:

1. Always keep in mind the importance of directly modeling and explaining responsive interaction techniques while observing parent-child interactions across daily routines and activities.

2. Plan to *demonstrate* activities and strategies. Showing is more effective than merely telling or describing. Honor the concerns and priorities of families by asking them what they would like to work on. When choices are offered, parents' interests and time demands can be accommodated.

3. Sometimes an older child can be helpful. Teach brothers and sisters appropriate activities. Often they can participate with the parent and the child for whom the activity was planned. Including other children serves two purposes: They are usually excellent teachers, and including them can prevent jealousy and feelings of being left out.

4. Call attention to the importance of teaching at the child's level. It will come as a surprise to many parents that children learn little by failing. It is crucial to show parents how to develop activities at which their children can succeed. At first, home interventionists must be very explicit about the need to avoid activities that result in failure for the children. Showing parents how to prompt their children and then gradually reducing and fading the prompting is important. This strategy is basic to successful home intervention. Give the parents specific guidelines such as those noted in Exhibit 3–2.

5. Be nonjudgmental. Some parents will be embarrassed about their homes or will be afraid of criticism. It is important to be blind to the things that are not relevant to working with the children and to notice things parents are proud of, especially things that they have done for their children.

6. Refer to the child's individualized education program (IEP) or individualized family service plan (IFSP) regularly. Help parents to see how the home program relates to the goals and objectives on the IEP.

7. Help parents to develop behavior management skills. Many parents are concerned about their child's inappropriate behavior and attribute it to the disability. Usually the basis of the problem is not the disability itself, but rather not knowing how to communicate effectively with the child. If inappropriate behavior is reported at the supermarket, plan some intervention there. The interventionist's demonstration of effective controls can be immensely helpful to parents who are frightened and worried.

Directions for managing the behavior of young children should be explicit. The interventionist can give reasons for what is suggested in a manner and language that parents understand. Exhibit 3–3 shows how this is achieved. Role playing, with the parent taking the part of the child, will help parents master the needed management skills. Most important, the interventionist must explain that behavior is learned. Changing habits and behavior patterns may not be easy, and improvement may not be made overnight. Parents may be helped by talking about their problems with other parents who have successfully learned improved child management skills.

8. Never forget that parents know their children better than the professional does in some ways. Most parents are accurate observers of what their children do and do not do. But their interpretation of the observed behavior is often inappropriate. For example, a child who screams and has a tantrum when denied something that he or she wants may be described by the parents as "bad" or "just like Uncle Will." Usually children who behave in this way have been rewarded by receiving the things they want when they cry. This cause-and-effect relationship is not well understood by many parents. The professional cannot explain it in a 5-minute lecture!

Chapter 7 enumerates some of the ways early interventionists can help parents in this essential task. The goal is to assist parents in reinterpreting the behaviors they have called "bad" as something the children have learned and not something "in" them. By the interventionist's example and explanations, parents can learn to think about their children more constructively.

EXHIBIT 3–2

Activity Guidelines for Parents

1. *Be ready to praise.* Praise your child's efforts and successes. Use hugs, pats, smiles, and positive words readily.

2. *Correct with care.* When your child makes mistakes, do not tell him or her that he or she is wrong. Instead, gently show or tell him or her the preferred response. For example, if your child hands you a spoon instead of the requested fork, say, "You've handed me a spoon. Now hand me the fork," instead of "That's not a fork. I asked for the fork."

3. *Find an appropriate time and place.* Do not remove a child from an activity in which he or she is involved. Keep the activity short, from 5 to 15 minutes. Be certain your child is wide awake, not hungry or "keyed up." Prepare a place to work where the child is comfortable and not distracted by sound or sight.

4. *Do not use force.* Do not force your child to continue an activity. Attention spans vary with the child and with the activity. Treat your child with the same consideration you would give your friends. If your child senses that you are tense, angry, or critical, he or she will learn to dislike the activities.

5. *Be flexible.* Vary the activity and methods to fit the child's needs. If one approach does not work, try another. Some learn more quickly while being active; others prefer being more passive. Use as many senses as possible, especially if one or more of the senses is impaired.

6. *Speak clearly.* Don't talk too fast.

7. *Be prepared.* Assemble materials and prepare the working space in advance. Do not waste the child's attention on preparation activities. Consider taking the phone off the hook during the short activity period.

8. *Be enthusiastic.* Do not under any circumstances let your child feel that you are working with him or her because "you have to." If you do not feel like working with your child, he or she will feel your tension. Reschedule your activity. By selecting a rather consistent time each day, you will find it easier to manage your time. If you find you are not enjoying your involvement, talk this over with your child's teacher or other professional. An adjustment in the activities or the approach may bring greater enjoyment.

9. Playfulness and the expression of enjoyment are essential if children are to achieve their potential. Let the parents observe activities during which the interventionist is expressing these feelings. Be willing to play with children, enjoying the games they like. This is very effective interaction. Avoid being too serious.

10. Introduce parents to other parents who have similar interests and needs. Even if most of the intervention is done in the home, plan occasional get-togethers for parents who have similar needs and interests.

11. Be aware of cultural influences on parents' communication styles and locus of decision making. (See Wayman, Lynch, & Hanson, 1991.)

12. Communication with all caregivers is essential. In some cases, the early interventionist may plan activities in the home to supplement the child's *regular* preschool or day care center program. When this is the case, a system of reporting what is done can be very useful. Common goals and objectives are essential. Methods of communication include the following:

a. Phone calls to the child's regular early childhood teacher, usually brief, to report on what was accomplished and to suggest carryover activities.

b. Written goals and objectives, with copies given to parents and to the preschool or day care teachers.

c. A passport notebook with comments and observations made by all concerned. This passport

Directions to a Parent for Managing a Behavior Problem

Scene: It is time for Ms. McLynn's second home visit. Danny's mother has asked her to help with Danny's screaming. When things don't go exactly the way he wants, he just screams. The neighbors are complaining. Several of them call their children in when Danny comes out.

Mrs. Dickson: "Hello, Ms. McLynn. I'm so glad you could come again so soon."

Ms. McLynn: "Well, I try to go to all of my parents in turn. But if one asks me, I can always return more quickly. Now, let's think about Danny's screaming together. You remember, last week I emphasized that especially with these young children we must work as a team. Unless we are consistent in the way we discipline him at home and at school, he will be even more confused."

Mrs. D.: "Oh yes, I do understand that. That's why I asked you to come back. The morning I visited the classroom he didn't scream once. Here he screams several times every hour!"

Ms. McL.: "The first few days he screamed at school, too. My aides and I have a routine when this happens. Many children try to control us by screaming. One of us picks the child up with no comment, and carries him or her to a small room that has only one chair. Then, the adult puts the child down, shuts the door, picks up a book, and sits down. No matter how loud the noise is, the adult just reads. As soon as the noise stops, the adult says matter of factly, "If you are ready, we can go back to the room." Because of Danny's hearing problem, it helps to gesture toward the room, too. Nothing more is said. Sometimes children begin to scream again, so it's back to reading the book. As soon as the child is quiet, the statement is made again."

Mrs. D.: "How long does it take?"

Ms. McL.: "Some children need to return to the room two or three times in the first week. Rarely more often."

Mrs. D.: "Do you explain to them why?"

Ms. McL.: "Only very briefly. Usually something like 'We can't play if you scream in our room, so we go to our special place until you feel better.'"

Mrs. D.: "That's all?"

Ms. McL.: "That's all. Talking won't do it. Our consistent responses will. Whoever takes the child to the little room remains very quiet, never appears upset, and does not scold."

Mrs. D.: "And how do I do that?"

Ms. McL.: "The first time, do it on faith. After you see it work a few times, you will fully expect it to be effective. Danny will sense this. Remember, you are not punishing him. You are simply communicating that when he screams, he has to go to a certain place alone or with you until he is quiet."

Mrs. D.: "Then, I should stay with him, too?"

Ms. McL.: "Whatever you think is best. Some parents pick the children up and isolate them in a special place, often their own room. If you feel that is safe, it serves the same purpose. But never put him into a dark or dangerous place. Remember, you want to communicate just two things: (1) When you scream, you will never get what you want, and (2) When you scream, it bothers us, so you must be away from your friends until you are quiet."

Mrs. D.: "But how will he understand if he can't understand the words?"

Ms. McL.: "He screams because in the past it got him what he wanted. Now, he just has to learn that won't work anymore."

Mrs. D.: "Ok—Please, can I call you if it doesn't work?"

Ms. McL.: "Of course. I'll check back in 3 days."

notebook may travel with the child and be used by all who are responsible for care and teaching. An example of a page from such a passport notebook is illustrated in Figure 3–2. Shea and Bauer (1991) offered the following guidelines for writing notes in the passport:

1. Be brief. (Parents and teachers are busy.)
2. Be positive. (Parents know their child has problems and need not receive constant negative reminders.)
3. Be honest. (Don't say a child is doing fine if he or she is not. However, write noncommittal comments or request a face-to-face or telephone conference in place of negative notes.)
4. Be responsive. (If a parent or teacher asks for help, respond immediately.)
5. Be informal. (All participants are equals.)
6. Be consistent. (If the passport is the communication system of choice, use it consistently and expect the same from other participants.)
7. Avoid jargon. (Parents may not understand educational jargon, and even professionals may use jargon at cross-purposes.)
8. Be careful. (No one should project personal feelings or the frustrations of a bad day onto the child, parent, or teacher.) (p. 1181)

Parents in the Early Childhood Center

Involving parents in daily center activities can be useful in a variety of ways. The center staff is able to model preferred techniques of teaching specific skills and effective approaches to behavior management. Many parents will then be able to translate some of what they have observed into more useful interactions in the home environment. Parents with specific skills or talents such as in music or art can feel good about the contributions they can make to the center. Parents who accompany classes on field trips to familiar places such as the grocery store can observe and, ideally, generalize ways of using everyday activities to teach their child. Finally, many parents will feel that their child is more like other children than different from them. As they observe progress over time, they will feel encouraged and more hopeful. The first few times parents come to the center will be difficult for them and for their children. Some parents will feel compelled to direct and correct their own children constantly. They may be deeply distressed by every small infraction of

Dec. 10, Mrs. J. (Susan's mother):

Susan wouldn't eat her breakfast this morning. She didn't seem sick, just not hungry. Could you give her an early snack, please?

Dec 10, Ms. S. (Susan's teacher at daycare):
Susan _was_ hungry when she got here. Two glasses of juice and a piece of toast disappeared right away. And then she _asked_ to go "potty." We are making progress. No accidents today! Hooray.

Dec. 11, Mrs. J.:

Ms. R., Susan's home teacher, came yesterday afternoon. She suggested that we continue to work on teaching Susan the names of her clothes. I'm going to put her clothes on the bed, and then tell her to bring me each thing, one at a time. Could you help with this at school, please?

Dec. 11, Ms. S.:

We surely can. Susan brought me her boots and her tote bag when I asked her today. Progress is good.

Figure 3–2 A passport page used by the day-care teacher, parents, and the home interventionist. This page was chosen from notes written during the fourth month of center attendance. Susan is 3 years old and has been described as "developmentally delayed." She uses two-word "sentences" that are partially intelligible. She has frequent "accidents," wetting and soiling herself at home and at school.

the rules. Tears and tantrums are the outward signs of the distress of the children. Nervousness and apologizing for the child's "badness" may be the parents' reaction. With careful planning, the center staff can prevent or at least minimize most of these problems.

First Step: Parents Meet Other Parents. Before parents begin to observe or participate, they can benefit by meeting with "veteran" parents. Parents from previous years, whether or not their children are currently enrolled, can be called on to help. If these experienced parents assist with planning and presenting the program, it will be much more believable and useful to the new parents. The opportunity to talk with other parents who have been through the program is the best preparation for beginners.

Centers should plan the orientation program *with* parents, not *for* them. Parents themselves can plan the agenda, choosing items to be discussed and points to be emphasized. Both the nature of the community and the characteristics of the children will influence what needs to be done.

A letter of invitation from the parents who are planning the meeting is more effective than a letter from the center. One parent group sent handwritten notes to each new parent 1 week in advance. A follow-up phone call, including an offer to pick up the new parents, resulted in nearly 100% attendance.

Although traditionally mothers have come to school, fathers can be especially helpful. Having one father call another helps to make it seem less strange. Other family members should be included whenever practical.

Evening meetings are usually more convenient for parents. Parents who do shift work or who work at night, however, can be encouraged to come to the center during the day. Properly welcomed, parents have even been known to take a vacation day to attend.

The orientation meeting. For the orientation meeting, the chairperson should be a parent. If at all possible the program presenters should also be parents. Refreshments made by the children are best. Cookies are fun to make and decorate, and concen-

trated punch is easy to stir. A special touch is added by having the children snip the edges of construction paper or scribble pictures to make placemats.

During the first meeting, program presenters can suggest the advantages of parent participation in the center. This includes observation visits, conferences, meetings, and regular volunteer work in the center. Parents who are genuine believers in the value of their classroom participation communicate this effectively. A sign-up sheet for classroom involvement should be placed in a conspicuous place. First visits should be short—30 minutes to 1 hour is sufficient. It will surprise most parents that coming to the center as often as once a week is desirable. This may not be possible for some, but all parents should be encouraged to come at least once a month.

The center may present specific participation guidelines. An example of a letter used for this purpose is found in Exhibit 3–4. Some parent groups prefer to have a roundtable discussion, talking about each item of the guidelines. Other groups prefer films or videotapes.

Relaxing and getting acquainted. After the planned meeting, a social time provides the opportunity for the center staff to introduce parents to each other. Name tags, including the name of the child who attends the center, are helpful. Although staff members will want to greet each parent individually, they will also want to encourage parents to talk to each other. Professionals will need to be wise in sharing their time equally among parents. This is not the time for in-depth parent conferences. An announcement to this effect just before the social time begins may prevent problem discussions.

Follow-up. The day after the meeting a letter from the center thanking the parents who participated and pointing out how much was accomplished is necessary. If these are handwritten and mailed, instead of sent with the children, the effect is much greater. In addition to the notes, a summary of what happened should go home with each child. This summary should be sent to each family, whether or not

EXHIBIT 3–4

Sample Center Participation Guidelines

Dear Parents,

As you know, it is very important for you to come to our center regularly to help us in the classroom, and to learn more about working with your children at home. But some of you have told me that you felt a little uncomfortable—that you really were not sure what to do sometimes. So I asked one of our "experienced mothers," Laura, to jot down some guidelines that will help you feel more at ease. Laura and I talked about these guidelines and she helped me to understand how you feel. Both Laura and I hope you will suggest other things that will make your time at our center more useful and enjoyable. These suggestions are just a beginning. Here they are:

Guidelines for mothers (fathers, grandparents, and aunts, too)

1. *Don't panic.* The children are allowed to do *some* things at the center that they cannot do at home, or that they do not normally do at home (using scissors, putting things into the refrigerator, or helping another child).

2. *Don't get "up tight."* If your child "shows off" because you are there, that is perfectly normal, and nobody will blame you.

3. *Don't talk in front of the children (either at home or at school).* Even if you do not think they will understand, never talk about them when they can overhear.

4. *Take time. Try what the teacher suggests.* It might seem the teacher's way makes matters worse, and sometimes it will, at first. But time (lots of it) will make a difference. Ms. McLynn says that with our children we are not just working for this minute. We want them to learn how to use self-control and good judgment. And this takes experience with "logical consequences" of things they do.

5. *Learn the class rules.* Find out what is a "no-no" and what's all right. For example, Hot Wheels—no riding inside, but the balance toys are okay. Moving the kitchen stuff around is okay, just like we change the room arrangement at home sometimes. Yelling is a "no-no." (That is an "outside voice.") Putting stuff away after you use it is also a rule. But some of them have not learned that yet.

6. *Ask.* If you are not sure what to do, ask. If you do not know why the teacher does things her way, ask. And do not be afraid to say how you feel. She will listen. Sometimes she misses something that happens, and it helps if you clue her in. (Remember, do not let the children overhear.) If you have a problem with your child, ask to talk about it with the teacher. She will find a way to talk to you so your child will not overhear. It is also important to tell the teacher if you do not agree with what is happening. Find out why it is happening. The reason will probably make it feel better.

7. *Talk.* Talk to the teacher and the children in the regular way. Ms. McLynn wants you to have "conversations" with the children except during "circle time." These conversations help the children learn. Those words on the bulletin board behind her desk are the cues for words they are working on. Try to use them often while you are talking to the children. Don't try to make them say things "the right way." Conversations should be fun. They help to teach language. Speech lessons are at a separate time, unless Ms. McLynn says otherwise, because trying to make a child correct a speech sound can make things worse. The child may just stop talking to you.

8. *Play with your child and other children at playtime.* You will learn, just as they will. Remember, someone else will be playing with your child. It averages out.

9. *Don't feel silly or useless.* It is really important to be there. Cutting stuff, helping clean up, or just listening are all important. Lots of things are important for the children to learn before kindergarten.

10. *Have an open mind when the teachers correct your child.*

Courtesy Laura Bridgeman

they attended the meeting. The guidelines distributed at the meeting can also be sent home at this time. If at all possible, parents who attended the meeting should contact those who did not come. Knowing they were missed is important to many parents.

Parents as Observers. All parents will feel unsure at first, even if they hide their feelings well. They will wonder what their children will do and will expect the worst. Often their children will oblige. Center staff must strive to make parents feel comfortable and welcome, giving their children specific things to do to keep them from seeking attention in undesirable ways.

Interacting with their own child. The center should encourage parents to greet their own child and allow their own child to show them around. These social skills must be taught to many children. Initial awkwardness can yield quickly to confidence and security if the center staff sets the stage and does a bit of managing. Cues such as "Show Dad where we keep our big blocks. I'll bet he can build a tall tower," or "Show Mother where we keep the easel and the markers. I wonder if she knows how well you can draw," may be effective. Naturalness, friendliness, and a comfortable feeling for all should be the goal.

If the parents indicate that they would enjoy it, encourage them to play a game with their own child and one or two others. A demonstration by a center staff member starts the game, but then the professional should be busy with others to allow the parent the opportunity to develop his or her own style. The intent is to set the stage for parents and children to have a good time and feel at ease.

Keeping the visit short. The time schedule should be understood by everyone before the visit begins. Parents should be encouraged to vary the time of day they visit to create a more complete understanding of their child's involvement in the program.

Providing observation guidelines. Staff can help parents become astute observers by telling them what to look for. A short list of focus points might be helpful. For example, an interventionist may wish a parent of Danny, a child with a hearing disability, to observe his reaction to sound in the classroom. She could prepare the following short list:

1. What does Danny do when someone calls his name?
2. Does Danny act differently when I stand directly in front of him and speak to him than when he cannot see my face?
3. Does Danny respond to noises made behind him or anywhere out of sight?

Such a list of focus points makes it easier to discuss the observations with everyone focusing on the child's behavior rather than on more subjective aspects of the child, such as personality. An interventionist could prepare the following list to help the parent of Vicky, a child who is hyperactive, understand his or her concerns:

1. What was the first thing Vicky did? What was the second?
2. Approximately how long did Vicky stay with each activity?
3. Which activity held Vicky's attention the longest?

A sample of a parent observation form that helps to focus the parent's attention is presented in Exhibit 3-5.

Parents as Participants. In some centers, parents are encouraged to participate as aides. Chapter 11 is designed to assist professionals in making effective use of parent volunteers. When parents are able to participate only occasionally, the interest checklist also found in Chapter 11 may be helpful in motivating their involvement. Some parents will be willing to assist the professional in individual center activities. Such experiences provide excellent opportunities for the professional to model desired strategies for working with young children.

It is often helpful to ask parents to play a game or direct a small group activity. Children love repetition. If they have experienced the activity before, it will be easier for the parent to facilitate their involvement. The activity should be one that is useful for the

◆ ◆ ◆

EXHIBIT 3–5

Parent Observation Report

Date: _____

Who was involved in this experience? _____

What happened first?

Then what did the child do?

What did you do, or what did another adult caregiver do?

What were the results?

Do you think you or the other adult caregiver might have done something better? Why or why not?

---

parent's own child. Suggestions such as the following can be put in a parent handout and can be posted or distributed when parents choose to participate:

1. Plan for success for both the parents and the children.
2. Choose an activity that can be demonstrated easily. Provide a brief written description of the objective and procedures of the activity.
3. Keep the group small (two or three children).
4. Explain the purpose of the activity. Be specific.
5. Emphasize that learning should be fun even if it is also hard work.

6. Do not emphasize "winning." Little children just like to play. Winning and losing are artificial concepts and interfere with learning.
7. Select a game or activity parents can use at home. Most commercial games or lessons can be duplicated with things found in most homes. Whenever possible, choose an activity that will benefit the child and interest his or her parent.
8. Specifically explain how to manage children's errors and misbehaviors. Demonstrate and talk about various techniques. A mistake or "failure" is merely a clue to try another way.

Conferences with Parents

Individual conferences with parents can and should be one of the most effective methods of parent involvement. Inherent in this approach is flexibility. Either the parent or the professional can request the conference. It can be held at the center or at home at any convenient time as long as parents feel the comfort of privacy and confidentiality. The content varies with the needs of the parents, the child, and the professional. The professional can individualize the specific suggestions made and the level of language used. With conferences, parents who cannot read or understand written comments do not miss important information about their child's progress.

Effective conferences with families involve the development of the following important skills:

1. The ability to be culturally sensitive and develop rapport with all the family members.
2. The ability to obtain information without appearing to be intrusive.
3. The ability to understand what information the family needs and desires.
4. The ability to provide the desired information in everyday language.
5. The ability to collaboratively problem solve.
6. The ability to summarize, help identify new objectives, and make appropriate recommendations.

By being aware of the need to develop competence in these important behaviors, professionals who are new to the field can focus on developing habits conducive to successful conferencing.

Preparing for the Conference. The objectives for conferences should be planned with situational needs in mind. For some the objectives will be general, such as merely becoming acquainted and helping to assure the parents that their child is well cared for and progressing. Another conference may be requested by the parent or the professional because of a specific concern. For example, an interventionist may need to know whether Vicky is as inattentive and active at home as she is in the center. If he under-

stands her parents' attitudes and reactions, he may be able to work with her family in developing consistency between school and home. Of course, objectives will have to be flexible enough to accommodate the families' concerns and priorities as well.

The professional should be prepared to provide parents with adequate information. Consider the information gathered through the various observation techniques discussed in Chapter 4. Samples of the child's work, anecdotal records, tape recordings, logs, and assessment data should be readily available on request. Special care must be taken to discuss this information in layman's terms.

When conferences are initiated by professionals, personal invitations should be extended by telephone or through letters. A xeroxed note is not very personal. Whenever possible, parents should be given a choice of date and time. A quiet, uninterrupted setting must be prepared with comfortable, adult-size chairs. The professional should not be seated behind a desk because this puts a distance between him or her and the parent, who may already be tense. Offering a beverage can make the parent feel more relaxed. Babysitting may need to be arranged because the presence of children distracts the conversation and destroys the confidentiality necessary. Scouts and aides can help out by taking the child and siblings to the playground or to another room.

Beginning the Conference. Often the initial few minutes of a conference are the most uncomfortable and are perhaps the most critical in building the necessary rapport. Initial impressions can create defensiveness that gets in the way of objective thinking and the creation of a productive relationship. Greetings, a handshake, and thanking the parent for coming help the parent to see that the professional appreciates his or her effort in coming. To help the parent feel at ease, it is helpful to begin with nonemotional topics, although these must be brief because the parent is usually anxious to get to the purpose of the meeting.

A time limit for the conference should be made clear so that the parent will not feel rejected when it is necessary to close the conversation. A statement such as the following can establish the time limit of a conference and clarify the purpose of the meeting: "I am so happy, Ms. Jones, that you are able to share the next 15 minutes with me today. I have so much to tell you about Jamie's progress, and I want to hear how you feel about it."

If the parent has initiated the conference, the professional might say: "I am so glad, Ms. Dickson, that you felt free to request this conference. I will be free until 4:00 and am eager to know where you would like to begin." If the parent hesitates, the professional should try not to become tense. If the silence or apparent reluctance of the parent to speak seems to go on too long, the professional should then make a facilitating comment such as "It is sometimes hard to express what we are thinking or feeling." All the while the professional should try to show by body language that he or she cares, is ready to listen, and is not pushy.

Conducting the Conference. Once the purpose of the conference is clarified, the parent should be encouraged to talk if he or she has said very little. The professional can make a facilitating comment such as "I thought you might share some of your observations and concerns about Mary so that we might plan a way to work together to help her progress." The professional should then listen very carefully to whatever the parent says. Parents usually express their primary concerns at this time. The professional is also given a glimpse of the sophistication level of the parent and can gear his or her language to that level.

Listening carefully. Listening carefully is absolutely critical in the development of productive relationships with parents. Simpson (1996, p. 117) states: "Indeed, listening is the sine qua non of a healthy interpersonal relationship as well as the key to effective communication." He further acknowledges that listening is a difficult skill that takes effort to master. However, it is well known that the most effective means of establishing rapport is to show interest in others through attentive listening. Attentive listening not only encourages parents to express themselves but also demonstrates the professional's acceptance and concern. Simpson (1996) discussed the following six attending skills as basic to effective listening: (1) door-opening statements, (2) clarifying responses, (3) restatements or paraphrasing, (4) reflection, (5) silence, and (6) summarization.

Minimal encouragers to talk are expressions and nonverbal cues that let the speaker know you want to hear more of what he or she has to say. These are often referred to as *door-openers.* Typical of these are such comments as "un-huh," "yes," "that's interesting," and "hmmm." These can be useful in getting parents to continue talking, but they should not become overused or be used stereotypically. The professional should be certain not to interrupt the parent with these or other comments. Leaning somewhat forward is usually a sign of listening and trying to focus on what is being said.

Clarifying responses help the listener to understand the parent or family member when, for some reason, one is unable to follow what has been said. Responses such as "I'm not sure I understand exactly what you mean. Could you say that again." elicits clarification. Such responses encourage the speaker to elaborate and demonstrate the professional's interest and concern. They can also be used when the professional isn't sure the information he or she has given has been clearly understood. For example, one might ask: "What is your understanding of what you have been told?"

Paraphrasing occurs when the professional attempts to restate to the parent in revised form what he or she has said. This demonstrates that what the speaker said has been heard and gives the speaker the chance to clarify any misunderstanding the professional may have. Often parents are more able to absorb and understand their own thoughts and motivations when heard from another person. This process can also help secure agreement between what is being said and what is perceived. A professional might say, "If I understand correctly, you are afraid other children will not play with Sarah because she cannot talk clearly."

Reflection involves comments that let the parent know the professional has heard and understood what the parent is saying. It helps to focus the parent's comments by recognizing a specific comment. It is a cue to parents to elaborate on that specific idea, concept, or question. If the reflection also includes the *feeling* that is perceived, then the professional will be demonstrating *active listening.* Consider the following example of a partial reflection and a reflection involving feeling necessary to active listening (Valand, 1975):

Parent: "I had thought that when he began speech therapy, his talking would improve."
Teacher: "Would improve?" or "You're feeling pretty discouraged."

Exhibit 3-6, which depicts a home conference, illustrates the skills involved in effective communication.

Active listening allows the listener to show sensitivity to the feelings and emotions being expressed as well as the content. It legitimizes the speaker's feelings and communicates that the emotions being expressed are acceptable. Active listening is "a profound way to communicate a willingness to hear, to understand, and to have empathy with someone who is isolated and struggling to be heard" (Lichter, 1976, p. 68). Considering the emotional needs of parents of children with disabilities, it is well worth the time to invest the energy necessary to become a good active listener.

Silence can serve to facilitate listening. It allows the listening to concentrate on listening and observing nonverbal signals rather than talking. It may communicate a willingness to listen. Skillful use of silence periods can stimulate conversation and contribute to an effective listening environment (Simpson, 1996).

Questioning. Morgan (1977, p. 4) suggested using questions for only two purposes: (1) to obtain

◆ ◆ ◆

EXHIBIT 3–6

Dialogue: A Home Conference Between Parent and Teacher

Scene: Matt is a 4-year-old who has been described by his mother as "never still" and by his father as "all boy." In the last week, the mother reports that several of her favorite plants have crashed to the floor as Matt walked by. "He never does anything mean or on purpose," she said. He bumps into things and is surprised when adults complain or he breaks things.

It is time for Ms. McLynn's first home visit. Matt's mother, Ms. G., greets her at the door.

Ms. G.: "Hello. Matt has been so excited about your coming, and when he heard you knock, he hid under the bed!"

Ms. McL.: "Good to be here, Ms. G. At school Matt is so helpful. I can always count on Matt to see what needs doing and to do it. He seems to sense the other children's needs, as well as mine."

Ms. G.: "But he is so rough. And always breaking something. My neighbors say he is hyperactive."

Ms. McL.: "What does that mean to them?"

Ms. G.: "Oh, you know, never still. He just can't seem to be quiet for a minute."

Ms. McL.: "But he has been very quiet since I've been here."

Ms. G.: "He's still hiding under the bed. Oh, he can be quiet when *he* wants to be."

Ms. McL.: "So you feel he really does have control of how active he is?"

Ms. G.: "Yes, I guess so. But just tell him to sit still and he bounces all over the place."

Ms. McL.: "You feel he is too active."

Ms. G.: "Yes. And he won't listen when I tell him to sit still. That burns me up. "

Ms. McL.: "His constant moving annoys you."

Ms. G.: "You bet it does. What can I do to make him behave? I've tried spanking, but he forgets right away."

Ms. McL.: "From watching at school and with what you told me, I'd like to suggest that we both try something. Let's catch him being quiet and gentle."

Ms. G.: "When? How?"

Ms. McL.: "At school I'll keep a special paper on my desk. Every time he is quiet or gentle, I'll say something like, "Matt, I like the way you helped Missy with her coat. You were so gentle," or "Matt, you are doing a good job with that puzzle. You are so quiet that I can hear the birds singing outside." Then, I'll make a quick note—for example 9:03—Quiet and gentle. Helped Missy with coat. 9:10—Worked puzzle. Quiet 3 minutes."

Ms. G.: "Well, it can't hurt."

Ms. McL.: "I'll call you in 2 days to see how it's working." And 2 days later when Ms. McLynn called, she was not surprised that Ms. G. could report more quiet and gentle times than noisy ones. So could Ms. McLynn.

specifically needed information or clarification, and (2) to direct the parent's conversation when it runs astray. Questions such as "Can you tell me exactly what Susie did that bothered you so much?" help to focus the conversation and provide additional information. Such an open-ended question, which cannot be answered with a "yes" or "no," encourages a reluctant parent. On the other hand, a closed question, which can be answered with a "yes" or "no," helps to narrow the focus of a disorganized parent. Since professionals need to avoid interrogation, they should practice becoming skilled in using productive questions.

Recognizing and accepting parents' concerns. This chapter has been emphasizing the importance of a warm, caring attitude that conveys understanding. Of course, this attitude and the skills to convey it are absolutely essential for an effective parent conference. Professionals must expect parents to be reluctant at first. They must be given time to learn that the professional cares. Reflective listening is one way to let parents know that their concerns have been heard and understood. Another is by being prepared and honest. If parents ask a question and the professional does not know the answer, he or she should kindly say so. The early childhood interventionist is not a medical doctor or a psychotherapist and must not pretend otherwise by giving misleading information. He or she can and should be prepared to make appropriate referrals. A file or notebook listing names and telephone numbers of local agencies can be helpful. It is important not to be biased in referrals or to endorse anyone in particular. It is a good idea to obtain a list from the local special education regional office, school psychologist, social worker, nurse, or principal.

Describing childrens' progress. The professional should be organized and positive in describing children's progress, giving specific examples of a child's skills or behavior whenever possible. The professional should encourage parents to discuss individual points of progress and to ask questions and should not overwhelm them with information or use jargon. Evasiveness or "fortune telling" are to be avoided. The professional can only discuss what the child will be doing in the center, what the child has accomplished, and what might be expected in the immediate next step. He or she cannot predict how the child will be functioning next year or the year after.

Summarizing. At periodic intervals, the professional should offer summarizing statements that respond to both perceived content and affect. This allows family members to, once again, verify the accuracy of the professional's perceptions. A summarizing comment might be as follows: "Can we say, then, that you are feeling very uncomfortable with Shane's placement in the early intervention program as you don't understand just what he will get out of being there every day?" In addition to summarizing content and affect, the family should be asked if they have additional concerns. Reticent families may be more able to share emotionally laden concerns because of the rapport built in the earlier stages of the conference. Of course, the professional must have the time to listen if, indeed, additional concerns are solicited.

Closing the Conference. The professional has the primary responsibility for ending the conference in conformity with the time limit. Comments such as, "Given the few minutes we have left, could you explain. . . ?" or "It is about time to call it a day; do you have any additional questions?" are gentle reminders that the conference must come to an end. Arranging for future contacts ("Let's see, our next regularly scheduled meeting is . . .") and thanking parents for their time certainly helps to bring a conversation to a close. By standing or by closing the child's folder, it is easy to demonstrate that time is up. Finally, switching back to social conversation, the professional can lead the way to the door.

After the Conference. Professionals need to allow enough time between conferences to record what has occurred during the conference. This record retains vital information, documents the visit, and helps create continuity between meetings. Although occasional notes may be taken during the conference, extensive notetaking is unwise because it interferes with listening and often makes parents uncomfortable. Parents should be apprised of any notes that are taken and the purpose they will serve. Only information that can directly be used to improve the instruction of the child is worth recording.

Involving Parents in Group Meetings

In many communities, parent involvement is synonymous with group meetings. If parents are invited to attend scheduled group meetings, then the center has fulfilled its commitment to parent involvement. Little attention is given to whether or not the planned meetings meet the needs of those invited to participate. Such meetings are usually designed to provide educational information to relatively large groups of people. Professionals are invited to speak, films are shown, books are displayed, and refreshments are served. The level of vocabulary used may or may not be understood by the audience. Eager parents may be able to resolve their confusion only by taking advantage of the question-and-answer period. As a result, parents who manage to attend one meeting may not return for the next.

In a study attempting to identify factors that cause parents to avoid involvement, Stile, Cole, and Garner (1979) reported factors such as (a) meetings held at inconvenient times or in inconvenient locations, (b) parent participation in planning not encouraged, (c) programs not aimed at "social" needs of parents in addition to skill deficits of children, (d) parents not allowed to organize or run their own programs, and (e) parents threatened by professionals or by situations. While these factors were identified over 20 years ago, the same factors exist in many situations today.

To maximize the value of group meetings, professionals will need to keep these factors in mind. They should realize that group meetings will meet the needs of some, but not all, parents. Group meetings are often welcomed by parents who wish to meet and talk with other parents who have children with similar disabilities. Other parents attend primarily to seek the knowledge of the experts in the field. Some rather shy parents may enjoy not being the focus of attention, while other shy parents may be too inhibited to come in the first place. Whereas those parents who linger on are obviously enjoying the experience, some parents may feel awkward socializing or feel pressure to hurry home. Because of the great diversity of individual needs, meetings should provide a balance between educational concerns and social involvement. Not all parents can be expected to be equally involved in all activities. Professionals must observe carefully and try to plan activities that will meet the needs of all of the parents at least some of the time.

Rationale for Parent Education Groups. If parents of children with similar problems are brought together, a supportive climate can be developed for families to learn about and share feelings concerning their children with disabilities. Parent education groups also enhance the opportunity to provide par-

ents with knowledge in specific skill areas such as home-based teaching and child management. Alternative approaches to childrearing can be presented. Parents can more readily become acquainted with local community resources. Finally, professionals have an opportunity to get to know parents in a setting that can be more relaxed than the parents' home or the child's classroom. Figure 3–3 provides a sample of topics typical of programs designed for parents of young children.

Guidelines for Developing Successful Group Meetings. A review of the literature indicates that parents are increasingly requesting a true partnership in all aspects of the education of their children and themselves (Turnbull & Turnbull, 1997). Parents who feel they have a voice in selecting topics, speakers, times, dates, and hours of meetings are usually more actively involved. This is why the suggestion was made earlier to involve parents in developing the orientation meeting. Parents who help plan have a tendency to recruit other parents to attend to realize the fruits of their labors. Note that Figure 3–3 not only presents possible program topics but also illustrates one way to assess the interests of parents.

Frequency of meetings. Because large-group meetings should be only a part of the total parent involvement program, they should not be called too frequently. Parents cannot handle more than one such meeting a month. If small-group meetings involving parents with very similar needs have been developed to offer social and emotional support, more frequent meetings may be desirable. If these meetings are being organized by the parents with the professional acting as a consultant, the parents will probably create the needed flexibility for these more informal meetings.

Notification of meetings. Large-group meetings must be advertised at least 1 month in advance. Multiple media should be used. Written flyers or notes sent home with the children, telephone calls through a calling chain, newspaper articles, and cable television and local radio announcements will be

Dear Parents:

Listed below are a number of topics that can become the focus of one or more parent meetings. Because we would like to arrange meetings that will be helpful to you, we would appreciate your cooperation in filling out this questionnaire. Please indicate by checking the appropriate spaces below which meetings would interest you enough for you to take the time to join us. Your comments and opinions are really needed. Please complete this form today and return it with your child by Friday.

Sincerely,

Your Parent Planning Committee

	Yes	No	Maybe
1. How children grow and develop			
a. Learning to talk	[ ]	[ ]	[ ]
b. Learning to think	[ ]	[ ]	[ ]
c. Getting along with others	[ ]	[ ]	[ ]
2. Understanding my child's special needs			
a. A pediatrician's views	[ ]	[ ]	[ ]
b. A physical therapist helps	[ ]	[ ]	[ ]
c. Other: _____	[ ]	[ ]	[ ]
3. The importance of play			
a. Helping your child learn to play	[ ]	[ ]	[ ]
b. Choosing appropriate toys	[ ]	[ ]	[ ]
4. Living with your child			
a. Eating hassles	[ ]	[ ]	[ ]
b. Bedtime nuisances	[ ]	[ ]	[ ]
c. Toileting troubles	[ ]	[ ]	[ ]
d. The babysitter search	[ ]	[ ]	[ ]
e. Brothers and sisters	[ ]	[ ]	[ ]
f. Other: _____	[ ]	[ ]	[ ]
5. Nutrition	[ ]	[ ]	[ ]
6. Safety/first aid	[ ]	[ ]	[ ]
7. Community resources	[ ]	[ ]	[ ]
8. Helping my child behave	[ ]	[ ]	[ ]
9. Parent effectiveness training	[ ]	[ ]	[ ]

10. What we need the most is:

_____

_____

11. The best day(s) for meetings are:

_____ ____A.M. ____P.M.   _____ ____A.M. ____P.M.

Figure 3–3   Sample parent program topics (interest checklist).

necessary for maximum participation. Follow-up notices approximately 1 week before the meetings will be helpful. Of course, small-group meetings with the responsibility for planning rotated among the interested participants will not take such elaborate notification. Usually one telephone call to each participant is sufficient.

Content of meetings. The content of meetings is where the active participation of an advisory group of parents is critical. Parents know what they need and should be encouraged to express their needs. Besides a written needs assessment as illustrated in Figure 3-3, professionals can be alert to needs expressed during home visitations, parent conferences, or informal conversation. Speakers need to be dynamic and able to speak on a comprehensible and assimilable level. The best recommendations usually come from the parents. Whenever possible a speaker should be heard before his or her assistance with a parent group is requested. Films or videotapes should also be previewed ahead of time.

Child involvement. Involving children's work or the children themselves can lure the parents into attending. Parents will come to see their child in a presentation, their child's work displayed, or their child on a film or a videotape. One early childhood center that had difficulty getting parents to form an advisory group planned an Easter egg hunt for the children. While the children were hunting eggs with the supervision of aides, the director offered the parents refreshments and conducted a brief but successful orientation and organizational meeting.

Variety. The need for variety is an important factor. Not every meeting should focus on a very serious topic that calls for the complete attention of the parents. Humor and fun are a necessary part of the learning of many parents who must face serious problems every day. Each meeting should involve some socializing, and some meetings should be purely social. Some groups of parents will plan and enjoy an occasional potluck dinner involving just the parents or even whole families. Workdays can be a very productive means of fostering informal communication.

Some parents will feel much more comfortable in informal clothes, painting classroom furniture or making educational toys. Still other parents would gladly organize and conduct a garage sale with proceeds to benefit their children.

Child care and carpools. The need for child care and carpools is another important factor. Research has already indicated that parents of children with disabilities suffer from a lack of relief from physical demands and time constraints. It is irresponsible to expect such parents to use their limited babysitting resources to attend a parent meeting. The planning committee must arrange child care through local service clubs, high school students, or other volunteers. Carpools or other transportation arrangements may also increase the attendance at meetings. Such practical matters can be all important to parents who may already have more than they need in the way of problems.

Evaluation. Evaluation is of crucial importance. The atmosphere during group meetings of any size must reflect friendliness, caring, and relaxation. If staff members are tense, then parents will find themselves responding to this tension. Professional staff must be alert to activities that lessen tension, bring smiles to faces, generate questions, prompt people to lean toward action, and are talked about positively during the socializing period. Attendance itself is only one form of evaluation. Evaluation can be informal anecdotal records or logs focusing on the items just mentioned, or it can be formal written reactions by the parents. Formal evaluations should be kept to a minimum.

Parent Support Through Family Resource Centers

Professionals and parents involved in the planning phases of early intervention services are finding that parents' needs assessment survey results show a strong desire for increased emotional support and counseling. One of the most economical and effective ways to provide needed support is through the development of parent support groups. One example of an effective group is Parents Helping Parents, which is described in Exhibit 3–7. This program provides parent-run support groups for families with a variety of needs; it also has become a well-established model parent resource center. Not only should early interventionists become familiar with whatever groups may be available in their areas, but they should also be prepared to assist in the development of such groups if none is available.

WORKING WITH CULTURALLY DIVERSE FAMILIES

Maria Diaz, the early interventionist from Centro de Niños, is knocking on the door of the Ramirez family to do her weekly home visit with Elena, a 30-month-old girl with severe cerebral palsy. The family of seven (including grandmother) came to the United

---

◆ ◆ ◆

EXHIBIT 3–7

Parents Helping Parents, Inc.

In 1976, two mothers of children with Down syndrome co-founded Parents Helping Parents. With help from local agencies, PHP became incorporated and a United Way agency. Financial support is realized through individual donations, grant receipts from local foundations and corporations, memberships, and various fundraising projects. Until 1985, it was an all-volunteer agency.

PHP philosophy: The most important thing a child with disabilities needs is well-informed, emotionally balanced, caring, accepting, and assertive parents. Parents Helping Parents gives to kids with special needs what they need most—special parents.

PHP purpose: To help children with disabilities receive the care, services, education, love, hope, and acceptance they need to enable them to become all they can be, through direct services to their parents.

PHP desire: To collaborate with professionals committed enough to the benefits of peer support that they themselves call and make the referrals. Their devastated clients should not be left to follow through on a suggestion and/or brochure laid in their unsure hands.

Like many parent support groups, PHP started because:

1. Other parents had much vital information about available resources as well as about the disability being confronted.

2. Peer counseling, with its immediate credibility and empathy, was paramount to working through the grief/loss process and on to recovery.

3. Many professionals lacked adequate knowledge about community resources and also lacked sensitivity to the financial, social, and emotional problems faced by entire families.

4. There was no easy way for new parents to meet experienced parents. Such meetings were too important to be left to chance.

Services include visiting parents, family rap or guidance sessions, newsletters, telephone counseling, information packets, gifts to newborns with special needs, workshops for parents in the IEP process, peer counseling, a speakers bureau, symposiums, sibling fun days, and workshops for medical professionals in better ways of helping families cope with the advent of a child with special needs.

Parents Helping Parents distributes manuals to assist other groups in the development of similar programs throughout the world. Family groups include any kind of physical, mental, emotional, or learning disability due to birth defects, illnesses, accidents, and developmental delays. Divisions include parents of near drownings, preemies and intensive care nursery support parents, an information and support network for individuals with learning disabilities, and help for those who have experienced neonatal death.

Interested individuals may contact Mary Ellen Petersen, Executive Director, Parents Helping Parents, Suite #3041 Olcott Street, Santa Clara, California 95054. Telephone (408)727-5775 & (800)397-9827.

States from Mexico to obtain help for Elena. They are all currently living in a converted garage in a neighborhood known for gang activity, drugs, and high unemployment. As Maria waits for the door to open, she thinks of the risks in this area as well as the extensive number of concerns this family has. At this home visit Maria will help set up a corner chair for Elena to use so that she can sit on the floor and play with the other children. She will also listen to Mrs. Ramirez expressing disappointment at Elena's progress and the desire to seek services of a "curandera" (folk healer) rather than return to the hospital clinic. Mr. Ramirez is in agreement, but he is even more concerned about finding work.

Besides working with Elena at home and school, what is Maria's responsibility to this family? How do culture, values, language, and resources of the Ramirez family enter into the interactions between the family and Maria, other early intervention team members at Centro de Niños, and community agencies?

There are probably few early education programs in the United States at present that do not include families and children from diverse cultural and language groups. Over the past 15 years, thousands have arrived in the United States from Mexico and

Central America, Southeast Asia, and the Mideast. Hanson, Lynch, and Wayman (1990), in their discussion of demographics, indicated that 36% of infants born in the United States in 1984 were born to ethnolinguistically diverse families. It is estimated that by the year 2000, 38% of children in the United States under age 18 will be members of nonwhite, non-Anglo-European groups. In many parts of the country the percentages are even higher. Because of economic and cultural barriers to prenatal care and environmental support, it is reasonable to assume that a number of young children from these groups will need early intervention services. Thus the challenge for professionals working with young children, whether in early intervention for high-risk infants or in a migrant worker's day-care center, is to be responsive to individual family cultural and language difference.

All families assume the role of socializing children to become part of the larger community. An examination and understanding of the differences between "mainstream" values of communities and specific families within these communities are a critical part of the ecological approach to intervention (Vincent, Salisbury, Strain, McCormick, & Tessier, 1990). The role of early interventionists must include acknowledging different cultural perspectives and learning how to work effectively within the boundaries that are comfortable for the family, while increasing the family's understanding of and improving their ability to work within the larger mainstream culture.

Cultural Influences on Childrearing Practices

Insights into how parents view children and their upbringing are critical in developing working relationships with families. Beliefs about issues such as adult-child interactions, feeding, toileting, sleeping, and discipline will emerge as the early interventionist gathers information about the child and family. "Regardless of the developmental and functional goals that provide the cornerstones for early intervention, the cultural preferences of the families form the primary basis for program planning" (Hanson, Lynch, & Wayman, 1990, p. 118). In fact, having inappropriate cultural expectations for a child's family could create more problems than the child's actual disability.

It is important for early interventionists to understand that parents do the best they can within the context of their own values and beliefs and within the constraints of their resources. Norton (1990) states: "Human beings raise their children to fit into the society they know. Childrearing practices reflect what parents know about life in their community, what they believe will be useful, and what they recognize as realistic aspirations for their children" (p. 3).

Attitudes toward childrearing vary in many ways. Below are examples of some of these variations.

Values of Independence and Autonomy Versus Interdependence and Obedience. According to Levine (1974), as societies become more affluent they tend to value autonomy and independence. Working class and poor families are more likely to value obedience because the kinds of employment available to them require obedience for success (Kohn, 1977).

Certain Western industrialized societies, especially the United States, value the characteristics of independence and assertiveness. Most other cultures emphasize the family values of interdependence, obedience, harmony, and respect. These differences result in very different childrearing attitudes and practices. For example, in the United States, the young child's abilities to initiate verbally, to use language to make requests, and to carry on a conversation with adults are seen as important and positive skills. They are often included in the goals and objectives identified for young children with special needs. In many other cultures, however, such behavior in children is viewed as inappropriate. American middle-class children are often viewed by other cultures as disrespectful, aggressive, and overindulged. Children should be "seen and not heard." They should not initiate interactions with adults, should not assert their preferences and desires. Consider the conflict that may result for a family with such values when the early childhood teacher indicates they should be helping their child initiate requests. In this situation, it is important for the professional to explore the family's degree of comfort with such a goal and to communicate why this goal might be important for success in the mainstream culture.

Another related area of difference is often referred to as "individualistic" versus "collectivist" views of personal development and behavior. Being an individual is highly esteemed in mainstream U.S. culture. Phrases like "rugged individualist" and "pursuit of individual freedom" are considered positive and basic to the "American way." Many cultures, particularly Asian cultures, which are influenced by Confucian values (Chinn & Wong, 1992), revere harmony, proper behavior, and maintenance of social order (e.g., conformity and hierarchical lines of authority). Family and community members must learn their proper roles. The extent to which a child or adult carries out his or her expected role is a measure of success and family pride.

Discipline Approaches. Discipline is another area that varies widely across cultures and is often an area of cultural mismatch between families and early childhood professionals. The greatest variance between mainstream U.S. culture and many other cultures can be found in authoritarian versus egalitarian (democratic) parenting styles. In authoritarian families, the parent is the absolute and final authority. In such families the use of corporal punishment tends to be more common. The more democratic views of childrearing and discipline are less likely to use corporal punishment and the rules are less fixed. Children are given the opportunity to give their side of the story, and sometimes may even participate in the selection of a specific punishment. Parents with an extreme egalitarian approach would be unlikely to say "Do it because I say so." Authoritarian families place great emphasis on obedience and respect. For them the mark of a good parent is one who punishes children for disrespectful behavior, or for not conforming to their expected role. Physical punishment or "shaming" are common disciplinary strategies (Harry, 1992).

Variation can also be seen in the age at which discipline becomes appropriate. For example, in some Asian cultures there is an abrupt shift in discipline practices which may occur around the age of 4 years (Chan, 1992; Chhim, 1989). While parents may be very indulgent and not use discipline at all in the early years, the 4-year-old is expected to begin to conform to adult expectations. Harsh consequences may be used to facilitate this learning.

Also, there may be significant gender differences in how young children are disciplined. Boys may be indulged while girls are punished more severely, or vice versa. In many cultures boys are given very special status relative to girls.

Attitudes Toward Disability. Another area of cultural influence and variation is in the family's attitude toward disability. Religion frequently plays a part in how families view a child's disability. A child's disability may be seen as God's punishment for some earlier wrongdoing of the parent. Thus, in some cases the family will be shamed by the child since the child's condition serves as a visible pronouncement of the parent's guilt. In other cultures, because the disability is seen as God's will, there may be a reluctance to intervene. Parents may be torn between the early intervention program's pressure for them to take an active role in facilitating the child's development, versus their feeling that trying to change or "fix" the child is questioning God's authority.

The Influence of Racism. Racism is a very real phenomenon in American society. While racism and prejudice are experienced to some extent by all minority groups in the United States, no racism is as profound as that which is experienced by African American families. Racism can have a major impact upon childrearing practices. According to Peters (1985), African American parents must prepare their children to cope and survive in a racist society. Many parents express this as being their most important parenting responsibility. Children are often taught that life will not be fair and that a good education can provide one means of surmounting racial barriers. White middle-class professionals often view such attitudes as paranoid and may believe that parents are setting their children up to feel oppressed. And yet, research on children's self-esteem suggests that African American children do *not* demonstrate lower self-esteem than their white peers (Gibbs, 1985; Powell, 1985). According to Boykin and Toms (1985) parents must struggle to help their children reconcile three different influences in their lives: the racism experienced by being a minor-

ity culture, the heritage and traditions passed down by their African roots, and the values and behaviors dictated by U.S. mainstream culture.

Family Structure. Another area of cultural difference often encountered by early childhood professionals is in family structure. The middle-class ideal (although certainly no longer the norm) is the "nuclear family." The nuclear family consists of two parents and their children, living in relative isolation from other family members. Actually, other kinds of family structure are becoming much more common in the United States. Single-parent households, especially those headed by divorced or never-married women, are increasingly common. Also, many minority families include numerous extended family members: grandparents, great grandparents, sometimes aunts and uncles and cousins, and spouses of grown children and their children. Such large family units, often living in relatively small quarters, seem chaotic and confusing to professionals who have grown up in nuclear families. They may be concerned about overstimulation of the young child, or inconsistent, unpredictable childrearing practices. In many cases, however, extended family households provide important support for parents and young children. Minority culture parents are often uncomfortable leaving their children with strangers or may not be able to afford day care. Extended family members provide trusted, culturally compatible care for their children while parents work. Extended family members also provide important opportunities for child interaction and nurturance.

Parents' Roles. There are interesting cultural differences in how parents see their roles vis-a-vis their children's development. Middle-class parents clearly view themselves as teachers of their children. They teach their children concepts and vocabulary and help them learn to solve problems. Some parents also see themselves as teachers of their children, but what they teach are morality and proper behavior, including self-help skills. For some families there is a strong focus on not spoiling children. This often entails not being overly responsive or indulgent. For some the goal is to teach children—especially boys—to "be tough" and be able to defend themselves. Still other families may believe that all skills simply evolve as a normal developmental course and view their roles as teachers or intervenors as minimal.

Caregiver-Child Communication. Another area of great cultural variation which has major implications for early intervention is parent-child communication. In middle class U.S. society, *talking* is highly valued. By the standards of other cultures, Americans are excessive talkers. This talking carries over into their interactions with young children. Parents typically respond *verbally* even to very young infants long before they have any intentional communication. It is not unusual for a parent to respond to an infant's burp or sigh as though he has just said something very profound! Parents also value early development of language skills and verbal assertiveness in young children. Very young children are expected to be able to label, explain, and initiate and maintain a conversation. Parents also believe that they can play an important role in helping children learn these skills.

This kind of verbal interaction is unusual in many cultures. In some cultures, very young children are not consistently responded to until they can talk intelligibly. As mentioned earlier, in cultures where respect and obedience are emphasized, it may not be considered appropriate for young children to initiate; thus, being responsive to young children's communications would not be a high priority.

Common strategies suggested by early intervention professionals to facilitate children's development of communication skills include asking parents to consistently label objects, follow the child's lead, and expand on the child's utterance. For some parents, such interactions will be unnatural. It will not only require learning a new skill, but a skill which may be contrary to the practices of their culture. In such cases it will be important for the professional to explain to the parents that while these may be unfamiliar interactions, they can prove very beneficial to the language development of their child with special needs.

Medical Practices

Differing views on medical practices may be a significant source of family and professional conflict. Families from a wide range of subcultures may hold on to traditional health practices. Faith healers, herbs, massage, animal rites, and other rituals are often a part of treatments that lead to misunderstandings. For example, some Vietnamese parents have been reported for child abuse when using the technique of "coining" to treat conditions such as colds, sore throats, and headaches. The process involves applying a medicated salve and then stroking the affected area with a hot coin. The superficial red marks raise suspicions of abuse. Such judgments often grow out of the assumption that these families are not concerned about or caring for their children. Vincent and colleagues (1990) reminded us that we often judge parents to be uncaring when they actually care *differently* for their children.

Language Differences

Perhaps the most obvious difference among subcultures is communication, both verbal and nonverbal. The inability to communicate directly with families in their primary language creates a great deal of frustration for both parents and professionals. It is often the source of misunderstanding and an inadequate transmission of information. The need for translation in both spoken and written communication is critical in any early intervention program serving other than English-speaking families. Some suggestions for working through a translator are found in Exhibit 3–8. It is equally imperative that materials such as reports, newsletters, and home programs be prepared in parents' languages.

One way to break through the language barrier and enhance the family's involvement in a child's program is to provide support and encouragement from other parents. The Multicultural Training of Trainers program (Chan & Mahseredgian, 1989), in the Los Angeles area, recruited and trained bilingual parents of children with special needs to work with non–English-speaking parents in their communities. This form of peer counseling assists other parents in understanding "the system" and community resources while offering much-needed emotional support. (See Exhibit 3–9.) Special conferences such as "Fiesta Educativa" for Spanish-speaking parents and professionals has been another effective means of reaching the growing population of Hispanic and Latino families (I. Martinez, personal communication, October 17, 1990).

◆ ◆ ◆

EXHIBIT 3–8

Communicating Through a Translator

For the Professional:

1. Spend a few minutes with the translator, prior to the meeting, discussing topics to be covered. Make sure the translator understands the concepts.
2. Your translator should be someone you trust, especially with confidential or sensitive information.
3. In a group situation, sit next to the translator.
4. Use simple words. Talk slowly and in a few sentences at a time.
5. Look at and talk to the parent, not the translator.
6. Use nonverbal communication when talking. Observe the nonverbal communication used by the parent.
7. Allow sufficient time for the meeting.
8. After the meeting, ask the translator for his or her overall impression of the meeting.
9. In families with both English- and non–English-speaking members, be aware of the tendency to ignore members who do not speak English.
10. When young family members speak English and adults do not, avoid using children as translators if possible.

For the Translator:

1. Develop reference materials for medical, educational, and psychological terminology.
2. Make it a point to understand the culture and beliefs of the families.
3. Ask clarifying questions if the meaning of statements is unclear.
4. If line-by-line translation is not clear, use your own words, verifying changes with the professional and the parent.
5. Be aware of both verbal and nonverbal communication.

As Maria Diaz discovered in her home visits with the Ramirez family, the effectiveness of her work is clearly tied not only to understanding the unique values of the family but also to her own cultural biases and values. Although Maria speaks Spanish fluently, her upbringing in an upper middle class family in Spain has little relation to the experiences of the Ramirez family. Conversations have raised a number of differences in the way they view issues such as health, childrearing, and education. Maria feels that in recognizing their differences she has begun to work within the boundaries that are comfortable to the family while sharing with them information about the ways of the larger culture.

In her ongoing experiences with the Ramirez family and other parents in the intervention program, Maria and the rest of the early intervention team must continually use caution in making prejudgments based on attitudes toward and stereotypes of certain subcultures. As Hanson, Lynch, and Wayman (1990) suggested,

The effectiveness of programs often will depend upon the development of ethnic competence and behavioral changes by the service providers . . . becoming ethically competent requires early interventionists to engage in four tasks. First, they must clarify their own values and assumptions. Second, they must gather and analyze ethnographic information regarding the cultural community within which each family resides. Third, they must determine the degree to which the family

◆ ◆ ◆

EXHIBIT 3–9

Suggestions for Working with Culturally Diverse Families

1. Make sure that program staffing reflects the cultures and languages of the children and families in the program.
2. Provide ongoing staff training related to family differences.
3. Encourage families to share their beliefs and traditions. Invite speakers to discuss all aspects of the culture and its relationship to disabilities, child rearing, medical practices, and so forth.
4. Network with other community resources that are meaningful to families such as churches, community advisors from subcultural groups, and the media (local television, radio, newspapers, etc.).
5. In addition to using trained interpreters for all parent interactions, provide written materials in the language of the participating families. Be sensitive to the comprehension and reading levels required. Be creative in addressing the needs of parents with limited reading ability. Bilingual curriculum materials and activities should also be an integral part of the child's program.
6. Learn at least a few words of the languages represented in the program, especially common greetings and phrases used in speaking to children.
7. Avoid stereotyping. Within cultural groups, recognize individual differences in background experiences, coping styles, interests, economic levels, and so forth. Parents from the same cultural group do not always have the same needs. Meet individual families at their own level of need and life experience. Remember that *"Families are different, not deficient"* (Mendoza & Cegelka, 1988).

operates transculturally; and finally, they must examine each family's orientation to specific childrearing issues. (p. 126)

WORKING WITH SPECIAL FAMILY POPULATIONS

In addition to the challenges encountered in working with all parents, many professionals who work with young children will discover that they are working with parents who have unique needs themselves. The nature of the circumstances or disabilities of these parents will vary widely. Although overt behaviors may appear to be similar, concerns can be very different. It is unwise and dangerous to generalize. Each parent is an individual with unique needs. In some way, each one can be assisted.

Parents with Developmental Disabilities

Children of parents with developmental disabilities are often enrolled in early intervention programs be-

cause they are considered at risk, rather than because they have a diagnosed disability. While all of the suggestions already made for working out partnerships with parents are appropriate for working with parents with developmental disabilities, there are two specific goals to keep in mind (Hanson & Lynch, 1995). These include helping the parents to become the most effective parents possible while also carefully monitoring their children's progress. In order to achieve these goals, the following guidelines may be useful:

1. *Establish priorities.* To help parents with developmental disabilities develop effective parenting skills, professionals must work with these parents in choosing their priorities carefully. The first priority may be to determine whether parents would benefit from assistance in managing the basic needs of daily living. Many parents with developmental disabilities are in the lowest socioeconomic bracket. Both resources and skill in budgeting may be limited. The early interventionist may be called on to help parents

plan budgets and to connect with available community resources. Assistance may also be needed in such daily living skills as selection and storage of food, in developing daily routines for both themselves and their children, and in securing transportation and attending to medical needs.

2. *Coordinate help.* As soon as possible, discover which other agencies are extending help to these families. If there are several, the development of a collaborative intervention plan with frequent communication among all those involved is essential.

3. *Make frequent, brief contacts.* Telephone calls are better than notes, and 10 minutes with the parent in the home can pay quick dividends.

4. *Avoid lengthy explanations.* Be brief. Be explicit. Show parents what to do and how to do it. They are usually willing to try, if they understand what is wanted.

5. *Require little or no reading.* Send only one request or direction in notes, if they can read. A list of things to do will probably be ignored.

6. *Model appropriate parent-child interaction.* As parent-child interaction may be limited, the early interventionist may need to model responsiveness to children's cues. Teaching parents simple "baby play" games such as peek-a-boo will help these parents become more involved with their children.

7. *Help parents interpret child's behavior.* Parents with developmental disabilities may misinterpret their children's behavior and see them as "bad children" who need to be punished.

8. *Involve parents with developmental disabilities.* Whenever possible, include these parents in center observations, volunteer activities, parent conferences, and meetings. Answer their questions in short sentences and with simple language. Supervise their activities closely. It is helpful to remember that they are with their child far more than the professional. If their interaction skills and behavior management can be improved, both parent and child will benefit.

Teen Parents

Although much attention has been given to the increasing numbers of teen pregnancies, little is found in the literature about the needs of young teen parents of children with disabilities. The developmental level of the teenager who, in many ways, is still a child herself must be considered. All teen parents appear to need emotional support and specific instruction in "parenting" while they are being helped to set and reach toward some realistic goals for themselves. Providing this emotional support in a way that enhances the teen parent's self-esteem is often a significant challenge, as early interventionists may represent authority figures at a time when teens tend to turn toward peers as their primary source of self-esteem and goal setting.

Teen parents who have, themselves, suffered from poor parenting will benefit from the same careful approaches to providing information and modeling "parenting best practices" discussed above. In addition, teen parents need to be linked to education, child-care services, social groups, and agencies that provide a wide range of support so they can develop the life and vocational skills necessary to be able to provide a stable environment for themselves and their children. To be effective, early interventionists must be accepting and able to provide consistent emotional support to a group of parents whose history is generally lacking in this essential element of healthy development.

Foster Caregivers

Foster care is increasing by staggering proportions across the United States. For example, in California, between 1985 and 1989, the number of all children in out-of-home care increased by 65% while the number of children less than 4 years of age increased by an amazing 165% (County Welfare Directors Association

of California et al., 1990). These children, including both those with and without disabilities, were placed because of existing laws related to abuse, neglect, and abandonment. Prenatal substance abuse is now considered one of the leading causes of the high infant out-of-home placement.

The foster child, in addition to possibly having developmental disabilities, often has overwhelming social-emotional needs. Caregivers and early interventionists must be concerned about such issues as attachment, diminished use of adults for comfort, passivity, inappropriate emotional responses, impulsivity, and fearfulness in their efforts to provide developmentally appropriate support to the young child. Because of the complexities associated with a child's removal from his or her natural parents, a team approach to placement, care, and reunification (when possible) is critical.

The implications for early interventionists are in working with foster families and encouraging participation in home and center activities. Intervention needs of the child with a developmental disability are developed with foster parent input as well as with the biological parent (as appropriate). In addition, the foster parents are encouraged to be a part of parent groups to take advantage of ongoing emotional support, training, and educational opportunities.

The next chapter will provide an overview of the current issues, trends, and controversies related to assessment. It will also elaborate on the role of interventionists in light of changing philosophies and practices.

Summary

Properly trained professionals will recognize and actively work toward involving families in a partnership of responsibility for their child's development. One of the first steps in bridging a link between parents and professionals is for the professional to recognize the emotional needs of families with children with disabilities. Parents often react to the realization that their child has a disabling condition in stages similar to the emotional adjustment encountered with the

loss of a loved one. The alert and informed professional can help parents work through each stage from initial feelings of shock, disbelief, and denial through anger and resentment, bargaining to make it go away, depression and discouragement, and on to acceptance. Understanding the family as a system is essential to true parent-professional collaboration.

Children and members of the extended family can be included in the process of emotional and educational adjustments. Siblings are an especially valuable ally, as children typically accept a child who has disabilities without jealousy or anxiety. Especially in early sessions with family members, it is important to avoid jargon and technical concepts. Test results should be explained in terms of common behaviors.

A variety of methods of parent involvement are surveyed, such as home-based instruction, observations, passports, and meetings. For effectiveness in home visits and instruction, teachers learn to use two-way communication, taking time to listen and observe, as well as to inform and demonstrate.

Guidelines are provided for working with parents within the center under a variety of purposes. With planning, it is possible to create a developmental approach for bringing parents into contact with other parents of children with disabilities (the more

seasoned veterans), orienting them to observation and eventual participation within the center. Parent education groups and parent-teacher conferences can be viewed as requiring special teacher skills rather than simply as an opportunity to meet.

Special consideration is given to working with culturally diverse families. Understanding cultural practices and language differences is essential to successful early intervention.

Finally, professionals are reminded that some parents of children with disabilities may have special needs themselves. These include parents who themselves have disabilities, teen parents, and foster parents. Throughout the chapter, sufficient details have been provided to encourage professionals to pick and choose the type and extent of involvement most appropriate for their parents, their children, and themselves.

Discussion Topics and Activities

1. Do additional reading and research into the emotional needs and feelings of parents of children with disabilities. Discuss these feelings with class members. If possible, try to empathize with these feelings.

2. Make a list of the public and private institutions in your area whose purpose is to help families of children with disabilities cope with their problems. Organize the list as a referral file including contact person, telephone number, and cost and type of services.

3. Assume the role of parent of a child with disabilities and do a local telephone survey. Describe your child's condition and ask for information as to where and how to obtain help. Record this information in a file and share it with classmates. Try to get some idea of how parents might feel when in this situation.

4. Review and discuss why parents may feel fearful about their meetings with center personnel. What can professionals do to help relieve these feelings?

5. Prepare and role play an orientation meeting. Try to be as convincing as possible when giving the reasons why you would like to get your children's parents involved.

6. Develop a questionnaire that you can use to determine the interests and needs of parents for parent involvement. Try it out on a few parents. Compare it with that of classmates and revise when necessary.

7. Collect magazine, newspaper, and journal articles about working with parents. Make a file of useful ideas.

8. Role play a home visit with classmates. Share constructive criticism.

9. Consider and discuss the possibility of a values collision between a home visitor and a family. How can such a collision be avoided? Have you ever been involved in such a situation?

10. As a class, discuss issues of confidentiality, privileged communication, and conversation in the teacher's lounge in relation to parent involvement.

11. Gather and discuss newsletters from local early childhood centers. Develop one that may be appropriate for an early intervention program.

12. Develop a "happygram" to be sent home to parents.

13. Spend some time walking in a variety of neighborhoods. Learn what resources are or are not available to families living there.

Annotated Bibliography

Emotional Needs of Families of Children with Disabilities

Blacher, J. (1984). Sequential stages of parental adjustments to the birth of a child with handicaps. *Mental Retardation, 22,* 55–68.

Blacher examines the literature for patterns of parental reaction to the birth of a child with special needs. Most important, he presents both sides of the question of whether parents follow a sequence of adjustment and raises practical questions to guide future research.

Buscaglia, L. (1983). *The disabled and their parents: A counseling challenge.* Thorofare, NJ: Charles B. Slack.

Everyone who works with children with disabilities and their parents should read this classic book seriously. In a direct writing style, the author makes a demand for competent, reality-based, and sensible guidance. He offers practical, down-to-earth suggestions for improved counseling. Most of all, the author considers disabilities to be made, not born.

Kübler-Ross, E. (1969). *On death and dying.* New York: Macmillan.

With warm sensitivity, the author depicts the delicate subject of people who are terminally ill and the struggle to accept death. This seasoned, remarkable book not only helps the reader to face the inevitable end of life more professionally and personally but also lends insight into the stages through which some parents of children with disabilities may pass.

Lambie, R., & Daniels-Mohring, D. (1993). *Family systems within education contexts: Understanding students with special needs.* Denver, CO: Love Publishing.

This text provides major concepts and research findings to help professionals understand the family life cycle, family interactions, and other environmental factors that may be affecting children with special needs. Special populations, including families of divorce and remarriage and abusive and addictive families, are discussed, and specific strategies for working with these families are presented.

Lobato, D. J. (1990). *Brothers, sisters, and special needs.* Baltimore: Paul H. Brookes.

This book not only describes the psychological basis for understanding needs of siblings but also offers practical activities to assist them in coping constructively with a brother or sister who has developmental disabilities or a chronic illness.

Luster, T., & Okagaki, L. (Eds.). (1993). *Parenting: An ecological perspective.* Hillsdale, NJ: Lawrence Erlbaum.

This volume is appropriate for the student who wishes to pursue the research on parents and children that addresses parenting from the perspective of the ecological paradigm articulated by Bronfenbrenner over 15 years ago. It addresses the influences on parenting behavior of one's own childhood experience, the development of parental beliefs, the ecology of teen-age parenting, children's temperamental characteristics, the marital relationship, social networks, parental work, and the neighborhood and community.

National Center for Clinical Infant Programs. (1985). *Equals in this partnership: Parents of disabled and at-risk infants and toddlers speak to professionals.*

The purpose of this booklet is to help voices of parents reach a wider audience. It contains direct contributions of parents of young children with special needs as well as addresses delivered at the 1984 Conference on Comprehensive Approaches to Disabled and At-Risk Infants held in Washington, DC.

Seligman, M. (1991). *Family with a handicapped child: Understanding and treatment.* Needham, MA: Allyn and Bacon.

This book focuses on helping families to cope with their children who have chronic disabilities. Through examination of the many variables that affect a family from internal family issues to external social pressures, the reader gains an appreciation for families of children with disabilities. They also gain a deeper understanding of the complexities of working with these families.

Options for Family Participation

Alper, S. K., Schloss, P. J., & Schloss, C. N. (1994). *Families of students with disabilities: Consultation and advocacy.* Needham Heights, MA: Allyn and Bacon.

This text is designed to enable professionals to assist families in becoming full partners in the educational process. It addresses family dynamics, roles of various family members, counseling and communication techniques. An emphasis is placed on empowering teachers and parents with advocacy techniques, including problem solving and consultation, so they can better access resources.

Anderson, P., & Fenichal, E. S. (1989). *Serving culturally diverse families of infants and toddlers with disabilities.* Washington, DC: National Center for Clinical Infant Programs.

This astute publication may serve as a guide to understanding the major cultural groups within the United States. It provides important considerations for working within our multicultural society.

Bakley, S. (1986). *But I wasn't trained for this: A manual for working with mothers who are retarded.* San Diego, CA: San Diego State University.

This manual provides insight into the characteristics of parents with developmental disabilities as well as useful techniques and suggestions to help meet their unique needs. This manual may be ordered from the San Diego State University Foundation, San Diego State University, Department of Special Education, San Diego, CA 92182.

Dunst, C., Trivette, C., & Deal, A. (1988). *Enabling and empowering families: Principles and guidelines for practice.* Cambridge, MA: Brookline Books.

This book is designed to assist professionals working with families in early intervention settings in carrying out the intentions of P.L. 99–457. Focus is on *enablement,* or creating opportunities or activities that strengthen family functioning and empowerment. The intent is to support families in their efforts to realize intrafamily mastery and control over important aspects of family functioning. A number of assessment forms are included in the appendixes.

Dunst, C. J., Trivette, C., & Deal, A. (Eds.). (1994). *Supporting and strengthening families: Vol. 1. Methods, strategies and outcomes.* Cambridge, MA: Brookline Books.

This collection of papers updates the thinking discussed in the editors' 1987 volume, *Enabling and Empowering Families.* It focuses on theory, practice, and outcomes that foster empowerment of families, allowing them to capitalize on their own resources and leading to a strengthening of individual and family functioning.

Gollnick, D. M., & Chinn, P. C. (1990). *Multicultural education in a pluralistic society.* Englewood Cliffs, NJ: Merrill/Prentice Hall.

Using culture as a basis for understanding multicultural education, the descriptions of seven microcultures to which Americans belong are included in this informative text.

Chapters discuss the microcultures of class, ethnicity and race, gender, exceptionality, religion, language, and age. The concept of pluralism and how to use it effectively in centers and schools is helpful.

Klass, C. S. (1996). *Home visiting: Promoting healthy parent and child development.* Baltimore: Paul H. Brookes.

This handbook for home visitors offers functional, field-tested guidance techniques for working with parents and children. Firsthand accounts of actual home visits address issues such as how to work with families from varying cultural backgrounds, how to teach parents about their children's development, what to do when parents or children are unresponsive, and how to use personal strengths to reinforce the parent-visitor relationship.

Lacy, A. (1981). *Project Hope—Inservice manual for home teachers.* San Diego, CA: San Diego County Superintendent of Schools.

This helpful manual should be in the library of anyone involved in working with parents in the home. It includes a parents' needs assessment procedure, step-by-step implementation procedures, self-quizzes, and "Dear Mom and Dad" letters, which are given to parents to help them understand normal child development.

Lynch, E. W., & Hanson, M. J. (Eds.). (1998). *Developing cross-cultural competence: A guide for working with young children and their families.* Baltimore, MD: Paul H. Brookes.

This comprehensive resource perceptively and sensitively explores cultural, ethnic, and language diversity in human services. It offers cultural understanding and helpful interaction strategies accompanied by easily referenced charts and a variety of case examples. The geographic and historical origins, values, beliefs, language, contemporary issues, and recommendations for effective cross-cultural interaction are described for eight cultures.

McWilliam, P. J., & Bailey, D. B. (Eds.). (1993). *Working together with children and families: Case studies in early intervention.* Baltimore, MD: Paul H. Brookes.

The 21 case studies in this book are based on actual experiences of professionals working in early intervention. Each case study includes discussion questions for use by instructors of students in independent study. These case studies attest to the need to individualize services for children and families.

Seligman, M., & Darling, R. B. (1989). *Ordinary families, special children.* New York: Guilford.

Parents and professionals alike will profit from this systems approach to working with children with disabilities and their families. Authors include an important chapter on cultural reactions to childhood disability and subcultural variations. Practical applications are noted throughout the text.

Shea, T. M., & Bauer, A. M. (1991). *Parents and teachers of children with exceptionalities. A handbook for collaboration.* Needham Heights, MA: Allyn and Bacon.

Shea and Bauer's comprehensive text explores the potential of parents to be full participants. The first section discusses the reactions and rights of special parents ending with a model for parent-teacher collaboration. Worksheets, forms, lesson plans, examples of handouts, and personal anecdotes are included to help the reader grasp the continuum of cooperative activities for full parent participation. A full chapter is devoted to transition issues.

Simpson, R. L. (1996). *Working with parents and families of exceptional children and youth: Techniques for successful conferencing and collaboration.* Austin, TX: Pro-Ed.

The central theme of this edition is that educators and professionals must be involved in helping families to cope with the various issues they routinely confront when raising and living with a child who has disabilities. It provides role-playing activities and strategies in an effort to help learners learn by doing. Practice in initial interviewing, IEP meetings, and resolution of conflicts are included.

Turnbull, A. P., & Turnbull, H. R. (1997). *Families, professionals, and exceptionality: A special partnership.* Englewood Cliffs, NJ: Merrill/Prentice Hall.

This text is based on the family systems approach and offers ideas for individualizing relationships between individuals with exceptionalities, families, and helping professionals. Unlike most texts, this one speaks to the needs of the family throughout the lifespan of the individual with special needs.

Turnbull, A., Patterson, J. M., Behr, S. K., Murphy, D. L., Marquis, J. G., & Blue-Banning, M. J. (Eds.). (1993). *Cognitive coping, families and disabilities.* Baltimore, MD: Paul H. Brookes.

This book is the result of a combination of scientific knowledge and experiential knowledge. It relates the combined knowledge of families, service providers, researchers, and theorists as they address giving birth to and/or raising a child with a developmental disability over the entire life span. Cognitive coping is said to involve thinking about a particular situation in ways that enhance self-esteem, allowing one to feel in control and experience a sense of meaning.

Vincent, L. J., Salisbury, C. L., Strain, P., McCormick, C., & Tessier, A. (1990). A behavioral-ecological approach to early intervention: Focus on cultural diversity. In S. J. Meisels & J. P. Shonkoff (Eds.), *Handbook of early intervention* (pp. 173-195). New York: Cambridge University Press.

In this scholarly text, there is an effort to bring together the best in current research and practice in early intervention. This chapter speaks to the issues of an ecological approach to early intervention with an emphasis on cultural diversity. The stated implications of a wide range of family differences suggest the critical need to understand the diverse values and approaches necessary to working with families and children in today's society.

Wasik, B. H., Bryant, D. M., & Lyons, C. M. (1990). *Home visiting: Procedures for helping families.* Newbury Park, CA: Sage.

In this book, home visiting is defined as the process by which a professional or paraprofessional provides help to a family in its own home. It provides a comprehensive history and philosophy of home visiting along with discussion of the skills essential for an effective home visitor. The authors speak from practical experiences gained from involvement in two early intervention programs.

Wolery, M. (Ed.). (1992). Family diversity. *Topics in Early Childhood Special Education, 12*(3).

This entire issue is devoted to identifying and discussing some of the challenges and tensions resulting from the diversity professionals encounter among the families and children they serve. Accepting diversity as a reality, readers are reminded that heterogeneity is the norm even within any given cultural group. They are challenged to understand their own cultural assumptions in order to be responsive to the inevitable challenge of the ever changing characteristics of families in today's society.

References

Anderegg, M. L., Vergason, G. A., & Smith, M. C. (1992). A visual representation of the grief cycle for use by teachers with families of children with disabilities. *Remedial and Special Education, 13,* 17-23.

Barber, P. A., Turnbull, A. P., Behr, S. K., & Kerns, G. M. (1988). Family systems perspective on early childhood special education. In S. L. Odom & M. B. Karnes (Eds.), *Early intervention for infants and children with handicaps* (pp. 179–198). Baltimore: Paul H. Brookes.

Berry, J. O. & Hardman, M. L. (1998). *Lifespan perspectives on the family and disability.* Boston: Allyn and Bacon.

Blacher, J. (1984). Sequential stages of parental adjustments to the birth of a child with handicaps. *Mental Retardation, 22,* 55–68.

Bowe, F. G. (1995). *Birth to five: Early childhood special education.* New York: Delmar Publishers.

Boyd, D. (1950). *The three stages.* New York: National Association for Retarded Children.

Boykin, W., & Toms, F. (1985). Black child socialization. In H. P. McAdoo & J. L. McAdoo (Eds.), *Black children: Social, educational and parental environments.* Beverly Hills: Sage.

Bristol, M. M., & Gallagher, J. J. (1982). A family focus for intervention. In C. T. Ramey & P. L. Trohanis (Eds.), *Finding and educating high-risk and handicapped infants.* Baltimore: University Park Press.

Cansler, D., & Martin, G. (1974). *Working with families: A manual for developmental centers.* Reston, VA: The Council for Exceptional Children.

Chan, S. (1992). Families with Asian roots. In M. Hanson & E. Lynch (Eds.), *Developing cross-cultural competence: A guide for working with young children and their families.* Baltimore, MD: Paul H. Brookes.

Chan, S., & Mahseredgian, H. (1989, May). *Cultural competence: Effectively serving ethnic minority children and families.* Workshop presented at the Infant Conference-89, Los Angeles.

Chinn, P. C., & Wong, G. Y. (1992). Recruiting and retaining Asian/Pacific American Teachers. In M. E. Dilworth (Ed.), *Diversity in teacher education.* San Francisco: Jossey-Bass.

Chhim, Sun-Him (1989). *Introduction to Cambodian culture.* San Diego, CA: San Diego State University Multifunctional Service Center.

County Welfare Directors Association of California et al. (1990). *Ten reasons to invest in the families of California.* Published by a grant from the Edna McConnell Claru Foundation.

Gallagher, P. A., & Powell, P. H. (1989). Brothers and sisters: Meeting special needs. *Topics in Early Childhood Special Education, 8*(4), 24–37.

Gargiulo, R. M. (1985). *Working with parents of exceptional children.* Boston: Houghton Mifflin.

Gibbs, J. T. (1985). City girls: Psychosocial adjustment of urban black adolescent females. *SAGE: A Scholarly Journal on Black Women, 2,* 28–36.

Hanson, M. J., & Lynch, E. W. (1995). *Early intervention.* Austin, TX: PRO.ED.

Hanson, M. J., Lynch, E. W., & Wayman, K. I. (1990). Honoring the cultural diversity of families when gathering data. *Topics in Early Childhood Special Education, 10*(1), 112–131.

Harry, B. (1992). Developing cultural self-awareness: The first step in values clarification for early interventionists. *Topics in Early Childhood Special Education, 12*(3), 333–350.

Hodel, M. B. (1981, January 16). Parents learn to share with son. *The Intelligencer* (Edwardsville, IL), p. 2.

Kirk, W. (1979). A parent's perspective. *Illinois Regional Resource Center Newsletter, 2,* 5–6.

Kohn, M. L. (1977). *Class and conformity* (2nd ed.). Chicago: University of Chicago Press.

Kübler-Ross, E. (1969). *On death and dying.* New York: Macmillan.

Lepler, M. (1978). Having a handicapped child. *The American Journal of Maternal Child Nursing,* 32–34.

Levine, R. A. (1974). Parental goals: A cross cultural view. In H. J. Leichter, (Ed.), *The family as educator.* New York: Teachers College Press.

Lichter, R. (1976). Communicating with parents: It begins with listening. *Teaching Exceptional Children, 8,* 66–71.

Mendoza, J., & Cegelka, P. (1988). *Parents and professionals advocating for collaborative training.* San Diego, CA: San Diego State University.

Morgan, W. (1977). *Skills in working with parents* (1240). Champaign, IL: University of Illinois, Institute for Research on Exceptional Children.

Mori, A. A. (1983). *Families of children with special needs.* Rockville, MD: Aspen.

Moses, K. (1987, Spring). The impact of childhood disability: The parents' struggle. *WAYS,* 6–10.

Moses, K. (1992). *The dynamics of transition & transformation: On loss, grieving, coping & growthful change.* Evanston, IL: Resource Networks, Inc.

Norton, D. G. (1990). Understanding the early experience of Black children in high risk environments: Culturally and ecologically relevant research as a guide to support for families. *Zero-to-Three, 10*(4), 1–7.

Peters, M. (1985). Racial socialization of young black children. In H. P. McAdoo & J. L. McAdoo (Eds.), *Black children: Social, educational and parental environments.* Beverly Hills: Sage.

Powell, G. J. (1985). Self-concepts among Afro-American students in racially isolated minority schools: Some regional differences. *Journal of American Academy of Child Psychiatry, 24,* 142–149.

Powell, R. (1986). Parent education and support programs. *Young Children, 41,* 47–53.

Poyadue, F. (1998). Helping families travel an unchosen path. (In press).

Public Law 102-119. And 105-17, Washington, DC: U.S. Government Printing Office.

Roos, P. (1975). Parents and families of the mentally retarded. In J. M. Kauffman & J. S. Payne (Eds.), *Mental retardation: Introduction and personal perspectives.* Englewood Cliffs, NJ: Merrill/Prentice Hall.

Sameroff, A. J. (1987). The social context of development. In N. Eisenberg (Ed.), *Contemporary topics in developmental psychology* (pp. 273-291). New York: Wiley.

Shea, T., & Bauer, A. (1991). *Parents and teachers of exceptional students: A handbook for involvement.* Rockleigh, NJ: Allyn and Bacon.

Simeonsson, R. J., & Bailey, D. B. (1990). Family dimensions in early intervention. In S. J. Meisels & J. P. Shonkoff (Eds.), *Handbook of early childhood intervention* (pp. 428-444). New York: Cambridge University Press.

Simpson, R. L. (1996). *Working with parents and families of exceptional children and youth: Techniques for successful conferencing and collaboration.* Austin, TX: Pro-Ed.

Stile, S. W., Cole, J. T., & Garner, A. W. (1979). Maximizing parental involvement in programs for exceptional children. *Journal of the Division of Early Childhood, 1,* 68-92.

Turnbull, A. P., Summers, J. A., & Brotherson, M. J. (1983, October). *Working with families with disabled members: A family systems approach.* Lawrence: University of Kansas, Kansas University Affiliated Facility.

Turnbull, A. P., & Turnbull, H. R. (1997). *Families, professionals, and exceptionality: A special partnership.* Englewood Cliffs, NJ: Merrill/Prentice Hall.

Valand, M. C. (1975). Conducting parent-teacher conferences. (Mimeographed paper). Chapel Hill: The University of North Carolina, Chapel Hill Training-Outreach Program.

Vincent, L. J., Salisbury, C. L., Strain, P., McCormick, C., & Tessier, A. (1990). In S. J. Meisels & J. P. Shonkoff (Eds.), *Handbook in early childhood intervention* (pp. 173-195). New York: Cambridge University Press.

Wayman, K. I., Lynch, E. W., & Hanson, M. J. (1991). Home-based early childhood services: Cultural sensitivity in a family systems approach. *Topics in Early Childhood Special Education, 10*(4), 56-75.

Chapter 4

Recognizing Special Needs
and Monitoring Progress

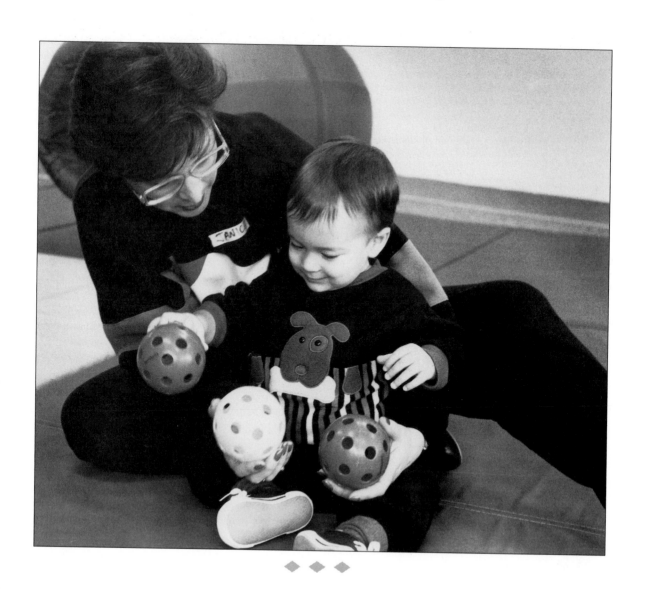

Key Concepts

♦ Developmental assessment is a process designed to deepen understanding of children's competencies and the environments most likely to help them reach their full potential.

♦ Philosophy and practices in identification, assessment, and evaluation are changing rapidly.

♦ A move toward an ecobehavioral approach to assessment facilitates understanding of environmental influences as well as the complex interactions of young children with their caregivers.

♦ Professionals must understand the usefulness and limitations of both criterion-referenced and standardized assessment measures, as well as the critical role of informal measures such as observation of the child in natural settings and the use of parent interviews.

♦ Assessment should be an ongoing process that builds on multiple sources of information gathered, whenever possible, during authentic daily activities such as playtime.

♦ Observers of children's progress should be trained; they should choose to observe within relevant and typical environmental contexts and should focus on describing functional needs (i.e., those behaviors needed by the child in order to participate in meaningful and purposeful daily activities).

♦ When children with special needs are included in class, certain information must be recorded, kept up to date, and made available to parents and others on the child's program planning team. Progress must be monitored on an ongoing basis.

♦ ♦ ♦

There continues to be much debate and discussion regarding assessment in early childhood. Several texts are available that provide comprehensive information related to approaches and procedures for assessment of infants and young children across developmental domains. These include *Interdisciplinary Assessment of Infants* by Gibbs and Teti, 1990; *Infant-Toddler Assessment* by Rossetti, 1990; *Assessing Young Children with Special Needs* by Benner, 1992; and *New Visions for the Developmental Assessment of Infants and Young Children* edited by Meisels and Fenichel, 1996. Descriptions of these resources can be found in the annotated references at the end of this chapter. The purpose of this chapter is not to present a thorough consideration of the topic of assessment, but rather an overview of the issues, trends, and controversies in the field. It will begin with a currently accepted definition of developmental assessment and a discussion of the purposes of assessment.

The following key issues will be considered: changing philosophies and practices; issues related to the use of standardized tests with infants and young children; current approaches to assessment, such as "authentic" assessment, including play-based assessment, parental and natural observations, and portfolio assessment; and techniques for becoming skilled observers of children.

WHAT IS DEVELOPMENTAL ASSESSMENT?

According to deliberations of outstanding early intervention specialists assembled by the National Center for Clinical Infant Programs, "Developmental assessment is a process designed to deepen understanding of a child's competencies and resources, and of the caregiving and learning environments most likely to help a child make fullest use of his or her developmental potential." These experts further state that "assessment should be an **ongoing, collaborative process of systematic observation and analysis**" (Greenspan & Meisels, 1994, p. 11). Assessment is conducted in order to assist parents and professionals make a series of informed, evaluative decisions. The choice of the tool or process of observation and analysis must depend on the type of decision that is required. The type of decision to be made will determine the nature of the information to be obtained and, therefore, the purpose of the assessment process. The purpose will then guide the process. The following section will discuss typical purposes for the use of assessment activities with young children.

IDENTIFICATION

In order for eligible children to receive the free appropriate early intervention services to which they are entitled, they must be found and identified. Therefore, **identification** involves both the child-find and screening activities that locate and identify disabling conditions in children who either are not receiving early intervention or are receiving inadequate intervention services.

Child-Find. The process of **child-find** includes finding and identifying children with disabling conditions. Educational regions within states often hire child-find teams that are usually interdisciplinary in nature. These teams are responsible for planning and conducting a public awareness campaign to inform and educate community members concerning the right to a free and appropriate education for all chil-

dren. A primary goal of the public awareness campaign is to generate referrals for screening. In most communities there are numerous possible sources of referral. If public awareness activities are sensitive to community characteristics, a significant number of first contacts may be made by families, themselves. Other referral sources may include staff from the hospital neonatal intensive care unit (NICU), local physicians, child-care workers, social service agencies, and family resource centers.

Screening. **Screening** is the initial step in the assessment and intervention process intended to assist children in receiving an appropriate education. "The purpose of developmental screening tests is to identify at an early stage those children who have a high probability of exhibiting delayed or abnormal development" (Meisels & Wasik, 1990, p. 612). Screening is a limited procedure. The intent is to identify those children who *might* have a problem that should be investigated thoroughly. Children with obvious or severe disabling conditions who have been located through child-find procedures should not be involved in the screening process. These children should be referred directly to the local department or agency responsible for thorough diagnosis of the disabling conditions.

Role of the Early Interventionist. Currently the role of the interventionist in the processes of child-find and screening varies with local areas and professional expertise. In some areas teachers and therapists have been asked to assist in public awareness activities and in conducting screening programs. At the very least, all educators of young children are expected to be able to recognize high risk or danger signals of disabling conditions in the children within their classes. (See Appendix D).

Professionals who consent to participate in screening young children should do so realizing the responsibilities involved in the process. Even though great efforts are usually taken to ensure that the screening process is fun for children, it is, nevertheless, a time of anxiety. Parents, especially, need support and encouragement to realize that screening is only a preliminary step and does not determine the definite existence of a disabling condition. Caution must be taken to avoid labeling children.

Although there is a tendency to replace standardized screening tests with information provided by parents and medical personnel as well as informed clinical observation, screening tests are still used. Extreme care must be taken in the selection of any screening tests. To begin with they must be used in relation to the definition for eligibility adopted in any local area. For example, if a state uses a very broad definition of developmental delay that would include children with even mild delays, then the screening criteria for referral for diagnosis to determine eligibility must be more liberal than in a state where the definition includes only children with severe developmental delays.

The selection committee must consider the following factors when selecting a screening instrument:

1. Qualifications of individuals who will use the test.

2. Reliability (consistency or stability) of the test.

3. Validity of the test (extent to which the test screens what it is supposed to screen).

4. Provision of items that cover the major functional areas, including language skills, cognitive skills, fine and gross motor skills, and social-emotional development.

5. Similarity of the children used to establish the norms to those being screened.

6. Degree to which the screening instrument discriminates against minority groups or specific disabling conditions.

7. Cost and time factors.

Publications mentioned in the annotated bibliography at the end of the chapter can be used as guides to prepare professionals for involvement in the process of test selection.

DETERMINATION OF ELIGIBILITY FOR SERVICES

Assessment processes may be performed in order to confirm or disconfirm the existence of a problem severe enough to make a child **eligible** to receive early intervention services. By clarifying the nature and extent of the problem through a multidisciplinary evaluation, a definitive **diagnosis** as to the **etiology** or cause of the condition may be made. In many cases, however, a specific cause of the delay cannot be identified. In such cases, the purpose of the diagnostic assessment is to determine whether the child is, in fact, sufficiently delayed to be eligible for services. Of course, this decision will depend on the local area's set of criteria specifying precisely how eligibility will be determined. Legally, states are discouraged from reporting or serving young children according to a disability category label. Therefore, many states have adopted criteria based on number of months of delay. This allows children to be made eligible according to their degree of *developmental delay* rather than by being placed in a disability category. It should be noted that Part C of P. L. 105-17 uses the term **evaluation** to refer to the assessment procedures used in determining a child's eligibility for services. This process of evaluation will be discussed in Chapter 6.

Determination of Services

The interagency team, in collaboration with the parents, will use the information derived from the multidisciplinary assessment of the child's current level of performance to decide what service options are most appropriate for the child and family. In making this decision, consideration must be given to a match between the needs, abilities, and priorities of the child and family and the services available. Such decisions must be dynamic in that they may be changed quickly if deemed necessary by continuing, ongoing assessment of child and family needs.

It must be realized that during a child's early years, there are several critical points when placement decisions must be made. Of course, the number of decision-making points will depend on the characteristics of the child's disability and when this disability becomes apparent. For example, service decisions may have to be made when the child is being discharged from the hospital, a few months later when delay is clearly recognized and an infant program is deemed appropriate, when the child transfers into preschool services, and when he or she becomes eligible for kindergarten.

The Role of the Early Interventionist

Historically teachers were not seen as active participants in decision making about children with problems. Increasingly, teachers are expected to be astute observers and communicators of their observations. Teachers are included as part of the multidisciplinary diagnostic team. This is especially true of teachers or therapists who have been asked to serve as service coordinators. Their careful observations are helpful in corroborating or refuting formal test results. Current practice requires that teachers understand what each specialist is saying and recommending. Teachers today must be alert to recognize conflicting advice, the failure of a specialist to use tests that take into account multiple problems, or the need to coordinate conflicting opinions and directions. It is critical that *all* information, whether derived from formal testing, parental interviews, or informal observations, be integrated and synthesized. It is often the teacher who must assume this responsibility in an effort to see that a comprehensive picture of the child's level of functioning is obtained.

Take the case of a child with a mild hearing problem who was judged to be severely cognitively delayed by a psychologist using norm-referenced IQ tests that required understanding and use of language. Because of the hearing loss, language was limited, scores were low, and an inappropriate diagnosis was made. This same child, tested by another psychologist who based decisions on performance testing (nonverbal IQ tests), was again described as being severely delayed. Even though the test scores were in the range of retardation, both the parents and the teacher were unconvinced that the child was indeed severely delayed. Fortunately, the second psychologist noted, "Vision should be checked."

A thorough visual examination revealed severe myopia (nearsightedness)! Provided with glasses and teaching adapted to both vision and hearing problems, this 3-year-old began to learn. In this case, if the teacher had not observed that specialists were not communicating, and if the teacher had not persisted in encouraging the parents to see that all of the team members had all of the information, the diagnosis of severe cognitive delay might have been accepted. The child's precious early learning years might have been lost.

Interventionists are expected to be completely familiar with the environmental aspects of their own classrooms. If asked whether or not a child would benefit from placement in their particular classrooms, teachers should be able to answer with confidence.

Teachers can also develop understanding of their own personal teaching styles and the atmospheres they develop only through willingness to be honest and to seek feedback from others who observe them. They should initiate dialogues with directors, school psychologists, speech therapists, and nurses to help gain as objective a picture as possible of the characteristics of the classroom in which they teach. Use of audiotapes and videotapes may help teachers (a) determine whether they seem to have greater patience with one type of disability than with another; (b) see whether they seem to reinforce children differentially by age or sex; (c) assess the degree of structure they impose in a classroom; and (d) discover their most effective techniques of child management. Just as children differ, so do teachers and parents. Honesty and objective observation will help create the learner-environment match that is increasingly being encouraged in the literature.

ASSESSMENT FOR PROGRAM PLANNING

Historically, there has tended to be a mismatch between the information obtained from a thorough di-

agnosis and the information needed by early interventionists to plan and provide direct services. Originally, it was thought that information gathered during diagnosis would be useful in the development of instructional programs. However, such information is usually provided only on a very general level. Therefore, most early intervention programs require additional **assessment** upon program entry. "Although [assessment] uses and builds upon information gathered in the diagnostic assessment, its purpose is to provide a more detailed description of the child's strengths and needs" (Hanson & Lynch, 1995, p. 148). Greenspan and Meisels (1994) emphasize that "The process of assessment should always be viewed as the first step in a potential intervention process" (p. 22).

Assessment is an *ongoing* process. Initially it is necessary to use various informal and formal techniques to carry out in-depth observation in an effort to pinpoint each child's skills and deficits. What the child can or cannot do, and under what circumstances, must be determined to select appropriate behavioral objectives and effective instructional strategies. As the child's program progresses, ongoing assessment data need to be collected to update individual objectives and intervention procedures.

The Role of the Early Interventionist

Historically, teachers followed an adopted curriculum and activity plans. Although good teachers have always individualized activities to some extent, current practice requires much more thorough initial assessment, increased ongoing assessment, and continuous adaptation of activities.

Assessment is essentially the first task of the teacher in developing the individualized instruction program required for each child with disabilities. Useful assessment draws information from a variety of sources. It begins by carefully listening to parents and encouraging them to share the wealth of information they have about their child. Assessment requires frequent observation of children in a variety of situations. Observation may be done with the help of standardized (formal) or informal teacher-made techniques of measurement. This observation helps to confirm or refute diagnostic testing results; at the same time, concerns are pinpointed and a basis for individualized planning is developed.

Program assessment procedures must be directly related to program objectives, which emanate from the program curriculum adopted. (The process of developing program objectives is discussed in Chapter 5.) As Bricker and Veltman (1990) pointed out, the major differences in assessment activities are in the types of tools and procedures used. They offer the example of Piagetian-based programs, which logically choose to use the Infant Scales of Psychological Development (Uzgiris & Hunt, 1975). Readers are referred to the annotated bibliography at the end of the chapter for guidance in selecting materials for an in-depth study of assessment tools and processes.

PROGRAM EVALUATION

As noted earlier, federal law does use the term evaluation to refer to the process used to determine eligibility for services (see Chapter 6). Although the term *evaluation* is sometimes used interchangeably with the terms *assessment* and *diagnosis,* evaluation is considered here as separate and vital to the development of quality programs for young children with special needs. There are generally two purposes for **program evaluation:** (1) to collect evaluative information that is used as the basis for ongoing program decision making and (2) to provide evaluative information for external support agencies such as the Office of Special Education and The Danforth Foundation.

Evaluative information is used in making value judgments as to whether or not an instructional program produced the desired results. Evaluators discuss two types of evaluation: formative and summative. With **formative evaluation,** data on the progress of children are collected periodically and used to make ongoing program changes. **Summative evaluation** is concerned with the overall effectiveness of a program. It is a final accounting of program success. Testing typically is done at the beginning of an instructional program and at the end to determine whether or not desirable learning changes have occurred.

The Role of the Early Interventionist

Often teachers in early intervention programs have had little input into curriculum planning and program evaluation. Present practice, demanding teacher accountability, makes their participation in these areas a necessity. Teachers may or may not be directly involved in the process of gathering information to determine the effectiveness of a program. Some programs choose to acquire assistance from an outside agency to conduct the evaluation. These evaluations are usually summative in nature.

However, evaluation procedures must be planned at the beginning of a program to ensure ease of information gathering and to avoid the hazard of gathering data that are not relevant to the instructional program. Information gathered during the formative or ongoing assessment of a child's progress is usually appropriate in making summative program evaluations. Whenever ongoing assessment information is used to make value judgments about a program's effectiveness, teachers are most certainly involved. Therefore the more organized, objective, and thorough a teacher is when observing and recording, the easier program evaluation will be.

CHANGING PHILOSOPHIES AND PRACTICES

Practices in identification, assessment, and evaluation are changing rapidly. New systems for describing special education services and the children who need them are evolving. It should be recognized that practices in some communities may vary somewhat from those described here.

The trend has shifted away from categorical descriptions such as *retarded* and *learning disabled,* toward descriptions that convey an understanding of the intervention needs of children. The emphasis is not on diagnosis of a problem to be found in the child but on (a) analysis of the specific instructional needs of the child, (b) determination of services required to meet these needs, and (c) avoidance of the stigma that can accompany traditional labeling. Both the kinds of tests used and the interpretations made of resulting information are changing. Greater care is given to recognizing the effects of ethnic background, previous experiences, daily environment, and the stress placed on children during testing.

The recognition of the child's interaction with the environment has added a vital dimension to the assessment picture. Ulrey and Rogers (1982) used the phrase "the ecology of assessment." The **ecological approach** includes community and cultural influences as well as the complex interactions young children with disabilities have with family and others in their life space. Barnard and Kelly (1990) emphasized the need for systematically observing structured and unstructured interaction between the child and parents, siblings, teachers, or clinicians. Reinforcing the principle of contextualization, Greenspan and Meisels (1994) stated "Knowledge and an understanding of the cultural context of a young child's caregiving environment is essential to understanding the meaning of the child's repertoire of skills, knowledge, and personality characteristics" (p. 14). Efforts to provide a more realistic view of the child, the family, and the environment should lead to a more meaningful intervention plan.

In the past, many developmental assessments focused on singular areas of functioning and used rigidly administered standardized tests. As these tests lack breadth and depth, they led to fragmented views of a child's functioning and neglected to consider the larger environmental context in which the child functions (Parker & Zuckerman, 1990). It was, then, difficult to construct a comprehensive intervention plan based on incomplete information. Currently, assessments are being designed to address a wider range of child and parent caregiver behaviors and to be viewed within a broader context of a child's experiential world.

Ecological Validity

This move toward an ecobehavioral approach to assessment allows for understanding of the community and cultural influences as well as the complex interactions young children have with family and others in their life space (Barnett, Macmann, & Carey, 1992). Greater effort is being made to observe children in settings with which they are familiar. Children are being followed as they behave in the context of normally occurring routines such as eating and playing. Parents are included as interacting partners to help ensure the **ecological validity** of the observations. Ecologically valid assessments not only help the interventionist understand what skills are demonstrated by the child at home but also give clues to those behaviors that are functionally relevant to the family. This practice allows parents and professionals to agree on intervention goals that have meaning and relevance within the child's real-life environment of home and community.

Ecologically valid assessments would not allow a stranger to conduct assessment activities in unfamiliar settings, a traditional practice. Instead, parents would be included as significant partners in the assessment process. As Bailey and Wolery (1989) pointed out "assessment should focus heavily on naturalistic observation of children's behavior in the context of normally occurring routines, such as when eating, playing with peers, or performing other regular activities to ensure that professionals are aware of the extent to which children actually use skills" (p. 16).

Greenspan and Meisels (1994) elaborate on the tendency for reliance on structured tasks or questions to produce error in interpretation of young children's capacities:

- Young children have a restricted ability to comprehend assessment cues.

- Young children's verbal and perceptual-motor response capabilities are limited.

- Some types of questions require complex information-processing skills that young children do not possess.

- Young children may have difficulty understanding what is being asked of them in an assessment situation, and they may not be able to control their behavior to meet these demands. (p. 3)

Unfortunately, professionals who are under pressure to make quick decisions too often revert to their experiences with procedures and instruments developed to assess competencies in older children. This tendency to assess functioning of infants and young children with tests or scales already in existence tends to underestimate the abilities of children in those areas that are hard to measure, such as social skill development and functioning of a child within the context of his or her family.

THE EARLY INTERVENTION TEAM

Today, the team approach is considered to be an essential component of good early intervention programs. The number and type of professional team members vary with the perception of the needs of the child and family, the approach taken, and the financial resources of the program (Widerstrom, Mowder, & Sandall, 1991). A brief description of the roles various specialists play on early intervention teams is found in Table 4-1. It must be remembered that parents or other caregivers are an essential part of the team throughout all aspects of the early intervention process. To be effective, the team approach requires participants to collaborate fully with one another. To do so, they must possess good communication skills, the ability to solve problems, and knowledge of available resources. Most of all, team members must demonstrate respect for one another.

A review of the literature reveals three primary approaches to team development. The most traditional model is the **multidisciplinary approach** in which each professional conducts his or her own assessment and intervention in isolation. Although professionals may confer with one another, consultation is not necessarily systematic and planned. Team members who work as part of an **interdisciplinary team** often work together in the same environment. While

Table 4–1 Roles of specialists on intervention teams

Specialist	Description	Specialist	Description
Audiologist	Conducts screening and diagnosis of hearing problems and may recommend a hearing aid or suggest training approaches for children with hearing disabilities.	Orthopedist	Conducts screening, diagnosis, and treatment of diseases and injuries to muscles, joints, and bones.
Early childhood	Conducts assessments and implements individualized programs for young children with special needs; is concerned with all aspects of the child's development that impact upon learning and successful daily living.	Otolaryngologist	Conducts screening, diagnosis, and treatment of ear, nose, and throat disorders; is sometimes known as an ENT (ear, nose, and throat) physician.
Early interventionist	Any professional who is a primary service provider for infant and toddlers with speical needs and their families.	Pediatrician	Specializes in the diseases, problems, and health care of children.
Neurologist	Conducts screening, diagnosis, and treatment of brain and central nervous system disorders.	Physical therapist	Conducts an evaluation of a child's muscle tone, posture, range of motion, and locomotion abilities; plans physical therapy programs aimed at promoting self-sufficiency primarily related to gross motor skills such as walking, sitting, and shifting position; helps with special equipment such as wheelchairs, braces, and crutches.
Nurse	Oversees the overall medical well-being of the child and family. May initiate preventive procedures as well as take responsibility for specific treatments such as management of a gatrostomy tube.	Psychiatrist	Conducts screening, diagnosis, and treatment of psychological, emotional, developmental, or organic problems; prescribes medication; is alert to physical problems that may cause nervous disorders.
Nutritionist	Conducts an evaluation of a child's eating habits and nutritional status; provides advice about normal and therapeutic nutrition and information about special feeding equipment and techniques to increase a child's self-feeding skills.	Psychologist	Conducts screening, diagnosis, and treatment of children with emotional, behavioral, or developmental problems; is primarily concerned with cognitive and emotional development.
Occupational therapist	Conducts evaluation of children who may have difficulty performing self-help or other preschool activities that use arms, head, hand, and mouth movements; suggests activities to promote self-sufficiency and independence.	Social worker	Provides counseling or consultative services to individuals or families who may be experiencing problems.
Ophthalmologist	Conducts screening, diagnosis, and treatment of diseases, injuries, or birth defects that limit vision.	Speech-language pathologist	Conducts screening, diagnosis, and treatment of children with communication disorders.
		Technology assistant	Assists with development and maintenance of adaptive equipment and devices.

Adapted from Project Head Start, *Head Start: Mainstreaming Prescboolers Series*. Washington, DC: U. S. Department of Health and Human Services, Office of Human Development Services, Administration for Children, Youth and Families, 1978.

each member carries out his or her own assessment and intervention, there is frequent communication and planning within the team.

A model that has recently received considerable emphasis is the **transdisciplinary team approach.** Transdisciplinary team members share their expertise and may cross the boundaries of their professional disciplines. All team members become sensitive to understanding the professional perspectives of other team members. Transdisciplinary team members must be open to sharing their expertise with others and open to learning new skills. By doing so, they are in a position to maximize what they can offer to a child and his or her family. For example, a physical therapist may carefully instruct an infant educator in appropriate positioning techniques for a child with a particular disability. The infant educator can then use those techniques in the future with a child whose disability is similar. Of course, the educator would always consult with the physical therapist before employing techniques learned earlier.

Characteristics of Transdisciplinary Team Assessment

Administrators, specialists, and parents must meet to agree on a set of common attitudes and values regarding what makes up a good assessment. The team's philosophy will determine the goals of the assessment process and the procedures used. After clarifying priorities, team members will define their roles and responsibilities in relation to one another. Teams may choose to conduct **arena assessments,** in which active spectators observe while the parent or a specialist guides the child through prescribed activities. The observers take notes and complete assessment tools appropriate to their disciplines. On occasion, team members may interact directly with the child or request that specific tasks be attempted. Parents are encouraged, throughout, to comment and to validate the child's performance (Widerstrom, Mowder, & Sandall, 1991).

Family-Directed Child Assessment

When family members participate actively on early intervention teams, family-based assessment is more likely to occur. **Family-directed child assessment** involves selecting assessment questions that are important to the family. It also means choosing assessment procedures that can answer these high-priority questions and incorporating family input throughout the assessment process. Practitioners in the field of early intervention must be certain to develop procedures that will enable assessment of a family's concerns, priorities, and resources along with the child's strengths and needs without being too intrusive into the family system. This topic will be covered in greater depth later in this chapter.

USE OF STANDARDIZED TESTS WITH YOUNG CHILDREN

Early intervention specialists are increasingly looking to observation of the child in interaction with trusted caregivers and appreciation of the child's core functional capacities as the cornerstone of assessment (Greenspan & Meisels, 1994). The use of standardized tests is increasingly being criticized, as these structured test approaches look at what a young child can and cannot do only in relationship to a defined set of stimuli. This "snapshot" of the child's capabilities taken with a particular instrument is not representative of the child's usual functioning in the context of everyday living.

Contributing to this move away from routine standardized testing are (a) the lack of reliability and validity of standardized tests for use with young children; (b) the need to obtain information that can easily be transformed into individualized instruction plans; (c) the cultural biases built into many standardized instruments; and (d) the influence of situational factors on test performance. Therefore, we agree with those experts who believe that structured tests should be used only if absolutely needed and only as one part of a comprehensive approach to assessment. Even then, structured tests should be appropriate and used only if they provide additional meaningful information.

These concerns can be demonstrated in the following scenario. Imagine you are 4 years old. Your mother, who seems nervous, takes you to a place that sort of reminds you of the doctor's office.

A strange man introduces himself to me and says he would like to play with some toys and show me some pictures. He asks my mother to sit off to the side. Though I can't really see her, I know she is still worried about something.

The man talks funny. Though he says some words like my mother does, many words are unclear. The man shows me some toys which look kind of interesting, but I have trouble figuring out what he wants me to do with them. I have the feeling I need to be very careful, and not do the wrong thing. He seems in a hurry because he only shows me each toy for about a minute or so. I turn around to check on my mother. She gives me a funny look. Is she upset?

Next the man shows me some pictures. Though I enjoy my picture books at home, these pictures are new to me, and I'm not sure what to call them. He asks me different questions like "What is that?" or "What do you do with this?" I'm surprised that he doesn't know the answers to these questions. If he doesn't know, I'm pretty sure I don't! I'm only 4.

The room seems hot; my new shirt is scratchy, I would like to leave now. It seems like hours since I got on the bus with my mother to come here.

This scenario is not exaggerated. Though we can see gradual changes in our approaches to assessment, standardized instruments are still in common use. Most young children do not perform optimally in situations that are not familiar to them: unfamiliar adults, perhaps speaking an unfamiliar dialect or language; unfamiliar materials; unfamiliar rooms and furniture; and unfamiliar emotions and behavior exhibited by their parents. Many young children will not perform on demand in such situations. Standardized tests constrain children's natural curiosity and initiative, placing them in a responsive mode.

Also, such tests focus only on specific skills or products rather then on the processes of learning. Process characteristics such as cognitive style, locus of control, interaction style, mastery motivation, and tempo are rarely the focus of traditional assessment.

Cautious Use of Norm-Referenced Tests

Standardized tests are instruments designed to be administered by a trained examiner following specified procedures. Depending on the purpose, standardized tests or assessments could be completed by psychologists or psychometrists; speech, language, and hearing clinicians; pediatricians; or social workers. Typically these examiners report test scores and norm-referenced information.

Norm-referenced test scores reflect comparison of the performance of the child being tested with performance of other children of the same chronological age (CA) who took the test when norms were being established. Thus a child with a mental age (MA) of 3 years and 6 months (3–6) is said to have performed on the norm-referenced tests, such as the Stanford-Binet test, in a way that most children do at CA 3 ½. If that child were, in fact, age 2 ½, his or her IQ would be 132. This child would be identified as superior in intellectual functioning. On the other hand, a child with a CA of 5 years with the same MA of 3–6 would have an IQ of 67 and would be considered to have mild developmental delays if deficits in adaptive behavior were also evident.

Instruments such as those that assess MA are of little value when assessing the performance of children with disabilities or those from a minority culture if the normative standards do not take into account the influence of the children's unique conditions or the nature of their development. *Children who have developed in a different manner by virtue of having disabilities or being bilingual or deprived cannot be compared logically to children who have been raised in what society considers to be normal circumstances.* Only when used with caution by a skilled examiner can standardized, norm-referenced tests provide information worthy of consideration for planning individualized instruction programs.

For example, norm-referenced tables typically are used by speech, language, and hearing clinicians as a comparison for a child's receptive and expressive language skills. Usually children have internalized most of the rules of grammar and syntax by age 4. Those who do not speak distinctly and in grammatically correct ways by that age are described as having delayed speech and language development. Useful information can be gained about the specific nature of a child's delay by analyzing performance on individual items of standardized, norm-referenced tests. Practitioners who are skilled in analyzing performances on individual test items will note patterns in development and behavior that may contribute to instructional goals and objectives.

Exhibit 4–1 details some special considerations in assessing infants and toddlers, while Exhibit 4–2 lists techniques for assessment that are culturally fair.

EXHIBIT 4–1

Special Considerations in Assessment of Infants and Toddlers

1. Although standardized instruments are available for assessment of various aspects of infant and toddler development, they *must* be accompanied by extensive use of informal measures as well.
2. Infants and toddlers must be assessed within the context of their families, ideally within their natural home environment.
3. Special considerations must be given to infant behavioral and physiological states, which may change quickly and dramatically due to factors such as hunger, fatigue, and lability. Assessment sessions may need to be rescheduled several times. Also, infant state considerations will require that infants be observed on more than one occasion, at different times of the day.
4. Parents must play a key role in the assessment of infants and toddlers, in terms of both the information they can provide to the professionals and the need to observe the infant's behavior in the most optimal environment—that is, with the caregiver.

EXHIBIT 4–2

Techniques to Accomplish Culturally Fair Assessment

1. Use multiple assessment techniques within naturalistic settings, involving the parents or other caregivers as significant partners in the process.
2. Examine test items to be certain they are not biased against children or families of a certain cultural background.
3. Examine test manuals to determine whether the group to which the child is being compared is culturally compatible.
4. Give directions in the child's native language.
5. Use a multidisciplinary or transdisciplinary process so that more than one professional, along with the parents, can contribute to hypotheses developed from the observations.

Awareness of specific task performance can also be helpful to the teacher who has an understanding of the thinking and acting processes involved in test items missed. Knowledge of weaknesses will allow the teacher to use informal observational techniques to observe the child doing similar tasks. This observation will create increased understanding of how or why the child missed the items. The opportunity to refute or corroborate the original test results is thus provided by observation.

When observing her student, Ms. McLynn, another teacher, had the uneasy feeling that Danny could not hear well, even though he had passed the auditory screening test. (See Exhibit 4–3.) She decided to play games with Danny, such as asking him to point to the source of sound when blindfolded and to repeat simple sentences. Danny had much more difficulty with these tasks than the other 4-year-olds in the room. Ms. McLynn became even more convinced that Danny must have a complete audiological examination. She spoke to Danny's parents, who agreed to take Danny to the speech and hearing clinic at the nearby university.

These illustrations emphasize that it is the responsibility of the teacher to determine whether or not a child's test scores are an accurate reflection of abilities. Only observation on a day-to-day basis can confirm or refute examiner conclusions based on test performance. In this regard, Hare and Hare (1977) offered valuable advice to teachers of young children:

A critical factor for the teacher to remember is that test scores should not determine an educational program; they are contributing bits of information. All standardized tests provide only a sample of the child's behavior at a specific point in time. . . . The teacher also should be aware that traits are not immutable, and even what we call intelligence varies during the life of an individual. (p. 31)

Considerations for Interpreting Standardized Test Results

Educators need to be alert to hidden penalties that may understate test results of children who have disabilities and those who are culturally different. What amounts to impossible response requirements for some children distorts even further the inappropriateness of single-test normative samples. A recent example comes to mind. Consider the validity of a norm-referenced IQ on a child with severe visual disabilities who was given a Stanford-Binet test with no accommodations for the visual impairments. What is even more disturbing is the fact that the child's mental capacity was classified and reported according to the score received.

It is the teacher who may need to confirm or refute the face validity of test results. Do scores seem reasonable when reality tested against the teacher's observational experiences with the child? To provide assistance to teachers who will be expected to interpret the results of tests or reports filed by diagnostic specialists, selected measurement terms can be found in the glossary at the end of this text. An understanding of these helps teachers to explain the results of assessment procedures to parents and/or instructional aides, just as they help in the use of test information for the development of instructional strategies.

But even before becoming involved in the assessment process, teachers should talk with the specialists involved in their children's multidisciplinary assessment. They should discuss the assessment procedures used by these specialists and techniques for interpretation and translation of diagnosis into instructional outcomes and goals. Such a discussion helps the teacher to understand the situational factors that may influence the performance of children observed by these specialists.

Importance of Reliable and Valid Tests

Tests developed for young children usually lack rigor in terms of reliability and validity. Therefore it is difficult to use norm-referenced tests in developing educational plans with any confidence. The term **reliability** refers to the consistency or dependability of a testing procedure. It is the degree to which a child's score is a true score. That is, little or no error in measurement is present. The reliability of a test is often determined by comparing results from repeated administrations of the test (test-retest), by giving

♦ ♦ ♦

EXHIBIT 4–3

Ms. McLynn's Observation

Ms. McLynn teaches a preschool class of 4-year-olds. For several weeks she has been puzzled about Danny. He just won't pay attention. Sometimes when she calls him he comes right away. Other times he pays no attention until she raises her voice and speaks firmly. Often he acts as if he hears her call, but then he looks for her in the wrong direction. Or when she tells him to do something he does something else. Then he just gives her a blank look when she explains all over again what she wants him to do. (At first Ms. McLynn had wondered whether he had a hearing problem, but the nurse said he had passed the hearing screening.) Today she has decided to observe him carefully and take notes. Her aide, Ms. Cain, is playing a game with 4 children, while 10 others, including Danny, are playing with various toys and games. Here is what she wrote.

April 1, 1999

Danny is playing in the corner with some toy animals. Another child called him but he didn't turn, so Susan poked him. He turned, surprised. Tim said, "Danny, I want that little duck." When Danny gave him the dog, Tim said, "Not dog, you silly. I want the duck.". Danny obligingly gave him the toy truck! So Tim went over and picked up the duck.

Danny walked over to the clay table and began to pound the clay. He hit it with all his 4-year-old's vigor.

Remember to ask Danny's mother about allergies. His nose always seems to be dripping. Even though he passed our screening, he just doesn't seem to be hearing.

equivalent forms of the test, by comparing the results from each half (split-half), and by noting the consistency in rating between two or more scorers (interscorer). Even though it is essential to be certain that results do not reflect considerable error, many test manuals do not report results from efforts to determine the reliability. Consistency in any performance is not characteristic of young children, but attempts must continue to be made to ensure as much reliability as possible when assessments are made.

When a test is reliable, it may not necessarily be valid. **Validity** refers to what a test measures and how well it does so. Does it measure what it is supposed to measure? For example, if a teacher wishes to determine a child's level of problem solving, then he or she must require the child to solve problems. Asking a child to identify pictures by pointing to those named and recording a resulting MA score does not tell a child's potential for solving problems. A valid problem-solving test has not been given. Instead , a valid test for assessing a child's level of receptive language and ability to associate a verbal symbol with a visual symbol has been given.

Three types of validity are usually discussed: construct validity, content validity, and predictive validity. Of the three, **construct validity,** or the ability to determine how well a test measures the conceptual idea behind its construction, is the most difficult to determine. Today many question whether or not intelligence tests actually measure the abstract quality called intelligence. **Content validity** assumes that the test has a representative sample of the behaviors it is supposed to measure. Tests of eye-motor coordination that omit eye-foot tasks do not include a truly representative sample of test items. **Predictive** or **criterion-related validity** is concerned with whether or not performance on the test items can predict actual achievement on another test that is supposed to measure related skills or future performance in related life skills.

Predictive validity is an issue of considerable concern to developers of screening or readiness tests. The very attempt to predict difficulties that have not occurred has long been known to be risky (Keogh & Becker, 1973). Furthermore, ethical considerations interfere with attempts to determine validity. Children are not expendable! If we know how to help children, it is unthinkable to withhold the help.

When concerned adults learn of a child's potential learning problems through the diagnostic interpretation of testing, they feel compelled ethically to implement remedial or preventative actions as soon as possible. Therefore, the researchers are prevented from conducting long-term studies to find out whether or not the predicted problems actually did occur. That is, if the remedial program has been successful, then children suspected of having learning problems would not be expected to continue to exhibit the predicted problems. As a result, the ability of tests to predict the actual existence of future problems is questionable.

Rather than prevent children from obtaining the services they need, educators are choosing to rely less on test results and more on professional and parent observation and judgment. Increasing recognition of the serious lack of substantial reliability and validity characteristic of available instruments has left professionals little choice.

Criterion-Referenced Techniques

Comparing a child's performance to that of other children the same age is the traditional norm-referenced assessment. By contrast, **criterion-referenced assessment** compares the child's performance to a standard or expected mastery of a skill. A few criterion-referenced instruments that provide information directly transferable to program objectives are the Carolina Developmental Profile, Boehm Test of Basic Concepts, Brigance Diagnostic Inventory of Early Development, and the Hawaii Early Learning Profile. However, directors and teachers of preschools often choose to develop their own criterion-referenced measurement instruments. They have the advantage of being able to tie the assessment devices to the program objectives.

It should be readily apparent that criterion-referenced devices facilitate daily planning for children. Appropriate tasks are sequenced, and the child is requested to perform each item, beginning with the most difficult. Instruction begins with the first item a child cannot complete in a sequence. It is said that we assess from the top down, or the hardest to the easiest, and teach from bottom up, from the easiest to the hardest. When assessing, concern is not with how well a child did in comparison to other children but with determining the next appropriate skill for a child to master. This process is discussed thoroughly in Chapter 6.

Cross and Goin (1977) enumerated the strengths and weaknesses of criterion-referenced tools. As strengths they cited (a) the measurement of intraindividual progress; (b) the ease in developing program objectives as a result of sequentially developed devices; (c) the fact that such devices usually cover many developmental areas and often have more items than norm-referenced techniques; and (d) the greater flexibility of administration necessary for use with children who have disabilities. Weaknesses of criterion-referenced instruments include (a) the tendency

to design techniques for specific groups of children; (b) the inclination to test very specific skills that may not give a picture of the total child; and (c) the characteristic of measuring skills in acquisition rather than generalization. For example, there is a big developmental difference between a child who happens to place items correctly on a form board through trial-and-error and one who places the items correctly with obvious ease. Even considering the weaknesses of criterion-referenced tests, Salvia and Ysseldyke (1985) concluded:

When tests are administered for the purpose of assisting the classroom teacher in planning appropriate programs for children, criterion-referenced devices are recommended. When planning a program for an individual student, a teacher obviously should be more concerned with identifying the specific skills that student does or does not have than with the knowing how the student compares to others. In criterion-referenced measurement that emphasis is on assessing specific and relevant behaviors that have been mastered. Criterion-referenced tests treat the student as an individual rather than simply providing numerical indexes of where the student stands on a variety of subtest continua. (p. 30)

Curriculum-Based Techniques

Curriculum-Based or **-Referenced Assessments** are similar to criterion-referenced techniques. Curricular objectives are used as the standard against which performance is judged. The child's performance is observed on tasks requiring skills that are targets of the curriculum. Curriculum-based assessments are popular because they provide direct linkage between assessment and the development of curriculum-related intervention goals and objectives. **Task analysis** is the procedure often used to break the curriculum-related skills into "testable" and "teachable" steps. This process is also discussed in detail in Chapter 6.

CURRENT APPROACHES TO THE ASSESSMENT OF YOUNG CHILDREN

The previous discussion points out only some of the serious issues that exist with regard to the validity and appropriateness of use of standardized assessment instruments with infants and young children with special needs. A position statement of the National Association for the Education of Young Children decried the use of formal standardized instruments with young children who have no disabilities (NAEYC, 1988). Such arguments are even more valid for young children with disabilities.

A more appropriate assessment model being described in the literature is dynamic assessment. **Dynamic assessment models** are concerned not with a child's current performance output but rather with understanding learning styles and potential through careful observation of how children learn in a dynamic, interactive setting.

Also more appropriate are **authentic assessment strategies,** which strive to obtain information from multiple sources (e.g., direct observation, parent report, child interviews, samples of the child's work, etc.). The argument is presented that young children cannot possibly be understood and appropriately described on the basis of a single, highly structured, performance-based test.

Building Assessment on Multiple Sources of Information

Early intervention specialists readily agree that the assessment process must build collaboratively on information derived directly from families. Part C reinforces this approach by requiring that the process begin with a thorough understanding of the family's concerns, priorities, and resources. Professionals are expected to seek from the parents a detailed description of their child's developmental history and current capacities in all primary areas of development. After listening carefully to parents' views of their child's strengths and challenges, it is recommended that there be direct observations of the child. These observations should include interaction with caregivers and unstructured play in a familiar setting. Greenspan and Meisels (1994) further suggest that interaction between the child and clinician be arranged, if appropriate. Then, specific assessments of individual functions can be scheduled if enough information to fulfill the purpose of assessment has not already been obtained.

By following this additive approach, a picture of the "whole" child can be developed by integrating the data obtained from multiple sources. Using a developmental framework, professionals and families can, through open dialogue, create an understanding of the child's competencies within the caregiving and learning environments that will lead to optimal program planning.

Using Naturalistic Observations

Naturalistic observation or **direct observation** is a method of gathering information about children that is currently being favored over gathering information through formal tests. Naturalistic observation occurs when assessment information is gathered about a child through careful, systematic observations of that child in his or her natural environment. Recordings about various aspects of a child's behavior can be gathered during one observation period. For example, by stepping back and watching children as they naturally play with one another, or with a familiar adult, information can easily be gathered about aspects of behavior such as expressive communication, social skills, motor skills, and task persistence. Exhibit 4–3 illustrates one such naturalistic observation.

A major advantage of direct observation is that skills observed are not artificially divided as they are with traditional testing procedures. Direct observation allows the assessor to learn directly just how a child is capable of functioning when faced with the everyday demands of his or her environment. The guidelines in this chapter are included to help interventionists develop critical observation skills.

The term **performance assessments** represents procedures that require multiple observations within natural settings. Performance assessments refer to any methods "that allow children to demonstrate their knowledge, skills, dispositions, and other aspects of development and expression through solving problems, acting on their environments, interacting with individuals in their settings, experimenting, talking and moving" (Meisels, 1996, p. 37). Such procedures allow for multiple observations upon which to judge a child's performance from a more holistic, functional point of view. It allows us to make hypotheses built on observations during the process or within the context of intervention. We can then learn how to intervene more effectively.

Play-Based Assessment

One type of assessment considered to be more "authentic" than standardized tests is play-based assessment. Play-based assessment addresses some of the concerns raised about the appropriateness of standardized tests for young children with disabilities.

According to Linder (1993), play-based assessment offers a more authentic alternative to traditional formal assessment using standardized tests. An inviting play environment is created in a preschool classroom or child-care center, or even in the child's own home. Various interesting toys and materials are used, and children are encouraged to explore and initiate their own play actions and interactions. In the transdisciplinary model of play-based assessment (Linder, 1993), only one professional and the parent interact with the child during the assessment. Other professionals may observe the interactions, but they do not directly conduct their own assessment. (This is an example of "arena assessment.") As mentioned earlier, the examiner in the play-based approach is a "facilitator"—someone who is highly skilled in encouraging and observing children's play.

The Linder model is not simply an open-ended free-play session. Rather, it is an organized sequence of play situations in which very specific observations are made across all developmental domains (i.e., cognition, communication, social-emotional, and sensorimotor). Linder recommends that the assessment be videotaped. The child is carefully observed by the transdisciplinary team in the following situations:

1. *Unstructured facilitation.* In this situation the child is free to play in any area. The facilitator follows the child's lead, occasionally attempting to encourage the next higher level of play.

2. *Structured facilitation.* Those skills which were not demonstrated in the first phase can be encouraged in this phase of the assessment. The facilitator becomes somewhat more directive; however, the flavor of the activity is still responsive and interactive.

3. *Child-child interaction.* In this phase of the assessment another child who is familiar to the target child (if possible) is brought into the play area. The facilitator again assumes a responsive rather than a directive mode. If the two children do not interact with one another, the facilitator may attempt to encourage interaction, e.g., through the introduction of an interesting toy or cooperative game.

4. *Parent-child interaction.* In this situation the parent is asked to engage the child in ways that would be typical of what they would do at home. While the primary purpose of this phase is to obtain more typical responses from the child as he or she interacts with a familiar adult, it can also be used to observe the quality of parent-child interaction.

5. *Motor play.* In this phase the child is directed to the available large motor play equipment and encouraged to climb, ride a bike, crawl, etc. The occupational or physical therapist may wish to be directly involved with the child at this point in order to better assess muscle tone, balance, and other physical factors.

6. *Snack.* The final phase of the assessment is a snack. The child included in the child-child phase should also be included in the snack activity, as is the parent. This activity provides opportunity to observe various self-help skills, as well as oral motor skills and social interactions.

Limitations of Play-Based Assessment. Clearly, play-based assessment as described above offers a richness of qualitative information that cannot typically be obtained through standardized testing. In addition, such information can be used directly in program planning for the child. However, as with any single approach, there are limitations to consider. Play-based assessment is often time consuming and requires the coordination and cooperation of several professionals. Also, some areas of development, for example receptive language or auditory processing, may be difficult to assess in a play situation and may still require more formal standardized measure. Children with severe physical disabilities may require more detailed assessment by a physical therapist. Finally, some of the very criticisms of standardized assessment may also be issues for play-based assessment. Some children from culturally different backgrounds may not be familiar or comfortable with many of the toys. Some children are not object oriented and do not typically play with "things." Also, some children will not play comfortably with a stranger, or with several people watching. Children with severe cognitive disabilities, with multiple sensory disabilities, or with severe behavioral difficulties may not respond well to unstructured, unfamiliar play settings.

Despite these cautions, the shift toward more play-based assessment models in the field of early childhood special education is an important one. It will no doubt significantly improve the quality and usefulness of assessment information and make the interface between assessment and intervention a much more seamless link.

BECOMING A SKILLED OBSERVER

As previously stated, the target, setting, time, and conditions should be determined by the purpose of the observation. Informal observations help provide a more comprehensive view of the child than the observations obtained solely with the aid of structured inventories, checklists, rating scales, and tests. The focus of the observation is limited only by the imagination and time of the observer. It is important to observe a variety of situations during different times of the day. The focus should be more general when teachers are assessing the overall development of a child.

On the other hand, if teachers are trying to determine whether a child has accomplished a particular objective, they will narrow their observation to a very specific behavior under specified conditions. Most teachers will refer to a written objective to guide their observation. For example, if the IEP requires the child to learn to button a coat, the observer will watch specifically to see whether the child can button a coat, under what conditions, and with what degree of skill.

Observing How Children Perform a Task

The primary purpose of most teacher observation is to determine the strengths and weaknesses in children's learning repertoires in order to develop instructional goals and strategies. The teacher should not be concerned with etiology (investigation of causative factors) or assignment of diagnostic labels. The teacher must instead be concerned with exactly what children can (and cannot) do and how they do it. In closely analyzing task performances the teacher observes children's processes or styles of performance, in addition to determining whether or not children can perform specific tasks.

For example, when asked to describe what is happening in a picture, does a child respond impulsively? Or does he or she give a more deliberate or reflective response, taking time to note details while carefully scanning the picture? When copying a figure does the child seem to study the picture and plan? Or does he or she start drawing with only a brief reference to the drawing presented?

Consider the Special Challenges when English is the Child's Second Language

Too many children are considered to be developmentally delayed because observers do not have sufficient experience with culturally and linguistically diverse children. Careful observation must include information about the child's development, the sociocultural context of his or her family, and a comparison of the child's development to the developmental patterns of other children from a similar background. (McLean, 1998). A variety of observation procedures must be used including observation in natural environments, observation of play in comfortable, familiar setting and interviews with family members and care providers.

Realizing Environmental Influences

Various researchers have discussed the importance of focusing on the interaction of the child with the environment rather than focusing on either the child or the environment independently (Rogers-Warren, 1982). Stoneman and Gibson (1978) found the assessment performance of preschool children with developmental disabilities improved when they were tested by familiar figures and away from classroom distraction. The influence of situational factors again suggests that the teacher must vary the conditions of observation to get the most comprehensive view of a child's learning strengths and weaknesses.

Recognizing the Interrelationship of Skills

Finally, observers must be aware of and attuned to the interrelationship of skills. Children who are concentrating on the development of a motor skill may or may not exhibit what might be considered to be normal verbal or social interaction with other children during that period. On the other hand, children who are skilled in the motor activity may exhibit greater verbal fluency because of their confidence in their motor skills and lack of verbal inhibition.

Young children do not develop skills in isolation. The most obvious example of the interdependence of

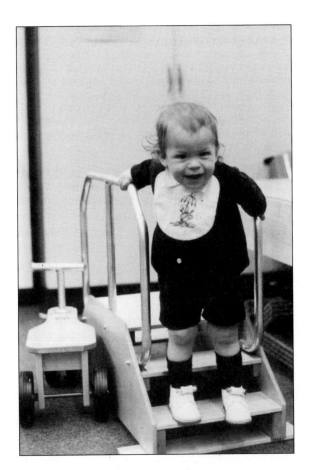

skills development is noted by psycholinguists in their study of language development. Chapter 9 elaborates on the importance of realizing that the potential for language development is present during every waking moment, assuming the child does not have severe impairments and is in a relatively stimulating environment. The teacher then must be aware of the child's total performance even when focusing on a single aspect of behavior.

In summary, observation is a complex, critical skill that can be developed only through systematic practice. The importance of becoming skilled in objective, systematic observation was made clear by a study conducted by the Illinois State Board of Education (1980). The study found that the most frequently used technique for child performance evaluation by teachers of young children with disabilities was observation of the child's behavior. In addition, national model programs also reported making frequent use of observational data. Therefore it is imperative that teachers strive to incorporate the following six abilities into their observational repertoire.

1. In-depth understanding of what is considered to be normal behavior.

2. Skill in recognizing high-risk behavior or danger signals.

3. Ability to follow the guidelines for responsible observation.

4. Ability to choose types of observational techniques appropriate to the purpose of the observation.

5. Awareness of the influence of performance styles, motivational factors, environmental variables, and extraneous behaviors on the judgments to be made about children's strengths and weaknesses.

6. Continuous practice of professionalism through respect for confidentiality, restraint from labeling, and attempts to counteract any tendencies toward placing stereotyped expectations on children.

Guidelines for Successful Observation

Observation is the skill of deliberately listening to and watching children's behaviors. They can be observed alone or in a group, at any time of the day, and under a variety of circumstances. While observing, the teacher notes aspects of appearance or behavior. Specific behaviors to be observed are determined by the purpose of the observation. Observers differ considerably in the process of recording information. Teachers often just make mental notes of what they see or hear. But use of an organized record-keeping form results in more systematic recording procedures. If the purpose of the observation is to assess the child's progress in an individualized program, systematic recording is essential to ensure objective, comprehensive data collection. The following guidelines help prepare teachers to become systematic, objective observers.

1. *Focus on observing exactly what the child does.* Record special, detailed observations of precisely what the child *does* and *says.* Use action verbs. Note the date, time, setting, what preceded the child's action or reaction, and what followed the behavior. *Do not* record inferences or opinions. Write down what is actually seen or heard.

2. *Record the observational details as soon after the observation as possible.* With practice, teachers develop the ability to participate and observe simultaneously by making mental notes. However, it is important to plan schedules so that recording of details can be done as quickly as possible. Details are important and are easily forgotten.

3. *Observe in a variety of settings and at different times during the child's day.* Changes in time and setting will often provide clues about children's interests. For example, children who are not comfortable on the playground may seek the solitude they never seek when in the classroom. Or they may become bullies on the playground, whereas they are self-controlled within the classroom. Children may be overly active when playing with other children

but not so when playing alone. There may be a certain time of day, perhaps just before lunch, when some children are especially irritable. Identifying these times and circumstances makes it possible to plan needed changes that create a smoothly run day. Watching for patterns often leads to an explanation of behavior.

4. *Be realistic in scheduling observations.* When the purpose of the observation is to determine the developmental level at which a child is functioning, it is critical to be able to observe and make notes as often and in as many situations as necessary to get a complete record of the developmental areas under concern. Observations that are haphazard or incomplete jeopardize the correctness of any resulting hypotheses. Be realistic when planning observation time. Be certain that there is a chance the observation will actually occur. On some days the only available observation time might be free-choice time.

5. *Begin by focusing on one child at a time.* Focusing on one child at a time and using checklists or rating scales will help to develop observational skills without running the risk of missing or forgetting information.

6. *Avoid being obvious.* Avoid calling attention to the child being observed or the fact that the observation is taking place. Interact as naturally as possible. Be seated in a place normal for the teacher to be during the activity that is being observed. For example, when observing playground activities, teachers usually post themselves in a spot providing optimal visibility. Stand or sit in the usual position when observing any activity.

7. *At all times, ensure confidentiality.* Notes must *never* be left around; a system of coding names should be developed to ensure privacy. *Never* discuss observations in front of other children or parents of other children. Read and become familiar with The Family Educational Rights and Privacy Act of 1974 (P. L. 93–380), because it is important to be aware of the parents' rights to read the records created. Never send or give data collected from observation or test

scores to outside agencies or individuals without written parental permission.

8. *Choose a workable recording system.* Teachers often need to experiment with file cards, notebooks, and three-ring binders to determine exactly what process is most convenient for them. Of course, the system used depends on the purpose and method of the observation. Well-organized, easy-to-review notes will facilitate the detection of patterns of behavior that may be extremely vital to real understanding of the child.

9. *Share your observational reports with parents as appropriate.* Objective evidence of child progress is always welcome.

The Portfolio and Its Use with Young Children

Teachers have always gathered together samples of students' work and assembled them into folders to display to parents at evening "open-house" gatherings. This process has become known as **portfolio assessment** and is receiving attention as a form of authentic assessment. Arter and Paulson (1991) define a portfolio as a purposeful collection of a child's work that portrays his or her efforts in one or more areas. For a young child, a portfolio might include records of various forms of systematic observation, video or tape recordings, photographs, and samples of a child's productive efforts such as drawings. In short, a portfolio (contained in a folder, box, expanding file, etc.) includes the visual evidence of the types of observations described below.

Decisions about what items to place in a portfolio will depend on the purpose of the portfolio. Grace and Shores (1991) suggest that portfolios should contain a statement of purpose along with a wide variety of work samples. Whenever possible, children should be involved in choosing the items to be included. All items should be dated and can be arranged according to curriculum area or category of development (Meisels & Steele, 1991).

As an assessment technique, portfolios can be used to document an individual child's progress over time and can be compared with a standard of performance that is consistent with the curriculum and appropriate developmental expectations. Portfolios are, obviously, a terrific tool for facilitating communication with parents. The types of observation techniques that follow provide valuable information to be included in portfolios.

Types of Observation Samples

Teachers should observe children in a variety of situations with as many purposes as they have objectives for the children. The particular technique chosen should relate directly to the purpose established. The following list describes some of the more common types of observation. As the list progresses, the techniques become more standardized (formal), requiring greater systematic planning and structure from the observer.

1. *Photographs.* Photographs provide a quick, easy method of obtaining children's reactions to various lessons. They provide an automatic record of involvement. These pictures can be taken at planned intervals to demonstrate sequential development. A dual purpose is served when the snapshots are used to stimulate language development, as discussed in Chapter 8. Using photographs in bulletin board displays offers repeated chances to encourage the development of self-esteem.

2. *Videotape and cassette recordings.* With the advancement of instructional technology, more and more classrooms commonly employ videotape and cassette recorders. Teachers have the advantage of participating directly in the activities and can later review the children's responses to their unique teaching styles. However, care must be taken to prevent the presence of recording equipment from distorting the observation. Children thoroughly enjoy observing and listening to themselves. Again, such techniques provide ideal opportunities for language

stimulation and allow the teacher to collect language samples. Moving pictures have often been used to provide evidence of development in areas such as motor coordination and social interaction. Local service clubs are often willing to make donations to help with film and processing costs.

3. *Collection of children's work.* Although early childhood education is usually process oriented rather than product oriented, there are opportunities to collect children's work. Collecting samples of such things as a child's paintings, tracings, cuttings, and attempts to print his or her name allows the teacher to analyze progress and to make this obvious to parents.

4. *Activity lists.* Programs that provide activity centers with some degree of free-choice time may post lists of children's names to be dated or checked off at each center area. By listing each child's name and the length of participation, the child's interests and level of involvement can be determined. The teacher will need to decide whether choices should be limited or children should be encouraged to broaden their participation.

5. *Anecdotal records, diaries, and logs.* Teachers record specific details of their observation, including exact behavior; precisely what precedes the behavior; and any reactions to the behavior, time, setting, and individuals involved. Care is taken to avoid making judgments, choosing isolated events, or overgeneralizing from atypical incidents. Systematic and regular recording allows the teacher to study patterns of behavior.

6. *Passports.* The passport (Shea & Bauer, 1991) is an ordinary spiral notebook that the child carries daily to and from home and the intervention program. An example of a passport is found in Chapter 3. All adults who work with the child are encouraged to make observational notations in the passport. Records are required to be brief, positive, honest, and consistent. The objective of the passport is to promote positive parent-teacher communication and cooperation.

7. *Time sampling and event recording.* In time sampling the observer selects specific behaviors that are readily observable and occur often. A few behaviors are chosen, and their occurrence is recorded on a prepared recording sheet during regularly scheduled, short observation periods. Unlike time sampling, event recording is not restricted to specific preplanned time intervals. A targeted behavior such as temper tantrums is recorded on occurrence. This method is often used with infrequently occurring behaviors.

8. *Checklists and rating scales.* Checklists and rating scales help specify exactly what the observer is to be observing. Use of such instruments makes it possible to vary the observer and still maintain consistency in the behavior that is observed. Illustrations of checklists and developmental scales are included throughout this text and in most texts in the field of early childhood special education. However, teachers are encouraged to design their own to ensure that the behavior observed is related to the goals and objectives of their program.

9. *Criterion-referenced tests.* Criterion-referenced devices or tests are designed to compare a child with a set of standards rather than with other children. Commercial tools usually establish the set of standards by selecting and sequencing items from several standardized developmental scales such as those developed by Bayley (1968) and Gesell (1940).

10. *Norm-referenced tests.* Norm-referenced tests provide the most standardized information-gathering opportunities for observation. The intent of norm-referenced measurement is to compare a child's performance to the performance of other children who are the same chronological age. Few norm-referenced instruments are useful in planning individualized programs for children. These tests tend to be less reliable with young children. "Norm-referenced tests are most useful for screening and classification, while criterion-referenced measures identify what to teach" (Smith, 1983, p. 325). However, funding agencies sometimes do require norm-referenced tests to complete program evaluations. Cautions when using such tests were discussed earlier in this chapter.

MONITORING CHILDREN'S PROGRESS

Record keeping in early childhood programs is not typically detailed with regard to specific learning objectives or training procedures. Nor is it individualized for each child. However, when children with special needs are included in the class, certain information must be recorded, kept up to date, and made available to parents and other members of the child's educational team. In other words, progress must be monitored on an ongoing basis. Record keeping must be designed to facilitate constant fine-tuning and adjustment of programs and procedures. Doing this in the simplest manner possible is very important. Unwieldy systems are either time consuming or simply not used. The goal of designing a record keeping system is that it be simple, efficient, and functional.

Data collection and record-keeping systems must be designed to fit specific training needs. Particularly challenging training objectives often require very specific and careful data collection. This is especially true if the child's progress is slow and/or inconsistent. In such cases it may simply be impossible to determine whether progress is actually being made without painstaking data collection efforts. For example, a plan for toilet training a child with multiple disabilities or reducing the destructive tantruming of a child with a severe behavior disorder would require very careful and frequent data collection of the type shown in Figure 4-1. The form in Figure 4-1 is being used to try to determine Jon's urination pattern and help him learn to urinate in the toilet. During the first part of the week he is checked every half hour to see if he is wet or dry. In addition, he is placed on the potty when he vocalizes because his mother reports that recently at home he has begun to signal when he is wet by vocalizing. Gradually Jon's urination pattern emerges. He is often wet around 8:30, and again around 11:00. If he is dry at these times, he is placed on the potty and praised if he urinates there. His vocalizations continue to be recorded to determine whether he is actually using vocalization as a signal that he is wet or that he needs to go to the bathroom.

Use of carefully planned motor prompts and hand-over-hand procedures to help a child who is blind learn to eat with a spoon might require keeping records of how much assistance was required on each bite during a meal, as shown in Figure 4-2. At the beginning of each meal, seven trials are recorded to determine the level of assistance required. Examining the data sheet we see that early in the week Sharon required total motor prompts (total assistance) on all seven trials. Though her performance is somewhat inconsistent, we see that by Thursday Sharon appears to be needing less total assistance and increasing the number of independent bites.

For keeping track of progress made across all IEP (IFSP) goals (outcomes), weekly or bi-weekly anecdotal record keeping may be more useful. One simple strategy is to make a single page for each child, listing the IEP objectives in each domain along one side of the form and leaving ample space to write comments next to each objective (see Figure 4-3). Several copies of this sheet are made for each child and placed in the child's folder. Each week one of the sheets is used to summarize progress and problems for each objective. This provides a running narrative of progress across all objectives. It also ensures that each objective is reviewed by the teacher and assistants weekly. Data sheets for specific problem behaviors as described above can be attached to these anecdotal overview sheets.

The important point about record keeping is that *it must be done.* No matter how competent the early childhood professional is, it will not be possible to carefully monitor the child's progress and the effectiveness of intervention procedures without such records.

This chapter has presented the primary sources of information used in recognizing children's special needs and in monitoring their progress. It has also discussed changing philosophies and practices, and raised cautions to be considered when using standardized instruments. The next chapter will consider how assessment information can be used in determining eligibility and in developing individualized service plans and programs.

PROGRESS DATA

NAME: _Jon_

OBJECTIVE: _Jon will urinate when placed on potty_

KEY: D = dry   W = wet   V = vocalized
P = placed on potty
+ = urinated in potty   — did not urinate in potty

Time	MONDAY	TUESDAY	WEDNESDAY	THURSDAY	FRIDAY
8:00	D	D	D	D	D
8:30	W	W	P—	VP+	P+
9:00	D	D	W	D	D
9:30	D	D	D	D	D
10:00	D	VP-	D	D	D
10:30	VP—	D	D	VW	VP+
11:00	W	W	VP+	D	D
11:30	D	W	D	D	D

Figure 4–1 Progress Chart

PROGRESS SUMMARY

NAME: _Sharon_   **WEEK:** _Nov 9-13_

OBJECTIVE: _Eat with spoon independently at lunch_

KEY: + = bring spoon to mouth independently
     ⊕ = support at elbow
     A = total assistance required

Trials	MONDAY	TUESDAY	WEDNESDAY	THURSDAY	FRIDAY
1.	A	A	⊕	A	
2.	A	A	A	A	
3.	A	⊕	A	⊕	
4.	A	⊕	⊕	+	
5.	A	A	+	+	
6.	A	A	A	⊕	
7.	A	A	A	⊕	

Figure 4–2   Progress Chart

STUDENT PROGRESS

NAME:_____   DATE:_____

OBJECTIVES	COMMENTS
Social Skills 1. 2. 3.	
Communication 1. 2. 3.	
Motor Skills 1. 2. 3.	
Self-Help 1. 2. 3.	

Figure 4–3   Progress Chart

Summary

There has been a movement away from categorical descriptions of children with disabilities toward an analysis of specific instructional needs of the child. Typically a multistage process is involved that consists of (a) initial identification of children with problems, perhaps involving observational comparisons against a developmental checklist and screening for medically related problems; (b) diagnosis resulting in multidisciplinary staff development of an IFSP or IEP; (c) teacher observation and determination of daily activities; and (d) monitoring of the child's progress on a continuous basis for the purpose of updating the child's program and periodically to review success of the overall program.

Several phases in the process of recognizing and accommodating a child's special needs require assistance of numerous specialists. But the early interventionist plays an instrumental role in the continuous success of the child's efforts. To be successful at this, part of the educator's role is to know what constitutes so-called "normal" behaviors. Armed with such knowledge, the teacher can then systematically observe for high-risk signals that might indicate the need for referral to specialized personnel or agencies. Guidelines and suggestions are given for how to strengthen this observational process.

Early childhood educators should be particularly cautious when using standardized tests as part of the assessment process. Norm-referenced tests that compare a child's scores with norms established by groups of children of the same age may distort a child's capabilities if disabilities or unique needs are not considered. Criterion-referenced assessment compares a child's performance to a developmental standard or sequence of skills to be mastered. But increasingly, play-based, teacher-developed techniques serve as the basis for assessment and evaluation.

This chapter emphasized that the ultimate responsibility for assessment, choice of daily activities, and effective teaching remains with the teacher. This is a responsibility for which few teachers feel prepared. To become skilled in the techniques of observation, formal and informal testing, and programming, practice and patience are essential.

Finally, this chapter has attempted to clarify some of the ambiguities in the whole arena of evaluation, bring to light some of the critical concerns surrounding evaluative procedures, and encourage study and practice.

Discussion Topics and Activities

1. Differentiate identification, diagnosis, assessment, and evaluation. Give the purposes of each process.

2. Select or construct your own developmental rating scale. Observe at least two children. If possible, observe a child suspected of having a disability and a child with no known deficits. Check and compare their performances according to your rating scale. Write a summary of the educational strengths and weaknesses you observed. Be certain you have parental permission, and observe all aspects of confidentiality.

3. Design a few informal assessment procedures that you can use to determine the educational strengths and needs of a young child with disabilities. Note the behaviors you would look for in order for the procedure to be useful to you in writing plans for the child being assessed.

4. Differentiate norm-referenced and criterion-referenced tests, and give the advantages and disadvantages of each type of test.

5. Use the Buros *Mental Measurements Yearbook* to thoroughly research a commonly used assessment

instrument such as the Peabody Picture Vocabulary Test. Present a critique to your classmates. Be certain to research important factors such as reliability, validity, and the characteristics of the normative sample.

6. Select a specific child with a severe disability. Plan what you would include in a portfolio to demonstrate the child's progress over a 6-month period.

Annotated Bibliography

Bondurant-Utz, J. A. & Luciano, L. B. (1994). *A practical guide to infant and preschool assessment in special education.* Boston: Allyn and Bacon.

This book provides basic guidelines for the use of a variety of evaluation instruments. Chapters include discussion of qualitative observations, family involvement, the team process, cultural diversity, special considerations for working with children with severe disabilities, ecological and behavioral assessment, and program evaluation.

Cohen, L. B., & Spenciner, L. J. (1994). *Assessment of young children.* White Plains, NY: Longman.

This volume is an introductory guide to assessment of children from birth to 8 years of age. It intends to provide a basic understanding of the assessment process, contribute to the development of assessment skills, and point the way to linking assessment results to planning for intervention. It includes separate chapters on the role of the family in assessment, observation of children in natural environments, assessment through play, and use of alternative assessment instruments.

DeStefano, D. (1991). *Best practices: Evaluating early childhood special education programs.* Tucson, AZ: Communication Skills Builders.

This resource provides information on best practices and follow-up procedures using a self-evaluation form to help programs identify their strengths and weaknesses. It covers curriculum programming, organization of the learning environment, social skills, use of support services, family involvement, and transitions.

Gibbs, E. D., & Teti, D. M. (Eds.) (1990). *Interdisciplinary assessment of infants: A guide for early intervention professionals.* Baltimore: Paul H. Brookes.

Contributors from a wide range of disciplines provide a broad resource of current domains, methods, and procedures in infant assessment. Topics include a history of assessment, exploration of measurement issues, assessment of neuromotor integrity, oral-motor development, sensorimotor competencies, infant information processing, language assessment, social and temperament development, play as-

sessment, parent-child interaction, family assessment, and use of a transdisciplinary approach.

Keogh, B. K., & Daley, S. E. (1983). Early identification: One component of comprehensive services for at-risk children. *Topics in Early Childhood Special Education, 3*(3), 7–16.

Even though many years old, this article is still essential reading for anyone involved in the process of early identification. Of particular interest are the cautions surrounding screening. Six questions critical to a professional approach to early identification are posed and discussed. The argument that early identification must be viewed as a comprehensive set of services, not just a test or assessment procedure, should be uppermost in the minds of all who have at heart the interests of young children with special needs.

Impara, J. C. & Plake, B. S. (Eds.). (1998). *Thirteenth mental measurements yearbook.* Lincoln: Buros Institute.

The purpose of these yearbooks is to present comprehensive reviews of a large variety of assessment instruments. Critical reviews from professionals both question and support claims made by test authors and publishers. Before using any instrument, these yearbooks should be consulted. Recent publications may not be included, whereas older tests may be found in previous editions of the yearbook. These yearbooks are found readily in the reference section of college and university libraries.

Linder, T. W. (1993). *Transdisciplinary play-based assessment: A functional approach to working with young children.* Baltimore, MD: Paul H. Brookes.

This intriguing book is intended to be a guide to a flexible new model for conducting assessment and intervention for children who are developmentally functioning between the ages of 6 months and 6 years. Intended for use by a transdisciplinary team, this book contains descriptive observation guidelines for assessing a young child's cognitive, social-emotional, communication, and sensorimotor development through child-directed play interactions. The requirement for parent participation results in a session that is less stressful for the child and less intimidating to the family.

McLean, M., Bailey, D., & Wolery, M. (Eds.), (1996). *Assessing infants and preschoolers with special needs.* Englewood Cliffs, NJ: Merrill/Prentice Hall.

This comprehensive text addresses issues, considerations, and procedures in assessing infants and preschoolers with disabilities. It is intended for professionals who are responsible for designing and implementing individualized intervention programs for young children with special needs. It serves as a valuable resource for the variety of professionals who are requested to collaborate in meeting the special needs of young children and their families.

McLean, M. (1998). Assessing young children for whom English is a second language. *Young Exceptional Children, 1,* 20–25.

A much needed review of what we need to know when assessing children who are acquiring a second language. Essential strategies are offered to help us understand it is not "business as usual."

McLoughlin, J. A., & Lewis, R. B. (1994). *Assessing special students.* Englewood Cliffs, NJ: Merrill/Prentice Hall.

The fourth edition of this text strives to show future teachers how to really use assessment results to improve education for children with disabilities. It provides an introduction to psychoeducational assessment and is an excellent resource for those who wish to gain a deeper understanding of testing in the broader context of assessment. Of particular interest is the chapter devoted to special consideration for early childhood and family assessment.

Meisels, S. J. & Fenichel, E. (Eds.) (1996). *New visions for the developmental assessment of infants and young children.* Washington, DC: Zero to Three.

This comprehensive volume stresses the importance of understanding a child's skills and abilities within the context of his or her learning and living environment. It is the elaboration of the principles and guidelines for developmental assessment developed by the Zero to Three's multidisciplinary work group on assessment.

Meisels, S. J. & Atkins-Burnett, S. (1994). *Developmental screening in early childhood: A guide.* Washington, DC: National Association for the Education of Young Children.

The purpose of this book is to clarify some of the issues and practical components necessary for the design of an effective developmental screening program for young children. Critical decisions involved in planning the screening program, selecting instruments, and involving parents and the community are discussed. Included is an annotated bibliography of appropriate readings.

Mindes, G., Ireton, H., & Mardell-Czudnowski, C. (1996). *Assessing young children.* New York: Delmar Publishers.

This text considers the major issues related to assessment of young children. It focuses on the importance of involving parents and in practicing astute observation. Alternative assessment strategies, the location of assessment, and special issues related to testing very young children are considered.

National Association for the Education of Young Children. (1991). Guidelines for appropriate curriculum content and assessment in programs serving ages 3 through 8. *Young Children, 46*(3), 21–38.

These guidelines are essential to all practitioners faced with buying assessment materials and determining assessment procedures. The guidelines first address the primary use of assessment as a tool for planning instruction and communicating with parents. Then guidelines for screening and program evaluation are offered. Finally, a framework for determining age-appropriate and individually appropriate curriculum is discussed.

Robinson, C., & Fieber, N. (1988). Cognitive assessment of motorically impaired infants and preschoolers. In T. Wachs & R. Sheehan (Eds.), *Assessment of young developmentally disabled children.* New York: Plenum.

This chapter considers issues involved in and procedures available for the assessment of infants and preschoolers with motor impairments. Problems in the use of traditional approaches in assessment of motorically disabled young children are discussed thoroughly. The process approach is presented as an alternate assessment procedure for infants and toddlers with physical disabilities. Well-documented case studies illustrate the process.

Rossetti, L. M. (1990). *Infant–toddler assessment: An interdisciplinary approach.* Waltham, MA: College-Hill.

The purpose of this text is to provide an introduction to the assessment of infants and toddlers. After discussing historical implications for assessment and an overview of the characteristics of the children who should be involved in assessment, the author uses the three teaming models (multidisciplinary, interdisciplinary, and transdisciplinary) to illustrate various approaches to assessment.

Assessment Within the Center or Classroom

Allen, K. E., & Marotz, L. (1994). *Developmental profiles: Birth to six.* New York: Delmar.

The purpose of this handbook is to provide a brief yet comprehensive guide to the development of young children from birth to 6 years of age. This is a nontechnical presentation intended to supplement a basic text on child development. Included are concise profiles of developmental areas, descriptions of daily activities and routines typical of children at each level, and appendixes containing growth charts, reflex schedules, and a sample health history form.

Beaty, J. J. (1997). *Observing development of the young child.* Englewood Cliffs, NJ: Merrill/Prentice Hall.

This attractive textbook offers students a method of observing and recording natural development of children ages 2 to 6. Its primary purpose is to teach nonspecialist observers to understand child development through the assistance of objective data gathered by observation in natural settings. Each of 12 chapters is devoted to a different aspect of development. A "Child Skills Checklist" made up of eight or nine specific items from each area systematically guides observations. Of particular value are the helpful intervention techniques given with each set of items to be observed.

Benjamin, A. C. (1994). Observations in early childhood classrooms: Advice from the field. *Young Children, 49*(6), 14–20.

This article offers practical, field-tested advice for incorporating observation into the daily life of early childhood programs. It provides guidelines to help practitioners prepare the environment for successful observations. Focus is on clarification of observational goals, organization, record keeping, confidentiality, and the involvement of children in the process.

Boehm, A. E., & Weinberg, R. A. (1997). *The classroom observer: Developing observation skills in early childhood settings.* New York: Teachers College Press.

This book focuses on skills that will enable early educators to make appropriate, valid inferences and to arrive at decisions based on objective observation gathered in natural learning environments and diverse educational settings.

Cohen, D. H., Stern, V. & Balaban, N. (1997). *Observing and recording the behavior of young children* (4th ed.) New York: Teachers College Press.

This book carefully presents and discusses the details of observing and recording while maintaining the quality of interaction. The reader is treated to a multitude of examples of what to look for and how to look for it throughout daily activities.

Meisels, S. J. (1993). Remaking classroom assessment with the work sampling system. *Young Children, 48*(5), 34–40.

Meisels offers an alternative to product-oriented, group-administered achievement tests for young children. This alternative, The Work Sampling System, assesses and documents children's skills, knowledge, behavior, and accomplishments through the use of developmental checklists, portfolios, and summary reports. Teachers learn to be better observers through this form of authentic assessment, and parents are invited to become participants in the assessment process.

Nicolson, S., & Shipstead, S. G. (1998). *Through the looking glass: Observations in the early childhood classroom.* Upper Saddle River, NJ: Merrill/Prentice Hall.

This book focuses on the importance of understanding the close relationship between observing, understanding what is being observed, and using results to improve curriculum and the environment. It includes many examples and applications in its practical approach.

Parks, S. (1992). *Inside HELP: Administration and Reference Manual for the Hawaii Early Learning Profile.* Palo Alto, CA: VORT Corporation.

This manual is a comprehensive administration and reference guide to be used in conjunction with all of the HELP curriculum and assessment materials. It includes clear definitions, assessment guidelines, and credit criteria for each of the 685 developmental skills and behaviors included in all of the HELP products. Of special importance are the special assists that enhance opportunities to be in compliance with Part H. For example, family-friendly definitions of the underlying concepts of developmental skills are offered, along with specific questions to facilitate family-directed assessment.

Sugai, G. (1986). Recording classroom events: Maintaining a critical incidents log. *Teaching Exceptional Children, 18,* 98–102.

This article contains a simple procedure for documenting critical classroom occurrences. The resulting log provides accurate and specific information about critical behaviors and events occurring in the classroom. It is the author's opinion that this systematic procedure can be extremely useful to professionals who may be called on to provide testimony in support of their instructional decisions.

Wortham, S. C. (1996). *The integrated classroom: The assessment curriculum link in early childhood education.* Englewood Cliffs, NJ: Prentice Hall.

This text is about integrating assessment and learning as an interactive process. It also fosters the integration of curriculum and instruction that is designed to be age appropriate, group appropriate, and individually appropriate. It specifically addresses cognitive, language, social, and physical development.

References

Arter, J., & Paulson, P. (1991). *Using portfolios of student work in instruction and assessment.* Portland, OR: Northwest Regional Educational Laboratory.

Bailey, D. B. & Wolery, M. (Eds.). (1989). *Assessing infants and preschoolers with handicaps.* Englewood Cliffs, NJ: Merrill/Prentice-Hall.

Barnard, K. E., & Kelly, J. F. (1990). Assessment in parent-child interaction. In S. J. Meisels & J. P. Shonkoff (Eds.), *Handbook of early childhood intervention* (pp. 278–302). New York: Cambridge University Press.

Barnett, D. W., Macmann, G. M., & Carey, K. T. (1992). Early intervention and the assessment of developmental skills: Challenges and directions. *Topics in Early Childhood Special Education, 12*(1), 21–43.

Bayley, N. (1968). *Bayley infant scales of development.* New York: Psychological Corporation.

Benner, S. M. (1992). *Assessing young children with special needs: An ecological perspective.* White Plains, NY: Longman.

Bricker, D., & Veltman, M. (1990). Early intervention programs: Child-focused approaches. In S. J. Meisels & J. P. Shonkoff (Eds.), *Handbook of early childhood intervention* (pp. 373–427). New York: Cambridge University Press.

Campbell, P. H. (1991). Evaluation and assessment in early intervention for infants and toddlers. *Journal of Early Intervention, 15*(1), 36–45.

Cross, L., & Goin, K. W. (Eds.). (1977). *Identifying handicapped children: A guide to casefinding, screening, diagnosis, assessment and evaluation.* New York: Walker.

Gesell, A. (1940). *The first five years of life.* New York: Harper & Row.

Gibbs, E. D., & Teti, D. M. (1990). *Interdisciplinary assessment of infants: A guide for early intervention professionals.* Baltimore: Paul H. Brookes.

Grace, C., & Shores, E. F. (1991). *The portfolio and its use: Developmentally appropriate assessment of young children.* Little Rock, AR: Southern Early Childhood Association.

Greenspan, S. I., & Meisels, S. (1996). Toward a new vision for the developmental assessment of infants and young children. In S. J. Meisels and E. Fenichel (Eds.), *New visions for the developmental assessment of infants and young children.* Washington, DC: Zero to Three.

Hanson, M. J., & Lynch, E. W. (1995). *Early intervention: Implementing child and family services for infants and toddlers who are at-risk or disabled.* Austin, TX: Pro-Ed.

Hare, B. A., & Hare, J. M. (1977). *Teaching young handicapped children: A guide for preschool and the primary grades.* New York: Grune & Stratton.

Illinois State Board of Education (1980). *Early childhood education for the handicapped: Special study.* Springfield: Illinois State Board of Education.

Keogh, B., & Becker, L. D. (1973). Early detection of learning problems: Questions, cautions, and guidelines. *Exceptional Children, 40,* 5–11.

Linder, T. W. (1993). *Transdisciplinary play-based assessment.* Baltimore: Paul H. Brookes.

McLean, M. (1998). Assessing young children for whom English is a second language. *Young Exceptional Children, 1,* (3) 20–25.

Meisels, S. (1996). Charting the continuum of assessment and intervention. In S. J. Meisels and E. Fenichel (Eds.), *New visions for the developmental assessment of infants and young children.* Washington, DC: Zero to Three.

Meisels, S. & Fenichel, E. (Eds.) (1996). *New visions for the developmental assessment of infants and young children.* Washington, DC: Zero to Three.

Meisels, S. J., & Wasik, B. A. (1990). Who should be served? Identifying children in need of early intervention. In S. J. Meisels & J. P. Shonkoff (Eds.), *Handbook of early childhood intervention* (pp. 605–632). New York: Cambridge University Press.

Meisels, S., & Steele, D. (1991). *The early childhood portfolio collection process.* Ann Arbor: Center for Human Growth and Development, University of Michigan.

National Association for the Education of Young Children. (1988). Position statement on standardized testing of young children 3 through 8 years of age. *Young Children, 43,* 42–47.

Parker, S. J., & Zuckerman, B. S. (1990). Therapeutic aspects of the assessment process. In S. J. Meisels & J. P. Shonkoff (Eds.), *Handbook of early childhood intervention* (pp. 350–369). Cambridge, England: Cambridge University Press.

Rogers-Warren, A. K. (1982). Behavioral ecology in classrooms for young handicapped children. *Topics in Early Childhood Special Education, 2,* 21–32.

Rossetti, L. M. (1990). *Infant-toddler assessment: An interdisciplinary approach.* Waltham, MA: College-Hill.

Salvia, J., & Ysseldyke, J. E. (1985). *Assessment in special and remedial education.* 3rd ed. Boston: Houghton Mifflin.

Shea, T. M., & Bauer, A. M. (1991). *Parents and teachers of children with exceptionalities: A handbook for collaboration.* Boston: Allyn and Bacon.

Smith, C. R. (1983). *Learning disabilities: The interaction of learner, task and setting.* Boston: Little, Brown.

Stoneman, Z., & Gibson, S. (1978). Situational influences on assessment performance. *Exceptional Children, 45,* 166–169.

Ulrey, G., & Rogers, S. J. (1982). *Psychological assessment of handicapped infants and young children.* New York: Thieme-Stratton.

Uzgiris, I., & Hunt, J. M. (1975). *Assessment in infancy: Ordinal scales of psychological development.* Urbana: University of Illinois Press.

Widerstrom, A. H., Mowder, B. A., & Sandall, S. R. (1991). *At-risk and handicapped newborns and infants.* Englewood Cliffs, NJ: Prentice Hall.

Chapter 5

Developing Individualized Intervention Plans and Programs

Key Concepts

♦ The Individuals with Disabilities Education Act (IDEA) requires that an Individualized Family Service Plan (IFSP) be generated for infants, toddlers, and their families. Individualized Education Programs (IEPs) be developed for preschoolers.

♦ Families should be seen as the primary decision makers in the individualized planning processes.

♦ The IFSP and IEP documents are of secondary importance to the **process** the team uses in developing them.

♦ Essential to the planning processes is a belief in collaboration among families and service providers.

♦ Identification of family concerns, priorities, and resources should be guided by a family-directed approach.

♦ Family concerns should be directly reflected in functional IFSP outcomes and IEP goals and objectives.

♦ Service coordination is a newly mandated service for infants and toddlers that can potentially enable parents to become their own advocates as their child enters into public school services.

♦ A multidisciplinary assessment team is expected to collaborate with the parents in determining appropriate goals and objectives for the IEP.

♦ Annual and periodic reviews of the IFSP and IEP should be a vehicle for continuous improvement of services.

♦ In order to minimize family stress, careful consideration should be given to planning steps in transition to the next educational environment.

♦ ♦ ♦

The previous chapter introduced some of the major issues surrounding the processes of identification, diagnosis, assessment, and evaluation. Attention was given to preparing professionals for their primary role as astute observers of children's behavior. The options available for assessment within the classroom were discussed. This chapter will focus on the process of developing individualized programs and plans.

THE INDIVIDUALIZED FAMILY SERVICE PLANNING (IFSP) PROCESS FOR INFANTS, TODDLERS, AND THEIR FAMILIES

The Individualized Family Service Plan (IFSP) is the written document specified in IDEA to guide the implementation of early intervention services for children from birth to age 3 and their families. It is to be developed through **collaborative interchanges** between families and the professionals involved in assessment and service delivery.

The purpose of the IFSP is to identify and organize formal and informal resources to facilitate families' goals for their children and themselves. The IFSP is a promise to children and families—a promise that their strengths will be recognized and built on, that their needs will be met in a way that is respectful of their beliefs and values, and that their hopes and aspirations will be encouraged and enabled. (Johnson, McGonigel, & Kaufmann, 1989, p. 1)

The written document, in and of itself, is not considered to be as significant as the *process* involved in the development of the written product. Service providers are expected to form partnerships with families built on trust and respect that are expected to be a viable part of each child's program throughout the critical first few years of the child's life. The IFSP process is intended to support the natural caregiving role of families. In keeping with the family systems dynamics outlined in Chapter 3, young children with special needs can be understood only within the context of their families. In this way, the IFSP is viewed differently from the IEP to be discussed later in this chapter. The IFSP process is *family centered,* while the IEP tends to be child centered. The IFSP approach takes into account the fact that infants and toddlers are uniquely dependent on their families for physical and emotional sustenance.

The IFSP Process

The process for developing the IFSP consists of the gathering, sharing, and exchange of information between families and staff to enable families to make informed choices about the early intervention services they want for their children and themselves. (Johnson, McGonigel & Kaufmann, 1989, p. 11)

Families may move through the dynamic process differently according to their concerns, desires, and choices. However, several key activities are expected to occur. These include the following:

1. *First contacts and screening for eligibility.* As discussed in the previous chapter, when a child is referred for early intervention services, an evaluation is conducted to determine a child's eligibility for services. Criteria for eligibility must be consistent with each state's definition of developmental disability. Assessment plans are developed with the family to determine the child's status in each of five developmental areas: physical development, including vision, hearing and health; cognitive development; communication development; social or emotional development; and adaptive development.

2. *Assessment of the family's resources, priorities and concerns, and the child's strengths and needs.* Child and family assessment involves interviews with caregivers designed to elicit family-directed expression of family resources, priorities, and concerns. Families are also encouraged to identify the supports and services necessary to enhance the family's capacity to meet the developmental needs of their child.

3. *Development of a service plan document.* A meeting must be held within 45 days of referral to develop the initial Individualized Family Service Plan (IFSP) document. The meeting must be held in settings and at a time convenient for families. It is required to be conducted in the native language of the family. An ongoing service coordinator is also designated at this meeting.

4. *Implementation and monitoring.* Services for an eligible child and family are expected to be implemented as soon as possible after the IFSP meeting. The service coordinator is responsible for coordinating, facilitating, and monitoring the timely delivery of early intervention services. A review of the IFSP must be completed every 6 months or more frequently if deemed appropriate. In addition, a full evaluation of the IFSP is to be conducted on an annual basis.

Participants in Initial and Annual IFSP Meetings

Participants in the initial and annual IFSP meetings usually include the following:

1. The parent or parents of the child.

2. Other family members as desired by the family.

3. An advocate or person outside the family, if the parent requests that the person participate.

4. The service coordinator who has been working with the family since the initial referral or who has been designated by the public agency to be responsible for the implementation of the IFSP.

5. A person or persons directly involved in the assessment process.

6. As appropriate, persons who will be providing services to the child or the family.

If any of these persons are unable to participate, arrangements are to be made to include their involvement through other means, such as arranging a telephone conference call; employing the services of a knowledgeable, authorized substitute representative; or making available pertinent records.

Identifying Family Concerns, Priorities, and Resources

Although P. L. 99–457 originally required identification of family strengths and needs as related to enhancement and development of the child, professionals are increasingly wary of the use of the term *needs,* which implies that families may need to be fixed. The term *concerns* is now used here in an effort to encourage the view that families are competent and able to make choices based on their concerns and priorities. It is not that families are just "needy" and we must help. It is *not* appropriate for early childhood special education professionals to decide what areas of family life should be assessed to determine family strengths and concerns. Therefore, the law specifically states that there must be "a *family-directed* assessment of the resources, priorities, and concerns of the family . . . ." (Section 636, P. L. 105–17).

When general problems in family functioning are suspected, it is appropriate to explore with the family the possibility of referring them to appropriate professionals for counseling or other forms of assistance. Only families can decide for themselves which aspects of their functioning are relevant to their ability to help their child develop optimally. As Vincent (1990) pointed out, we need to understand the concerns and priorities of the family from the family's point of view and then identify the concerns and priorities from the professional's point of view. Through collaboration, concerns are then prioritized before resources can be identified.

Florene Poyadue, former Executive Director of Parents Helping Parents (see Chapter 3), has referred to **CPR (concerns, priorities, and resources)** as the lifeline of families who have children with special needs. Once concerns are prioritized, the responsibility of both the professional community and families is the identification of viable resources. It is important that professionals assist families in identifying and building on their own resources and strengths while at the same time helping them to link up with appropriate community resources. It must be remembered that only resources that are easily accessible to families are useful.

Considerable discussion has been generated among professionals and families as to the least-intrusive way to help families identify their concerns, priorities, and resources. It is clearly acknowledged that professionals need training and experience in a more **family-centered approach to assessment** in order to balance their needs for specific information to determine eligibility and programming against families' priorities and concerns. As communities work through implementation of Part C, they must be creative in designing data-collection methods that maintain the integrity of each family as **primary decision makers.** This means that whenever there is doubt about a family's concerns or a child's need, the opinions of the family should be sought first. Whether families complete interview forms or provide information

through descriptive stories about their children, they must be given a choice in the assessment procedures used. Essential to success of the whole process is a relationship between families and professionals built on trust and respect.

Bailey (1987) listed five basic skills professionals need to develop in order to work collaboratively with families. These include the ability to (1) look at families from a systems perspective; (2) identify relevant family needs; (3) use appropriate listening and interviewing techniques; (4) negotiate thoughtfully with families to reach consensus on solutions; and (5) help families match their concerns with available resources.

THE INDIVIDUALIZED FAMILY SERVICE PLAN DOCUMENT

In written form, the IFSP must contain the elements that are listed here. One important difference from the IEP includes a statement of "outcomes expected to be achieved for the infant or toddler and the family" (Section 677) rather than goals and objectives. These **outcome statements** are to reflect changes family members want to see for their child or themselves. Each outcome is to be stated functionally in terms of what is to occur (process) and what is expected as a result of these actions (product).

Even though an example format is shown in Figure 5–1, readers are cautioned that formats differ from state to state and within states. A telephone call to health, education, and social service agencies should be able to direct interested individuals to the right sources to obtain copies of the format used locally. Whatever formats are chosen, the following contents are required (Sec. 636).

1. A statement of the child's present levels of physical development (including vision, hearing, and health status), cognitive development, communication development, social or emotional development, and adaptive development based on objective criteria.

INDIVIDUALIZED FAMILY SERVICE PLAN (IFSP) for Children Birth to Three Years   SANTA CLARA COUNTY

Child's name: _Cathy Rae Wright_   Birth Date: _11-15-97_ Age: _26_ months   Sex: _F_

Parent(s)/Guardian(s): _Martha and Gary Wright_   Address: _1414 Coolidge Drive Cupertino_ Zip: _95014_

Home phone: _398-2461_ Work phone: _408_ _554-2490_ Primary language of the home: _English_ Other languages _____

Date of this IFSP _1/15/00_ Projected periodic review _7/15/00_ Projected annual review _1/15/01_ Tentative IFSP exit _11/15/00_
                            (at 6 months or before)

Service Coordinator Name	Agency	Phone	Date Appointed	Date Ended
Sandy Drohman	_Regional Center_	_408-461-2192_	_12/10/99_	_/ /_
			_/ /_	_/ /_

Family's strengths and preferred resources (With the family, identify the family strengths and the resources they might find helpful in addressing family concerns and priorities.) Mr. and Mrs. Wright are well-educated and constantly seek additional information about Cathy's condition. They are anxious to help Cathy in any way possible. Mrs. Wright's family is very supportive. They provide child care for Cathy's older brother.
Because of Cathy's tendency to be medically fragile, Mr. and Mrs. Wright prefer a home based early intervention program. They appreciate receiving written materials to help them understand how to work with Cathy. Mrs. Wright wants to be home when the home visitor comes so she can learn from her.

Family's concerns and priorities (With the family, identify major areas of concerns for the child with special needs and the family as a whole.) Mr. and Mrs. Wright are very concerned about Cathy's delays in walking, using her fingers to pick up things, and in talking with other children. They also worry about her small size. Cathy is their second child and was born at 24 weeks gestation. Mr. and Mrs. Wright would like to have more information on the issues of prematurity and they would like to find an appropriate support group for themselves.

Page _1_ of _6_ total IFSP

Figure 5–1 Example of an IFSP.

139

INDIVIDUALIZED FAMILY SERVICE PLAN (IFSP) for Children Birth to Three Years   SANTA CLARA COUNTY

Child's name: _____ Cathy Rae Wright _____   Chronological Age: _____ 26 _____ months

CHILD'S STRENGTHS AND PRESENT LEVELS OF DEVELOPMENT

With the family, identify what the child can do and what the child is learning to do. Include family and professional observations in each of the following areas:

PHYSICAL *Based on parent report and HELP Strands

Health _____ Cathy is said by her parents to be healthy but is very petite. Her parents are working with a nutritionist to
_____ help Cathy gain weight. _____

Vision _____ Cathy has had corrective surgery for strabismus. _____

Hearing _____ She has had numerous ear infections and currently has tubes in her ears. _____

Gross Motor (large movement) _____ Cathy stands on tiptoes, runs on toes, makes sharp turns around corners when running,
_____ walks upstairs with one hand held _____

Fine Motor (small movement) _____ Cathy grasps crayon adaptively and points with index finger; imitates horizontal
_____ strokes, builds 6 block tower, turns pages one at a time; has trouble picking up small objects. _____

COGNITIVE (responsiveness to environments, problem-solving) _____ Cathy finds hidden object; attempts and succeeds in activating
_____ mechanical toy; demonstrates use of objects appropriate for age _____

COMMUNICATION (language and speech)

RECEPTIVE (understanding) _____ Cathy points to body parts when asked; obeys two part commands. _____

EXPRESSIVE (making sounds, talking) _____ Cathy names 8 pictures, interacts with peers using only gestures;
_____ attempts to sing songs with words _____

SOCIAL/EMOTIONAL (how relates to others) _____ Cathy expresses affection, is beginning to obey and respect simple rules,
_____ tends to be physically aggressive _____

ADAPTIVE/SELF-HELP (sleeping, eating, dressing, toileting, etc.) _____ Cathy can put on socks and shoes, verbalizes need to use
_____ the toilet, but is not potty trained, feeds self _____

DIAGNOSIS (if known) _____

_____

Figure 5–1 (continued)

INDIVIDUALIZED FAMILY SERVICE PLAN (IFSP) for Children Birth to Three Years   SANTA CLARA COUNTY

Child's name: _____ Cathy Rae Wright _____

IFSP OUTCOMES

With the family, identify the goals they would like to work on in the next six months. These should be directly related to the family's priorities and concerns as stated on page one.

OUTCOME: Cathy will increase her attempts to vocally communicate in order to make her needs known and to positively interact with others.

	Service Type (Individual = I Group = G) Location	Frequency of sessions Length of each session	Start Date	End Date (anticipated)	Responsible Agency/ Group Including payment arrangements (if any)
Strategy or activity to achieve the outcome (Who will do what and when will they do it?) AIM Infant Educator will model for Mr. and Mrs. Wright techniques to solicit Cathy's vocalization efforts. **Criteria** (How will we know if we are making progress?) Increased vocalization will be observed by parents and infant educator.	I – Home-based infant program	1 hour each week	1-23-00	11-10-00	AIM (funded by SARC) Family
Strategy or activity to achieve the outcome (Who will do what and when will they do it?) Mrs. Wright will take Cathy to play with neighborhood children and will invite children to her home. She will encourage play and vocalization. **Criteria** (How will we know if we are making progress?) Mrs. Wright will observe and note extent of interaction	G – Home and in the neighborhood	once each week for at least 30 minutes	2-1-00	ongoing	Mrs. Wright
Strategy or activity to achieve the outcome (Who will do what and when will they do it?) Cathy will be assessed by a speech pathologist by 2-15-00 and followed on an as needed basis. **Criteria** (How will we know if we are making progress?) A follow-up report will be submitted.	I – Regional Center Speech and Language Clinic	1 hour play based assessment	2-1-00	as needed	Sandy Drohman will make arrangements (funded by SARC)

Page __3__ of __6__ total IFSP

Figure 5–1 (continued)

141

INDIVIDUALIZED FAMILY SERVICE PLAN (IFSP) for Children Birth to Three Years   SANTA CLARA COUNTY

Child's name: _____ Cathy Rae Wright _____

IFSP OUTCOMES

With the family, identify the goals they would like to work on in the next six months.
These should be directly related to the family's priorities and concerns as stated on page one.

OUTCOME: _Cathy will increase her weight in order to maintain health and continue a developmentally_
appropriate growth pattern

	Service Type (Individual = I Group = G) Location	Frequency of sessions Length of each session	Start Date	End Date (anticipated)	Responsible Agency/ Group Including payment arrangements (if any)
Strategy or activity to achieve the outcome (Who will do what and when will they do it?) Mr. and Mrs. Wright will continue to work with Mrs. Breez to improve Cathy's nutrition intake. **Criteria** (How will we know if we are making progress?)	Kaiser Hospital Clinic	30 min. each month	ongoing	as needed	Mrs. Breez (Kaiser funded)
Strategy or activity to achieve the outcome (Who will do what and when will they do it?) **Criteria** (How will we know if we are making progress?)					
Strategy or activity to achieve the outcome (Who will do what and when will they do it?) **Criteria** (How will we know if we are making progress?)					

Page __4__ of __6__ total IFSP

Figure 5–1 (continued)

INDIVIDUALIZED FAMILY SERVICE PLAN (IFSP) for Children Birth to Three Years   SANTA CLARA COUNTY

Child's name: ___Cathy Rae Wright___

IFSP OUTCOMES

With the family, identify the goals they would like to work on in the next six months.
These should be directly related to the family's priorities and concerns as stated on page one.

OUTCOME: Mr. and Mrs. Wright will join Parents Helping Parents *in order to receive peer parent support and learn more about Cathy's condition.*

Strategy / Criteria	Service Type (Individual = **I** Group = **G**) / Location	Frequency of sessions / **Length** of each session	Start Date	End Date (anticipated)	Responsible Agency/ Group Including payment arrangements (if any)
Strategy or activity to achieve the outcome (who will do what and when will they do it?) Sandy Drohman will provide all referral information to Mr. and Mrs. Wright and will accompany them to their first meeting if they desire.	G – Parents Helping Parents	(up to parent's discretion)			Sandy Drohman Mr. and Mrs. Wright Parents Helping Parents
Criteria (How will we know if we are making progress?) Mr. and Mrs. Wright will find satisfaction in increased support and knowledge.					
Strategy or activity to achieve the outcome (who will do what and when will they do it?) AIM Infant Educator will assist Mr. and Mrs. Wright in obtaining additional information about Cathy's condition.	I – Home	ongoing	2-1-00	11-10-00	AIM Infant Educator
Criteria (How will we know if we are making progress?) Mr. and Mrs. Wright will express satisfaction over the assistance received in becoming more informed.					
Strategy or activity to achieve the outcome (who will do what and when will they do it?)					
Criteria (How will we know if we are making progress?)					

Figure 5–1 (continued)

INDIVIDUALIZED FAMILY SERVICE PLAN (IFSP) for Children Birth to Three Years   SANTA CLARA COUNTY

Child's name: ___Cathy Rae Wright___

TRANSITION PLAN — This child's transition at ___36___ months will be accomplished by completing the following steps:

1.) At 30 months, Mrs. Wright will meet with the district program specialist to review placement options.

2.) Mrs. Wright will visit the sites with Sandy Drohmann.

3.) Mrs. Wright will state her preference and will sign enrollment forms.

4.) Mrs. Wright will attend the orientation with Cathy.

STATEMENT OF ELIGIBILITY — The IFSP team determines that assessment results demonstrate that the family and child are eligible for services under Part H of the *Individuals with Disabilities Education Act* — ☒ Yes or ☐ No. Percentage of time child is in natural environment ___N.A.___ %.

FAMILY — I (We) had the opportunity to participate in the development of this IFSP. It represents my (our) concerns, priorities, and outcomes for my (our) child and family. I (We) ☒ do ☐ do not give permission for this plan to be implemented. I (We) understand that this IFSP plan is in effect through ___11/15/00___.

_____   _____Mrs. Martha Wright_____   ___1/15/00___
Date   Parent(s)/Legal Guardian(s) Signature(s)   Date

OTHER IFSP PARTICIPANTS — The following individuals/agencies participated in the development of the IFSP either by attending the meeting or giving input by telephone or in writing and agree to carry out the plan as it applies to their role in the provision of entitled early intervention services.

Name, Title & Phone		Agency	Gave input by telephone or writing (Person receiving input initial here)	Date
Mr. and Mrs. Gary Wright		Parents		1-15-00
Sandy Drohman	461-2192	Regional Center		1-15-00
Julie Maze	460-6190	Public Health Nursing		1-15-00
Margaret Breez	642-8314	Kaiser Nutritionist	JD	1-10-00
Rosalie Martinez	648-2941	AIM Infant Program		1-15-00

Notes for consideration at next review: ___Consider relationship between Cathy and her older brother, John.___

Page __6__ of __6__ total IFSP

Figure 5–1 (continued)

2. A statement of the family's resources, priorities, and concerns related to enhancing the development of the child.

3. A statement of the major outcomes expected to be achieved for the child and family and the criteria, procedures, and timelines used to determine the degree to which progress toward achieving the outcomes occurs.

4. A statement of the specific early intervention services necessary to meet the unique needs of the child and the family, including the frequency, intensity, and method of delivering services.

5. A statement of the natural environments in which early intervention services shall appropriately be provided, including a justification of the extent, if any, to which the services will not be provided in a natural environment.

6. Projected dates for initiation of the services and the anticipated duration of those services.

7. The name of the service coordinator who will be responsible for the implementation of the IFSP and coordination with other agencies and persons.

8. Steps to be taken to support the transition of the child, upon reaching age 3, to the next program of services recognized to be appropriate.

9. The contents of the IFSP shall be fully explained, and informed written consent from the parents or guardian shall be obtained prior to provision of early intervention services described in the plan. The case of Cathy, which is given in Figure 5-1, illustrates one format that encompasses the requirements.

Developing Outcome Statements

The IFSP team is expected to develop **outcome statements** that will guide the choice of services to be delivered. It is important to remember that these statements should have a direct connection to the concerns and priorities expressed earlier by the family. These statements will document the changes families hope to see for their children or themselves as these changes relate to the developmental needs of their child. Outcome statements are to be functionally stated in the language of the family whenever possible. They should refer to practical activities that fit into a family's daily life and represent skills that enhance the child's ability to cope with daily environmental demands.

Phrasing the statements as "*in order to*" statements makes it easy to understand the functional purpose of the action to be encouraged. For example, parents who are anxious for their child to learn to walk may not be satisfied with an outcome statement that is written as "Josh will pull to standing," unless an addition is made so that it reads: "Josh will pull to standing *in order to* begin the process of walking." This formula, as advocated by Deal, Dunst, and Trivette (1989), allows the result (product—walking) of the process (pull to stand) to be readily understood. That is, action A will be encouraged in order to realize outcome B. Activities or strategies should, then, flow directly from the outcome statements. For example, advice from a physical therapist should be sought to determine the most appropriate strategies to encourage Josh to pull to standing.

Figure 5-1 illustrates three outcome statements chosen by Mr. and Mrs. Wright for their daughter, Cathy. Others could have been included, but Cathy's parents decided that these three were of the highest priority at the time of the initial IFSP.

It is important to realize that the IFSP does not take the place of a **program plan.** The IFSP identifies *services* and desired *outcomes.* It does not identify a complete list of specific objectives, strategies, and activities to be used in bringing about the outcomes. Though not required by law, all service providers should prepare a written plan of specific long and short-term objectives (including teaching steps and strategies) for reaching each outcome. (See Chapter 6 for detailed information related to writing instructional objectives.)

SERVICE COORDINATION

Public Law 99–457 and now P. L. 105–17 mandate that a **service coordinator** be designated to ensure the full development of the Individualized Family Service Plan (IFSP) for birth to 3-year-olds and their families. The law intends that professional assistance be provided to support optimal family functioning. Thus service coordination is considered to be an integral part of the IFSP process. Part C rules and regulations state that service coordination consists primarily of activities designed to assist and enable an eligible child and the child's family to receive the rights, procedural safeguards, and services that are authorized to be provided through each state's early intervention program. The service coordinator who is assigned during the IFSP meeting is responsible for coordinating all services across agency lines and is to serve as the single point of contact in helping parents to obtain appropriate services.

Service coordination is to be an active, ongoing process that involves helping parents to gain access to services identified in their IFSP, coordinating these services, and facilitating timely delivery of appropriate services throughout the duration of the child's eligibility. In many areas, early childhood special education teachers may be expected to become service coordinators. Those who have not had training in family systems theory, in understanding the requirements of federal and state legislation, and in local service delivery systems must seek this training before accepting such a responsibility.

Specific functions of service coordination include (a) coordinating the performance of evaluations and assessments; (b) facilitating and participating in the development, review, and evaluation of IFSPs; (c) assisting families in identifying available service providers; (d) informing families of the availability of advocacy services; (e) coordinating with medical and health providers; and (f) facilitating the development of a transition plan to preschool services, if appropriate.

Although specific service coordination activities are listed, it is understood that these activities are fluid, interrelated, and always individually determined in collaboration with families. Activities that are help-ful to one family may be irrelevant or undesired by another. Even activities that are appropriate for a family today may not be suitable for that family tomorrow. Effectiveness of service coordination will depend on the competencies of the service coordinator, including his or her ability to actively involve families in helping to get their own needs met.

Who Can Become Service Coordinators?

While the law does mandate the involvement of someone responsible for service coordination, it allows flexibility in the choice of service coordinator and in the model of service coordination implemented. It is the intent of the law that the person best qualified to meet the needs of the family and the child should become the family's service coordinator. Optimally, the service coordinator will be selected on the basis of the desires of the family and can be from any agency. Service coordinators will change as the needs and appropriate services for the family change. Parents do have the right to reject service coordination entirely.

Models of Service Coordination

In reviewing the history of service coordination, Dunst and Trivette (1989) discussed three models of service coordination: *role-focused, resource procurement,* and *client empowerment.* The first two originated from traditional social work practices and perceive the client as incapable of self-help. The *role-focused model* originated from the deinstitutionalization movement in the 1960s, when the service coordinator's (termed *case manager*) role was as a guardian for clients with mental disabilities who were thought to be unable to help themselves. The disadvantage of this model is that it discourages families from defining their own goals and becoming active in making appropriate choices to achieve these goals. Such discouragement may result if service coordinators interpret the law literally and focus on their role as one of only ensuring that the family service plan is implemented. Families can easily become passive recipients of services rather than active service seekers.

The *resource procurement model* centers around identifying family needs and procuring resources to meet these needs. "The assumption is that because the young client is incapable of getting services without help, and because the service-delivery system is so confusing, professional assistance is required to make the system work" (Bennett, Nelson, & Lingerfelt, 1992, p. 148). This assumes that families are unable to advocate for themselves and no effort is made, in this model, to help families become self-sufficient.

The *client-empowerment model,* or family-empowerment approach, is an enabling model visualizing families as capable people who, given guidance, can help themselves. The emphasis is on enabling families to take control of the intervention process to the extent they are able to do so. This is a family-support model that assumes families are able to set goals, make decisions, assess their needs, and determine what is best for themselves. Family-support approaches are also in keeping with the ecological model of development espoused by Bronfenbrenner (1979) and advocated throughout this text. Children cannot be seen as separate from their family systems, and families must be understood within the context of their community and its service system.

THE ENABLING MODEL OF SERVICE COORDINATION

The enabling model, well-articulated by Dunst and Trivette (1987, 1988), is conducive to a family-centered approach to service coordination. While it does emphasize coordination and integration of services, it also encourages families to function as independently as possible and to be actively involved in the service coordination process. Instead of independently coordinating the services, the service coordinator is more likely to arrange for service providers to be more responsive to family needs. They will not decide for a family what they need, but will help families to clarify their own concerns and articulate their own needs. They will first "coach" families to recognize and

mobilize resources closest to themselves such as within their extended family and neighborhood. Then, they will assist families in understanding how to access community public and private resources.

This model is essential given that the law does not require the designation of service coordination after the child reaches age 3. Framers of the law clearly wanted families to become as capable as possible in meeting their own needs and those of their children. The word *enable* was added to the federal regulations to underscore the need to strengthen the ability of families to make decisions and carry out actions in their own behalf. In truth, service coordination will be effective only to the extent that it enables families to become competent enough to function effectively as their own service coordinators throughout the remainder of their caregiving days.

PROMOTING ESSENTIAL INTERAGENCY COLLABORATION

Educational programs that serve young children with special needs can provide all the services that children and families require only through collaboration with other programs and agencies. **Community networking** describes the efforts involved in coordinating services among agencies. Community networking can reduce fragmentation, avoid duplication, and help families gain easy access to needed services.

Families of children with disabilities under the age of 3 years will be assigned a service coordinator whose responsibility will be to faciliate interagency collaboration in behalf of families' needs. Older children or children whose disabilities are not severe enough to be deemed eligible for service coordination will look elsewhere for assistance in navigating the service delivery maze. The most appropriate professionals to be of assistance are the early intervention specialists and early education teachers with whom families are in daily contact.

Therefore, in order to develop efficient and effective interagency collaboration, programs must involve a variety of networking activities. Networking activities vary because of differences in resources or community needs and geographic and cultural factors. Early education specialists need to *develop a clear understanding of the needs of each child and family and a thorough knowledge of the available resources.* A personal evaluation of programs and personnel fosters a useful match between needs and services. Attention should be paid to the quality, breadth, and cost of services. Families will need help in complying with referral procedures and support during waiting periods. Ideally, networking efforts will result in formal or informal interagency agreements that extend services to meet the special needs of children and their families.

Collaboration also includes involvement in activities that create awareness of the early education program and its contribution to the process of networking. Open houses, personal contacts, media coverage, brochures, presentations at meetings, and participation on community advisory councils develop public awareness. Even though networking activities will change with time, they remain essential to the delivery of a successful early intervention program.

DEVELOPING AN INDIVIDUALIZED EDUCATION PROGRAM (IEP) FOR PRESCHOOLERS

Current federal guidelines require children who will receive any special education services to be seen for a diagnostic study by members of a multidisciplinary team before services can begin. They do not specify the professionals to be included. However, it is expected that choice of the members for a specific team will be determined by the characteristics and suspected disabling conditions of a particular child. For example, in all cases of suspected speech and/or language delays, the child should be seen by a speech-language pathologist. This pathologist should also be present at the subsequent meeting or "staffing," at which time the IEP is developed. Other people who attend this meeting include the following:

1. One or both of the child's parents.

2. At least one regular education teacher if the child is participating in a regular education program.

3. At least one special education teacher, or where appropriate, at least one special education provider of such child.

4. Any member of the school staff, other than the child's teacher, who is "qualified to provide, or supervise the provision of, specially designed instruction to meet the unique needs of children with disabilities" (Section 614).

5. An individual who can interpret the instructional implications of evaluation results.

6. An administrator who has the authority to make commitments on behalf of the school district.

7. Other individuals whose expertise may be desired by the parent or school.

The Multidisciplinary Diagnostic Team

The **multidisciplinary diagnostic team,** including the parents as valid members, considers the child's current educational needs. Priorities are chosen. **Goals** are specified and **behavioral objectives** written for each goal. The team, with critical input from the family, determines what services will be received and where the services will be offered. These will be written on the program plan.

Referring Professional's Preparation. In preparation for the multidisciplinary staffing, the teacher would write observations of the child in several different settings and circumstances. She would summarize any information gained from informal or formal classroom assessment and gather relevant samples of the child's work. She must be prepared to give evidence of the child's present level of functioning. Questions based on her concerns should be prepared. The following are examples:

1. Sometimes he seems to hear us and at other times we get the feeling he doesn't want to pay attention. Does his hearing change from time to time?

2. He seems to pay more attention to a man's voice than to a woman's. Why is this?

3. It is very difficult to understand Danny. He can't be deaf. He loves to sing, and he keeps on pitch as well as the others do. But his speech is nearly unintelligible. Why is this?

4. If we show him how to do something, he is quick to learn. Why is he so slow when we tell him what to do?

The teacher would be ready to present any information she has about the child and would be prepared to answer any questions other team members would have. Of course, she would have obtained a signed "release of information" from the child's parents. She would also plan to report any intervention she has already tried with the child, including any special materials or methods.

Finally, the teacher would be prepared to state as clearly as possible exactly what she needs to know to develop an appropriate intervention program. Her prepared questions will help her gain the information she needs. Having her questions and concerns written down ahead of time will help her to be certain that no important consideration is overlooked. Professionals must actively seek all the information they feel necessary for the planning and implementation of the services listed on the IEP form. The professional's responsibility in this role cannot be overemphasized.

Specialists' Preparation. Whenever possible, the specialists who evaluate young children ask to see reports of observations made by others, including teachers and parents. Often a screening test is used as a preliminary to in-depth evaluations.

Each specialist will choose assessment procedures judged to be relevant to the suspected problems. During the diagnosis it may become apparent that additional tests are needed. If one specialist obtains information that suggests that additional specialists need to be included in the multidisciplinary diagnostic team, it is his or her responsibility to request the necessary additional diagnosis. The chairperson of the staffing in which the IEP is developed often is the person referred to in the law as the representative of the local educational agency. This person may be responsible for collecting all assessment information and being certain that no important aspect of the diagnostic process is overlooked. Professionals involved must be prepared to relate test results, their level of confidence in the child's performance, and recommendations for placement and services to the chairperson. They should make every possible effort to translate their findings into information directly useful to program and activity planning.

When participating in the multidisciplinary staffing, professionals should be prepared to speak in language that parents understand. They must remember that parents, as well as professionals, are to be included as active, vital members of the team.

Parents' Preparation. Parents will be expected to organize any information they have received from previous examiners. They have the responsibility of honestly and accurately sharing information about their child's behavior and perceived strengths and concerns. Parents serve as the child's advocate.

Professionals can be very helpful in assisting parents to prepare information they wish to share as well as in developing a list of questions to be asked of specialists. Parents should be given any assistance they need to fully understand the program and services being proposed. In some cases translators or multilingual specialists will have to be included as part of the multidisciplinary team. It is especially important for professionals to understand exactly which intervention goals are important to each child's parents. A questionnaire or interview asking parents to identify those skills that they would *most* like to see their child accomplish in the coming year, behaviors that would reduce stress in the family, increase independence, and so on, is an effective way to ensure parents' *active participation* in selecting and prioritizing goals for their children. Parents' goals should take highest priority on the list of objectives to be achieved. For example, the parent may think the child's becoming independent in feeding is more important than making eye contact with the staff. It is more important that the child be accepted by significant others throughout the day than by those who work with the child at preschool. While professionals tend to feel that they know what is most important for the child to learn and achieve, the needs and desires of the parents should take precedence whenever realistically possible. Initial understanding and genuine acceptance by parents of services to be offered can save many hours of discussion or even the necessity of changes later on.

Sending home a rough draft of goals and objectives for the family to review and react to *prior* to the IEP meeting is another way to solicit active parent participation in setting priorities. This approach may also help to relieve parental anxiety.

THE CASE OF DANNY

The following narrative gives insight into the background and proceedings of one child's multidisciplinary conference.

Background Information

Danny's parents are worried. Twice they have been asked to withdraw him from child-care centers. Now the private preschool that he has been attending has called them in for a conference. Both parents work, and they want the best possible placement for Danny. Several friends have told them that they know he would not be accepted in the public school kindergarten next year. He rarely talks, and when he does, it is very difficult to understand him. He is also stubborn. Many times when they tell him to do something, he acts as if he does not hear them unless they yell at him. They are worried that he might be placed in a special classroom.

October 21, 1999. Danny has now been enrolled in a private preschool for 3 weeks. Ms. McLynn and Ms. Johnson are anxious to discuss their observations with Danny's parents, the Dicksons.

Ms. Johnson: Thank you for coming. We are enjoying Danny and hope he is enjoying us. We have observed Danny in a variety of situations and would like to discuss our observations with you.

Mrs. Dickson: We are so pleased that Danny is coming to your program. We are grateful for the help you have given Danny and are anxious to hear about how he is doing.

Ms. Johnson: Well, as you know, it is sometimes difficult for us to understand what Danny is saying, and it seems that often he doesn't understand us. When we try to tell him to do something, he just seems so confused. We can get him to pay attention by standing in front of him and talking directly to him. He also seems to have trouble with the names of things like colors and body parts.

Mrs. Dickson: We have also noticed some of the things you are talking about. His pediatrician examined him, as you suggested, and he said he is fine. He told us that many children don't learn to speak clearly until they are in school.

Mr. Dickson: Our friends the Joneses have a little girl who the psychologist said is very slow. She doesn't talk clearly either, and they put her in a special class. We really don't want Danny put in a class with children who have problems or can't learn. Danny isn't dumb.

Ms. McLynn: I agree with you, Mr. Dickson. Danny isn't dumb. But something is wrong. He misunderstands us most of the time, and we can't understand him. He doesn't know the names of lots of things the others know.

Ms. Johnson: We feel that we aren't helping Danny enough. He needs special kinds of help that we aren't trained to provide. We are hoping that you will agree to have specialists test Danny to help us find the best ways to work with him.

Mr. Dickson: I'm not sure. Are you sure that Danny needs all of this help? We can understand him.

Ms. Johnson: Yes, I believe you can understand Danny and he is obviously bright in many ways. He does the most difficult puzzles easily and builds wonderful towns with blocks. We would just like to find out what is causing Danny's communication problems and how we should be working with him.

Mr. Dickson: Okay. Who do we call?

As Mr. and Mrs. Dickson left the preschool, they still felt somewhat frightened. Mrs. Dickson remembered that one preschool teacher had said her son had a "dull expression" and another said that he seemed "bewildered." But when they spoke to friends and relatives, they all reassured them that Danny was just a late bloomer. In spite of their fears, they did call their local public school office, and an appointment for a diagnostic interview was made. They had to sign papers to release information from the preschool and to confirm that they agreed to the testing.

January 15, 2000. A multidisciplinary team staffing conference is in progress at the Special Education Office. In addition to Danny's teacher from the private preschool and his parents, a school psychologist, nurse, social worker, speech-language pathologist, and supervisor of special education are present. The supervisor has reviewed the background information.

Mr. Dickson: I am eager to hear what the psychologist has to say, first.

Psychologist: Danny worked very hard and seemed to want to try everything. Because Danny seemed to understand so little speech and language, and I had a hard time understanding him, I gave him two kinds of tests. Well, really three. First, I tried a vocabulary test. For that test, I show pictures and name them. All Danny had to do was point to the picture that I named. There are four pictures on each page, and only one is correct. On that test, Danny responded by naming or pointing to a few pictures correctly. He often seemed confused. He couldn't identify as many pictures as most children his age. Then, I attempted to use a standardized intelligence test that requires Danny to listen to me and answer questions and point to things, too. Again, he was unable to do most of the items that other 4-year-olds can do. So, next I used a nonverbal performance test. On this test, Danny had to listen to only a few directions and did not have to talk to me. He did have to watch me carefully, and then imitate some of the things I did. And here he was more successful. He seemed to enjoy these activities. His confused expression disappeared and he looked more interested. Danny was able to match the colors very well. He could do difficult puzzles, complete copying designs, and put pattern pieces together. When he finished, he grinned at me and seemed to want to do more.

Ms. McLynn: That's the way he is at school, too. He can color and draw better than most of the other children. He is quick to learn how to make things.

Speech-Language Pathologist: My tests indicate that Danny says most of the vowels correctly, although the short vowels as in p*i*n, p*a*n, p*e*n, and p*u*n aren't distinct. He can imitate the voiced consonants, for example, /b/, /d/, /g/, /m/, and /n/, and he uses them in some words but he often omits them on the ends of words. He says ba*w* for ba*ll* and d*aw* for d*og*, for example. When he tries to make sentences, he leaves off /s/, /t/, and /z/ at the ends of words, so he cannot "signal" past tense as in hopp*ed* and look*ed*. He doesn't use plurals, as in car*s* and truck*s*.

When I asked him to listen to me say a sentence and point to the picture that showed what I had said, he was really confused. One picture page has a little boy looking into a mirror seeing himself and another picture where he is looking at a shelf. Danny had no idea what I wanted him to do. When I said "He sees himself," he pointed to both pictures. Also, I recorded more than 50 things that he said while we played with some cars and trucks and a toy garage. He really enjoyed that. When I analyzed what he said, I found that he is using three- and four-word sentences, although the words are not clear. He tried to ask me for things, too.

Nurse: Danny responded very quickly and accurately to my vision screening test. I showed him just once what I wanted him to do. He was all business, paid close attention, and quickly demonstrated that he has good eyesight. But the hearing testing was another story! He wiggled and giggled. He said he heard the tones when the audiometer was off. At 25 decibels, the loudness level used for hearing screening, he heard 500 and 1000 Hertz in one ear, but he did not respond to the same loudness at higher frequencies. In the other ear, he did not answer correctly at all at 25 decibels. So, I referred him to our speech and hearing center for a complete hearing evaluation with more sophisticated equipment. The audiologist, a specialist in evaluating hearing and recommending needed remediation, reported that Danny exhibited a high-frequency sensorineural hearing loss in both ears.

Speech-Language Pathologist: Danny has problems hearing the difference between the high-frequency sounds in particular. He had trouble with other auditory processing tasks, too.

Mr. Dickson: But if he can't hear, how come he can hear us when he wants to? He can be sitting in front of the TV and just pay no attention when I tell him something. But if I get angry, he jumps right away.

Speech-Language Pathologist: When you get angry, you probably speak louder, and your tone of voice changes.

Mr. Dickson: You bet it does.

Speech-Language Pathologist: He can hear those changes, because the vowels are in the lower frequencies, and he hears them almost as you and I do. He can hear the change in your tone of voice for the same reason. What he cannot hear is the consonants. All those years he must have been hearing things with the most important parts missing. For instance, with the reported hearing loss he hears "Come to supper" as "um oo u er."

Mrs. Dickson: Why, that is exactly what he says when he tells someone it is time to eat!

Speech-Language Pathologist: So, you see, he has been saying what he has been hearing.

Mr. Dickson: So what do we do now?

Ms. McLynn: Is there someone who can help us to teach him what he needs to know? We really want to help Danny.

Speech-Language Pathologist: The first thing we must do is have the audiologist evaluate Danny for hearing aids. Then, I can work with him regularly. I'll give his teacher many special activities to help him to learn in spite of his hearing loss. He can learn to use his hearing better, and he can learn to supplement what he hears through lipreading.

Mr. Dickson: I'm ashamed for all of the times I've punished him for not listening. But he always heard his brother's motorcycle when he was half a block away. And he was always the first to run outside to look for jet planes. He loves the stereo and sings right along with the tunes. You are telling me he can hear all that but not hear the speech sounds like /p/ and /t/?

Speech-Language Pathologist: Right. And I can teach him how to make those sounds and to recognize them when he sees them on people's lips, even if his hearing doesn't improve. Of course, we will expect that it will.

Ms. McLynn: We've noticed he seems to hear a man's voice best. Should he be placed in a man's class?

Speech-Language Psychologist: Not necessarily. But it will be helpful if you speak more slowly and in shorter sentences. Be close to Danny, and be sure that you have his attention before you tell him something. Avoid having sources of bright light such as a window behind you when you talk to him. He will need to see your lips and mouth. Even though he is not dependent on lipreading, he will be taught to use visual as well as auditory clues. If the light is in his eyes, it is harder to see your lip movements.

Ms. McLynn: What should we do when we don't understand Danny?

Speech-Language Pathologist: Use all the situational cues available. Sometimes tell him to tell you again. If you still don't understand, ask him to show you. Encourage him to use gestures. When you do understand, let your face show your pleasure. Then, say what Danny was trying to say. Look expectant. Be pleased if he repeats your model, but don't insist. Make no corrections of his articulation at this time. You are striving to motivate him to talk more and to keep trying.

After the discussion, the members of the multidisciplinary team wrote the IEP that is illustrated in Figure 5–2. His parents agreed that it was an excellent plan. They were grateful for the care with which everyone had evaluated Danny. They felt that the specific suggestions met his needs very well.

Required Contents of the IEP

The IEP is a written plan that must contain the following elements:

1. A statement of the child's present levels of educational performance (based on results of norm-referenced and criterion-referenced tests).

2. A statement of annual goals and related benchmarks or short-term behavioral objectives.

3. A statement of the specific special education and related services and supplementary aids to be provided to the child, and a statement of the program modifications or supports for school personnel that will be provided.

4. An explanation of the extent, if any, that the child will not participate with nondisabled children in the regular class.

5. The projected dates for initiation of services and the anticipated frequency, location, and duration of services.

6. The appropriate objective criteria and evaluation procedures.

7. The schedules for determining whether the short-term instructional objectives are being achieved (each child's program must be evaluated at least once each year).

Although the precise written format may differ from area to area, the required content must be included. Figure 5–2 is an example of a typical IEP report form.

Purposes and Limitations of the IEP

The **annual goals** included in the IEP describe what a child with disabilities can be expected to accomplish within a specified period. Usually the allotted

INDIVIDUALIZED EDUCATIONAL PROGRAM

I. STUDENT INFORMATION
Date   Jan. 15, 1999

Student name	Dickson Danny R.		Sex __M__
	Last First Initial	Grade placement	M-F

Birth date   __June 6, 1994__   Parents   __John and Mary Dickson__   Phone 463-9546
         Mo   Day   Yr

Address   __61 Lakeside Road__   __Lincoln__   Zip   __69745__
            Street   City

District of residence   __Lincoln__   Receiving school/agency   __Lincoln__

II. MEDICAL INFORMATION

A. Vision screening	Nov. 5, 1998	Ms. Land, R.N.	Passed
	Mo Day Yr	Examiner	Results
B. Hearing screening	Nov. 5, 1998	Ms. Land, R.N.	Failed
	Mo Day Yr	Examiner	Results

Comments   Failed screening at 25 db. Referred to Speech & Hearing Center

III. LEVEL OF CURRENT PERFORMANCE
(Based on achievement, diagnostic, and criterion-referenced testing and teacher observation.)

A. Achievement			
Spelling level	Pretest	Posttest	Date
Math level	Pretest *not appropriate*	Posttest	Date
Reading level	Pretest	Posttest	Date

B. Mental ability	Test	Date
MA 3-0 IQ 65 (CA 4-6)	Stanford-Binet	Nov. 25, 1998
Perf. IQ 92	Wechsler Preschool and Primary Scale	

C. Psychomotor	Test	Date
VMI age 4-4	Beery-Buktenica Test of Visual Motor Integration (VMI)	Nov. 25, 1998

D. Social behavior	Test	Date
As reported by parents, age appropriate, except for severe tantrums	Teacher observation	Nov. 5, 1998

E. Speech-language	Test	Date
Articulation—multiple omissions and substitutions	Goldman-Fristoe Articulation	Nov. 13, 1998
Language age—approximately 30 mo.	Environmental Language Inventory	

F. Other (Self-help, vocational, etc.)
Self-help—superior for age

IV. PROGRAM ELIGIBILITY *(Check appropriate item[s].)*

[ ] A. EMH	[x] E. Speech impaired (SI)	[ ] J. Deaf-blind (DB)
[ ] B. THM	[ ] F. Visually impaired (VI)	[ ] K. Physical handicap (PH)
[ ] C. BD	[ ] G. Autistic (AUT)	[ ] L. Educational handicap (EH)
[ ] D. LD	[ ] H. Deaf (D)	[x] M. Early childhood (EC)
	[x] I. Hard of hearing (HH)	[X] N. Other (specify)

Figure 5–2   An example of an IEP.

Student name   <u>Dickson,   Danny   R.</u>

                          Last   *First*   *Initial*

V. PROGRAM PLACEMENT *(Enter information in columns following listing.)*

	Date	Duration	Extent of participation in percentages
A. Waiting list			
B. Regular class			
C. Regular class with consulting	2/1	90 days	50% (2½ hours daily)
D. Regular class with supplementary intervention			
E. Regular class with rest room			
F. Part-time special class	2/1	90 days	50% (2½ hours daily)
G. Full-time special class			
H. Residential school			
I. Special day school			
J. Hospital school			
K. Hospital-treatment center			
L. Alternative school			
M. Homebound			

VI. SUPPORTIVE SERVICES *(Enter item[s] in columns following listing.)*

	Date	Duration	Extent of participation in percentages
A. Counseling	2/1	90 days	Weekly — 1 hour
B. Individual psychological counseling			
C. Group psychological counseling			
D. Speech therapy	2/1	90 days	Consulting and individual
E. Occupational therapy			
F. Hearing aid evaluation			
G. Adaptive physical education			
H. Regular physical education			
I. Parent-infant education			
J. Remedial reading			
K. Social work			
L. Braille-large print			
M. Orientation-mobility			
N. Adaptive equipment			
O. Barrier-free environment			
P. Diagnostics			
Q. Physical therapy			
R. Audiological therapy	2/1	90 days	Consulting — evaluation only
S. Hearing therapy	2/1	90 days	Consulting — twice weekly
T. Vision therapy			
U. Physically disabled-mentally disabled			
V. Behavior therapy			
W. Supportive materials			
X. Other (specify)			

Figure 5–2   (continued)

p. 3

Student name   <u>Dickson,   Danny   R.</u>
                              Last   *First*   *Initial*

Primary language   <u>English</u>

VII. IEP TEAM

Mrs. L. Wilson, Supervisor

Mrs. N. Hess, Speech-language pathologist

Ms. A. Neff, Social worker

Ms. C. Land, Nurse

Mr. B. Decker, School psychologist

Ms. McLynn, Preschool teacher

VIII. REVIEW SCHEDULE

[   ] A. 30 days   [✗] C. 90 days *1st review*

[   ] B. 60 days   [✗] D. Annual

IX. ASSESSMENT CRITERIA

Review for appropriateness of plan after 90 days. Review again after 1 year

X. ANNUAL GOALS (CHILD)

A. To develop attention and concentration skills.

B. To improve expressive language skills.

C. To develop the ability to imitate speech sounds.

D. To increase vocabulary.

E. To improve articulation of phonemes and syllables.

F. To reduce temper tantrums.

XI. ANNUAL GOALS (FAMILY)

A. To gain a better understanding of Danny's hearing and speech problems.

B. To learn to utilize strategies for facilitating Danny's speech and receptive language skills at home.

C. To learn how to deal with Danny's temper tantrums.

XII. PARENT CONSENT

I have been involved in the preparation of this individual plan and

[✗] *I am in agreement with it.*

[   ] *I disagree with its contents.*

I realize that this is an educational plan and not a binding legal contract.

John Dickson   Mary Dickson
Signature of parent(s) guardian(s)

Figure 5–2   (continued)

p. 4   Student name   Dickson,   Danny   R.
                                                                   Last   First   Initial

XII. SUMMARY OF SERVICES RECOMMENDED BY THE MULTIDISCIPLINARY TEAM AT THE IEP CONFERENCE, JAN. 15, 1999

Because Danny's parents both work, they need him to be cared for throughout the day. The early childhood special education class maintains a daily program for 2½ hours each day. As a result, it was decided to plan Danny's day as follows:

AM: The school bus will pick Danny up at his home at 8:50 and take him to the public school near his home for a 2½-hour session. His program will include all of the planned curriculum appropriate to his present level of performance, as well as the specific goals and objectives in his IEP. Each week he will receive two 20-minute speech and language lessons with three other children. In addition, the speech-language pathologist will plan and monitor a developmental speech and language program at both his preschool center and the special education class. This pathologist will also provide guidance to his teachers and parents with regard to his special needs as a child with mild hearing impairment.

PM: The preschool center will pick Danny up at his public school at 11:30 each day. He will be served luncheon at that center. After a nap time, he will participate in the activities at the center. The speech-language pathologist will be available for consultation with Danny's teachers there. Twice each month, Danny's special education teacher will contact the preschool center for consultation. Teachers from the preschool center will visit the special education class to observe Danny after 1 month.

XIII. INSTRUCTIONAL OBJECTIVES FOR ANNUAL GOALS INCLUDING EVALUATION CRITERIA AND DATE

A. Given a two-stage direction in one utterance, Danny will (1) attend to the speaker, (2) wait until directions are completed, and (3) do the activities in the order presented within 1 minute.

B. During a 30-minute activity period Danny will converse with the teacher or another child at least five times. He will use three- or four-word sentences. The conversation will fit the situation and be spontaneous, not directed.

C. When the teacher models a sentence for Danny, he will imitate her, using the same number of syllables (up to four syllables) and with partially intelligible articulation.

D. When shown five pictures in each of five categories—(1) clothing, (2) toys, (3) foods, (4) transportation, and (5) furniture—Danny will name them correctly, with no more than one error within each category.

E. During a structured speech lesson, Danny will imitate the teacher's production of all vowels and these consonants in isolation and syllables: /p/, /t/, /k/, /f/, /m/, /b/, /d/, and /g/.

F. During a 30-minute play period, Danny will not have any temper tantrums. During the complete school day, he will have no more than one outburst of anger.

Figure 5–2   (continued)

time is one school year. However, the scheduled period may be as little as a few weeks or months.

There must be a direct relationship between the child's present level of educational performance and the goals, objectives, and services to be provided.

However, the IEP is *not* intended to be detailed enough to be used as a complete instructional plan. The written goals and objectives are expected to state skills that are most needed based on assessment of a child's level of achievement. They are designed to target remediation of particular developmental lags or to accelerate learning. The intent is to focus attention and teaching effort on critical areas that are listed by priority and area of need.

The IEP is intended to serve as a basis for the subsequent development of a detailed, individualized instructional program that encompasses the complete curriculum. For example, although Danny's IEP focuses on his goals and objectives in speech and language, his complete instructional program would include social development, gross and fine motor skills, cognitive development, and school readiness activities. In all of these areas Danny would be expected to participate and learn. Adaptations to meet his needs would be made in the process of instruction.

Considerations Beyond the IEP

Interpreters of the law recognize that special education teachers have primary responsibility for implementation of the IEP. These teachers are expected to monitor each child's progress. If at any time they feel that plan is no longer appropriate, they are expected to request another meeting to review the IEP. Parents may also request a review of the individual program.

When children with special needs attend regular classes, even part time, their mainstream teachers should have copies of the IEPs. The special education teacher should explain the contents of each plan. This teacher should be available to serve as consultant to the classroom teacher. Consultations should include a mutual sharing of concerns and information, suggestions for behavior management, materials, and teaching strategies.

WRITING GOALS AND OBJECTIVES

The obvious reason for writing goals and objectives is that the law requires them to be included in educational plans for children with special needs. However, there are even more compelling reasons. These reasons are contained in the following characteristics of a well-written behavioral objective:

1. What is to be taught is described precisely and accurately. Anyone reading the objective knows what to do and the conditions in which it is to be done.

2. What the children will be doing when the objective has been achieved is defined and described.

3. The time allowed to complete the task is stated. How well the child must perform (the criterion) is clearly identified.

4. Because the task, the performance expected, and the criterion for success are clearly stated, accountability is facilitated.

In addition to these advantages are the following two less obvious but equally important benefits:

1. After writing objectives and working with them, teachers often discover that they are able to analyze learning problems more efficiently. They recognize the critical importance of small changes in what they are doing. These seemingly small changes, sometimes referred to as *branching*, can make enormous differences in teaching success. In effect, practice in thinking in the manner required to write behavioral objectives enhances teaching skills.

2. Once a series of performance (behavioral) objectives has been developed, it can be used to teach other children with similar needs. A well-written file of objectives can be a tremendous time saver in lesson planning.

Basics of Writing Behavioral Objectives

It is difficult to select the most efficient route to a destination unless you know what your destination is.

Behavioral (or performance or instructional) objectives require that the teacher state the destination precisely. "Fuzzy" terms are appropriate in goals. They are not allowed in behavioral objectives. For example, a correctly written *goal* might read, "To teach the colors red, yellow, and blue." But the *objective* related to the goal must contain the following three components:

1. What the teacher will *provide, restrict,* and *do.*

2. What the learner will be *doing* or *saying* when the objective has been achieved (a behavior that can be seen or heard).

3. *How well* or *how often* the learner must perform in this manner to convince the teacher that the task has been learned (within what time frame this performance must occur).

An example of a correctly written objective related to the goal "To recognize the colors red, yellow, and blue" might be "When the teacher points to any one of 15 different items (5 of each color red, yellow, and blue) and asks 'What color is this?' the children will answer within 20 seconds, stating the color correctly on 80% of the trials." Exhibit 5–1 illustrates terms useful in writing goals and objectives.

The standard that must be achieved to accomplish this objective is 80% of the trials. This standard is referred to as the **criterion.** Eight of 10 (or 80%) correct performances are usually described as "proficiency" on the task. Ten of 10 or (100% accuracy) are defined as "mastery level." (The level required must vary with the needs of individual children. Some cannot be expected to reach 100%.)

The following is an example of an objective and goal related to a social skill:

Goal: Increase social interaction with peers.

Objective: When placed in a situation where she has the only items essential for cooperative play, Alisa will share spontaneously during at least five consecutive play sessions.

In some cases a time limit becomes part of the criterion for judging successful performance, for example, within 2 minutes.

EXHIBIT 5–1

Appropriate Verbs for Writing Behavioral Objectives

1. Goals

The verbs suggested in this category are useful for writing goals but are *not* appropriate for writing behavioral objectives:

To decrease	To discover	To improve	To practice
To develop	To demonstrate	To increase	To understand

2. Behavioral objectives

The verbs suggested in this category are useful for writing behavioral objectives and can be used to describe observable behaviors:

To answer	To follow	To name	To recall
To color	To hold (as directed)	To pick up	To say
To complete	To imitate	To place together	To sort
To cut	To list	To point to	To use
To draw	To look at		

Guidelines for Choosing and Writing Behavioral Objectives

Teachers will want to write objectives to meet particular needs. Norm-referenced tests and preschool curriculum guides suggest similar goals for all early childhood classes. However, each class and each program are unique and special.

The following procedure has been useful in writing objectives for preschool children. Each objective must contain the basic components, but the manner in which they are recorded may vary. Several different forms are suggested, but the process of choosing them and sequencing them remains the same.

1. *Identify a particular goal.* Goals should state in general what you want the children to learn. Examples of goals include to improve self-esteem, to express feelings, and to develop expressive language. Goals are not specific. They do not describe what teacher or child will do.

2. *Decide what you want the children to learn in relation to the goal.* Choose the most difficult task you want them to be able to do. Visualize exactly what they will be doing when you look at them doing it and say "Now they *know* that." Write a description of what you have visualized in your mind's eye. This will be the observable behavior.

3. *Think about what you will give them and tell them when you want them to perform this observable behavior.* This will become the part of the objective that identifies what the teacher will do, provide, or restrict. Often this section begins with "Given" or "When the teacher."

4. *Write what you have visualized in the form you have chosen.* At first, it seems helpful to write the objective in one long sentence that includes all of the components. Later, you may prefer the shorter versions. Each must be complete. It is important to state a criterion or standard within each objective. Each criterion must be reasonable, and it must fit that particular objective.

5. *Begin task analysis.* So far you have chosen a goal, decided on the most difficult of the objectives

you want to achieve in relation to the goal, and written all of this in the form you have chosen. What you have written is the terminal objective. Next, think about what you would need to do if the children could not achieve this objective in the way you have written it. Assume that it was too difficult for any of them. But you do want all of them to achieve it at least by the end of their experience in your program. How could you make it a little bit easier? Write this slightly easier en-route behavior (one of the objectives on the route to the terminal objective). Sometimes it is helpful to actually do the task yourself or carefully watch another do it to determine the en-route objectives.

6. *Continue task analysis as suggested in the previous guideline.* Write en-route behaviors that are simple and include so many prompts (cues) that you are certain every child you teach will be able to do at least the easiest one.

7. *Do not try to write every possible step.* Choose steps between objectives that you feel the majority of the children will be able to take. (Analyze the samples offered with this consideration in mind.) If you have a child who can perform a specific objective but seems unable to do any part of the next one in your sequence, you may need to plan another *branch.* That is, for an occasional child it may be necessary to insert additional objectives. Usually these need not be added to your sequence but rather recorded separately on the child's record. If you discover that you need this particular branch for a number of the children, add it to your sequence. (As noted earlier, keeping each en-route behavior on a separate card makes it easier to add or delete objectives.)

8. *Assemble your objectives.* At first, putting the en-route behaviors on individual cards makes it easier to arrange them in sequential order. Later, as your skill in task analysis grows, it becomes less necessary. However, if the en-route behaviors are on separate cards, it is easier to insert additional steps for children who need tasks broken into tiny steps. After assembling the en-route behaviors (objectives), it is helpful to actually do the task as outlined to verify the initial sequence and detect any missing steps.

Write the goal at the top of the form you have chosen. Beginning with the simplest one, write the objectives in sequence from the easiest to the most difficult. Remember, the most difficult one is your terminal objective. All of the others are called en-route behaviors. They are similar to en-route destinations on a trip. The terminal objective is your final destination, and the other objectives are specific places you will proceed through on your way to this destination. When you are headed toward a particular place on a trip, it may be your "target" for that day or week. In the same way, you may refer to a particular objective for a certain child as a target behavior. This process of analyzing terminal objectives and discovering and sequencing en-route behaviors is referred to as the process of **task analysis.**

9. *Identify the entry behaviors of each child.* Each of the children will enter your preschool or center with some awareness of the information or behavior you have chosen to teach. A few will be able to demonstrate the skills described in some of your terminal objectives the very first day. Others will be completely unaware of any facet of that particular target behavior. This is why you must analyze the terminal objective and write the en-route behaviors. Attempts are then made to determine which of the en-route behaviors each child can do (assessment). Dates must be recorded. When this is done, each child's entry behavior has been identified. Now you know where to begin.

10. *Provide a variety of equivalent practice.* Use many different materials and toys until you feel your criterion has been achieved. Don't rush. At first, some children will progress very slowly. When you feel confident that an individual has achieved criterion on the entry behavior (the objective this child was able to do when entering your class), record the date next to the name and begin working on the next objective in the sequence.

11. *Provide as much equivalent practice as necessary.* The sequence of the objectives is intended to be useful to you in planning for all of the children. Some of them may learn quickly. Do not be surprised

if some children move through a whole series of en-route behaviors and right through the terminal objective in a very short time. Others may take days or weeks on each en-route behavior. For accelerated children, a variety of activities and materials should be provided. Maintain the same level of difficulty your written objective states as you provide this equivalent practice.

Your written objective describes particular materials to be used in checking for criterion performance (at least in some instances). But you should *feel completely free to use any materials you choose in lessons, games, or spontaneous play.* The intent is to provide each child with many successful experiences (equivalent practice) on each level. The critical task is to *maintain the appropriate level of challenge.* A well-planned sequence of behavioral objectives serves as a very helpful frame of reference for working effectively and efficiently with individual children.

12. *Use the objectives you have written as the basis for daily lessons.* As soon as you have written your first goals and objectives, use them. Experiment with them. Use them as the basis for lessons with individual children. Try using them with a small group of children who are working on adjacent en-route behaviors. Next, attempt working with a larger group, all of whom are working on two or three adjacent objectives. Gradually, as you feel comfortable with this new way of planning lessons, attempt to include one or two children who are working toward the same terminal objective but are working on widely separated en-route behaviors.

13. *Evaluate your objectives continuously as you use them.* Writing a series of objectives becomes easier with practice. Trial and error can be an efficient teacher. However, failure by the children must be interpreted by the teacher as an indication that the objectives must be changed in some way. Asking the following questions can be helpful if problems occur:

a. Could the children do any part of the task?

b. Did they listen and look, or were the directions too long?

c. What modality or modalities were involved in the teacher's directions; that is, visual, auditory, tactile-kinesthetic, or combinations of these?

d. Which modalities were required in the response?

e. What distractors interfered?

f. What additional cues might have helped?

g. Did both the teacher presentation and the expected response allow for individual adaptations because of disabling conditions? For example, if the child had a visual impairment, were auditory and tactile-kinesthetic clues provided? If the child had a hearing impairment, were visual and tactile-kinesthetic clues available?

h. Was the time allotted adequate?

i. Was the content limited and specific to avoid misunderstanding?

j. Were the related subskills well learned before the presentation?

In practice, children should be able to demonstrate proficiency performance or 80% accuracy on one objective before proceeding to the next. The new objective should be partially achievable on the first try. That is, if the next en-route behavioral objective is a total mystery to the children (or to any one child), more branches or tinier steps are needed. A well-written sequence allows for continued success experiences. A limited amount of failure can be instructive. It can lead the children to use their mistakes as clues in the discovery of what they need to do differently. But for children who have experienced a great deal of it, failure must be kept to a minimum for a long time.

14. *Add new goals and objectives to the curriculum as the need for them appears.* Remember, your goals and objectives are your curriculum. You will want to add to them regularly. You will also want to delete or remove some from time to time. As you become accustomed to thinking in terms of what the children say and do (or do not do) as a result of your teaching, you will feel more effective as a teacher. Planning will be simplified. Individualizing lessons, based on the en-route behaviors you have written, will be much easier. En-route behaviors that do not work can be deleted. More steps can be inserted, if needed, for some children. Many children will be able to achieve each en-route objective rapidly. When the steps are small enough for the slowest to "climb," many children will achieve each level within a brief time.

FACILITATING TRANSITIONS

Transitions mean change and change normally means increased stress for children and families. As the Individuals with Disabilities Education Act (IDEA) makes a major distinction between services required for infants and toddlers (birth to age 3) and preschoolers (3- to 5-year-olds), transition from program to program is inevitable. There is also an inevitable change as children and families move from preschool services to those provided by the public schools for school-age children. Part C does recognize the need to assist families and to ensure continuity of services. It requires that plans for transition be specifically spelled out in IFSPs and that service coordinators assist families during these vulnerable periods of change. Interagency coordination and written agreements clarifying local transition procedures are being developed throughout the country.

While stress may be unavoidable, it can be lessened through careful planning that should begin as early as possible. Service coordinators and other interested professionals should be certain that transition plans are made and implemented only in the context of a partnership with the child's family. Transitions are normal life events that require well-planned steps in order to effectively cope with the changes required. Parents who are taking a newborn infant home from the NICU or are realizing they are leaving the comfort of the infant program behind may be feeling very anxious. Professionals, through the development of well-articulated transition plans, can help parents turn these anxious moments into opportunities for growth.

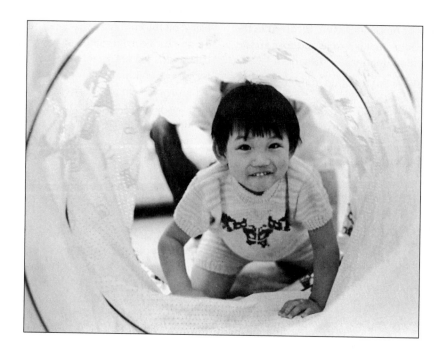

Steps in Transition to Center-Based or Public School Services

Bennett, Nelson, and Lingerfelt (1992, p. 105) offer helpful suggestions to service coordinators as they discuss the following eight steps that are essential to the development of smooth transitions:

1. Discuss the objectives of the transition and the roles and responsibilities of each member of the child's team.

2. Develop a transition timeline so that transitions proceed in a timely, step-by-step manner.

3. Accompany family members as they view and evaluate program options.

4. Discuss program options with family members.

5. Encourage the family to select a program.

6. Arrange for the exchange of all pertinent records and paperwork in a timely manner.

7. Assist the child and family in making the transition.

8. Encourage reciprocal follow-up between sending and receiving programs.

The Role of the Early Intervention Specialist in Facilitating Transitions

Early intervention specialists are in a unique position to help families and children make the move from programs for infants and toddlers to programs for preschool-age children. Families who are coping with their children's special needs in a demanding environment can be especially stressed in times of transition. They have many questions and are faced with the unknown. Teachers and other early intervention personnel can encourage parents to visit and become familiar with possible new settings for their child. They can directly prepare children and families by first understanding the environmental expectations of the placement possibilities. Whenever possible, children can be exposed to new routines and requirements ahead of time. Exiting teachers can work directly with receiving teachers in person, via telephone, and through reports to smooth the way and provide reassurance and support to parents. Putting parents in direct touch with parents who already have children in the new environment can be invaluable. These same concerns and strategies should be used when children move from preschool programs into public elementary school programs and beyond.

The focus of this chapter was on the process of developing individualized intervention plans and programs. Families were seen as central to these planning processes and to the success of their implementation. Chapter 6 will address effective intervention strategies for realizing the outcomes, goals, and objectives detailed in the individual plans. Attention is given to describing generic instructional strategies while recognizing the importance of play as a primary context for learning.

Summary

Before intervention strategies can begin, either an Individualized Family Service Plan or an Individualized Education Program must be developed. In developing either document, it is essential to remember that the process itself is much more important than the documents. Families must be the primary decision makers in determining how they wish to be involved and what outcomes or goals and objectives should be included. Both processes do require multidisciplinary team assessment and involvement in determining services and strategies. This team considers the child's current development level in determining eligibility for services. Each process requires annual reviews.

While IFSPs and IEPs are similar in intent, currently there are some important differences. First, the IFSP is family focused while the IEP is still more child focused. Rather than functional outcome statements, the IEP includes goals and objectives. To date, only the IFSP process provides for service coordination and definite steps to smooth the stress of transitions. Readers may wish to watch closely to see if the IEP process becomes more like the IFSP process as families become used to a family-centered approach to service planning.

Discussion Topics and Activities

1. Consider the following problems: The IEP conference for David has concluded. The parents are pleased with the suggestions made by the multidisciplinary team. These include continued placement in your preschool class for 3-year-olds. An early childhood special education teacher has been assigned to help you plan activities for David. Test results indicated that David is lagging in all developmental areas. What questions will you want to ask the special education teacher when he or she visits you the first time?

2. Interview parents who have participated in an IEP or IFSP meeting. Try to find out how they felt about the experience. Did they feel comfortable? If not, what bothered them about the process? Ask them what advice they would give to a new early interventionist for making families feel welcomed and a true part of the team. Share your findings with class members.

3. Work with your instructor in setting up an opportunity for you to sit in on an IFSP or IEP meeting. Try to determine just what the teacher and others

do to make parents feel that their opinions are important and that they are critical to the decision-making process. If possible, interview the early childhood special educator to ask the questions that occurred to you throughout the meeting.

4. Ask your instructor for assistance in determining whom to contact in your local area to become involved in the Part C implementation process.

5. Compare the IFSP process with that of the IEP. Determine what would be necessary to carry over the family-focused approach into the IEP process.

6. Become thoroughly familiar with the local agencies that provide services to young children with special needs in your area. With a class member, visit at least one local agency to become familiar with how services are accessed, exactly what services are available, and what the eligibility criteria are. By collaborating with class members, develop a directory of services useful to parents as well as early intervention professionals.

Annotated Bibliography

Arena, J. (1996). *How to write an I.E.P.* Novato, CA: Academic Therapy Publications.

Included in this clearly written book are samples of the ways that goals and objectives can be written to facilitate effective programming. Also included are activities for parent use outside of the classroom.

Bailey, D. B., & Simeonsson, R. J. (1988). *Family assessment in early intervention.* Upper Saddle River, NJ: Merrill/Prentice Hall.

This innovative text is designed to provide the information needed to assess family needs and plan goals jointly with families. Thorough coverage of the entire assessment procedure is offered, together with specific strategies for assessing family concerns and family communication, determining and stating family goals, and evaluating family services.

Bennett, T., Lingerfelt, B. V., & Nelson, D. E. (1990). *Developing individualized family support plans.* Cambridge, MA: Brookline Books.

This training manual is based on the text *Enabling and Empowering Families* by Dunst, Trivette, and Deal (1988). It provides a compact package of functional and practical materials to train professionals about implementing family-centered IFSPs.

Mager, R. F. (1997). *Preparing instructional objectives: A critical tool in the development of effective instruction.* Center for Effective Performance.

Here is a classic that provides the tools necessary to state clearly what the desired outcomes of intervention will be. It is a systematic guide to identifying, selecting and writing well-stated objectives. Fifty practice exercises are included to sharpen one's skills in writing comprehensive, functional objectives.

McGonigel, M. M., Kaufmann, R. K., & Johnson, B. H. (Eds.). (1991). *Guidelines and recommended practices for the Individualized Family Service Plan* (2nd ed.). Bethesda, MD: Association for the Care of Children's Health.

This monograph represents a consensus about the best practices for providing family-centered, comprehensive early intervention services. It is not a blueprint for implementation. Rather, it suggests a philosophy and conceptual framework for the IFSP and provides recommendations for practices and procedures that are consistent with the intent of federal law.

McNamara, B. E. (1986). Parents as partners in the IEP process. *Academic Therapy, 21,* 309–319.

To enhance communication between professionals and parents this article presents strategies that can be employed prior to, during, or after the IEP conference. Included are questionnaires to help teachers gain insight into their own attitudes toward parent involvement and to help evaluate the success of parent participation in IEP meetings.

Olson, J., & Kwiatkowski, K. (1995). *Planning family goals: A systems approach to the IFSP.* San Antonio: Communication/Therapy Skill Builders.

This practical manual will assist professionals in recognizing and addressing the choices and priorities of family members. It builds on family stems theory, family stress theory and the ecological approach in showing how to plan and provide early intervention services. Sample IFSPs are provided.

Strickland, B. B., & Turnbull, A. P. (1990). *Developing and implementing Individualized Education Programs.* Upper Saddle River, NJ: Merrill/Prentice Hall.

This book is designed to help educators answer the question, How can I effectively carry out my responsibilities associated with the IEP? It is organized into three major parts: (1) procedural guidelines for IEP development, (2) mechanics of IEP development, and (3) implementation of the IEP. Also included is a comparative description of the IFSP.

TenBrink, T. D. (1986). Writing instructional objectives. In J. M. Cooper (Ed.). *Classroom teaching skills.* Lexington, MA: D. C. Heath.

This chapter serves as an excellent resource for those wishing to perfect their skills at writing behavioral objectives. Written in a self-teaching format, it allows the reader to use exercises that help in the selection of appropriate instructional objectives from available sources, and it teaches how to write these objectives in a useful and well-defined manner.

Woods, J. J. (1995). *A family's guide to the Individualized Family Service Plan.* Baltimore, MD: Brookes Publishing Co.

The purpose of this video is to help families negotiate the IFSP process. It outlines the roles of professionals, describes what happens during the IFSP meeting, discusses relevant legislation and explains how services, resources and desired outcomes are to be documented.

Zipper, I. N., Weil, M., & Rounds, K. (1993). *Service coordination for early intervention: Professionals and parents.* Cambridge, MA: Brookline Books.

This monograph is intended to help build effective systems for service coordination. It covers topics such as identifying and prioritizing the variables influencing implementation of service coordination, the functions of service coordinators, necessary competencies, and approaches to strengthening parent/professional partnerships.

References

Bailey, D. B. (1987). Collaborative goal setting with families: Resolving differences in values and priorities for services. *Topics in Early Childhood Special Education, 7* (2), 59-71.

Bailey, D. B., & Simeonsson, R. J. (1988). *Family assessment in early intervention.* Upper Saddle River, NJ: Merrill/Prentice Hall.

Bennett, T., Lingerfelt, B. V., & Nelson, D. E. (1990). *Developing individualized family support plans.* Cambridge, MA: Brookline Books.

Bennett, T., Nelson, D. E., & Lingerfelt, B. V. (1992). *Facilitating family-centered training in early intervention.* Tucson, AZ: Communication Skill Builders.

Bronfenbrenner, U. (1979). *The ecology of human development: Experiments by nature and design.* Cambridge, MA: Harvard University Press.

Deal, A. G., Dunst, C. J., & Trivette, C. M. (1989). A flexible and functional approach to developing individualized family service plans. *Infants and Young Children, 1*(4), 32-43.

Dunst, C. J., & Trivette, C. M. (1987). Enabling and empowering families: Conceptual and intervention issues. *School Psychology Review, 16*(4), 32-43.

Dunst, C. J., & Trivette, C. M. (1988). *Enabling and empowering families: Principles and guidelines for practice.* Cambridge, MA: Brookline Books.

Dunst, C. J., & Trivette, C. M. (1989). An enablement and empowerment perspective of case management. *Topics in Early Childhood Special Education, 8*(4), 87-102.

Johnson, B. H., McGonigel, M. J., & Kaufmann, R. K. (Eds.). (1989). *Guidelines and recommended practices for the individualized family service plan.* Bethesda, MD: Association for the Care of Children's Health.

Montessori, M. (1972). *Dr. Montessori's own handbook.* New York: Schocken Books.

Public Laws 94-142, 99-457, and 102-119. Washington, DC: U.S. Government Printing Office.

Vincent, L. (1990, October 6). *Collaborating with families: A challenge of the 90's.* Keynote address delivered at Santa Clara University, Santa Clara, CA.

Chapter 6

Implementing Intervention and Instructional Strategies

Key Concepts

- The content of curriculum must be functional and ecologically relevant.

- Curriculum content should also focus on the development of the underlying cognitive and psychoemotional processes that enable children to engage in self-directed learning and establish positive human relationships.

- Programs should use an "activity focus" by working on several objectives simultaneously in the context of a pleasurable and motivating activity.

- Identification of motivations is critical to successful intervention with infants and young children with special needs.

- Young children must be motivated to act upon the environment and to initiate interaction.

- Adults play a crucial role in facilitating the development of infants and young children through responsivity to children's cues, use of communicative interactions, and social mediation of experiences.

- Creating a predictable environment through the use of routine and repetition is essential to children's learning and adjustment.

- One of the most important contexts for learning in the early education program is children's play.

- Careful arrangement of the physical environment is necessary to accommodate the physical needs of young children with disabilities.

- Thoughtful scheduling of daily activities through the time-use plans provides for desired consistency and for a wide range of abilities and interests.

- Specific steps should be taken to prepare for the inclusion of young children with special needs.

- In addition to certain generic strategies, the early childhood special education professional must also have a thorough understanding of disabilities and must master intervention strategies specific to each disability.

Up to this point, we have been concerned with issues preparatory to the delivery of direct intervention services such as the philosophical basis for inclusion of young children with special needs, history and legal precedents for early intervention, understanding and collaborating with families, assessment of child needs as mediated by family concerns, and the development of individualized service plans and programs.

The purpose of this chapter is to suggest practical, generic instructional strategies that can provide the methodological foundation for intervention programs for all children. The overall approach presented in this chapter makes it possible to include children with disabilities or developmental delays in a wide range of early education programs. One such program is discussed in Exhibit 6-1.

◆ ◆ ◆

EXHIBIT 6–1

A Child-care Center Where Children with Special Needs Are Welcomed

Until recently many public and private child-care centers were reluctant to accept children with special needs. They said that they were neither trained nor equipped to help them. Other centers accepted children with disabilities but simply took care of their physical needs.

Ms. Johnson and Ms. McLynn want to provide the best possible services for the children with special needs who come to their center. They begin by listening carefully to the parents' requests and descriptions of their children. Then they observe the children in their preschool environment.

These teachers find the following sequence helpful:

1. Before a child is enrolled, parents meet with the director and the teacher. Information, parent concerns, and available services are considered. The enrollment form includes questions about previous experiences as well as a health history. The child's developmental level is discussed.

2. For the first few weeks the child is observed throughout the day. Special needs are identified. Ms. McLynn and Ms. Johnson discuss these with the parents at a second conference.

3. During this second conference inquiry is made into what other services the child might be receiving and appropriate release of information forms are signed.

4. After a child has been evaluated and recommendations for intervention services and procedures have been received at an IEP conference, Ms. McLynn and Ms. Johnson incorporate the suggestions and activities into the child's daily program.

5. Regular contact with parents and others working with the children is maintained through telephone conversations, conferences, and written reports.

This child-care center includes several children with disabilities during each session. If these children require a great deal of extra time and attention, an additional aide is provided.

Today this child-care center and others accept the challenge of including children with special needs. Wise teachers refuse to merely "love and take care of children." They are aware that the most critical years for learning occur before the traditional school entrance age of 5 or 6. As a result, they cooperate with parents and involved professionals by including children with special needs in their centers. They are careful to meet individual needs appropriately

CURRICULUM

Definition

Curriculum has been defined in various ways. Wolery (1983) defined it as an organized description of what to teach. It should also include basic strategies and activities for teaching, but the primary emphasis of a curriculum definition is generally on what to teach. Mori and Neisworth (1983) suggested that an acceptable early childhood curriculum is not simply a hodge-podge of objectives. It should provide a clear plan for programming; meet the needs of the child, parent, ethnic group, and general culture; and match teacher style and theoretical approach.

Vincent (1988) has aptly described curriculum as a "road map"—a tool that helps us know where we are going and how to get there. The desired outcomes for children and families are the destination. The instructional objectives and teaching strategies are the routes by which we get there.

Choice

Many types of curricula have been developed for infants and young children, both with and without special needs. Many curricula have been designed in a comprehensive way and include criterion-referenced assessments, detailed, step-by-step behavioral objectives, and suggested activities and materials. These are often commercially available as packaged programs. It is important for early intervention professionals to understand, however, that such so-called "self-contained" curricula may or may not meet the needs of children in their particular programs. First interventionists must clearly identify their own, as well as parents' educational goals for their children. Second, they must examine the strengths and learning styles of children, as well as their own instructional styles. A clear conceptualization of both the desired program outcomes and the best intervention strategies must be generated before a curriculum is selected. Early childhood special educators will find that packaged curricula need modifications and adaptations in order to meet unique needs of a particular group of children. They may also choose to design their own curricula.

Philosophy of this Text

In practice, most programs for young children with special needs combine elements of several curriculum models. The philosophy of this text is based on the following assumptions.

1. The content of the curriculum must include goals that are meaningful and relevant to each child within the context of his or her home and community. That is, they must be **functional** and **ecologically relevant.** (Refer to Chapter 4 for a review of these concepts.) In addition, curriculum content will also include the development of children's underlying cognitive and psycho-emotional processes, which enable them to eventually engage in self-directed learning and establish positive human relationships.

2. Intervention strategies will evolve around **activities** that provide direct instruction on specific skills within the context of functional and normal daily activities. Using functional behavior to enhance skills will promote generalization through the natural utilization of these skills.

3. The designing of specific behavioral objectives and **en-route** behaviors will consider information related to the stages and processes of typical **development.** In addition, principles and techniques from the field of behavior analysis (e.g., task analysis) will be used as tools when necessary within the activity-based intervention.

4. Teaching strategies used to reach targeted goals will reflect a strong **social-transactional** approach, with the primary method of instruction being rooted in the social interactions between children and significant adults (i.e., teachers and caregivers) as well as between children and their peers.

GENERIC INSTRUCTIONAL STRATEGIES

A wide body of research and theoretical work in fields such as developmental and experimental psychology, child development, neuropsychology, and education has generated an extensive knowledge base from which we can develop a catalog of principles and strategies for early intervention. These strategies and principles are generic in that they apply not just to young children with special needs, but to all children. They are based on several key principles that describe how children learn. Students wishing to develop expertise in the field of early childhood special education cannot hope to do so without understanding, first, how all young children learn, and second, how teaching strategies can be adapted and fine tuned to meet the needs of children with special needs.

Motivation

One of the most powerful keys to learning is **motivation,** one of the oldest notions in the field of psychology (Maslow, 1998). Motivation is an incentive or inducement to action. Human organisms behave and act on the environment for certain reasons. Young children with no disabilities are typically easily motivated; early childhood educators may not need to spend a great deal of conscious effort identifying and understanding the motivations of such children. For young children with disabilities, however, the identification of high-preference objects, people, and activities is crucial to intervention success.

It is helpful to view motivation as being of two types: external and internal. The techniques of behavior analysis and behavior modification rely primarily on externally provided motivators. These might include primary **reinforcers** such as food and water or socially conditioned reinforcers such as praise or tokens. In addition to external motivation is "effectance motivation" which is thought to be dependent on internal motivational factors.

Behavior Modification

The contributions of techniques of **behavior analysis** and **behavior modification** to the field of special education have been substantial. The ability to describe behavior objectively, analyze antecedent events and consequences, and shape children's behavior is a basic skill requirement for all educators. While space does not allow a thorough presentation of the principles and applications of behavior modification in this text, early interventionists must acquire competence in the use of techniques such as successive approximations, the use of cues and prompts, and the provision of contingent reinforcement (see Walker & Shea, 1999).

Briefly, this approach is based on the principle that immediate consequences of a specific behavior can either strengthen or weaken that behavior. Consequences that are pleasurable are called *reinforcers.* Consequences that are unpleasant or aversive are called *punishers.* The use of punishers or aversive control is not appropriate for infants and very young children. However, the use of **positive reinforcement** can be very helpful in increasing the strength and frequency of certain behaviors. For example, giving a thirsty child a sip of juice each time he or she makes a sound might help increase vocalizations.

Whenever possible, the positive reinforcer should be a logical or "natural" consequence of the particular behavior, rather than an artificial one. An example of a natural reinforcer for making the correct sign for a favorite toy would be providing the opportunity to play with the toy rather than receiving a piece of candy. Another example would be giving the child a glass of juice for saying "juice," rather than telling the child "Good talking."

Another key component of behavior modification is the planning and selection of specific cues and prompts. Again, whenever possible, the child should learn to respond to natural rather than contrived cues and prompts. Earlier behavior modification programs utilized highly structured programs aimed at so-called "errorless learning." Teaching of specific skills was broken down into many small steps, beginning with highly contrived prompts that were to be faded gradually until the child could perform the behavior without prompts. Unfortunately, such procedures often produced children who were "cue bound," that is, they continued to be extremely dependent on specific prompts. Generalization to other settings was difficult. For example, a child could be taught to say the word "cookie" in response to the prompt "Say cookie," but would not spontaneously request a cookie without a cue in another setting. Thus, more recently emphasis has been placed on teaching children to recognize the appropriate situation in which to use the behavior, respond to more-natural cues such as an adult's expectant look or saying "Is there something you need?", and teaching in natural contexts.

Another key component of behavior modification is reinforcement of the child's **successive approximations.** This is a solid principle of learning based on recognition of the importance of starting with whatever the child can do and gradually encouraging closer and closer approximation to the correct behavior. For example, initially a child may only be able to swipe at a paper with a colored marker. Gradually the child can be reinforced for behavior that comes closer and closer to making a circle.

Behavioral principles are also very useful in our attempts to understand certain behaviors by carefully observing both the **antecedents** of the behavior (i.e., the events that occur immediately prior to the behavior) and its **consequences** (i.e., what occurs immediately following the behavior). For example, a child who has tactile defensiveness (i.e., is very sensitive to touch) may have frequent episodes of crying. Careful recording may reveal that these episodes are brought on by situations in which the antecedent event is the child's being crowded by other children. Observation may also reveal that the usual consequence of this crying is for the child's favorite adult to start talking to him. A simple intervention that may reduce the crying and increase the child's tolerance for crowding would be the following: When the favored adult notices the antecedent situation (crowding) occurring, she could approach the child *before* *he* begins to cry, commenting on how she is pleased he's having such a good time with the other children. Such a rearrangement of **contingencies** (i.e., what behavior or event follows or precedes what other behavior or event) both reinforces the child for participating and not crying, *and* conditions the child to associate crowded situations with the pleasant experience of being talked to by a friend.

Behavior modification techniques can be powerful influences on children's behavior. It is extremely important that they not be used in isolation from a thorough understanding of the *whole* child. For example, one would not use behavior modification strategies to control tantrums without also exploring all possible causes of these tantrums (e.g., medication effects, pain, or fear).

Effectance Motivation

The classic theory of **effectance motivation** holds that all young children innately have an internal drive toward effectance or achievement (White, 1959). Children internalize or feel personally responsible for the mastery they have over their own behavior and the resulting effect on their environment. If free of disabling conditions, children can more easily feel pride in accomplishments they can attribute to their own effort or ability (Cook, 1986). It is this personal feeling of control over one's self and pride in one's efforts that provides inducement to act (motivation).

The existence of an internal drive to have an effect on one's environment suggests the importance of encouraging young children to initiate interactions with both the animate and inanimate world around them. For nondisabled children, the key to this type of motivation lies both in the opportunity for self-initiation and exploration and in the existence of a responsive environment. For children with special needs, teachers and caregivers must be able to read cues that are often ambiguous and may occur infrequently. These cues must be perceived in order to identify situations in which a child with disabilities is attempting to act upon the environment. It may also be necessary to manipulate the child's environment in ways that increase the likelihood that the child will initiate an interaction and experience success.

The teacher may have to, verbally and in other ways, call the child's attention to the fact that his or her actions really do make a difference. Only when the success of an action is attributed to one's own efforts can pride resulting in motivation or the desire to try again be realized (Cook, 1986). The following examples may help illustrate the importance of understanding children's motivations.

Johnny is a healthy, energetic, typical 4-year-old. Most of his interest is in large muscle activities. He loves being outside, riding tricycles, and climbing. One rainy day he wandered over to the cupboard where the play dough was kept, managed to climb precariously up on the counter, and opened the cupboard. Mrs. Hunt's first inclination was to reprimand Johnny for climbing, but instead she said, "What are you looking for? Can I help you?" She then realized that he was trying to get the play dough. This was uncharacteristic of Johnny, since he typically had no patience for this kind of fine motor activity. So Mrs. Hunt decided to encourage his interest, and she provided him with the play dough. She also stayed close to him while he rolled it into balls and "snakes," assisting him and praising him occasionally. Thus she was able to encourage participation in a new activity by taking advantage of Johnny's own drive to act upon his environment.

Another child, Robert, has cerebral palsy. He has very limited movement in all four extremities. He cannot walk and is just beginning to reach and attempt to grasp objects. Even though he has severe physical impairments, he has a great sense of humor and loves attention. During free-play time, he is placed prone on a bolster so he can watch two of his nondisabled peers, Maria and Jeff, playing with blocks. The teacher enters the group and begins to build a block tower just within Robert's reach. She demonstrates to Robert that if he reaches and contacts the block tower, he can knock it down. She pretends to be dismayed by the destruction of the tower. Robert beams. Now the teacher rebuilds the tower and, without prompting, Robert reaches to knock the tower down again, thoroughly enjoying the game. Very shortly, Maria and Jeff want to get into the game, each building towers for Robert to knock down.

These scenarios demonstrate the use of motivation and the importance of having an effect on one's environment. In the first example, the teacher recognizes Johnny's interest in the play dough and responds to that interest, thus allowing him to have an impact on the objects and people around him. She then assists his development in a new skill area. In Robert's case, he becomes motivated by his effect on both the physical and the social environment. He experiences *effectance* by successfully making the tower fall down and also by initiating a turn-taking game (social interaction) with both his teacher and his nondisabled peers. This is a result that is often difficult for young children with disabilities to achieve.

Social Mediation of Experience

The literature in the field of developmental and cognitive psychology is rich with both theoretical explanations and empirical descriptions of ways in which adults mediate (i.e., assist in making meaningful) the environment and the events that young children experience. Feuerstein, Rand, Hoffman, and Miller (1980) referred to these phenomena as **"mediated learning events"** or MLE, in which adults carefully enhance a child's understanding and mastery by translating events both physically and verbally as the child experiences them.

Another theorist, Vygotsky (1980) stated that cognition develops within a social context. He described that "zone of proximal development," which

is the realm of abilities that the child is able to exhibit while interacting with a significant adult but cannot perform independently. As sensitive adults interact with young children they become aware of this "zone" and are able to facilitate development by providing just the right degree and type of support necessary to assist the child's progress toward independent mastery of a task. Bruner (1982) referred to this as **scaffolding,** or the providing of graduated cues to assist a child through problem solving. Such social mediation of the child's experience is important for all infants and young children, regardless of their particular capabilities. Note the two examples that follow.

Jose is a highly gifted, somewhat rambunctious 3-year-old. He is trying to use three blocks to build a sort of archway for his truck to go under, but it is too narrow. He glances around briefly for a solution but quickly gives up and starts to move on to something else. His teacher notices and says, "Gee, the space is too narrow, isn't it? The truck can't fit through there. The truck is too big. Hmm. What can we do?" While making these comments, the teacher finds a long piece of cardboard, which, if substituted for the block across the top, will make it possible to widen the opening. She does not say this, but simply offers the piece of cardboard to Jose. She waits, giving him the opportunity to discover the solution himself, which he promptly does. He pushes the truck through, and his teacher comments, "Oh, good. Now the opening is big enough for the truck to go through."

A second child, Min, has severe developmental delays and multiple disabilities. She is blind and non-ambulatory. She is able to reach and grasp but does so infrequently. Her favorite activity is eating. She appears to be sensitive to food aromas, because she becomes much more alert as lunchtime approaches and food carts are moved through the hallways. Her teacher helps Min organize and understand her experiences around lunchtime, mediating the environment around her. As the teacher notices Min becoming alert to the smell of the approaching food, the teacher says "Lunch! It's lunchtime, Min. Let's get ready." The teacher first introduces Min's bib, encouraging her to touch and feel it, saying "here's your bib."

The teacher puts on the bib, encouraging as much independence as possible by getting Min to push her arms through the holes. Next, as the cart enters the room, she taps its side so Min can hear it, then moves her close to it so she can feel it. The teacher says, "Good, our food cart is here. Now we can eat. I'll push you over to the lunch table."

In this way, the teacher is mediating what might otherwise be simply a confusing blur of sounds, smells, touches, and position changes. By doing this consistently, the teacher will eventually assist Min in understanding and anticipating these events.

Adult-Child Communication Strategies

As can be seen in the preceding examples, another critical factor in assisting children's learning is the use of language. How adults and older children talk to infants and young children has a major impact on their development, particularly in the areas of language and cognition. These strategies will be discussed in some detail in Chapter 9. However, it is appropriate to summarize them here as well.

1. *Use referential language.* That is, use the names of things and actions; be specific and concrete. For example, a child is enjoying rolling a ball down the slide. Teacher A might say something like "Wow! That's neat. Look at it go." While this is an enthusiastic and positive response to the child's involvement, it is not referential. This comment would have a less-positive effect on the child's language development than would teacher B's response: "Wow! the ball's rolling down. Down the slide. The ball's rolling down fast!"

2. *Use redundancy and repetition of key words and phrases.* It is not sufficient to refer to something only once. Language needs to be redundant, mentioning key concepts and events several times. In addition, repetition of key words and phrases is important. Redundancy and repetition are important to all children, and even more important for children

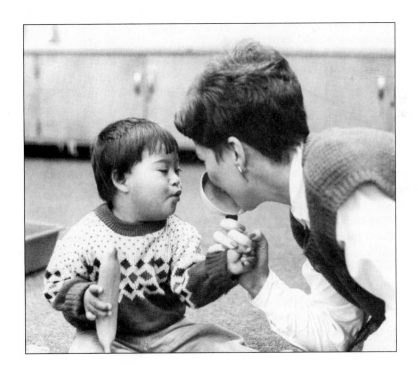

with disabilities. In the example above, the word "ball" is used two times; "down" is used three times; and "rolling" is used twice. Ideally, these three concepts would be introduced again during the play situation, in a slightly different context. For example, the teacher could roll a different ball down an inclined board, or the children could roll themselves down a hill, and so on.

3. *Utilize routines.* Some degree of routine and predictability is important for all children. For children with special needs, the careful use of routines becomes an important teaching strategy. Repetition of key words and phrases within a familiar sequence of daily events facilitates language development. Both play routines and caretaking routines are effective strategies for encouraging many areas of children's development and will be discussed in more detail later.

4. *Provide comprehensive input.* The importance of comprehensive input was first described by MacNamara (1972). It is important for children to be tuned in to and understand what you are talking about, even if they don't actually understand all the words. Several strategies facilitate this. For example, adults can follow the child's lead and talk about what the child is paying attention to and experiencing. Sometimes this is called "mapping language onto experience" (McLean & Snyder-McLean, 1978, p. 193). Another strategy is to talk about concrete things that can be seen, felt, or heard. In this way words can be associated easily with their referents.

5. *Match adult language to the child's language level.* For children who are just beginning to learn language, adult language input must be short, consisting of one- and two-word utterances and short, simple sentences. As the child's language develops, adult language can become more complex. MacDonald (1989, p. 173) referred to this as **progressive** matching. For example, John has just begun to use single words. As he is playing catch with his teacher, she says "Catch. Catch the ball. Catch the ball, John." John's friend Theo, who speaks easily in simple sentences, joins the game. The teacher says, "Here Theo. Catch the ball, then throw it to John." In this way, the teacher models more complex utterances for Theo.

6. *Establish turn taking.* For very young children or children with severe disabilities, it may be necessary to first establish turn-taking skills before the strategies previously listed can be used effectively. Turn taking provides the social basis upon which communication skills develop. In a nondisabled child, turn-taking skills are well established within the caregiver-infant dyad in the first 3 or 4 months of life. For some children, however, this may need to be established as a specific teaching goal. Several strategies can be used to establish turn taking: (a) imitating something the child is already doing; (b) engaging in a pleasurable activity and then interrupting that activity and waiting until the child makes some kind of response; or (c) physically prompting the child to take a turn. Chapter 9 will elaborate on other ways to develop communication skills.

Routines

Daily living routines are important in designing educational programs for young children. For infants, daily living routines may be referred to as *caregiving routines.*

Daily Living Routines. Daily living routines are the kinds of routines that occur as part of carrying out the daily activities of life. Families may vary in the extent to which their lives are characterized by a predictable routine or schedule. While some home environments may be quite predictable (e.g., wake up, eat breakfast, go to school, come home from school, have a snack, take a nap, play with Dad, eat supper, watch television, take a bath, read a story, go to bed), others may be chaotic and unpredictable. Some degree of predictability is thought to be important to young children. It helps them feel secure and gives them a sense of mastery and control over their environment. As will be discussed in Chapter 7, it facilitates both emotional and cognitive development.

Daily living routines are also important in the center or classroom for the same reasons that they are important at home. In addition, they provide useful contexts for teaching language and cognitive concepts. A familiar routine is a necessary background against which children with disabilities can experience novel and special events. For these children, such events can be attended to and processed more easily when they are experienced as different from the norm. On the other hand, when such events occur as simply one of many unexpected and unfamiliar events in a day, they are meaningless at best and probably confusing.

Play Routines. Play routines provide another way to utilize repetition and routine in the classroom. Play routines can be designed specifically to teach language and concepts, and social skills. A play routine often revolves around a pretend play theme, such as going shopping, going on a camping trip, finding something lost, hunting for treasure, and so on. The possibilities are endless. The purpose of a play routine is to provide a familiar activity sequence within which to teach specific concepts, vocabulary, social behaviors, or pragmatic communication skills. The play routine requires a great deal of work and planning initially, but as the routine is repeated over and over it becomes easier to implement while it also becomes more powerful as a teaching strategy. The complexity and content of the play routine will be dependent upon the needs and characteristics of the children in the class.

Exhibit 6-2 demonstrates how the generic strategies discussed here can be incorporated into the medium of play, the context that is most normal to young children.

PLAY AS AN IMPORTANT TEACHING CONTEXT

Skilled use of the strategies described here presents a significant challenge to the early childhood special education professional. There is no better context in which to use these strategies than the context of play. In fact, in many ways play is probably the single most important concept in early childhood special education. It is important both as a teaching context and as

an end in itself. Play is an important skill. Typical young children can often learn play skills with little guidance from adults. Many children with special needs, however, must be assisted in learning these skills. Thus the teaching of play as a social skill is considered an important part of the early education curriculum. This aspect of play will be discussed further in Chapter 7.

Play is an ideal context in which to discover and mobilize children's motivations. It also creates a rich environment where teachers can use the interaction and mediation strategies described earlier.

Within the field of early education there is a strong historical precedent for a focus on play. Froebel, a German educator in the 1800s, believed that the principles of early education include the following:

1. Education should primarily protect and nurture.

2. It should not prescribe and control.

3. Play should constitute the heart of the curriculum.

4. Play is the means by which children gain insight.

5. Play is the means of mental development.

This is a strong endorsement of the role of play in education, and it has continued to influence the field of early education throughout its history (Weber, 1971).

It is equally important to apply this concept to the field of early childhood *special* education. This application requires some refinement. First, as mentioned before, some children with special needs do not engage in play easily. Thus teachers must develop strategies not only for utilizing play as a context but also for encouraging its occurrence. Second, it is necessary to understand how the elements of play can be achieved for all children.

There are some 40 definitions listed in the dictionary for the word *play.* An operational definition that might be useful for our purposes would be the following: *Play* is a situation in which an infant or child is actively engaged with his or her environment—either animate or inanimate—but for which there is not an intended or predetermined outcome or goal.

EXHIBIT 6–2

Use of Generic Instructional Strategies During Playtime

Event	*Strategy*
The children in Mr. Curtis's class have finished lunch. Mr. Curtis announces that it is time to clean up the tables and go to recess.	Signal for transition
The children are very familiar with this routine, so with little assistance they throw away their napkins and milk cartons and bring their cups and plates to the sink.	Use of routines
Andrea, a 4-year-old who has Down syndrome, heads out to the playground. On her way she notices the bottle of bubble soap on the shelf. She loves blowing bubbles and tries to grab the bottle.	
Miss Chinn, the aide, notices and asks, "Would you like to take the bubble soap outside?" "Okay. Can you get the bottle for us?"	Response to child's interest
Andrea reaches with one hand, but has difficulty getting hold of the bottle. Miss Chinn gently moves Andrea's other hand toward the bottle, encouraging her to grasp with both hands.	Scaffolding
Andrea gets the bottle and carries it outside.	Child experiences success
Andrea's friend Alex notices that she has the bubble soap. He comes over and offers to help her get the top off. He blows some bubbles, then hands the wand to Andrea so she can try.	Peer interaction
The teacher approaches and sits down on the grass with the children. He says, "Andrea, look at these bubbles. Many, many bubbles! Oops! One popped. The bubble popped. Pop! Pop!"	Use of short sentences Repetition of key words
Andrea looks at Alex pointing to a bubble on the ground, saying "Buh!" Alex says, "Bubble. Right!" Then the bubble pops and Andrea says "Pop! pop!"	Child responds and is heard
Later that same day, Miss Chinn finds a balloon. She brings the balloon to Andrea, saying, "Let's blow up the balloon." Andrea does not seem interested at first, but she becomes intrigued as Miss Chinn starts to blow. She blows it up a little bit, then stops. She looks expectantly at Andrea.	Redundancy Generalization practice
Andrea waves her hand toward the balloon. Miss Chinn says, "Shall I blow some more?" Andrea says, "More."	Reading child's nonverbal cues
The aide finishes blowing up the balloon. Then she says, "I'm going to *pop* the balloon." "I'm going to *pop* it."	Responsivity Foreshadowing events
Andrea looks at her quizzically. Miss Chinn then takes a pin and pops the balloon. She says, "It popped!" Andrea claps her hands excitedly. She runs off to find her friend Alex at the sand table. She looks at Alex and says, "Pop!"	Social interaction Use of language to describe past events

There are several key elements in this definition that parallel the principles and strategies discussed earlier and that demonstrate why play is such a powerful teaching and learning context. First, the child must be engaged. This suggests that, at the very minimum, there must be some information processing occurring; the child is paying attention to something. Furthermore, active engagement requires initiating and acting upon the environment in some way. The term *environment* refers not only to the physical world of objects, space, and sensory stimuli but also (and perhaps more important) to the social environment. The social, or animate, environment consists of the people (and pets), communication, emotions, facial expressions, touches, and so on, that impinge in some way upon the infant's or child's experiences.

The element of play that perhaps most distinguishes it from other contexts or activities is the final element: There is no predetermined outcome or goal. In play, goals may emerge and unfold or arise spontaneously; outcomes are discovered through exploration and trial and error.

Given this definition of play, it can range from the simple exploratory behavior of the infant to the complex pretend scenarios of the preschooler. Playing peek-a-boo or putting blocks in a can may be play for one child, while pretending to be an alien from outer space is play for another.

Thus play must be viewed as an important and necessary component of early childhood special education. It is, of course, not the only component. Routine daily living events are equally important contexts for learning. For busy parents, these contexts are possibly more important than play. There is also an important place for more structured, traditional learning contexts, particularly as children reach preschool age or are enrolled in behaviorally designed programs that focus on particular skills or behaviors. But the hallmark of the competent professional in the field of early childhood special education will be the ability to unleash the full potential of play not only to facilitate learning but also to enhance the joy and quality of life for young children with special needs.

ARRANGING THE PHYSICAL ENVIRONMENT TO MAXIMIZE LEARNING

There is substantial evidence that the social environment, as reflected in the preceding discussion, has great effect on children's development. It is also important to consider how the *physical* environment can influence both children and adults in ways that will enhance children's opportunities to learn and to interact socially with one another. Generally, physical arrangements and facilities that are effective for typical young children will be suitable for children with special needs. However, some adjustments may have to be made, depending on the nature of the children's special needs. There may also have to be greater space within the classroom area to accommodate a larger number of adults, especially if active participation of family members is expected. A two-way mirror is very helpful in allowing unobtrusive observation by families and teachers in training. The discussion that follows is meant to further highlight some of the unique considerations that might accompany integration of young children with special needs.

When integrating children who have physical challenges, ramps may have to be provided and enough space made available for children who need to maneuver equipment such as walkers or wheelchairs. Some may even need special positioning devices, which take additional space within the classroom. Materials should be at eye level. Shelves and tables must be sturdy enough to support children who have difficulty standing and maintaining balance. Sand and other activity tables should be set away from walls so that children may get to them from all sides. Tables with semicircular "bites" out of them and rims around the edges allow children to get closer to materials while also preventing items from rolling to the floor. In some cases, materials should be put on the floor. Nonslip floor coverings are necessary to prevent tripping or catching crutches. Adaptable equipment will be necessary to ensure full participation of all children.

For centers attended by children with visual impairments, room arrangements should be fairly fixed. Clutter must be eliminated. When changes must be made, it is important to assist children with visual impairments with adaptations to these changes. Routes from one area to another should be direct, minimize cross traffic, and be free of obstacles. Doors should be either fully open or completely shut. Sharp edges of tables should be padded. Auditory or tactile cues should be used to designate areas. For example, a carpet might mark the quiet corner while the bubbling of an aquarium signifies the science center. Groups should be kept small and noise levels controlled to allow for maximal use of hearing. Noisy, chaotic environments reduce opportunities for children with visual impairments to learn.

It is usually not necessary to make adaptations in facilities or equipment for children with cognitive, health, communication, or social-emotional differences. Children who are experiencing difficulties in self-control or overactivity do require more clearly defined limits and greater consistency in caregiving in order to feel safe. Opportunities for as much natural social interaction as possible are essential to the success of an integrated program. Teachers will find that while acting as guides they can use flexibility of setting and materials to help children develop social skills.

Special Considerations for Infants and Toddlers

Some special concerns for infant and toddler environments are worthy of note. Health and safety issues are of primary importance. Floors need to be padded, sharp edges and table corners eliminated, and elevated areas no more than 2 feet in height. Sinks and soap for handwashing and diapering must be conveniently located to encourage good hygiene. Diapering areas should not be located near food preparation centers. Carpets of short pile material will facilitate ease of cleaning. Storage areas that are easily accessible help to avoid clutter and hazards in traffic areas.

Environments for infants and toddlers should be designed to encourage movement and interaction with one another. Movement can be facilitated by providing carpeted steps and ramps that lead to interesting play areas. Places to crawl through, such as tunnels, and cozy spaces to crawl into, such as a specially designed box or cubby, will serve to motivate movement. Use of multiple elevations also encourages easier interaction between very young children and their caregivers by facilitating eye contact. Water beds set on the floor are effective movement motivators and can be comforting at the same time. Adult

rockers and couches not only provide additional places for toddlers to climb into but also encourage adults' holding, reading, and talking to infants and toddlers. "Adopted grandparents" might be just the right people to provide needed encouragement to move and verbalize.

Providing choices for infants and toddlers whose disabilities may be confining is essential. They need incentives for body movement and a variety of toys. Toys and other interesting objects should be displayed clearly on shelves that are neutral in color so that the objects stand out. To avoid visual confusion, only a few toys should be visible at any one time. However, it is wise to keep some interesting toys in cupboards or on high shelves to encourage children's communicative behaviors as they request objects that they cannot reach.

Room acoustics can be optimized by use of absorptive materials on floors, walls, and ceilings to reduce resonance and ambient noise. Many children with and without disabilities (as well as many adults) find noisy environments distracting and disorganizing. This may be especially true of those who have visual impairments and those who are easily overstimulated. Constant background noise from radios and record players encourages children and adults to talk louder, thus increasing the overall noise level in the classroom. This, in turn, increases stress and fatigue. Of course, it is important that efforts be made to reduce environmental noise without inhibiting children's exuberance. Readers are referred to Bailey and Wolery (1999) for an excellent presentation of guidelines for assessing environments.

Before including young children with special needs, directors would be wise to assemble an advisory panel made up of a physical therapist, an occupational therapist, a child psychologist, a speech and language pathologist, a nurse, and an early childhood special educator. This committee can make recommendations for adaptations to be made in the physical setting and the program. Figure 6–1 illustrates one very satisfactory environmental arrangement. Note that the library corner or block area may be conducive to "circle time."

Figure 6–1 Room arrangement. (Reprinted with permission from Teaching Research Division, Western Oregon State College.)

SCHEDULING INTERVENTION ACTIVITIES

When including young children with special needs, early interventionists must select and schedule activities that allow for a wide range of abilities as well as interests. If such activities focus on the process of involvement rather than on products per se, then there is much greater flexibility and choice within the activity. That is why activities that originate out of natural play behavior are so appropriate. For example, children can practice self-help skills in the dress-up

corner, where they can learn naturally from their peers as the process of dressing and undressing occurs. In such an activity, each child's unique needs can be accommodated. One child can be encouraged to put on colorful socks, while another is attempting to button a shirt, and a third is tying shoes. All through the activity, children have the opportunity to socially interact. This is even more likely if the teacher has contrived a purpose for the dress-up, such as "going out for lunch."

When scheduling center-based activities, balance is the key: There should be a balance of large-group, small-group, and individual activities; structured and unstructured activities; active and passive activities. Activities should address all areas of children's development.

Scheduled Plans Promote Desired Consistency in Routines

As discussed earlier, daily routines provide the consistency necessary to help young children feel secure and realize a sense of mastery and control over their environment. Scheduled plans are one means of regulating activities and providing for consistency through the establishment of daily routines. We acknowledge that teachers planning for a group of preschoolers rarely have the luxury of hours for planning on school time. Teaching young children is demanding work at best. It is important to develop efficient, effective ways to plan. This requires a well-organized curriculum.

The first step in planning is to ask the following questions:

1. How will the day be divided into the various activities?

2. How much time will be allowed for each activity?

3. Which routines and activities will be repeated daily (for example, greeting the children as they arrive, circle time, bathroom routines, playtime, and outdoor time)?

4. How will themes be used to provide focus for the activities?

5. What use will be made of small and large groups for specific teaching?

6. Which activities must be repeated frequently over time to allow for increasingly complex skill development?

7. Who will have to follow these activity plans?

By answering these seven questions, a system appropriate for the classroom will emerge. First, consider question 7: Who will have to interpret and follow your activity plans? Teacher aides and volunteers will need to understand what is being done and

why. So while writing plans, you should consider the answer to question 7 continuously. Ms. McLynn's unique planning considerations are discussed in Exhibit 6–3.

Next, how the day will be divided and how much time will be spent on each activity (questions 1 and 2) should be considered. To avoid having to fill in a blank space each week with repetitive comments such as "Greet children individually" or "Take care of bathroom needs" or even "Sing the Clean-Up Time Song," it is helpful to write a schedule that can be used for many weeks. Any activities that are repeated daily should be included. Enough detail should be included so that a substitute will be able to have a clear picture of what is expected during each time segment. Exhibits 6–4 and 6–5 give examples of time-use plans.

In addition to the scheduled plan, a lesson plan form with spaces to write specific activities, strategies and vocabulary for each day is also important.

Regardless of the materials used or specific activities, teaching will be guided by the specific objectives for each child. For instance, if the teacher chooses to teach colors this week by baking cookies and icing them with the colors being taught, he or she will conform to the objectives by asking some children to "Show me the blue icing" or "Use the yellow icing." For children who have demonstrated that they can *recognize* colors (for example, "Show me") the teacher will be ready to ask, "What color did Joe use on his cookie?" This, of course, reflects individualizing because Joe is asked to *recall* the color, a more difficult objective than to merely recognize it when the color is named. When the teacher plans in this way, it becomes unnecessary to write objectives for each different activity because the teacher is providing **equivalent practice.** That is, the teacher is expecting each child to perform on the level identified on his or her individual plan.

However, some activities will involve cooking, whereas others involve dressing the doll, sorting different color toys, or choosing paper for a fine motor project. While teaching, the teacher is continually assessing the individual performances. He or she can be very creative in the activities chosen but will not need to write each one in detail.

◆ ◆ ◆

EXHIBIT 6–3

A Week's Plan and Individualized Activities

Ms. McLynn plans activities a week in advance. She is careful to choose things that the children are able to do and will enjoy.

Vocabulary, concepts to be emphasized, and gross and fine motor activities as well as music and stories are chosen in relation to a theme. For example, if the theme is "See signs of spring and learn about them," she will plan a walk to look at buds and spring flowers, plant seeds, do a craft (fine motor) activity such as make crepe paper flowers, and learn a song about spring.

Many of the objectives for each child require practice over time. Each day, Ms. McLynn chooses materials and games that promote these skills. This equivalent practice makes it possible for the children to do many different things at essentially the same skill level. They are not bored, even though they are practicing the same skills daily. The needed repetition never becomes meaningless drill.

Ms. McLynn found it difficult to include each child's individual objectives on the weekly lesson plan. She prefers to list the activity, such as "numerals and counting," on the plan. Then, she uses her checklist and objectives to provide individualized lesson targets for each child. This does not mean that she works with them one at a time. She conforms her directions and questions to each child on the basis of individual skills during the group activity.

Ms. McLynn's friend Ms. Watts has less experience in teaching young children with different individual needs. She prefers to have a separate page for each child. She writes the specific objective for each part of the weekly plan on the individual child's plan. Then, she writes a comment each afternoon about the effectiveness of her planning. In this way she is learning to evaluate and adjust her planning. Each of these teachers chooses a theme and plans individualized activities within group lessons. However, they prefer different systems for organizing and record keeping.

PROVIDING A VARIETY OF ACTIVITIES TO ACCOMPLISH ANY ONE OUTCOME OR OBJECTIVE

In choosing appropriate activities to achieve any one outcome or objective, educators are limited only by their imagination and creativity. For example, the following objectives might be chosen to achieve the goal "To learn the names of body parts":

Terminal objective:

When the teacher points to any body parts (eyes, ears, nose, mouth, arms, hands, or feet) and says, "Tell me what this is called," Danny will name them correctly 80% of the time. Each body part will be checked on a doll, the child, and another child.

Individual objectives:

1. When the teacher points to any of the body parts listed and says, "This is a_____," Danny will imitate the teacher's spoken model.

2. When the teacher points to any of the body parts listed and says, "Is this the _____?" Danny will name the part.

3. When the teacher says, "Show me your _____," Danny will point to his own named body part.

4. When the teacher asks, "What is this?" while pointing to his or her own, another child's, or a doll's features, Danny will name the features correctly.

The following list of activities could be used to provide equivalent practice on any of the objectives just described.

EXHIBIT 6–4

Example of a Daily Plan: Preschool Classroom

Time-use plan and description of daily routines for both morning and afternoon classes*

8:30 A.M.   *Greeting.* Children are greeted individually as they arrive. Welcome by name, encourage to respond with eye contact, and use a smile and "Hello" or "Good morning." Help them only as much as necessary to hang up their coats and get ready for their special work. Ask whether they have brought a note from home. Some (as needed) go to the bathroom.

    Active conversation with them about everything they are doing is a must, since their primary need is to develop social, language, and cognitive skills about their everyday experiences. Encourage them to look into the mirror to see whether they are neat and ready for school. During the first 30 minutes children will appear to be playing, some alone and some in small groups of *their choice.* This open classroom is an important teaching time, because children choose "lessons," games, or toys. Teachers, aides, and parents may play or work with them, but it is each child's option to choose what to do. Encourage children to choose carefully, complete an activity, then return toys and games to the shelves. They are not required to share what they have chosen and may play alone if they prefer. It is important to enjoy conversation with children about what they are doing, although this will be a bit one-sided at first. Interactive conversation (which includes the adult's listening) is the optimum way to teach speech and language skills.

    Concepts to emphasize are listed on the weekly theme page and on the *concept board* behind the teacher's desk. The intent of the concept board is to provide a "prompt sheet" for adults in the classroom to use these words continually in appropriate ways throughout the day. Contrive occasions for children to use these concepts correctly. Spontaneity is important. Repeated use is requisite.

8:45 A.M.   *Clean-up time.* Children take turns ringing the bell to announce the end of play time. Sing the "clean-up" song. All participate in cleaning up and moving chairs to form a semicircle facing the bulletin board. Reward with praise those who arrive first with their work completed.

    Circle time. Sometimes children sit on their own carpet squares on the floor or under a tree to allow for variety. The purpose of this period is to give children practice in participating, listening, and controlling themselves in a large group. This takes time. "Dailies" include a review of the weather, days of the week, the calendar, learning names, recognizing who is absent, and "show and tell." These activities not only help children become socially aware but also help develop their language expression, memory, and just plain everyday knowledge.

9:00 A.M.   *Small-group time.* Children choose from activities previously set up by the teacher. These usually include a fine motor activity, language activity, problem-solving activity, and combination activity such as cooking, which builds fine motor skills, language, and concepts. Some children may work individually with the teacher, aide, or therapist at this time. For children with special needs, choices may be narrowed to develop target behaviors such as cleaning up, toileting, and washing hands.

9:30 A.M.   *Snack time.* A wide variety of nutritious foods are eaten to encourage conversation and understanding of differences, for example, in color, texture, taste, and shape. As children finish, they brush their teeth and select a book from the shelf.

◆ ◆ ◆

EXHIBIT 6–4

9:50 A.M.	*Story time.* Sometimes all children "read" to themselves. At other times, some read to themselves while others join an adult to listen to a story. When enough adults are available, several stories may be listened to in small groups around the room.
10:10 A.M.	*Movement time.* Depending on the weather, movement activities may be inside the room, in the gym, or outside. Music may accompany such activities. The physical therapist may work with some children.
10:30 A.M.	*Music and art time.* Music and fingerplay activities may be done in the group circle. Art activities are usually done in small groups. Sometimes parents will share special interests with children at this time. Choice is given, when possible.
10:50 A.M.	*Dismissal preparation.* Children clean up and then join others in the circle. One at a time, children get their belongings and put on their coats while others exchange feelings about the day and sing the closing song.
11:00 A.M.	*Dismissal.* Children are released to parents or bus drivers.

*Note: Times suggested are approximate. Young children should not be rushed. Flexibility is necessary to capture "teachable moments" and to accommodate special events such as field trips.

1. Bathing a doll.
2. Dressing a doll.
3. Washing hands and faces.
4. Doing a puzzle (that includes body parts).
5. Drawing at the chalkboard.
6. Drawing on paper.
7. Making a jack-o'-lantern.
8. Pasting features on a teddy bear made of construction paper.
9. Singing a song ("Made up" chants are fun, for example, "I touch my nose and blink my eyes. I clap my hands and say 'Surprise!' ").
10. Making a gingerbread man.
11. Telling stories, and encouraging the children to act them out.
12. Puppet plays.

As illustrated in the following dialogue, these activities will allow children to work on different en-route behaviors while participating in an activity together.

The Activity: Bathing a Doll

Equipment: Aprons, warm water, soap, wash cloths, towels, a doll bathtub, and a dirty doll.

Teacher: Sally, will you help me wash our doll? She is so dirty. Look at those hands and feet. (Pointing.)

Sally: I get the water and soap.

Danny: Wa-er (water).

Teacher: Get the towel, Danny.

Vicky: Where? (Grabbing the doll.)

Teacher: Hold her very carefully, Vicky. Be gentle. (Pointing to the arm.) See, her arm is all wet.

Danny: Dere no (nose). (Pointing.)

Teacher: Right Danny, that's her nose.

Danny: Wha da? (What's that?)

Teacher: That's her ear (Pointing.) Can you find her other ear?

Danny: Dere (There.)

Teacher: Right!

Using the objectives, the teacher can individualize any activity by applying the expected level of performance (criterion) requirements to the activity.

Evaluating the Effectiveness of Each Activity

The usefulness of any activity is determined largely by its appeal to children. In addition, the activity should

EXHIBIT 6–5

Example of a Daily Plan: Infant Toddler Center

B. Ammons	D. Tison
Teachers	*Physical Therapist*
A. McKail / C. Rodriquez	M. Briggs
Assistants	*Speech Therapist*

DATE: Sept 20

Time	Daily Activities	Notes
9:00	1. Arrival	1. Staff will greet bus and assist children and parents in coming to classroom.
	2. Facilitated Play • Puzzles • Blocks • House Play • Mirror activity: old hats • Manipulative toys	2. • Optional areas: floor, table, and room areas. • Assistance given to individual children or small groups—Encourage participation. • <u>Objectives</u>: language, socialization, fine and gross motor.
9:25	3. Transition	3. • Give signals/cues to end play. • Allow time to leave play areas. • Bring chairs to circle. • Assist in positioning children who need help.
9:30	4. Large-group circle A. <u>Music</u> (with guitar) "Good Morning"/"Buenos Dias" "Where Oh Where?" (Sing each child's name) "Wheels on the Bus" B. <u>Activity</u> "What's in the Box?" (Balloons hidden in decorated box.) Blow up balloon and pass around.	4. A. • Parents may be encouraged to sit with the children. B. • Objectives: language concepts, social interaction, attention, motor activity, problem solving.
9:45	5. Outside Play yard: facilitated and self-directed play: • Sand box • Water play • Trikes, cars, wagons • Playground equipment (slides, ladders, swings, etc.)	5. • <u>Objectives</u>: gross motor, social interaction (encourage children with disabilities and those without to interact with toys, games, equipment); exploration through movement and space. • Parents are encouraged to participate.
10:15	6. Small-group activity (4-5 children in each group). • Make pudding (choose flavor, open box, mix, taste)	6. <u>Objectives</u>: lanuage concepts, choice, taste, social interactions, fine motor.
10:40	7. Clean-up Toilet	7. This is time for children to help clean up—wash pans and hands. As clean-up proceeds, 2-3 children go to "potty room." This is an important time for teaching self-help skills, language, etc.
11:00	8. Lunch Clean-up	8. Good teaching opportunity: • Encourage self-help, language, socialization. • Attention to positioning and feeding techniques (as needed).
11:45	9. Closing: Large-group (three classes) music/activities	9. Parents, children, and staff join together in music, rhythms, rhymes, and relaxation. Bilingual songs and games.
12:00	10. Going home	10. Staff assists parents and children in going to bus.

Important Components Underlying Daily Program

1. Physical Therapists and Speech Therapists work in classrooms throughout the morning.
2. Parents participate in classroom or observe through one-way mirror or socialize with other parents in parent room.
3. Bilingual interactions throughout morning activities.
   • Spanish/English
   • Chinese/English
4. Each child has individual goals within daily activities.
5. Signal transition times.

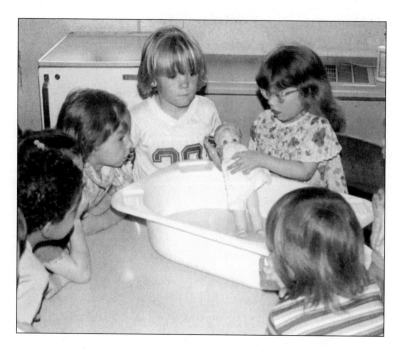

lend itself to repetition with minor variations. (Children enjoy a meaningful amount of repetition.) Each activity should be chosen to develop skills in ways that are a challenge but do not overwhelm the least capable child in the group. Participation is a prerequisite for effective learning with young children. "Just watching" is a useful beginning for some very shy or young children. With gentle encouragement these children can be helped to become full participants.

Using an Activity to Achieve More Than One Objective

Bricker (1998) suggested using an **"activity focus"** for program planning. This approach suggests that programs must be built around activities that are *appropriate* and *motivating*.

Most activities can be used to achieve several objectives at the same time. For example, learning to follow two- and three-stage directions is an important skill. Counting and learning colors and other concepts are goals included in every preschool curriculum.

In bathing the doll, teachers might say "Get the blue towel. It is under the sink" (emphasizing color

and the preposition *under*). She might say, "Take off both socks. See, one sock is on her foot, and the other is on the floor" (emphasizing one-to-one correspondence, foot, and the preposition *on*).

Of course, most preschool teachers do many of these things spontaneously and without much conscious planning. However, when the program includes children with special needs, this important emphasis on specific skills cannot be left to chance. These children require explicit examples, meaningful repetition, and a variety of related experiences. One experience is inadequate. The ability to generalize from one experience to the next must be conscientiously nurtured.

PREPARING THE WAY FOR SUCCESSFUL INCLUSION OF YOUNG CHILDREN WITH SPECIAL NEEDS

The following suggestions are based on the belief that teachers play the central role in the development of programs to successfully include children with special needs. The tone of the classroom is set through the teacher's attitudes and actions. Therefore teachers are strongly encouraged to acknowledge their own fears and apprehensions before initiating an inclusive program. It helps to remember that every child is more like others than different from them. Understanding that all children can have adjustment problems because of their stage of development makes it possible for teachers to recognize that some deviant behavior is just plain normal. Learning something about each specific disability will alleviate many fears and make the teacher feel less helpless. Preparation and planning will go a long way in smoothing the transition for children, families, and staff. The following suggestions are general and can be considered only in light of each specific situation:

1. *Meet with the child's parents before including him or her in the program.* Besides seeking vital parental support, you can explore special interests, specific problems, and solutions. Unpleasant times may be avoided through preventive advice. Some teachers find it helpful to have the child visit the classroom either as a guest for a short time during the day or after the other children have departed. Arranging such a visit before a regular day of enrollment relieves the fears of many children.

2. *After the brief visit just described, phase children in slowly.* A parent may need to be present in the beginning. Adding only one child with special needs at a time will allow you the opportunity to give as much individual attention as necessary.

3. *Prepare already enrolled children in advance.* Be honest in dealing with children's questions. It is extremely important to understand and deal with the fears and concerns of the children who are not disabled.

4. *Be honest in dealing with children's questions.* Give short, truthful answers. Avoid making a big production about introducing the child or explaining his or her differences. Remember, children are more alike than different. To the child who asks, "Why does Susie talk so funny?" you can reply, "Susie had an operation so that she can learn to talk just like you.

Perhaps you will be able to help her make new words while you are playing with the puppets today."

5. *Deal with fears and concerns of parents.* In general, parents of young children tend to favor inclusion. However, they often do have concerns as to whether children will receive adequate attention in integrated programs and question the adequacy of staff training. Parents of children with disabilities also express concern that integrated settings may result in social rejection of their children. Staff must be adequately trained to deal with fears and concerns of parents. Facilitating meetings between parents of disabled and parents of non-disabled children can be helpful. Parents also appreciate receiving information from clear, relevant, and readable materials that address their concerns and questions.

6. *Give all parents support and encouragement.* They will need it. They especially want to be kept informed of their child's progress. Be positive and encourage them to participate as much as possible.

7. *Be positive.* Focus on the attitudes and behaviors you wish to see in children. Be what you want to see expressed.

8. *Be realistic.* Do not expect too much or too little. Go slowly. Get to know the child well. By thoroughly understanding the child's developmental strengths and weaknesses, you can be realistic.

9. *Do not be afraid to be structured.* Young children need clear, firm guidelines for behavior. Identify specific safety rules. Tell and show the children what to do from the first day when safety and cleanliness are involved.

10. *Develop guidelines for classroom behavior* with *the children whenever possible.* Keep the rules simple and few in number. Do not expect the child with special needs to understand and follow all rules immediately. Tell other children that they must help the new child learn by showing him or her how to behave.

11. *Highlight the strengths of the child with special needs.* These need to be real. For example, a child may know how to operate a computerized

communication device, or may be artistic or good at drawing detailed designs (e.g., child with autism). Express enthusiasm and pleasure as each milestone (no matter how small) is achieved. Be genuine. Do not exaggerate.

12. *Be sure the child with the disability is not always the recipient of assistance.* Create opportunities for him or her to help others.

13. *Seek to change the environment, not the child.* Be creative in designing strategies to support participation in all activities.

14. *Train staff to facilitate peer social interactions.* As social interaction between disabled and non-disabled children does not happen automatically, staff must be trained to facilitate this interaction. Resources in the form of consultants and curriculum guides such as those described at the end of the chapter are helpful. Assigning "special buddies" for all children is a very effective technique for seeing that children with disabilities become socially included. The typical peer buddies should be trained so that they will understand how the disabled child communicates—how to read that specific child's cues. The typical peer can be given definite strategies for initiating and responding to the child with the disability. Other useful strategies such as small group "cooperative learning" activities and physical proximity control are discussed in Chapter 7.

15. *Most of all, do not expect too much of yourself* or *of the situation.* Progress takes time.

CONSIDERATIONS FOR ADAPTING CURRICULA FOR CHILDREN WITH SPECIFIC SPECIAL NEEDS

It must be remembered that a child with disabilities is first a child. The suggestions given here are designed to help teachers, parents, and other caregivers meet those special needs that can get in the way of a child's opportunity to experience the best possible childhood. These ideas are suggestions to be accepted, rejected, or modified to meet each child's unique needs. Of course, only some of the many possible considera-

tions are included here. Numerous others can be found in appropriate sections throughout this text. We hope they will serve as a stimulus to the development of many other successful adaptations.

Health Impairments

Common chronic health problems include allergies, anemia, asthma, cancer, cystic fibrosis, juvenile diabetes, epilepsy, heart defects, hemophilia, pituitary problems, juvenile rheumatoid arthritis, muscular dystrophy, and sickle-cell disease. No attempt will be made here to describe each of these problems in detail. A number of them are defined in the glossary. For more details, readers are referred to medical and nursing reference books. The suggestions made here are appropriate for almost any child with chronic health impairment, regardless of its specific nature.

Caregivers must work very closely with health care providers not only to ensure coordination of care of the primary disorder but also to assist in the maintenance of general health. Remember that children with health impairments are more prone to common illnesses such as colds, ear infections, or diarrhea than are typical children. Children with chronic health needs usually miss more school, spend more time convalescing at home, and are hospitalized more frequently than are children with most other disabling conditions. Repeated separation and trauma create emotional and physical stress.

Much greater responsibility is placed on parents, who must continually monitor the child's health, chauffeur the child to and from appointments, endure the anxieties of medical routines, and sometimes perform daily therapy. In addition, some chronic health problems are life threatening. Caregivers must, then, be more sensitive and supportive than usual.

Specific Intervention Strategies for Working with a Child with Health Impairments.

1. Find out as much as possible about any health problems experienced by children in your program. Read widely and personally visit health

care agencies. Ask questions and record answers. Pay attention to the role of diet, medication, possible side effects of medication, physical restrictions, and behaviors indicating that a chronic illness is becoming acute.

2. Consult the child's parents and the primary care physician in planning the child's program. Become aware of what may cause a health crisis such as a seizure or insulin reaction. Caregivers must be completely prepared to deal with any such health-related crisis. They must know what warning signs to look for, what accommodations are appropriate, and how to follow through on emergency measures.

3. Prepare classroom aides and other children for the possibility of crisis events so that no one will be frightened and everyone will receive appropriate care. Perhaps a curriculum unit can deal with emergencies, including fire protection, earthquake procedures, and so forth. Then the child who has a health impairment is not made to feel different.

4. Prepare a list of typical classroom activities. Ask the parents and the physician to note which activities should be avoided and to suggest adaptations so the child can participate as fully as possible.

5. Encourage the child to be as independent as possible.

6. Some children fatigue rapidly. Arrange the class schedule so that vigorous activities are followed by less strenuous ones. Do not restrict a child unless there is a clear physical or emotional danger.

7. Help children to understand the implications of their health problems. Be open and encourage them to discuss or act out (in play) their fears and anxieties. Children who understand what foods they can or cannot eat, what activities they must avoid, and so on can begin to make decisions for themselves and thus feel more in control of their lives.

8. Develop a plan for keeping in touch with children who must be absent for long periods of time. Telephone calls, cards, and tape recordings

can go a long way toward helping children cope with isolation.

Hearing Loss

A hearing loss ranges from mild (hard of hearing) to profound (deaf). Specialists (audiologist, otologist, speech and language pathologist) can assist caregivers in understanding the degree to which development of communication skills will be affected by the disabling condition. Parents should be consulted to determine how much hearing capacity the child does have and which teaching methods and communication system (oral vs. total communication) to use with those who have more severe impairments. Early developmental milestones will be similar to those of the hearing child. The impact of a hearing impairment is most obvious in language development. Actual cognitive ability is hindered only to the extent that performance depends on language comprehension and use. Children with hearing impairments may exhibit inappropriate behavior due to lack of understanding or resulting socialization problems.

Specific Intervention Strategies for Working with a Child with Hearing Losses.

1. Seat the child up close for good visibility of teacher, activity, or other children.

2. Experiment to find out or ask parents how close a speaker must be for the child to hear.

3. Provide the child with experiences that make use of residual hearing.

4. Speak at normal speed and volume without exaggerating lip movements.

5. Avoid speaking with your back to the child or with a bright light behind you. Don't inadvertently cover your mouth when speaking. Realize that moustaches and beards do interfere with visibility of lip movements. Lipstick may enhance visibility.

6. Use normal vocabulary and sentence structure. Be prepared to repeat, rephrase, point out, or demonstrate if the child does not understand.

7. When seeking the child's attention, be certain to use his or her name. Teach the child to attend to your face, and do not give any directions until the child is obviously attending.

8. When teaching the child, use visual and tactile aids. Model the desired behavior whenever possible.

9. Learn to change a hearing aid battery and/or cord.

10. Encourage speech in group activities by allowing time for the child to start and finish speaking.

11. Work closely with the audiologist and speech and language specialist in planning programs for any child with a hearing impairment.

12. Adaptations made for children with speech and language delays will also be effective with children with hearing impairments.

Difficulties in Learning

Children with learning impairments are those who may be at risk for the development of learning disabilities or who for some reason learn "differently." Such children may exhibit excessive motion, find it difficult to attend or concentrate, lack coordination, experience difficulties in visual or auditory processing of information, have poor memories, and have difficulty in abstract reasoning and in making generalizations. Such disabilities are often difficult to detect and accept because they may be invisible.

Specific Intervention Strategies for Working with a Child with Difficulties in Learning.

1. Be consistent in the use of behavior management techniques to increase or decrease movement. Structure and consistent classroom organization helps these children to feel secure and to respond appropriately to their environment.

2. Present content in short segments using a multisensory approach (audio, visual, manipulative). Provide for as much overlearning or repeated practice as necessary.

3. Analyze tasks. Break them down into as many small steps as needed for success. Use short sentences and simple vocabulary.

4. Use concrete examples when presenting new concepts. Choose functionally important concepts, not just those next on the developmental scales.

5. Praise the child's progress, no matter how small.

6. Concentrate on each child's strengths, not weaknesses.

7. Be patient when it is necessary to show a child how to do something many times. Don't expect children to generalize easily.

8. Give directions one at a time until a child can handle more than one. Provide physical help if necessary.

9. Consult with speech and language specialists in planning the child's program. Suggestions for the children with hearing impairments, visual impairments, and speech and language impairments are also useful for those with learning impairments.

10. Help parents to understand that such children are not just "dumb" or stubborn. Encourage the establishment of consistency and opportunities for multisensory learning experiences at home. Help parents to recognize their children's small successes.

Physical Disabilities

Orthopedic impairments (of the bones, joints, or muscles) may be the result of conditions such as arthritis, cerebral palsy, muscular dystrophy, spina bifida, and spinal cord damage. Characteristics will vary by the nature and severity of each condition. Children with physical impairments acquire information and manipulate the environment through other sensory modes. Children who are severely involved communicate and signify learning through breathing changes and eye blinks.

Of course, the most obvious developmental disabilities are in the motor area. Such children may attain motor milestones at a different rate or in a qualitatively different way than typical children. Some will never attain certain milestones. Certain aspects of language and cognitive development will be delayed due to motor impairment. For example, inability to grasp and manipulate the environment contributes to delayed problem solving. Alternative responses using adaptive equipment may be necessary to enhance cognitive development.

Delays in postural control and inability to use the muscles necessary to imitation may hinder development of communication skills. Speech itself may be directly affected. Children with physical impairments who are unable to cuddle with their caregivers may not receive the positive interaction so necessary to all aspects of early development. Frustration may be a major part of life for both children and parents.

Specific Intervention Strategies for Working with a Child with Physical Disabilities.

1. Review the suggestions made for working with the child with health impairments.

2. Proper handling and positioning of the child is extremely important. The child needs to feel comfortable and well balanced to be able to concentrate. Consult the parents and physical therapist in order to determine appropriate positions. For example, a prone position over a bolster will allow the child to make visual contact with the environment. A side-lying position may assist arm and leg movements. Each child's position will usually need to be changed every 20 to 30 minutes.

3. Arrange activities and the environment so that minimal movements will produce effects on the environment.

4. Use adaptive equipment that allows the child to interact with the environment as much as possible. Consult specialists in making the most appropriate physical adaptations to the classroom and its equipment.

5. Become proficient in the use of wheelchairs, crutches, braces, artificial limbs, and other mechanical aids.

6. Consult speech and language specialists in order to identify a successful response mode for the child. Special language boards will need to be constructed for some children.

7. Work toward realizing the goal of maximum physical and social-emotional independence for each child. Positive self-regard may be the key to future motivation and self-fulfillment.

8. Do not underestimate a child's capabilities; do be realistic.

Visual Impairments

Legally, a person who is partially sighted is one with corrected visual acuity between 20/200 and 20/70. The term *partially sighted* is used when there is enough usable vision for learning with the help of magnification. A person who is legally blind has corrected visual acuity no better than 20/200 in his or her better eye. Such a person sees at 20 feet what those with normal vision see at 200 feet. Vision loss may result from common refractive errors (nearsightedness or farsightedness) or from impairments such as amblyopia (lazy eye), cataracts, cornea damage, detached retina, glaucoma, and retinitis pigmentosa.

Many of the children enrolled in mainstreamed programs will have some functional vision. Visual impairments do affect other areas of development. Delays have been noted in motor milestones that require self-initiated mobility, such as elevation of self by arms, raising to a sitting position, or running. Delay in the use of the hands results in delay of concept development. Language differences may become more noticeable after the age of 3 years, approximately. Many children with severe visual impairments experience difficulty with personal and possessive pronouns. In general, both cognitive and language development are hindered by lack of stimulation.

Specific Intervention Strategies for Working with a Child with Visual Impairments.

1. Consult with the child's parents and vision specialists to determine just what the child can see.

Many children can at least see shadows, color, and sometimes large pictures.

2. For some children, peripheral vision may be best. Therefore, do not assume that a turned-away head means inattention.

3. Be aware of lighting conditions and their effect on the child.

4. Orient the child to the classroom layout and materials location. Give a new orientation whenever changes are made.

5. Areas of the classroom can be identified by different floor coverings, different mobiles, and so on.

6. Provide the child with a rich variety of tactile, manipulative, and auditory experiences.

7. Facilitate auditory localization, reaching for sound, and auditory discrimination skills.

8. Try to keep the general noise level down, since a child with visual impairments relies heavily on auditory cues.

9. Encourage independence both by your actions and in the way the room is arranged. For example, giving the child the cubbie at the end of the row will make it easier to find. Experiment with bright, shiny, and lighted objects of various sizes and shapes.

10. Encourage children to identify themselves when they approach a child with severe visual impairments.

11. Be alert to the need for physical prompts. When teaching new self-help skills, work from behind the child and gradually reduce the help given.

12. Before beginning a new activity, simply say what is going to happen.

13. Consult with specialists to develop aids for the child who is partially sighted. For example, black pen marks on the edges of paper will help the child to know the boundaries of the drawing pad.

14. Be creative in finding ways to help the children develop a positive concept of self.

The principles and strategies described in this chapter are powerful and effective for *all* children. They represent some of the basic competencies of all early educators. Because this is a text in early childhood *special* education, there are additional skills and methods that must be mastered by the early childhood special education professional. These include environmental manipulations, use of special methods and adaptive devices for children with specific disabilities, microanalysis of children's behavior and of teaching effectiveness, and, especially, parent-professional partnership in the design and implementation of programs for children with special needs. These will be addressed throughout the remaining chapters of this book.

Having focused on strategies common to all high-quality early education programs and on specific adaptations for those with unique needs, in the next chapter we will discuss techniques for promoting healthy social and emotional development.

Summary

Curriculum can be considered to be a clear description of what we teach (goals) and how we teach (strategies). Goals and strategies are to be developed in accordance with a clearly defined philosophy based on assumptions about human nature and how young children learn. The philosophy of this text assumes that goals must be functional and ecologically relevant. Strategies will be built on what we know about each child's development and the most appropriate techniques for helping each child reach his or her goals. Instruction is thought to be rooted in the social interactions between children and significant others in their environment.

A wide body of research has contributed to the catalog of principles and strategies that make up what can be called generic instructional strategies.

The strategies that can be adapted and fine-tuned to meet the needs of children with special needs have been outlined. No matter the strategy, play is seen as the most natural and important teaching context.

It is important not only to arrange the social environment but also to consider how the physical environment can influence both children and adults in ways that will enhance children's opportunities to learn and to interact socially with one another. Considerations special to arranging the environment for infants and toddlers were worthy of note.

Time-use plans promote desired consistency through routines and assist the staff in accommodating special needs within their daily activities. Finally, numerous specific suggestions were made for adapting curricula for children with unique special needs.

Discussion Topics and Activities

1. Observe a teacher in an early intervention program. Describe how she or he utilizes each of the generic strategies discussed in this chapter.
2. Visit a center where children with special needs are included. Observe the children during play activities. Follow a particular child and note the materials, physical arrangement, and number of children. Try to determine whether or not the child is really engaged in the play activity. Make a hypothesis or two as to why the child is or is not engaged. Discuss your observations with your classmates.
3. Observe an inclusive preschool program and make a sketch of the physical environment. After comparing with the drawing in the text, determine the strengths and weaknesses of the observed layout.
4. Develop a time-use plan for a program involving infants and toddlers. Include prompts for accommodating children with special needs within the overall daily plan.
5. Develop a file or notebook where you can add additional suggestions for adapting curricula for children with specific special needs.

Annotated Bibliography

Bricker, D. D. *An activity-based approach to early intervention* (Baltimore, MD: Paul H. Brookes, 1998).

This book clearly outlines an activity-based approach to intervention that relies on natural and relevant events to teach young children of all abilities. It offers charts, case studies, and useful appendixes to help interventionists take advantage of natural interactions. It is especially useful to special educators and therapists who have had little experience with the natural activity-based approach often familiar to those with experience in regular early childhood education.

Cripe, J., Stentz, K., & Bricker, D. D. *AEPS curriculum for birth to three years* (Baltimore, MD: Paul H. Brookes, 1993).

The AEPS curriculum includes a complete set of learning activities to facilitate the infant and toddler's acquisition of functional skills as they are linked to IFSP/IEP outcomes and goals. These activities are easily integrated into children's daily routines. Helpful teaching strategies, instructional sequences and recommendations for environmental arrangements accompany each activity.

Bricker, D. D., & Waddell, M. *AEPS curriculum for three to six years* (Baltimore, MD: Paul H. Brookes, 1996).

This easy to implement curriculum offers a flexible set of strategies and activities related to the diverse ways in which preschool-aged children acquire new skills. It is organized into sequential goals and offers additional programming strategies.

Division for Early Childhood, Council for Exceptional Children. *DEC recommended practices: Indicators of quality in programs for infants and young children with special needs and their families* (Reston, VA: The Council for Exceptional Children, 1993).

This set of DEC-recommended practices was compiled by a cadre of DEC members in hopes that early intervention personnel might use them to examine the practices they employ in their programs. These practices can also serve as a guide to those who are developing programs and selecting practices for their programs. Family members may also use this booklet as a "consumer" guide for selecting a program for their child with special needs. To be selected as recommended practices, each indicator had to reflect or be compatible with the following criteria: research- or value-based, family-centered, multicultural emphasis, cross-disciplinary participation, developmentally/chronologically age appropriate, and conducive to normalization.

Furuno, S. *HELP activity guide.* (Palo Alto, CA: VORT Corporation, 1985).

This valuable resource offers thousands of practical, task-analyzed curriculum activities and intervention strategies indexed by the 685 HELP skills found on the HELP charts. In addition, VORT offers *HELP at Home,* which includes 540 pages of unique, reproducible, ready-to-use parent handouts suggesting activities in six major developmental areas. Another practical resource is *HELP for Special Preschoolers* compiled by professionals from the Santa Cruz County Office of Education and made available through VORT. This binder covers over 600 skills in 28 goal areas.

Johnson-Martin, N. M., Jens, K. G., Attermeier, S. M. & Hacker, B. J. *The Carolina curriculum for infants and toddlers with special needs.* (Baltimore, MD: Paul H. Brookes, 1996).

This user-friendly curriculum guide covers 26 subdomains of development of children from birth to 24 months developmental age. It offers detailed intervention sequences, daily routine strategies, sensorimotor adaptations, and a sample assessment log.

Johnson-Martin, N. M., Attermeier, S. M, & Hacker, B. J. *The Carolina curriculum for preschoolers with special needs.* (Baltimore, MD: Paul H. Brookes, 1996).

This comprehensive curriculum guide picks up where the first guide leaves off by addressing the needs of children between the developmental ages of 2 and 5. It provides detailed teaching and assessment techniques for 25 subdomains of child development. A sample assessment log for charting individual child progress is also included.

Linder, T. W. *Transdisciplinary play-based assessment: A functional approach to working with young children.* (Baltimore: Paul H. Brookes, 1996).

This book presents a practical and innovative guide to assessment and intervention within the context of play. It is appropriate for infants and young children developmentally between the ages of 6 months and 6 years. The book contains descriptive observation guidelines for assessment and program planning in the areas of socioemotional, cognitive, communication, and sensorimotor development through child-directed play. It is intended for use by a transdisciplinary team.

MacDonald, J. D. *Becoming partners for children: From play to conversation* (San Antonio, TX: Special Press, 1989).

This book describes play and conversation-based strategies for facilitating the development of social and communicative competence in young children with disabilities. The book is intended as a guide for professionals for planning intervention programs, as well as working with parents. Techniques are based on turn taking and communicative interaction within a play context.

Noonan, M. J., & McCormick, L. *Early intervention in natural environments* (Pacific Grove, CA: Brooks/Cole, 1993).

This practical resource offers "how-to" guidelines and examples of how to provide early intervention services in natural environments such as child-care settings, homes, and preschools. It deals with a significant number of the issues facing early interventionists today. Of particular value is its sensitivity to families.

O'Brien, M. *Inclusive child care for infants and toddlers* (Baltimore, MD: Paul H. Brookes, 1997).

This resource includes practical information on handling daily care tasks. Suggested play activities and intervention approaches that foster the development of all young children are presented. Users will appreciate the check forms, parent report forms, and feeding/play schedules.

Odom, S. L. & McLean, M. E. (Eds.) *Early intervention/early childhood special education: Recommended practices* (Austin, TX: Pro-Ed., 1996).

This contributed volume contains discussion of issues of standards and recommended practices in early intervention and early childhood special education. Topics include development and implementation of IFSPs and IEPs, recommended practices in communication intervention, favored preservice and inservice practices, and general intervention strategies to promote social, emotional, and motor skills.

Peck, C. A., Odom, S. L., and Bricker, D. D. (Eds.) *Integrating young children with disabilities into community programs.* (Baltimore, MD: Paul H. Brookes, 1993).

This perceptive book investigates the issues that energize and shape the movement toward integration and the diverse factors that affect all those involved. Each chapter offers a review of the pertinent literature, a synthesis of research results, and recommendations for practice. It is appropriate for advanced students who wish to bridge the gap between research and practice.

Peters, J., and the staff of the Teaching Research Early Childhood Training Department of Western Oregon State College. *Supporting children with disabilities in community programs* (Monmouth, OR: Teaching Research Publications, 1992).

This very useful manual was written as an outgrowth of 6 years with children ages 3–5 in the Child Development Center at Western Oregon State College. The authors' purpose for writing was to share their experiences and learning with others who are serving preschoolers with disabilities within community programs.

Rab, V. Y. & Wood, K. I. *Child care and the ADA: A handbook for inclusive programs* (Baltimore, MD: Paul H. Brookes, 1995).

This direct guide includes all of the main points about the Americans with Disabilities Act (ADA) as it relates to community programs. It provides specific strategies to assist in understanding the regulations, making appropriate changes to comply with the law, preparing staff, and locating community support. A resource list and descriptive strategies are included.

References

Bailey, D. B., & Wolery, M. (1999) *Teaching infants and preschoolers with disabilities.* Upper Saddle River, NJ: Merrill/Prentice Hall.

Bricker, D. (1998) *An activity-based approach to early intervention.* (Baltimore, MD: Paul H. Brookes, 1998).

Bruner, J. (1982) The organization of action and the nature of the adult-infant transaction. In E. Tronick (Ed.), *Social interchange in infancy: Affect, cognition and communication* (pp. 23–35). Baltimore, MD: University Park Press.

Cook, R. E. (1986) Motivating children to succeed. *Santa Clara, 28,* 7–10.

Feuerstein, R., Rand, Y., Hoffman, M., & Miller, R. (1980) *Instrumental enrichment* (Baltimore, MD: University Park Press.

Klein, M. D., & Briggs, M. (1987) Facilitating mother-infant communicative interaction in mothers of high-risk infants. *Journal of Childhood Communication Disorders, 10*(2), pp. 95–106.

MacDonald, J. (1998) *Becoming partners with children: From play to conversation* San Antonio, TX: Special Press.

MacNamara, J. Cognitive basis of language learning in infants. *Psychological Review, 79,* 1972, pp. 1–13.

Maslow, A. H. (1998) *Toward a psychology of being.* New York: Van Nostrand Reinhold.

McLean, J., & Snyder-McLean, L. (1978) *Transactional approach to early language training.* Upper Saddle River, NJ: Merrill/Prentice Hall.

Mori, A., & Neisworth, J. (1983) Curricula in early childhood education: Some generic and special considerations. *Topics in Early Childhood Special Education, 2*(4).

Vincent, L. *Curriculum development.* Inservice training for early childhood special education teachers, Los Angeles Unified School District, 1988, March.

Vygotsky, L. (1980) *Mind in society: The development of higher psychological processes.* Cambridge, MA: Harvard University Press.

Walker, J. E., & Shea, T. M. (1999) *Behavior management: A practical approach for educators.* Upper Saddle River, NJ: Merrill/Prentice Hall.

Weber, L. (1971) *The English infant school and informal education.* Upper Saddle River, NJ: Prentice Hall.

White, R. (1959) Motivation reconsidered: The concept of competence. *Psychology Review, 66,* pp. 297–333.

Wolery, M. (1983) Evaluating curricula: Purposes and strategies. *Topics in Early Childhood Special Education, 2*(4), pp. 15–24.

Chapter 7

Promoting Social and Emotional Development

With Contributions by Carol Cole

Key Concepts

- A strong, positive attachment to a primary caregiver appears to be the key to the development of a healthy personality.

- A healthy environmental climate is conducive to the prevention of social and emotional problems.

- Specific intervention strategies should be employed to assist young children in the development of positive social skills.

- Play is not only an important context for development, but it is also a critical social skill that can be facilitated.

- Children with behavioral difficulties can be positively managed through careful environmental planning.

- Children who have been abused and neglected need consistency, predictability, and an opportunity to become attached to a primary care provider.

- The effects of prenatal exposure to substances are unpredictable; while some children suffer a variety of ill effects, others show no effects.

- Many intervention techniques that may be effective with young children who suffer effects of prenatal substance exposure are the same techniques that have been effective with other high-risk populations. Labeling or segregating these children reflects inappropriate practices.

- The problems of children who have been abused or prenatally exposed to substances and their families are complex and must be dealt with by a collaborating multidisciplinary team.

The promotion of social and emotional development means helping children to develop a healthy personality and a sense of self. Numerous attempts have been made to describe the attributes of a healthy personality. The work of early theorists such as Erik Erikson, as well as the more recent work of Stanley Greenspan and Daniel Stern, provide useful foundations for the understanding of infant and child emotional development. From the initial attachment to a primary caregiver in infancy through the establishment of mutually responsive interaction patterns and communicative strategies, the emotionally supported preschooler achieves a strong and healthy sense of self and the ability to express and understand a wide range of emotional experiences and ideas.

With this emotional strength and healthy autonomy, the young child begins to develop effective social skills. For many children, preschool is their first experience in a group setting. They may need assistance in handling this new experience. All children are in the process of learning to recognize and to cope with their feelings in environments that require that they also learn to regulate their own behavior.

This chapter aims to help professionals and parents understand how adults can assist children to become emotionally and socially well adjusted. We present techniques for dealing effectively with emotional and behavioral needs. We recognize the influence of the environment and emphasize the importance of play in the creation of a secure, growth-producing early education experience.

DEVELOPING A HEALTHY PERSONALITY

Understanding emotional development and the growth of personality in infants and young children must begin with a careful look at the process of **attachment.** The infant's strong, positive feeling for a primary caregiver provides the seed from which all aspects of development can grow. For children with special needs—children with disabilities as well as those at risk due to factors such as maltreatment and prenatal drug exposure—the establishment of a strong caregiver-infant attachment relationship may be threatened. It is important for early education professionals to understand the nature of the attachment process and to be able to facilitate its development.

Attachment

Over the years, the development of an attachment bond between the child and the caregiver has been thought by developmentalists to be perhaps the most pervasive early social and emotional event in the child's life (Ulrey & Rogers, 1982; Greenspan & Weider, 1998). Attachment is most commonly assessed using the Ainsworth Strange Situation paradigm (Ainsworth & Wittig, 1969). In the "strange situation," the infant's response to a series of separations and reunions with a stranger and parent are carefully observed. The paradigm consists of the following seven 3-minute episodes:

1. The mother brings the infant to the playroom and puts the infant down.

2. A stranger enters the room and attempts to play with the infant.

3. The mother leaves the room.

4. The mother returns and the stranger leaves.

5. The mother leaves the infant alone.

6. The stranger returns.

7. The mother returns and greets and picks up the infant.

As a result of early studies conducted by Ainsworth (1973) and her associates, three categories

of attachment were defined. Group B infants greeted parents in an unambiguous manner upon reunion. For example, the child might smile, greet, approach, or establish physical contact. These infants were considered to be *attached.* Group A infants demonstrated pointed avoidance of the caregiver upon reunion, characterized by aborted approach, averted eye gaze, or ignoring. These infants were labeled *insecurely attached-avoidant.* Group C infants could not be comforted by caregivers, and upon reunion they directed angry, resistant behavior at the parents through behaviors such as pushing away, kicking to be put down, or refusing a toy. These infants were described as *insecurely attached-resistant.* Some more recent researchers have suggested the existence of a fourth group of infants who are disorganized and demonstrate both avoidant and resistant behaviors (Lyons-Ruth, Connell, Zoll, & Stahl, 1987).

Ainsworth (1973) described the insecurely attached infant as a child who becomes greatly distressed when separated from the caregiver; at the same time, this child is not easily comforted by the caregiver. It is as if the child's sense of trust has been disturbed or never fully developed. More securely attached children, on the other hand, fuss less when left and cease crying more quickly. There is an interesting parallel between Thomas, Chess, and Birch's (1968) descriptions of easy and difficult children (discussed later in this chapter) and Ainsworth's description of securely and insecurely attached children. Some children, then, may be predisposed by temperament to influence the attachment process negatively or positively.

Over two decades ago, Connor, Williamson, and Siepp (1978) offered a glimpse of the importance of the reciprocal relationship between the young child and the primary caregiver: The baby signals his need for some kind of caretaking by crying or fussing; the mother responds by picking up the child; the child responds in turn with some kind of bodily reaction such as cuddling. The baby's bodily adjustments signal to the mother that he is ready for the next step, be it diapering, feeding, bathing, or just cuddling and stroking. The baby responds to the caregiving by quieting, which reinforces the mother's caregiving.

The importance of such a chain of cues and responses is readily apparent. Any breakdown in the signaling and response system may affect the whole bonding and attachment process. Fraiberg (1974), in her classic research on blind infants, notes that their mothers frequently have difficulty feeling attached because of the lack of eye contact and delay in the development of the infant's social smile. Other disabilities and difficult temperament can delay the attachment process. Children with cerebral palsy may not be able to give warm reinforcement to the caregiver, since cuddling may be more difficult. Children with hearing impairments cannot respond with eye contact and other attachment signals when the mother uses her voice. Resultant attachment patterns, then, are an end product of a complicated interactional process. Not only do the child's innate mannerisms influence the response of the parents, but, of course, the adult's natural tendencies help determine the child's view of self and environment. The self-esteem of one affects and is influenced by the other.

One of the goals of many early intervention programs is to encourage and support the development of a strong affectional bond between caregivers and children, especially in those instances when disabling conditions adversely affect attachment. Educators can help parents become tuned in to the child's cues so that their responses can produce an enjoyable response in the child. When parents can learn to understand unclear or confusing cues from their child who has special needs, they have a chance to respond in appropriate ways, allowing them to develop higher parental self-esteem. Bromwich (1997) has developed a process of identifying the level of mutually positive and pleasurable interactions between parent and child. Teachers can use such an observation technique as they plan intervention strategies that may include modeling of recognition, sensitivity, and responsiveness to young children's signals and cues.

Erikson's Stages of Psychosocial Development

In his classic developmental outline, Erikson (1993) discussed three stages of psychosocial development thought to be characteristic of the young child. Each stage includes the solution of a problem involving conflicting feelings and desires. The resolution of the central problem of each state creates a favorable disposition for adjustment at the next developmental stage. Table 7–1 presents Erikson's stages of personality development along with adult behaviors that can

Table 7–1   Adult behaviors to promote child's personality

Erikson's Stage	Appropriate Adult Behaviors
1. To promote sense of *trust*	Be consistent and sensitive in caretaking.
	Play trust-building games (playful repetition such as peek-a-boo).
	Provide prompt relief of discomfort.
	Provide genuine affection.
	Establish climate of stability and predictability.
	Avoid showing favoritism.
	Provide for choice making.
2. To promote sense of *autonomy*	Allow opportunities to explore.
	Forbid only what really matters.
	Couple firmness with tolerance.
	Avoid shaming.
	Let child set pace, try developing skills.
	Be accepting of individuality.
3. To promote sense of *initiative*	Provide leeway for imagination.
	Encourage role playing.
	Serve as an appropriate model.
	Hold punishment to a minimum.
	Talk about feelings and dreams.
	Answer questions.

help children come to a healthy solution of each stage's problems of conflicting desires and feelings.

Sense of Trust Versus Mistrust. The first year of life was considered by Erikson (1993) to be the crucial time for the development of a sense of trust. During this time, an environment characterized by consistency and dependability fosters the development of trust in those responsible for the child's care. The quality of caregiving is more important than the quantity of food or love given. Caregiving that is basically consistent and sensitive to an infant's needs promotes a view of the world as dependable and safe. Negative, inconsistent, or insensitive caregiving, by contrast, stimulates a fearful, suspicious view of the world.

The child's development of a sense of trust (or mistrust) in the world is only one of the personality attributes developed during infancy. Erikson also discussed the importance of children's perceptions of their ability to control their own body movements. Through actions such as continuous repetition of grasping and holding objects, children learn that they can depend on their bodies to do their bidding. It is not difficult to imagine the frustration experienced by children with physical disabilities during their quest to develop a sense of trust in their own bodies. A curriculum that incorporates specialized body movement activities encourages even children with disabilities to become more trusting in their body control.

Interventionists who provide an atmosphere of consistent, sensitive caring help to further a young child's development of trust in the environment. Conversely, helter-skelter experiences in the program can make a fearful child even more fearful or a basically secure child question his or her relationship to others. A trustful atmosphere is easily developed through establishing reasonable, enforceable rules of conduct, the regularity of a basic schedule of activities, and sensitive, immediate responses to children's needs.

Sense of Autonomy Versus Shame and Doubt. From the end of the first year of life through the sec-

ond and third year of life most children are busy exploring their environment and trying to establish some independence. Children who are primarily trustful usually do not hesitate to join "the terrible twos" if encouraged to develop skills at their own pace. Children of this age who are given opportunities to make simple choices, to exercise their expanding sensorimotor abilities, and to experiment with their new-found verbal skills will become confident enough to assert themselves appropriately.

Children who are shamed (e.g., being called a "bad boy") or told "no" continuously will begin to doubt themselves and their abilities. They may react by defiance or act ignorant of authority. Children who are not allowed to make choices when they are young may become overdependent and fearful when they need to make major life choices. Some children may withdraw into their feelings of worthlessness, whereas others may strike out aggressively.

Interventionists can assist children in developing **autonomy** with a reasonable degree of self-control by creating opportunities for young children to explore, to make decisions, to ask questions, and to exercise appropriate self-restraint. Curricula and room arrangements that provide centers with materials to manipulate and activities from which a child can choose ideally promote autonomous, confident behavior. Establishing firm, reasonable guidelines for classroom exploration and conduct encourages autonomy while not letting children become overwhelmed by their need for independence and by their lack of mature judgment. Children of this age who are readily propelled by their more mature large muscles may be easily frustrated when their smaller muscles do not react so efficiently. Interventionists must lend assistance that does not create conditions for loss of self-esteem. Children with disabilities may need special incentives to venture into the activities so easily enjoyed by unencumbered children.

Although controls and gentle firmness are essential protections for young children, these controls must have meaning. In this regard, Erikson (1971) suggested that the most constructive rule an adult can follow is "to forbid only what really matters and, in such forbidding, to be clear and consistent" (p. 126).

Sense of Initiative Versus Guilt. Children who have developed a basic trust in their environment and in themselves and who have experienced a growing self-confidence in their ability to explore and experiment are ready to develop a **sense of initiative.** Around 4 or 5 years of age, children experience a heightened period of imagination and fantasy. It is a time for reaching out and intruding both physically and verbally. Children with healthy personalities and healthy bodies vigorously try out their developing ideas of themselves. They are great imitators, as evidenced by their "superhero" play and their use of any and all four-letter words.

Children of this age are also beginning to develop what is termed a *conscience.* Since they often have difficulty separating fantasy from reality, they may feel guilty about merely thinking unkind thoughts. Teachers who are aware of this tendency try to avoid overreacting to a child's characteristic statement of "I hate you." When difficulties occur in the home such as death or a divorce, children need to be helped to realize that their actions or thoughts did not cause the unpleasant event to happen. This is also an age of nightmares and dreams. These children need extra comfort and reassurance in separating fantasy from reality.

Teachers who allow leeway within secure guidelines for children's developing sense of initiative can contribute significantly to their motivation to achieve. This motivation is important to the next stage of industry versus inferiority, and it is necessary to the development of self-esteem and the desire to try out the freedom to explore, to imagine, to question, to help plan, to make choices, to participate in meaningful activities, to create, and to engage in role-playing behavior. Teachers of young children with special needs must be aware of the need to teach some children to explore, to play, and to attempt what may be difficult. Children whose abilities or environments are limited may have to be helped directly if they are to develop feelings of trust, autonomy, and initiative. Usually these qualities develop sponta-

neously in nondisabled children through nurturing environments.

Greenspan's Model of Affective Development

Stanley Greenspan has been an important contributor to the understanding of infant/child emotional development. His work has been particularly important because he has addressed the specific needs of infants and young children with disabilities and developmental differences, including children with autism (Greenspan, 1990; Greenspan & Weider, 1998). Like Erikson, Greenspan has proposed a "developmental structural model" of the stages of emotional growth (Greenspan, 1992) that are summarized here. Greenspan's model parallels Piaget's stage theory of cognitive development in many ways.

There are six basic stages represented in Greenspan's model. It should be noted that in more recent writings, the last three stages (Complex Sense of Self, Emotional Ideas Representation, and Emotional Thinking) are each divided into two substages. In most cases, the second substage simply represents greater elaboration of the particular emotional capacity being addressed. Thus, for the sake of simplicity, only the six basic stages are described below.

Self-Regulation and Interest in the World. During the period from birth to approximately 3 months, healthy infants develop the ability to regulate their internal states in ways that allow them to take in and attend to the world around them. Through sight, vision, sense of touch, and smell, infants experience their environment. This experience is best achieved when they are in a calm, alert state.

Babies who are neurologically overresponsive and are easily overstimulated may experience great difficulty maintaining a calm, alert state. As a result, such babies will have less opportunity to take in the world around them. They may not develop a natural interest in their world if that world is painful or irritating.

Babies who are hyperirritable will need special handling techniques that assist them in self-regulation and maintenance of a calm, alert state. For example, swaddling them, placing them in a tucked and flexed position, applying firm pressure to the chest, using deep pressure massage (rather than light stroking), and rocking can be helpful in calming hyperresponsive infants. Some premature babies, babies who have been exposed to certain drugs prenatally, and babies who have experienced certain neurological insults may benefit from the use of such techniques.

Some infants may be hyporesponsive, that is, they are difficult to arouse. They have trouble becoming fully awake and maintaining an alert state. They are sleepy and passive. Such babies may respond more to certain types of sensory stimulation than to others. For example, a baby might remain sleepy through parents' exhaustive efforts to interest him or her in their sounds and funny faces. Such a baby might be more aroused by touch and kinesthetic stimulation (movement and position). Thus it may be possible to assist the baby in reaching an alert state by massaging or tickling and frequently changing his or her position. Once in an alert state, the baby may find voices and faces more interesting.

In summary, during this early stage of development, infants must be supported in their efforts to achieve a calm, alert state and to experience the sensations provided by the world around them without being overwhelmed.

Falling in Love (Attachment). During the period from approximately 2 to 5 months, infants who have been successful during the first stage in regulating internal states (homeostasis) will begin to be very familiar with their primary caregiver. In addition, they begin to associate sensations of the primary caregiver—face, voice, odor, touch—with pleasurable sensations of being cuddled and fed. As a result, as Greenspan said, the babies "fall in love" (Greenspan & Greenspan, 1985, p. 16). This is the essence of infant attachment. The reciprocal of this experience for a caregiver, as an infant responds to the caregiver's presence and behaviors, is what is called **bonding.** As a caregiver bonds with the infant, he or she be-comes more responsive to the infant, both behaviorially and affectively, and, in turn, strengthens the infant's attachment. As discussed earlier, the development of attachment and bonding progresses over time and is dynamic and interactive. Each partner influences the other in powerful ways.

Infants who have disabilities such as blindness or deafness or who have difficulty responding in positive ways to caregivers' behaviors (e.g., infants who are born very prematurely or who have been affected by prenatal exposure to drugs) may be in some jeopardy during this stage. For example, an infant who is hyperirritable may cry or turn away when his mother brings her face close or talks to him. He may look at her only fleetingly and may avert his gaze when she smiles. Such an infant may have difficulty developing a preference for the human world, which is an important outcome of this stage of attachment. According to Greenspan (1988, p. 16), parents of such infants may need special assistance in learning how to "woo" their infant in order to ensure this attachment process.

Intentional Two-way Communication. From approximately 3 to 10 months of age, as their behavior consistently elicits feedback from significant caregivers, one can observe the gradual development of intentionality in infants. They learn that they can do things that have an effect on the environment, and particularly that they can use actions to communicate with the social world. Caregiver responsiveness to this intentional communication is crucial to infant development.

Specifically related to children's healthy emotional development is a type of caregiver response referred to as **affect attunement.** By the time infants reach 9 or 10 months of age, the nature of their caregivers' interactions begins to include mirroring of the infant's affect (emotional state). Parents no longer simply imitate or respond to the baby's behavior, but also accurately reflect the baby's feelings. When the baby is happy, Mother smiles and reflects this feeling. When the infant is crying and upset, Mother may furrow her brow and frown, saying "Oh, poor baby." When the infant is startled or surprised, Mother may

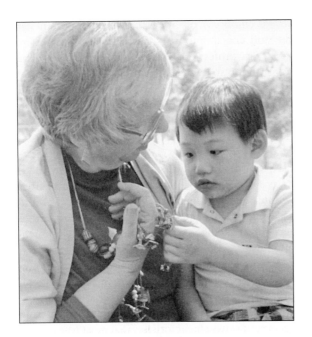

pull back quickly, with her eyes opened wide, saying "Oh, my goodness!" In this way, the infant can begin to learn that it is okay to express a wide range of emotions. As caregivers match and reflect their emotions, infants also learn to recognize emotions in others. Most important, they learn that not only their behavior, but also their feelings, can influence others.

It is extremely important that adults learn to read the affective cues of infants with disabilities. For example, an infant with severe motor impairment may have difficulty giving clear cues of joy or sadness. Parents may be extremely frustrated by not being sure whether the child finds an experience pleasurable or not. Sometimes only the greatest extremes of emotions, such as anger, can be understood easily. Early interventionists from several fields may need to work together as a team with parents to help make this kind of emotional communication clear so that parents can respond appropriately. Failure to do this enhances the risk that the infant will give up and become passive and withdrawn. Such a reaction will significantly interfere with the child's ability to fully realize the next stage of emotional development—an **organized sense of self.**

The Emergence of an Organized Sense of Self. The period from 9 to 18 months (the transition from infancy to toddlerhood) is an important period of development in which infants achieve a clearer sense of themselves as individuals who are separate from others. They begin to be able to move away from caregivers by using **distal communication.** That is, they can crawl across the room and look back at Father who, in turn, smiles and vocalizes to them. In this way, toddlers learn that they can be separated from caregivers but still experience their love and support. Thus, they eventually learn that it is safe to be separated by physical space and that they, themselves, are separate beings.

Children with certain disabilities may need special assistance during this stage. For example, a child who is blind may need to be assisted in learning to communicate distally and in learning that he or she has a separate identity. A toddler who has been in neglectful environments or who has had multiple placements may have been thwarted at every stage of emotional development. If the toddler's social environment has been unresponsive and he or she has not been successful in expressing and understanding a wide range of emotions, development of a sense of self will be significantly threatened.

As toddlers develop a sense of self, they become increasingly able to associate and utilize more complex chains of behavior around emotional events. For example, when their mothers return home, toddlers do not simply smile, but they smile, vocalize, toddle over, and reach their arms up to be held. They initiate and carry out these behaviors in competent ways. Their sense of ways of interacting in various circumstances begins to be internalized and organized. Their self-image is forming.

Emotional Ideas (representation). From 18 to 30 months of age, toddlers become increasingly able to represent ideas and experiences internally (mentally). By 24 months, the toddler can create a mental image of basic feelings and needs (e.g., happiness, sadness, anger, fear). By 30 months, the child can mentally represent and express a wider range of needs and emotions as well as two or more emotions in one play episode or expression (e.g., baby's tired; baby hugs mommy). The emotionally healthy toddler develops a clear mental image of what these basic emotions feel like, as well as what they look like in other people. For example, the infant can create a mental image of his own feeling of fear or anger, as well as create images of mommy or daddy when they are angry or happy.

During this period toddlers are becoming much more independent. They develop a more sophisticated understanding of themselves as emotional beings and of the emotional characteristics of significant others. That is, not only can they see themselves as "sometimes naughty and sometimes nice," but they also know that although mommies are sometimes happy and sometimes sad, they are still the same person.

Emotional Thinking. From 30 to 48 months, the child begins to understand and think about the logical connections between ideas. For example, the child understands causal relationships such as "The girl is sad because her mother is angry." Or, "If I kiss my baby sister she will be happy.", etc. The child learns that certain ways of behaving will make mommy mad and others will make her happy. Children who have not experienced consistent reactions to their behavior, or who have not been allowed to express a range of emotions, will be hampered in this stage of development.

During this stage, children's participation in pretend play plays an important role in their development of emotional thinking. Pretend play is also a critical educational and therapeutic activity. Through pretending, a child can act out his or her own range of emotions as well as practice elaborated relationships between mothers and fathers, parents and children, brothers and sisters, and so on. Pretend play can provide the child with the opportunity to learn to say "I'm really mad at you!" rather than hitting someone to express anger.

Children can also act out their own emotional crises and frustrations. Children from abusive and neglectful environments may learn important coping strategies by playing out themes of abandonment or violence. For these children, as well as children with

severe emotional disorders, it will be important for the early educator to work in collaboration with mental health professionals in determining appropriate intervention strategies.

BUILDING A HEALTHY ENVIRONMENT

Early education specialists have shifted their focus away from a skill-based approach to a more interactional view recognizing the importance of the child-environment fit. This **ecological perspective** recognizes the need to create a healthy environmental climate conducive to preventing emotional and behavioral problems. Such a climate not only can prevent the occurrence of problems but also can be the major factor in resolving conflicts that develop between children and their environment. The following sections discuss characteristics that most researchers consider essential to optimum growth during the early childhood years. These are highlighted in Figure 7–1.

Consistency

Long ago, Blackham (1968) pointed out why reasonable consistency is an absolute prerequisite to effective teaching: "Nothing upsets a child more than not knowing what is expected of him and what he can expect from his teacher" (p. 109). Consistency means predictability. In instructing parents and teachers in techniques for effective child management, predictability can be equated with the feeling of being safe. Maslow recognized the expectation for safety as a basic bodily need. When we cannot predict what will happen next, we are usually constantly ready to defend ourselves. "If our predictions come true, we feel safe. If they don't come true, it is upsetting—we become angry. If we can't make any successful predictions at all, we are in a constant state of turmoil" (Maslow, 1968, p. 7).

From a practical point of view, caregivers must be consistent for children to learn the rules of conduct for social acceptance. Children are as baffled by

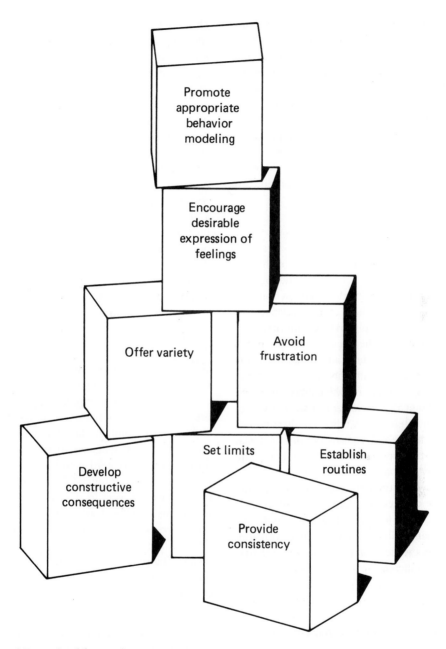

Figure 7–1 Building a healthy environment.

inconsistent rules as we would be if we were trying to learn the rules of baseball and the batter sometimes ran to third base instead of first base after a hit. If it is sometimes all right for a child to jump up and down on the sofa and if other times a reprimand results, the rule the child learns is to "try and see."

Instead of the "terrible twos," we should call toddlers the "testing twos." Given consistent responses to their testing, they learn the rules and usually try to function within them. At the same time, consistency fosters their understanding of the basic relationships between cause and effect.

Routines

To develop Erikson's sense of trust or the feelings of being safe, professionals must plan carefully. Routines or schedules that allow children to predict within reason what will happen next help them to relax and to handle transitions from one activity to another with relative ease. Although schedules should not be so rigid that teachers cannot take advantage of "teachable moments," children can be prepared for changes in routine and for the times between activities when movement, a change of pace, or grouping is required.

Misbehavior often results when children do not know when or how to change to the next activity. Children should be given a signal such as a flick of the lights or a soft word that they will soon need to stop the activity in which they are engaged. Young children need time to become uninvolved just as they need time to become involved. Teachers should discuss obvious changes in the daily schedule with children so that they can develop the understanding that change can be predicted.

Limits

Reasonable limits or rules help provide consistency. Rules or limits not only contribute to children's emotional needs for security but also create conditions for bodily safety. While children have a strong need to be autonomous, they lack the cognitive judgment to control their own behavior enough to avoid harming themselves or others at times. Behavioral limits offer

children guidelines they can imitate and internalize in their development of appropriate self-control. As pointed out earlier, teachers must establish a delicate balance between necessary limits and the freedom to explore.

Only rules that are absolutely necessary to a positive learning environment for both children and teachers should be established. Too often teachers and parents establish so many rules that none can be learned or enforced consistently. Teachers should remember that if children are to follow a rule or a direction and have no choice, they should not be given a choice. Inadvertently, adults sometimes make the mistake of saying something such as, "It is time to go home. Wouldn't you like to put your coat on?" What if the child replies "No"?

In a well-quoted text on child management, Smith and Smith (1976) suggested that a good rule should fulfill the following three requirements:

1. *It must be definable.* Rules have to be at the developmental level of the children both in vocabulary and expectations. They must state specific behaviors that are expected or not allowed. For example, we often hear parents or teachers tell children to "be good." What does "be good" mean to the child or to the adult? To the child it may mean not running in the building because that is what he or she got into trouble for yesterday. To the parent it may mean eating all his or her lunch because the parent has noticed many leftovers in the lunch pail. Rules or expectations must be clearly stated in behavioral terms. If teachers want children to stay within a certain area while sitting on the carpet, then they should mark the area with a piece of tape so the child knows exactly what the limits are. Concrete, visual aids help young children learn rules of conduct just as they help them develop cognitive skills.

2. *It must be reasonable.* Teachers must judge the developmental level of children before rules can be established. It is not reasonable to expect many 2 ½-year-olds to share to the extent that many parents and teachers would like them to. A constant reference to developmental norms is necessary. It must be remembered that children with developmental delays

require extra patience as they learn to adapt to limits that others may adapt to more easily. For example, some children may be able to listen to a story for only 5 minutes, whereas other children may still be engrossed 20 minutes later.

3. *It must be enforceable.* Teachers and parents must assume that not all children can or will adhere to all limits. Some rules will be broken. For limits or rules to help children feel safe and trustful, any established rule must be enforceable. When children observe that teachers cannot or will not do anything about a broken rule, they cannot predict what will happen and become anxious. Children seek and enjoy limits. Some will break a rule just to see whether they can indeed predict what will happen. This is generally called "testing the limits," and it happens in every classroom. As suggested earlier, teachers should see a certain amount of this as normal in children's establishing predictability. Teachers should react firmly, consistently, and calmly. This reaction will define for children the consequences of their behavior. It will tell them what will happen if rules are broken. Seeking to avoid the consequences will motivate them to control their behavior. They feel secure when others are helping them to develop self-restraint. Of course, only developmentally appropriate rules can be enforced. If a special circumstance causes a teacher to change the rules or limits, a discussion with the children will help them to understand the need for flexibility within consistency.

Constructive Consequences

An effective means of helping children to develop social responsibility is through the use of natural and logical consequences. **Natural consequences** occur when an adult does not interfere at all and a child learns from what naturally happens in a situation. For example, children who do not cooperate when games are played soon learn that other children avoid playing with them. If a child does not eat the prepared snack, becoming hungry may help him or her to learn to eat when food is available.

Logical Consequences. Logical consequences, conversely, are those developed by adults who find that natural consequences either are not readily available or are harmful. These usually help to keep or to restore order and avoid chaos. For example, children who insist on throwing sand must be removed from the sandbox. Consequences that help children to learn to control their own behaviors must be both logical and immediate. If a consequence does not bear any logical relationship to the misbehavior, then it will be difficult for the child to learn the logical relationship between cause and effect. A consequence that occurs long after the misbehavior will not be associated with it by the child. If the child cannot remember what it was that caused the consequence, then he or she will not make the link between cause and effect. This is one of the reasons why the threat "Father will punish you after he gets home" does not work.

Logical Connections. A **logical connection** between an act and its consequences provides a number of advantages to establishing and maintaining a healthy relationship between children and their environment. Children who are denied the use of materials after being careless with them are less likely to see the teacher as arbitrary than when they are told to sit in the corner for being careless. Children will only feel "picked on" if ordered to sit in the corner. Removing the materials, however, can be seen as necessary to the protection of the other children. A logical connection also helps children to focus on the behavior to be changed, making it easier to interpret the misbehavior as the cause of the consequence.

A child who is also given some control over the extent of the consequence will be more likely to feel the ability to do something about terminating or preventing such consequences in the future. For example, children who are asked to remove themselves from the group for being disruptive, and told they may return when they feel they can control themselves, have an opportunity to take part in their own rehabilitation. They can learn not only that disruptive behavior will cause removal but also that self-control can earn the chance to return. Conversely, children who are told to sit in the "time-out" area for 20 minutes or until the teacher comes for them feel that immediate self-control will not help and that only passage of time changes events.

Variety

Careful planning to include a change of pace during the day is essential to motivating children to learn. A variety of both individual and group activities consistent with the children's developmental level should be included. Young children need to have active involvement interspersed with quiet activities. Children whose senses or physical mobility are limited will fatigue more quickly and need an opportunity for rest. Others may need additional opportunities to move freely to release inner tension.

By nature, young children generally have short attention spans. (Of course, there are exceptions.) This needs to be considered carefully when planning the daily schedule. If children's attention wanders and they are bored or frustrated, they become restless. This restlessness can become contagious, influencing the behavior of a number of children. This is one of the reasons why learning theorists recommend that practice of any kind be distributed over time.

Finally, a change of pace also means including activities that are just plain fun and full of laughter. Most adults are guilty of being in too much of a hurry or so intense that they miss the occasional opportunities to laugh with children or to turn a mistake into a learning experience. Even shoes on the wrong feet often appear funny enough for a chuckle and for encouragement to try again rather than the usual response of "Your shoes are on the wrong feet."

Avoiding Frustration

Teachers who are astute observers of children are able to plan and implement a therapeutic environment. They are alert to individual signs of frustration and stress. Understanding the developmental level of each child makes it possible to plan appropriate activities. Even the best matched activities, however, can produce frustration in a tired, hungry, or sick child.

Teachers should quickly recognize warning signs such as fussing, crying, nail biting, sighing, fidgeting, thumb sucking, and tantrums. Usually a prompt change of activity will reduce the frustration and thus *prevent* disruptive behavior.

Frustration can be avoided by teachers' reducing clutter and noise, keeping directions simple, providing meaningful activities that are relatively short, and being available if the child needs help. They should analyze tasks and break them into manageable subskills that are appropriately sequenced. Efforts, regardless of outcomes, should receive recognition. Competition should be avoided. Activities that guarantee success can not only make a child's day but also make the day of the teacher.

Transition times can be periods of frustration for children if not smoothly organized. Distractible children can become unruly if left to wander or wonder. Withdrawn children may become fearful. Routines for transition times must be explicitly taught. As discussed earlier, signals such as flickering the lights help children to wind down from one activity to get ready for the next. Hurrying young children only frustrates the teacher who forgets that preschoolers have not developed the inner time clocks that often become the bosses of adults. Scheduling major activities to end at natural breaks during the day makes transitions smoother. For example, it is easier to gain children's cooperation in cleaning up art materials if they know lunch will follow.

Encouraging Desirable Expression of Feelings

In spite of an appropriately planned schedule of activities, consistency, and well-defined limits, unpredictable things do happen. Children need to learn to cope constructively with feelings that arise from interpersonal situations. Anger, jealousy, depression, fear, and other unpleasant feelings are common interpersonal emotions. Teachers choose either to provide an opportunity for helpful expression or to insist on at least temporary suppression. The success and choice of teachers' approaches often depend on how well they can handle their own unpleasant feelings.

Teachers who have confidence in their abilities to handle negative feelings and have carefully created a trustful relationship with their children can handle stressful situations in ways that promote emotional growth (Biehler & Snowman, 1996).

Sensitive teachers find many opportunities to help children accept and express their feelings appropriately. Practically any unpleasant experience in the classroom can be a source of discussion. Young children cannot assimilate long lectures explaining feelings or behavior. Short statements or a warm physical touch will help a child to know that having feelings is all right. A simple acknowledgment of feelings and inquiry about coping behaviors will help a child understand and express emotions appropriately while feeling accepted. For example, the teacher might say, "It is okay to be mad when Johnny rips your paper, but I can't let you hit him. Can you think of another way to let Johnny know how angry you are?"

Numerous well-written books are available that help children learn to cope effectively with their developing feelings. Even difficult topics such as death and divorce are subjects of sensitive presentation. Puppets, role-playing activities, art activities, punching bags, and imaginative, unstructured play also give children opportunities to work through their feelings acceptably. Figure 7–2 and Exhibit 7–1 illustrate some lessons that can be planned to help children learn to understand, label, and constructively express their feelings.

Promoting Appropriate Behavior Modeling

Young children with disabilities often learn new and more adaptive behavior through imitating their nondisabled peers. The modeling effect is a strong argument for integrating children with and without disabilities in early education programs. In her often-cited rationale for inclusion, Bricker (1978) emphasized that "children can acquire new responses from observing and modeling others' behavior; however, the opportunity for watching and imitating more complex behavior must be available" (p. 19).

The teacher's responsibility is to understand the dynamics of learning through imitation and to ensure that appropriate models of desired behavior are available. A number of variables help determine whether or not a child will reproduce the observed behavior. Researchers have found that simply placing children with and without disabilities together does not necessarily result in the desired peer imitation (McLean & Hanline, 1990; Jones & Rapport, 1997). In fact, it appears that teachers who directly reinforce children for imitating appropriate behavior and who manipulate the environment to ensure desired peer interaction increase the chances for positive social behavior (Chandler, 1998).

FACILITATING SOCIAL SKILLS

The development of positive social skills is critical to the successful inclusion of children with special needs in community-based settings. Social skills are also essential to the emotional well-being of young children, as such skills enable them to develop friendships and self-esteem. Guralnick (1993) states that "it currently is generally agreed upon that the ability to establish appropriate and effective relationships with one's peers constitutes a critical developmental milestone for children during the preschool years, one that has important implications for children's cognitive, communicative, and overall social development" (p. 345). Cavallaro, Haney, & Cabello (1993) stressed the importance of environmental structuring and peer mediation in the facilitation of full social participation of young children with disabilities. Examples of environmental structuring follow.

Use of Environmental Structuring

1. *Keep the groups relatively small* (from two to four children) when structured learning activities are involved. Small groups make it possible for teachers to facilitate ongoing positive social interactions without interrupting them.

Animal friends
Some children find it easier to talk about relationships between animals rather than between people. Copy pictures of animals "being friends" to poster size and display them in the room. Use coloring books, magazines, and storybooks for ideas. You may want to read stories about animals and then make posters about them.

Monster day
Plan a monster day. Have each person (including yourself) create a monster. Hang them and discuss them. Include a discussion of fears and nightmares as well as those unexplained monsters (UFO's and Loch Ness) and the friendly ones (Cookie Monster and monster books).

Happy-sad face
To help a child identify and label the way he or others may be feeling, make happy-sad faces. Draw eyes on a paper plate, attach a smile-frown with a paper fastener, and rotate the mouth to express feelings. This may work well with children who have trouble verbalizing their feelings.

Personality mirrors
Cut an oval shape from poster board and cover it with foil. Have the child put his name on it with letters cut from construction paper. Then let him find magazine pictures of things that he likes to do or eat. Display them for all children to see.

Apartment windows
Make an apartment, house, or store from poster board. Attach "windows" using pictures cut from magazines or newspapers. Discuss what rooms the occupants are in or what they are doing or feeling.

Slides
Make a slide presentation of people's faces that are expressing feelings, communication signals, or different ways of handling situations.

Figure 7–2 Affective domain activities. (Reprinted with permission of Cathi Effinger Steinmann, St. Louis.)

EXHIBIT 7–1

Teaching Thoughtfulness

Goal:

To create daily opportunities to nurture thoughtfulness in children.

How to begin:

1 *Be* what you wish to see children express. If you want them to be thoughtful, be thoughtful yourself.
2. Notice nearly every expression of *that* quality. Call attention to the child who expresses it in a spontaneous way. Do not make a major production of it. Rather, touch the child gently or hug lightly. Say "That was thoughtful. You helped Susie with her coat," or "That was thoughtful." You may think that the other children are not paying attention but they are. In no time they will try to figure out ways to get you to tell them how they are being thoughtful. And of course they will be learning the subtle meaning of "thoughtful."
3. Avoid calling attention to thoughtlessness. Ignore it.

After a few days:

1. Reduce the frequency with which you call attention to the target quality. Continue to do all of the things suggested above, just less often.
2. Make up short stories about children who are thoughtful. Use puppets, flannel boards, or Polaroid pictures. Catch a child expressing thoughtfulness. Paste the picture on one page and write a brief story below it telling what happened: "Susie couldn't get by. Tommy moved his chair. Then she could get through. That was thoughtful."
3. Read stories and comment about examples of thoughtfulness as you read. ("Little Red Riding Hood was thoughtful. She shared her cookies with her Grandma.")
4. Occasionally with puppets and stories, mention lack of thoughtfulness (or whatever quality you are focusing on at the time). Then ask the children to suggest a thoughtful thing to do. Be careful. At this point, do not lecture. Do not try to relate it to something they should have done.

NOTE: Remember, you are not only nurturing thoughtfulness, but you are also helping the children to learn the names of their feelings and actions. All too often adults tell children to "be thoughtful," or "That was a thoughtless thing to do." Children may not have the slightest idea what they are talking about. Labeling the good behaviors makes it easier for children to express them spontaneously and purposefully.

From then on:

1. Continue to call attention to examples of the qualities you wish to see expressed. Of course, as these qualities increase in number, it becomes impossible to call attention to each of them constantly. It also becomes unnecessary. There seems to be a special magic to the expression of positive qualities. If a once-established quality seems to be diminishing, however, merely begin to call attention to it again, and do so on a regular basis.
2. Introduce new targets regularly. Watch them expand. You may discover quickly that even some of the naughtiest children express some of the target qualities from the first day. You may not have noticed before.

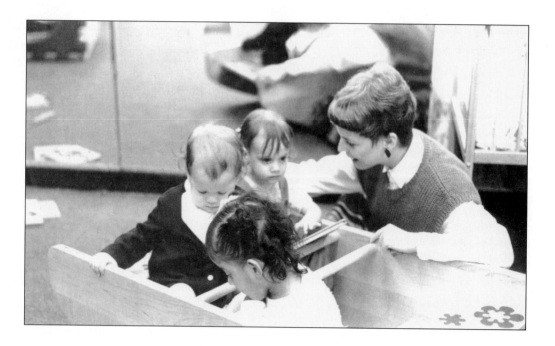

2. *Provide materials appropriate to the skills or interaction desired.* Children must learn to use play materials before they can be expected to play with them in cooperative situations. Children who become frustrated because they do not have the skill to use a material may become disruptive or withdrawn. Research has also revealed that some materials are more conducive to positive social interaction than others. For example, simple table games such as Lotto or Candyland, with specific rules, may be more conducive to cooperative play than more unstructured play materials such as sand. Children with disabilities who have not developed imaginative play may need to move gradually from structured to unstructured play when positive interpersonal relationships are a high-priority goal. Teachers will need to observe carefully to determine which materials are most conducive to fostering the desired behavior.

3. *Make sufficient materials available to promote cooperation and imitation.* When children outnumber the materials available, cooperative play obviously is dependent on children's willingness to share. If sharing is not one of the priorities for the play activity, then abundant materials should be available. Imitation is also not immediately possible and cannot be reinforced if children must wait to use the materials.

4. *Plan definite activities that require cooperation.* Hewett and Taylor (1980) described a number of tasks that require at least two children to communicate and cooperate to reach a mutual goal. Each one's actions are indispensable to the other. For example, the pan-sorting task requires one child to sit on each side of a screen. Each has three different-colored pans and a number of objects. One child is the dispatcher, who describes what he or she is doing as objects are placed in the pans (e.g., "I am putting the yellow car in the red pan"). The other child attempts to follow these directions to imitate the actions of the dispatcher. Such an activity is particularly helpful to children who have difficulty cooperating and paying attention long enough to follow directions. Of course, the more verbal the children, the easier the task. Remember, some children must be taught how to imitate or to model the behavior of others.

Use of Typical Peers as Mediators of Social Skills

Several authors (Cavallaro, Haney, & Cabeallo, 1993; Noonan & McCormick, 1993; & Chandler, 1998) described strategies for using peers as mediators of social skill development. Such strategies include asking a peer to demonstrate a skill or activity for the child with special needs, and training or prompting children (both with and without disabilities) to *initiate* interactions with one another.

ENCOURAGING DEVELOPMENTAL PLAY BEHAVIOR

Although research on the significance of play for children with disabilities is limited, the contention that play is an important contributor to their development is widely accepted. Recognizing the critical role of play in the enhancement of every aspect of a child's development, researchers are now investigating play behavior from a variety of viewpoints.

The Importance of Play

The importance of play has been noted in the early literature as far back as Plato and Aristotle (Cherry, 1976). Freudians view the repetition of experiences in play as a means of gaining mastery over painful events. Eriksonians consider play to be a method by which children organize and integrate life experiences. Piagetians see play as an essential means of mastering one's environment. Play develops creativity and increases the child's repertoire of responses. The importance of play as a context for teaching and learning was discussed in Chapter 6.

In addition, the crucial role of play in the development of skills leading to social competence is receiving considerable attention (Umansky & Hooper, 1998). Teachers are directed to become social engineers who can help young children play appropriately with others as a means toward ensuring the development of acceptable social skills.

The importance of creating an environment that promotes spontaneous and appropriately directed play cannot be underestimated. Early childhood educators have long realized the need for play activities as a part of all preschool curricula. The issue of accountability, however, has jeopardized the role of spontaneous play in some classrooms. Teachers feel pushed to judge the value of a play activity by what is learned. Perhaps the challenge now is to create a three-way balance among less-structured creative activities, freedom of choice, and directed tasks designed to remedy developmental deficits.

The Nature of Play

Piaget (1963) placed play into three broad categories. First, *practice play* accompanies the sensorimotor stage of cognitive development. Practice play is characterized by the exploration and repetition involved in mastering an activity. The game of taking things out and putting things in is typical practice play.

Symbolic play describes the second type of play, which occurs during the preoperational stage of cognitive development. Preschool children involved in symbolic play can be seen using one object to represent or symbolize another. A child might attribute the qualities of a camera to a small wooden block and go around "taking pictures." The child's increased verbal ability allows imitating and reenacting experiences, thus facilitating pretending and dramatic play. The third kind of play is referred to as *games with rules,* which requires more complex communication and cooperation. Whereas some children may engage in rule-oriented play during preschool, interest in this behavior is thought to heighten during the concrete operational stage of cognitive development near 7 years of age.

Development of Social Interaction Skills Through Play

A review of the literature readily suggests that investigators have shifted their focus from emphasis on the cognitive competence of children with disabilities as a predictor of future functioning to concern for social development. Despite the good intentions of inclusion, we find again and again that "Positive peer interactions for children with special needs and/or social delays may not develop without specific experiences or interventions" (Chandler, 1998, p. 14). Special programming strategies are necessary to increase interaction and promote social skill development of children with special needs. They are just less adept at developing the interpersonal skills typical children may acquire through usual play behavior. To understand the developmental levels of social play behavior, we will discuss a variation of the classic work of Parten (1932). Parten's seven levels of social participation provide a sequence for reference, but they need more empirical support to be followed without caution. At least they do provide guidelines for observation and selection of intervention strategies. The following discussions of each level elaborates on the work of Bailey (1978):

1. *Unoccupied behavior.* At this level there is no interpersonal interaction. The child may watch anything that attracts his or her attention. Some children will engage in self-stimulating behavior. Even at this level, children should be placed near other children and reinforced for manipulating a toy and staying within the social environment.

2. *Solitary independent play.* Again the child plays alone and with toys that are probably different from those being used by other children. He or she may be within speaking distance of other children but is unlikely to interact with them. Teachers should encourage involvement with toys even if the child is not interacting with others. Toys must be carefully chosen and reinforcement given for appropriate use. Not only will encouragement of appropriate use of toys and objects help children enhance their cognitive skills, but it will make them better prepared to become socially integrated.

3. *Onlooker behavior.* On this level, children are definitely observing the play of others and may even engage in conversation with them. As a step toward actual involvement with others, adults should place children where they can clearly observe and should encourage any attempts at interaction. One promising approach to increasing the social interaction of

young children with disabilities has been to teach nondisabled peers to be the initiators of social exchanges (Strain and Kohler, 1988; Chandler, 1998). McHale and Olley (1982) reported that "peers even briefly trained to use behavioral procedures can elicit social responses during play from young children with a variety of handicaps" (p. 84). However, generalization to new settings is still questionable (Guralnick & Neville, 1997). Thus, these authors suggested that a more effective procedure might involve play with an untrained nondisabled peer who possesses the "natural" initiations to which the children with disabilities might respond.

4. *Parallel activity.* Behavior on this level includes independent play among children that utilizes toys like those used by the other children. To move children toward complete involvement, the teacher should encourage the nondisabled children to share toys with the children who have disabilities and to ask for toys from the children with disabilities. In this way the nondisabled children act as initiators of involvement. Children with disabilities should be placed clearly within the group and not on its fringes.

5. *Associative play.* On this level, children are playing with other children. There is borrowing, loaning, sharing, engagement in similar activities, and interest primarily in association rather than activities. To facilitate such involvement, teachers must deliberately structure the environment. They must provide toys and objects such as blocks, dress-up clothes, and games that encourage interaction. Space must be adequate, as crowding tends to lead to disruptive play. Nondisabled peers should be reinforced for conversation and sharing with playmates who have disabilities. Children with disabilities may need extra reinforcement and redirection if they begin to wander from the group.

6. *Cooperative or organized play.* On the final level of Parten's continuum, children play in a group that is organized in some way. There are common goals and a division of labor. All members usually feel part of the group even though it is led by one or two players. Typical activities include building structures during block play and dramatization. The teacher's role in facilitating cooperative play centers around

preparation of the environment and providing appropriate space and "social" toys requiring cooperative interaction between two or more children.

Some Ways to Get Children to Play. Education usually emphasizes structured, teacher-directed play because some children do not appear to learn readily through spontaneous play. There is increased recognition of the environmental factors that can impact on children's involvement in play. For example, inappropriate toys and play materials may contribute to the limited play behavior of children with disabilities. Toys that are not durable fail to withstand rough treatment, and toys such as dolls designed for symbolic play are not developmentally appropriate for some children. Children who still need to engage in practice play must be provided with toys strong enough to accommodate repeated use. Children who lack attending skills, imitation skills, or communication skills cannot be expected to share or take turns. Developing these abilities takes time and is taught deliberately through modeling and reinforcement. Teachers need to assess a child's developmental strengths and weaknesses to encourage the most appropriate play activities.

Once the teacher notes that a child has begun to explore the environment and effectively uses a variety of different toy objects, Wehman (1978) encouraged the development of "(a) more sophisticated and sustained toy play and (b) greater frequency of social interaction patterns" (p. 284). Exhibit 7–2 suggests some guidelines to enhance productive free-choice play.

Imagining and pretending may be difficult for many children. Granting this freedom to be somebody else or something else is often a good way to lead a withdrawn child out of his or her shell. Dress-up clothes, an assortment of hats (fireman, cowboy, train conductor, or nurse), and old costumes left from Halloween are appealing. Pretending to be animals during story times and participating in musical activities allow many children to romp and move freely. With freedom of movement comes greater ease in being around other children.

A large box with holes for windows provides a sense of protection. As the children crawl in and out

they discover new ways of looking at things. Looking through the window in the box restricts the view in unexpected ways. Moving becomes purposeful. Seeing what is inside intrigues some children. If the box is large enough, a small carpet and a place for a snack will encourage some children to enter.

Teachers may want to tell short stories using a flannel board or pictures. Then, as the teacher provides simple props and withdraws from the center of the activity, children usually accept the suggestion to "play the story."

Role playing is a form of pretending and imagining. An apron and play kitchen equipment make it possible for children to be Mom or Dad. A plastic hammer or a wrench enables a child to be a carpenter or a garage mechanic. Some children pretend to be their big brothers and sisters.

Much insight into fears and frustrations can be gained by encouraging role playing without evaluating it. Of course, the insights gained may not be pleasant.

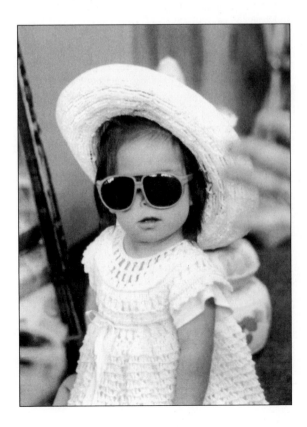

EXHIBIT 7–2

Setting the Stage for Productive Free Playtimes

A. *Arrange the play area thoughtfully.*

1. Provide adequate space indoors and out. Avoid crowding.

2. Arrange small play spaces separated by shelves or other dividers. Puzzles, books, and other things to do alone should be available.

3. Prepare larger spaces for cooperative play with blocks and other building materials.

4. A play kitchen in a corner encourages group play. Provide some full-size pans and spoons and child-sized equipment.

5. Maintain the same basic room arrangement over time, but vary the play materials available. Have a storage area where toys may "rest." Sometimes allow the children to choose what will be stored and what will be available.

6. Include clay and easels, but monitor their use.

7. Puppets, dolls and doll houses, and barns and animals should be regularly available. These imagination stimulators require set-up space, whether used alone or with a group.

8. Remove toys that appear to encourage an activity or noise level incompatible with the best interests of all the children. In small areas, large cars and trucks usually generate too high an activity level for safety.

9. Plan to alternate indoor and outdoor play whenever possible. Outdoor areas should provide safe climbing and running spaces, as well as tricycles and structures for crawling in, over, and under.

10. Be alert for special needs. Provide special equipment for children with physical disabilities.

B. *Establish rules or guidelines from the beginning.*

1. Keep the rules simple and limited in number.

2. Telling children rules is important, but not very effective. They will need to learn the guidelines by observation and experience. But the teacher should have the rules firmly in mind.

3. Rules should be designed to establish thoughtful, kind, and courteous behavior. The following are some we have found useful:

    a. The child who chooses a toy first may decide whether he or she wants to play alone or with others. The child's decision will be respected.

    b. Sharing is not required, especially if the item to be shared belongs to a particular child. Sharing is, however, encouraged.

    c. Children wanting to join an established group must be invited to join. The newcomer may ask to play, but cannot move in without a welcome.

    d. Good manners are modeled and expected. "May I," "please," and "thank you" are routinely used by teachers. Children absorb these courtesies quickly.

    e. When a child or a group is finished with an item, the item must be returned to its place on the shelf before a different toy or game is chosen.

    f. Sometimes children like to just watch for awhile. This wish is respected. A rocker and a beanbag chair are often used by watchers.

    g. Just as child newcomers may not barge into an established group, so adult (teacher or parent) newcomers must ask permission and be accepted.

EXHIBIT 7–2

C. *Some attitudes for teachers and parents during free play.*

1. Respect the children's ability to choose an activity suited to their present learning needs. By providing a range of materials and possible activities, the teacher allows the self-knowledge of each child to function.

2. Trust each child to use good judgment. Interfere only if real danger or unkindness is imminent. Anticipate and prevent trouble rather than punishing it after the fact.

3. Be aware of what is happening throughout the room. Even when attending to a particular child, the teacher must be alert to everyone and everything. Evidence of this awareness from the beginning leads children to follow the rules consistently.

4. Avoid overprotecting the child who lacks assertiveness. By "making" more aggressive children share, the teacher rewards the child who fails to assert himself or herself for this lack of assertiveness. Rather, suggest to the quiet ones that they ask for a turn. If they begin fussing, remove the object of the argument for a time. Explain that they will have to find a way to resolve the problem.

5. If an unacceptable behavior persists, reevaluate the whole situation. If things are being thrown in the wrong place, find a place where it is appropriate to throw and move the throwers there. If loud noises inside are a problem, be outside more often.

6. Avoid making children self-conscious. Calling everyone's attention to a mistake or a mess is unkind.

7. Avoid comparisons. Respect uniqueness consistently.

Judgment about how to use such knowledge requires compassion, understanding, and wisdom.

Puppets are therapeutic and fun for most children. A box with a "stage" cut out, an old television with the insides removed, or a table with a curtain becomes the puppet theater. Of course a real puppet stage can be constructed by a willing parent. The puppets can be made from socks or sewn from a simple pattern. Commercial puppets are enchanting, although most are expensive. Children enjoy merely playing with the puppets, but if a teacher puts on the first show, they will have a better idea of how to be puppeteers.

It is not unusual for withdrawn children to say their first words with a puppet on their hands. Often they will find it necessary to use the puppet for days whenever they want to talk. A change of puppets should be offered with care. If a particular puppet is effective, the teacher should not rush into expecting the child to assume many roles with other puppets. Some children require prolonged encouragement before they can venture out.

Peers and play often draw children out of their shells. Suggesting that one child help another by picking up a spilled puzzle leads to later spontaneous kindnesses. Some children notice the needs of other youngsters more completely than most adults believe. Consider this experience of Lance and Carla:

Lance was enrolled in kindergarten, but over a period of several months he stood quietly and firmly in one corner of the room. The kindergarten teacher was patient and experienced, but with 32 other children, the situation was overwhelming to Lance. Because of Lance's continued withdrawn behavior, his parents placed him in a preschool. When he entered school his eyes were unsmiling and his lips were taut. For several days the other children played around him. He refused snacks, special treats, and all efforts to involve him in play. Then Carla took over. She was 4 years old. She walked right up to Lance and said, "I like blocks. Play with me." Without further ado she pulled Lance abruptly to the floor, pushed the blocks to him, and began to build. Smiling and chatting away (definitely a monologue) she told him all about the wonderful house she was building. Lance stared emotionless, but Carla was not disturbed. After a while Carla said, "Help put the blocks back. We'll do a puzzle." Lance did not move. A few minutes later Carla announced, "Lance likes grapes." The teacher did not discover how Carla knew of Lance's liking for grapes, but promised to bring the fruit the next day.

The following day, Carla asked for some grapes "for Lance." Carrying the grapes with one hand and dragging Lance with the other, she moved to the puzzle corner. She said, "We'll do a puzzle first." With the grapes plainly in sight, but out of Lance's reach, they began a puzzle. "When we finish we eat grapes," said Carla. Lance smiled and slowly pushed a puzzle piece to Carla. He also ate grapes with Carla.

Carla's mothering continued for weeks as she ignored Lance's rebuffs. She regularly told everyone, "Lance is my friend," and busily planned things to do with him. She alternately insisted and cajoled. Frequently, when Lance ignored her she walked away, only to return as if nothing had happened a few minutes later. Carla literally planned and executed therapy for Lance. No doubt, Carla's natural inclinations accomplished more than many well-planned teacher-directed lessons.

Facilitating Play and Social Skill Development in Children with More Severe Disabilities. Children with obvious or more severe disabilities may have had little opportunity to play with other children. Some may have spent a lot of their short lives in hospitals, while others may have been overprotected by parents who fear their child might experience ridicule or rejection. Of course, many disabling conditions by their very nature make it difficult for children to play in ways that lead to social skill acquisition. For instance, children with severe hearing, speech, or cognitive impairments may not have the language necessary to make their needs known or to engage in appropriate verbal interchange. Children with physical disabilities or lack of behavior control may have problems making friends because their behavior or necessary adaptive equipment has become a barrier to social interaction. Therefore, caregivers

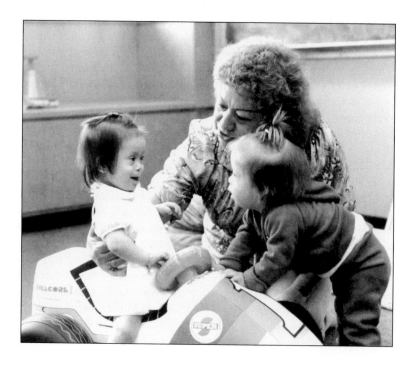

must make special efforts to facilitate effective involvement of children with more special needs.

Instructors from Texas Tech University listed the following target skills to be given special consideration when working with children with more severe disabilities:

1. Start and sustain play with other children.

2. Follow another child's lead or model.

3. Pretend in creative dramatic play.

4. Share materials and take turns.

5. Let other children know what they think and feel. (1984, p. 104)

Several strategies for developing these skills have already been discussed. Of course it is necessary to begin by carefully observing to find out what social skills each child already has and which ones need to be developed. In addition, Fewell (1984) developed an assessment scale especially designed to evaluate play behavior of children from birth through age 3. More recently, Linder (1993) compiled guidelines for an approach to assessment of observation of play.

Physical Prompting and Fading. Sometimes children with more severe disabilities do not become involved because they do not know how to play with the available toys or respond to others. When they do not react, there is no play behavior for the caregiver to reinforce and encourage. The caregiver, then, may have to physically guide the child through the desired response. For example, if the game is to roll a ball from one child to another, the caregiver or a trained peer may manually guide the child's hand until the child can approximate the behavior on his or her own. The guiding hand should be gradually removed as the approximation becomes closer and closer to the desired behavior. If during this fading or gradual removal of the physical prompting, the child becomes upset or apparently is not ready to continue alone, the fading should be discontinued temporarily. Such an approach can be very effective with children who experience severe physical, visual, hearing, or mental impairments. It is much easier for these children to follow directions illustrated through physical prompting.

Initiating and Sustaining Play. Sometimes physical prompting is not enough. Children may need to be given the words they need to initiate and sustain play behavior. When a child doesn't seem to have the words to invite another to play, the caregiver must supply them for the child. For example, when Danny wanted Brad to help him build a road in the sand, he kept looking and motioning to him. Brad, who often does not follow nonverbal cues, did not respond. Then Ms. McLynn said, "Danny, go and say to Brad, 'Come help me build the road.'" Danny modeled Ms. McLynn who, in turn, reinforced both Danny and Brad as both began to build a road. When another child began to step on the road, Ms. McLynn said to Danny, "Say, 'Stop!'" Danny again modeled Ms. McLynn, and the children played on.

HELPING CHILDREN WITH EMOTIONAL AND BEHAVIORAL CHALLENGES

No matter how consistent and positive a teacher and the environment are, there will be children who continue to need additional help as they strive to develop a healthy, well-adjusted personality. There will also be behaviors that we perceive to be challenging just because our unique set of past experiences, values, instructional practices and institutional guidelines lead us to perceive certain behaviors to be challenging (Strain and Hemmeter, 1997). Perhaps further understanding of the normalness of individual temperamental traits will help us to be less stressed in the face of challenging behaviors.

Individual Temperament

Like Thomas, Chess, and Birch, we believe that "the personality is shaped by the constant interplay of temperament and environment" (1970, p. 2). Through intensive parent interviews and observation of children, these researchers identified nine characteristics of temperament, which they clustered into three basic types describing approximately 65% of the children studied. The other 35% just did not show a basic constancy of temperament or style of behavior.

Developmentalists have long paid attention to the descriptions of temperament made famous by Thomas, Chess, and Birch (1970). They described the *easy* child as one whose behavior is low in intensity and who is adaptable, approachable, predictable in bodily functions, and positive in mood. This kind of child easily makes parents believe they are good at parenting. Obviously, such a child (who accounted for approximately 40% of the sample studied) would be a pleasure in the classroom.

The second type of temperament is that of the *difficult* child, who made up approximately 10% of the sample studied. This type of child is often negative in mood, adapts slowly to change, has unpredictable biological functions, and often exhibits intense reactions to environmental demands. Such a child not only requires that teachers and parents exercise extra effort and patience to keep the child's self-esteem intact but also behaves in such difficult ways that the self-esteem of involved adults is often threatened. When adults are unable to provide firm guidance by building the environment discussed throughout this chapter, they may experience a sense of helplessness when such children appear unhappy or out of control. The threat of becoming burned-out caregivers is very real. This possibility is even more acute in the case of at-risk children who have exhibited early developmental delays. When children are unable, due to disabling conditions or prematurity, to give forth the early social signals necessary to establish early attachment, their difficult behavior later on is even more of a threat to parents who may already be feeling uneasy about their parenting skills.

The third type of child discussed by Thomas, Chess, and Birch is the *slow-to-warm-up* child, who accounts for approximately 15% of the sample. Such a child typically exhibits negative responses to new situations but, given time and patience, eventually adapts. Patience and understanding of the child's tendency to withdraw seems to be the key to helping this child become well adjusted.

The stability of these temperamental traits is thought to be dependent on particular experiences of the individual. Thomas, Chess, and Korn (1982) stated that "the concept of difficult temperament as a within-the-infant characteristic in no way implies a fixed immutable trait . . . but can be modified or altered by post-natal genetic or maturational influences, situational context, or the effect of the child-environmental interactional process" (p. 15).

It is the responsibility of caregivers to influence the child-environment interactional process so that difficult temperamental traits can be modified toward healthy adjustment to environmental demands now and in the future. Therefore the following sections suggest some practical methods of giving additional assistance to children whose behavior interferes with learning or can be described as disruptive or harmful.

Children Who Lack Sufficient Self-Control

Children who lack sufficient self-control are usually thought of as aggressive, hostile, overactive, impulsive, or hyperactive. Such children find it difficult to follow the classroom rules of conduct. Some, such as hostile and aggressive children, may deliberately strike out at others or damage equipment. Others, such as hyperactive or impulsive children, may merely be unable to control extraneous movements. While these behaviors are certainly challenging, it is important to remember that any behavior that continues over time is "working" for the child exhibiting such behavior. Such behaviors have a purposeful, communication function. Strain and Hemmeter (1997, p. 4) suggest that such behaviors may be attempting to communicate messages such as the following:

a. You're asking me to do something that is too difficult.

b. I don't understand what you want.

c. I want a certain thing, and I want it now.

d. I'm bored, pay some attention to me.

It is our responsibility to try to recognize what the child is trying to communicate and assist them in learning socially acceptable ways to communicate their thoughts and needs. We are, further, encouraged to try to prevent undesirable attempts at communication by anticipating needs and preventing such behavioral episodes. Efforts at prevention include making sure activities are developmentally and individually appropriate and requests are clearly understood, using highly desirable toys and activities, and providing positive feedback.

Some children with challenging behaviors may be labeled as having **attention deficit disorder (ADD)** or **attention deficit with hyperactivity disorder** (ADHD). ADHD is characterized by the inability to maintain normal levels of attention, extreme impulsivity, and may have high levels of activity. While many young children normally exhibit these behaviors, children with ADHD exhibit inappropriately high degrees of these behaviors (Blackman, Westervelt, Stevenson, & Welch, 1991). Children who are definitely ADHD cannot be made to behave as children without disability. The onset of ADHD is before the age of 5, and it occurs more often in boys. Degrees of severity differ, and symptoms can be exacerbated or ameliorated by environmental factors. Early intervention specialists should be careful not to automatically ascribe the ADHD or ADD label to every child who exhibits extreme problems with behavior control. Only through complete, multidisciplinary diagnosis is the diagnosis of ADHD warranted.

Some children may be eligible for additional community resources through special education if they can be referred as learning disabled, seriously emotionally disturbed, or otherwise health impaired. Parents can be helped to realize that these labels are necessary evils to obtain funding for available additional services such as family counseling or behavior management consultation. However, as noted throughout this textbook, labels usually do more harm than good. The basic problem for the classroom teacher or parent is the same—helping the child to control his or her own behavior. Many of the same techniques for behavior control can be used effectively with all children who have these problems. Some children, however, will need individualized help. We will begin with those techniques that will be useful with a number of children and then follow with special considerations.

Pick Your Battles. Teachers and parents should pick only the most disruptive and aggressive behavior

as targets for control. They should be willing to tolerate a higher level of activity than is normally preferred. Otherwise, their negative reactions will exacerbate the child's behavior (Blackman, Westervelt, Stevenson, & Welch, 1991).

Do Not Permit Aggressive Behavior. Not permitting aggressive behavior should be the first rule toward helping children control the expression of unacceptable, possibly harmful behavior. From the very beginning, adults must make it perfectly clear that hitting, kicking, pushing, and shoving will not be allowed. Then teachers and parents must act swiftly in the face of the expression of such behavior to demonstrate consistently and firmly what the consequences of such actions will be. Children thus learn that such acts will not be tolerated, as they lead to nonpunitive but effective consequences. Firm consistency helps children develop trust in themselves and in others.

Despite the teacher's best efforts toward preventive discipline, aggressive acts do occur and must be dealt with immediately. The key to dealing with aggressive children is to be nonaggressive oneself. Nonhurtful discipline, such as a time out, is considered by many to be effective. Children learn that aggressive behavior will not be tolerated of anyone, not even of the teacher. They also learn that the teacher can be trusted to be nonhurtful. If teachers are to give attention, they should give it to nonaggressors. That is, the teacher should give attention to the victim rather than to the aggressor. Throughout this chapter, other examples of nonaggressive methods of behavior control are discussed. These merit consideration.

Prepare the Child's Environment. Teachers need to prepare the child's environment. Children who are hyperactive, anxious, or angry often find it almost impossible to sit still, to take turns, or to wait for explanations. They may constantly squirm, turn, or wiggle. Such children may be easily overstimulated if they have difficulty filtering out extraneous sounds or sights. Teachers must take care to limit the noise level in their classrooms and the visual stimuli surrounding these children. Centers that have minimal space or are associated with different activity or noise levels may create too much confusion. Inabilities to filter out extraneous stimuli and to control impulses may be the reason some of these children can be so difficult for parents to handle when shopping in department or grocery stores. Conversely, Zentall (1977) found that some hyperactive children may actually need *more* stimulation. Zentall hypothesized that some children produce their own stimulation through activity because they are understimulated. Such different views again require that teachers be astute observers to consider each child's needs when preparing the environment.

Concentration can be improved by providing a quiet place to work free from distraction. Ample equipment and materials should be available so that these children do not have to do too much waiting or sharing. Teachers should limit the use of toys or games with many small pieces to manipulate that can create frustration. They must space tables or desks far enough apart so that extraneous movements will not bother others. They should eliminate toys, such as guns and soldiers, that elicit aggressive behavior. They should place impatient children in a position to receive snacks or working materials relatively early in the waiting time. As these children show signs of increasing their capacities for self-control, waiting time can be increased.

Carefully Consider Curriculum Implementation. Teachers must carefully consider curriculum implementation. When children are appropriately involved in activities with materials or people, they usually are demonstrating appropriate behavior as well. Children who find it difficult to concentrate may fall behind in developing pre-academic skills and may be labeled as learning disabled later on. Sometimes their speech is so fast that words and thoughts become a jumble, resulting in excessive use of gestures. Children's frustrations may develop into aggressive behavior and a loss of self-esteem from being ashamed of their lack of self-control. To avoid these frustrations, directions must be extremely clear and given one by one; often with visual aids. Teachers should analyze tasks and present them in sequential steps so they can reinforce success intermittently and frequently. Materials and activities must be interest-ing. Using the child's name often while working with a group helps the child to focus his or her attention. A calm voice is a must. A raised voice will only create anxiety and heighten the child's level of activity.

Unstructured free playtimes or transition times can be especially difficult for impulsive children. Choices for these children may have to be limited. It helps to establish definite procedures for transition times, such as those suggested in Exhibit 7–3. A teacher or paraprofessional will need to stay with the most impulsive children until they have become involved in their new activities. Hewett and Taylor (1980) described "order tasks" that can be especially useful in "helping children learn to adapt to routines, follow directions, complete assignments, and control their behavior" (p. 189). These are tasks that usually involve eye-hand coordination and are simple enough to complete so that children can readily realize success. Examples include picture puzzles, pegboard designs, and bead stringing. When children are losing control during either free play or work time, they can be directed to these order tasks to help them gain composure acceptably and nonpunitively.

Using loud, lively records during music time can be upsetting for children who have difficulty with control. Some activity records require children to be able to process auditory information quickly to participate. For children who lack self-control, these records may be inappropriate or can be used for only a very short time. Teachers must remember that many behavior problems are simply children's responses to overstimulation or frustration. Why create or accentuate such problems?

Teachers can use visual aids to help children control themselves. Carpet squares or pieces of tape on the floor give them a definite, visual, and tactile space in which they are to keep themselves. Having a definite location for their belongings is also important to all children. It helps them to control their things and themselves. While on field trips, overactive children should be in small groups and close to adults. If they are verbally engaged, they usually have better body control. Similar-style name tags for groups of two or three help these children to feel a manageable sense of belonging to a small group.

EXHIBIT 7–3

Daily Activity Transition Techniques

A. *When children are playing (free play or free choice activities):*

1. Five minutes before clean-up time, quietly say, "It's almost clean-up time." Speak to small groups and individuals—do *not* make a group announcement.

2. Have a child ring a bell to signal "Clean-up time, now."

3. Sing a "clean-up song."

4. Move among the children, helping them find containers and properly sorting and replacing toys. As children learn where things belong, teacher assistance should be reduced.

   SUGGESTIONS: Early in the year, have a limited number of toys and games available. As the children learn to replace those correctly, add new ones and remove some things. Avoid clutter. Provide variety, that is puzzles, games, blocks, beads, or coloring materials. Have a specific container for each kind of toy. Provide a particular place to which each container is returned as the children clean up.

B. *Transition from circle time or a group activity to another directed activity such as a small-group lesson, snack time, or individual lessons:*

1. As the activity in progress draws to a close, tell the children, "It's almost time for _____."

2. Establish brief eye contact with each—a look and a smile at the same time. Then say, "Listen for the directions. It is _____'s turn."

3. Give each child in turn specific directions for moving to the next lesson or activity location. For example:

   Teacher: "Matt, clap your hands two times, touch your ear, and walk backward to the table for a snack." (Others watch as Matt follows the directions. The directions are given in one long sentence. Matt must wait until the teacher finishes speaking before he begins.)

   Teacher: (To Danny, who has a learning problem): "Danny, jump two times." (Danny's directions are shorter and spoken more slowly.)

   When the teacher gives specific directions for going to the table or the next activity location, children learn to listen to and follow directions while being able to "let off a little steam." The transition occurs in an orderly way and enhances a sense of appropriate behavior.

Deescalate Play Behavior. Children need to be helped by active adult participation to deescalate their play when it gets out of hand. To illustrate the need to help children refocus their play when they become too involved, Caldwell (1977) described the all-too-familiar sandbox scene. Children begin innocently making sand pies and then one child steps on or otherwise destroys a child's product. Then hostility erupts and aggression occurs. Caldwell suggested that involved adults should not only catch the behavior before it escalates but also return children to positive playfulness by not making judgments and reading intent into every aggressive act.

Use Time Out Effectively. Marion (1995) discussed a number of steps that should be considered when developing effective time-out procedures. These include the following:

1. Simply explaining to the child that he or she will be placed in time out every time the unacceptable behavior occurs.

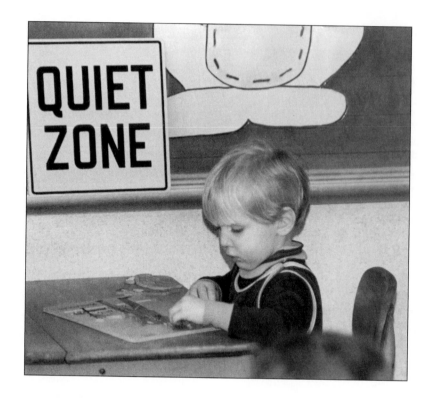

2. Designating a nonfrightening time-out area away from activity but within view of the teacher.

3. Calmly insisting that the child take a time out if resistance is shown.

4. Praising the child who participates in a time out as planned.

5. Keeping the time out short.

6. Rewarding positive behavior when the child returns to an activity after a time out.

Several conditions increase the likelihood of success of this approach: Teachers are cautioned to warn the child only once; to describe the child's probable feelings with kindness; to restate clearly the broken rule; to make the child responsible for knowing when he or she is once again in control; and to actively assist the child's return by helping him or her become involved in the ongoing activities. Hewett and Taylor (1980) added the importance of allowing the child to return without lecturing or attempting to obtain promises to be good in the future. They also sug-

gested that when the child returns the teacher should make an effort to engage him or her in a task in which the child is interested and can be successful.

Maintain Physical Proximity and Touch Control. An adult's physical proximity or a gentle touch will help some children maintain control over their behavior. This is especially useful when young children are placed in situations that require extra efforts at control. Many public-supported early childhood programs are placed within elementary schools. As a result, children may be expected to stand and walk in lines and to control their behavior in ways that usually are not expected until they reach kindergarten age. Teachers may even need to take the hands of some children to help them maintain the needed control. This should not be done as a punishment for misbehavior, but should be done before problems arise, as a help to the child. If the teacher uses handholding as a punishment, the teacher might become an aversive stimulus and the child might feel less worthy.

Use Signal Interference to Prevent Loss of Self-Control.

Signal interference can be very effective with impulsive children if teachers have observed carefully to see what usually "sets off" such children. Sometimes patterns in behavior are obvious, such as excessive frustration or activity just before a snack, during circle time, or near the time to go home. Environmental factors such as overstimulation, lack of sufficient movement space, or lack of time to complete a task might be a part of the patterns. Nonverbal (and sometimes verbal) signals such as a nod or a wink can be especially effective if used in the beginning stages of misbehavior and with children who are capable of understanding them and can remember why the signal is being given.

Signals must be used before a child becomes so emotional that he or she is unable to stop the behavior. A warm relationship between the teacher and the child contributes to the effectiveness of this approach. As children mature, they can be taught to understand their own signs of impending loss of control. They can then be encouraged to signal the teacher that they need a time out or a change in activities.

Deal Consistently with Temper Tantrums.

Temper tantrums that are only bids for attention may go away when they are consistently ignored. If the tantrums persist, then the child becomes a candidate for the six-step time-out process just outlined. Nonthreatening statements are preferred, such as, "It seems that you are unable to play with us right now. I hope you will be able to work with us after some time in the 'thinking corner.'" Once the child is back and participating appropriately, reinforcement should be given for the constructive behavior in progress.

Mutual cooperation with parents is essential to establishing firm, consistent guidelines. Above all, adults must be certain that a tantrum does not result in the child's getting his or her own way if that way is inappropriate. The child's day should be programmed so that numerous opportunities exist for the child to get attention in constructive ways.

Help Overactive Children to Feel Good About Themselves.

Many children who overact are angry underneath and expend energy covering up feelings of inferiority or fears of being vulnerable. P|mary objective for such children is to |themselves as worthwhile people capab|ing self-control. Experience has show|these children begin to feel like responsible individuals, their need for negative behavior is diminished.

Healthy young children enjoy pleasing adults whom they can trust. When these children misbehave, teachers should ask themselves whether something they are doing or not doing is causing the problem. Have the children been allowed to change activities frequently enough? Is too much being demanded? Are the children being allowed to constructively express their feelings verbally and physically by pounding clay or knocking down tenpins? Is the reward-to-punishment ratio at an optimum level? The teacher's responsibility is to prevent children from losing control of their behavior. Loss of control creates shame, guilt, and lowered self-esteem.

The curriculum needs to be reviewed periodically to ensure realistic and developmentally/individually appropriate expectations. Experts caution educators to beware of stressing academics to the detriment of social and emotional development. It is suggested that early educators avoid emphasizing academics during the preschool years. Instead they are encouraged to concentrate on certain prerequisite skills such as listening, being able to relate past experiences to present activities, and using and respecting the tools of learning.

Finally, helpful teachers will (a) express their acceptance of children's feelings, negative and positive; (b) reassure overactive children that one of the teacher's jobs is to protect children from harming others or themselves; (c) exhibit confidence in children's abilities to improve self-control; and (d) demonstrate that children will be allowed greater opportunities to control their own behavior as they exhibit increased self-restraint and appropriate expressions of feelings.

Scheduling

As discussed earlier, predictable routines are essential to supporting young children's socially acceptable behavior. Schedules must be reasonably consistent in order for children to learn expected routines. By knowing what to do and when to do it, children are less likely to exhibit challenging behaviors. Predictability in type of activity, rather than sameness, is the key.

A Word About Medication: Caution

Perhaps the most controversial method of handling children who lack sufficient self-control involves using psychotropic drugs. Stimulants such as methylphenidate hydrochloride (Ritalin) and dextraamphetamine sulfate (Dexedrine) seem to have a paradoxical effect on children who are overactive. Such drugs do not actually act as a sedative because they do not slow down or suppress a child's initiative. Instead they "may inhibit production of substances that interfere with the normal work of neurotransmitters" (Swanson & Reinert, 1984, p. 142). The child is then able to focus on meaningful stimuli and organize bodily movement. Possible side effects include insomnia, stomach upset, dizziness, and nervousness.

Tranquilizers such as chlorpromazine hydrochloride (Thorazine) and thioridazine hydrochloride (Mellaril) are used with some children. These drugs seem to decrease aggressive and destructive behavior, but they can create drowsiness (Swanson & Reinert, 1984). Response to medication is specific to the individual child. It is extremely important to remember that very young children tend to have a greater variability of response and a greater incidence of behavioral and cognitive side effects than do older children. The most commonly reported side effects are insomnia, stomachaches, decreased appetite, and weight loss (Stevenson & Wolraich, 1989).

Considering the diagnostic difficulties involving young children and lack of sufficient treatment studies, a cautious approach to the use of stimulant medication is definitely warranted. Medication should never be used as the only treatment. Its use should be considered only when the hyperactivity is extreme and when medication is part of a well-designed and well-monitored, multimodal management program.

Children Who Are Reluctant to Participate

Children who are reluctant to participate are rarely a bother to teachers and classmates. Shy or timid children are easily overlooked. Special attention is important for children whose behavior ranges from timid and inhibited to completely withdrawn; otherwise their needs may go unnoticed. Such children usually separate themselves physically, avoid group activities and verbal interaction, seem afraid to try new tasks, sometimes appear disinterested, and may seek comfort through self-stimulation (e.g., rocking, twisting their hair, or thumb sucking). Kauffman (1985) described these children as those who lack the very behaviors that bring them into social contact, such as looking, talking, playing with, and touching. He saw them as "lacking in responsiveness to others' initiations of social contact" (p. 207). Teachers often find themselves responsible for helping these children to develop approach and responsiveness behaviors.

In addition to lacking social contact behavior, some of these children may be preoccupied with self-stimulation or with daydreaming and fantasy. By being so absorbed in their imaginations or their repetitive acts of sensory stimulation, they miss social cues. This lack of attention prevents them from the social learning available to children who are not isolated either physically or emotionally. Children who also experience language delays are at an even greater disadvantage. Even if they are paying attention, they may not be able to understand directions or to ask necessary questions. They have or take few opportunities to demonstrate what they know and understand. Skill and patience are absolutely necessary to help these children develop the trust they so desperately need.

Prepare the Child's Environment. Swap (1974) sought to explain the tasks of teachers working with these overly controlled children to prepare their environment by combining the theoretical approaches of Hewett (1968) and Erikson (1963). This combination encourages teachers to help children develop trust in themselves and their environment at the same time they are being taught how to listen and respond.

"On the one hand, the teacher needs to establish a climate of safety, predictability, and consistency. . . . On the other hand, the teacher needs to extend . . . an acceptance of his [the child's] responses, however limited, and provide nurturance, nourishment, and individual attention regardless of the quality or quantity of the child's initial output" (p. 165).

Children who are reluctant to participate will appreciate a small, safe place into which they can retreat. The place must not be like the time-out area. The child should be able to view the classroom activities from the safe place. Many inhibited children learn a great deal from watching others. Through watching they may develop the confidence necessary to attempt a new or different task.

As the child becomes more trustful, the "watching chair" can be moved closer to the ongoing activity. At an intermediate point, identical play materials can be placed within the child's reach. The teacher should not coax the child. No attention should be given to the child unless he or she attempts the activity either alone or with the others. If this occurs, then positive reinforcement should be given quietly and inconspicuously. The teacher must know what the child enjoys. A smile, rather than a public announcement of the child's participation, would probably be more appropriate.

These children will feel more secure if materials are kept in the same place day to day. They want a definite place for their own objects, including crayons and coats. The teacher should not force them to share until they are ready to do so. Consistency in routines and procedures helps them to predict and therefore feel more comfortable. The child must be prepared in advance for any new or strange situations such as visitors, field trips, or tornado drills.

Promote Peer Assistance. Seating nonparticipating children near relatively quiet but competent children can do wonders in promoting peer assistance. Experience has shown that extremely shy children often respond to another child much more quickly than to an adult. Caring, concerned children who do not move too loudly or quickly are excellent models and they do not threaten the insecure child. Such children can be prompted to invite the reluctant child to participate without begging for involvement. As noted earlier, in the story of Lance, sometimes the best approach is for the child or perhaps the teacher to ask for help, for example, "Johnny, will you please help me clean up this paint," or "Please hold the picture." Help can begin with an independent activity such as passing snacks and can graduate to a cooperative activity such as two children going to get the juice. Helping others gives the child an easy basis to establish relationships; at the same time self-esteem can be enhanced.

Consider Curriculum Adaptations. Like most children, inhibited children need a predictable schedule that includes both group time and individual time. Group size can be increased as the child builds confidence. Some children who are unwilling to express themselves in conversation will join in a song because they feel less conspicuous. They may sit on the edge initially. The teacher should not rush them. In the beginning, peripheral involvement such as holding pictures rather than naming them can be encouraged. Many of these children will participate physically before they will participate verbally. If a story is being read and followed by questions, call on the reluctant child last and then do not coax. Teachers must remember that the child must set the pace.

Many young children will interact with pets before they will interact with people. Letting such children take care of pets helps them to feel they are contributing to the welfare of the pets and to the classrooms. Their involvement also gives them a chance to receive the approval they seek.

Socially isolated children often respond to the social learning principles of modeling and imitation. Teachers should therefore seriously plan opportunities for these children to observe positive, pleasant social interaction as discussed earlier.

Individual attention is sometimes the key to getting reluctant children to participate in instructional activities. Teachers should approach them calmly, speaking slowly and clearly, and state exactly what they expect. They should present activities that they are reasonably certain are interesting to the child. Teachers must try to couple their attention to the child with something pleasant. They should help children to be reminded of good things when they see or think of their teacher. If the child refuses to become involved, then the teacher should merely place the materials nearby and let the child watch. This procedure should be followed at snack time as well. The teacher should not become anxious if the child does not eat. The more uncomfortable attention the child receives, the less he or she is likely to eat.

Walsh (1980) offered the following suggestion for helping isolated children become a part of the group: Begin by standing close to the isolated child. Then suggest that he or she join a group: "Tim and Laura could use someone to help build a bridge. . . . Why not give them a hand, Bob?" At this point, the teacher should move away, returning to give more attention only if the child acts on the suggestions. (p. 11)

Teachers then may wish to give additional suggestions if they seem to facilitate involvement.

Provide Opportunities for Expressing Feelings.

As mentioned earlier, the expression of a full range of emotions is essential to healthy emotional develop-ment (Greenspan & Greenspan, 1985). Inhibited, withdrawn children typically experience many unex-pressed emotions. Special encouragement thus must be given to self-expression. Drawing, painting, pup-petry, clay, water play, fingerpainting, and music can provide opportunities for this expression. Of course, these children must not be forced, and their efforts must be rewarded without regard to their products. As trust develops, teachers can gradually encourage verbal expression by asking questions such as "Is the girl in your picture very upset or unhappy today." Like active listening, this approach helps children to feel understood and accepted. They can attribute their unpleasant feelings to the object in the drawing and thus find these feelings to be less threatening.

Pictures, especially photographs of the children themselves, are especially useful when talking about feelings. Pictures that show clear facial expressions, definite gestures, or obvious effects of the child's ac-tions on others should be chosen. Such pictures help the child to perceive how another may feel and to dis-cover cause-and-effect relationships. Guided discus-sion should focus on describing what is happening, what will happen, and how those in the picture might feel. Review Figure 7-2 for other suggestions.

Help Reluctant Children Feel Good About Themselves. Above all, teachers must be conscious of the need to help reluctant children feel good about themselves so that they may find the courage to develop the social contact and attention skills critical to healthy social involvement. The teacher should begin with step-by-step presentations of noncompetitive tasks that can be achieved by the child. Nonthreatening rewards for effort coupled with a trusting relationship developed through dependability are essential. When children participate little, it is extremely difficult to manipulate the environment to ensure an optimal reward-to-punishment ratio. Avoiding punishment may be the most efficient means toward helping the child build confidence and trust in the beginning. Reinert (1980) listed the following five methods that do *not* work with reluctant children:

1. Forcing the child to become involved.
2. Embarrassing the child.
3. Ignoring the behavior.
4. Asking the child why he or she does not want to take part.
5. Comparing the child to other children. (p. 137)

Because a child's inhibited, withdrawn pattern can be a developmental pattern later associated with serious disturbance, it is imperative that teachers work closely with parents, counselors, and psychologists. When a child's severe reluctance persists after a couple of months of consciously structuring the environment and creating nonthreatening opportunities for involvement, the teacher should not hesitate to seek help. After giving the child a reasonable time to become adjusted, considering the child's age and previous experiences (or lack of them), the teacher takes careful observational notes. The teacher should study these carefully to see whether any progress is being made, and he or she should discuss minimal progress with the school psychologist or with some other mental health worker to determine whether additional evaluation or a change in programming is necessary.

USE OF REINFORCEMENT

Research suggests that lack of achievement may be related to children's failing to link acceptable performance with their own efforts or abilities. They may instead attribute their successes to chance, task ease, or powerful others (Cook, 1986). Given this tendency of some children to attribute successful performance to external causes, teachers must be extremely careful in phrasing their praise.

Give Credit Where Credit Is Due

The praise must describe in specific terms the behavior that the teacher wishes to have repeated either by the child being praised or by those who are watching at the time. Furthermore, the praise must give the child credit for his or her efforts or abilities. Consider these statements: "Danny, you should feel happy. You listened carefully to my directions and then tried to do exactly what you were asked to do." Such statements point out to others what behavior is expected at the same time Danny is helped to realize that his efforts are important. Note that effort rather than outcome was emphasized.

Young children, and especially young children with special needs, must be encouraged to focus on effort rather than on outcome. After all, they may be able to control their efforts even though successful outcomes are sometimes out of reach. Consider this statement: "Danny, I'm so glad you have a new hearing aid. You were able to follow my directions." Danny now feels that he could succeed because of the hearing aid, not necessarily because of his effort. He may or may not put forth effort in the future, especially once his hearing aid is no longer a novelty.

Minimize the Use of Negative Consequences

To minimize negative side effects of any form of punishment, teachers and parents must make careful efforts to control each child's **reward-to-punishment (R-P) ratio.** According to Kirkhart and Kirkhart (1972), rewards are considered to be any action or statement that builds a child's self-esteem or anything that makes the child feel good about himself or herself. Punishment may refer to any action or statement that decreases a child's self-esteem or makes him or her feel less worthy.

Kirkhart and Kirkhart (1972) clearly pointed out the importance of the reward-to-punishment ratio in the development of a healthy personality:

A reward to punishment ratio of five rewards for every one punishment is about optimal in guiding and directing a child's behavior. However, when the R-P ratio falls down to only two rewards for every one punishment, neurotic symptoms begin to develop, especially those of inferiority and inadequacy and a generalized fear of failure. (p. 152)

They further stated that predelinquent behavior is often observed in children whose reward-to-punishment ratio falls to one-to-one or below.

Observations of classrooms readily suggest that many teachers are unaware of the reward-to-punishment ratio they are using. This is especially a problem when a child does very little that merits reward and functions as if negative attention is better than none at all. To control the reward-to-punishment ratio, teachers must plan carefully to ensure that such children are attempting tasks for which their efforts can be rewarded.

Preventive observation is essential. When a teacher sees children begin to lose control or interest because of frustration, fatigue, or hunger, the teacher must quickly change the child's activity. The reward-to-punishment ratios can approach optimal levels by preventing punishment and by increasing reward. Teachers can develop special nonverbal signals such as a nod or a wink to be given as reminders to children who seem about to misbehave. Then immediate reward or reinforcement can be given when a child increases the effort to control his or her behavior.

Ignore Minor Disruptive Behaviors

Some irritating behaviors will disappear if they receive no attention or reward from anyone. Teachers must be astute observers. Even though a teacher may ignore a behavior, it does not mean that other children are not giving attention to it. Simply ignoring the

behavior will not work in such a situation. The child is getting attention of some kind and is possibly modeling inappropriate behavior for other children.

Some children will use troublesome four-letter words, stick out their tongues, or tap their tables merely to get a reaction from the teacher. Observant teachers usually guess when this is the case. Ignoring behavior can be effective as long as the teacher realizes that the child may go on until some kind of attention is given. The answer is to find a way to give the child positive attention. This can be done by directing the child into an activity while simultaneously ignoring the undesired behavior. Depending on the child, ignoring alone may just bring on more disruptive behavior.

Keep Negative Consequences to a Minimum

As discussed earlier, punishment needs to be kept to a minimum to assure a satisfactory reward-to-punishment ratio. Punishment is thought only to decrease the rate at which inappropriate behaviors occur and can also produce negative side effects such as fear, tension, and withdrawal. Any aggressive acts by an adult also provide undesirable models for children to imitate.

Punishment in the form of logical and natural consequences can have an informative effect if used wisely. Punishment that is part of rule setting in the classroom can be a natural consequence predicted by those who do not follow classroom rules. When linked directly to their behavior, they can see the relationship between their causative act and the resulting effect.

If children know that hitting others or otherwise fooling around during circle time will cause them to be asked to go to the time-out seat, then they will see the punishment as justified and directly caused by their behavior. They will not see the teacher as arbitrary or themselves as unresponsible for the outcome. They will know how to prevent the punishment in the future if the teacher has specifically stated why they were punished. The teacher might say, "Vicky, you must take time out. You have hit Susie and we cannot hurt others."

Walker and Shea (1999) offered the following guidelines to those who find it absolutely necessary to use punishment:

1. Specify and communicate the punishable behavior to the children by means of classroom rules for behavior.

2. Post the rules where the children can see them, and review them with the group frequently.

3. Provide models of acceptable behavior.

4. Apply the punishment immediately.

5. Apply the punishment consistently, not whimsically.

6. Be fair in using the punishment (what is good for Peter is good for Paul).

Of course, these rules have to be adapted for use with very young children. Picture symbols might be used instead of words when listing the rules. Walker and Shea also listed 14 reasons why teachers should avoid using either physical (spankings) or psychological (derogatory statements) punishment. Basically, other forms of behavior management are more effective and avoid damaging effects. More important, punishment bruises the already fragile developing self-images of children.

Punishment that is in any way derogatory or demeaning should be avoided at all costs. Only punishments that are logical, natural, and unattached to the child's person or personality should be used. Table 7–2 illustrates the importance of this suggestion. Acceptable punishments, when kept to a minimum and used as a last resort, include deprivation of privileges (including time out) and compensation for intentional wrongdoing such as picking up deliberately spilled puzzle pieces. It should be remembered, however, that any form of punishment should be administered with firm kindness to avoid becoming derogatory or demeaning.

SPECIAL CONSIDERATIONS FOR WORKING WITH CHILDREN WHO HAVE BEEN ABUSED AND NEGLECTED

Probably the single most important intervention strategy for children who have been abused and neglected is the establishment of a predictable and safe environment. Over a period of time, a responsive, predictable environment may provide the child with the support necessary to enable him or her to explore the physical environment as well as relationships with others. Earlier discussions of classroom routines, both

Table 7–2   Logical consequences versus punishment

The Behavior (What Happened)	Logical and Natural Consequence	Punishing the Personality
Child spills milk	Child clean up spill	"You are so clumsy." "Don't you ever watch what you're doing?" "You messed up again."
Child grabs another child's toy	Returns the toy	"You're a brat again." "Must you be so bad?" "You're always the selfish bully."
Child "forgot" to hang up coat	Hangs up coat	"Can't you remember anything?" "How many times have I told you. . . ?"
Child yells loudly in supermarket	Softly say, "Let's practice a soft voice." Return to market and practice being quiet	"Shut up; you're a bad girl." "Good girls are quiet in public." "I'll never take you to the store again."

◆ ◆ ◆

EXHIBIT 7–4

Recognizing Signs of Physical Abuse

1. Be alert for signs of sadness or anger, as well as bruises, burns, and cuts. Listen to what the children say. Be especially alert for changes in behavior that cannot be explained by impending illness or a happening at school. Begin *at once* to record specific details of your observations. Be certain to make a written note of the date, time, and manner of observation. These may be necessary if a report must be made to authorities. Keep these confidential and under lock and key.

2. Cigarette burns are usually round. Small round burns should always be investigated.

3. Bruises on legs and buttocks can be the result of falls. The frequency and the severity of the bruises are useful criteria. Even clumsy children stay unbruised most of the time. If the child is nearly always bruised, be suspicious.

4. Black eyes do result from bumping into things. So do bumps on heads. Again, the severity and the relative frequency of the bruises dictate the degree of teacher concern.

5. Little children usually "tell all," but even 3-year-olds can be frightened into lying about how they were hurt. It is not unusual for parents to tell little ones that if they say that mommy and daddy hurt them a big bad person will come and take them away. When this happens, the children's explanations are usually and obviously "dictated." If the story changes, be suspicious.

◆ ◆ ◆

EXHIBIT 7–5

Follow-Up

1. After a report to the proper authorities has been made, the teacher should seek help and guidance from the principal or the director of the school. Next steps with the parents should not be decided by the teacher alone. Home visits should be discontinued at least for some time. This is a needed safety precaution for both the teacher and the parents.

2. On subsequent visits, after conferences with persons who are competent to advise the teacher on what to do and how to do it, the teacher should not go alone to the home. An aide should accompany the teacher and should be alert to what is said. Confidential notes made by the teacher after the meeting should not become part of the child's file but should be kept in the teacher's personal possession. These can be destroyed when the need for them is ended.

3. Regardless of the nature or severity of the case, if the child continues to attend school, it is the teacher's responsibility to continue to try to encourage the parents to participate in parent meetings and volunteer at school. The teacher should have the help of persons trained and skilled in helping these parents. If the school or center does not offer this service, the teacher should insist on receiving it from some public or private source. Skill in teaching does not imply that the teacher must be all things to all people. Trying to be so can result in disaster.

in this chapter and in Chapter 6, provide important suggestions for designing and implementing predictable environments. Programs that depend primarily on children's own self-direction or that require children to accept major responsibility for their use of time may provide too much freedom and ambiguity for children who have been maltreated. For children with attachment disorders, it will be important to assign a **primary provider**—one person who is consistently available to the child to greet the child, assist with self-help skills, and especially to be available in moments of frustration and loss of control.

It is also important for children to learn how to influence people and events in appropriate and effective ways. Other important program goals for these children will be to assist them in learning how to self-control and to express and understand a wide range of emotions. Children who have been maltreated will often engage in disruptive behavior that interferes with the learning of others. Both punishment and sympathy should be minimized. The need for discipline should be prevented when possible. Coercion and power struggles should be avoided. When negative consequences are necessary, they should be predictable, consistent, mild, and brief.

Discipline should be carried out in an affectively neutral environment so that positive expressions are not paired with negative consequences. Children who have been abused and neglected often receive mixed messages from caregivers. For example, a parent may be physically abusive one moment and overly solicitous the next, or the parent may assume a false sweetness to induce the child to comply or perform some task. Thus, a teacher should not apply a discipline strategy such as removal from an activity while at the same time saying something positive such as "You know I love you very much."

In addition, staff members should be clear and consistent in their expression of such emotions as happiness, sadness, or fatigue. This will assist the child who has been maltreated in understanding human emotions and will provide models for the child's expression of his or her own emotions.

Cicchetti and Toth (1987) have emphasized the importance of a **transactional model of interven-**tion for maltreating families. In a transactional model, all elements of the system (i.e., child, family, and environment) are viewed as exerting reciprocal influences on one another. A transactional model does not isolate one element of the system, such as the child, for intervention. Rather, such a model attends to all components of the dysfunctional family system, including child, family, and environmental characteristics. Thus it will be necessary for the classroom teacher to work in close collaboration with other team members and social service agencies to meet the many needs of the child who has been maltreated and his or her family. Exhibits 7–4 and 7–5 provide information on recognizing signs of physical abuse and following up after a case of abuse has been reported.

SPECIAL NEEDS OF CHILDREN INFLUENCED BY PRENATAL SUBSTANCE ABUSE

Unfortunately, terms such as *drug babies, crack babies,* and *crack kids* have almost become household words in our society. It is important for early educators to avoid using these highly pejorative labels, which reveal virtually nothing about an individual child's characteristics or developmental patterns. It is also important for professionals in this field to be careful to avoid stereotyping these children and to understand and express the complexity of the problems associated with this population. The following is a summary of issues and concerns presented by Poulsen (1989):

1. While the maternal use of drugs during pregnancy places the fetus at risk, there is no one-to-one relationship between either type of drug or frequency of use and the child's developmental outcome.

2. The developmental outcome of infants who have been exposed to drugs prenatally may range from no or little effect to significant developmental, learning, behavioral, or psychosocial problems. Other factors that influence outcome

include inherent vulnerability of the fetus, prenatal care and nutrition, gestational age at time of drug exposure, and additional prenatal and perinatal risk factors such as maternal infection.

3. The developmental outcome is affected as much by the postnatal social environment as it is by the original perinatal insult. Group homes and multiple placements can also provide compounding psychosocial risks.

4. Children prenatally exposed to drugs, as a group, are neither homogeneous nor unique. Many of the characteristics of these children are similar to those of other children labeled as high risk, including those who were born prematurely or small for gestational age (SGA).

5. Since these children are more like other at-risk children than they are a separate category, programs should *not* be designed that segregate and label them.

6. All children at biological risk will be more vulnerable to adverse environments than non-risk children will be. Many natural and foster mothers cannot meet the needs of these children for predictable, consistent, and responsive caregiving without special intervention support.

7. If the child is placed in foster care, there should be only one placement until reunification with the natural parents or relinquishment takes place.

8. Substance-abusing parents will often have many additional life stresses that interfere with parenting, such as drug recovery, poverty, housing issues, and domestic violence.

9. The problems of the infant who has been exposed to drugs prenatally and his or her family are complex and must be addressed via a collaborative interagency team.

Fetal Alcohol Syndrome

One substance which is clearly related to an identifiable long-term outcome is alcohol. Phelps and Grabowski (1992) found that children born to women who are chronically alcoholic manifest many of the following symptoms:

1. Deficiency in both prenatal and postnatal growth.

2. Facial malformations such as microcephaly, short palbebral (eye) fissures, fronto-nasal alterations, thin upper vermilion (lip) border, flat midface, and hypoplastic maxilla and/or mandible (jaw).

3. Central nervous system effects, such as cognitive disability, motor problems, tremulousness, and/or hyperactivity.

This syndrome is referred to as **fetal alcohol syndrome.** In order for a diagnosis of fetal alcohol syndrome (FAS) to be made, a child must demonstrate symptoms from all three categories (Phelps & Grabowski, 1992). A child who exhibits some of these features but not enough to be diagnosed with FAS is referred to as demonstrating **fetal alcohol effects (FAE).**

Studies comparing the performance on intelligence tests of children exposed to alcohol in utero versus unexposed children found that the exposed group obtained lower scores than the non-exposed group (Coles et al., 1991; Conry, 1990). However, those exposed children who were *not* diagnosed as FAS scored within the "average" range.

*Characteristics of Infants and Young Children Prenatally Influenced by Drugs**

Babies who have been exposed to substances prenatally may have regulatory difficulties (Chasnoff, Lewis, Griffith, & Willey, 1989) such as poor eating and sleeping patterns. Some may be hypersensitive to touch, sound, and light. They are easily overstimulated and difficult to soothe. Some may lack organized responses to environmental stimuli and have poor arousal, depressed interactive abilities, and few vocalizations. Still others display tremors, decreased quality of movement, and hypertonia. As discussed earlier,

*The authors wish to thank Carol Cole, Early Intervention Specialist, Los Angeles United Public Schools, for contributing the essence of this section.

Greenspan's model suggests that these characteristics affect parent-infant attachment and how an infant learns about people, objects, and events in the world.

The variety of drugs used, amount and time of use during pregnancy, and individual constitution all influence fetal outcome. Many children who have been exposed to drugs prenatally have also been abused and/or neglected. The characteristics presented in the previous section on maltreatment may also be present in these children (Weston, Ivins, Zuckerman, Jones, & Lopez, 1989). Fetal development may also be affected by other toxic substances, such as alcohol, and some infants may experience developmental and learning problems due to lead poisoning. These conditions will be discussed in Chapter 10.

While there is no typical profile of children prenatally exposed to drugs, there seems to be a developmental continuum of vulnerabilities that persist into the preschool years. Some children are identified as having moderate to severe disabilities before 3 years of age. They often receive early intervention services through programs developed for children with disabilities. However, other children who were prenatally exposed appear to be typical in their acquisition of major developmental milestones during the first 3 years of life.

Some children display fine motor difficulties. Many children appear disorganized. They seem unable to focus on classroom tasks and are impulsive and easily distracted. Such children may eventually be labeled as having learning disabilities or attention deficits.

Children who have been prenatally drug exposed may be chronically irritable. Often how they try to soothe themselves may not be seen as acceptable classroom behavior. For example, a child may simply remove himself or herself from an ongoing classroom activity, even when there is a teacher directing the activity. Some of these children insist on carrying an object with them wherever they go, often manipulating and twisting it. Others may tap their fingers, jiggle their feet, or suck their thumbs when they are overly stressed. These behaviors do not have to be stopped before an activity can proceed.

During the preschool years, regulatory difficulties may persist. Some children continue to be easily overstimulated and often have difficulty modulating their behavior. For example, giggles can turn into uncontrolled laughter, pleasant moods into sullen ones, independence into extreme dependence. Particularly in the area of social-emotional development, these children may show delays and exaggerated reactions to events. For example, they often display more difficulty with transitions within the school day (e.g., changes in routine and changes in staff) than is expected for children their age.

While a subgroup of children who have been prenatally exposed to drugs do appear to exhibit the characteristics just described, it is important for the early childhood educator to realize that *most* prenatally exposed children do not present this picture (Chasnoff, Griffith, Freier, & Murray, 1992; Cohen & Erwin, 1994). A recent study compared the behavioral and social characteristics of exposed and non-exposed preschool children in special education programs. Over half of the exposed children were indistinguishable from non-exposed children. Only 25% of the exposed children displayed behaviors resembling the extremely difficult behavioral profiles usually attributed to these children (Cohen & Erwin, 1994). It is also the case that the research describing the effects of prenatal drug exposure is often methodologically flawed because of the difficulty controlling for the environmental factors which often co-occur with drug exposure (Carta, et al, 1994). These include factors such as poor prenatal nutrition, prematurity and birth complications, maternal attachment problems, and multiple placements. A longitudinal study of literacy development of young, cocaine-exposed children was reported by Barone (1993). The majority of these children followed the normal course of early literacy development. Exceptions were those children who experienced traumatic events such as child sexual abuse and serious illness. It was concluded that " . . . children who are in stable, emotionally supportive families, regardless of their prenatal drug history, appear to be developing into literate individuals" (p. 3).

According to Neuspiel (1991), no independent long-term effects of prenatal drug exposure (other than alcohol) have been conclusively demonstrated. "In light of this fact the labeling of these children is completely unwarranted" (Schutter & Brinker, 1992). Much research remains to be done in this area. However, it continues to be clear that whatever the effects of prenatal exposure to drugs, the childrearing environment is of critical importance in the outcome of these children. (Hawley & Disney, 1992)

Classroom Strategies for Managing Children Who Have Been Influenced by Prenatal Exposure to Drugs

There are several strategies that can be very helpful in working with young children who have been influenced by prenatal drug exposure. The strategies are useful for many children with special needs.

1. Be aware of the kinds of situations and events that trigger inappropriate behaviors:
   - Inconsistent, unstructured environments
   - New situations
   - Overstimulation
   - Internal changes, such as illness or extreme fatigue

2. When misbehavior occurs attempt to understand what triggers the behavior as well as what consequences may be maintaining the behavior.

3. Increase predictability and consistency in classroom routines. Prepare children for what comes next.

4. Avoid making cognitive and social demands that are far beyond the developmental level of the child.

5. Provide extra support during new or difficult tasks; teach in small steps.

6. Reduce unnecessary stimulation, especially background noise.

7. Respect children's play and work space by keeping unnecessary interruptions at a minimum.

8. Limit the number of rules; communicate them clearly and enforce them consistently.

9. Expect setbacks and regressions; be aware that home events, particularly family or neighborhood violence, caregiver changes, and dependency court dates, can have a major impact on children's behavior and learning.

Use of the above strategies, over time, strengthens children's self-control and sense of mastery over the environment.

Additional Considerations for Working with Children Influenced by Prenatal Exposure to Drugs

It is important for professionals to avoid stereotyping and labeling children who have been exposed to drugs. Each child is unique. Without stigmatizing labels, many prenatally drug-exposed children might not be thought of as different from other normally developing children. When providing services for this population of children, care must be taken to suspend moral judgments as to why they are at risk. However, it is important to understand each child's past experiences. After birth, the infant may be moved abruptly to a foster home. Frequent changes of caregivers are the rule rather than the exception for this population. Often, just as attachment and trust begin to develop, the infant is moved again, increasing mistrust and behavioral unpredictability. Young children being raised in group care with multiple caregivers can show a decrease in appropriate use of adults for support and indiscriminate expressions of affection. Languishing in the court system until permanent placement is determined can delay them from receiving the kind of stable environment they need for optimal growth. Children who have been maltreated often have similar early experiences with multiple caregivers and dependency court processes.

By the time these children reach preschool age, the short 1,095 days since birth often have been complicated by environmental instability. Children have feelings about these experiences that must be acknowledged as real, important, and legitimate by the early intervention staff. It is important to remember that children behave and misbehave for a reason, even if it cannot be figured out. In responding to misbehavior, the first priority should be to acknowledge what the child seems to want and feel before dealing with the misbehavior. Doing so allows the child to recognize that feelings are real and valid. Being understood facilitates self-esteem and promotes a willingness to function within prescribed limits.

Developing a working home-school partnership in which professionals share their expertise but also listen to what caregivers want and need is essential. Through this partnership, the teacher learns an individual child's story. As with children who have been maltreated, a team-based, transactional approach is crucial to working with these families. Family, child, and environmental characteristics are all interrelated, and they *must* be viewed as a system. Caregivers who continue to use drugs may have little energy for meeting the needs of their children. Drug addiction is all-consuming. Caregivers may be enslaved by both the physical addiction and their debilitating lifestyle.

Viewing children within the larger ecological system helps teachers frame reality when engaging in mutual discussions with them. They should let the child's history and actions guide the kind and intensity of reassurance, support, and intervention to be provided. Children who have experienced disrupted attachment or sudden changes in caregivers will test limits repeatedly. Their background must be remembered when teachers respond. Isolating a child for misbehavior may convey the wrong message. Teachers may be more successful dealing with these episodes if they recognize when children may be

seeking reassurance that they will not be removed. If a child's home placement is to be changed, teachers can help by preparing the child emotionally for the move and by providing support to the receiving caregivers. Maintaining a child's early education placement during such moves may be of great assistance. Acknowledging reality validates the child's experience and feelings while enhancing his or her ability to deal with whatever stress reality brings. Ignoring a child's reality will not make it go away.

In working with this population, as with children who have been maltreated, it is important to accept the child and family as having unique strengths and needs. Most are doing the best they can. The solution is not to be punitive or to demand that the child catch up quickly, but to work with the child and the family. Early childhood special educators can make a difference, even though the problem is great. It is important to remember that while we may not be able to remediate organic deficits caused by prenatal exposure to drugs or inoculate children against adverse childrearing conditions, we can create intervention services for children and families that can significantly improve children's self-esteem, self-control, and ability to solve problems in the real world.

As thoroughly discussed in this chapter, children who have developed healthy self-concepts through nurturing environments will develop more readily in all areas. The next chapter will, however, outline the concerns most essential to the promotion of motor skills.

Summary

This chapter provided an overview of the essential elements of a home and school climate conducive to developing healthy personalities. Some of Erikson's (1963) growth stages were reviewed to emphasize the interaction between forces within the child and conditions from without. These necessitate early warmth and consistency in caregiving, encouraging

autonomy within reasonable guidelines, and developing initiative tempered with gentle direction.

More recent theory proposed by Greenspan has described five major stages of emotional development: self-regulation, attachment, intentional communication, an organized sense of self, and emotional thinking. Greenspan stressed the importance of a responsive environment and the infant's need to learn to express and recognize a wide range of human emotions. Using a Piagetian framework, such cognitive milestones as intentionality and pretend play assume important roles in affective growth.

The essential blocks that build a growth-producing environment were illustrated and described. Teachers were urged to prevent inappropriate behaviors by building security through the use of a number of behavioristically oriented principles, including establishing limits, routines, variety, constructive consequences, avoidance of frustration, behavior modeling, and opportunities for appropriately expressing feelings.

Some children arrive at preschools and child care centers with behaviors and emotional characteristics that interfere with learning. They may be too active or too withdrawn. They may be impulsive. Some are overly dependent on adults for direction, whereas others refuse all directions from their teachers. Techniques for working with unique ways of behav-

ing were suggested. These range from effectively using time out to using puppets and play. Throughout, the role of positive reinforcement and appropriate modeling of behavior was emphasized. Enhancing self-esteem is an ever-present goal.

Guidelines were offered to assist teachers in creating an environment that fosters the development of spontaneous play behavior considered to be essential in the development of emotional well-being.

The final section addressed the characteristics and needs of children who have been abused and neglected and/or influenced prenatally by exposure to drugs or alcohol. Issues and concerns related to the dangers of stereotyping and labeling these children were presented, and the complexity of problems and circumstances related to these children and their families were described. Specific behavioral and learning characteristics observed in some of these children were considered, as were specific teaching and intervention strategies.

Discussion Topics and Activities

1. Make a list of necessary center limits or rules. Be certain that each is definable, reasonable, and enforceable. Role play the explanation of these limits to determine whether they are indeed definable.

2. List and discuss any special adaptations that will have to be made in classroom structure and management for children with disabilities.

3. Develop a workable classroom schedule that provides a balance between active and passive involvement, experiences that require visual attention, those that necessitate auditory attention, and group and individual activities. Exchange constructive criticism with classmates.

4. Make a chart of as many natural and logical consequences for behavioral difficulties as you can think of. Keep the chart handy. Observations in classrooms should help you expand your list. A review of one of Dreikurs's excellent books will

convince you of the importance of these alternatives to punishment.

5. Role play how you would deal with a parent who insists his or her child should settle arguments by fighting.

6. Try to identify toys that might be frustrating to some children. Make a list of these toys and the types of children who might have difficulty with them.

7. Develop a repertoire of techniques to effect smooth transitions. Role play some of these with classmates.

8. Study one of the many excellent texts on behavior management techniques. Conduct a behavior management project to increase or decrease a designated behavior. Report the results of your project in graphic form to your classmates.

9. Visit a school supply center or obtain catalogs from toy companies. Develop a list of "social" toys and a list of "isolate" toys. Share with your classmates in the development of a master list for all to keep.

10. Observe children engaged in pretend play. Describe the range of emotions expressed.

11. Observe the caregiver-infant interaction of three dyads. Identify the stage of emotional development of each infant. Cite the behavioral evidence for your conclusions.

Annotated Bibliography

Developing a Healthy Personality

Chess, S., & Thomas, A. (1996). *Temperament: Theory and practice.* New York: Brunner-Mazel.

This comprehensive volume contains the wisdom of decades of research and clinical practice. It stresses the importance of dynamic, interactive understanding of temperamental and environmental factors, with particular emphasis on the "goodness of fit" between parents and children. Of particular interest are the sections on understanding temperament in infancy and toddlerhood and in the child with disabilities. Methods of assessment, intervention, and handling difficult children are most valuable.

Erikson, E. H. (1993). *Childhood and society.* New York: W. W. Norton.

Erikson, E. H. (1971). A healthy personality for every child. In R. H. Anderson & H. G. Shane (Eds.), *As the twig is bent: Readings in early childhood education.* Boston: Houghton Mifflin.

These readings contain original source material offering the reader a glimpse of Erikson's eight stages of man that are considered to be the impetus for much of today's lifespan research. The 1971 reference is extremely well written and a fascinating digest of a major contribution to the understanding of children's emotional development.

Greenspan, S., & Greenspan, N. T. (1994). *First feelings: Milestones in the emotional development of your baby and child.* New York: Viking Penguin.

This book is written primarily for parents of children from birth to 4 years of age. It presents the stages of emotional development as conceptualized by child psychiatrist Stanley Greenspan. The book describes how to recognize key stages of a child's emotional growth and how to enhance and support that growth. It also includes examples of strategies for optimally supporting the development of infants who vary in neurophysiological make-up (such as the hyperresponsive infant) and temperament.

Greenspan, S. I., & Weider, S. (1998). *The child with special needs: Encouraging intellectual and emotional growth.* Reading, MA: Addison-Wesley.

The authors have integrated their research and clinical experience into a guide for those who work with children exhibiting developmental problems. They offer a unique understanding of challenges such as autism, language and speech delays, Down syndrome, cerebral palsy, and ADD. They offer techniques to help children with disabilities reach key milestones through playful interactions. The recommendations are illustrated through case studies that reflect compassionate understanding of the stresses and rewards involved in raising a child with special needs.

Hendrick, J. (1996). *The whole child: Developmental education for the early years.* Upper Saddle River, NJ: Merrill/Prentice Hall.

This comprehensive textbook offers sound philosophy and practical suggestions in a number of critical areas for teachers of young children. Of particular interest are the sections on nourishing emotional health and fostering social development. Topics such as self-esteem, helping children master emotional crises, what to do about aggression, and the establishment of self-discipline are addressed. An overview chapter on working with exceptional children is also included.

Zeanah, C. H. (Ed.) (1993). *Handbook of infant mental health.* New York: Guilford Publications.

This book will serve as a comprehensive resource to a wide variety of professionals interested in infant mental health. It thoroughly covers models of development, risk conditions and protective factors, and social policy considerations, along with assessment, evaluation, and diagnosis for children from birth to 3 years of age.

Promoting Positive Social and Emotional Development

Brenner, A. (1997). *Helping children cope with stress.* Lexington, MA: Jossey-Bass Publishers.

Given the assumption that the range of everyday stressors children experience has broadened, this book seeks to provide caregivers both understanding and techniques to enable children to cope more effectively. A variety of viewpoints and strategies is presented for the reader to adapt to children's specific needs. Situations discussed range from low-level stress to more acute stresses such as abuse, parental alcoholism, divorce, and death. It is a well-organized, useful reference book.

Eddowes, E. A., & Ralph, K. S. (1998). *Interactions for development and learning: Birth through eight years.* Upper Saddle River, NJ: Merrill/Prentice Hall.

These authors articulate ways that positive interactions are related to each area of child development. Activities that promote positive interactions are offered according to six age groups within the early childhood range. New teachers will appreciate the practical applications.

Essa, E. (1998). *A practical guide to solving preschool behavioral problems.* Albany, NY: Delmar.

This "how-to" manual uses a situational approach for solving specific behavior problems that commonly occur in the preschool setting. Each behavior is discussed in a separate chapter, with step-by-step recommendations provided to correct the problem. The reader is encouraged to consider the influences of developmental, environmental, and health factors on children's behavior.

Hanson, M. (1994). Substance abuse and early intervention. *Topics in early childhood special education, 14*(2), 1–291 (entire issue).

This issue is devoted to examining a number of important issues around the topic of infants and young children who are prenatally drug exposed. Two articles offer excellent literature reviews. Both of these emphasize the extent to which child outcomes are mediated by environmental variables. In addition there are articles that document the wide range of behavioral and social characteristics of preschool children who have been prenatally exposed, as well as articles that make policy recommendations related to meeting the needs of these children and their families.

Hendrick, J. (1997). *Total learning: Developmental curriculum for the young child.* Upper Saddle River, NJ: Merrill/Prentice Hall.

The in-depth text helps the reader to more fully understand regular early childhood education. It introduces a developmentally based curriculum emphasizing multicultural/mul-tiethnic education. The chapters on play, designing a supportive environment, achieving emotional and interpersonal competence, and the sense of self are of particular interest.

Hildebrand, V. (1998). *Guiding young children.* Upper Saddle River, NJ: Merrill/Prentice Hall.

This book is designed for students who are learning to communicate and interact with young children. Readers learn how to handle ordinary daily routines to cope with behavior problems, and to guide children toward self-direction. One section is devoted to the mainstreaming of young children with disabilities.

Honig, A. S. (1986). Stress and coping in children. *Young Children, 41*(4), 50–63; (6), 47–59.

This most welcome two-part review of research examines the components and stages of stress in young children. Research findings are used to illustrate varieties of intrapersonal, ecological, catastrophic, and interpersonal stress factors in the lives of children. Some measures of stress are also given. Of greatest value are the suggestions offered to help caregivers recognize, prevent, and alleviate child stress while enhancing children's coping skills.

Johnson, D. W., & Johnson, R. T. (1994). *Learning together and alone: Cooperation, competition, and individualization.* Englewood Cliffs, NJ: Allyn & Bacon.

Although this is an older book, it still fosters the current interest in engaging children in cooperative learning. The basic principles are adaptable to all age levels and to almost any school situation. The advantages of cooperative over competitive or individualized learning activities are clearly supported by research. Cooperative learning experiences appear to promote far more positive interaction between children with disabilities and those without than do more traditional approaches to classroom structure. The essential components and implementation steps of cooperative learning are presented by Johnson and Johnson in the April 1986 edition of *Exceptional Children.*

Kauffman, J. M. (1996). *Characteristics of emotional and behavioral disorders of children and youth.* Upper Saddle River, NJ: Merrill/Prentice Hall.

This text is designed to provide insight into the problems and characteristics of children who are emotionally disturbed. It is intended for the student interested in theory and research related to behavioral disorders. Although it is not a "how-to" methods book, there are examples of how to control disruptive behavior throughout the book.

Katz, L. G. & McClellan, D. E. (1997). *Fostering children's social competence.* Washington, DC.: National Association for the Education of Young Children.

This volume gives an overview of young children's developing social competence and offers suggestions on how teachers can actively support it. Many examples and vignettes illustrate principles and strategies to strengthen children's social skills. It also discusses common practices such as continual praise and heavy reliance on time-out that actually undermine the development of social competence.

Marion, M. (1995). *Guidance of young children.* Upper Saddle River, NJ: Merrill/Prentice Hall.

This well-written, brief paperback is based on the assumption that adults want to help children learn to control themselves; to like and value themselves; and to be humane, caring, competent, independent, assertive, cooperative, and helpful. The child, the adults in his or her life, and the environment are considered the essential components in the guidance system. The book is enormously helpful to anyone involved in early childhood education. It is soundly based on theory and research while offering a great variety of well-received practical suggestions for guiding young children.

Marion, M. (1997). Guiding young children's understanding and management of anger. *Young Children 52*(7), 62–67.

This review of research addressed three basic questions: What do we know about the development of children's feelings and expression of anger, what factors contribute to the management of anger and how can caregivers assist children to express their feelings in nonaggressive ways? Readers will appreciate the amount of wisdom presented in few pages.

Morris, L. R., & Shulz, L. (1989). *Creative play activities for children with disabilities.* Champaign, IL: Human Kinetics Books.

This book includes 250 games and activities designed to help children from infancy through age 7 grow through play. Many activities incorporate special adaptations for children with visual, hearing, emotional, and mental challenges.

Musselwhite, C. R. (1986). *Adaptive play for special needs children.* Austin, TX: Pro-Ed.

All categories of disability are addressed in this practical and comprehensive resource book. The primary focus is on the therapeutic and educational value of play for children and adolescents with disabilities. The author surveys empirical research and theoretical articles and discusses the practical applications of the theory, giving specific play strategies to meet specific goals. Methods of organizing toy lending libraries, adaptive toy workshops, annotated bibliographies, and a resource list make this a highly valuable reference book.

Neisworth, J. T., & Fewell, R. R. (Eds.) (1991). Emerging trends for child behavior disorders. *Topics in early childhood special education, 11*(2), 1–103 (entire issue).

This issue is devoted to examining current issues, trends, and strategies related to the prevention and management of behavior problems in young children. Articles address topics such as management of behavior problems through appropriate arrangement of the caregiving environment; examination of the effects of a play-based developmental intervention program on children with behavior disorders; effects of self-monitoring on on-task behavior of preschool children; parents as partners in treating behavior problems, and management of children with ADHD.

Reynolds, E. (1995). *Guiding young children: A child-centered approach.* Mountain View, CA: Mayfield.

This text provides child-care providers with practical problem-solving techniques that exclude the use of punishment, blame, or guilt. It focuses on the importance of environment first and then progresses to listening skills, negotiating, and setting limits. Examples and case studies are included.

Schutter, L. S., & Brinker, R. P. (1992). Conjuring a new category of disability from prenatal cocaine exposure: Are the infants unique biological or caretaking casualties? *Topics in Early Childhood Special Education, 11*(4), 84–111.

This is an important article which questions the appropriateness of labeling children who have been prenatally exposed to cocaine. The article briefly reviews the research literature and discusses the methodological difficulties that characterize the research. The authors discuss the importance of and barriers to establishing partnerships with parents of young children who have been drug exposed. The article also includes a good overview of intervention approaches and stresses the importance of ecologically valid interventions designed specifically with reference to the needs of each family.

Smith, G. H., Coles, C. D., Poulsen, M. K., & Cole, C. K. (1995). *Children, families, and substance abuse: Challenges for changing educational and social outcomes.* Baltimore, MD: Paul H. Brookes.

This carefully researched text provides early education professionals with accurate information and innovative strategies to help children reach their full potential. It includes compelling case studies and emphasizes collaborative service delivery.

Sparks, S. (1992). *Children of prenatal substance abuse.* San Diego, CA: Singular Press.

A guide for professionals who work with children exposed prenatally to alcohol and cocaine. Helpful prevention, assessment, and intervention strategies are included. Points are illustrated through case studies. Readers are assisted by the charts that illustrate physical and behavioral characteristics.

Strain, P. S., & Hemmeter, M. L. (1997). Keys to being successful when confronted with challenging behaviors. *Young Exceptional Children, 1* (1) 2–8.

Very practical suggestions are offered to assist professionals to define challenging behaviors, become more comfortable with how to effectively react to challenges, understand how the challenging behavior "works" for the child, and how to prevent such behaviors. Specific preventive suggestions on how to modify the physical environment, daily schedules, and activities are included.

Streissguth, A. (1997). *Fetal alcohol syndrome: A guide for families and communities.* Baltimore, MD: Brookes Publishing Co.

The author anthologizes 25 years of her research with potent case studies, photos, and empirical data. This readable and informative guidebook offers understanding and techniques for working with those who experience fetal alcohol syndrome and fetal alcohol effects.

Columbus Trawick-Smith, J. W. (1994). *Interactions in the classroom: Facilitating play in the early years.* Columbus, OH: Merrill/Prentice-Hall.

Here is a book that focuses on the role teachers have in children's play. It shows future educators how to construct a play-based curriculum. Children are expected to guide their own learning while teachers serve as play facilitators. Early childhood curriculum is defined as a way of interacting with children as much as it is a collection of lessons or learning materials.

USA Toy Library Association, 5940 W. Touhy Avenue, Chicago, IL.

This is a rather new organization designed to provide play experiences and materials that stimulate growth and development. Individual and institutional memberships are available. Members receive monthly newsletters detailing new toys and toys adapted for children with special needs. Included are a toy library operator's manual, discounts on toy purchases, an annual membership meeting, and workshops on toy library operations, therapeutic play, and intervention programs.

Walker, J. E., & Shea, T. M. (1999). *Behavior management: A practical approach for educators.* Upper Saddle River, NJ: Merrill/Prentice Hall.

The specific purpose of this text "was to provide experienced teachers, teachers-in-training, and paraprofessionals with a guide for the application of behavior modification techniques in special and general educational settings" (p. ix). The authors have managed to translate the often misunderstood principles of behavior modification into classroom practices readily usable by practitioners. This is a handy tool for those wishing to become more-effective managers of behavior.

Zeitlin, S., & Williamson, G. G. (1994). *Coping in young children: Early intervention practices to enhance adaptive behavior and resilience.* Baltimore, MD: Paul H. Brookes.

These authors provide a resource that explores how to help children cope more effectively by promoting social interaction, self-initiation, regulation of emotions, problem solving, and generalization of learning. It is a step-by-step, comprehensive guide to implementing early intervention services with a coping perspective. Intervention practices are recommended for difficulties such as low frustration tolerance, limited task persistence, and hyperactivity.

References

Ainsworth, M. D. (1973). The development of infant-mother attachment. In B. M. Caldwell & H. Riciutti (Eds.), *Review of child development research* (Vol. 3, pp. 1–94). Chicago: University of Chicago Press.

Ainsworth, M. D., & Wittig, B. A. (1969). Attachment and exploratory behavior in one-year-olds in a strange situation. In B. M. Foss (Ed.), *Determinants of infant behavior* (Vol. 4, pp. 129–173). London: Metheum.

Bailey, E. W. (Ed.). (1978). *Ongoing data collection in the classroom.* Seattle, WA: Western States Technical Assistance Resource.

Barone, D. (1993, June). Literacy development of children prenatally exposed to crack/cocaine. *Perinatal Addiction Research and Education Update,* pp. 2–4.

Biehler, R. F., & Snowman, J. (1996). *Psychology applied to teaching.* Boston: Houghton Mifflin.

Blackham, G. J. (1968). *The deviant child in the classroom.* Belmont, CA: Wadsworth.

Blackman, J. A., Westervelt, V. D., Stevenson, R., & Welch, A. (1991). Management of preschool children with attention deficit-hyperactivity disorder. *Topics in Early Childhood Special Education, 11*(2), 91–104.

Bricker, D. D. (1978). A rationale for the integration of hand-icapped and nonhandicapped preschool children. In M.J. Guralnick (Ed.), *Early intervention and integra-tion of handicapped and nonhandicapped children.* Baltimore: University Park Press.

Bromwich, R. (1997). *Working with parents and infants: An interactional approach.* Baltimore: University Park Press.

Caldwell, B. M. (1977). Aggression and hostility in young chil-dren. *Young Children, 32,* 4-13.

Carta, J. J., Sideridis, G., Rinkel, P., Guimaraes, S., Grenwood, C., Baggett, K., Peterson, P., Atwater, J., McEvoy, M., & McConnell, S. (1994). Behavioral outcomes of young children prenatally exposed to illicit drugs: Review and analysis of experimental literature. *Topics in Early Childhood Special Education, 14*(2), 184-216.

Cavallaro, C. C., Haney, M., & Cabello, B. (1993). Developmentally appropriate strategies for promoting full participation in early childhood settings. *Topics in Early Childhood Special Education, 13*(3), 292-307.

Chandler, L. (1998). Promoting positive interaction between preschool-age children during free play: The Pals Center. *Young Exceptional Children, 2*(2), 14-19.

Chasnoff, I. J., Lewis, D. E., Griffith, D. R., & Willey, S. (1989). Cocaine and pregnancy: Clinical and toxicological im-plications for the neonate. *Clinical Chemistry, 35,* 1276-1278.

Chasnoff, I. J., Griffith, D. R., Freier, C., & Murray, J. (1992). Cocaine/polydrug use in pregnancy: Two-year follow-up. *Pediatrics, 89,* 284-289.

Cherry, C. (1976). *Creative play for the developing child.* Belmont, CA: Fearon.

Cicchetti, D., & Toth, S. L. (1987). The application of a trans-actional risk model to intervention with multi-risk mal-treating families. *Zero-to-Three, 7*(5), 1-8.

Cohen, S., & Erwin, E. J. (1994). Characteristics of children with prenatal drug exposure being served in preschool special education programs in New York City. *Topics in Early Childhood Special Education, 14*(2), 232-253.

Coles, C. D., Brown, R. T., Smith, I. E., Platzman, K. A., Erickson, S., & Falek, A. (1991). Effects of prenatal alcohol expo-sure at school age. I. Physical and cognitive develop-ment. *Neurotoxicology and Teratology, 13,* 357-367.

Connor, F. P., Williamson, G. G., & Siepp, J. M. (1978). *Program guide for infants and toddlers with neuromotor and other developmental disabilities.* New York: Teachers College Press.

Conry, J. (1990). Neuropsychological deficits in fetal alcohol syndrome and fetal alcohol effects. *Alcoholism: Clinical and Experimental Research, 14,* 650-655.

Cook, R. E. (1986). Motivating children to succeed. *Santa Clara, 28,* 7-10.

Erikson, E. H. (1963, 1993). *Childhood and society.* New York: Norton.

Erikson, E. H. (1971). A healthy personality for every child. In R. H. Anderson & H. G. Shane (Eds.), *As the twig is bent.* Boston: Houghton Mifflin.

Fewell, R. R. (1984). *Play assessment scale.* Seattle, WA: University of Washington Press.

Fraiberg, S. (1974). Blind infants and their mothers: An ex-amination of the sign system. In M. Lewis & L. Rosenblum (Eds.), *The effect of the infant on its care-givers.* New York: Wiley.

Greenspan, S. I. (1988, September). Fostering emotional and social development in infants with disabilities. *Zero-to-Three, 9*(1), 8-18.

Greenspan, S. I. (1990, September). An intensive approach to a toddler with emotional, motor and language delays: A case report. *Zero-to-Three, 1*(1), 20-26.

Greenspan, S. I. (1992). *Infancy and early childhood: The practice of clinical assessment and intervention with emotional and developmental challenges.* Madison, CT: International Universities Press.

Greenspan, S. I., & Greenspan, N. T. (1985). *First feelings: Milestones in the emotional development of your baby and child from birth to age four.* New York: Viking Penguin.

Greenspan, S. I. & Weider, S. (1998). *The child with special needs: Encouraging intellectual and emotional growth.* Reading, MA: Addison-Wesley.

Guralnick, M. J. (1993). Developmentally appropriate prac-tice in the assessment and intervention of children's peer relations. *Topics in Early Childhood Special Education, 13*(3), 344-371.

Guralnick, M. J. & Neville, B. (1997). Designing early inter-vention programs to promote children's social compe-tence. In M. J. Guralnick (Ed.), *The effectiveness of early intervention* (pp. 579-610). Baltimore, MD: Paul H. Brookes.

Hawley, T. L., & Disney, E. R. (1992). Crack's children: The consequences of maternal cocaine abuse. *Society for Research in Child Development Social Policy Report, 6*(4), 1-22.

Hewett, F. M. (1968). *The emotionally disturbed child in the classroom.* Boston: Allyn and Bacon.

Hewett, F. M., & Taylor, F. D. (1980). *The emotionally dis-turbed child in the classroom.* (2nd ed.) Boston: Allyn and Bacon.

Jones, H. A., & Rapport, M. J. (1997). "Research to Practice in Inclusive Early Childhood Education," *Teaching Exceptional Children, Vol. 30,* no. 2, pp. 57-61.

Kauffman, J. M. (1985). *Characteristics of children's behav-ior disorders.* Upper Saddle River, NJ: Merrill/Prentice Hall.

Kirkhart, R., & Kirkhart, E. (1972). The bruised self: Mending in early years. In K. Yamamoto (Ed.), *The child and his image* (pp. 121–177). Boston: Houghton Mifflin.

Linder, T. (1993). *Transdisciplinary play-based assessment: A functional approach to working with young children.* Baltimore: Paul H. Brookes.

Lyons-Ruth, K., Connell, D. B., Zoll, D., & Stahl, J. (1987). Infants and social risk: Relations among infant maltreatment, maternal behavior and infant attachment behavior. *Developmental Psychology, 123*(2), 223–232.

Marion, M. (1995). *Guidance of young children.* Upper Saddle River, NJ: Merrill/Prentice Hall.

Maslow, A. H. (1968, 1998). *Toward a psychology of being.* New York: Van Nostrand Reinhold.

McHale, S. M., & Olley, J. G. (1982). Using play to facilitate the social development of handicapped children. *Topics in Early Childhood Special Education, 2*(3), 76–86.

McLean, M., & Hanline, M. F. (1990). Providing early intervention services in integrated environments: Challenges and opportunities in the future. *Topics in Early Childhood Special Education, 10*(2), 62–77.

Neuspiel, D. R. (1991). Cocaine and infant behavior. *Developmental and Behavioral Pediatrics, 12*(1), 55–64.

Noonan, M. J., & McCormick, L. (1993). *Early intervention in natural environments.* Pacific Grove, CA: Brooks/Cole.

Parten, M. B. (1932). Social participation among preschool children. *Journal of Abnormal and Social Psychology, 27,* 243–269.

Phelps, L., & Grabowski, J. A. (1992). Fetal alcohol syndrome: Diagnostic features and psychoeducational risk factors. *School Psychology Quarterly, 7,* 112–128.

Piaget, J. (1963). *Play, dreams, and imitations in childhood.* New York: Norton.

Poulsen, M. K. (1989, December). *Perinatal substance abuse: Social policy and service delivery issues.* Paper presented to the California Early Intervention Technical Assistance Network Work Group, Sacramento, CA.

Reinert, H. R. (1980). *Children in conflict.* Upper Saddle River, NJ: Merrill/Prentice Hall.

Schutter, L. S., & Brinker, R. P. (1992). Conjuring a new category of disability from prenatal cocaine exposure; are the infants unique biological or caretaking casualties? *Topics in Early Childhood Special Education, 11*(4), 84–111.

Smith, J. M., & Smith, D. E. (1976). *Child management.* Champaign, IL: Research Press.

Stevenson, R. D., & Wolraich, M. L. (1989). Stimulant medication therapy in the treatment of children with atten-tion deficit hyperactivity disorder. *Pediatric Clinics of North America, 36*(5), 1183–1197.

Strain, P. S., & Hemmeter, M. L. (1997). Keys to being successful when confronted with challenging behaviors. *Young Exceptional Children, 1*(1), 2–8.

Strain, P. S., & Kohler, F. W. (1988). Social skill intervention with young children with handicaps: Some new conceptualizations and directions. In S. L. Odom & M. B. Karnes (Eds.) *Early intervention for infants and children with handicaps.* (pp. 129–144). Baltimore: Paul H. Brookes.

Swanson, H. L., & Reinert, H. R. (1984). *Teaching strategies for children in conflict.* Upper Saddle River, NJ: Merrill/Prentice Hall.

Swap, S. M. (1974). Disturbing classroom behaviors: A developmental and ecological view. *Exceptional Children, 41,* 163–172.

Texas Tech University. (1984). *The special child: Student laboratory manual.* Lubbock, TX: Home Economics Curriculum Center.

Thomas, A., Chess, S., & Birch, H. G. (1968). *Temperamental and behavior disorders in children.* New York: New York University Press.

Thomas, A., Chess, S., & Birch, H. G. (1970). The origin of personality. *Scientific American, 223,* 102–109.

Thomas, A., Chess, S., & Korn, S. J. (1982). The reality of difficult temperament. *Merrill-Palmer Quarterly, 28,* 1–20.

Ulrey, G., & Rogers, S. J. (1982). *Psychological assessment of handicapped infants and young children.* New York: Thieme-Stratton.

Umansky, W., & Hooper, S. R. (1998). *Young children with special needs.* Columbus, OH: Merrill.

Walker, J. E., & Shea, T. M. (1999). *Behavior management: A practical approach for educators.* Upper Saddle River, NJ: Merrill/Prentice Hall.

Walsh, H. M. (1980). *Introducing the young child to the social world.* Upper Saddle River, NJ: Merrill/Prentice Hall.

Wehman, P. (1978). Play skill development. In N. H. Fallen & J. E. McGovern (Eds.), *Young children with special needs.* (pp. 77–303). Upper Saddle River, NJ: Merrill/Prentice Hall.

Weston, R., Ivins, B., Zuckerman, B., Jones, C., & Lopez, R. (1989). Drug exposed babies: Research and clinical issues. *Zero-to-Three, 9*(5), 1–7.

White, B. P., & Phair, M. A. (1986). "It'll be a challenge!" Managing emotional stress in teaching disabled children. *Young Children, 41,* 44–48.

Zentall, S. (1977). Environmental stimulation model. *Exceptional Children, 43,* 502–511.

Chapter 8

Helping Young Children Develop Motor Skills

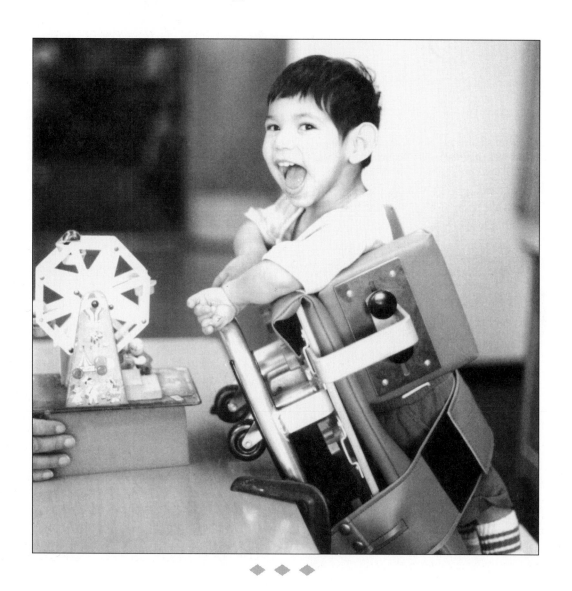

Key Concepts

♦ Infants learn from the sensations of movement, which come primarily from active rather than passive movements.

♦ Motor development follows a highly predictable sequential and overlapping pattern.

♦ Physiological maturation and environmental factors influence the rate and quality of physical and motor development.

♦ Assessment of motor skills is a team effort using a variety of approaches.

♦ Therapeutic intervention should encourage functional behaviors, including gross and fine motor skills, and their use in daily living.

♦ Positioning and handling are important considerations in normalization of muscle tone, prevention of deformity, and stabilization of the body.

♦ Adaptations of materials and environmental considerations should be a vital concern in program planning for children with motor impairments.

♦ Various strategies and aids are useful in teaching self-help skills. Including parents in the design and implementation is vital.

Working with young children to develop motor skills requires a special kind of planning. Competition and "winners," often associated with physical education in schools, are inappropriate. Infants and young children need to learn about their bodies. They need to develop balance and coordination. It is important for them to discover themselves in relationship to space. Care must be taken to help children develop an inner awareness of the difference between the two sides of the body, since moving through space requires both sides of the body to act as a team.

Coordination of movement skills contributes to children's development of confidence and trust in themselves and their bodies. This sense of bodily trust is considered to be important to the emergence of healthy personalities (Erikson, 1993). These are just some of the reasons that sensorimotor activities have held a dominant place in early education. For many children with motor problems or delays (cerebral palsy, mental retardation, orthopedic disabilities,

etc.), movement experiences are often limited. Additional instruction, therapeutic intervention, and encouragement are essential to minimize the disability and maximize children's potential in all aspects of development.

Motor skills are usually divided into at least two general categories. **Gross motor skills** refer to activities that involve the use of the large muscles of the neck, trunk, arms, and legs. Included are basic body movements such as lifting the head, rolling, crawling, creeping, walking, running, leaping, jumping, hopping, galloping, and skipping. Large muscle strength and endurance are also important in climbing, pushing, pulling, hanging, and lifting.

Fine motor skills involve more precise movements of the small muscles, especially those of the eyes, speech musculature, hands, fingers, feet, and toes. Movements such as blinking, focusing, sucking, grasping, releasing, pinching, and writing are considered to be fine motor activities. Many fine motor

247

skills, including cutting, copying, stringing beads, and pasting, require the eyes to direct the hands. These activities are referred to variously as those that require perceptual-motor, visual-motor, sensorimotor, ocular-motor, or eye-hand coordination.

This chapter reviews normal motor development, including gross and fine motor skills and perceptual-motor integration, and suggests activities to enhance development. Identification and problems of atypical motor development are emphasized, with suggestions for intervention. Special efforts are taken to encourage the integration of movement skills with other areas of the curriculum as well as in day-to-day functional activities.

THE DEVELOPMENT OF MOTOR SKILLS

Babies learn from the sensations of movement, which come primarily from active rather than passive movements. In this developmental process, the ability of the higher centers to mature is in part dependent upon sensory information brought to them. Sensory input (such as tactile, proprioceptive, visual, or auditory) is sent through the nervous system and integrated at appropriate levels of the brain and spinal cord. As messages are received and processed, responses are sent back in the form of motor acts. Voluntary motor activity is controlled by upper brain centers located in the cerebral cortex, while involuntary or unconscious muscle movements (e.g., digestion of food, eye blinking, reflex movements) are controlled by lower brain centers, that is, the cerebellum and parts of the brain stem.

In general, the development of motor skills proceeds according to the laws that govern the physiological maturation of the child, with the development of movement patterns progressing from simple arm or leg actions to highly integrated total body coordinations.

The rate of development is thought to depend not only on the quality of environmental stimulus but also on the stage of brain development. No distinction is usually made in the motor abilities of boys and girls

in infancy and early childhood because the differences are not very great. During the late preschool years, girls appear to perform better on tasks requiring manual dexterity, whereas boys are more adept when using large (gross) muscles. The extent to which this difference may be culturally determined is still being questioned. Parent's expectations and interactions with infants often differ according to the sex of the child. These expectations are reflected in play activities.

Environmental factors such as amount of sleep and exercise, quality of medical care, and adequacy of nutrition may influence the rate and ultimate degree of physical, and thus, motor development. In addition, childrearing practices that vary among cultures also should be taken into account when viewing differences in motor skill development. In general, a child's potential for motor skill development is considered to be the result of genetic origin and specific environmental influences.

By the time a child is 5 or 6 years of age, many motor behaviors have been established and require only refinement and mastery at a higher, more complex level. During these early years, motor development follows a highly predictable sequential and overlapping pattern. Although the rate at which typical children progress varies, the sequence remains fairly constant. The literature on motor development contains many descriptions and timetables for the stage/age at which motor abilities are attained. Variation in developmental rate is well documented. It is not unusual to hear mothers compare walking age variations from 8 to 18 months. For example, Figure 8–1 clearly shows the sequence and variation in postural control.

Sequential Trends of Motor Development

There are seven basic principles that govern the sequence of motor development:

1. *Cephalocaudal pattern.* Muscular development proceeds from the head to the foot. For example, infants have voluntary control over their heads

before lower parts of their body. Similarly, children can usually throw before they can catch.

2. *Proximo-distal pattern.* Growth and development tend to proceed from the spine (proximo) to the outer extremities (distal). That is, voluntary movement begins in the shoulder, then moves on to the elbow area, wrist, and finally, the fingers.

3. *Mass-to-specific pattern.* Body movement of young infants is undifferentiated, involving the total body. Later, specific patterns of movement develop out of these generalized mass movements. When learning new skills, it takes time for children to inhibit the unwanted extraneous movements.

4. *Gross-motor-to-fine-motor pattern.* Children usually gain control over large muscle activity before fine or small muscle activity. In addition, a child must gain differential control. That is, movement of muscles on one side of the body should occur without similar movement on the other side of the body, unless desired.

5. *Maximum-to-minimum-muscle-involvement pattern.* Like the mass-to-specific pattern, body movement becomes increasingly more efficient. With practice, children learn to eliminate unnecessary expenditures of energy. Where it once took a whole bodily effort to catch a ball, children learn to catch with the use of just one arm and hand.

6. *Bilateral-to-unilateral pattern.* Children progress from undifferentiated use of both sides of the body to unilateral preference, referred to as the *establishment of laterality.*

7. *Orderly development pattern.* Children differ in the rate of their development but do tend to follow a similar pattern if environmental conditions are adequate and no organic deficits are present.

Helping Parents to Understand

In teaching or talking to parents about various aspects of child development, early interventionists often find themselves caught up in lengthy, detailed descriptions of developmental domains. As a result of parents' requests for jargon-free explanations of sequential development, Lacy (1981) put together a manual describing development from the view of the growing infant. *Dear Mom and Dad* includes extensive recommendations for parent-child activities and is included here (Figure 8–2) as a summary of the area of early motor development.

Reflexive Development

Early motor activity of infants is structured by a variety of primitive and automatic reflexes. Primitive reflexes are evident in early infancy at or soon after birth. It is not known whether these reflexes are the framework for further motor maturation or must be inhibited for the development of coordinated voluntary control. There is a wide range of variation in reflex responsiveness among infants as well as within the same infant, depending on the behavioral states of the child being observed. These reflexes are expressions of the immaturity of the infant's nervous system and provide a basis for assessing the integrity of the developing neuromuscular system early in life.

Although the teacher may have difficulty understanding the complexities of neurological development, it is important to have some idea of how coordinated movement evolves and what factors may interfere with normal functioning. Appendix C summarizes major reflexes and potential problems. Concerned early interventionists may consult a physical or occupational therapist who is specifically trained to assess reflexive behavior.

Developing Gross Motor Skills

Gross motor skills refer to the involvement of the large muscles of the neck, trunk of the body, arms, and legs. Early childhood affords the time and practice for emerging skills to become accomplished before rapid bodily changes begin to occur. Children develop postural control and learn to walk, run, catch, and jump with relative skill. (See Figure 8–1 for progressions of change in postural control.) The extent to which children become proficient in these skills is dependent

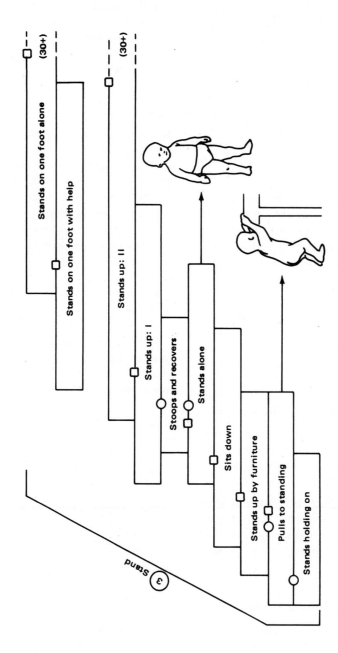

Figure 8–1 Progressions of change: Postural control. (*Source:* Keogh & Sugden, 1985)

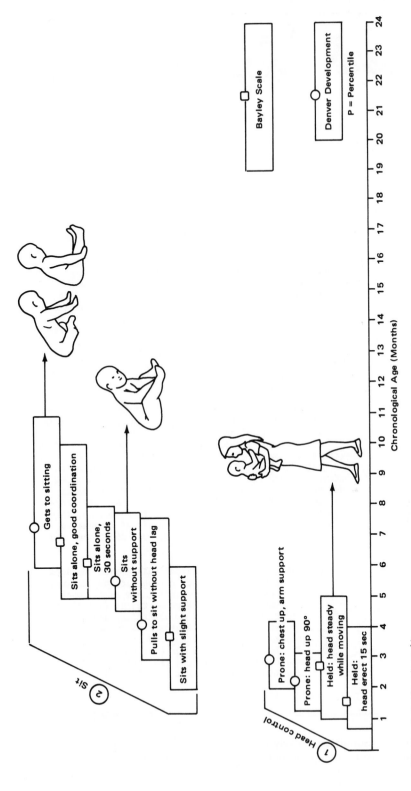

Figure 8-1 (Continued.)

Dear Mom & Dad

a baby's Letters to her Parents

(Gross Motor Development)

Dear Mom and Dad,

I'm sure that one of the first things you noticed when I was born was that I came out moving and haven't stopped yet! Those early movements weren't really planned out by me, though. A lot of that thrashing about was because of my immature nervous system and getting into certain positions was because of reflexes. Remember how you used to put me on my back to change me and I would jump? Well, that was my startle (Moro) reflex. And also that position on my back where I looked like a fencer (head turned toward bent arm and leg-- opposite ones straight)? Well, that was my ATNR reflex. I really began to notice things around me with my senses before I could act on them with my body, and that was frustrating--let me tell you!

As I did get going, though, I developed from my head down to my toes and from the center of my body to the outside muscles--"head down" and "inside out" is how I remember it. You see, my control was first with eye muscles, then with facial, on to neck, and finally down to trunk, legs, and feet. So I could focus my eyes and make faces, then balance my head before my body, and after that drag my body on the ground before creeping on hands and knees, and finally pull up to stand before walking. The side- ways growth showed up in arm-waving, then batting, then using wrist, hands, and finally individual fingers to manipulate objects. (I'll tell you more about arms and hands later.)

In those early months, my physical performance depended a lot on whether I was crying, sleepy, active, or alert. I really wasn't tuned in too much back then. But you kept on trying just the right activities for my abilities, giving me opportunities for new growth by the way you placed my body, praising and encouraging me, but always you found out very early that the way I felt about myself (my self-concept) depended so much on how well I could move

Infant Development Program

Figure 8–2 (pp 270–272) Summary of early motor development. (With gratitude to Virginia McDonald, Ann Lacy, and Project Hope, Department of Education, San Diego County, California)

my body by myself. So, you used a "hands-off" policy when you could, helping me to crawl or walk with a towel around my waist, etc. Then I really began to feel that I could make things happen in my new world.

Well, that whole first year seemed to be a time of learning more and more about how to use my body. My social growing and use of objects and language weren't quite as important to me yet. But I was really doing some learning as I thought out and planned all of those movements. A couple of things were going on all at once. First of all, I began to take in (integrate) those reflexes that I mentioned earlier, and also some others and started doing motions that I had control over. At the same time, I was gradually changing from being sideways to being upright as I got control over my head and trunk and then arms and legs. This ability to move and choose my actions and to move toward being vertical in my second year affected all parts of my life. It helped me to explore more with objects and try out new experiences through my senses (fine motor and cognitive), I could see people better and get to know them (visual and social), and my inside breathing organs were in a better position to help me talk (language). The best part of all was being able to move about by myself and have many more chances to explore things that had been out of reach or range--and just be more independent on my own.

As I learned each new step, you must have wondered why I sometimes did things so slowly--and also the same thing over and over. Well, I went slowly because I really needed to concentrate on my new accomplishments. (Sometimes I even wanted to give up eating and sleeping, too, to concentrate on my new physical miracles.) And the reason I practiced so much is that I wanted to make sure that each movement really became a part of me so that I wouldn't forget it. Sometimes I tried a new movement, like standing, only once and then dropped it for awhile (maybe even two months) because my new independence frightened me.

No, it wasn't all easy. I went along first wanting to take on the world, then needing to slow down or stop, and sometimes even drop something I had learned. I know you

Figure 8–2 (Continued.)

could tell, Mom, as I often cried, clung to you and acted difficult, that sometimes this new independence brought by a new movement was a little scary; I needed to slow down and come back to you for some reassurance. You probably came to realize that my shakiness and unsureness was sure to pop up right before a new "motor milestone." Thanks, Mom and Dad, for understanding and going along with my difficult times of wanting to move away from you and then being scared and returning for the comfort and love only you could give.

Thanks, too, for finding that nice balance between freedom and limits. It must have been hard for you to give me the chance to explore and learn, while also teaching me about rules and dangers. But you did a great job of protecting me and also giving me a nice environment to want to learn about. And best of all, you watched my own individual signals and trusted me. From the top of my head to the bottom of my toes and from the inside out, I thank you.

Love,

Your Growing Child

Figure 8–2 (Continued.)

on muscle development as well as opportunity for muscle use. However, it must be remembered that even in the most optimal situations, large and uneven growth spurts do occur. To provide the stimulation needed, safe environments free from obstacles and full of encouragement are needed. References at the end of the chapter suggest how to facilitate the development of growth-producing play areas.

Proficiency in gross motor skills is influenced by changes in body proportions. The 2-year-old's head accounts for about one fourth of the child's height. By the time the child is 5 years old, it accounts for only about one sixth of the total height (Cratty, 1998). As children become less top heavy, their ability to balance themselves develops. Children entering kindergarten have usually experienced an increase in muscle tissue, creating a larger potential of muscle energy available for movement. (Keogh & Sugden, 1985)

Developing Fine Motor Skills

Fine motor skills involve small muscles. Most fine motor skills, as far as preparation for manual control is concerned, involve hands and fingers. (See Figure 8–3 for progression of change in manual control.) Coordination of hands and fingers is often described as requiring strength, flexibility, and dexterity. The coordination of eye-hand movement is referred to as a visual-motor skill.

Handedness. When observing children engaged in fine motor activities, the question of "handedness" or hand preference usually arises. Preschool teachers can relax, for research indicates that it is usual to find children frequently interchanging the use of hands throughout early childhood. Hand dominance is often not achieved until the age of 6. Even then, some children develop functional ambidexterity (Westphal, 1991). The fact that children tend to use their right hands more often in taught activities such as cutting and throwing suggests the influence of our cultural bias.

Practice Payoff. Long before a baby can walk, her mother may report, "Sally picked up a raisin today."

Surprised that the child could pick up something so tiny, mothers become more alert about leaving beads and other nonedibles around. Later, this ability to see small things and pick them up will become the foundation for grasping and holding crayons, pencils, and other small objects.

Although merely having things available to pick up is all that is necessary for most young children to learn important fine motor skills, they must have opportunities to practice. Building with small blocks, manipulating small toys, and using crayons, chalk, and scissors all lead to the improvement of essential skills.

Snap-together beads, geoboards, puzzles, beads for stringing, button and lacing boards, and large nuts and screws offer interesting and challenging fine motor practice for young children. Even cooking activities help children to develop skills such as stirring, cutting, pounding, and rolling, while learning a variety of concepts. A sample list of typical motor skill activities is found in Table 8–1. A chart of normative expectations can be found in Appendix A.

Developing Perceptual-Motor Skills

Much has been written about the integral relationship between developing motor and perceptual skills (perceptual-motor skills) as well as visual and auditory perception. To comprehend the dynamic role of sensorimotor and perceptual skills in a child's development and in typical preschool curricula, it is necessary to have a basic understanding of perception.

Perception. Lerner, Mardell-Czudnowski, and Goldenberg (1987) explained perception as follows:

Perception is an interpretive function of the brain. It is the translation of sensory impressions into some representational level that is easily stored and recalled. In reality, the functions of sensation, motor activity and perception are so closely related that it is difficult to separate one from the other. (p. 160)

Perception is a learned cognitive process. Encountering sensory stimulation of a particular kind for the first time, children *receive* (sense) the stimulation.

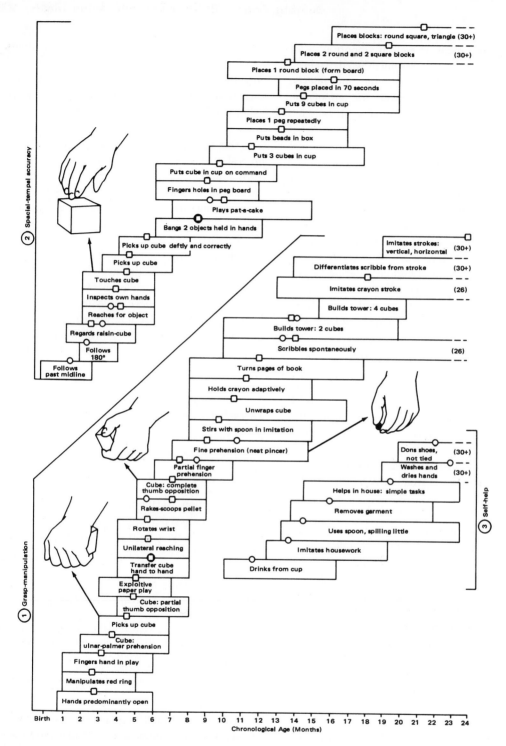

Figure 8–3 Progressions of change: Manual control. (*Source:* Keogh & Sugden, 1985)

Table 8–1   Typical motor skills activities

Gross Motor Development

Eye-Foot Coordination	Eye-Hand Coordination	Body Awareness	Balance
Kicking	Climbing	Crawling in and out of things	Standing (
Climbing	Hanging	Crawling through and around things	Walking the balance beam
Jumping	Striking balloons		Riding wheeled toys
Hopping	Throwing	Moving like an animal	Walking around tire edges or sandbox rails
Dancing	Catching	Mirroring activities	
Walking the balance beam	Using tools	Playing "Simon Says"	Moving and carrying something without spilling it
Jumping over ropes	Block building	Steering wheeled toys	Walking with bean bag on head or shoulder
	Rolling balls		
	Pounding		
	Stirring		

Fine Motor Development (Eye-Hand Coordination)

Cutting	Lacing	Outlining with stencils or templates
Coloring	Geoboards	Copying
Drawing	Tracing	Pasting
Sewing	Painting	Building block towers
Puzzle building	Paper folding	Stacking
Bead stringing	Copying designs	

Self-Help Skills

Dressing (buttoning, zipping, snapping, buckling)
Eating
Personal hygiene (brushing teeth, washing hands)
Toileting

Subsequent encounters usually result in their *perceiving* (interpreting) the stimulus. If any of the senses are impaired, even slightly, children may not be able to sense the initial stimulus accurately. If they do not receive an accurate first impression, later interpretations of that stimulus will be wrong or confusing to them.

Failure to develop accurate perceptions has been observed in children described as learning disabled. The early works of Strauss and Werner (1942) and Strauss and Lehtinen (1947) emphasized that perceptual deficits interfere seriously with all learning. Cruickshank (1967) also supported this belief.

Perceptual-Motor Skills. In an effort to enhance perceptual-motor skills (coordination of what is perceived with movement of body parts) or remediate deficits, there have been numerous teaching systems

and techniques proposed (see Cratty, 1998; Frostig, 1974; Ayres, 1972; Kephart, 1964).

In the past, perceptual-motor skill instruction was the primary focus of curricula in many special education programs. In summarizing his review of research on perceptual-motor instructional programs, Mercer (1983) warned:

Many of the perceptual-motor training programs commonly used, then, do not directly improve academic achievement or perceptual-motor development. Until further research, the inclusion of academic content in motor activities is desirable. (p. 278)

After considering more than 60 studies, Larsen and Hammill (1975) concluded that the relationship among visual, perceptual, and academic performance is not significant. Therefore Hammill and Bartel (1975) urged teachers "to implement perceptual-motor training on a remedial basis in only those few cases where improvement in perception is the goal" (p. 230). They further suggested that such training is more acceptable for preschoolers than for kindergarten or school-age children.

Or, as Piazza (1979) suggested,

If perceptual, motor, or psycholinguistic skills are to be trained they should be done for their own sake and not for some projected transfer to an academic area. Children do need to be taught the difference between the left and right sides of their bodies, and . . . such tasks as cutting. (p. 47)

It is for these reasons that we encourage the development of perceptual-motor skills as tasks in and of themselves, and in association with language and concept development.

Individualizing a Visual-Motor Activity

By writing the goal and objectives for cutting with scissors on one page, as illustrated in Table 8–2, the teacher has a helpful one-page reference to guide him or her in planning the lesson to be useful to a group of children with widely varying skills. The terminal objective is an appropriate skill for a 5-year-old, whereas lifting cotton balls with the tongs can be accomplished by most 3-year-olds.

However, some 5-year-olds with developmental delays may find it difficult to learn to use the tongs. They may require help and physical guidance as well as encouragement and verbal guidance for many days or weeks before they can proceed to the second objective. By being included in the activity with children

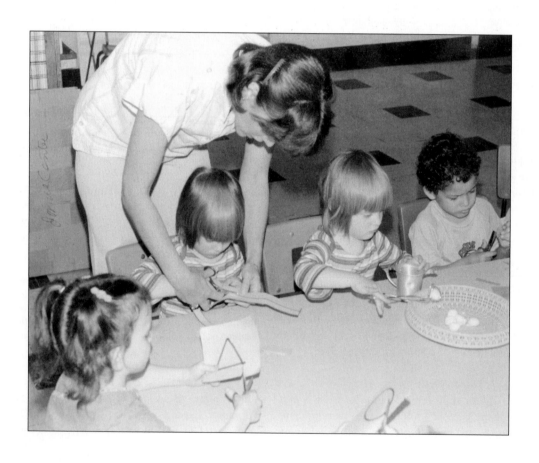

Table 8–2 Example of using goals and objectives to individualize an activity

Given (the teacher will provide or restrict)	The child will	Criterion
Goal: To develop cutting skills.		
Terminal objective: Blunt-tip scissors; paper with a 3-inch straight line, a 3-inch curved line, and a 3-inch-diameter circle; and directions to cut on the line and cut out the circle.	Cut as directed.	Cut within ¼ inch of lines within 5 minutes.
En-route objectives (least to most skilled):		
1. Tongs, 5 cotton balls, 4-inch bowl, teacher's guidance in placing fingers and thumb and forefinger in cutting position, and help in opening and closing tongs.	Open and close tongs around cotton ball, lift it to bowl, and release it into bowl, accepting teacher's assistance as needed.	Keep fingers in correct position and accept help.
2. Same as above, except restrict teacher's help to verbal directions, encouragement, and reminders.	Same as above.	Keep fingers in correct position and complete action (no time limit and no penalty for "dropped" cotton).
3. Same as above.	Same as above.	Maintain correct position, lift and drop cotton into bowl (no more than one ball outside bowl within 2 minutes).
4. Blunt-tip scissors and strips of construction paper 1 inch wide and 11 inches long.	Cut paper.	Cut at least 10 pieces within 5 minutes.
5. Same as above, with heavy black lines marked on paper at 1-inch intervals.	Cut paper on lines.	Cut within ¼ inch of lines, one cut per line (no time limit).
6. Blunt-tip scissors and construction paper 3 inches wide and 11 inches long, with heavy black lines at 1-inch intervals the width of the paper.	Make three cuts per line.	Cut within ¼ inch of lines, severing each piece within 10 minutes.
7. Same as terminal objective (except longer time criterion).	Cut as directed.	Cut within ¼ inch of lines within 10 minutes.
8. Same as terminal objective.		

Adaptations for children with physical disabilities include squeeze scissors instead of traditional scissors. For some children, scissors with four finger holes may be useful because they allow the teacher to cut with the child. Children with visual impairments should be provided buff-colored paper with a heavy brown line for necessary contrast.

who can do the more difficult tasks, they observe and discover that they also can learn.

It is critical to remember that one of the reasons for the sequence of carefully planned en-route behaviors is to provide each child with a task until criterion is reached. It is possible to develop difficult skills gradually and without the pain of failure.

Beginning by expecting each child to "cut on the line" guarantees failure for many of them.

To teach five or more children to cut on the line, it is necessary to provide each one with the materials needed, demonstration at his or her level of performance, and continued encouragement. In this way, no one fails; rather, each child succeeds. Most will recognize the challenge of the next step and be eager to try it.

In addition to the usefulness of the clearly written behavioral objectives to the teacher, as the lesson is planned and conducted, these same objectives help in pinpointing necessary **branching** or smaller steps.

The basic set of goals and objectives should be designed to be useful guides in teaching the majority of the children. But some children will need even smaller steps. By analyzing the existing objectives, the teacher can identify what these more precise steps should be.

The format of the page of objectives is a help in analyzing the task. If the child is not succeeding, where is the breakdown? Should a change be made in what the teacher is providing or restricting? Or is the quantity of work or time allowed inappropriate? Sometimes the en-route behaviors become more diffi-

cult because the task changes. At other times only the time limitations change. By evaluating the task, the criterion, and what the teacher does or does not do, it is possible to establish a much better sense of successful teaching for the teacher as well as the children.

Throughout all of the activities, teachers attempt to help children establish independence, accuracy, patience, and persistence. These qualities can be nurtured more successfully when en-route behaviors are clearly stated.

Recording Progress. Figure 8–4 illustrates an easy way to record children's progress when a group includes children with varying skill levels focusing on the same goal. By placing the en-route (expected behaviors) down the left side of the page and the names of the children across the top, it is easy to record progress and to identify each child's current en-route

CURRICULUM DOMAIN: Fine motor

Goal: To learn cutting skills

Key: + = Skill already established
☐ = Current target behavior
⌗ = Date achieved

	Meg A.	Mary C.	Danny D.	Bobby J.	Vicky M.	Eric R.
Tongs and cotton balls	+	+	+	+	+	+
1-inch snipping	10/95	9/95	10/95	+	☐	+
1-inch snipping on heavy line	☐	10/95	10/95	+		+
3-inch cutting on heavy straight line		☐	☐	10/95		+
3-inch cutting on heavy curved line				☐		10/95
Cutting out 3-inch-diameter circle, heavy line						☐

Figure 8–4

behavior. The teacher (or aide) simply records the date and level of accomplishment for each item. Some prefer to include only the date of achievement. Then, the next item on the list becomes the current enroute behavior to be practiced.

ATYPICAL MOTOR DEVELOPMENT

Atypical motor development or motor differences can occur for a variety of reasons. Brain damage, orthopedic problems, genetic defects, developmental delays and sensory impairments can potentially interfere with motor skill acquisition.

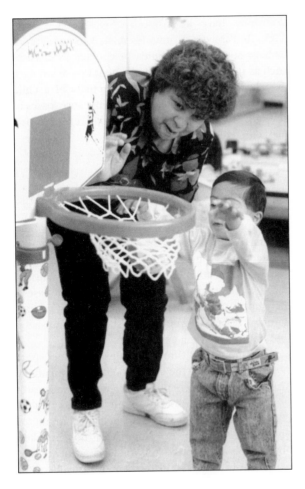

Deviations in movement patterns affecting the young child usually originate in the prenatal or perinatal period. Neuromuscular dysfunction originating in the central nervous system, specifically cerebral palsy (CP), is the most common motor disability among children of all ages. Cerebral palsy is a general term given to nonprogressive brain lesions. It generally causes complex problems in all aspects of development (Batshaw, 1997). Abnormal movement patterns seen in children with CP are related to primitive reflex retention and problems of motor incoordination and muscle tone. A continuum of motor dysfunction due to insult to the brain may include on one end a child with clumsy and awkward movements and on the other a child with CP who has such severe impairments that any coordinated movement is next to impossible. In between are varying degrees of movement problems.

Although the severe form of CP affects many other developmental areas, it is important to be cautious not to equate the degree of motor disability with cognitive deficits. According to Batshaw (1997), studies show that central nervous system insult is not an accurate predictor of cognitive growth and later academic performance.

Problems in Muscle Development

Muscle characteristics of tone, control, and strength are significant concerns in development and eventual intervention. Causes of problems vary from central nervous system damage and genetic disorders to nonspecific delays in development (Batshaw, 1997). Hanson and Harris (1986) discussed the deviations in muscle development that require consideration when programs are planned.

1. *Deficits in muscle tone.* The degree of tension in the muscle at rest defines muscle tone. Three types of muscle tone deviation are noted. The first, hypotonicity, describes low tension or flaccidity in muscles. The "floppy" child usually demonstrates generalized weak, flabby muscles, and often hypermobile joints, especially in shoulders, hips, and

ankles. The child with Down syndrome, Prader-Willi syndrome, or those classified as having ataxic cerebral palsy are good examples of "floppy" children. The hypotonic child is usually less active than his or her peers and may become fatigued easily by motor activities.

Motor milestones such as sitting, creeping, and walking are usually delayed because of the affected child's generalized low muscle tone. Other areas affected may be the chest and face muscles. Because of low muscle tone, breathing tends to be shallow. The child may also have difficulty sustaining sounds when attempting to cry, babble, or talk.

Conversely, the child with **hypertonia** has too much muscle tone. Another name for hypertonia is **spasticity.** A high percentage of children with CP have spasticity. The affected muscles are characterized as feeling stiff and rigid. For instance, when the child tries to passively extend the flexed arm, it feels "locked," and a slow, steady pressure at the elbow is necessary to perform this motion. In children with spastic hemiplegia, one side of the body is affected. In spastic diplegia, the legs are primarily affected, but trunk and arms may also be involved. In spastic quadriplegia, all four extremities and trunk are involved.

Children with hypertonia are frequently delayed in achieving motor milestones. They often have difficulty assuming and maintaining postures that go against gravity, such as sitting, creeping, and standing. Breathing may also be impaired due to decreased movement of the ribs and chest. If facial and oral muscles are involved, as is often the case in spastic quadriplegia, articulation, chewing, and swallowing also may be affected (Hanson & Harris, 1986).

Fluctuating muscle tone, which can be seen in children who are generally hypertonic or hypotonic. Usually in these cases, an attempt at voluntary movement sets off increased muscle tone. However, when the child is resting, muscles may be hypotonic. The incoordination of contraction and relaxation may be seen in *athetoid* movement patterns, which are repetitive, poorly coordinated voluntary movements. The most common type of motor disability in which fluctuating tone occurs is athetoid cerebral palsy.

2. *Deficits in muscle control.* Writhing movements, tremors, and fluctuating muscle tone are abnormal motor characteristics that interfere with voluntary movements. As the child with CP tries to do something, for example, not only is fluctuating tone present, but also uncoordinated movements and abnormal posture caused by increased or decreased tone. Involuntary facial movements (mouth opening and closing, the tongue moving in and out) are often related to general muscle tone fluctuation throughout the body. Attempts at fine motor activities tend to increase problems in overall coordination in some children with CP.

3. *Deficits in muscle strength.* There may be differences in muscle strength among and within children. Certain degenerative diseases such as muscular dystrophy have a progressive effect on muscle strength. Paralysis of muscles related to spinal cord damage such as spina bifida or contagious diseases such as polio often cause permanent loss of strength in certain muscle groups. The inactivity of a child wearing a cast for a broken bone will cause losses of strength and muscle tone that quickly return to normal with exercise and movement.

ASSESSMENT OF MOTOR ABILITIES

In educational planning or therapeutic intervention, it is important to assess the young child in all developmental areas and to determine how the absence or delay of motor abilities will affect overall learning and social interactions. No matter what type of assessment approach is used (observation checklist or standardized tests), the information should be translated into optimal learning experiences.

As emphasized throughout this text, the responsibility for assessing the child should be a team effort. The parent, teacher, physician, and allied health professionals all contribute information essential in identification, diagnosis, and remediation of motor problems. As with all assessment, care must be taken not to apply diagnostic labels until all pertinent information is obtained. The high-risk premature infant, for example, is too often given an early diagnosis of cerebral palsy based on symptoms characteristic of an immature but developing nervous system. Imagine the effects of that incorrect diagnosis on the parents!

Early education program staff often become coordinators and synthesizers of assessment information. Information from parents on early developmental milestones, family history, and current behavior, plus hospital records and diagnostic assessment from medical specialists, add up to a more comprehensive view of a child's physical development.

Infants and Toddlers

Probably the earliest assessment of motor development is performed routinely at 1 minute and at 5 minutes after birth. The newborn baby is assessed for appearance (color), heart rate, reflex irritability, activity, muscle tone, and respiratory effort to determine whether or not further medical assistance is needed. A practical scoring system usually used to assess these attributes is the Apgar score (Apgar & James, 1962). Table 8–3 shows the five criteria and point values used to measure the effect of loss of oxygen and damage to the circulation in newborns. Each characteristic is rated 0, 1, or 2 (2 being best). These are added together to obtain an overall score that varies from 0 to 10. The 5-minute score has been shown to predict future developmental progress quite accurately (Batshaw, 1997). More extensive observation of the newborn may be accomplished with an instrument such as the Brazelton Neonatal Behavioral Assessment Scale (Brazelton, 1996). The Brazelton Scale helps identify problems in the central nervous system and the sensory abilities of the newborn.

When infants or young children lack obvious or visible impairments, it is much more difficult to detect possible problems related to motor development. Usually a parent or early educator detects the more subtle behaviors that can be observed over time and are not seen in a short office visit with a medical specialist. Some of the behaviors that should be noted and considered as indicators of the need for referral include the following:

1. Delayed motor milestones. (Although delay is an important indicator, normal developmental variations must be kept in mind.)

2. Abnormal posturing of arms and legs during rest or activity.

3. Tremor of hands or arms when performing a task.

4. Significant difference in skill between right and left arms or legs.

5. Early hand preference (before 13 months of age).

6. Poor balance and equilibrium.

7. Difficulties in eye tracking.

8. Poor coordination in gross or fine motor activities.

9. Poor motor control of tongue, lips, or mouth muscles (e.g., drooling).

10. Inability to inhibit movements, as shown by jerking, mirroring, or fidgeting.

11. Poor visual-motor integrative skills, often seen in drawing.

12. Weakness or extreme fatigue during movement activities.

Table 8–3 Apgar scoring system

Points	0	1	2
Heart rate	Absent	Below 100	Above 100
Respiratory effort	Absent	Slow, irregular	Normal respiration
Muscle tone	Limp	Some flexion	Active motion
Gag reflex	No response	Grimace	Sneeze, cough
Color	Blue all over; pale	Blue extremities, rest of body pink	Pink all over

The more of these signs a child displays, the more likely he or she is to have some type of neurological dysfunction. Any of these behaviors should be noted and communicated to the child's primary care physician. In addition, various medications can cause side effects that may appear to be symptoms of neuromotor or attentional problems. Early childhood program staff and parents should know about the possible side effects of any medication a child may be taking.

Severe Motor Impairments

Young children with severe motor impairments present some difficult assessment problems—especially if cognitive or communication skills are also being evaluated. Because many assessment tasks require both fine and gross motor skills, the child with severe motor problems is penalized for inability to perform on standardized items. An understanding of primitive reflexes and abnormal movement patterns helps the educator to place the child in the *best position* for achieving optimum voluntary motor responses. A physical or occupational therapist can provide ways to help the child improve motor performance and demonstrate skills in other developmental areas.

Videotaped records of a child's behavior and performance in informal play settings can also be very helpful in understanding the qualitative aspects of his or her ability. The evaluator may require several sessions to properly assess the child's strengths. Because the child's psychological and physiological state can drastically influence muscle tone and coordination, movement abilities may differ considerably from day to day.

General Considerations for Assessment of All Young Children

Effective observation of motor skills requires observers to keep in mind that the *process* or *approach* to motor tasks is significant. How a child goes about trying to catch a ball is much more revealing than whether or not the ball is caught. There is a great difference in ability between (a) the child whose eyes are following the path of the ball and whose hands are working together to attempt a catch and (b) the child who seems not to be looking at the ball and whose hands hang loose or do not seem to work together. Although neither one may actually catch the ball, their differences in attempts must be carefully noted and considered. They are clearly at different levels developmentally. A child's lack of experience in activities such as climbing stairs or using scissors also influences performance. The child's level of excitement or fear of strangers and/or new tasks could be further inhibitors to motor processes.

Since the quality of performance is dependent on physiological maturation and experience, assessment for the purpose of developing instructional objectives must depend on individually referenced criteria. Although comparison with group norms can provide the early childhood educator with a general frame of reference, it cannot determine whether individual progress is adequate in light of changes that take place within that individual. For example, a 3-year-old who has the body height and weight of a 2-year-old cannot be expected to perform balance tasks with the ease of most 3-year-olds. Considering lack of balance to be a weakness and including objectives to teach balance would be inappropriate until a shift in bodily proportion takes place. In short, educators are expected to combine knowledge from normative tests with observation of individual differences and develop a set of *criterion-referenced* objectives.

Developmental Task Analysis. Once a teacher has used a developmental checklist derived from normative expectations and has observed very carefully while considering individual levels of maturation, interests, and experiences, program activities can be determined. The checklist may include only broad curriculum objectives that may be stated more as goals, or it may contain a more specific task analysis that breaks each broader goal into teaching steps. The checklist then becomes a teaching as well as testing or assessment tool.

In utilizing task analysis as an observational tool to establish appropriate motor goals and objectives, a sample formula may be helpful for both interventionists and parents. Hanson and Harris (1986) suggest five basic steps as illustrated in Exhibit 8–1. In the section on adaptive skills found on page 290, applications of task analysis are illustrated.

Play-Based Assessment

This approach provides many opportunities to observe a wide range of infants and young children in both structured and unstructured play activities. It is especially useful in observing movement behaviors. Linder (1996) and her colleagues have developed observation guidelines for sensorimotor development that encompass categories of (a) general appearance of movement; (b) muscle tone/strength/endurance; (c) reactivity to sensory input; (d) stationary positions used for play; (e) mobility in play; (f) other develop-

mental achievements; (g) prehension and manipulation; and (h) motor planning. The **sensorimotor observations** are integrated into the overall transdisciplinary play-based assessment, which includes cognitive, language, and social development.

THERAPEUTIC INTERVENTION

What is the purpose of therapeutic intervention? Who should provide the therapy? How is it used in home- or center-based intervention programs? Early childhood educators ask these critical questions when planning for children with physical limitations.

Therapists and teachers have shifted the focus from *developmental* goals to **functional independence.** Work on functional motor goals should begin

EXHIBIT 8–1

Example of Five Basic Steps in Task Analysis

BEHAVIOR: Child Rolls from Back to Stomach

1. **Decide which behavior you want to teach.**
   Debbie will roll from back to stomach without assistance.
2. **Decide on the cue you will use to prompt the child.**
   Say, "Roll over, Debbie," while physically assisting her. Favorite toys are lying out of reach in the direction Debbie will roll to encourage rolling.
3. **Decide on consequences to follow the behavior.**
   Debbie will pay with the toy obtained by rolling.
4. **Break the behavior into small steps and order the steps.**
   a. When Debbie is lying on her back, physically bring her arm across her chest and, by bending her at her knee, gently roll her all the way over from back to stomach.
   b. Debbie is physically rolled one half way over. She rolls the last half of the way on her own.
   c. Debbie rolls on her own from back to stomach.
   d. Debbie rolls on her own from back to front.
   Note: The verbal cue "Roll over, Debbie" is used during each step.
5. **Decide how well Debbie must do the behavior.**
   a. The number of seconds you will wait following the cue. Debbie will roll within 30 seconds of the cue.
   b. The number of times Debbie should perform correctly. Debbie will perform correctly 8 out of 10 times. When Debbie does this 8 out of 10 times for 3 days in a row, she can go on to the next step.

as early as possible, especially for young children with severe disabilities. Examples of functional goals might include picking up Cheerios, turning a doorknob, and holding a crayon. Such skills enable the child to be more independent or to better interact with his or her environment. Too often professionals persist in trying to "normalize" the muscle tone and movement patterns of young children with severe brain damage. We must relinquish responsibility for trying to "fix" this brain damage and instead work toward setting realistic functional goals for the child, the parents, and ourselves.

In planning intervention for an individual child, one should look carefully at the child's functional level, considering activities for daily living, interactions within home and community environments, skills needed to support other developmental areas (i.e., positioning for problem-solving activities or social interaction), and types of assistive devices needed to enhance performance. After reviewing this information, teachers have a better picture of the functional level and the type of motor goals to be initiated for the child.

Role of Therapists

As part of the team approach in early childhood special education, the therapist must help teachers and parents to understand the objectives and techniques for development of functional motor skills. In consultation with physicians, the occupational or physical therapist will provide the expertise for implementing gross and fine motor activities and offer advice on positioning and use of therapeutic devices (braces, wheelchairs, etc.) as well as facilitating the development of feeding and other adaptive skills. He or she will also work with families in both home and school settings to help integrate the therapy prescriptions into the daily routine of the child's care.

In working with infants and young children, there is considerable overlap in the roles of physical and occupational therapists. In institutional programs or in working with older children and adults, the **physical therapist** is usually concerned with large muscle movement and gross motor activities, while the **occupational therapist** is more often involved in evaluation and treatment of perceptual-motor (fine motor) functioning and activities of daily living.

The current trend in many early intervention programs is to have the therapist actually work in the center beside the teacher or in the home with the parents. In this way the therapist also demonstrates how the therapeutic activities can be integrated into the daily routine of the classroom or the home. In addition, the therapist can observe and participate in classroom or home activities that may lead to better understanding of other developmental concerns.

Therapy must be an integral part of the early childhood special education program, with the teacher understanding the rationale and serving as a promoter and translator of therapeutic objectives in the child's daily program. Ongoing staff training in the classroom or in special meetings should be a significant part of the therapist's responsibility.

Approaches to Therapy

There are a number of widely differing therapeutic techniques to improve motor performance of young children with physical disabilities, including exercise, skill instruction, use of adaptive devices, drug therapy, and often surgery.

Proper positioning, inhibition of abnormal reflexes, and facilitation of active movement are major concerns in working with a child who has cerebral palsy or other neurological disorders. Among several techniques for dealing with these, the most popular is the Neurodevelopmental Treatment Approach (NDT) developed by Bobath and Bobath (1975). Although skillful use of the NDT approach requires extensive training, the basic principles and practical application can be utilized by both teachers and parents (Stern & Gorga, 1988).

Other approaches to therapy are usually classified by the name of their promoter (i.e., Phelps, Rood, and Doman-Delacato). The Doman-Delacato approach has been popular with some parents of neurologically impaired children, but has been highly controversial among professionals. Techniques consist of several periods of daily "patterning" involving four or five adults to assist in carrying out specific movement patterns such as creeping or crawling.

One therapeutic approach that has had significant influence in the field of early intervention is sensory integration. In the following section, a brief explanation of important components is included.

Sensory Integration

Sensory integration is another approach used often in the therapeutic repertoire and training of the occupational therapist (Ayres, 1972, 1994). Williamson and Anzalone (1997) expressed the belief that learning disabilities are related to deficits in sensory integration. Many of the special activities are designed to provide tactile (touch) and vestibular (balance) stimulation. The therapist uses multisensory approaches that enhance the nervous system's abilities to organize and interpret sensory input in order to improve motor output effectiveness. Swings, rotary equipment, scooters, and other play equipment are used in the child's therapy.

In recent years, sensory integration has become a very popular—though often controversial—approach to working with young children with disabilities. There is much anecdotal evidence of its positive effect in working with a variety of disabilities, particularly with autism. However, there is as yet no widely accepted body of research demonstrating its effectiveness.

Sensory integration is the ability to take in information through the senses of touch, movement, smell, taste, vision, and hearing, to integrate this input with stored information (e.g., prior experience, memories, and knowledge) and then to organize an appropriate response. Difficulty processing and organizing sensory information can result in "sensory integrative dysfunction" Jean Ayres (1994, p. 51) describes sensory integrative dysfunction using the following analogy. "Good sensory processing enables all the impulses to flow easily and reach their destination quickly. Sensory integrative dysfunction is a sort of 'traffic jam' in the brain. Some bits of sensory information get 'tied up in traffic,' and certain parts of the brain do not get the sensory information they need to

do their jobs." Sensory integrative dysfunction may include the following:

Attention and Regulatory Problems. Some children may have difficulty screening out or inhibiting their response to extraneous nonessential sensory information, such as background noises or visual stimuli. Such children may be easily distractible and have difficulty inhibiting their attention to these irrelevant stimuli. Therefore, they have difficulty maintaining attention to appropriate information. Some children may also have problems with self-regulation. That is, they may overreact to stimuli and have difficulty calming themselves once they are in a highly aroused state.

Sensory Defensiveness. Most early interventionists are familiar with children who demonstrate "tactile defensiveness" or hypersensitivity to touch. These children resist touching or handling common materials and textures. In addition, children may also be highly sensitive to other sensory stimuli, resulting in auditory defensiveness (e.g., avoiding direct eye gaze or hypersensitivity to light), or vestibular defensiveness (intolerance of movement or unstable surfaces). Children can also be highly sensitive to oral sensations (e.g., certain food textures or temperatures) and to olfactory stimuli (e.g., negative reactions to strong odors).

Sensory defensiveness may result in social withdrawal, avoidance of certain objects (e.g., vacuum cleaners), foods, sounds, and social experiences. Children's motor movements may be greatly inhibited by fears such as walking up or down steps or on uneven surfaces. This can result in an insistence on certain routines and behavioral rigidity (e.g., insistence on wearing only certain clothing and eating certain foods; or insistence on highly predictable, "safe" daily schedules.

Activity Level as Possible Indicators of Sensory Integrative Dysfunction. The following are possible variations in activity level that may indicate problems in this area:

- Child does not explore environment; avoids manipulating objects or moving around

- Child is disorganized and lacks purpose

- Child lacks variety in play activities; engages in repetitive, stereotypic play

- Child appears clumsy, has poor balance, trips often; may lack protective responses

- Child has difficulty calming himself following rigorous physical activity or after becoming upset

- Child seeks excessive amounts of sensory input, e.g., excessive spinning, bumping into others, or jumping

Therapeutic techniques are based on complex theories of neurology and require very specific training to design and implement. Individuals who are most likely to have attained clinical competence in this area are physical and occupational therapists. Some advocates of "SI" therapy, as it is called, may be overzealous in their claims of broad applicability of this therapeutic approach in treating a very wide range of behavioral, educational, personality, and movement disorders. Nevertheless, sensory integration therapy appears to have significant promise in alleviating or managing certain attention and regulatory disorders.

Positioning and Handling

Although it is often important to encourage movement, there are times when the young child should remain in a static position. For infants and young children with motor impairments, one area of significant concern is positioning and handling. In order to modify excessive or insufficient muscle tone and to control the predominance of abnormal reflexes, certain positions and specific handling techniques should be integrated into the child's home and school or center activities.

Positioning is the placement of the child in carefully selected positions (e.g., side-lying, sitting, standing) in order to normalize muscle tone, prevent deformity, and stabilize the body (Copeland & Kimmel, 1989). Careful positioning will also allow a child to function more efficiently during toileting, feeding, play, and other functional activities. For ex-

ample, if a child's trunk is not stabilized for sitting, control of arms and hands for self-feeding and playing with toys may be compromised.

Handling, according to Copeland and Kimmel (1989), is a dynamic process with goals of normalizing muscle tone, preparing the child for movement, and facilitating movement.

Use of hands on an appropriate key point of the body can control or inhibit undesirable postures and movements. In addition to specific activities for the positioning and handling of individual children, Hanson and Harris (1986) have suggested the following general guidelines to consider in planning intervention:

1. *Key points of control* refers to parts of the body nearest the center of the body, including the *head and neck,* the *shoulder girdle,* and the *legs.* These are the key points to think about whenever you move, carry, or position a child. Paying close attention to these points will aid in normalizing muscle tone as well.

2. *Symmetry* of the child's body means that both sides of the body are positioned similarly so that one side is a mirror image of the other. Symmetry is also a consideration in developing muscle

tone, as well as in inhibiting primitive movement patterns.

3. *Midline positioning* is important. Many young children with motor impairments are unable to bring their hands together at the midline (the middle of the body). Activities using hands in midline will help develop motor and self-help skills. Side-lying positioning is one way to facilitate midline activities. Hanson and Harris (1986) and Finnie (1975) have offered specific techniques and equipment to encourage activities at the midline.

4. Use only *minimal support* when positioning and handling the child. Providing too much support will not allow children to use the muscle control they have already developed. For example, if a child has adequate trunk control to sit independently, a corner chair with a high back is not necessary. Using such a device will only inhibit trunk muscles and not provide the practice needed to develop strength and endurance.

Based on these guidelines, Copeland and Kimmel (1989) have suggested asking the following questions during assessment:

1. Is the head at midline and can the child visually focus on the desired target, e.g., toy, object, playmates?

2. Is the trunk symmetrical and well-aligned with the rest of the body?

3. Are the lower extremities properly aligned? If seated, kneeling, or standing, are the lower extremities bearing weight equally?

4. Are the upper extremities properly aligned and in functional positions for weight bearing or manipulation of objects?

5. Does this position promote the development of tightness, contractures, deformity, or pressure sores? (p. 48)

Whenever possible, parents and professionals should consult with the therapist to determine the child's individual needs for positioning and handling.

There are also several excellent resources that give detailed guidelines and activities. Some of these include Bigge (1991); Hanson and Harris (1986); and Ratliff (1998).

Proper Lifting

In using correct lifting and carrying techniques, especially with young children who have severe motor impairments, the early interventionist or parent has an opportunity to provide support as well as therapy. When a young child is lifted up correctly, abnormal reflexes are not stimulated, and the child appears more normal and actually is under less stress. Some important steps in lifting and carrying are as follows:

1. Speak to the child, telling him or her what you are going to do and where you are going.

2. Wait for some response and encourage the child to assist in the process (e.g., "You need to help. Give me your hand.").

3. Praise the child for any attempts to help.

4. Lift the child gently.

To protect yourself from injury, practice the following:

1. Bend your knees and keep your back straight.

2. Avoid twisting; approach the child straight on.

3. Keep the child's body as close to yours as possible.

4. Do not try to carry the child by yourself if he or she is too large or too heavy.

5. Give the *least* amount of help needed.

Proper and improper lifting techniques are shown in Figure 8–5.

Adaptive Equipment for Gross and Fine Motor Activities

Appropriate early intervention program planning for children with motor problems may involve a diverse array of equipment. Children may require *prostheses*

Figure 8–5 Proper and improper lifting techniques. (*Source of drawings:* From *Positioning for infants and young children with motor problems* [videotape manual], pp. 8–11. Courtesy of the University of Colorado School of Nursing, Marilyn Krajicek, Director, First Start.)

(aids designed to function as limbs), *orthoses* (aids for assistance), *mobility devices* such as walkers and wheelchairs, positioning aids, or *academic aids* to help function in a classroom. Copeland (1982), Bigge (1991) and Ratliff (1998) have illustrations of adaptive equipment.

It is especially important for teachers of children with severe disabilities to learn about and use **adaptive equipment.** Basically, the value and purpose of this type of assistance are to: (a) help maintain normalized muscle tone; (b) inhibit primitive reflexes; (c) allow the child to use voluntary movements; (d) provide optimal positioning to interact more effectively with the environment; and (e) encourage independence.

Equipment to aid in **positioning** is now commonly found in almost every program serving children with special needs. The wedge, the bolster, the prone board, and modified chairs are used in a variety of ways as required. These types of equipment can be

purchased commercially or made by a skillful teacher or parent. The choice of adaptive equipment should be made in consultation with a therapist, who can also help the teacher to identify its purpose, explain its use for a particular disability, and describe any special precautions to be observed while the child is using the equipment. (Inappropriate use of adaptive equipment can often do more harm than good.)

DEVELOPMENT OF ADAPTIVE BEHAVIOR SKILLS

Adaptive skills (toileting, feeding, grooming, dressing) comprise a large portion of the young child's daily living tasks. Providing for skill development and necessary adaptations are major considerations in early intervention programs. For children with delayed or limited motor skills the normal unfolding of adaptive skills is seriously compromised. Integration of functional activities that provide optimum opportunities for learning require an on-going team effort. The role of positioning, handling, and therapeutic approaches provide much of the framework for development to occur.

Certain motor skills, including a child's ability to control parts of his or her body, are important precursors for adaptive skill development. For example, the ability to pick up an object and bring it to the mouth is required for finger feeding and usually appears around the seventh month (Umansky & Hooper, 1998). Although there are differences in when adaptive skills are acquired, development appears to follow a developmental sequence. Knowledge of the steps in the adaptive domain is essential. This provides the basis for determining where to begin instruction and what prerequisite skills are needed. Table 8–4 presents the major milestones for adaptive skills.

Use of Task Analysis

Task analysis of adaptive skills is a process of breaking down a skill area into its component parts, as noted in Exhibit 8–1. Task subskills offer the specific information from which to assess and plan a developmental program for use by both parents and early interventionists. For example, when teaching a toddler to put on a T-shirt, the steps may be broken into single teaching units (Copeland & Kimmel, 1989, p. 204):

1. Hold shirt bottom open with right hand.
2. Insert left hand into shirt.
3. With right hand, pull shirt over left hand so hand comes through sleeve.
4. Hold shirt bottom with left hand.
5. Insert right hand into shirt and through sleeve.
6. Pull shirt over head.
7. Pull shirt down.

Copeland and Kimmel (1989) suggest that the number of steps and substeps may depend on the child's cognitive level, the amount of physical mobility, and response to praise or rewards.

If the goal is too difficult or requires participation beyond the young child's physical abilities, a **partial participation task analysis** may be an alternative. In this approach, steps are broken down into even smaller increments. This is to encourage the child with more limitations to participate in a meaningful way. Snell (1987) uses toothbrushing to describe partial participation task analysis. The child's participation involves opening his or her mouth for the caregiver to brush one quadrant of his or her teeth and swallowing a drink of water after each quadrant is brushed.

A unique feature of task analyzing adaptive skills involves the use of **chaining.** Chaining is based on the fact that one step must be accomplished before the next step can be performed. For assessment purposes **forward chaining** (beginning with step 1) yields the most useful information. **Reverse chaining** is more useful for teaching a skill. With reverse chaining the last part of the task is done first. Consider the example:

1. Child puts on sock when just above heel.
2. Child puts on sock when just below heel.
3. Child puts on sock when toes started in.
4. Child puts on sock when handed to him with heel in correct position.
5. Child puts on sock (heel in correct position).

Smiles and praise for each success combined with "you put your sock on" encourages self-help and builds language.

Dressing, toileting, and feeding are each a complex set of adaptive skills that are critical to independence. Therapeutic and instructional procedures are emphasized in the next section.

Dressing

Several guidelines suggested by Bailey and Wolery (1984), Snell (1987), and Copeland and Kimmel (1989) all point to the fact that success rate of self-dressing will be greatly increased when the following practices are included in the total plan. When at all possible, training should be done at appropriate times and in natural settings. Training should be done as often as possible in the child's home and during times when dressing and undressing normally occur. This will involve active family and staff participation in

Table 8–4   Developmental sequence of adaptive skills

Age in Months	Eating Skills	Toileting Skills	Dressing and Grooming
0–3	• Oral reflexes (e.g., sucking) present at birth • Coordinates sucking, swallowing, and breathing		
3–6	•Brings hand to mouth holding object • Begins to hold bottle with some assistance • May eat some solids—sucks from spoon • Begins to swallow from cup • Basic chewing begins to appear		
6–9	• Can hold bottle and bring it to mouth • Can hold and eat cracker • Uses tongue to move food in mouth • Eats infant food		
9–12	• More control over lips, tongue, and jaw • Holds spoon • Finger feeds	• Pays attention to acts of eliminating	• Holds arm out for sleeve
12–18	• Brings spoon to mouth • Drinks from cup with some spilling • Chews appropriately	• Indicates discomfort over soiled pants • Begins to sit on potty	• Takes off shoes and socks • Tries to put on shoes
18–24	• Sucks with straw • Scoops food, feeds self • Chews with rotary jaw movement • Uses cup with fewer accidents	• Communicates need to go to toilet	• Finds large armhole • Attempts to brush teeth
24–30	• Holds fork and begins to spear food	• Bladder trained during day	• Removes pull-down garments • Buttons large front button
30–36		• Becomes more routine and sets time for elimination • Uses toilet independently	• Attempts to wash hands • Uses toothbrush • Opens front and side buttons • Closes front snaps

defining the goals, teaching procedures, establishing several types of reinforcers, and designing an easy data-keeping system (Copeland & Kimmel, 1989).

As with all other adaptive areas, children with motor impairments have more difficulty learning dressing skills unless adaptations can be made. It definitely requires a team effort. Some suggestions made by Finnie (1975) and Copeland and Kimmel (1989) are:

- Training plans should begin with the easiest garments and follow the normal sequential development of accomplishing undressing before learning to put on clothes.

- Clothes used for training should be several sizes larger than the child's normal size for ease of manipulation and putting on and off. (This method has been found to be more successful than practicing with dressing form boards.)

- Children who have difficulty conceptualizing may benefit from dressing or performing dressing or grooming tasks in front of a mirror.

- Children who have poor balance can perform many dressing skills while lying down. The child, for example, may begin by side lying to put on pants and gradually turns as pants are raised to waist level. This positioning is especially useful when there is excessive motor tone.

- Children can sit in a corner or use a corner chair to provide more stability while dressing.

- If the supine position on the caregiver's lap, changing table, or floor does not reduce extensor tone, the child may be placed prone over the caregiver's lap. Lower and upper extremity dressing can be done in this position. (Always consult with the therapists.)

- Simple changes to a child's clothes may be the determining factor of the success level in self-dressing: use of Velcro in place of snaps or buttons; elasticized waistbands; adding a metal ring through a zipper's tab to make it easier to grasp and pull; tube socks to eliminate the need of getting the heel positioned correctly; and slip-on shoes or shoes with Velcro closures.

- For all young children, use the opportunity to verbally label and discuss each step of the process.

Toileting

Independent toileting skills are often an area of concern and frustration for both parents and child (and, yes, for the early interventionist). Children achieve bowel and daytime bladder control between 2½ and 3 years of age. Children with more severe developmental delay may not be ready until 5 years of age (Snell, 1987). This does not suggest that younger children with developmental disabilities cannot be toilet trained. It does, however, point out the need for a coordinated team effort and consistent follow-through for both home and center programs.

Prerequisites to training include neuromuscular control and the child's awareness of discomfort when he or she eliminates in his or her diaper. Then the child's pattern of elimination must be established. One way of doing this is to check the child every half hour to determine whether she is dry, wet, or has had a bowel movement. Over time, perhaps 7 days, a pattern of elimination may emerge if eating habits and activity levels have remained constant (Copeland & Kimmel, 1989). This pattern directs the trainer toward implementation.

According to Copeland and Kimmel (1989), other prerequisite skills that speed toileting control are the ability to walk with or without assistance, the ability to indicate a need to use the toilet, the ability to remain in a sitting position for at least 5 minutes, and the ability to comprehend and follow instructions.

While the child is learning the prerequisites, Noonan and McCormick (1993) suggest that toileting needs are most easily managed through "timed toileting." This involves placing the child on the toilet for a few minutes at a time until elimination occurs. If the child uses the toilet, provide reinforcement. If the child does not eliminate, remove him or her from the toilet without consequences. To further increase awareness of the toileting process each time the child eliminates, the trainer can label the process by saying, "Megan, you did number one (or two)," using whatever label the parents and teacher feel are appropriate. (Terminology should be consistent.)

Copeland and Kimmel (1989) recommend that for children who have difficulty in maintaining trunk control while sitting on a potty chair, adaptation can be made to the existing chair by adding back and side supports or hip and shoulder straps, or using a commercial potty seat that has these features. Fear or discomfort in sitting on a potty seat or potty chair will certainly make this process more of a "combat zone" than a natural, pleasurable experience. Relaxation can be achieved when the child feels secure with feet either on the floor or with some type of footrest.

Supportive adults willing to work through the ups and downs of the training period are essential. Potty time, as well as diaper changing, is an opportune time to engage in language development activities, including nursery rhymes and songs.

Feeding

An integral part of many early intervention programs is the consideration of teaching adaptive skills related to feeding, eating, and drinking. Mealtime is the natural time for teaching and reinforcing feeding skills as well as a time when prespeech skills can also be facilitated (Mueller, 1972). For young children with special needs, teachers, therapists, and parents need to coordinate efforts at all meals to reinforce newly learned skills and develop others. The family dinner time provides the best opportunity to integrate language, socialization, and motor skills learned during the day. Because of time and attention required by the parent to perform the task of feeding, it has been suggested by Copeland and Kimmel (1989) that the child with a disability be fed before the regular dinnertime. Then, during the meal, the child can be given dessert or a toy so that she or he may continue to participate and interact with the family without placing demands on parents' mealtime. As the child becomes more independent, this schedule would probably change.

For infants and young children with severe disabilities, individualized plans for feeding must be a necessary part of the team's recommendation. This is especially true when there is a neuromotor disability, such as cerebral palsy. Strategies may be needed to minimize the effects of oral-motor problems, including proper positioning and use of adaptive equipment. Positioning is critical in feeding the child with motor problems. If proper positioning techniques are not used during feeding, many children with abnormal muscle tone will have problems with gagging, choking, or swallowing (Copeland & Kimmel, 1989). Everyone who feeds the child must have an understanding of the child's movement patterns in order to respond appropriately to changes that may occur from day to day and hour to hour. Whenever possible, on-going consultation with the occupational therapist or physical therapist can offer very important assistance in this process. Figure 8-6 shows the most usual positions for feeding: lap, arm, or chair.

In addition, the following suggestions are adapted from Umansky and Hooper (1998), Bigge (1991), Copeland and Kimmel (1989):

Feeding Positions.

- Positions in which a child can be fed will depend on age, physical size, postural tone, and movement patterns—see examples in Figure 8-6.

To feed a baby with motor problems —
in your arms:

Put the baby into the crook of your arm,
with the head tucked;
Bring the arms forward; and
Be sure the hips and knees are bent.

In your lap:
Put your feet up on a stool or chair.
If necessary, use a pillow or wedge; and
Put the child on your lap facing you

To feed a child in a high chair:
Add rolls between the legs or at the sides
if necessary;
Put the lower part of the child's body
against the back of the chair; and
Use a safety strap;
Make sure that the feet are flat on a footrest.

Figure 8–6 Most common positions for feeding. (*Source of drawings:* From *Positioning for infants and young children with motor problems* [videotape manual], pp. 8–11. Courtesy of the University of Colorado School of Nursing, Marilyn Krajicek, Director, First Start.)

- Unless an infant is still being bottle- or breast-fed, he or she should be positioned as upright as possible.

- The child's head should be tilted slightly forward to encourage normal swallowing.

- Hand pressure on the back of a child's head while feeding may elicit a primitive reflex that causes the child's body to extend and, thus, should be avoided.

- While sitting in a highchair or adapted seat or highchair, the child's legs should be relaxed and feet flat on the footrest or on the floor.

- The food and trainer generally are positioned in front of the child unless oral-motor intervention is required.

Sucking and Swallowing.

- For bottle feeding, use nipples with regular-size holes. Larger holes in a nipple may cause choking if there is difficulty swallowing.

- When the child begins to suck on the nipple, "tug" gently at the nipple as if to pull it out. This can encourage the child to suck a bit harder. Also try thickening the liquid with a small amount of rice cereal for more suck resistance.

- A downward stroke on the cheek stimulates sucking.

- If there are problems with jaw control, assist by holding child's chin in cupped hand.

- Assist lip closure by placing index and second fingers above and below the child's lips using a "scissors" motion to close lips. If assistance for jaw closure is needed, support jaw with the baby finger.

- If there is a lack of normal swallowing, close the child's mouth (supported if necessary); stroke downward under chin.

- Encourage mouthing and sucking of toys, hands, and pacifiers during non-feeding times.

Self-Feeding.

- When beginning to teach chewing, use foods that a child can digest easily.

- Place small amounts of food between the child's teeth on the inside of the mouth. Use lip and jaw control as necessary to keep mouth closed. This should stimulate a chewing response.

- From pureed or baby foods, gradually introduce textured foods, e.g., bits of dry cereal, toast, soft cheese, diced potato, etc.

- Problems with finger feeding may require that the trainer place a hand over the child's and assist getting food into the mouth. Reduce support from hand, to wrist, to elbow, and finally to no support. Same routine when spoon is introduced.

- For a hypersensitive bite reflex, use a small, rubber-coated spoon for feeding. Place spoon on front third of tongue and apply downward pressure. Remove spoon at 45° angle and avoid scraping food off with teeth. Food should be removed with lips.

- Children with severe eating and drinking problems are at risk for choking. Food may easily obstruct airways. If a child is coughing, the airway is not totally obstructed. Allow the child to cough, and assist the child to lean forward.

- Safety reminder: Avoid bacon, peanuts, popcorn, hot dogs with skin, grapes, raw carrots, or any small, round food such as candy. These foods are easy to choke on.
- A nonslip rubberlike material, purchased by the roll, can be used for placemats under plates, toys, etc., to keep them in place.

Drinking.

- Offer broths or semi-sweet liquids (warm or cool) for the beginning stages of cup training. Milk and sweet liquids seem to impede the process.
- Place the rim of the cup on the child's lower lip. Placing the cup between the teeth causes abnormal swallowing.
- Use of a "cut out" cup helps to observe lip closure and avoids bending the child's head back.
- A wide range of cups and eating utensils is available from several adapted equipment companies. Consult with therapists on selection of most-appropriate items for individual children.

ADAPTING THE ENVIRONMENT

Because most disabling conditions require children to work extra hard to utilize the learning resources in their environment, most programs for children with special needs attempt to identify obstacles to learning and facilitate children's involvement in the learning process.

The Classroom

The integrated early education classroom is a dynamic system that includes both physical and social components. According to Rogers-Warren (1982), physical components include the actual classroom space, the arrangement of activity areas within the space, the furniture and fixtures, the play and work materials, the activities of the program and their sequence, the number of adult participants, the number

and types of children (with and withou and the grouping of staff and children. nents are the behaviors of adults and c classroom setting.

The classroom environment can facilitate movement and independence by providing opportunities for children to determine their own behavior and manage some of their own materials. Even a child with the most severe disabilities needs a chance to have some effect on the environment. Accessible bathrooms, drinking fountains, and play materials will encourage independence and learning. Rogers-Warren (1982) suggested a checklist to help teachers accommodate young children with physical disabilities in the classroom:

- How does the setting appear at a child's level? Are there interesting things to see and touch, such as windows, mirrors, mobiles, aquariums and toys?
- Is there room for a wheelchair-bound or awkwardly mobile child to negotiate in and out of spaces and turn around?
- Are shelves and tables at a comfortable level for a child's height? Is there a place (preferably more than one) that can accommodate a child in each activity area?
- Are shelves, tables, sinks, and other fixtures sturdy enough to hold the weight of a minimally mobile child who may need support?
- Are prosthetic devices (such as a standing cuff) easily accessible in the areas where children might gain practice standing or sitting without an adult's assistance while engaged in an activity?
- Are some of the materials and toys accessible to a child without assistance even if he or she is minimally mobile?
- Is the sound level and acoustic arrangement of the room satisfactory for a child with a hearing impairment or a hearing aid? Are there some special quiet areas for children to work with minimal noise distraction?

- Does the environment contain sufficient contrasts to attract the notice of a visually impaired child? Do color and light contrasts corroborate texture and height contrasts?

- Are the cues (use of color, change of levels, dividers) that designate different areas clear and consistent?

- How much of the environment is designed for self-management or self-engagement? How frequently do children use these opportunities? Does a child need training to use these opportunities?

- Does the arrangement of the room allow for quiet places and social places to meet the changing moods and needs of children? (pp. 29–30)

In an effort to make integrated classrooms appropriate for the young child with motor impairments, Safford (1989) suggested that activities involving movement should allow the child to be involved as much as possible without accentuating the inability to move well. For example, the leader can combine sitting activities with floor locomotion activities such as rolling or combat crawling. (These movement activities are enhanced by music or rhymes.) If a child is unable to perform movements

voluntarily, an adult should assist in motoring the child through the activities.

The Home

In home-based programs, the primary learning environment is the home and its surroundings. Although program staff may have little control over the child's home, the home interventionist may recommend ways to make the home safe and facilitate learning. Burns, cuts, falls, electrical shock, and poisoning are some of the major home hazards. An interventionist who reviews such hazards with the family and explains what to expect from children at different ages promotes safety concerns. Other things that the home interventionist may wish to explore with parents are:

1. The kinds of toys and objects in the home that stimulate exploration and learning.

2. Toys that are age and developmentally appropriate and can be adapted to accommodate special needs.

3. The level of visual and auditory stimulation in the home.

4. Modification to the environment that may allow the child greater independence and freedom of action.

5. Adaptive equipment such as chairs, prone boards, and self-help aids should be included in home-based programs to encourage opportunities for social interaction and participation in family life.

Exhibit 8–2 describes a model therapeutic home-based program.

MOVEMENT EDUCATION

Whenever infants and young children move any part of their bodies, there is potential for two kinds of learning to occur: learning to move and learning by moving. Bailey and Burton (1989) expanded on this:

EXHIBIT 8–2

Model Therapeutic Home Program

Since therapeutic intervention for young children with significant physical disabilities must include more than a once-a-month clinic visit or prescribed routines in a center-based program, emphasis on the integration of occupational and/or physical therapy into a functional home-based program seems critical to the provision of consistent, ongoing therapy. As suggested by Vincent, Salisbury, Laten, and Baumgart (1979), a desirable approach is for the therapist and family to work together to identify the times and contexts within which to apply therapeutic methods and work on therapeutic goals that are relevant for the child and realistic for the family. By assessing the family's typical routine, the therapist and family can identify naturally occurring teaching opportunities (Rainforth & Salisbury, 1988).

One approach to assessment and implementation is the Family Daily Routine model (Vincent et al., 1979). Rainforth and Salisbury (1988) have described the process in detail. An example of embedding home programming recommendations into existing family routines can be seen in the case of Frankie R.

Frankie is a 2-year-old boy with severe cerebral palsy (spastic quadriplegia). He is enrolled in a home- and center-based early intervention program where he receives physical therapy on a weekly basis. The therapist and Frankie's parents identified several goals for home and center. Two of the goals included in the family plan are:

1. To increase range of motion in shoulders and hips.
2. To establish symmetry and head control while sitting.

5:30 P.M.: Television, relaxing with Dad

Method: Position Frankie straddling Dad's leg, side-lying on the couch, or prone-lying over Dad's lap.

Rationale: Mr. R. agreed that these procedures would not conflict with his need to relax and also would provide an opportunity for him to interact with Frankie. The physical therapist indicated that both goals were being addressed.

7:00 P.M. Bath with Mom or Dad

Method: Stretch Frankie's shoulders and hips while bathing and drying him; also stretch his trunk by hip and shoulder rotation. Facilitate head control and reaching by playing in the water and touching body parts.

Rationale: The warm water and terrycloth towels tend to help Frankie relax, and, while he is undressed, this is a good opportunity to work on range of motion. Bathtime provides a natural motivation to maintain head control and to move arms in the water. It is also an excellent time for communication.

Adapting this type of model for all home activities allows the maximum benefit from parent-identified activities that, with minimal intrusion, can be used to provide practice of important developmental skills (Rainforth & Salisbury, 1988).

Learning to move involves the emergence and refinement of movement skills and the development of general movement abilities. Learning by moving consists of infants forming associations and making cognitive relationships. This is the process whereby they gradually construct their reality. (p. 1)

Thus, **movement education** as a critical component of early intervention and preschool programs should also be viewed as a means of providing growth in self-image, concept development, language development, perceptual discrimination, socialization, and recreation. This section will highlight adaptations in movement education and include the significant role music and imagination play in young children's development.

Adaptations in Movement Education

Popovich (1998) suggested the use of prompts (cues) when assisting children who are having difficulty developing motor skills that should be within their behavioral repertoire. If a child does not respond to a normal verbal direction and modeling of desired responses, the verbal direction is repeated and accompanied by gestures. If there is still no response or an inadequate one, the verbal request can be accompanied by physically helping the child to perform the act. Positive reinforcement is given at whatever level the act is attempted. Of course, physical or gestural prompts are removed (faded) as soon as possible. Other adaptations are included in the following list. [Some of these guidelines are based on those offered by Frostig (1974)].

1. Carefully plan lessons consistent with classroom guidelines for behavior.

2. Incorporate some degree of movement education into each day's plan.

3. Alternate vigorous activities with more relaxing ones.

4. Give attention to all attributes of movement. None should be left out in the total week's plan.

5. Vary body positions in on-the-floor activities as well as during activities that involve locomotion.

6. Intersperse activities in a group with activities alone or with a partner. This variation creates opportunities for cooperation without too much repetition.

7. Use equipment and music to allow for creative variations, but not as a part of every lesson. Children need time to concentrate on their own bodily actions.

8. Conscious teaching of concepts does not need to be included in every activity. Instead, integrate concepts logically into the day's schedule.

9. Take care to allow for repetition and modeling when giving directions to children who may have perceptual or linguistic delays. Move from the known to the unknown and from the simple to the complex. Do not expect transfer from one activity to another.

10. Use physical, tactile, and verbal prompting as needed. Break tasks into simple, sequential steps. Give positive reinforcement with each step of progress. Be patient with those who are slow or reluctant. Keep vocabulary within the children's level. Do not expect understanding of the verbal labels "left" and "right."

11. All young children, especially those who are medically fragile, need adequate rest periods. Do not try to cover too much at once or continue an activity for too long.

12. Provide varied but structured activities for children who have difficulty paying attention and/or controlling bodily movements. Activities should be simple and free from distractions. Maintain eye contact. Be gentle but firm. Do not give the child a choice if a choice is not intended. For example, saying, "Do you want to _____?" allows the child to say "No."

13. If a child has a visual impairment, be certain to use his or her name when verbally directing activities. Minimize eye strain by not standing where the child must look into a glare. Give the child an extra dose of body awareness activities.

14. Use visual cues such as "stop" and "go" signs in red and green not only as attention getters but also to assist those with hearing impairments. Also be certain children with hearing impairments can read your lips when giving directions. Be certain that shadows are not in your face, and stand relatively still. Be certain to get the child's attention before beginning an activity. Withdrawal or hyperactivity can be the result of not being able to distinguish words.

15. Include children with physical impairments whenever possible. For example, when others are running under a parachute, these children can be pushed under. When possible, substitute a sitting or lying position for a standing position.

16. Most important of all is the need for lessons to be enjoyed by everyone. Do not attempt activities that involve movement and noise if you are not in a mood to tolerate what they create.

Exhibit 8–3 provides an example of an adapted gross motor activity.

Movement and Aquatics

Aquatics or hydrotherapy is probably one of the most underused modalities for young children with delayed motor development. Because pools are not always accessible, it is rarely considered as a program component. It is worthwhile to look for pool facilities within easy travel distance from the center or from the child's home. Health Clubs, YMCA, and YWCA programs often include an aquatics program for young children.

Learning to swim may not be the immediate goal but there is great potential for physiological, psychological, social, and recreational gains (Doremus, 1992). Sensory and movement experiences for socialization, normalization, and relaxation are also important objectives. For children who are motorically involved or whose ability to move is otherwise limited, water offers a medium in which to experience a wide range of movement patterns, including range of motion, balance, active movements, and improved respiratory function. Doremus (1992) makes the following suggestions in program planning:

- Obtain written parental consent and instructions from child's physician regarding health precautions.

- Young children require one-to-one staffing in pool. Volunteer support may be needed.

- To promote comfort and relaxation, water temperature of 86° to 93° Fahrenheit is preferred.

- Length of each session will be determined by child's tolerance level, typically 30 minutes.

- In terms of frequency of sessions, at least every other week is recommended for children to practice and retain newly learned skills.

- To implement program, list each child's goals and objectives on a small card kept poolside in plastic zipper bag. Indicate any precautions such as "seizures," "tubes in ears," etc.

- Keep it fun at all times! (p. 10)

Movement Skills and Music

Dancing, marching, imitating, and imagining are often more enjoyable with music. Most commercially prepared records and tapes move a bit too fast for preschoolers, at least at first. If so, sing the songs without the records and say the directions first. Gradually, as the children's ability to listen and move quickly grows, the recording can be used. Some children feel lost with the recorded voice. Young children with mild hearing losses or perceptual problems, particularly, find recorded voices difficult to understand.

Rhythm bands, whether they include real instruments or pans with spoons, are exciting to children. Banging on something is an excellent way to develop awareness of body movement. The music may not be concert hall quality, but it certainly pleases the performers. Learning to make different kinds of noises by stamping feet loudly and then tiptoeing quietly leads to other kinds of body awareness.

A number of books are available to assist teachers in movement skills activities with the accompaniment of music. Because it is difficult to define dances or other rhythmic activities in terms of age, teachers must carefully think through their children's developmental characteristics. Even the most appealing jingle can frustrate children if the accompanying movements are too difficult. For children with special needs, Nelson has suggested beginning with the most simple and gradually working up to the more difficult songs or games. Reluctant children may need a personal invitation to join by offering them your hand. If they do not accept, they should

EXHIBIT 8–3

A Gross Motor Activity with Adaptations

Goal: *To develop body image; to increase awareness of moving in different directions (directionality).*
Objectives: Given directions to move forward, backward, and sideways, each child will do the following:

1. Do as directed when the teacher prompts (physically, with gestures, or with additional words, as needed).
2. As a member of a group, follow the teacher's spoken and gestured signal.
3. As a member of a group, follow spoken directions (no gestures).
4. Throughout this lesson, stop and remain still in the exact position he or she was in at that moment when asked to "freeze." (This condition helps children learn to inhibit unnecessary movements.)

Procedure: Begin with children sitting in a line facing the teacher. Then the activity may proceed according to the following steps (of course, variations will be determined by the individual needs of the children):

1. "Susie, come stand here" (point to a masking tape X on the floor).
2. "Good, now walk forward" (physically prompting and gesturing Susie).
3. "Right, you walked forward. Thank you. You may sit down. Tommy, it's your turn. Come stand on the X."
4. "Tommy, can you walk backward?" (Gesturing—but because Tommy begins to move backward, no physical prompting is needed.)
5. "Tommy, you did that just the right way. You walked backward."

Procedural notes: The teacher's enthusiasm and encouragement are of critical importance. The lessons will be individualized as each child's movements are observed. Physical prompts, gestures, and demonstrations will be faded as quickly as possible. Children will be encouraged to verbalize their understanding of their body movements through natural conversation as the activity progresses. Other considerations include the following:

1. Initially each child should be given a brief individual turn. Children will learn from watching. Begin with the child who is most likely to succeed with little or no help. This child serves as a model for the others to follow.
2. Next, pair two children at a time to follow the directions. The children may be given the same or two different directions, depending on their stage of development. (Keep the activity moving.)
3. As soon as possible (but for some children this may take several days), have groups of three to five children moving at the same time.
4. To add variety, a 4/4 march or dance rhythm can be introduced with records, a drum, or by singing. A square dance calling format can be included with the help of another adult. Guide children as needed, using modeling or prompting as well as calling the directions.
5. New directions should be introduced following this same sequence, before incorporating them into the dance.

Lesson adaptations:

1. For the child with a hearing impairment:
   a. Be sure the child can see your face and gestures.
   b. Place a child with normal hearing on either side.
   c. Let this child feel the drum or other musical instrument as the rhythm is played. It sometimes helps to set record players on the floor and let the child perform with bare or stocking feet.

EXHIBIT 8–3

2. For the child with a visual impairment:
   a. Use physical prompts until the verbal prompts can be followed. (Fade physical assists as soon as possible.)
   b. Assign a sighted partner. Holding hands will be helpful.
   c. Be certain the space used is free from tripping and falling hazards.

3. For the child with a motor impairment:
   a. Encourage as much participation as possible.
   b. Use supports (for example, walkers and crutches) as needed.
   c. Have an adult push a wheelchair, if necessary.
   d. Assign the child to be caller or drum beater.

4. For the child with learning delays:
   a. Continue the prompting as needed.
   b. Place excellent models beside the child.
   c. Give directions slowly and one at a time.
   d. Repeat directions as often as necessary (with kind enthusiasm).
   e. Demonstrate patience if the child cannot do what he or she could do the day before.
   f. Socially reward each small step of progress.

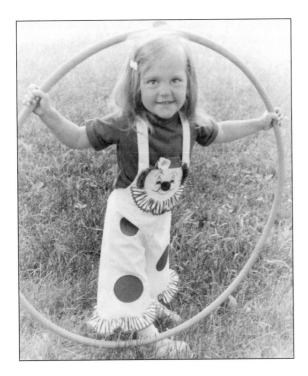

not be forced to join. Rather, she has suggested the use of song games that invite children to join by name.

Movement Skills and Imagination

Children often need help in imagining things, since some have had little opportunity to pretend. They enjoy pretending to be engineers on trains, bus drivers, animals, and robots. Dress-up clothes add to the fun but are not necessary. Films and filmstrips can start an idea. Stories and flannelboard materials can lead to stimulating ideas. Pretending to put out a fire with an imaginary hose is almost as exciting as the real thing, and much safer.

Children discover the motions people make through seeing a combination of real people, films, and pictures. Then they take turns pretending. Gradually, they become more creative. The fireman has to put out a fire on the roof, so he stretches up high. Next, the fire is in the basement, so he aims the hose down low. A robot, walking with stiff legs, may move very slowly. Then, as someone turns the controls, he moves faster or even more slowly. Although the teacher may need to suggest ways to move at first, the children's use of imagination improves quickly.

The purpose of the next chapter is to convey the complex nature of the development of communication skills. Focus will be on the importance of helping young children develop functional communication skills that will enable them to initiate and influence social interaction.

Summary

Professionals who work with children with a wide range of abilities and disabilities in various early intervention settings should understand physical and psychological factors that may interfere with the normal developmental process. Because infants are now in many programs, knowledge of the beginning behaviors is critical in planning intervention and assisting parents effectively. All early educators should study the development and interrelationship of the nervous system and motor skills.

The young child with a motor delay requires a team approach involving the physician, therapists, nutritionists, parents, and teachers to meet special needs at home and school. Observations and team planning ensure consistency and selection of appropriate intervention strategies. Mutual understanding of therapeutic and educational goals serves to strengthen motor skill development.

Adaptations of materials and environmental considerations should be a concern for all early education programs, but more specifically when children who are medically fragile or have motor delays are included. Finding ways for these children to interact, respond, and develop will require more than the few activities usually listed in curriculum guides. Gross and fine motor skills, adaptive skills, and movement experiences must be an integral part of each child's day-to-day home and school activities. Its relationship to other aspects of development makes movement an essential component of an effective early education program.

Discussion Topics and Activities

1. Thoroughly review at least three developmental checklists. Pay special attention to the sequential order of the motor skills. Adopt a checklist that seems to be complete or compile your own. Observe a typical child and a child with a disability or children of two different ages. Were you able to detect differences in skill development? If not, your checklist needs to be broken into smaller steps.

2. Now take a major skill such as throwing and break it into subskills as directed in Chapter 6. Sequence these skills. After your task analysis is complete, try to teach the skill to a friend or a child. What subskills did you leave out? Did the order of your skills need to be changed? With adults, skipping is a good skill to analyze.

3. Interview or ask a physical and occupational therapist to visit class. Ask for information, for example, about positioning techniques, adaptive equipment, and special teaching procedures. Be certain to ask the therapist to explain his or her view of motor development.

4. Investigate the relationship between motor skills and body awareness. Begin a file of activities specially designed to teach body awareness and contribute to self-esteem.

5. There are several suggestions in the literature that instruction in perceptual skills may not be defensible. Research this matter. Discuss and debate the issue with classmates.

6. Try to explain the sequential trends of motor development to another person, deriving and using specific examples. If you can explain them clearly to another, then you probably understand them well.

7. Research and discuss the various disabling conditions, such as cerebral palsy, muscular dystrophy, and visual impairment, that have an impact on motor skill development. If possible, invite a member of the community who has experienced difficulties from such an impairment to discuss ways teachers can be of assistance.

8. Plan a motor activity. Be creative. Consider parachutes, isometric exercises, and dances. Teach this lesson to your classmates. Discover the fun some movement activities really are. Do your lesson with children.

9. Design a playground that would be suitable for children with a variety of disabling conditions.

Annotated Bibliography

Bailey, P. W. (Ed.) (1997). *Active learning for children with disabilities: A manual for use with the active learning series.* Menlo Park, CA: Addison-Wesley.

The *Active Learning* series is made up of activity books for infants and 1 to 5-year-olds. For each age group there is a planning guide and four activity sections. For example, *Active Learning for Ones* includes the following sections, which contain ideas suitable for use with toddlers from 12 to 24 months: "Planning for Ones," "Activities for Listening and Talking," "Activities for Physical Development," "Creative Activities," and "Activities for Learning from the World Around Them." Included are over 300 activities that are easy to read and do with one toddler or a small group. Ideas on setting up environments for toddlers in this age group and an easy system for writing plans help caregivers set the stage for a good activity program. Developed at the Frank Porter Graham Child Development Center in Chapel Hill, NC.

Baker, M.J., Banfied, C.S., Killburn, D., & Shufflebarger, K.J. (1991). *Controlling movement: A therapeutic approach to early intervention.* Gaithersburg, MD: Aspen.

This looseleaf manual provides precise therapeutic activities for parents and early interventionists to use in systematic programs for infants and toddlers. It is easy to read and has excellent illustrations.

Batshaw, M.L. (1997). *Children with disabilities.* Baltimore: Paul H. Brookes.

This updated edition is an excellent reference providing in-depth descriptions of all the major types of disabilities in a style understandable by both parents and professionals. It has more than 200 detailed illustrations, a helpful glossary, and a thorough resource list.

Bigge, J.L. (1991). *Teaching individuals with physical and multiple disabilities.* Upper Saddle River, NJ: Merrill/Prentice Hall.

Although this book focuses more on school-age children with disabilities, it is highly recommended to early interventionists for the comprehensive, readable discussions on therapeutic management, adaptive and assistive devices, pre-speech and feeding techniques, and augmentative communication. Useful lists of resources are included throughout the text.

Blackman, J.A. (Ed.). (1997). *Medical aspects of developmental disabilities in children birth to three.* Rockville, MD: Aspen Systems.

This manual summarizes health information that is important in the day-to-day care of children with developmental disabilities. The authors give the description, cause, incidence, detection, course, accompanying health problems, usual medical management, and implications for education of approximately 40 developmental disabilities. Illustrations accompany its clear explanations.

Copeland, M.E., & Kimmel, J.R. (1989). *Evaluation and management of infants and young children with developmental disabilities.* Baltimore: Paul H. Brookes.

Since both authors are occupational therapists, the focus is on abnormal motor development and instructional methods designed for infants and young children with developmental disabilities. Detailed discussions on movement, feeding, toileting, and dressing are particularly useful. Excellent resource.

Curtis, S. (1982). *The joy of movement in early childhood.* New York: Teachers College Press.

This book includes a series of photographs exploring stages involved in each of the fundamental motor patterns—walking, running, jumping, kicking, throwing, and catching. It offers suggestions for incorporating these patterns into a total motor activity program and discusses other facets, such as setting up creative play spaces and making one's own equipment.

Diamant, R.B. (1992). *Positioning for play: Home activities for parents of young children.* Tucson, AZ: Communication/Therapy Skill Builders.

This is a collection of 70 reproducible activity sheets to teach parents therapeutic play activities to stimulate development of motor skills in young children, birth to 3 years. Emphasis is on proper positioning during play. Instructions and illustrations are clear and concise.

Endres, J.B., & Rockwell, R.E. (1994). *Food, nutrition, and the young child.* Upper Saddle River, NJ: Merrill/Prentice Hall.

This book focuses on nutrition as an integral part of early childhood programs. It stresses a team approach in which nutritionists, teachers, and parents work together to ensure an effective program. The section on nutrition discusses needs of the child from birth to 5 years of age. It includes excellent ideas for incorporating food and nutrition into the overall learning environment.

Fisher, A.G., Murray, E.A., & Bundy, A. (Eds.). (1991). *Sensory integration: Theory and practice.* Philadelphia: F.A. Davis.

Well-written text that presents a clear picture of sensory integration and its use with children. Topics include play theory and sensory integration, assessment, vestibular-proprioceptive system, tactile processing, and sensory defensiveness.

Geralis, E., & Ritter, T. (Eds.). (1997). *Children with cerebral palsy: A parent's guide.* Rockville, MD: Woodbine House.

This is a manual written for parents of young children with cerebral palsy. Though the language is simple it is not condescending. It offers information related to medical terminology and practices, types of services available, equipment, early intervention approaches, parent coping strategies, and legal rights. Information is given to help parents choose a pediatrician and to evaluate intervention programs. A glossary and reading list are also included. Chapters are written by both professionals and parents.

Hansen, M.J., & Harris, S.R. (1986). *Teaching the young child with motor delays.* Austin, TX: Pro-Ed.

This easy-to-read guide is written primarily for parents of children from birth to age 3 who have motor impairments.

The book provides information to parents on how motor development influences other areas of child development, teaching strategies, and therapeutic activities. Resource lists and diagnostic materials are useful to both parents and professionals.

Jaeger, L. (1987). *Home program instruction sheets for infants and young children.* Tucson, AZ: Communication and Therapy Skill Builders.

The home instruction sheets represent some of the more common exercises and activities for young children with motor dysfunction. The instruction sheets are generally used with parents as a reminder of recommended home activities generally prescribed by the physical therapist. Teachers may also use the positions and activities in the classroom.

Linder, T.W. (1996). *Transdisciplinary play-based assessment: A functional approach to working with young children.* Baltimore: Paul H. Brookes.

This book contains descriptive observational guidelines for assessing a young child's development through child-directed play. The chapter on sensorimotor development by Susan Hall provides an excellent framework for assessing both the qualitative and quantitative components of this area of development.

Morris, S.E., & Klein, M.D. (1998). *Pre-feeding skills: A comprehensive guide for feeding development.* San Antonio, TX: Psychological Corporation.

From anatomy and normal development to assessment and treatment, this comprehensive book provides a framework for developing therapy plans for a variety of feeding problems.

Parks, S., Furuno, S., O'Reilly, P.T., Takayo, I., Hosaka, C., Zeisloft-Folboy, B. (1988). *HELP ... at home.* Palo Alto, CA: Vort Corporation.

This is a very practical and useful collection of developmental activity sheets for professionals to give to parents of young children, birth to 36 months (updated and adapted version of the Hawaii Early Learning Profile Activity Guide). In addition to activities in all developmental domains, there is step-by-step instruction in areas such as positioning and feeding. Instructions for the activities are user-friendly.

Petrie, P. (1987). *Baby play: Activities for discovery and development during the first year of life.* New York: Pantheon.

This is a book to be enjoyed and used by all who are interested in infant development. Excellent illustrations and photographs are included, as well as valuable suggestions for developmentally appropriate activities and toys.

Ratliffe, K.T. (1998). *Clinical pediatric physical therapy: A guide for the physical therapy team.* St. Louis, MO: Mosby.

Primarily written for physical therapists, this book is useful for the early interventionists and the family. A unique feature of this text is that it redirects the reader's attention from the disability to the child as a whole within the context of the home, family and community.

Seaman, J.A., & Depauw, K.P. (1989). *The new adapted physical education: A developmental approach.* Mountain View, CA: Mayfield.

The authors present an extensive discussion of neuromotor development as a basis for understanding the needs of indi-

viduals with motor disabilities. Approaches to intervention provide a useful resource for early intervention specialists. The role of well-trained adaptive physical education specialists is clarified.

Zeitlin, S. & Williamson, G.G. (1994). *Coping in young children: Early intervention practices to enhance adaptive behavior and resilience.* Baltimore, MD: Paul H. Brookes.

This guide explains how to integrate a child's developmental skills with daily functional living. Step-by-step, this approach shows how to assess coping behaviors and plan appropriate intervention strategies.

Audio-visual Recommendations

Communication/Therapy Skill Builders—3830 E. Bellevue/ P.O. Box 42050-P93, Tucson, AZ 85733.

A number of videos on early intervention topics are available through this company, including some that would be pertinent to learning more about various aspects of motor development:

1. Normal Development of Reach and Grasp
2. Normal Infant Reflexes and Development
3. Normal Development of Walking
4. Sensory Integration Therapy

Human Development Series: Concept Media. P.O. Box 19542, Irvine, CA 92713.

1. Birth to 2½ (4 videos)
2. 2½ to 6 yrs (4 videos)

These recent video productions on human development provide an insightful look at the process of development from birth to 6 yrs. The videos (one from each set) on *Physical growth and motor development* serve as an ex-

cellent background for understanding of normal as well as atypical motor development. Useful for both parents and professionals.

Learner Managed Designs. 2201 K W. 25th St., Lawrence, KS 66046. *Positioning for infants and young children with motor problems.*

This is one of several training videos from the University of Colorado School of Nursing. This video is excellent for understanding basic principles and techniques of positioning and handling infants with motor problems.

Special Needs Project. 3463 State Street, Suite 282, Santa Barbara, CA 93105.

1. Potty Learning for Children who Experience Delay (video: 69 minutes).
2. Medical Issues Impacting Feeding and Swallowing (video: 15 minutes).
3. Sensory Integration Therapy (video: 20 minutes plus viewer's guide).

References

Apgar, V., & James, L.S. (1962). Further observations on the Newborn Scoring System. *American Journal of Diseases of Children, 104,* 419–428.

Ayres, J. (1972, 1994). *Sensory integration and learning disorders.* Los Angeles: Western Psychological Services.

Bailey, D.B., & Wolery, M. (1984). *Teaching infants and preschoolers with handicaps.* Upper Saddle River, NJ: Merrill/Prentice Hall.

Bailey, R.A., & Burton, E. C. (1989). *The dynamic infant.* St Paul, MN: Toys 'n Things.

Baker, B.L., Brightman, A.J., Blacher, J.B., Heifetz, L.J., Hinshaw, S., & Murphy, D.M. (1997). *Steps to independence: Teaching everyday skills to children with special needs.* Baltimore, MD: Paul H. Brookes.

Batshaw, M.L. (1997). *Children with disabilities.* Baltimore: Paul H. Brookes.

Bigge, J.L. (1991). *Teaching individuals with physical and multiple disabilities.* Upper Saddle River, NJ: Merrill/Prentice Hall.

Bobath, B., & Bobath, K. (1975). *Motor development in the types of cerebral palsy.* London: Heinemann.

Brazelton, T.B. (1996). *Neonatal behavioral assessment scale.* London: Cambridge University Press.

Copeland, M. (1982). Development of motor skills and the management of common problems. In K.E. Allen & E.M. Goetz (Eds.), *Early childhood education: Special problems, special solutions.* Rockville, MD: Aspen.

Copeland, M.E., & Kimmel, J.R. (1989). *Evaluation and management of infants and young children with developmental disabilities.* Baltimore: Paul H. Brookes.

Cratty, B. (1998). *Clumsy child syndromes: Descriptions, evaluation, and remediation.* Newark, NJ: Gordon and Breach.

Cruickshank, W. (1967). *The brain-injured child in home, school, and community.* Syracuse, NY: Syracuse University Press.

Doremus, W. (1992). Developmental aquatics. *Teaching Exceptional Children, 24,* 6–10.

Erikson, E. (1993). *Childhood and society.* New York: Norton.

Espenschade, A., & Eckert, H. (1980). *Motor development.* Upper Saddle River, NJ: Merrill/Prentice Hall.

Fallen, N.H., & Umansky, W. (1985). *Young children with special needs.* Upper Saddle River, NJ: Merrill/Prentice Hall.

Finnie, N. (1975). *Handling the young cerebral palsied child at home.* New York: E.P. Dutton.

Frostig, M. (1974). *Movement education, its theory and practice.* Workshop presented at The Marianne Frostig Center of Educational Therapy, Los Angeles.

Hammill, D., & Bartel, N. (1975). *Teaching children with learning and behavior problems.* Boston: Allyn and Bacon.

Hanson, M.J., & Harris, S.R. (1986). *Teaching the young child with motor delays.* Austin, TX: Pro-Ed.

Keogh, J., & Sugden, D. (1985). *Movement skill development.* Upper Saddle River, NJ: Merrill/Prentice Hall.

Kephart, N. (1964). Perceptual-motor aspects of learning disabilities. *Exceptional Children, 31,* 201–206.

Lacy, A. (1981). *Dear Mom and Dad.* San Diego, CA: Project Hope, Superintendent of Schools, Department of Education, San Diego County.

Larsen, S., & Hammill, D. (1975). The relationship of selected visual perceptual skills to academic abilities. *Journal of Special Education, 9,* 281–291.

Lerner, J., Mardell-Czudnowski, C., & Goldenberg, D. (1987). *Special education for the early childhood years.* Upper Saddle River, NJ: Merrill/Prentice-Hall.

Linder, T. (1996). *Transdisciplinary play-based assessment: A functional approach to working with young children.* Baltimore: Paul H. Brookes.

Mercer, C. (1983). *Students with learning disabilities* (2nd ed.). Upper Saddle River, NJ: Merrill/Prentice Hall.

Morris, S.E., & Klein, M.D. (1998). *Pre-feeding skills: A comprehensive resource for feeding development.* San Antonio, TX: Psychological Corporation.

Mueller, H. (1972). Facilitating feeding and prespeech. In P.H. Pearson & C.E. Williams (Eds.), *Physical therapy services in the developmental disabilities* (pp. 89–109). Springfield, IL: Charles C. Thomas.

Noonan, M.J. & McCormick, L. (1993). *Early intervention in natural environments.* Pacific Grove, CA: Brooks/Cole.

Piazza, R. (1979). *Three models of learning disabilities.* Guilford, CT: Special Learning.

Rainforth, B., & Salisbury, C.L. (1988). Functional home programs: A model for therapists. *Topics in Early Childhood Special Education, 7* (4), 33–45.

Ratliffe, K.T. (1998). *Clinical pediatric physical therapy: A guide for the physical therapy team.* St. Louis, MO: Mosby.

Rogers-Warren, A.K. (1982). Behavioral ecology in classrooms for young handicapped children. *Topics in Early Childhood Special Education, 2* (1), 21–32.

Snell, M.E. (1987). *Systematic instruction of persons with severe handicaps.* Upper Saddle River, NJ: Merrill/Prentice Hall.

Stern, F.M., & Gorga, D. (1998). Neurodevelopmental treatment (NDT): Therapeutic Intervention and Efficacy. *Infants and Young Children (1),* 22–32.

Strauss, A., & Lehtinen, L. (1947). *Psychopathology and education of the brain-injured child.* New York: Grune & Stratton.

Strauss, A., & Werner, H. (1942). Disorders of conceptual thinking in the brain-injured child. *Journal of Nervous and Mental Disease, 96,* 153–172.

Umansky, W., & Hooper, S. (1998). Young children with special needs. Upper Saddle River, NJ: Merrill/Prentice-Hall.

University of Colorado Health Sciences Center School of Nursing. (1988). Manual to accompany video-tape *Positioning for Infants and Young Children with Motor Problems.* Lawrence, KS: Learner Managed Designs, Inc.

Vincent, L., Salisbury, C., Laten, S., & Baumgart, D. (1979). *Designing home programs for families with handicapped children.* Unpublished manuscript. Madison, WI: University of Wisconsin, Department of Rehabilitation, Psychology, and Special Education.

Westphal, R. (Ed.). (1991). *Human development: 2½ to 6 years.* Costa Mesa, CA: Concept Media.

Williamson, G.G., & Anzalone, M.E. (April/May 1997) Sensory Integration: A key component of the evaluation and treatment of young children with severe difficulties in relating and communication. *Zero to Three, 17,* 29–36.

Chapter 9

Nurturing Communication Skills

with contributions from Virginia B. Armbruster

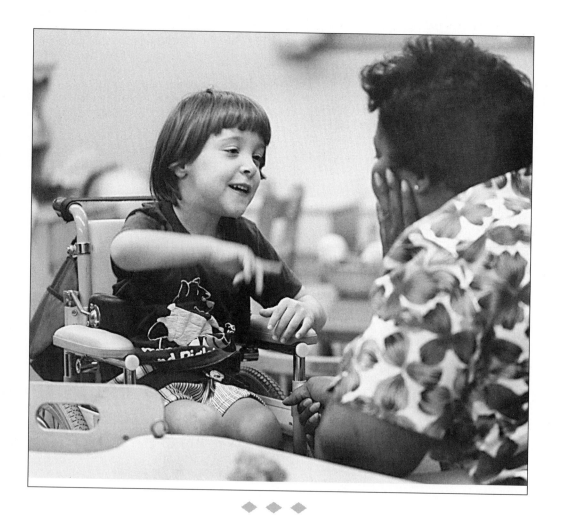

Key Concepts

- Communication and language are very complex skills that are best understood as occurring within a context of social interaction.

- Communication skills develop in predictable stages beginning at birth; the foundation of language is laid during the first year of life.

- The development of language during the preschool years consists not simply of more words and longer sentences, but of pragmatic skills that enable the child to communicate effectively and appropriately in a variety of social contexts.

- The focus of communication intervention must be on the development of functional communication skills that enable the child to *initiate* social interaction and influence his or her environment.

- Key adult behaviors that facilitate communication skills are listening and responding to children's communication attempts and carefully mapping language onto children's experiences.

- The learning of a second language proceeds in much the same fashion as the acquisition of the first language, and, like the first, the second language is best learned in interactive social environments.

- All children can communicate. For young children with severe and multiple disabilities, alternative modes of communication may have to be established.

- For children with hearing impairment, teachers must be aware of both the role of residual hearing and use of manual communication.

In recent decades, probably no aspect of child development has received more attention than the area of communication. Similarly, a great deal of interest has been generated regarding intervention strategies to facilitate the development and acquisition of speech and language skills. Much has been learned about which techniques and strategies best support the efforts of the young child with disabilities to communicate with those around him or her.

This chapter will consider several interesting areas of research and apply them to the design of early childhood curricula for children with special needs. However, we must first review some basic terminology used to describe the various subskills of language.

THE SUBSKILLS OF LANGUAGE

The complexity of language is impressive. Language is often referred to as the most complex human function. In order to manage this complexity in discussing language, it is helpful to use the conceptual framework originally described by Bloom and Lahey (1978). This framework defines three dimensions of language: **content, use,** and **form.** Each of these dimensions includes several traditional linguistic subskills, e.g., **phonology, semantics, syntax, morphology,** and **pragmatics.** These are described in the sections below.

Content, Use, and Form

Bloom and Lahey (1978) and Lahey (1988) described three dimensions of language: content, use, and form. The *content* of language is its meaning—what it refers to or what it is about. *Use* refers to the purpose or function of language—what it is used for. The *form* of language refers both to its syntactic and morphological structure (i.e., the order and forms of words) and to the phonological form (i.e., the particular sounds, or phonemes, and the sound sequences that occur in spoken language). Every utterance can be analyzed according to these three dimensions. Take for example the child who, hoping for a second helping of ice cream, looks at her mother and says, "Is there more ice cream?"

- The *content* of this utterance refers to the existence of a frozen, sweet dairy product called "ice cream."

- Its *use,* or purpose, is to obtain a second helping.

- The *structure* of the utterance is a five-word interrogative sentence.

This theoretical framework is helpful in making clear the multidimensional and complex nature of language.

Semantics

Learning the *meanings* of words (**semantics**) is very dependent on interactions with adults who make their meaning clear. For example, talking about the ocean to a child who has never seen one will result in little understanding of *ocean.* Young children do not learn word meanings through vicarious experiences. Things they see must be named while they are looking at them and touching them. Activities must be described while they are happening. And then children must have the opportunity to experiment with the words, to discover whether they have learned what each really means.

Bloom and Lahey (1978) described several **semantic relations** typically expressed in children's early two-word combinations. These include meanings such as *recurrence* (e.g., "more juice" or "'nother birdie"); *disappearance* (e.g., "cereal gone" or "no dollie"); *appearance* (e.g., "that Mommy" or "there ball"); *rejection* (e.g., "no want!" or "don't wash!"); *actions,* (e.g., "baby fall" or "push Daddy"); *locations* (e.g., "cookie 'frigerator" or "doggie bed"); *possession* (e.g., "Teddy mine!" or "Mommy shoe"); and occasional *descriptors* (e.g., "cereal hot" or "pants dirty").

Syntax

Learning the rules for correct word order in sentences is one aspect of **syntax.** Syntax includes knowing that it is correct to say "we are going to the ball game" rather than "game ball we are going to." Of course, children learning to utter syntactically correct sentences are really just trying to communicate. They are not consciously practicing the rules they are learning. But as they learn, children everywhere develop language in a similar sequence. Between ages 10 and 14 months, most typically developing children use single words to communicate. By age 2, they string two or three words together, and by age 4 they have mastered most of the syntactic rules and are creating grammatically correct sentences that follow the rules of the language they have been hearing and practicing.

Morphology

Children must also learn the rules for changing the *form* of individual words (rules of **morphology**). For example, they discover when to add *s,* when to add *es,* and when to change the word *man* to *men.* They discover how to form possessives and how to use number and tense in verbs (e.g., he walks, they walk, he walked, he is walking, or we walked). Children learn comparatives (long, longer, longest) and how to add prefixes and suffixes to alter meaning. They use pronouns as possessives (his or hers), as subjects (I, he, or they), and as objects (him or her).

As they learn these rules of morphology, children make many interesting mistakes. They overgeneralize, saying, "We wented" and "The mans." However, their errors are logical and confirm that they are not just imitating what they are hearing. They are learning rules. Exceptions to the rules, such as irregular verbs and irregular plurals, will be learned in time. Often very young children can be heard using irregular nouns and verbs correctly (men, ran, or fell). As they begin to internalize language rules, they may change to rule-governed forms (mans, runned, or falled). Then the adult models around them must help them to discover these exceptions to the rules all over again.

Phonology

Learning the rules of the sound systems of speech and language (**phonology**) involves not only the individual speech sounds, or *phonemes,* but also discovering that pitch and rhythm changes make a difference. The intonation patterns *("prosodic" or "suprasegmental" features)* are learned very early. Babies just a few months old babble in ways that sound almost like the patterns adults use. A conscientious listener can hear questions and statements in the intonation patterns of babies long before words can be heard. Careful listening will also detect exclamations!

As they near 6 months of age, many babies begin to babble in syllables that include some of the phonemes of the adult system. Their production is usually somewhat wide of the mark. By 1 year, they have learned to use some sounds accurately some of the time, and the first words begin to appear. However, the accuracy of children's production is highly dependent on being able to hear the sounds they are trying to produce clearly, accurately, and often. They do not need to hear the sounds in isolation or even in syllables. Hearing them in words and connected speech (phrases and sentences) appears to be enough. But they do need to hear the phonemes, and they do need lots of opportunity to practice them. Most children learn to produce nearly all of the 44 phonemes of English by the time they are 4 years old.

Pragmatics

Learning how to use language in appropriate ways within various contexts is crucial to the successful development of communication skills (Prutting & Kirchner, 1987). **Linguistic pragmatics** refers to rules and conventions that govern how language is used for communication in different situations. Pragmatic communication skills also include many nonverbal behaviors.

Speakers and listeners follow a set of unconscious guidelines as they talk to each other. These include behaviors such as looking at each other and looking away, and waiting for the speaker to pause before the listener begins to speak. These behaviors require attention to subtle cues. Facial expressions and body language appropriate to particular circumstances must be learned. Sensing this nonverbal communication, children are often quick to perceive insincerity.

The situation, the specific topic, the relation of listener to speaker, and many other variables determine *what* is said as well as *how* it is said. Children who have not acquired these pragmatic skills stand out as "different" in preschool groups almost as much as those whose speech is unintelligible. But it is more difficult for parents and teachers to pinpoint how and why they are different.

Hopper and Naremore (1978, p. 63) presented a useful introduction to pragmatics. They listed the following ways in which the situational context influences how a person communicates: (a) the people present; (b) what was just previously said; (c) the topic of conversation; (d) the task that communication is being used to accomplish; and (e) the times and places in which the communication occurs. Observation suggests that young children readily use these contextual clues to enable themselves to understand much more than words alone.

As Bates (1976) described it, the acquisition of pragmatic skills begins to develop well before children's first words. Bates described various prelinguistic communication acts such as pointing and reaching, combined with vocalizations and directed eye gaze. These behaviors, which typically emerge in young children around the 10th month of age, lay an important foundation for later language development.

CONTRIBUTION OF SOCIAL INTERACTION THEORY TO UNDERSTANDING EARLY COMMUNICATION DEVELOPMENT

The past 3 decades of research have reflected an important shift from emphasis on speech and language to emphasis on communication. Social interactionist theories maintain that language is learned primarily through social interactions (McCormick, Loeb, & Schiefelbusch, 1997). A second important shift of interest has been away from the child in isolation and toward the **dyad** (significant pair of individuals)—in this case the parent-child or teacher-child dyad. Research in these areas has revealed exciting new information—in addition to confirming many age-old intuitions—regarding the contributions of conversation and interaction to children's development of communication skills and the role of early caregiver-infant and caregiver-child interactions in children's development.

A third shift of focus in the study of children's development of communication has been away from the study of the form and structure of language toward the study of the purposes of children's communicative behaviors and the functional uses of communicative behavior within social contexts. This area of focus is referred to as **developmental pragmatics** (Bates, 1976; Ochs, 1979).

These areas of emphasis have generated information and theories with important implications for the field of early childhood special education. Several theories have evolved that reflect some aspect of this social interaction focus. Tannock, Girolametto, and Siegel, (1992) describe an "interactive model," which suggests that parent responsiveness, and the use of "motherese," are critical factors in the development of communication. This model also proposes intervention strategies based on the theory. These include following the child's lead, utilizing strategies such as increased wait time to encourage communicative initiation and turn taking, and certain language modeling techniques, including describing what the child is doing, repetition of key words and phrases, and syntactically and semantically expanding the child's utterances.

Elizabeth Bates describes the "functional" model (Bates & McWhinney, 1988). This theory suggests that grammar develops as a function of communicative use and meaning, and within the context of communicative interactions.

A third theory of this type has been proposed by Keith Nelson (1986). Nelson's theory is based upon the notion of the existence of a "rare event learning mechanism." In the course of children's interactions with others on occasion they will be particularly attentive to certain language inputs and to mismatches between their current grammatical skill and the adult's model. At such points children's cognitive processes of selective attention, storage, retrieval, and hypothesis testing are all activated, and the learning of new language structures takes place. Again, it is within the context of meaningful interactions with more competent speakers that this occurs.

A fourth theory is a familiar one. This is Vygotsky's theory of adult social mediation of children's learning experiences (Vygotsky, 1978). This theory, which is applicable to all learning, not just language development, suggests that more-capable adults or peers provide assistance to the child within social interaction contexts. When this assistance is provided within the "zone of proximal development" it provides the necessary "scaffolding" (Bruner, 1983) to enable the child to master a particular skill and achieve independence.

These social interactionist approaches have provided a much greater understanding of the precursors of language development occurring during the child's first year of life. Second, research and theories related to the effect of caregiver input and social interaction on children's development have important implications for intervention strategies and the design of early intervention curricula.

STAGES OF DEVELOPMENT OF COMMUNICATION SKILLS IN YOUNG CHILDREN

Early childhood special educators must thoroughly understand the development of communication skills in normally developing children. Several available texts provide detailed descriptions of typical communication development within each of the five subskills previously defined (see, for example, Owens, 1988). Table 9–1 also provides development information for the major language subskills.

The following section will briefly describe the major accomplishments in communication skills development from birth to 3 years of age. Because space does not allow a detailed description of this process, the section is intended only as a review. Students are encouraged to supplement their background with the readings listed in the annotated bibliography at the end of this chapter.

Prelinguistic Communication

It is important for early childhood special educators to recognize that the infant begins the process of learning to communicate long before the onset of true or conventional speech and language. Literally from the moment of birth, communication takes place between infant and caregiver. Research in the areas of mother-infant interaction and developmental

Table 9–1 (pp. 296–298)   Normal language development: expected sequence and approximate age norms*

Age in Months (Approx.)	Pragmatics	Phonology	Grammar Morphology-Syntax	Semantics
1	Gazing, crying, "comfort sounds"	Begins to play with pitch change		
3	Laughs, smiles when played with; looks at speaker; sometimes responds to a speaker by vocalizing	Vocalizes two or more syllables		
6	Babbles and smiles at a speaker; stops (begins turn taking) when someone speaks	Babbles four or more syllables at one time; plays at making noises; labial (/p/, /b/,/m/) consonants emerge; vowels		
8	Plays "peek-a-boo" and "pat-a-cake"; listens to adult conversations; turns toward speaker; understands gesture	Intonation patterns for questions and commands; jargon includes vowels and consonants (five or more of each)	(No real words, but vocalizing sounds as if forming a sentence or question)	Recognizes names of some common objects
10	Follows simple commands; enjoys clapping to music; begins to "send message" by pointing	Uses a varied jargon, with pitch and rhythm		Says first words; tries to imitate words
12	Responds to manner and attitude of speaker (e.g., joy, anger, or hurry)	Consonant-vowel and consonant-vowel-consonant jargon	Holophrasic speech (one word stands for a whole sentence)	Uses two or more words; learns new words every few days
12 to 18	Follows one- and two-step directions	Imitates noises and speech sounds	Some begin to use two-word sentences	Recognizes and points to many familiar objects; learns new words almost daily
18 to 24	Jargon and some echolalia; "dialogue" uses speech to get attention; "asks" for help	Uses /p/,/b/,/m/,/h/, /t/ and vowels	Two- to three-word sentences, but omits articles and most modifiers; begins to use personal pronouns; telegraphic speech	Says 10 to 20 words at 18 months, but some say as many as 200 words by 24 months; understands many more

Table 9–1 (Continued)

Age in Months (Approx.)	Pragmatics	Phonology	Grammar Morphology-Syntax	Semantics
24 to 36	At 2, speech is not used for social control, but at 2½ demands and attempts control By 3, language is linguistically and contextually contingent, and 70% of speech is intelligible, although articulation errors are still common. Short sentences (three to four words) are common. All vowels are correct, but /r/, /s/, /ch/, /j/, /v/, /l/, /x/ are often incorrectly spoken. Vocabulary ranges to as many as 1,000 words. Sentence types include agent-action, action-object, and agent-object	Many begin to use additional consonants; add /f/, /k/, /d/, /w/, /g/; vowels 90% intelligible	By 2½ grammatical morphemes begin to appear: -ing (present progressive) -s and -es (plurals) -ed (past tense) a, an, the (articles) my and 's (possessives) auxiliary verbs prepositions	Recognizes names and pictures of most common objects; understands 500 words
36 to 48	Social control; whispers; tells name; "explains" what happened; asks questions, sustains topic; systematic changes in speech depend on the listener; some role playing; metalinguistic awareness (ability to think about language and comment on it); "hints" at things through smiles and gestures as well as words	All vowels correct; although many children articulate most consonants accurately, articulation errors on the following are still within normal range: /l/, /r/, /s/, /z/, /sh/, /ch/, /j/, /th/; pitch and rhythm variations similar to adults, but this age enjoys extremes— yells and whispers	Expands noun phrases with tense, gender, and number; conjugates "to be" correctly; uses pronouns, adjectives, and plurals; near age 4, begins using longer and more compound and complex sentences; begins to interrelate clauses (uses and, because, when, and then)	Vocabulary grows rapidly; actively seeks to learn new words; likes to experiment and makes many charming errors; continues process of differentiating lexical types; knows between 900 and 1,000 words

Table 9–1   (Continued)

Age in Months (Approx.)	Pragmatics	Phonology	Grammar Morphology-Syntax	Semantics
48 to 60	Seeks information constantly; "why" is a favorite; becomes aware of behavior listeners attend to; begins to grasp relevance	Begins to use stress contours, pitch changes purposefully; articulation errors still common, but diminishing; nonfluency not unusual; blends difficult	Uses comparatives (big, biggest); uses all sentence types, including relative clauses; grammar approximates that of adults	Size of vocabulary varies widely with experiences; many know 2,000 or more words

*From Brown (1973), Bzoch and League (1970), Dale (1976), Hopper and Naremore (1978), Prutting (1979), and Wilkinson (1979).

pragmatics has suggested that the communication patterns established during the first year or two of life are crucial to children's later development in several areas, including language, cognition, and social skills.

During the first few months of life, the infant's communications are not really intentional. Nevertheless, they can be easily understood by those around the infant. For example, crying, smiling, cooing, looking, and eventually reaching are behaviors that often have great meaning for the infant's caregivers, even though the infant may not be doing them "on purpose." A term often used to describe these kinds of communicative behaviors is *perlocutionary* (Bates, 1976).

These perlocutionary behaviors are responded to and interpreted by caregivers as though they *were* intentions. As the infant gains greater control, voluntary behaviors eventually become intentional communicative acts. By 9 or 10 months of age, most children are engaging in a variety of intentional (but still unconventional) behaviors such as pointing, use of directed eye gaze, and use of vocalizations to get attention, to exclaim, or to accompany their own actions or expression of wants and needs.

Prelinguistic Functions. These types of intentional communicative behaviors are often referred to as *illocutionary.* Halliday (1975) described several categories of communicative functions that infants may use even prior to the acquisition of first words:

1. The *interactional function* is also referred to as the "you and me" function. By using this function the infant is attempting to elicit interaction and attention from others in his or her immediate environment. For example, an infant may look at mother, clap his hands, and vocalize in an attempt to play "pattycake." Or he may wake from his nap and call from his crib in order to get some company.

2. The *instrumental function* is also referred to as the "I want" function. Here the infant uses communicative behaviors to obtain something he or she wants from the environment, such as food or a favorite object. For example, an infant's looking toward his bottle, pointing, and saying, "Uh" is an instrumental communicative behavior.

3. The *regulatory function* is the "Do as I tell you" function; it is used by the infant to control others' behaviors. For example, an infant may be requesting someone to push her in her stroller, or pick her up.

4. The *personal function* is called the "Here I come" function. The infant uses this function to

simply express some emotion or to accompany his or her own actions. For example, an infant tastes a bite of ice cream and says, "Mmmm," or drops something and says, "Uh oh!"

5. The *heuristic function* is an important function because it sets the stage for the infant's use of communication to obtain information from adults in his or her environment. This is referred to as the "Tell me why" function. By use of strategies such as a vocalization with question-like rising intonation, or raised eyebrows, the infant learns to solicit additional information, such as a label or explanation, from people nearby.

6. The *imaginative function* may be used by some infants during this prelinguistic stage of communication development. The imaginative function is referred to as the "Let's pretend" function; it accompanies the older infant's pretend play activities (e.g., car sounds).

The Onset of Language

Somewhere around 1 to 1½ years of age, the infant learns his or her first "real" words. After this point, communication becomes symbolic and conventional. The toddler continues to use all the communicative functions just described, but now many of these functions are expressed using recognizable words such as *peek, bottle, up, oh oh, whaddat?* and *night night*. In addition, a new function is now added to the toddler's repertoire: the *informative function*. Halliday has called this the "Let me tell you" function, because the child can now truly share information via symbolic language behavior.

Around this same time, the child also begins to move toward a new stage of cognitive development: the **preoperational stage.** Now the infant becomes increasingly able to represent things mentally. As a result, he can also use his newly found symbolic behavior to refer to things that are not immediately present in the environment, and very shortly, to events that happened in the past.

Thus the onset of conventional speech and language skills also typically coincides with several other exciting milestones in the infant's development. The infant's communication is no longer tied to the here and now. In addition to using social interaction and manipulating her environment to meet her basic wants and needs, she can now share her experiences with others.

It should be noted that the speech of a toddler at the early one-word stage is often unintelligible to anyone not involved with the toddler on a regular basis. Some words may even be idiosyncratic, bearing little phonemic relationship to the conventional word (e.g., "da" for bottle). Real words may also be combined with jargon, or strings of unintelligible speech sounds (often consonant-vowel syllables such as "da" or "tee"). The toddler may sound as though she is uttering whole sentences, although she really is not.

Combining Words

Sometime around 20 to 24 months, when the infant has learned approximately 50 to 100 words, he will begin to put them together. Often his first combinations will be words he already uses. For example, instead of saying "juice" or "more" to get another glass of juice, he will say "more juice." Just why the infant begins to combine words in this way is not clear. For many years, child language acquisition research focused on this process of learning to produce longer and longer utterances that conform more and more closely to adult language.

The *structure* of language refers to the way in which words are combined into sentences (syntax) and the various forms of words (morphology). The young child must learn to say, "I want juice," rather than "Want juice I," and "The boys are running," rather than "The boys is run." There is much literature from the 1960s and early 1970s that described in some detail the evolution of children's grammar. While teachers of young children need not be familiar with all the specific details of children's grammatical development, it is important that they know the major stages of language structure development as described in the following paragraphs.

1. *Telegraphic language.* When children begin to combine words, they are most likely to use words that have the most meaning. In earlier writings on child

language acquisition, these utterances were called "telegraphic" because they appeared to omit unessential words. Utterances such as "Baby like bottle" are typical of children in this stage.

2. *Grammatical morphemes.* Around 2 years of age, children begin to include grammatical morphemes in their utterances. Words such as *the* and *an,* word endings such as plural *s,* present progressive *ing,* past tense *ed,* and others are gradually included. As a child first begins to use grammatical morphemes, she may often use them incorrectly. For example, she may say, "The boy runned" or "an apples." The teacher should be aware that incorrect use of grammatical morphemes nevertheless represents a more sophisticated stage of grammatical development than the earlier telegraphic stage in which grammatical morphemes were omitted altogether.

3. *Simple sentences.* Gradually, by the age of 3 years, children learn to produce sentences that resemble simple ones used by adults. These sentences will contain a subject and a predicate and will include the necessary grammatical morphemes, although still not always in the correct form. The 3-year-old says, "I want some milk, please," or "Let's go outside," or "My dollies is mad!"

The 3-year-old has also learned to make sentence transformations, that is, to ask questions ("Do you have my doll?") and give commands ("Give me my doll!"), as well as to make simple declarative statements ("This is my doll.")

4. *Complex language.* By the age of 4 years, young children can easily combine words into sentences and produce them intelligibly. In addition, they can produce complex sentences such as, "I don't want to go to the store if I can't buy a new toy." Perhaps even more important is their increasing linguistic flexibility. They can now adjust the structure and content of their language according to the nature of the situation and the age and status of the listener. For example, to his 2-year-old sister, the 4-year-old might say, "Give me the ice cream!" But when talking to an older adult he would change the structure of his language (e.g., "Could I have some more ice cream, please?").

The 4- or 5-year-old child is also capable of carrying on a conversation: the child can take turns, extend the topic, and return the conversational floor to his or her partner. The following dialogue demonstrates these conversational strategies, which are so crucial to the young child's development of social skills:

Danny: "Did you see 'The Simpsons' on TV last night, Erin?"
Erin: "No, 'cause I watch 'Sabrina.' "
Danny: "Bart got in trouble."
Erin: "How come?"
Danny: "He played a trick on his teacher."
Erin: "I like Sabrina better than 'The Simpsons.' "

Finally, the 4- or 5-year-old child can engage in *narrative*—stories that have a beginning, a middle, and an end. The child is now not only able to use language to manipulate the environment and obtain social interaction, but also to express emotions and to share his or her experiences and ideas with others. Language and cognition now become inextricably woven together as a means of problem solving and learning about the world.

Hopefully, the 4-year-old has acquired the kinds of linguistic skills that will also support academic achievement. These autonomous or literate-style language skills are discussed in Chapter 10. The child's words and sentences can now stand alone. He or she can tell a story or describe a situation clearly and successfully to a listener who has no previous knowledge or shared reference regarding the event being described.

Many of the milestones described in this section will be communication goals for young children with special needs. Strategies for helping children develop these communication skills will be described later in the chapter.

NECESSARY CONDITIONS FOR THE DEVELOPMENT OF COMMUNICATION SKILLS

Because of the tremendous complexity of speech and language skills, several necessary conditions must exist in order for these skills to develop normally.

First, the peripheral sensory system must be intact. Hearing is of greatest importance, of course, for the development of language. In addition, vision and oral sensation must function well.

The central nervous system must also be intact. Speech and language development depend on the ability not only to receive incoming auditory information but also to process, organize, and store it. Of particular importance in the development of speech production (i.e., articulation skills) is the motor system. The production of speech involves incredibly precise coordination of many muscles and muscle groups making up the speech production mechanism, including those involved in movement of the tongue, lips, jaw, velum, larynx, and muscles of respiration. The production of speech sounds in the rapid sequence necessary for the production of intelligible speech requires synergistic split-second timing and smooth control of these muscles. For children with motor impairments such as those associated with many forms of cerebral palsy, the production of speech is extremely difficult.

Cognitive abilities are crucial to the development of language skills. The content of a child's language is dependent on what the child is able to represent, organize, understand, and recall of the world around him or her.

Social/affective growth must also be normal in order for communication skills to develop. Communication development during the first year of life, and many of the precursors of language, depend on the infant's or young child's seeking out the attention of and interaction with others in his or her environment. The child who lacks this drive toward social interaction, as, for example, in many cases of autism, will most likely be significantly impaired in the development of communication skills.

Finally, the environment itself must be responsive to the infant's and young child's needs, and the linguistic input provided by caregivers must be appropriate to the infant's ability to process information. Recent research has suggested that several interaction strategies, particularly caregiver responsiveness, can enhance children's later development. These interaction strategies are also important to teachers in the field of early childhood special education, and they should be incorporated into the daily activities of the classroom. We will discuss these interaction strategies in more detail later in this chapter.

Characteristics That Can Interfere with Language Development

Characteristics of common communication disorders are summarized in Figure 9–1. The following sections discuss these disorders in more detail.

Hearing Loss. Hearing loss can interfere with both speech and language development. Even mild or intermittent hearing impairments such as those associated with otitis media can interfere with the learning of speech and language. Children who are hearing impaired can be taught to speak and to understand language, but the task is not an easy one and requires the help of parents and highly trained specialists. Frequently children with severe and profound hearing loss will need to use sign language as their primary mode of communication. Although children who are deaf are eventually identified, lack of language development in children with mild hearing losses frequently goes undetected.

Children with mild hearing losses cannot hear all phonemes with equal clarity. The distorted speech pattern they hear is inconsistent and incorrect. Bess and McConnell (1981) discussed the effects of mild, intermittent hearing loss and its long-term interference with language development. If a child fails to develop normal communication skills at expected ages, regardless of what other factors seem to be involved, the child's hearing should be checked and regularly rechecked by a competent audiologist. If any hearing deficit is detected, the causes should be discovered and removed. If this is not possible, parents should receive guidance, and the child's language development should be monitored and directed by a speech-language pathologist or a trained teacher of children who are deaf.

The family, taking into account input from professionals, must make a decision as to what

LANGUAGE DISORDERS

Delayed language: marked slowness in the onset
and development of language skills necessary for
expressing ideas and for understanding the thoughts
and ideas one hears or reads

Learning disabilities: something interfering with a child's ability to understand the
message that his eyes and ears receive

Aphasia: loss of speech and language
abilities after brain damage resulting
sometimes from a stroke or head injury

HEARING DISORDERS

Conductive: occur in the outer or
middle ear; speech and other sounds may be
heard faintly, often muffled

Sensorineural: occur in the inner
ear or auditory nerve and cause one to hear
speech sounds faintly and sometimes in a
distorted way; words may sound slurred or
lacking in clarity

Mixed: combination of
conductive and sensorineural losses

CAN HAVE ACCOMPANYING
CAN HAVE ACCOMPANYING

SPEECH OR HEARING PROBLEMS
SPEECH OR LANGUAGE PROBLEMS

LANGUAGE OR HEARING PROBLEMS

CAN HAVE ACCOMPANYING

SPEECH DISORDERS

Articulation: difficulties with the way sounds
are formed and strung together; characterized by
substituting one sound for another (wabbit for
rabbit), omitting a sound (han— for hand), and
distorting a sound (shlip for sip)

Stuttering: interruptions in the flow or rhythm
of speech; characterized by hesitations, repetitions, or prolongations of sound, syllable, word,
or phrase

Voice: inappropriate pitch (too high, too low,
never changing, interrupted by breaks);
loudness (too loud or not loud enough); or
quality (harsh, hoarse, or breathy)

Figure 9–1 Characteristics of common communication disorders. (From public information materials of the American Speech-Language-Hearing Association. Reproduced with permission.)

communication methods will be used: speech, sign, or a combination of the two. Children who are unable to hear normally during the first years of life may be disabled in all aspects of language and speech development. The longer the hearing impairment is undetected and untreated, the more serious will be the effects on the development of communication.

Auditory-Perceptual Impairments. Auditory-perceptual impairments are presumed to be the cause of specific language disorders in some children. A review of the literature on this topic by Lubert (1981) noted that a diversity of labels and assessment instruments has led to some confusion. This article reported that these disorders have been studied by researchers from several disciplines, including neurology, psychiatry, psychology, speech pathology, audiology, and linguistics. Terms used include *developmental aphasia, congenital aphasia, aphasoid children, developmental dysphasia, language deficit, language delay, learning disability, verbal auditory agnosia,* and *central auditory dysfunction.*

The perceptions and observations of the various specialists have led to different conclusions, theories, and remediation approaches. Lubert (1981) reported:

• The above research suggests that language-disordered children may be characterized by an impaired rate of processing for rapidly changing acoustic information. An obvious treatment implication is that the signal should be slowed down to facilitate its perception by the language-disordered child. (p. 1)

Thus, parents and teachers should avoid presenting stimuli too rapidly. Fast talking and chaotic environments may be difficult for some children to process, and they may be overwhelming. As a result, these children may eventually develop the habit of "tuning out" their environments, which can cause additional learning problems.

Visual Impairments. While visual impairment does not produce the same degree of interference as hearing impairment, it does affect concept and vocabulary development. If the child cannot see clearly, it is difficult to recognize the things and events being discussed. Because children who are blind, by virtue of their disability, have a deprived experiential base, they need special help to acquire speech and language. Like children with a partial hearing loss, children who are partially sighted have special needs that often go unnoticed. Fraiberg (1977) has offered specific and useful information to aid early identification of children with visual impairment. Chapter 4 lists warning signs of possible visual impairment.

Cognitive Impairments. Mental retardation is presumed to be the cause of delayed speech and language in some children. Since many tests of intelligence rely heavily on verbal interactions between examiner and child, it is difficult to tell cause from effect. Qualified examiners should be able to make this distinction, but many find it difficult. Thus a young child without speech and language may be judged to have developmental delays due to lack of communication skills.

Children with slower-than-average cognitive development need thoughtfully planned and carefully provided individualized opportunities and challenges. Children who have moderate and mild retardation will often be able to learn to talk and understand speech and language in the expected sequences, although at a slower pace. It is especially important to provide these children with a **language-nurturing environment** matching their linguistic age, rather than their chronological age. Thus, if they are just beginning to use two words, they should be talked to, listened to, and played with in a manner appropriate to that level of language development. Children who have been described as having retardation may need special help in the pragmatic skills of language, as well as with vocabulary, grammar, and articulation. Helping them to understand when to talk, as well as what to say, should be an important part of curriculum planning.

The child with more severe retardation poses very different problems and challenges for the early childhood special education teacher. When there is severe impairment of cognitive and perceptual processes, the impact on the development of communication skills is great. In many children who have severe or profound retardation, rule-governed sym-

bolic language skills may never develop. However, it is important to recognize that these children, too, must have some means of communication. We will discuss young children with severe and multiple disabilities in a later section.

Emotional Problems. Deviant language development or the refusal to communicate at all may result from emotional problems. Although these problems require the skillful and caring therapy of persons especially trained to help children and their parents, much can be done to support mental health in a preschool environment. Chapter 7 offers a number of classroom support strategies for children with emotional or social problems. Cooperation among therapists, parents, and teachers is especially critical in this area.

Autism. One of the identifying characteristics of children who have autism is the atypical development of social skills and language. Current theories regarding etiological factors in autism suggest that its basis is neurophysiological; that is, that there are differences in how the child's central nervous system responds to incoming stimuli. These differences result in serious information-processing deficits (Rutter, 1986).

Many children with autism are particularly sensitive to tactile and auditory stimuli, which can result in major interference with the processes of attachment and social interaction as well as development of communication skills. In addition, the problems with social responsiveness typical of these children also contribute to particular difficulties with the development of functional uses of communication.

Lack of Stimulation. Lack of appropriate stimulation limits communication development. Recent studies in many areas support the importance of loving, emotionally satisfying stimulation from birth. However, some parents simply do not know how to talk to their young children. It is not uncommon to have them say, "What can you say to a baby?" or, "My friends will think I'm crazy if I talk to a 2-year-old."

It is usually assumed that people who speak a language, children as well as adults, instinctively know how to talk to children. This is not always true. Later, suggestions for teaching parents and others how to talk to their children will be given. In any case, when a child is not talking, be alert to help parents create a language-nurturing environment.

Parents can learn to use everyday experiences to teach communication skills. Cooking, cleaning, and gardening are excellent experiences for children. Conversation during these activities becomes an excellent language-teaching time. Washing the car or working with tools provide additional excellent opportunities to foster speech and language learning. But parents need encouragement, effective examples, and thoughtful reminders if they are to make their child's language-learning environment stimulating.

Characteristics That Interfere with Speech Development

Structural Abnormalities. Craniofacial deformities of any kind interfere with speech skill development. A child who cannot imitate and reproduce speech sounds will be less skilled in using language as well. For example, if deviant mouth structure precludes placing tongue and teeth in the correct position to pronounce /s/, as in boys and shoes, the child cannot use the language rule "Add /s/ to form plurals."

Hypernasality, often associated with cleft palate, also interferes with learning speech. Only three English speech sounds are intended to have this characteristic nasal quality: /m/, /n/, and /ng/ (as in ring). When most of the sounds of speech are nasalized, listeners usually characterize the speech as unintelligible. Conditions other than cleft palate can cause this. If a child seems to be "talking through the nose," the causes should be discovered and corrected.

Motor Problems. Normal control of the muscles necessary for speech is needed for correct articulation. This develops so spontaneously in most children that its significance is not recognized. Playing the violin skillfully is far less complex than pronouncing a word correctly. To appreciate this muscular achievement, shut your lips lightly and pay attention to your tongue as you say, "Look at Larry's new green coat." (Shutting your lips helps to focus on the tongue activity.)

Cerebral palsy interferes with muscle coordination. Injury, other physical problems, and certain drugs also interfere. Teachers will want to work closely with therapists when children have problems of this kind.

Voice Disorders. The effect of a cleft palate and/or lip may result in a nasal voice even if a surgical repair was accomplished early in the child's life. Children who have frequent respiratory infections may lack nasal resonance. Children who scream a lot may be hoarse. All of these problems deserve skillful attention and remediation from professionals.

Stuttering. Stuttering is a disturbance in the rhythmic flow of speech. When a speaker repeats a sound or syllable, prolongs it more than is typical of other speakers, or blocks (completely halts the speech flow), many people describe this as stuttering. Some stutterers develop patterns of grimaces and gestures in an effort to avoid disturbing their flow of speech. Sometimes described as *secondary characteristics,* these behaviors are often thought of as habits that reflect the speaker's anxiety and an effort to break tension, or motor behaviors that become conditioned responses overtime.

Stuttering usually begins between the ages of 2 and 4, although it may happen later. All speakers normally repeat, hesitate, and sometimes prolong sounds. This is especially true of young children. They are in a hurry. Finding the right word is difficult for little children, and this is reason enough for them to hesitate and repeat.

Some speech-language pathologists believe that calling attention to the perfectly normal disfluencies of young children may result in more repetitions. Telling children to slow down or to think before they speak may cause them to stumble even more. Then parents become even more anxious and so do their children. The following suggestions may be useful to both parents and teachers of young children who are beginning to stutter:

1. Reduce the pressure to communicate.

2. Slow down your own rate of speech.

3. Avoid watching the child's effort to speak in obvious ways.

4. Avoid reacting with alarm to speech blocks or repetitions.

5. Do not make comments such as "stop and start over" to a stuttering child.

6. If the stutterer is so disturbed by the disfluency that a reaction from you is expected, say something like, "That was a hard word," or "Sometimes my words get stuck too."

7. Refuse to feel anxious yourself. It won't help.

NURTURING SPEECH, LANGUAGE, AND CONCEPTUAL SKILLS

There is a large body of information available to the early childhood special education professional regarding ways of facilitating the development of communication skills in young children. Some of this information will be presented in the following sections.

The Important Role of Caregiver-Child Interaction

The importance of the early caregiving environment, and particularly caregivers' use of responsive communicative interactions, has been well established. Earlier research in the field of developmental psychology (e.g., Clarke-Stewart, 1973; Yarrow, Rubenstein, and Pedersen, 1975) and more recent research with populations with special needs (e.g., Mahoney, Finger, and Powell, 1985) have clearly demonstrated relationships between certain kinds of caregiver-infant/child interactions and the development of young children. A longitudinal study reported by Coates and Lewis (1984) demonstrated relationships between mothers' interaction behaviors with their infants at 3 months and the children's school achievement and cognitive skills at 6 years of age. As

many studies of this type have found, maternal responsivity appeared to be the strongest factor.

Particularly important to the development of children's language skills are caregivers' uses of certain **communicative interactions,** which will be described in the following section. For more detailed understanding of this important area, students are referred to descriptions of several intervention programs designed to assist parents of children with special needs in developing and refining these skills (e.g., Klein & Briggs, 1987; Klein, Briggs, & Huffman, 1988; MacDonald, 1989; Manolson, 1985). Figure 9–2 gives examples of the kinds of interactions often targeted for infants and very young children.

The caregiver-child interactions described in the following sections are equally important for teachers and other early interventionists. Early interventionists must not only develop the ability to recognize and encourage the use of interactive behaviors between parents and children but, just as important, they must be

OBSERVATION OF COMMUNICATIVE INTERACTION (OCI)
Mother-Infant Communication Project

Infant's Name _____ Birthdate _____ Age _____

Setting _____ Date _____ Adjusted Age _____

Observer _____

	Rarely/Never	Sometimes	Often	Optimally	Not Applicable
1. Provides appropriate tactile and kinesthetic stimulation (e.g., gently strokes, pats, caresses, cuddles, rocks baby).	1	2	3	4	N/A
2. Displays pleasure while interacting with infant.	1	2	3	4	N/A
3. Responds to child's distress.	1	2	3	4	N/A

   a. changes verbalization
   b. changes infant's position, attempts to distract.
   c. provides positive physical stimuli (e.g., patting, rocking).
   d. avoids negative physical or verbal response.

	Rarely/Never	Sometimes	Often	Optimally	Not Applicable
4. Positions self and infant so eye-to-eye contact is possible (e.g., facing and 7 to 12 inches away).	1	2	3	4	N/A

   a. attempts to make eye contact.
   b. reciprocates eye gaze.

	Rarely/Never	Sometimes	Often	Optimally	Not Applicable
5. Smiles contingently at infant.	1	2	3	4	N/A

   a. consistently returns infant's smile.
   b. smiles in response to infant vocalization.

	Rarely/Never	Sometimes	Often	Optimally	Not Applicable
6. Varies prosodic features.	1	2	3	4	N/A

   a. uses higher pitch.
   b. talks more slowly.
   c. exaggerates 'intonation'.

	Rarely/Never	Sometimes	Often	Optimally	Not Applicable
7. Encourages "conversation".	1	2	3	4	N/A

   a. uses rising intonation questions.
   b. waits after saying something to infant, and looks expectantly, providing infant turn.
   c. imitates child's vocalizations, or words
   d. repeats own sounds, words or phrases (e.g., "Here's the bottle. Bottle.")
   e. answers when infant vocalizes (e.g., "Oh, yeah?", "Okay.", "Is that right?").

	Rarely/Never	Sometimes	Often	Optimally	Not Applicable
8. Responds contingently to infant's behavior.	1	2	3	4	N/A

   a. touches or responds with facial expression within 2 seconds after infant vocalization.
   b. vocalizes within 2 seconds after infant moves arms, head, etc.
   c. vocalizes within 2 seconds after infant vocalization.
   d. stops own activity or verbalization in response to interruption by infant's vocalization or movement.
   e. responds vocally to infant from a distance of more than 2 feet.

	Rarely/Never	Sometimes	Often	Optimally	Not Applicable
9. Modifies interaction in response to negative cues from infant.	1	2	3	4	N/A

   a. changes activity.
   b. reduces intensity of interaction.
   c. terminates attempts at interaction.

Figure 9–2 Communicative interaction checklist. (Source: Klein & Briggs, 1997)

---

10. Uses communication to teach language and concepts.   1   2   3   4   N/A

    a. interprets infant's behavior appropriately (e.g., ''Oh, you're hungry, aren't you.'')

    b. re-casts own sentences (e.g., adult says, ''Shall we turn on the light? Turn on the light. There's the light.'').

    c. comments on infant's attention to immediate environment and *labels* objects (e.g., ''You see the doggie? That's the doggie.'')

    d. matches infant's vocalization, or word with slightly more elaborate language (e.g., baby says, ''Ball'', and adult says, ''That's a ball.'' or ''Big ball.'')

Figure 9–2 (Continued.)

able to demonstrate and consistently use these strategies themselves.

Encouraging Conversation. The literature on so-called "motherese" and mother-infant interaction has described several specific strategies mothers use to encourage and maintain a dialogue with their infants (Cross, 1984). These include behaviors such as (a) use of rising intonation "yes/no" questions (e.g., "Wanna eat now?" or "Is baby tired?"); (b) pausing expectantly after each utterance to give the infant a turn; and (c) imitating the infant's vocalizations or responding to the infant's vocalizations as though they were intelligible (e.g., "Oh yeah?", "Is that right?", "No kidding!", etc.).

Responding Contingently to Child's Behavior. Maternal responsivity has frequently been found to be a robust correlate of later development in young children. Particularly important for the early childhood special educator is a sensitivity to all communicative attempts on the part of the child. For example, a child with severe disabilities who is non-verbal and rarely initiates interaction or attempts to get attention should receive *immediate* attention for any communicative effort, including gestures, changes in body position, vocalizations, and so forth. The child who communicates only by crying or pulling the teacher's sleeve should receive an enthu-

siastic response for making a grunting sound or pointing to get a drink of juice, because this is a new behavior for the child. MacDonald (1989) described an interaction strategy called "upping the ante," in which the teacher or parent encourages a slightly more sophisticated response than the one the child typically uses.

Modifying Interaction in Response to Negative Cues. Another important aspect of maternal responsivity, albeit a more subtle one, is the ability to change or terminate interaction with an infant in response to such cues as gaze aversion, changes in body tension and facial expression, or lack of response from the infant. Interventionists, too, must be able to read children's cues of disinterest, overload, or distraction. Continuing a particular cue or prompt, such as "Show me the doll," when the child is clearly not attending to the stimulus is wasted effort and may eventually teach the child to "tune out" as a generalized strategy to overwhelming or meaningless stimulation.

Using Communication to Teach Language and Concepts. Much has been written about the maternal language patterns that are typical of middle class mothers as they interact with their young children. Some of these communicative interaction strategies appear to be correlated with later language development (Nelson, Bonvillian, Denninger, Kaplan, & Baker,

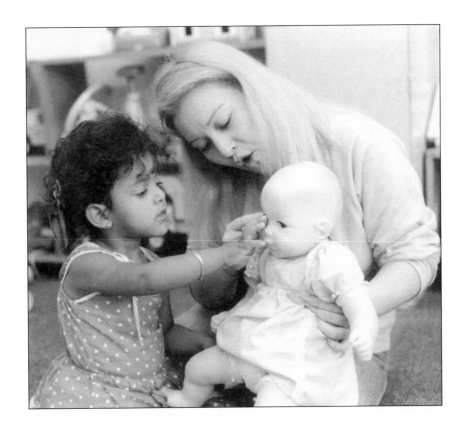

1984). Caregivers and professionals should use these language behaviors in response to the infant's or toddler's interest and attention, as demonstrated by the child's eye gaze, gestures, and vocalization or words. These interaction strategies include:

1. *Commenting* on what the infant or child appears to be attending to (e.g., "Oh, you hear that doggie barking, don't you?"), also referred to as "parallel talk" (McCormick et al., 1997).

2. *Re-casting* one's own words or phrases in different ways in order to emphasize important words (e.g., "*Doggie.* That's the *doggie.* Hear the *doggie? Doggie!*").

3. *Matching* the child's vocalization or word with a slightly more elaborated response, thereby inter-preting the utterance (e.g., the child says "buh" and the teacher says "Bottle, yes bottle"). This is also referred to as "progressive matching" by MacDonald (1989).

4. *Expanding* the utterance syntactically (e.g., the child says "cookie" and the teacher says "That is a cookie"); or *semantically extending*, that is, adding meaning to the utterance (e.g., the child says "doggie" and the teacher says "Yeah, that's a *big* doggie!").

Several instructional programs have been designed around the interaction strategies described here. For more information, refer to MacDonald (1989), Manolson (1985), Mahoney and Robinson (1992) and Giralometto, Verbery, and Tannock (1994).

CLASSROOM STRATEGIES THAT FACILITATE COMMUNICATION

The social interactionist theory of language development and knowledge about the stages and major achievements of language acquisition generate a useful approach to early language intervention. Before describing some of the strategies suggested by this approach, let us consider three important principles related to the development of communication skills.

1. *Interaction* is the first key to the development of communication skills (Reike & Lewis, 1984). Infants and young children must learn to experience the pleasures of turn taking and reciprocal interaction.

2. True communication skills must be *functional* for the child. The ability to provide rote answers to stereotyped questions is not really communication. Infants and children must have opportunities to *initiate* communication. Observation of early childhood special education classrooms reveals that children are too often placed in a respondent role. That is, they are taught to respond to specific prompts and cues provided by the teacher. Communication used only in this way cannot be a learning tool for children. They must be encouraged to initiate interaction, to use language and other communicative behaviors to appropriately manipulate the environment, to ask questions and obtain information, and to solve problems. Children must learn to use language for purposes other than simply answering questions.

3. Language develops best in a *responsive environment.* The teacher who is most sensitive to the infant or child's communicative intentions will be most successful in facilitating language development. Many specific ways of responding are suggested by the literature describing *"motherese"* (the speech and language characteristics typical of mothers' communication with infants and young children described earlier).

Beginning Where the Child Is

Our understanding of appropriate practices in nurturing receptive and expressive language suggests that teachers should attend to children's levels of development. Thus, if 4-year-old Sean does not yet try to tell adults anything, one thing to nurture is the "telling" of things as very young children do. If Susie cannot produce any speech sounds distinctly, she may need to be encouraged in simple vocal play and babbling. If Tommy does not try to ask for things, perhaps he should be expected to make some kind of sound before he is given what he wants.

Developmental scales of speech and language can be checked to determine whether a child has a developmental lag. Speech and language pathologists can assist as questions arise. Table 9–1 can be used as a basis for constructing a checklist for evaluating language development. However, instructional objectives for language development should also be based on the *functional needs of the child;* they should not be limited to items on a developmental checklist.

The Importance of Conversations

Conversations about familiar things that interest young children are a critical tool in helping them to learn communication skills. Nelson (1974) reported that children's first verbal labels or names are of objects, people, events, and actions they know and can associate with. Unless they are truly interested and can make associations, they will not attend. And attention is a prerequisite for learning anything.

Choosing What to Talk About

Communication skills develop around objects and events that interest children. For the really reluctant talker, food can be a good place to begin. For example, while sitting around a table with other children the teacher can cut an apple into pieces and describe such things as the name of the fruit, the smooth, red skin and small, black seeds, the sharp knife, and how the apple will taste. Pragmatic skills also can be nurtured in this "social situation" (e.g., turn taking and use of polite requests).

Any game, dollhouse, play kitchen, or toy barn can be used as the conversational focal point. At first, the teacher should join the children in an ongoing activity with toys they have chosen, following the children's lead. Later, when rapport has been well established, the teacher may choose the activity. Introducing variety is important. But at first, joining into the children's choice of things to do is best.

The following are general suggestions for engaging in conversations with young children:

1. Listen attentively. Even if the things children are saying are unintelligible, look at them with interest and listen.

2. Speak slowly and distinctly, using natural or slightly exaggerated intonation patterns (the prosodic features).

3. Keep sentences short, no more than three or four words. Sometimes use single words. Repeat frequently.

4. Avoid one-sided conversations, which may result from asking too many questions. Questions asked one after another do not constitute conversation. In fact, just as with adults, too many questions result in no conversation. But good questions *can* facilitate learning.

5. Talk mostly about the here and now. Make sure references to the past and future are very clear, and contrast them with references to the present. For example, "Today it's raining, but *yesterday* it was sunny" or, "*After* we finish our snack, *then* we will go outside."

6. Use a calm and pleasant tone of voice. Bring fun to every conversation.

7. Use words the children are interested in, because they can see or understand what they refer to as you talk. Tell them the names of actions as well as things.

8. Pause between sentences. Don't be in a hurry.

9. As the children understand and speak more, gradually make your sentences longer and use a larger vocabulary.

10. For children who have mastered simple sentence structure, model complex relationships through more complex sentence structure, e.g.,

"Oh look, now the sand sticks together *because* we mixed it with water." "*If* we put one more block on top *then* what will happen?"

Listening

Adults should listen to children with great interest. This is especially true if the children have not developed speech and language skills at the expected rate. Communication on their part requires a great deal of effort. The reward most likely to accelerate the growth of speech and language is an interested listener. Presenting an alert facial expression, remaining quiet, and giving the child your patient, undivided attention are important strategies.

Developing Pragmatic Skills

Pragmatic skills are the social skills of language. Taking turns during a conversation, refraining from interrupting, and saying the appropriate thing cannot be learned in isolation. Children require social experiences and are dependent on social interaction. By modeling correct pragmatic skills, adults can direct attention to courteous and effective ways of conversing. Also, role playing is a very useful strategy in helping children develop such pragmatic skills as use of polite forms, initiating conversations, and topic extension.

Expanding Skills

Ideally, children's language skills are expanded through increasingly complex conversations using more complex sentences and vocabulary. MacDonald (1989) has referred to this strategy as "progressive matching" (p. 174). Exhibits 9–1 and 9–2 suggest ways to promote children's syntactic development.

FACILITATING COMMUNICATION IN CHILDREN WITH SEVERE AND MULTIPLE DISABILITIES

Children with severe and multiple disabilities demonstrate very few communicative behaviors. Many of these children may never develop the use of

EXHIBIT 9–1

Some Ways to Promote Syntactic Development

Tony uses many two- and some three-word sentences, and he loves to talk. Both his parents and his teachers have many conversations with him throughout the day. They *listen* to him with obvious interest. Some of the time they *expand* what he has said. When he says "Falled down," they may say "Your big tower fell down. That was noisy." They do this in a way that suggests "You're right, it fell down," never in a manner that indicates "Now, say it the right way."

As the adults do things while Tony is present, they may use *self-talk*. They talk about what they are feeling and doing, as they do it. "Time for supper. I'll take the plates to the table, now. The meat and the green beans are almost ready, and it's time to make the salad. I'll cut the carrots, first." Of course, the speaker pauses after each sentence and *listens* if Tony starts to say something.

Sometimes his teachers and parents use *parallel talk*. They talk about what Tony is doing. "Tony, you put the toys on the shelf just the right way. I like the way you are picking up those blocks. You put the biggest ones on the bottom."

When Tony says something incorrectly, they rarely correct him directly, but they do use *corrective echoing*. If he says "Her throwed dat ball," they might say "You saw Susie. *She threw* the ball." And although they may exaggerate the "she" and the "threw" slightly by saying them slowly, they are really just confirming that they understood.

◆ ◆ ◆

EXHIBIT 9–2

Arrival Time to Build Language Skills

The Scene: Children are arriving, and the teacher and aide are greeting them individually.

The Teaching Strategy: A warm greeting and a brief conversation with each child are designed to make each child feel welcome and expected. Modeling, expanding what the children say, and listening to them are some of the strategies to be used to promote communication skills. Direct correction of articulation errors or grammatical mistakes will be avoided.

Ms. McLynn: Good morning, Sally. I am so glad you brought your doll. Do you want to take her coat off?

Sally: Me do. Coat dirty.

Ms. McLynn: I know you can take her coat off. Her coat *is* dirty, isn't it? We can brush the dirt off.

Sally: Wed shoes. (Pointing to her new shoes)

McLynn: I like those new red shoes. They are shiny.

Timmy: Hey, looka dat! Dat nose wiggles.

Ms. McLynn: I see our rabbit. She *is* wiggling her nose!

Nancy: Ms. McLynn, my mommie said that she couldn't come today but she will call you afterwhile. She has to go to the supermarket 'cause we're having company tonight.

Ms. McLynn: I'm glad you told me she couldn't come. Would you like to pretend that you are at the supermarket, too? We have lots of things in our store, too.

intelligible speech. Some may never be able to use any formal symbolic system of communication such as signing or graphic symbols. Nevertheless, these children *can* learn to communicate using nonverbal, nonspeech systems of communication.

In planning communication instruction programs for children with multiple disabilities, it is perhaps easiest to consider two types of children. The first group includes those who have the cognitive skills necessary for the development of language (i.e., some formal system of symbolic communication) but do not have the fine *oral-motor skills* required for the production of intelligible speech. The largest number of children in this group would be those with severe forms of cerebral palsy but without mental retardation.

The second group of children are those whose disabilities produce a poor prognosis for the development of any formal symbolic system. The group includes children with severe and profound cognitive disabilities and some who demonstrate multiple sensory impairments (e.g., a child with deafness, severe visual and motor impairments, and moderate mental retardation). For such children, the goals of intelligible speech production and any formal symbolic system of communication, such as sign language or graphic symbols, may be unrealistic. However, they *can* learn to utilize specific behaviors in functional ways to communicate basic wants, needs, and feelings.

A classroom teacher who is unfamiliar with children who have severe multiple disabilities is often initially overwhelmed with the apparent difficulty of working with such children, especially in the area of communication skills. Again, while space does not permit a thorough description of intervention strategies for this group of children, several keys to facilitating communicative behaviors are presented in the following sections. In addition, the strategies included in Exhibits 9-2 and 9-3 can encourage communication in *all* children, regardless of the nature of their disabling conditions.

Verbal Input Strategies: Communicating with Children Who have Severe Disabilities

Respond to Child's Behavioral Cues. Many of the input strategies discussed earlier are also appropriate for children with severe disabilities. When an infant or young child demonstrates a low response rate (i.e., just doesn't seem to "do much"), the teacher's immediate and consistent *response* to the child's cues of interest and attention, and to any attempts to communicate, becomes crucial. Teachers must be more vigilant with such children and be ready to respond with appropriate communicative input.

For example, let us consider a child who has severe motor and visual impairments. The child's voluntary behavioral repertoire consists of moving his head from side to side and a few vocalizations. He does not appear to understand any verbal input, but he does respond to sudden loud sounds, to the sound of his mother's voice, and occasionally to food odors as lunch is prepared. The teacher must be very alert to cues from this child that he is recognizing and processing some incoming stimulus. For example, if another child in the classroom drops her tray on the floor, the child with severe disabilities is startled and begins moving his head from side to side. The teacher should provide some verbal input appropriate to the situation and its meaning to the child. In this case, the teacher might say something like, "Oh oh! That was loud, wasn't it? That was a loud crash! Maria dropped her tray." In this way, the teacher comments on the most salient aspect of the situation (in this case the sound, since the child cannot see well), repeats his or her comment in a slightly different way, and semantically extends his or her own comment by adding information about the source of the sound.

Use Repetition and Predictable Schedules. Repetition, redundancy, and responsiveness are important input strategies in working with infants or young children with severe disabilities. Certain key words and phrases should be used repeatedly to make significant the events of the day. Certain verbal cues should always be associated with certain actions and events. In this way the teacher establishes **verbal routines** (Snow, Midkiff-Borunda, Small, & Proctor, 1984), which are important as children begin to learn to decode language. Snyder-McLean, Solomonson, McLean, and Sack (1984) discuss the strategy of establishing "joint action routines" in which the adult engages jointly in an action with the child while associating key words and phrases with the activity.

For example, the greeting activities that begin the classroom day should include parts that are always repeated. The transition from music time to lunch should always be accompanied by many predictable cues, such as "OK, who knows what time it is now? It's lunch time. It's time to eat," followed by a sequence of predictable events (e.g., chairs moved, bibs put on, table set, etc.). After lunch, the input might be, "OK, we're all done. All done eating. Let's go outside. We'll play outside." Tables are cleaned, chairs pushed in, coats put on, and so forth, while appropriate verbal input strategies accompany these key events.

Techniques for Teaching Communicative Behaviors: "Output Strategies"

Careful verbal input (in response to cues provided by the child that indicate interest and attention or attempts to communicate) is an important key to facilitating communication development. However, for children with severe disabilities, input strategies are not enough. For these children, it is also necessary to manipulate objects and events in the environment to create the opportunity and the need to communicate. Some of the strategies for doing so are described as follows.

Identifying High-Preference Objects and Activities: Making Communication Functional.

Typically developing young children first develop communicative behaviors around the objects, activities, and persons they are most interested in and most desire. The young child's call for "Mama" and requests for "bottle" and "cookie" reflect the importance of high-preference events as motivators for the development of communication skills. The desires and preferences of the typical child are numerous and easily identified. However, identification of **high-preference items and events** for a child with severe disabilities can often present a major challenge. Nevertheless, designing an environment that creates a need to communicate is not possible without first determining those things about which the child is most likely to communicate.

Thus it is necessary to devote time to the systematic identification of high-preference items and activities for each child. To do this, parents should be interviewed carefully with regard to their child's schedule and activities at home. This effort may uncover clues related to possible preferences. In addition, the teacher should devote time to systematically identifying high-preference items and activities. Food is often assumed to be a high-preference item, and indeed it often is for many children. But the teacher should be aware that there are many other objects, persons, and activities that may motivate the child who has severe disabilities to communicate. Table 9–2 lists some examples of these. The teacher must also be aware that, as with all individuals, children's preferences change over time and vary with circumstances. The search for high-preference, motivating objects, activities, and persons to use in teaching functional communication skills must be a continuous process in any program that includes children with severe and multiple disabilities.

High-preference objects and activities can be identified and verified using a number of strategies. These same strategies can simultaneously be used to determine what voluntary behaviors a child with severe disabilities may be capable of using in a communicative way. The teacher must realize that the mere presentation of a potential high-preference object or activity will not necessarily evoke a positive response from the child. In many cases, interrupting or with-

Table 9–2 Examples of High-Preference Activities for Preschoolers with Severe Disabilities

Motor/Kinesthetic	*Manipulables*
Bouncing	Playing with cause/
Riding in a wagon	effect toys
Swinging in a blanket	Operating knobs
Auditory/Visual	*Setting changes*
Singing	Going outside
Listening to records	Reduction of discomfort
Listening to radio	*Tactile/Physical*
Watching television	*Interaction*
Operating a music box	Stroking
Playing with percussion toys	Hugging
Listening to tapes of	Tickling
familiar voices	Brushing hair
Watching flashing lights	Blowing air
Watching mobiles	Playing with water
Playing with a Jack-in-the-box	Playing with sand

holding an item or activity will be much more effective in determining the child's desire for it.

Identifying Behaviors That Can Be Used Communicatively

Whether to activate some augmentative communicative system or simply to find a communicative signal, the teacher must identify which behaviors the child can voluntarily control. Even in a child with the most severe disabilities, there is probably some behavior that can be voluntarily controlled, such as directed eye gaze, head turning, reaching, or vocalization. *Any* behavior can be used as a communicative signal.

Three simple procedures can be utilized to determine which behaviors the child may be able to use by creating "communicative context" (Constable, 1983).

1. *Presentation.* An obvious technique is simply to present an object to the child and observe the child's behavior. However, the presentation of an object or event, even if desired by the child, may not evoke any voluntary response.

2. *Interruption.* Another way is to present an object or activity believed to be high preference,

and then to stop the activity or remove the object. For example, a child who enjoys being pushed in a wagon is pushed for a moment or two; then the wagon is stopped. The child's behavior is carefully observed, in the event that she attempts to reinstate the activity. She may vocalize, move her head, change her body position or tension, attempt to reach out, and so on. The teacher can systematically observe which behaviors are under some degree of voluntary control.

3. *Withholding an anticipated event.* If there are regularities and predictable events in the child's daily life that he or she enjoys, and if the child is able to anticipate those events given certain cues, then withholding such an event may also be a way of evoking the same kinds of behaviors as those described in item 2. For example, assuming that snack time is a high-preference activity for that child, seating everyone else at the snack table and "forgetting" the child would provide another opportunity to observe potential communicative behaviors.

Such procedures are sometimes referred to as "violations of routine events" (Raver, 1987, p. 229).

Another strategy that can be used to create motivation for spontaneous communication is called "violation of object functions" (Raver, 1987, p. 230). An example would be using a shoe to brush your hair or putting a cup on a doll's foot. Such ridiculous situations can often serve as powerful elicitors of communicative behavior. Raver has also suggested that such a strategy may promote the development of humor.

Teaching Communicative Behaviors: Creating Opportunity and Need for Communication

The simple strategies just described are powerful basic tools for both assessment and beginning intervention. Presentation, interruption, and withholding of an anticipated event provide simple, systematic procedures to be used not only to identify and verify high-preference items and activities but also to begin *teaching* rudimentary communicative behaviors. When a child's preferences have been inventoried and at least one voluntarily controlled behavior identified, the environment can be systematically manipulated and designed to provide opportunities for the child to use the important communicative function of *requesting*. Teachers should keep in mind that, in most children, the use of language or gestures to request some desired object, event, or person emerges long before the use of language or gesture for the purpose of labeling or sharing information.

Because space prohibits giving detailed descriptions of many specific intervention techniques and procedures, the reader is encouraged to refer to other resources related to this area (e.g., Rogers-Warren & Warren, 1984; Klein et al., 1981). Here is a brief description of several techniques.

1. Even a child with the most severe impairments can be taught to request more of a desired object or activity, as described previously. It is not necessary that the child make this request again and again in each setting. For example, the child need not request every single bite of a favorite food. Rather, four or five opportunities could be provided several times per day. There is some evidence that this *distributed practice* is more effective than intensive training blocks of what are called *massed trials.*

2. Another important technique is to provide *choices.* In as many situations as possible throughout the child's day, give opportunities to make choices. Choices of activities, food items, toys, and people can easily be incorporated into classroom programming.

3. Pausing and *waiting* for a child to initiate communication to request a highly desired object or activity is one of the most powerful techniques to encourage functional communication. This technique is referred to as a "time delay" procedure (Alpert & Kaiser, 1992). All too often teachers bombard children with questions, commands,

prompts, and cues without giving them ample time to respond. Many children with severe disabilities require a longer time than others to process incoming information and organize a response. An expectant look on the teacher's face accompanied by silence can often be an amazingly powerful provocateur for communicative behavior.

4. Finally, it is extremely important to make sure that the child with severe disabilities, particularly the nonambulatory child, is provided with some means of getting adults' attention. The child who is at the mercy of others to initiate communication cannot really engage in functional dialogue. Many children will be unable to produce an audible vocal signal as an attention-getting device, and they will need to be provided with some other type of auditory signal such as a bell or buzzer. The ability to *initiate* communication is critical to the success of any communication instruction program.

Use of "Milieu Teaching" Techniques in Shaping Specific Communicative Behaviors

Milieu teaching is a term used to refer to a variety of behavioral techniques that are used in the natural environment to teach specific communication skills. Milieu techniques include three basic elements: (1) arranging the environment in ways which increase the need for a particular type of communicative behavior; (2) identifying specific target behaviors; and (3) applying specific teaching procedures (McCormick, Loeb, & Schiefelbusch, 1997). Some authors have described sequential communication training steps to be used in the natural environment. Wulz, Hall, and Klein (1983) have described a sequence of cues and prompts that may be used with any of the situations and strategies just described. These steps are similar to those described by Rogers-Warren and Warren (1984). Similar techniques have been referred to as "*mand*-model technique" (Halle, 1982), "incidental teaching" (Warren & Kaiser, 1986), and "time-delay procedure" (Peck, 1985). An excellent description of each of these procedures can be found in Beukelman and Mirenda (1992).

1. *Create the need or opportunity to communicate.* Using the kinds of strategies just described, manipulate environmental variables to encourage attempts to communicate. Keep in mind that identifying the objects, persons, and events that interest and motivate the infant or young child is a critical prerequisite to this step.

2. *Pause and wait.* Give the child an opportunity to initiate communication. For children with severe disabilities, this may take 10 to 20 seconds (as opposed to individuals without disabilities, who can organize and produce a behavior in 1 or 2 seconds). There are two ways in which the pause and wait strategy can be used. Early in teaching it is often helpful to look expectantly at the child. Many teachers will find it very difficult to look at a child without saying anything for 10 to 20 seconds. However, in some cases the use of this time delay can produce previously unseen communicative behaviors. (See Halle, Alpert, & Anderson, 1984.)

When the child has acquired the behavior, (e.g., directed eye gaze, pointing at an object, pointing at a picture, etc.), instead of looking expectantly at the child during the wait period, the teacher can move or turn away as though busy doing something else. This procedure can be used to encourage the use of an attention-getting behavior such as vocalizing, or activating an AAC switch. Initially, this procedure will require two teachers: one teacher to implement the delay while another observes the child's unsuccessful attempts and provides prompts and cues.

3. *Provide a natural cue.* Initially in teaching a communicative behavior, cues and prompts can be provided when the child is unable to respond or responds inappropriately during the pause period. It is important, however, that cues and prompts *not* be provided every time, lest the child learn to simply wait through a series of prompts to eventually obtain the desired communicative consequence. Occasionally, the opportunity to communicate should simply be terminated until a later time during the day. This is particularly appropriate for optional situations such as choosing a toy or a dessert.

When a child does not respond during the pause period, employ a *natural* cue. A natural verbal cue is one that is likely to occur in the natural environment, for example, someone asking, "What do you want?" or "Can I help you?" or "Tell me what you want to do now." If the child still does not respond, prompts may be used.

4. *Use prompts and assistance.* A wide variety of prompts may be used to assist the child in communicative behavior. Many of these are borrowed from behavioral teaching strategies. Perhaps the most commonly used prompting strategy is the use of **modeling.** Modeling can be an effective prompt for children who have a generalized imitation strategy, and who will attempt to imitate the teacher's model. Unfortunately, many children with severe disabilities do not have a generalized ability to imitate a model. For these children, physical prompting and shaping may be necessary.

Physical prompting involves physically guiding the child through the behavior. For example, if you are teaching a child to reach or point toward a desired object, a physical prompt moves the child's hand and arm through the motion of pointing. Using traditional behavioral methods, gradually fade this physical prompt until the child can produce the behavior on his or her own.

To use physical prompting effectively, the "topography" of the behavior must be accessible. Unfortunately, vocalization—one very important communicative modality—does not lend itself to physical prompting. Control of vocalization is completely internal. A teacher cannot force or assist a child in vocalizing other than by use of an imitative prompt. Thus, it is important to realize that when physical prompts must be used, communicative behaviors other than vocal behaviors must be selected.

5. *Comply with the communicative request.* Within this sequence of steps, provide the desired object or activity at any point at which the child produces an acceptable approximation to the targeted

communicative behavior. That is, the child should get the toy, be moved to a favorite location, have the record player turned on, or whatever is desired.

In addition, the teacher should always accompany his or her compliance with the appropriate verbal input. The input strategies described earlier are very important here, particularly the use of repetition and re-cast sentences. As the teacher provides the desired item, he or she should say, "Oh, you want the *doll*, huh! Here's your *doll*. What a cute doll." If the child then appears to be paying attention to the doll, the teacher can semantically expand these utterances by adding a bit more information. For example, "Oh, the *doll* has a new *dress*. Look."

The use of these steps increases the likelihood that several necessary conditions will be met for effective communication instruction. First, the child is *actively processing* incoming information and recognizes the *need* to communicate. Next, the child *initiates,* or is helped to initiate the communicative interaction and is not forced to wait for a specific stimulus to which to respond. Third, the child's communicative behavior has an *impact* upon the environment, because the teacher complies with the request. The child thus experiences *effectance,* perhaps the most powerful reinforcer of all. Finally, the opportunity is created for the teacher to use verbal input to map language onto the child's experience.

Use of the strategies described earlier with regard to natural environments and daily routines is referred to as a milieu approach. According to Warren and Kaiser (1988) the term *milieu approach* represents an array of approaches characterized by (a) distributed practice rather than massed trials, (b) following the child's lead, (c) teaching within conversational contexts, and (d) teaching within natural communicative situations.

While the strategies and approaches described in this section have been most frequently reported in association with children with more severe disabilities, they can be equally effective with children who have mild to moderate disabilities.

Some specific strategies for encouraging young children to talk are given in Exhibit 9–3.

Facilitating Social Communication Between Children with Special Needs and Nondisabled Peers

In order for successful social interaction to take place between a child and his or her peers, two components must be in place. First, the child must be able to *respond* to a peer's initiation in an appropriate way. Second, the child must be able to *initiate* interaction in a way that is likely to obtain a positive response (Odom & Strain, 1986).

Some children with disabilities may lack these skills, and they may need direct instruction related to these important social communication behaviors. Odom and colleagues (1988) have developed a curriculum that is specifically designed to socially integrate preschoolers with special needs and their typical peers. An important section of the curriculum describes procedures for direct instruction of social skills.

Familiar procedures of modeling, prompting, and reinforcement are used. The teacher first talks to a small group of children about appropriate play behaviors, demonstrating "good" and "bad" social behaviors and familiarizing the children with classroom behaviors related to playing together cooperatively. Both children with disabilities and those without can then be taught to initiate (e.g., "Jose, can you ask Mary to help you with the tower?") and respond appropriately (e.g., "Jose, Mark is sharing his cookie with you. Tell him 'Thank you.' ") in actual play situations. Initially, children's appropriate social behavior may need to be reinforced externally by the teacher (e.g., saying, "Jose, that was very nice of you to say 'Thank you' to Mark," giving the child a sticker for being polite, etc.). However, these contrived reinforcers should be discontinued as quickly as possible. The goal ultimately is for the natural consequence of the child's appropriate interaction and communication to be its own reward.

EXHIBIT 9–3

Promoting Specific Reasons for Talking

Using Language for Finding Out About Things

Curiosity is expected of young children. Hide something in a box or bag, and then encourage them to guess what is inside. Ask, "Is it round?" "Can it swim?" Offer the opportunity to teach how asking questions leads to answers. If "why?" and "how?" questions are not being used by some children, games and experiments with different toys can initiate them.

Using Language for Getting Involved

As young children often play beside each other rather than with each other, sand, water, and block play encourage "getting involved." As they learn to express intentions, tell others what to do (directing), and report what has happened, they learn new language quickly. Combining verbal children and those who speak less well provides a natural language learning opportunity.

Using Language for Getting Help

Wanting something that is put away or too high to reach provides the need to ask for it. Zippers that stick and shoes that come untied create the need to ask for help. This becomes the opportunity for you to act as if gestures, helpless looks, and even tears do not communicate. However, any attempt to say something should be rewarded. (Of course, for the child who usually does not even use nonverbal attempts at communication, *any* effort should be rewarded.)

Modeling "Tie my shoe" and accepting the child's "Tie oo" at first encourages greater effort. Gradually, if you are absolutely certain that the child is able to say it better, you may appear to be puzzled until the child makes a better attempt.

Using Language to Get Attention or Approval

Some children poke and pull at adults as well as other children. Children need something to take the place of a habit that needs to be changed. The words "Look" or "Watch me" can be used in many situations. Each time they attempt to get attention in other ways, avoid responding immediately. Turning away, ask "Do you want me to look?" (pause) "Tell me (pause) *look*." Then, refuse to watch unless they say *something*.

Using Language to Tell Something

If there are interested listeners, most children want to tell them something. Asking parents to write a note about interesting events at home is helpful. Then, you can initiate the discussion. Sometimes a picture or a favorite toy from home serves this purpose. Formal show and tell is not usually effective with young children, but informally telling the teacher or a friend is popular.

Using Language to Defend Themselves

"Stop that" needs to be learned early. "Move, please" is better than shoving. Teaching children how to defend themselves verbally instead of with a push or shove results in more pleasant homes and classrooms. They will need examples, models, and teachers' insistence that saying something is better than just shoving.

◆ ◆ ◆

EXHIBIT 9–3

Using Language to Learn New Things

Children who know how to express themselves in one way are quicker to learn other ways to talk about things. When a wide range of new experiences are provided throughout the year, new ideas and new words are learned. The vocabulary of taking care of the science corner is not the same as the vocabulary for music time. For children with very limited speech and language, initially focus on things they need to know and say in the classroom and at home, and then expand the horizon.

Using Any Utterance to Begin Communication

For some children with severe disabilities, any attempt to make a sound will need to be rewarded with instant encouragement. If it appears that a child wants something and is attempting to ask for it, give it to the child immediately. If you know what word was attempted, model (say) it to confirm that you understood. First efforts should never be the occasion for an attempt to improve the child's production. That comes *much* later. But letting the child know that he or she has in fact communicated is rewarding in itself.

AUGMENTATIVE AND ALTERNATIVE COMMUNICATION SYSTEMS

For many children with severe and multiple disabilities the development of an **augmentative** or **alternative communication system** will be necessary. Such a system involves the use of non-speech communication strategies. Examples of these include signing, pointing to pictures, use of electronic communication boards and computerized speech synthesizers, and so on. The system can "augment" existing communication skills and behaviors or may provide an "alternative" to speech production for a child who has no means of communication. Thus the term *augmentative and alternative communication* is used (also referred to as **AAC**).

In recent years AAC has come to be associated in many peoples' minds with high technology equipment such as adapted computer keyboards, which can be activated by a touch or laser beam to produce a communication printout or synthesized speech.

(For a list of resources related to AAC technology, see Appendix G.)

It is important to understand, however, that AAC can include both high tech and "low tech" systems, and are often multi-modal (ASHA, 1991). Low tech systems are non-electronic. They include strategies such as simple adaptations of manual signs, use of photos or black and white line drawings arranged on a communication board or in a communication book, and letters of the alphabet printed on a card.

Particularly for very young children it is important to begin training with very simple, low-tech strategies and devices. It is easy for the early intervention professional to be somewhat in awe of the many computer hardware components, and the hundreds of software programs designed for young children. However, for many children, low-tech strategies and devices are more appropriate for their individual needs. And even for those children who will eventually benefit from computerized systems, early training in simple strategies such as touching pictures or di-

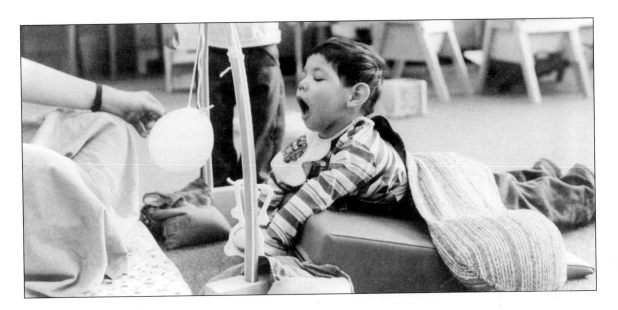

rected eye gaze will make the transition to high-tech devices much easier. Early interventionists should not wait to see whether or not efforts to teach speech to the child with multiple disabilities are going to be successful before beginning augmentative communication instruction. There is currently no evidence that teaching non-speech communication strategies interferes with speech development. Such instruction may actually facilitate vocalization and speech development (Klein, 1985). In addition many of the skills necessary for successful use of an AAC system are also beneficial for children who are not severely disabled, for example, use of pictures or line drawings as representations of real objects and activities, and use of computer keyboards.

The development of an AAC system for a particular child requires a team approach: ideally such a team might include the parent, early childhood educator, occupational or physical therapist, and speech-language therapist. In addition, if high-tech devices are being used, a technician would also be an important member of the team.

While space does not allow a thorough discussion of the strategies and procedures for developing an AAC system, the following briefly outlines the sequence of necessary steps.

Steps in Developing an AAC System

1. *Determine the child's communicative needs and opportunities.* Together with the child's family it is important to determine in what situations and for what purposes the child currently needs or attempts to communicate. (If the child does not *attempt* to communicate, then the primary goal becomes creating motivation necessary to encourage communicative attempts.)

2. *Determine the child's current communicative repertoire.* If the child does attempt to communicate, how does he or she do it? What does the child do to express wants and needs, express emotions, or share information? What movements can the child voluntarily control? Does he use his eyes, vocalizations, or gestures such as reaching or pointing?

3. *What are the barriers to successful communication?* Determine why the communication is not

successful. Are vocalizations unintelligible? Are hand gestures poorly controlled? Is the child trying to refer to things that are not immediately present, such as something that happened yesterday?

4. *Determine the best "indicating response" to be used.* What behavior does the child have the best control of? For many children with severe physical disabilities, eye gaze may be the only reliable voluntary movement. Other children may be able to touch or point to a picture successfully. Some children may not be able to use their hands, but may have sufficient head control to point with a head stick (pointer) mounted on a head band, or may be able to move the head to activate a switch.

5. *Determine the best "symbol system."* The symbol system will depend largely on the child's cognitive level. Some children will need to begin with the actual object, moving step-by-step to more abstract representations, while others may be able to begin immediately with black-and-white line drawings of very concrete objects.

6. *Design the "display."* Once the indicating response and the symbol system have been determined, it is then necessary to determine how the symbols will be displayed. For the child who cannot walk, but who can point to pictures, a common display would be a communication board mounted on a wheelchair. For a child who uses eye gaze as an indicating response, the most common display would be pictures arranged on a clear plexiglass frame called an "E-tran" board. For a child who is mobile, the display might be a picture book, or laminated cards on a large ring.

7. *Design training steps.* Teaching a child to use an augmentative communication system requires careful planning of training steps. Exhibit 9–4 is an example of the training steps used to teach a young child with cerebral palsy to use directed eye gaze. More detailed information on the development of AAC systems can be found in recent texts (e.g., Baumgart, Johnson, & Helmstetter, 1990; Beukelman & Mirenda, 1992; Reichle, York, & Sigafoos, 1991).

Classroom Strategies That Facilitate Augmentative Communication Skills

Several activities that facilitate the development of augmentative communication skills can be built into the everyday activities of an early childhood program. These activities can be both fun and meaningful for all children, not just for the child with severe disabilities. Examples of these include:

1. *Use of switch operated toys.* Battery-operated toys can be included among the play materials in the classroom. The switches can be adapted to be more easily operated by children with severe motor impairments. Cause-effect toys can be adapted with pressure switches, large toggle switches, heat-sensitive touch switches, and so on. Such switches are intriguing to all children and facilitate the learning of cause-and-effect relationships. In addition, for the child with severe motor impairments, they provide the motivation and opportunity to practice the fine motor movements required for eventually activating various communication devices.

2. *Use of computers.* It is important for all children to become comfortable with keyboard operations and monitor displays. Hundreds of software games and activities are available that are interesting and appropriate for very young children. These should be included in the early childhood classroom and every effort should be made to familiarize the child with disabilities with the operation of the keyboard and the relationship to the monitor display. This is a particularly good activity for peer interaction and modeling.

3. *Use of picture representations and symbols.* An important skill in the development of a successful AAC system is the ability to recognize that pictures and abstract symbols have representational meaning, i.e., that they stand for some real object or activity. Many young children, with and without disabilities, have not acquired this understanding. Obviously this

EXHIBIT 9–4

Training Angie to Use an AAC System

Angie was a 2½-year-old girl with spastic cerebral palsy. There was severe involvement of all parts of her body. She was unable to sit unsupported, to reach or grasp, or bring her hands to midline. She also had some difficulty with head control. She was unable to produce speech sounds, though she occasionally vocalized. One day her mother mentioned to her early interventionist that Angie had recently begun to stare intently at things she wanted. Together, the early interventionist and parent, in consultation with a speech-language specialist trained in augmentative methodology, planned the following intervention.

1. *Carefully describe current communicative behavior.* In Angie's case the most reliable communicative behavior was "directed eye gaze."

2. *Identify high-preference and low-preference objects and activities.* Angie loved to eat, so favorite foods were identified as high-preference items, especially strawberry yogurt, ice cream, and orange juice. One low-preference activity identified was having her face washed, which she had always hated.

3. *Establish "indicating response."* The logical indicating response in Angie's case, since she really had no other consistent communicative behavior, was the use of eye gaze. Angie's mom began to give her lots of practice using her eyes to track her glass or spoon before giving her a bite or drink.

4. *Offer choice of high- or low-preference item.* Angie's mom or her teacher would hold up two items: a glass of juice and a washcloth, saying "Which would you like Angie: Juice or washcloth?" Whichever item she looked at for more than a fleeting glance was the one she received. Initially she would occasionally stare at the washcloth. She immediately got her faced washed a bit, even though her mom knew this was not what she really wanted. This step was necessary to help her understand the communicative nature of her eye gaze. Quickly she learned to scan the items quickly to look for the item she wanted, and then fix her gaze on that item.

5. *Offer choice of two high-preference items.* The next step was to offer her a choice of two high-preference items. This represents a true communication situation. Her communication partner really does not know which of two foods she wants. Her eye gaze communication puts her in control of the choice.

6. *Pair pictures with items.* Next, the objects, e.g., a glass of juice and a bowl of yogurt, were paired with pictures. In Angie's case, black and white line drawings of a glass and a bowl were used. (Photos of the objects could have been used, but Angie's mom felt she could learn to recognize the line drawings easily, and they were easier to produce than photos by simply using a magic marker on a 3 × 5 index card). The name of the item was printed at the bottom of the picture.

7. *Fade objects.* Gradually the items were removed from sight and only the pictures were presented. Angie learned that the picture *represented* the object. This was the beginning of Angie's comprehension of symbols, which is an important cognitive skill for the use of an augmentative communication system.

8. *Reduce picture size and design display.* Now the pictures could be made somewhat smaller and placed on a see-through plexiglass board which could be attached to her wheelchair. The teacher and occupational therapist experimented to determine the best position of the board and how far apart the pictures needed to be to reliably tell what Angie was looking at.

9. *Add vocabulary; expand system.* From this point on it was a fairly easy matter to add new pictures representing key vocabulary (e.g., "bathroom" and "TV") and whole sentences (e.g., "What's your name?") Eventually Angie developed better control of her hands and arms and learned to activate an adapted keyboard to produce synthesized speech.

symbolic representation skill is necessary for the eventual development of literacy (see Chapter 10), as well as for the development of augmentative communication systems.

Thus, whenever possible, functional use of pictures and symbols (including printed words) should be demonstrated in the classroom. For example:

- Black-and-white line drawings can be pasted on cupboard doors and boxes indicating their contents.
- Bathroom signs should be similar to adult bathroom signs.
- Lunch menus should be posted and referred to.
- Children can choose a favorite toy by choosing the appropriate laminated card or by pointing to a picture on a grid that corresponds to that toy.

Visual discrimination and matching skills can also be encouraged by use of picture matching games and name recognition. (For more cognitively advanced children shapes and letters could be matched.)

4. *Conversation starter strategies.* Several suggestions have been made in the literature (e.g., Musselwhite, 1990) of ways to assist non-speaking children in sharing information and experiences with others. These strategies are very important because it is easy to overemphasize the communicative function of requesting. This is because it is relatively easy to teach a child to request wants and needs; thus, this is the communicative function that is most often emphasized in work with children with severe disabilities. It is also important for young children to have ways of sharing information with others. Beukelman and Mirenda (1992) describe three conversation starter strategies:

Collections

Children can be encouraged to collect things of interest to them, such as bracelets, toy cars, pictures of friends, etc. Both teachers and peers can be encouraged to notice and comment on the items in the collection, as well as new additions to the collection. Again, this is an activity that all children can enjoy. For the non-speaking child it provides an excellent communicative context in which others can easily participate.

Remnant Books

Remnant books provide a way for the non-speaking child to share past experiences. For example, a child may save various scraps and reminders—"remnants"—from a weekend trip to the zoo. The teacher and parent should help the child construct the book. The remnant book might have a postcard with a picture of the zoo, a ticket stub with the price of admission, a hamburger wrapper from lunch, photos of the most interesting animals, and a parking ticket next to a drawing of the family car. The book should be easily accessible so that the experiences can be shared at any appropriate time.

Topic Setter Cards

For children who have difficulty initiating conversations, topic setter cards may be useful. A simple line drawing or symbol that has meaning for the child is drawn on an index card. On the back of the card facing the prospective communication partner there is a message. For example, "What's your favorite TV show? Mine is 'Power Rangers.' "

Using the Picture Exchange Communication System (PECS)

In recent years a simple low-tech system of picture communication has become popular, particularly for developing early communication skills of children with autism who do not have functional oral language. The Picture Exchange Communication System, or PECS (Frost & Bondy, 1994), uses behavioral techniques to teach the child to use pictures to obtain desired objects or activities, or to make comments. The system begins with careful observation of the child in order to determine high-preference objects and activities. Whenever a highly motivating activity or object is identified, a photo or black-and-white line drawing is produced and placed on a card or in a binder with Velcro.

Unlike more typical AAC picture systems, the child does not *point*. Rather, the child is taught to remove a Velcro-attached picture from a book or binder, approach another person, and hand the picture to the person. The person receiving the picture responds with appropriate language and gives the child the desired object or activity. Careful physical prompts (not verbal prompts) are provided until the child learns the following sequence:

1. Finding the correct picture
2. Removing the picture
3. Approaching the adult
4. Handing the adult the picture
5. Waiting for the adult's response/compliance with the request.

A significant advantage of the PECS system is that it requires *social interaction* for the communication to be successful.

WORKING WITH CHILDREN WITH HEARING LOSS

A preschool teacher whose class includes a child with a hearing loss must work in close collaboration not only with the child's parents but also with specialists trained to work with infants and young children with hearing loss. These specialists may include an audiologist (if the child wears a hearing aid), a speech pathologist trained to work with children with hearing loss, or a teacher of the deaf.

A very important decision for every family of a child with a significant hearing loss will be the selection of a primary communication modality: i.e., speech or manual sign (or a combination of both). Approaches that emphasize speech (sometimes referred to as "oral" or "oral English" approaches) stress the importance of teaching the child with a hearing loss to produce intelligible speech and to be able to understand the spoken language of others. Within

this approach, some emphasize the use of both auditory (via the use of a hearing aid to maximize the use of the child's residual hearing) and visual input (e.g., lipreading). Ling (1984) advocates a "unisensory" approach that relies only on auditory cues in an effort to maximize the child's ability to use auditory information and residual hearing. Proponents of the oral approach believe that the individual with a hearing loss must be given the skills to function comfortably in a hearing world.

The signing or "manual communication" approach is strongly endorsed by members of the Deaf community, as well as by many teachers of deaf students, who believe that manual communication is the most easily and naturally acquired language for children with significant hearing losses. For these children the process of teaching speech skills is often slow and tedious (Hunt & Marshall, 1994).

There are several different systems of sign language. American Sign Language, or ASL, is the system preferred by most members of the Deaf community. ASL is a language in its own right. Its structure does not correspond to the structure of English: rules of word order are different and there are no signs for grammatical markers such as *-ing* or *-ed*. Because of the belief that ASL does not facilitate the learning of spoken English and literacy skills, other sign systems have been developed that more closely match the grammar and vocabulary of the English language. These systems can be signed simultaneously with speech. Examples of such systems (referred to as "manually coded English") are Signing Essential English (SEE I), and Signing Exact English (SEE II). Another interesting system is called "cued speech." This system manually supplements speech production through the use of hand signs made near the mouth; these signs provide supplementary information about the vowels and consonants being spoken (Schwartz, 1987).

The controversy over which approach is best has raged for over 200 years and continues to be an emotionally charged debate. Overall, the research findings on efficacy are mixed. One consistent finding has been that for deaf children of deaf parents the early use of ASL (American Sign Language) clearly facilitates language development. Adults who are deaf and who identify strongly with the Deaf community are proponents of the notion that children who are deaf should not be viewed as deficient or having a pathology, but as members of a different culture that has its own language, traditions, values, and literature (Hunt & Marshall, 1994). Most individuals within the Deaf community view ASL as their native language; spoken English is an optional second language.

The decision regarding the language modality to be used with the child who is deaf or hard of hearing must be made by the parents. If parents have already made this decision, it is the responsibility of the early childhood professional to understand and support that approach. In those cases where parents are in the process of trying to decide which approach is best, the early childhood professional can direct them to specialists who can give them accurate and reliable information about the characteristics of each approach.

Suggestions for Working with Children with Hearing Loss

The following are general suggestions for early interventionists or early childhood professionals whose classes may include a young child with a hearing loss.

1. For children learning to sign, ask parents to teach you signs used at home; teach parents new signs introduced at school.

2. Teach signs for key words such as "Help" or "All done" to all children in the program.

3. Be sure that windows or other light sources are not behind you or shining into the eyes of the child. In order for the child to read lips or signs the light must be on the speaker or signer, not in the child's eyes.

4. As often as possible include adults and older children with hearing loss in your classroom. It is important for all young children (not just the child with a hearing loss) to observe role models who wear hearing aids and/or use sign language. Such an individual might sign and speak a story or song, or simply assist with daily routines.

5. Include in your classroom books that include the signs for key words in the story. (Many such materials are available from Gallaudet University Press in Washington, D.C.)

6. When the child does not appear to understand, repeat the sentence, or say it in a slightly different way. Then add visual cues, e.g., gestures, facial expressions, or pointing to an object or picture.

Facilitating a Child's Ability to Lip-read and Comprehend Speech

Use the following suggestions to facilitate the development of the child's ability to lip-read and comprehend speech:

1. Don't talk too fast. You may need to slow your speech rate slightly, but be careful not to distort the rate and rhythm of your normal speech pattern.

2. Do not exaggerate lip movements or pause after each word. This will not make lipreading easier and provides inappropriate speech models for the child. However, do avoid mumbling, chewing gum, or keeping your hands in front of your mouth

3. Stand or sit still. It is hard for children to focus on a moving target!

4. Don't ask "Do you understand?" (Children will often say "yes" regardless.) Rather, discover how much has been understood by asking questions or giving directions and observing the child's responses.

5. If the child does not appear to understand, repeat the sentence or say it a different way. Then add visual cues such as facial expression, gestures, or pointing to an object or picture.

6. Be aware of the child's potential for use of residual hearing. Help the child learn the meaning of various sounds in the environment by drawing his attention to them, e.g., the sounds of musical instruments or the sound of a timer bell.

7. Perhaps most important, follow the suggestions made in this text for nurturing the development of speech and language in all children.

Hearing Aids

It is critical that the early childhood professional be aware of the child's potential for the development of **residual hearing.** Even children with the most severe losses usually have some hearing, and with assistance can eventually learn to use this hearing. The *meaning* of sounds must be learned and does not happen automatically.

Ideally, the young child with a hearing loss will have been fitted with a hearing aid in infancy in order to maximize the use of residual hearing. The challenge of supporting the very young child's use of a hearing aid is an important one. With the assistance of the audiologist, the teacher and parent must work together to insure optimal use of the hearing aid. *Ensure that the child wears the hearing aid consistently in the center and help the family to expect the same at home.* Also, consult with the audiologist to determine the types of sounds the child can most easily perceive.

The following suggestions may be helpful in encouraging the child's use of a hearing aid. (Luetke-Stahlman & Luckner, 1991):

1. Check the batteries daily; have extra batteries on hand.

2. Cover the controls on the hearing aid so they remain set at the proper levels; keep cords from being twisted.

3. Keep earmolds cleaned (do not clean with alcohol); keep the receiver away from water or extreme heat; avoid dropping the receiver.

4. Work with parents to teach preschool children to care for and insert their own aid as part of their daily self-care routine.

5. At home have a special place where the aid is always kept, away from pets and siblings.

6. For infants and very young children, behind-the-ear aids may need to be taped on.

7. Be aware of the acoustic characteristics of your classroom and the child's home environment. For optimal use of amplification, the acoustic environment must be appropriate, i.e., relatively free of extraneous noise (such as background music, playground or hallway noise, etc.) and reverberating surfaces. When speech sounds are reflected off hard surfaces they are more difficult to comprehend. Dampen noise by use of carpets, wall hangings, acoustic tile, etc. (Leavitt, 1984).

Children with Intermittent Hearing Losses

Often young children have hearing losses that come and go. Fluid in the middle ear, wax in the ear canal, and frequent colds, no matter how mild, may result in a hearing loss that comes and remains awhile. Usually physicians are unaware of this condition unless parents report it to them. And parents are unaware because the child is not complaining. However, they often report that "Johnny has been so stubborn this week. He doesn't come and do what I tell him unless I yell at him." Or they may say, "Sandy has been so grumpy all week. She won't listen. She just pretends not to hear me." (See Naremore, 1979)

WORKING WITH CHILDREN WITH VISUAL DISABILITIES

Much has been learned in the past decade regarding the development of communication skills in children with severe visual impairments (see, for example, Anderson, Dunlea, and Kekelis, 1984). Considerable attention is being given to facilitating communicative interactions between young children who are blind and their caregivers (Dote-Kwan, 1991).

It is important that early intervention professionals work collaboratively with specialists in visual disabilities to ensure that optimal adaptations are made. It is wise to involve orientation and mobility specialists as well as those who specialize in teaching children with visual disabilities. The following suggestions may be helpful in facilitating communication skills in children with visual impairments:

1. Utilize the strategies already described in this text.

2. During vocalizations, touch the child to let him or her know you are there listening. Converse or interact with the child verbally, just as you would with any other youngster of the same language development level.

3. Use auditory and tactile cues to help the child *anticipate* what will happen next; e.g., before you wash the child's face, touch his hand with the washcloth and say "Let's wash your face now."

4. Talk about what you are doing and what the child is doing as it happens. Label actions as well as things, using key words that are appropriate for the child's level.

5. Be certain the child uses vision to the maximum extent possible, and then combine looking with touching and talking.

6. Be certain that children with visual impairments see and feel all parts of an object and understand the relationship of parts to the whole.

7. Spatial relations are difficult to demonstrate. Place the child in various positions and encourage touching and manipulating. Sometimes use toys to demonstrate concepts such as on-off, up-down, and in-out.

8. Use language and the auditory modality to facilitate children's beginning understanding of directionality and distance, e.g., "I'm across the room, far away." "Now I'm coming closer!"

9. Avoid "bombarding" the child with too much talk. Pause frequently and avoid talking too rapidly.

10. Teach the child to localize sounds and recognize their source, direction, and distance.

Chapter 4 also includes a list of high-risk signals of possible visual impairments. Such a checklist should be readily available and studied frequently.

WORKING WITH THE CHILD WHO HAS AUTISM

In establishing communication intervention goals and strategies for children with autism, professionals first must consider the possible need to manage problems of tactile defensiveness and auditory sensitivity. Assistance should be sought from occupational or physical therapists in designing strategies to reduce and manage tactile sensitivity. In addition, staff members should work with parents to identify and understand the child's aversions and sensitivities to certain sounds.

The primary intervention goal related to communication interaction will be helping children develop the important early social interaction skills that are crucial to the later development of language skills. Especially important are turn taking, social initiation, and the development of instrumental and regulatory functions of communication, that is, using gestures and vocalizations to express wants and needs and to influence the behaviors of others. (See Prizant & Wetherby, 1988.)

The use of traditional modeling approaches to language instruction that rely on elicited imitation may be problematic, since children with autism often develop so-called "echolalic" speech (i.e., the immediate or delayed exact repetition or "parroting" of another person's speech). While they may respond easily when the teacher models a cue such as "say 'cookie,'" generalizing the response to functional and meaningful spontaneous use of the word *cookie* is often extremely difficult. Techniques that may be more helpful include a combination of modeling and environmental manipulation techniques such as those presented earlier in the discussion of strategies for children with severe disabilities. (For a discussion of the uses of echolalia by children with autism see Prizant, 1983.)

Children with autism often handle visual/graphic information more easily than auditory/verbal information. One successful approach to developing communication behaviors is the use of PECS, the Picture Exchange Communication System described earlier in this chapter. This approach has several advantages for children with autism (Bondy & Frost, 1994):

- It focuses on *functional* communication

- It *requires* social interaction and exchange

- It relies more on visual information than on auditory

- It provides an acceptable "replacement behavior" for children whose communicative behaviors have become disruptive and inappropriate.

Ogletree and Oren (1998) stress the importance of designing communication intervention programs for children with autism that are both structured *and* functional, rather than one or the other. They point out that historically, approaches have emphasized one or the other. For example, Lovaas's "discrete trial" approach (McEachin, Smith, & Lovaas, 1993) has been criticized because of it's lack of generalization across partners and situations, its emphasis on the child as a respondent rather than an initiator, and its focus on specific language forms rather than on functional communication skills. On the other hand, more child directed transactional models (see for example Wilcox, Kouri, & Caswell, 1991) implemented in natural play environments have not been particularly successful with children with autism (Ogletree & Oren, 1998). A combined approach is both structured and functional. In this type of approach functionality is established by working with the child within meaningful contexts such as play and daily routines, and identifying high-preference, motivating activities. In addition, a communicative need is established through strategies such as delay of an expected event, placing desired items out of reach, and use of "environmental sabotage" such as forgetting to give the child a spoon, or putting a lid on too tight. When the child indicates a desire for an item, then structured direct teaching steps are used, including expectant waiting, verbal prompts, modeling, etc.

There are many approaches and therapies recommended for children with autism. Unfortunately, there is no "magic bullet" or cure and there is much disagreement among professionals as to the most effective communication intervention. There are however, certain strategies and considerations that are well established. Children with autism have great difficulty communicating, regardless of their cognitive abilities. Often they are extremely hypersensitive to auditory and tactile stimuli and may handle visual/graphic forms of communication better than auditory/verbal. They are often easily overwhelmed by changes in daily routines and have great difficulty learning in chaotic, noisy, unpredictable environments. Predictable daily schedules, with ample visual cues signalling transitions, will create an environment in which the child's energy and attention can be made available for learning. Behavioral techniques that provide repetition and clear cues and predictable consequences can be utilized within natural daily activities to teach functional communication and social interaction skills.

WORKING WITH THE CHILD WHO HAS LANGUAGE DIFFERENCES

The English spoken by the majority of people in the United States is usually called standard American English. Realistically, there is little question that people who speak standard English have advantages in school and in the job market. Ideally, speakers of nonstandard dialects can also learn standard English. Similarly, children from different language backgrounds should be encouraged to develop both their native language and English as a second language. As will be described in Chapter 10, in the discussion of literacy, there are also important differences in how families *use* language.

Because demographics in the United States are changing so dramatically, it is imperative that professionals working with young children be prepared to respect and celebrate diversity, while at the same time preparing children to succeed in the mainstream.

Dialectal Variations

Through the years, delineating which dialect speakers have speech and language disabilities and which are merely "different" has become a recognized necessity (Mattes & Omark, 1984). Teachers are being encouraged to consult with speech-language pathologists to separate language deficiencies from language differences before initiating a program of language development. In turn, the speech-language pathologist is expected to be aware of the limitations of culturally biased tests currently used in determining whether or not a child has a language deficiency.

In 1979, a federal judge in Michigan's Eastern District Court ruled that the Ann Arbor School District must develop a plan for teaching standard English to dialect speakers while respecting differences in dialect (Bountress, 1980). This decision was in response to African-American parents' contention that their children were experiencing academic difficulties as a result of teacher insensitivity to the students' dialects. "The best recommendation appears to be that the teacher should respect the black child's dialect just as she respects the Mexican or Puerto Rican child's Spanish, yet while doing this, also make it possible for him (or her) to learn standard English" (Hendrick, 1980, p. 239).

There is growing awareness of various social dialects, and attempts are being made to assist children in the development of both their native dialect and standard English (Taylor, 1986). Adler (1979) has been an avid proponent of **bidialectalism,** which is an approach to the teaching of standard English while maintaining the native dialect. According to him, "the espoused goal of such programs is to increase language skills *in general*—to teach children to use standard English in appropriate contexts while respecting and maintaining the native dialect" (p. 125). The intent is to teach children to be competent in any social situation by being able to use whatever form of language is appropriate to the participants and the setting.

English as a Second Language

The same degree of respect is necessary for children who are learning English as a second language. In addition to learning the vocabulary, grammar, and syntax of the new language, these children must discover acceptable social behaviors in the new culture. Learning two sets of social-language interactions as well as two languages can result in confusion and discomfort.

More and more programs expect either the teacher or an assistant to be bilingual. When this is not possible, teachers should study the basic social differences and hold conferences with parents and others who can explain the cultural expectations. For example, one difference often noticed is the degree to which speakers of different languages expect or avoid eye contact. Teachers who do not understand social differences may accuse the Indian or Puerto Rican child of not paying attention when actually the child is avoiding eye contact in an effort to show respect to adults. This is only one of many pragmatic differences which are influenced by culture.

Learning a New Language

Richard-Amato (1988) has emphasized the notion that second language learning must be an *interactive* process. It should be clear that the strategies already described in this chapter can make important contributions to children's learning a second language.

The most efficient way to help children learn a second language uses conversations about the things they are interested in throughout the day. Tough (1977) and Krashen and Terrell (1983) have contended that the same principles that undergird the fostering of language in all children should be the basis of teaching. They emphasized that the dialogue between teacher and child should be in situations that maintain the child's interest and attention. However, they pointed out some important differences in the way the teacher might use the same situation with a first and a second language learner. The teacher may help the child who is already using the language (first language learner) to think and speak beyond the immediate situation. Such a child can be reminded of similar past events or helped to anticipate future similar situations. On the other hand, a child who is learning a new language may need to focus only on present situational clues to understand what is being said. The teacher should use language that makes the meaning clear for each specific time and place.

As we have emphasized throughout this chapter, consideration of each child's unique needs is necessary, whether the child is a first or second language learner. Similarly, "other conditions that help the child learn his first language seem likely also to help a child learning a second language" (Tough, 1977, p. 84). The conditions referred to by Tough include giving the child ample opportunity to hear the same phrases again and again; encouraging practice of well-formed phrases at appropriate times; modeling and expanding; and concentrating on a small number of phrases at first, and then extending the variety and precision of what the child is able to say and understand. (For an excellent summary of current approaches to facilitating communication skills and literacy in the bilingual, bicultural child, see Bunce, 1998.)

COLLABORATIVE CONSULTATION WITH SPEECH AND LANGUAGE SPECIALISTS

Nurturing the development of communication skills in young children requires a team approach. Major contributions can be made by a qualified speech and language specialist who has received training in early intervention. The speech-language specialist can make a particularly important contribution in the area of assessment, using both formal and informal measures.

In the field of communication disorders, growing emphasis has been placed on the use of **collaborative consultation models** (Marvin, 1987, Montgomery, 1992).

A collaborative consultation model differs from a more traditional "expert" model of consultation, in which the consultant assumes the role of a professional who provides information or services that the teacher does not possess. The collaborative model emphasizes the parity between the teacher and the speech-language specialist, who work as a team and contribute different skills and information to the processes of assessment, planning, and intervention, as well as solving specific problems. The following are examples of the types of collaboration that might occur in such a model.

As part of the assessment, the speech/language specialist would carefully interview the classroom teacher regarding the child's communicative behavior and observe the child in the classroom. Communication goals and objectives would be generated as a team, involving the parents, who meet with the teacher and the speech-language specialist together. Innovative teaching strategies and activities might be demonstrated in the classroom by the speech/language specialist, who would receive feedback and suggestions for adaptation from the classroom teacher.

Collaborative consultation models are also becoming increasingly important to the success of efforts to mainstream children in all types of educational environments. In such programs, collaboration must also take place between special educators and regular classroom teachers. For further information related to the growing area of collaborative consultation, the reader is referred to Heron and Harris (1999).

Although some professionals might argue that cognitive skill development precedes development of language skills, we chose to discuss the development of communication skills first. It is fitting, then, that the next chapter will concentrate on techniques for encouraging the development of cognitive skills and literacy. Understanding of the dynamics of language development will assist in obtaining insight into children's developing mental capacity as they journey toward becoming literate beings.

Summary

Communication, language, and speech are highly complex skills that develop as a function of many underlying processes, including cognitive, fine motor–perceptual, and especially social interaction. There is perhaps no area of development as crucial to the young child with special needs as communication skills.

The early education teacher, in close partnership with parents, can have a major impact on this area of development. For the child who has less severe disabilities, providing language input finely tuned to the child's perceptual and cognitive level, in a style that follows the child's lead and within a context of social interaction, can greatly facilitate communication skills development.

For the child who has more severe and multiple disabilities, in addition to these input strategies it will also be necessary to structure the environment in ways that encourage the child to communicate his or her basic wants and needs. Once this important motivational factor has been provided, specific communicative behaviors can be shaped. Often these are not conventional speech or language behaviors. Nevertheless, they can be used in functional ways and can form the basis of augmentative communication systems.

With careful planning, the strategies that facilitate communication can be incorporated into all classroom activities. Furthermore, monitoring of children's communicative behaviors within a variety of *naturally occurring contexts* can provide the most meaningful assessment of progress.

Discussion Topics and Activities

1. Using a good quality tape recorder, record conversations of mothers and young children. Look for mothers who have more than one preschool-age child. Record the verbal interactions with each child, alone. How are they similar? How do the conversations differ?

2. Analyze the children's responses to mother's speaking pattern. Consider length, grammar, and syntax, using tapes made for Activity 1.

3. Record your own conversations with children 1 year, 2, 2½, 3, and 4 years of age. Attempt to interact intuitively with these children. Then analyze what you have done in response to the feedback from the children.

4. Bring the tapes to class. Listen to them and critique the appropriateness of the adult's utterances with the children. Consider vocabulary, length of sentences, speed, pauses, interest to the children, and the effect on the children's vocalizations.

5. Record a 15-minute conversation with one 4-year-old and an adult as they make cookies or do something similar. Play the tape for the class. What *new* concepts were introduced?

6. Record the conversations of several 4-year-olds as they play together. Analyze the speech and language used from the frame of reference of each of the subskills of language.

7. Write dialogues to demonstrate appropriate conversations with children from ages 2 through 5.

8. Select a child who has severe and multiple disabilities. Conduct interviews with the child's teacher and parents to try to identify three high-preference activities or objects. Systematically present each to the child and observe his or her behavior. Also, observe the child's behavior as you take the object away or as you interrupt an enjoyable activity. What behavior can you identify that could be used by the child as a communicative system?

Annotated Bibliography

Baumgart, D., Johnson, J., & Helmstetter, E. (1990) *Augmentative and alternative communication systems for persons with moderate and severe disabilities.* Baltimore: Paul H. Brookes.

This is a straightforward, easy-to-understand text dealing with designing augmentative communication systems. The text includes separate sections for preschool-age, elementary-school-age, and adolescent students. Particularly helpful are case studies included in several chapters that demonstrate successful planning and implementing of augmentative communication systems.

Bernstein, D.K., & Tiegerman, E. (1985). *Language and communication disorders in children.* Upper Saddle River, NJ: Merrill/Prentice-Hall.

This text provides an excellent review of the social and cognitive bases of language development, as well as the stages of language acquisition in children. It focuses on types of communication disorders in children, including those associated with mental retardation, autism, hearing impairment, and learning disabilities. Two chapters on intervention are also included.

Beukelman, D.R., & Mirenda, P. (1992). *Augmentative and alternative communication: Management of severe communication disorders in children and adults.* Baltimore, MD: Paul H. Brookes.

This is a very understandable text describing the basics of AAC, including the descriptions of the system components and types of AAC, as well as intervention issues and strategies appropriate for different populations. Particularly useful are clear explanations of both high- and low-tech AAC systems for children with severe disabilities, and for very young children.

Cazden, C.B. (Ed.). (1981). *Language in early childhood education.* Washington, DC: National Association for the Education of Young Children.

This is an excellent reference for anyone who works and plays with young children. The various authors cover nearly every facet of language development and suggest numerous ways to promote oral communication. A section about daycare programs includes useful ideas for working with children whose language style or dialect is different.

Chen, D., Friedman, C.T., & Calvello, G. (1989). *Parents and visually impaired infants.* Louisville, KY: American Printing House for the Blind.

These are excellent materials for parents of infants who are blind. They offer strategies for helping parents observe their own infants and set parent-infant interaction priorities. Included are an excellent section on strategies for assessment of infants' communication, sections on hearing and vision screening, and assessment of the infant's interaction with objects. The program is unique in that it allows parents to take primary responsibility for goal setting and observation.

Cheng, L-R.L. (1991). *Assessing Asian language performance: Guidelines for evaluating limited-English-proficient students.* Oceanside, CA: Academic Communications.

This text, while not aimed specifically at very young children, not only contains valuable information related to the characteristics of Asian languages and dialects but also includes discussion of the culture and history of the various Asian groups. Strategies and materials for non-biased informal assessment of communication skills and language background are provided. Appendixes include a variety of helpful resources such as questionnaires, language elicitation pictures, checklists, and so on. This book should be useful for both speech/language pathologists and teachers.

Cole, E. (1992). *Listening and talking: A guide to promoting spoken language in young hearing-impaired children.* Washington, DC: A.G. Bell Association for the Deaf.

Provides detailed strategies for working with young hearing impaired children. These include general strategies for encouraging language and communication, as well as techniques for developing children's listening skills and speech production skills.

Flexer, C. (1994). *Facilitating hearing and listening in young children.* Washington, DC: A.G. Bell Association for the Deaf.

This book is a guide for developing hearing and listening skills in young children. Specific strategies are provided to design and maintain optimal listening environments through practical auditory and acoustic management. The book also discusses writing IEPs and programs for early intervention.

Fraiberg, S. (1977). *Insights from the blind: Comparative studies of blind and sighted infants.* New York: Basic Books.

Careful observational research, thoroughly described, forms the basis for this classic book. The effects of visual deficits on the child's organization of early experience and on ego development are reported. Specific suggestions for promoting the mental and physical development of infants and young children are explicit. The section on language acquisition is a must for anyone working with children who have visual impairments.

Hendrick, J. (1994). *Total learning: Developmental curriculum for the young child.* Upper Saddle River, NJ: Merrill/Prentice Hall.

Chapter 15 concentrates on developing verbal competence. In addition to offering many useful ideas, the book provides specific lesson plans. Particularly helpful is the section on African-American English and bilingualism. Resources, including books, music, and poetry are abundantly presented.

Klein, M.D., Briggs, M.H., & Huffman, P. (1988). *Facilitating caregiver-infant communication: A model program to facilitate positive communicative interactions between caregivers and their high-risk infants.* Los Angeles: Division of Special Education, California State University, Los Angeles.

This publication provides specific guidelines, techniques, and materials for carrying out a program designed to facilitate positive communicative interaction between caregivers and their high-risk infants. The program is particularly helpful in working with high-risk families. It includes specific strategies for observing the infant in the neonatal intensive care unit, establishing center-based groups, developing a home visit program, and using videotape feedback as an intervention technique. The program also includes simplified handouts for parents related to caring for and playing with their infants, the Observation of Communicative Interaction (OCI), a parent booklet entitled *Help Your Baby Learn to Talk,* and two videotapes: "Talking to your Baby" and "Talking to Toddlers."

MacDonald, J.D. (1989). *Becoming partners with children: From play to conversation.* San Antonio, TX: Special Press.

The work of this author during the past 20 years has provided the basis for numerous language intervention programs developed in the past decade. In this text, he presents a detailed description of a communication assessment and instructional program that applies many of the strategies found in typical parent-child interaction. The program includes the following levels of instruction for parents and their children: play, turn taking, communicating, using language, and becoming conversational partners. This text provides an excellent rationale and literature review as well as detailed descriptions of each level of instruction. It is soundly based on social interaction theory and developmental pragmatics.

Manolson, A. (1985). *It takes two to talk*. Toronto: Hanen Early Language Resource Center.

Built on the work of Dr. James MacDonald, this is a program for parents of young children with disabilities. It is designed as a step-by-step instructional program to teach parents to encourage their own children's language development through the careful use of certain caregiver-child interactions such as turn taking, following the child's lead, and prompting for better turns.

McCormick, L., Loeb, D. & Schiefelbusch, R.L. (1997). *Supporting children with communication difficulties in inclusive settings*. Boston, MA: Allyn & Bacon.

This is an excellent text on language intervention aimed at teachers and beginning communication specialists. It provides an easily understood review of language acquisition and disabilities, as well as descriptions of intervention strategies, including strategies designed for infants and preschool children. Included are excellent chapters on ecological assessment, bilingualism, literacy, augmentative communication, and strategies for working with children who have severe disabilities.

Odom, S.L., Bender, M.K., Stein, M.L., Doran, L.P., Houden, P.M., McInnes, M., Gilbert, M., Deklyen, M., Speltz, M.L., & Jenkins, J.R. (1988). *The integrated preschool curriculum*. Seattle: University of Washington Press.

This is a curriculum specifically designed to facilitate the social interaction of preschool children with and without disabilities. It contains detailed strategies and activities that can be used to encourage social interaction and play. It is appropriate for use with children with all types of disabilities.

Owens, R.E., Jr. (1995). *Language development* (4th ed.). Columbus: MacMillan/Prentice Hall.

A comprehensive text describing communication and language development, this book contains a good chapter reviewing research in the area of "motherese" and mother-child communicative interaction. Children's functional language use and pragmatic skills are considered in all stages of language development. Also included is a chapter on dialects and bilingualism.

Phillips, A.L., & Cole, E. (Eds.). (1993). Beginning with babies: A sharing of professional experience. *Monograph of the Volta Review*. Washington, DC: A.G. Bell Association for the Deaf.

This monograph addresses a wide range of issues related to infants with hearing loss. These include assisting the early intervention professional in parent support, multicultural issues, and audiological concerns. Also included is a discussion of the legal issues around provision of services to infants who are deaf or hard of hearing.

Prizant, B.M., & Wetherby, A.M. (1988). Providing services to children with autism (ages 0 to 2 years) and their families. *Topics in Language Disorders, 9*(1), 1-23.

This is an excellent article describing the characteristics of and communication intervention strategies for young children with autism. The article discusses the potential of early intervention as prevention. Practical and meaningful suggestions related to assessment are provided. Intervention approaches described in the article focus on facilitating functional communication skills and on the important social relationship between caregiver and child.

Reed, V.A. (1994). *An introduction to children with language disorders*. Upper Saddle River, NJ: Merrill/Prentice Hall.

This text is appropriate for a first course in language disorders in children. It devotes considerable attention to assessment and intervention, and links language behaviors directly to the educational system. Covered is the relationship between language and a variety of disabilities such as autism, cognitive impairment, hearing impairment, and visual impairment.

Reichle, J., York, J., & Sigafoos, J. (1991). *Implementing augmentative and alternative communication: Strategies for learners with severe disabilities*. Baltimore: Paul H. Brookes.

This text describes strategies for planning and implementing augmentative communication systems for individuals with severe disabilities. It includes a section on decision making related to planning an augmentative system and conducting ecological inventories of functional communication behaviors and needs. Five chapters are dedicated to strategies for facilitating initiating behavior, particularly requesting and rejecting. Also included are sections related to communicative exchanges and generalization. The last section of the book deals in some detail with specific instructional strategies for students with particular kinds of needs, such as those who have very severe physical disabilities.

Rice, M.L., & Wilcox, K. (Eds.). (1995). *Building a language-focused curriculum for the preschool classroom*. Baltimore: Paul H. Brookes.

This is the first book of a two-volume set providing the theoretical background and practical strategies needed to create an effective language intervention program. It centers around the language-focused curriculum developed and implemented at the University of Kansas Language Acquisition Preschool. Case vignettes demonstrate techniques in practice. The second volume is a planning guide by Betty Bunce. This detailed guide provides activities and ideas for creating a language-focused curriculum.

Richard-Amato, P.A. (1988). *Making it happen: Interaction in the second language classroom.* New York: Longman.

This is an important text in the area of teaching English as a second language. It takes a strong position supporting an interactional, context-based approach to language learning. The text is unique in that it provides an excellent review and critique of existing theories regarding second language learning as well as detailed suggestions for practical classroom applications. While it does not focus exclusively on the preschool-aged child, it is an excellent resource for anyone wishing a current review of this field.

Schulman, B. (Ed.). (1987). Making the collaborative consultation model work: The speech-language pathologist as consultant and teacher in mainstream education. *Journal of Childhood Communication Disorders, 11*(1).

This entire journal issue is devoted to articles describing various ways in which the speech-language pathologist can work as a consultant in the classroom. Several articles address the role of the speech-language pathologist in working with the teacher to facilitate literacy.

Schuyler, V., & Rushmer, N. (1987). *Parent-infant habilitation: A comprehensive approach to working with hearing-impaired infants and toddlers and their families.* Portland, OR: IHR Publications.

This is a state-of-the-art and comprehensive text dealing with the development of infants and toddlers with hearing impairments. It describes an approach to early intervention that emphasizes the role of parent-infant interaction and relationship as the key to development and learning. Use of both speech and manual sign language are included, and the stress is on a highly individualized approach to each infant and family. The text includes chapters dealing with parental reactions to the infant with a hearing impairment and the importance of the parent-professional partnership. It provides strategies for helping parents develop observation skills and for using naturalistic interactions as opportunities for language teaching. The relationship between language and cognition is also discussed.

Snow, C., & Butler, K. (Eds.). (1984, Sept.). Language development and disorders in the social context. *Topics in Language Disorders, 4.*

This entire issue is devoted to the consideration of various applications of research on mother-infant interaction and language development within the social context. It considers remediation of communication disorders in young children who have visual impairments, hearing impairments, and language delays.

Warren, S.F., & Rogers-Warren, A.K. (1985). *Teaching functional language.* Baltimore: University Park Press.

This edited text first presents a functional communication perspective and then provides several chapters describing various intervention strategies used with children with severe disabilities who have autism, language delays, and are difficult to teach. Two chapters also discuss naturalistic and conversational teaching strategies. The final section of the book considers methods for facilitating and measuring generalization of language behaviors.

References

Adler, S. (1979). *Poverty children and their language: Implications for teaching and treating.* New York: Grune & Stratton.

Alpert, C.L., & Kaiser, A.P. (1992). Training parents as milieu language teachers. *Journal of Early Intervention, 16*(1) 31-52.

American Speech-Language-Hearing Association (ASHA) (1991). Report: Augmentative and alternative communication. *American Speech-Language-Hearing Association, 33* (Suppl. 5), 9-12.

Anderson, E.G., Dunlea, A., & Kekelis, L.S. (1984). Blind children's language: Resolving some differences. *Journal of Child Language, 11,* 645-664.

Bates, E. (1976). Pragmatics and sociolinguists in child language. In D. Morehead & A. Morehead (Eds.), *Language deficiency in children: Selected readings.* Baltimore: University Park Press.

Bates, E., & McWhinney, B. (1988). What is functionalism? *Papers and Reports on Child Language Development, 27,* 137-152.

Baumgart, D., Johnson, J., & Helmstetter, E. (1990). *Augmentative and alternative communication systems for persons with moderate and severe disabilities.* Baltimore: Paul H. Brookes.

Bess, F.H., & McConnell, F.E. (1981). *Audiology, education and the hearing impaired child.* St. Louis: Mosby.

Beukelman, D.R., & Mirenda, P. (1992) *Augmentative and alternative communication: Management of severe communication disorders in children and adults.* Baltimore: Paul. H. Brookes.

Bloom, L., & Lahey, M. (1978). *Language development and language disorders.* New York: Wiley.

Bondy, A., & Frost, L. (1994). The picture exchange communication system. *Focus on Autistic Behavior, 9,* 1-19.

facilitating language and communication development in the classroom. *Seminars in Speech and Language, 5,* 213-228.

Tannock, R., Girolametto, L., & Siegel, L. (1992). Language intervention with children who have developmental delays: Effects of an interactive approach. *American Journal on Mental Retardation, 97,* 145-160.

Taylor, O.L. (Ed.). (1986). *Treatment of communication disorders in culturally and linguistically diverse populations.* Boston: College-Hill.

Tough, J. (1977). *Talking and learning: A guide to fostering communication skills in nursery and infant schools.* London: School Council Publications.

Vygotsky, L. (1978). Mind in society: The development of higher order psychological processes. In M. Cole, J. Scribner, J. John-Steiner, & E. Souberman (Eds.) *Culture and thought: A psychological introduction.* Cambridge, MA: Harvard University Press.

Wilcox, M.J., Kouri, T.A., & Caswell, S.B. (1991). Early language intervention: A comparison of classroom and individual treatment. *American Journal of Speech-Language Pathology, 1,* 49-62.

Warren, S., & Kaiser, A. (1986). Incidental language teaching: A critical review. *Journal of Speech and Hearing Disorders, 51,* 291-298.

Warren, S.F., & Kaiser, A.P. (1988). *Research in early language intervention.* In S.L. Odom & M.B. Karnes (Eds.), *Early intervention for infants and children with handicaps.* Baltimore: Paul H. Brookes.

Weiss, R.S. (1981). INREAL intervention for language handicapped and bilingual children. *Journal of the Division for Early Childhood, 4,* 40-51.

Wilkinson, L.C. (1979). Theoretical bases of language and communication development in preschool children. In L. Taft & M. Lewis (Eds.), *Developmental disabilities in the preschool child.* Symposium presented by Rutgers Medical School, Educational Testing Service, and Johnson and Johnson Baby Products, Chicago.

Wulz, S.V., Hall, M.K., & Klein, M.D. (1983). An instructional communication strategy for severely handicapped children. *Journal of Speech and Hearing Disorders, 48,* 2-10.

Yarrow, L.J., Rubenstein, J.L., & Pedersen G. (1975). *Infant and environment: Early cognitive and motivational development.* New York: Wiley.

Chapter 10

Encouraging the Development of Cognitive Skills and Literacy

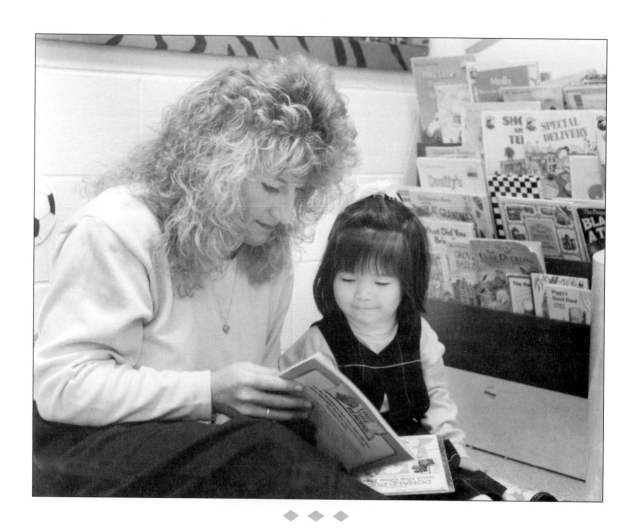

Key Concepts

- ◆ Understanding the development of thinking and reasoning, from the infant's first reflexes to the 5-year-old's problem-solving strategies, is critical to the effectiveness of the early childhood special educator.

- ◆ The three cognitive processes of attention, perception, and memory work together to enable the child's development of cognitive skills.

- ◆ The most significant single contribution to the understanding of children's cognitive development has been the theory of Jean Piaget.

- ◆ The early childhood special education professional must master techniques that facilitate critical cognitive skills such as intentionality, means-end discovery, trial-and-error exploration, object permanence, and imitation in infants and toddlers with special needs.

- ◆ Critical cognitive skills for the preschool child include symbolic representation (particularly pretend play), problem solving, cognitive subskills related to academic readiness, and expansion of referential language skills.

- ◆ Early childhood special education professionals must be able to utilize specific strategies for adapting learning environments for infants and young children who are cognitively different.

- ◆ Preschool programs should *not* emphasize the direct instruction of reading; rather, the preacademic focus should be on facilitating emergent literacy within naturalistic daily activities (i.e., an appreciation of and interest in the nature and purposes of writing and reading) and phonological awareness.

- ◆ Children's early experiences with literacy and literate oral language styles such as narrative will greatly influence their later academic success.

- ◆ Facilitating children's successful transition to kindergarten requires a thorough understanding of expectations of the receiving classroom (particularly with regard to school language skills and social skills), careful planning for the transition, and collaboration with parents and the receiving teacher.

◆ ◆ ◆

Kim: "When we talk on the phone how does our words get to the telephone pole wires and to our house?"

Mom: "Well, that is hard to explain. Our voice travels by what we call sound waves."

Kim: "Oh, it must be like on the ocean. Our talk rides like a surfer."

As this interaction between mother and child demonstrates, cognitive development of young children is evidenced in their attempts to use what they know to solve new problems. New information is taken in and related to what was learned earlier. New knowledge and old knowledge are adapted to solve problems more efficiently. Or, as Kodera and Garwood (1979) explained, "Acts of cognition are thought to represent an individual's attempts to make sense of experience" (p. 153).

WHAT IS COGNITION?

Cognition is defined in the dictionary as "the act of knowing." Piaget (1954) referred to the development of cognition as the child's **construction of reality.** These simple definitions belie the great complexity of human cognitive processes. How the young child develops the ability to mentally represent and understand the world around him or her is by no means simple. Understanding the evolution of thinking and reasoning, from the infant's first reflexes to the development of complex problem-solving strategies, is critically important to our effectiveness as educators of young children. Many children with special needs have cognitive impairments that interfere with the development of the conceptual and reasoning skills necessary for mastery of academic skills. The early childhood special education professional can recognize these challenges and provide the support necessary for the achievement of important cognitive skills and the "construction of knowledge" (DeVries & Kohlberg, 1987).

BASIC COGNITIVE PROCESSES

Three basic processes related to information processing are important to the development of cognition: attention, perception, and memory. Infants must be able to pay attention to the world around them; they must also be able to receive, recognize, and discriminate stimuli. Eventually they must be able to organize and interpret those stimuli and store them for later retrieval.

Attention

Attention is the focusing of the individual's perceptual processes upon a specific aspect of the environ-

ment. Learning cannot take place unless the individual is able to focus attention on the important elements of a task or situation. Attention is basic to many cognitive tasks and is a prerequisite for effective intervention. Attention in the form of concentration requires that the developing child learn to master two somewhat contradictory skills: (1) the ability to focus on those aspects of his or her environment that are relevant and have the greatest functional value to the task at hand and (2) the ability to ignore the multitude of irrelevant stimuli around him or her. *Selective attention* begins almost at birth, and the kinds of stimuli and the way babies look at them change in predictable ways. When a child attempts to attend and respond to too many irrelevant stimuli, the child is considered to be distractible.

Much recognition is given to what are sometimes called *attention deficit disorders* (American Psychiatric Association, 1980). Such disorders are very common and may be present when extreme inattention, impulsivity, and hyperactivity characterize a child's behavior. However, an attention deficit disorder may also be present when a child is withdrawn and unable to respond (Swanson & Reinert, 1984). This hypoactivity may be related to the child's tendency to become fixated on stimuli that are no longer relevant or to be preoccupied with some inner need that in extreme cases may be suggestive of autism.

Teachers of young children must consider these behavioral descriptions cautiously. The concept of normal development must be ever present as the model of reference. Young children are, by nature, very active, inattentive, and impulsive. Yet the inability to focus selectively on relevant stimuli is among the developmental learning disabilities discussed by Kirk and Chalfant (1984). These learning disability specialists offer a number of useful suggestions for children who are clearly more inattentive than what is considered typical. Some of these are described later in the chapter.

Perception

Perception is the "process of becoming aware of and interpreting objects and events that stimulate the

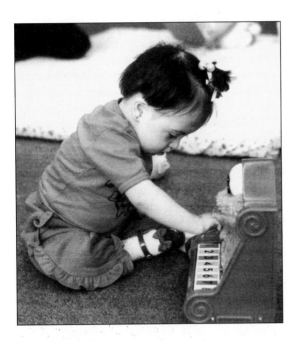

children will contribute greatly to the progress of children with perceptual disabilities, who usually have difficulty interpreting and obtaining accurate meaning from their environment.

Discrimination Abilities. "Discrimination is the process by which one perceives the likenesses and differences among related stimuli" (Kirk & Chalfant, 1984, p. 112). Children who learn to visually discriminate characteristics such as shape, size, distance, and color while in preschool will be prepared for the subtle discriminations between printed letters, numbers, and words necessary to success in kindergarten and first grade. Likewise, children who learn to perceive the differences and similarities in pitch, loudness, rhythm, melody, rate, and duration of sound will likely be successful in learning to read by phonetic methods. Most prereading activities, by design, assist children in developing discrimination skills. For example, when a child is asked to find a picture illustrating a spoken word, he or she is discriminating among details in the picture while also practicing sound discernment, association, and memory skills. A majority of the activities discussed in this book, found in early childhood methods books and highlighted in Appendix F, give children practice in developing perceptual efficiency and accuracy.

sense organs" (Silverman, 1975, p. 366). Perceptual abilities are dependent on the sensory systems of touch, taste, proprioception, smell, hearing, and vision. These systems actually develop in utero, thus enabling the newborn infant to begin the processes of perceptual development at birth. Each sensory system (tactile, visual, auditory, olfactory, and gustatory) is associated with a different mode of perception. For perception to occur, some information must be stored in the nervous system. Sensations are then interpreted in the context of stored information.

The interpretations or perceptions of individuals may differ, depending on what is stored and on the strength of the perception modality, such as visual and auditory, which develop unevenly. Thus one child may perceive more accurately through the visual channel while another may gather information more efficiently through the auditory channel. As stated earlier, young children may find it easiest to interpret physical cues, followed by visual and finally verbal cues. Unfortunately, most teachers tend to teach predominantly through talking and expecting responses to verbal directions. Teachers who attempt to match teaching input to the developmental needs of their

Memory

The third basic cognitive process is **memory.** Memory is the process by which information that is received through attention and perception is stored in the central nervous system. Atkinson and Shiffrin (1968) suggested the following model of memory:

1. Incoming sensation is perceived briefly (about 1 second).

2. If attended to, it will be placed in short-term memory, which can store information for 10 to 15 seconds.

3. Depending on a number of factors, some information will be placed in long-term memory, where it can be stored indefinitely.

Very young children have few memory strategies and may need repeated experiences of the same event or information before it can be stored in long-term memory. As children get older they develop so-called "rehearsal" strategies (Atkinson & Shiffrin, 1968). Information in short-term memory ies purposely repeated or practiced, which then assists in long-term storage.

The ability to learn is highly associated with memory. The most common kinds of memory include long-term, short-term, sequential, auditory, visual, rote, recognition, and recall. When assessing a child's difficulties in memory, several important questions must be considered. Are environmental conditions such as noise, excitement, emotional upset, or interpersonal problems interfering with retention? Is the content to be remembered meaningful, concrete, and short enough to be developmentally appropriate? What kind of response is required? Is it immediate or delayed? Does it require recognition or recall, a motor or vocal response?

For very young children, little in the way of rote memory should be expected. The developmental sequence prepared by Montessori (see Chapter 6) and this chapter's guidelines for facilitating concept development help in the preparation of memory-strengthening lessons.

As Thurman and Widerstrom (1990) pointed out, the three processes of attention, perception, and memory are interdependent. Individuals cannot pay attention if they are not able to perceive incoming stimuli; they cannot store information that they do not perceive; they cannot further develop perceptual skills of recognition and interpretation if they do not have information stored in memory, and so on.

DEVELOPMENT OF COGNITIVE SKILLS

The Developmental Theory of Piaget

The most prominent cognitive theorist to influence the fields of child development and early education was Jean Piaget, a Swiss scientist interested in episte-mology, or the study of human knowing. He was neither a learning theorist nor a maturationist. Rather, he combined these two views and believed that human cognitive development is a product of the interaction between the environment and the infant's biological capacities.

Two important concepts developed by Piaget's theory are the **schema** and the process of **adaptation.** The schema can be defined as a psychological structure that provides the individual with a template for action in similar circumstances (Piaget & Inhelder, 1969). Schemata, which are initially infant reflexes, gradually become differentiated, combined, organized, and under the child's control. They also eventually become internalized, that is, they become mental processes. This occurs through adaptation, a twofold process comprised of **assimilation** and **accommodation.**

During the assimilation part of adaptation, experiences are taken in by infants or young children through the application of existing schemata. For example, the infant applies his "sucking schema" to his thumb. However, not all experiences can be assimilated to existing schemata. For example, if the infant tries to apply his existing sucking schema to the corner of his blanket, he will not be successful. The infant must change, or "accommodate," his existing schema in order to adapt to this new situation. Thus, through the complementary processes of first using existing schemata and then modifying them to adjust to new experiences, the infant adapts to the world around him. In Piaget's view, this is the process of learning.

In addition to his important theory of cognitive development, Piaget also contributed an important research methodology that included naturalistic observations of infants and young children combined with presentation of situations in which to test his hypotheses. Information related to the sensorimotor and preoperational periods was based on his observations of his own children. His descriptions of the development of mental operations was based on his observations of school children.

Piaget described several stages in the development of cognition. Each stage of development builds upon the previous one. This is referred to as the "spiral of knowing" (Gallagher & Reid, 1981, p. 35). As children mature and interact with their environment, they construct and reconstruct reality through the processes of assimilation and adaptation, in accordance with their cognitive capabilities at each stage.

The Sensorimotor Stage. Piaget reportedly believed that the most creative period of an individual's life is between birth and 18 months of age (Anisfeld, 1984). The **sensorimotor stage** is divided into six substages. The first five of these stages lay the foundation for the beginning of representational thought—the mental representation of objects and events. The sixth stage, with its full achievement of object permanence, marks the transition from sensorimotor "knowing" through patterns of action to mental knowledge and symbolic ability.

Sensorimotor substage 1: use of reflexes (0–1 month). During the first month of life, the infant interacts with his world primarily through reflexes. As the nipple touches his lips, he sucks; he "roots" or turns automatically to the side of the cheek that is touched; sudden loud sounds or loss of support elicit a startle, or "Moro," reaction, and so on.

Sensorimotor substage 2: primary circular reaction (1–4 months). During the second substage, the infant's reflexive behavior leads accidentally to new experiences. For example, the infant discovers his thumb and assimilates this experience to his existing nipple-sucking schema. He accommodates to the new object (his thumb) and thus *learns* to suck his thumb. Such primary circular reactions are always centered on the infant's own body.

Sensorimotor substage 3: secondary circular reactions (5–8 months). During this substage the infant becomes increasingly interactive with events and objects in the external environment, outside his own body. Secondary circular reactions are those behaviors in which the infant engages in order to repeat an interesting event. For example, the infant accidentally hits a mobile hanging above his crib, which provides the visual experience of seeing the mobile move. The infant then tries to hit the mobile again to recreate this experience.

Sensorimotor substage 4: intentional adaptations (8–12 months). During this substage, the infant begins to utilize and coordinate his secondary circular reactions in order to achieve a specific goal. This represents a major milestone in the development of cognition: the development of **intentionality.** Now the infant can look at the mobile and utilize the "looking-and-swiping" schema acquired through his secondary reactions of substage 3 and *intentionally* activate the mobile. He now has the goal in mind *before* he engages in the behavior. He has discovered the means-end relationship.

Also during this stage, the baby demonstrates the earliest ability to search for hidden objects. However, he will search in the place in which he last discovered the object. For example, an interesting object is covered with a blanket, and the infant is assisted in rediscovering the object. In full view of the infant, the object is then hidden under a box. Despite observing this, the infant will again search for the object under the blanket. He does not engage in a systematic search based on where he sees the object disappear.

Sensorimotor substage 5: discovery of new means (12–18 months). In substage 5, rather than simply repeating a behavior in order to recreate an interesting event, the infant searches for novelty through tertiary circular reactions. He systematically changes his behavior and observes the effect. This is sometimes called **trial-and-error exploration.** The following is a familiar example of this type of behavior. An 8-month-old infant, sitting in a highchair, drops, and then tosses his food onto the floor, first from one side of the tray, then from the other. While parents may interpret this as willful naughtiness, it is actually evidence of the growing cognitive abilities of the infant. It enables him to learn about cause and effect. Through such trial-and-error behavior, the infant discovers new means, or strategies, for achieving goals. For example, the child learns that he can crawl *around* a barrier to reach something on the other side if he is unable to crawl *over* it.

Continued development of the concept of object permanence can also be seen during this substage. Now the infant will more systematically search for the object at the place where he sees it disappear. However, if the infant does not see the object being moved, he will not search for it.

Sensorimotor substage 6: rudiments of representational thought (18-24 months). Substage 6 marks the end of the sensorimotor period. By the end of this substage, the toddler has mastered the full concept of **object permanence.** He clearly understands that objects exist whether or not he can see them. He will search systematically for an object even when he has not seen it disappear. This important cognitive capability now frees the infant from his dependence on sensorimotor actions for discovery and understanding. It frees him from the "here and now" world and enables him to develop memory skills.

The 18- to 24-month-old toddler now has the capacity for **mental representation**—the ability to think. This mental representation ability is particularly evidenced in two types of behavior observed toward the end of substage 6: deferred imitation and pretend play. The ability to imitate something observed at an earlier time reflects the toddler's mental representation and memory for that event; deferred imitation also provides a mechanism for learning.

The ability to act out previously experienced events through pretend play (e.g., putting the doll to bed or pretending to serve breakfast) also is clear evidence of the ability to think about and remember such events. Like deferred imitation, pretend play provides important contexts in which to learn.

The Preoperational Stage. The second major stage of cognitive development in Piaget's theory is called the **preoperational stage.** This term simply reflects the fact that while preschool children are clearly more capable than sensorimotor infants, they are not yet able to perform the mental operations required of logical thinking and reasoning. Piaget was more intrigued with what the preoperational child could *not* do than with the important achievements of this period. In Piaget's later writing, this stage was divided into two periods: the preconceptual and the intuitive.

The preconceptual period (2-4 years). A major accomplishment during this period is the development of **symbolic ability.** The child learns that one thing can represent another thing. This symbolic ability is evidenced both in her pretend play and in increasing language development. The child can now use a block as a truck, or she can *imagine* that a cloud is a bear floating in the sky. Language becomes freed from the immediate context. Words as symbols can now be used to describe and share experiences that occurred in the past.

The intuitive period (4-7 years). During this period, the child makes an important transition into the period of concrete operations. She learns to categorize objects on the basis of certain features. Toward the end of this period, she begins to be able to **decenter.** That is, she no longer is only able to focus on one feature of an object at a time, but will begin to demonstrate the ability to consider more than one characteristic simultaneously, as well as some reversibility in her thinking.

The classic conservation experiment demonstrates this. Throughout most of the period from 2 to 7 years of age, the child is unable to respond successfully to the following experiment: Two identical beakers are filled with equal amounts of water. The water from one of the beakers is poured into a narrower, taller beaker. When asked whether the tall beaker now contains more or the same amount of water as the short, wide beaker, the child invariably responds "More," despite repeated demonstrations of pouring water back and forth. According to Piaget, the preoperational child lacks the ability to attend to both height and width and centers only on height (tallness). She also lacks reversibility of thought and cannot realize that the width of the shorter beaker would compensate for its lack of height and vice versa.

The lack of ability to decenter is also observed in the preschooler's egocentrism. She has difficulty taking another person's perspective and views the world in relationship to herself. She does not understand that someone else may not be able to see what she can see, and her language is often insufficiently referential.

During the **intuitive period,** the preschool child experiences a gradual shift in the ability to perform mental operations. Also during this period the child's thinking becomes more elaborated, as is particularly demonstrated in dramatic play episodes. The preschooler can orchestrate long and complex interpersonal sequences that provide opportunities for practicing social routines and solving problems. Another characteristic of children during this period is their inability to think logically. Children's thought is sometimes referred to as *transductive*. While truly logical thought is either inductive (proceeding from the specific to the general) or deductive (from the general to the specific), young children's thought often proceeds from the particular to the particular, with no logical connection. For example, a 4-year-old trips as she comes in the door and announces, "I just ate a whole candy bar so I can't walk too good!" Although the child cannot think logically at this stage, she clearly recognizes that events have causes and perceives the need for explanations.

The Stages of Concrete Operations and Formal Operations.

Once the child moves into the stage of **concrete operations** (which extends from the ages of 7 to 11 years), he has achieved the mental flexibility necessary to perform the operations required in reading and mathematics and the ability to think logically. This significantly enhances his problem-solving capability. The child in this stage of cognitive development is able to decenter and to consider many dimensions of an object or a problem simultaneously.

The final stage of **formal operations** is achieved somewhere between 11 and 15 years of age. The young adolescent is now capable of performing the mental operations mastered during the concrete operations stage on more abstract material. He can now think about complex moral dilemmas that often have more than one "right" answer, depending on the situation. He can also think scientifically, using processes of the scientific method such as hypothesis testing.

The developmental theories of Piaget and his associates are complex, and their development spanned a time period from the early 1930s to the 1970s. These works have been addressed here in the briefest manner. The student of early childhood special education is encouraged to examine texts such as Gallagher and Reid (1981), Piaget and Inhelder (1969), Ginsburg and Opper (1969), Piaget (1977), and Bell-Gredler (1986).

Alternate Views of Cognitive Development.

While the theory of Piaget continues to provide the cornerstone of our understanding of the intellectual development of young children, several theorists have offered alternative or supplementary views of development, particularly with regard to the preoperational period of development (Cole & Cole, 1989). For example, **neo-piagetian theorists** (Case, 1985) have suggested that Piaget's stages of development are domain specific—that sub-areas of development such as drawing, language, and mathematics may have their own developmental schedules. An **information-processing approach** developed by Klahr and Wallace (1976) used a model of development that is analogous to the processes of a computer: input, sensation, short-term memory, strategies for long-term memory storage, and retrieval and association. A **biological approach** suggests that the human brain consists of a vast collection of "mental modules" (Fodor, 1983), which are specifically tuned to respond and make sense of certain kinds of environmental input. Such modules might include number concepts, language, causality, and so on. Finally, the **cultural context view** has much in common with Piaget's views, but it places greater emphasis on the role of social context, and particularly on children's participation in "social scripts" that are created by adults (Nelson, 1986).

DEMONSTRATION OF COGNITIVE SKILLS THROUGH THE DEVELOPMENTAL STAGES OF CHILDREN'S PLAY

One of the easiest ways to observe the development of children's cognitive skills is through the observation of their play. There are many ways of categorizing play, some of which were mentioned in Chapters 6 and 7 in this text. Westby (1980) described strategies for assessing cognitive and language abilities through observation of children's play. She described 10 stages of play ranging from the intentional manipulations of the 9- to 12-month-old to the complex symbolic play orchestrations of the 5-year-old. Fewell (1984) developed a scale for the assessment of the stages of play. Linder (1990) described strategies for assessment of all domains of development through observation of play.

The stages of cognitive development can be readily observed using the following taxonomy: simple manipulation, exploratory play, functional play, and symbolic play.

Simple Manipulation. Simple manipulative behaviors such as mouthing, poking, waving, banging, or throwing are examples of secondary circular reactions that are typical of sensorimotor substage 3. As the infant reaches substage 4, around 8 to 10 months, these sensorimotor schemata become combined and under her intentional control. She now clearly *intends* to bang or throw. For example, the infant notices a ball and purposely moves toward it, picks it up, and throws it.

Exploratory Play. As the infant moves into the fifth substage of sensorimotor development, she engages in trial-and-error exploration. She notices some blocks and a can. She picks up the can and bangs it on the floor, then puts it on her head. She picks up the block and puts it in the can. She dumps the block out of the can. She is also capable of inventing new means to achieve her goals. For example, she can't reach a ball that has rolled under the sofa, so she takes her mother by the hand to solicit her help.

Functional Play. By the end of the fifth substage, the child can demonstrate appropriate object use. She pushes the truck, pounds with the hammer, dials the telephone, combs her hair, and so on. She may also demonstrate autosymbolic play, pretending to engage in some familiar activity such as sleeping or eating.

Symbolic Play. By the end of the sixth substage, the child has achieved the ability to represent objects and events internally and to engage in symbolic behavior.

Symbolic play develops through several stages from the end of the sensorimotor period through the preoperational period.

Initially, the child engages in pretend play activities in which she is the actor, engaged in some highly familiar activity such as going to sleep. During the next stage, she focuses the pretend play activity on some inanimate recipient of her actions such as a doll or teddy bear. Now she pretends to put the doll to bed or pour coffee for the bear. Next, the doll will be the agent, not just the recipient, of the child's actions (i.e., the doll washes herself, or puts the teddy to bed).

After 24 months, there is a gradual increase in the preoperational child's ability to use nonrealistic objects to represent real objects, as symbolic skills improve. Eventually, after 36 months, the child uses imaginary objects or people. There is also an increase in the length and complexity of pretend play sequences in the preoperational period. After 24 months the child can play the roles of different individuals and reenact events from the past. After 36 months the child begins to plan pretend scenarios in advance and organize who will do what. Play sequences begin to look more like a story, with a beginning, a plot that evolves (e.g., a problem to be solved or a special occasion), and an ending. By this stage, language becomes an essential element of play.

By age 4 or 5 the child begins to act out possible *future* scenarios (i.e., "what would happen if . . . ?" situations) and can act out multiple roles (e.g., play the mother who is also a doctor).

FACILITATING THE DEVELOPMENT OF COGNITIVE SKILLS IN INFANTS AND TODDLERS

Several cognitive milestones are particularly important targets for early intervention. Certain disabling conditions may begin to interfere with children's achievement of these important cognitive skills early in infancy. For example, a child who is blind may have particular difficulty with the achievement of object concepts and object permanence. A child with motor impairments may have difficulty discovering means-end strategies, and his or her opportunities to practice trial-and-error exploration will be limited.

The following section describes several key cognitive milestones during the period from birth to 3 years of age and provides suggestions for facilitating these cognitive skills. In addition, the reader is encouraged to review earlier chapters that have described generic strategies such as scaffolding (Chapter 6), communicative interactions (Chapters 6 and 9), and naturalistic milieu approaches to intervention (Chapter 9). These strategies are particularly effective in the development of cognitive skills. Many of the specific suggestions in this chapter reflect those approaches.

The reader is also again reminded that teaching must be activity-based. That is, intervention goals and objectives are integrated and incorporated into pleasurable, developmentally appropriate *play* activities. They are *not* isolated as bits of behavior to be learned.

Intentionality

As discussed earlier, somewhere around 8 to 10 months of age typically, developing infants achieve the ability to do things intentionally. They no longer must discover things by chance in order to repeat them. They can now perform an action on purpose. Achievement of **intentionality** is a prerequisite to almost every other skill. The ability to deliberately act upon the environment is an important key to continued development.

Some children with severe disabilities may need assistance in the development of intentionality. For such a child, the importance of intentionality cannot be overemphasized. Learning that the individual can produce a behavior volitionally and that such behavior has an effect on the world around him or her is a major accomplishment. The following strategies are examples of ways to facilitate this important cognitive milestone.

1. *Increase motivation by use of high-interest objects and activities.* Begin by taking a careful inventory of high- and low-preference objects, people, and activities. It will be necessary to in-

terview caregivers to obtain a good understanding of the child's likes and dislikes. Once these are identified they may be used to create the need or desire to act upon the environment in some way.

2. *Create the desire or need to perform intentional acts.* The following are examples of strategies:
   a. Place a high-preference object within the child's view but out of reach.
   b. Begin a pleasurable activity, then abruptly stop it. Wait for the child to do something in an attempt to continue the activity. For example, push the child in the swing, then stop the swing. Wait for some kind of signal from the child that he or she wants to continue, then resume the activity.
   c. Engage in an unpleasant activity such as washing the child's face, then discontinue the activity if the child indicates rejection (e.g., pushes your hand away).
   d. Interpret even unintentional cues such as head turning or arm waving as intentional; respond as though the child did it purposely. For example, if the child inadvertently moves his or her arm toward a toy, respond by handing the child the toy.
   e. Adapt favorite toys, tape players, television sets, and so on so that they can be activated by a switch requiring only minimal movement from the child.

3. *Allow ample time for the child to initiate a purposeful behavior.* Some children appear not to demonstrate intentional behavior simply because they have learned that there will not be enough time to organize a response. Adults frequently anticipate children's needs or perform actions for them, interfering with their initiation of intentional acts.

Means-End Behavior

As infants learn to act intentionally on their environment, they discover that these actions have certain effects upon objects and people. As they become

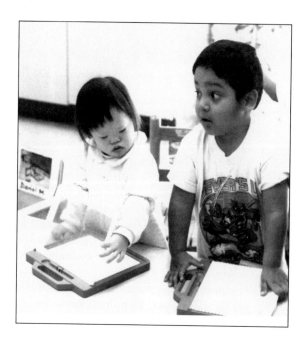

familiar with these causes and effects, they are able to engage in an action intentionally in order to bring about a desired end and, when necessary, to modify that action to create new means to achieve the desired end. For example, a child may use a stool to help her climb onto a counter so she can reach the cookies, or she may pull at mother's hand and take her to the counter to get the cookies.

These kinds of behaviors are important manifestations of the child's ability to cognitively associate certain events with their consequences. Children with disabilities often need assistance with both understanding these relationships and engaging in **means-end behaviors.** It may be necessary to structure the environment carefully in ways that clearly demonstrate cause and effect and consistently reinforce the child for attempts to achieve certain goals.

Simply constructed toys and devices that produce an interesting response to a specific type of manipulation can be effective. These include infant toys such as a "Busy Box," a "Jack-in-the-Box," and an easily activated musical toy.

Equally important is the contribution of a responsive social environment. Caregivers who respond quickly to an infant's signals of discomfort or to an older child's bids for attention will support the development of means-end behaviors.

Trial-and-Error Exploration

The ability to systematically explore objects and space is crucial to the development of the child's ability to learn from experience and develop problem-solving skills. Systematic manipulation of objects and modification of the individual's own actions lead to self-directed learning and the discovery of new behaviors and solutions.

In attempting to assist children in learning these exploratory strategies, teachers must understand that they are teaching a *process* rather than a specific behavior. For example, a jar containing pieces of candy is offered to a child. The jar has a tightly fitted lid. To teach the child to take off the lid would simply require task analyzing this skill and teaching it step by step until the child had mastered unscrewing the lid. On the other hand, encouraging **trial-and-error exploration** requires a different approach. It is necessary for the teacher to use several of the generic strategies described in Chapter 6. The teacher must assist the child in initiating different attempts to open the jar and reinforce *persistence,* not just success. The teacher must be able to read the child's cues of boredom or frustration and know when to finally scaffold successful unscrewing of the lid. Other opportunities must be created later on in which to generalize this trial-and-error process.

The following example demonstrates a way of encouraging trial-and-error behavior as a problem-solving strategy.

Nathan is sitting at the snack table with several nondisabled peers. Each child is handed a fruit roll in a wrapper as a special treat. The children eagerly tear open their wrappers. Nathan has motor coordination difficulties and typically cannot manage such a task. He has become accustomed to seeking help in such situations, so he hands the package to his teacher. This time, the teacher does not immediately open the package. She hands it back to him and says, "I'm sorry Nathan, I can't help right now. I'll help in a few minutes." She signals to the aide to sit next to Nathan. Nathan fiddles briefly with the wrapper, then looks at the aide, who says, "Well, try it this way." She turns it around and hands it back to him. He tugs at one end of the wrapper unsuccessfully. The aide says, "Boy, that's hard to do, isn't it?" He pulls at the other end of the wrapper, again to no avail, then bangs it on the table. At this point the aide takes the package and makes a small tear in one corner. She hands it back and points to the torn corner. Nathan pulls at that corner and opens the wrapper. The teacher then approaches Nathan, saying, "Well, you got that unwrapped all by yourself, didn't you!" Hopefully this child has learned something about the value of trying different solutions and the importance of persistence.

Object Permanence

The achievement of the concept of **object permanence** is critical to the child's continued development of important mental processes including memory and mental representation. Throughout the first year of development, children learn about the existence and properties of objects. As they continue through the sensorimotor period, they eventually discover, by the end of the second year, that objects and people continue to exist even when they are out of sight and their removal was not observed.

At this point, which marks the end of the sensorimotor period, children have the ability to represent objects and events internally. They can conjure mental pictures in their minds. They no longer must see an object to know it exists. This is obviously important for the development of memory skills.

There are many simple ways in which object permanence can be demonstrated for young children. Perhaps one of the first such activities introduced to infants is the game of peek-a-boo, a simple way to demonstrate that a person continues to exist even when the infant cannot see the person's face. Other ways to demonstrate object permanence include

searching for something missing from its expected storage container, playing hide and seek, or hiding cookies in your pocket and asking children to guess what you have.

Deferred Imitation

The ability to recreate an action observed at a previous time reflects the development of important cognitive skills. It requires an understanding of object permanence, the beginning development of memory skills, and the ability to mentally represent a sequence of events. **Deferred imitation** eventually plays an important role in the development of pretend play and language development.

The development of imitation skills, both immediate and deferred, may be encouraged by using the following sequence:

1. Begin by imitating the child's behavior, encouraging turn taking and then encouraging the child to continue the game. Children who have no disabilities will happily see this as a sort of "Simon Says" game.

2. Next, introduce a variation of the behavior to see whether the child will attempt to follow suit.

3. Once the child can do this easily, you can be the initiator of the imitation game, rather than imitating the child's behavior first. (Over the years, many programs have been developed that teach imitation at this level, using modeling, physical prompts, and reinforcement techniques.)

4. When the child has acquired a generalized imitative response (i.e., the child will attempt to imitate novel behaviors in addition to those that have been trained) and has developed the concept of object permanence, it may be possible to teach *deferred* imitation. The length of time between presentation of a model and imitation of the model can be increased gradually. For example, at recess, children can pretend to "walk like a duck." Later, you can say, "Can you remember what we did at recess?" This requires the child to use both memory and imitation skills.

FACILITATING THE DEVELOPMENT OF COGNITIVE SKILLS IN PRESCHOOLERS

Symbolic Representation

As children enter the preoperational stage of cognitive development, two major achievements reflect emerging symbolic skills: (1) increasing use of language to represent objects and events that are not present in the immediate environment or that occurred in the past and (2) the ability to engage in symbolic, pretend play. The topic of language, which was discussed in some detail in Chapter 9, will be addressed later in this chapter.

Much has already been said about play in this text. Play is important as a context for teaching (Chapter 6), as an end in itself in the development of social skills, and as means for facilitating healthy emotional development (Chapter 7). Through symbolic play, children express their understanding of the world around them and the interrelationships of people and events. In addition, symbolic play provides an important context within which to experience and express emotions, both one's own and those of others.

In this chapter we have discussed symbolic play as an important cognitive milestone. The ability to allow one thing to stand for something else, such as a block representing a car, or a tissue representing a blanket, is evidence of the child's developing symbolic representation skills. Other evidence of symbolic skills can be observed in drawing, language, mental images, and eventually in reading, writing, and mathematics.

It is important for the early childhood special educator to be aware of the importance of facilitating play skills in general, and particularly pretend play. As we discussed earlier in this chapter, symbolic play moves through various stages. The first is **autosymbolic play,** in which children themselves are the actors. These play episodes reenact highly familiar activities such as pretending to eat or go to sleep, and they incorporate materials that are real (e.g., a pillow) or that closely resemble real objects (e.g., a small plastic spoon or tiny cup from a tea set). For children who are functioning developmentally at the end of the sensorimotor period, these are the kinds of activities that can be modeled both by the teacher and by other children. The use of play routines discussed in Chapter 6 can be helpful in establishing this early type of pretending.

The simple level of pretending can also be encouraged in group activities. For example, the teacher can say, "Let's pretend to be a snake" or "Let's pretend to swim." For children with special needs, it will be important to select pretend activities that represent very familiar activities or concepts. Children cannot pretend to do or be something they have never experienced.

Gradually, the teacher should introduce pretend play scenarios that involve other actors, such as dolls and stuffed animals, as well as other children acting out familiar roles in relationship to one another. The classroom should include dramatic play centers that include materials that encourage pretending, such as dress-up clothing, a toy stove, a sink and cupboards, dishes, brooms, telephones, dolls and doll beds, and so on.

Also, the teacher should gradually encourage the use of objects that are more and more abstract. For example, instead of toy cars that crash and have to go to the Fisher-Price garage for repairs, wooden blocks can be used for cars and an upside-down box can become a garage. The ability to use the same blocks for a fence and the box for a doll bed represents the emergence of the kind of mental flexibility (i.e., reversibility and understanding of transformations) that is a hallmark of the next stage of cognitive development, the stage of concrete operations.

The following example demonstrates the facilitation of symbolic play skills in a child with severe disabilities.

Jason and Monique love to play house in the dramatic play center. Andrea, who has many autistic-like behaviors, loves to sit in the rocking chair in the classroom and rock. The teacher decides to move the rocking chair into the dramatic play area and suggests to Jason and Monique that maybe Andrea could be the mother today: she could help put the baby to bed by rocking her. After rocking for awhile, while Jason and Monique are "cooking," Andrea is encouraged to put the doll in her own bed. Now it is time for everyone to go to sleep. Jason and Monique lie down with their pillow, and they encourage Andrea to do the same. The baby then wakes up crying in the night, and, since Andrea is the mother, she must rock her back to sleep.

A scenario such as the one just described could also be worked into a play script, which is repeated several times. In this way, Andrea could be assisted not only with pretending but also with language development and cooperative play.

Problem Solving

As preschoolers face increasing demands to develop greater and greater independence, the cognitive skills that enable them to engage in **problem solving** become increasingly important. Typical preschoolers often have little difficulty *recognizing* problems to be solved; they may need help only with generating more effective solutions. Children who have disabilities or are at high risk, however, may need assistance not only in the development of problem-solving strategies, but also in recognizing that a problem exists and that they have the capability to solve that problem through their own focused efforts.

Problem solving is distinctly different from academic learning. Academic skills represent external knowledge that must be taught; problem-solving opportunities during early childhood encourage the child to create new mental relationships by interacting with the environment. Meaningful problems stimulate children's mental activity as they relate new understandings to previous ones (Goffin & Tull, 1985, p.28).

Conditions Necessary for Problem Solving to Occur. It is all too easy to structure activities with young children so carefully that they never have the opportunity to solve problems or to realize the relationship between cause and effect. Alert parents and teachers often prevent problems so consistently that young children seldom have the chance to recognize a problem, let alone solve it. Yet everyday activities at home and at school can offer many opportunities to teach children these important skills. Even if problem-solving opportunities are readily available, children will only respond when the following conditions are met.

Freedom from fear of failure. Taking risks is natural to young children. That is why they must be watched so carefully. But taking risks in trying new things requires courage for some children. This is especially true if their early explorations resulted in pain or punishment. Sometimes the punishment has been a part of their disability. The child with visual impairments may be physically insecure and may resist exploring. Some children with disabilities may be overprotected, and abused children may be excessively wary. Children who have had limited opportunities to play, to use a variety of different toys and materials, and to discover need help in freeing their natural talents and curiosity.

Opportunities to experience cause and effect. Young children readily learn the relationship between cause and effect through inquiry and experimentation. Teachers and caregivers must take time to listen to and act on children's questions. Safe conditions, inside and out, should allow for experimentation. Noise and mess often are a sign of cognition in action. Children learn when they can dig and pile up things. Pouring and stirring with sand and water teach new concepts. The opportunity to discover is controlled in part by what there is to discover. But the freedom to "do it myself" must be taught to some.

Encouragement and reinforcement. Encouragement and reinforcement are also necessary for cognitive learning. Cognitive learning is disrupted if children fear punishment. The natural consequence of making a mess should be cleaning it up, never a teacher's scolding or saying, "I warned you not to do that." Encouraging experimentation may merely require making the materials available, but some children need to be told repeatedly that it is all right to play with particular things that were (and perhaps are) forbidden at home. Both these children and their parents need to understand that some things are appropriate at school and not at home.

Teachers should be alert to provide social and tangible rewards for progress in expressions of curiosity and resilience and for the learning achievement. Just as structured, sequential lessons are needed for children to learn to recognize shapes and colors, so prompting and supporting are needed for children to learn qualities such as curiosity, experimentation, and problem solving (Zimmerman & Pike, 1972).

Problem-Solving Skills to Be Nurtured. In speaking of the problem-solving skills to be nurtured, Cook and Slife (1985) concluded that

Most research about problem solving suggests that the five steps are practically a universally endorsed process: (1) recognition of the problem, (2) analysis of contributing factors, (3) consideration of possible solutions, (4) choice of optimal solutions, and (5) evaluation of feedback to determine results. Not only is problem solving a natural logic, but the motivation to overcome obstacles appears to be natural as well. (p. 5)

Recognizing problems.   Recognizing problems in everyday situations as they occur is the first step in nurturing problem-solving skills. The child who stands helplessly waiting for someone to hang up a coat needs help in thinking about alternatives. The child who cries when the milk is spilled has a basic problem-solving opportunity misinterpreted as a threatening-punitive situation. If the teacher uses the words "We have a problem. What shall we do?" and then encourages the children to define the problem and to clean up the mess, progress can be rapid. Children basically enjoy solving problems.

Deciding where to have a snack or the best place for playing with clay presents opportunities to talk about why one place is better than another. This is the beginning of problem solving. "Staging" or contriving problems to solve is a useful addition to those problems that occur spontaneously. Having too few cartons of milk at snack time creates the need to count

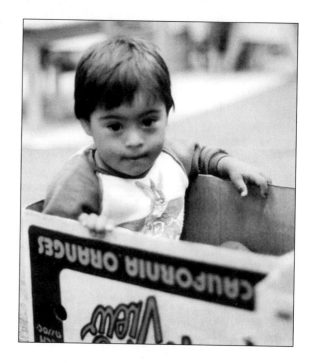

the children before going to get the milk. Losing pieces of puzzles can become the occasion to talk about how this problem could be avoided in the future. Children can then be helped to see that puzzles should not be put away unless they are finished and complete. Discovering that the taller children can reach things whereas others cannot leads to problem solving, an arithmetic lesson, and a lesson on concept comparatives (e.g., Who is tallest? John is tall, but Timmy is taller. Bill is the tallest child in the class).

Although problem solving itself is considered to be a cognitive (thinking) skill, it involves language learning, social awareness, and motor activities. The alert teacher sees the distinct opportunities to develop many skills from the simplest situations.

Defining problems.   Defining the problem is a skill that precedes effective problem solving. One afternoon in a classroom, the children complained of being hot. They were sitting around a table near a large west window playing with clay. It would have been easy for the teacher simply to say, "Oh, you are sitting in the sun. That's why you are hot. Here, I'll move the table into a shady spot." Instead she asked

"Why are we uncomfortable? I'm hot, too." (Note that she used the long word "uncomfortable" but coupled it with the word they knew, "hot.")

One of the boys responded, "That old window is stuck," but he did not add that it was bitter cold outside and energy conservation forbade opening windows. A little girl made the good suggestion that the heater should be turned off. But after the thermostat was turned down they were still uncomfortable. Finally, one announced, "We got too much solar energy in here." Earlier the teacher had told them about how the sun could be used to provide energy. She had explained that the sun heats water and other things. It was not long before the children were agreeing that solar energy was the reason (cause) they were hot (effect). They had defined the problem. They were ready to think of ways to solve it.

Attending to critical features and conditions. Facilitating attending to critical features and conditions of the problem is the teacher's role. In the case just mentioned, she suggested that one boy feel the table where the sun was hitting it. Before she could suggest it, another boy decided to feel the floor where the sun was not hitting it. He reported it was cold. Then three children at once saw the solution. "Move the table into a spot where the sun wouldn't hit the table," they offered. But the little boy who had made the first comment about solar energy had another idea. "Let's sit under the table. It's cool down there." And they did.

Sitting under the table would not have occurred to the teacher. It was a temporary solution but a good one. The children were very pleased they had thought it up themselves.

Considering alternative solutions. Children can consider alternative solutions as soon as they have learned how to recognize and state a problem. Creative thinking is a result of thinking about alternatives.

According to Raudsepp (1980)

The importance of creativity to professional and personal success cannot be overestimated. Professionally, creativity plays a fundamental role in the problem-solving and decision-making that are intrinsic to technical and managerial activities. Personally, creativity supplies the insight and variety that help make life interesting and meaningful. (p. 73)

Raudsepp was not talking about preschool! He was describing the importance of nurturing creativity in business managers and engineers! He pointed out the need to overcome personal and environmental factors that inhibit the development of creativity.

1. *Creativity.* If creativity is so essential, it should be systematically cultivated from earliest experiences. Raudsepp suggested playing games that develop the ability to discover principles linking different situations and things. He emphasized that recognizing simple solutions (such as sitting under the table to avoid the sun) is a skill that can be taught.

One of the games Raudsepp suggested is Tangram, which originated in China around 1800. The game consists of a seven-piece set of "tans." With these seven pieces over 1,600 designs can be arranged! Very young children enjoy doing this, and with encouragement they create fascinating figures. After a few experiences with Tangrams, they begin to play more creatively with blocks, clay, and all other manipulables. The mere awareness that the same pieces can be put together in different ways creates a mental set that establishes the habit of thinking creatively.

2. *Divergent thinking.* Seeking divergent solutions is important in developing problem-solving skills. Divergent thinking (Guilford, 1967) is a form of creative thinking involving an opportunity to go off in different directions exploring various strategies to solve problems. After one group of 4-year-olds had grasped the knack of divergent thinking, a whole carton of milk spilled on the floor. One creative thinker quickly suggested that the best solution was to find a hungry cat. Another used the concept of osmosis and suggested placing a terrycloth towel in a pan with one corner placed into the puddle. She had previously noticed that when her towel had just one corner in the bathtub the water "climbed up the towel" and made a mess on the floor. She translated this observation into a way to clean up the spilled milk.

3. *Brainstorming.* Brainstorming in preschool is exciting. As soon as children understand that the teacher really respects their ideas and will adopt them, they express unbelievable creativity. We find it useful to let them watch us write their suggestions on the chalkboard in a column. After they have made a number of suggestions, we read them together to see whether one is better than the others. If all of the suggested solutions to a problem are similar, the teacher may offer a very different idea, even an obviously silly one.

Choosing the best alternative.   Discussing the suggested alternative solutions to a particular problem provides opportunities for developing language, vocabulary, and cognitive skills. As children talk about the different ways of meeting a particular need, they become engrossed in what they are thinking about and add new ideas. But one alternative must be chosen and given a fair trial. Reasons for the choice should be discussed. Verbal children usually take the lead in telling their ideas. Even nonverbal children, however, can be encouraged to suggest different ways to solve a problem.

One teacher who contrived a problem placed the tumbling mats beside a shelf so that, to get around them, everyone had to walk several feet out of the way. The teacher even pretended to stumble over them several times. Then she announced, "Boys and girls, we have a problem." Fifteen pairs of feet marched over to see what was happening. The teacher explained, "These mats are in the way, and we don't have any place to put them away. What shall we do?"

Silence. Then, one very small boy announced, "We could open 'em up and walk on them."

"No," said another child. "They'd get dirty."

Another boy said, "Let's just frow [throw] them away." (He did not enjoy tumbling.)

A little girl who could speak very little pointed up and said, "Up dere." She had noticed that the top shelf had some space. Everyone quickly agreed that "up dere" was indeed an effective answer.

Evaluating results.   Evaluating the "up dere" solution did not take long. When they tried to get the

unwieldy mats to the top shelf, they discovered it would not work. Just as adult engineers go back to the drawing board, so did the children. They reviewed all of their ideas. None seemed useful. So they decided to think about it some more. The next day one little girl came bouncing into the room. "I'se got sootion" she said. "Puts dem over dere by da books. Den we can sit soft while we read." And they did.

Developing flexibility and independence. Teaching effective problem solving requires teachers to accept some solutions that do not seem appropriate to adults. Surprisingly, children quickly develop a sense of things that will work and things that will not. But at first they must be encouraged to try the things that occur to them. The boy who suggested that the cat should clean up the milk forgot one thing: the school did not have a cat! When this was remembered, he suggested more conventional means of mopping up spilled milk. But if she had had any way of anticipating his suggestion, the teacher vowed that she would have brought a cat to school that day. Rewarding creative thinking causes it to blossom. The reward is as simple as seriously accepting the suggestions and trying them.

Avoiding critical attitudes and fault finding. If a teacher does not laugh at or ridicule a suggestion, neither will the children. If one child observes, "That's a dumb idea," the teacher may quickly respond, "There are no dumb ideas around here. Remember, we're brainstorming." If the teacher uses this term for a few days, the children will add it to their vocabularies, but more important, they will add it to their way of thinking. They will learn to withhold critical judgment until several ideas are expressed.

Nurturing affective development through conflict resolution.   If children are accustomed to thinking in terms of alternative solutions, they will transfer this learned skill to the task of solving personal problems. If two children are determined to play with the same toy, problem-solving skills should be brought to bear on the resolution of this "problem." If they are used to thinking in terms of alternatives, it will not be long before you will hear them calmly suggesting that they can "take turns," play together, or find something else to do for awhile.

Nurturing language and reasoning through problem solving. Nurturing language and reasoning through problem solving is as simple as encouraging a great deal of discussion about "what to do." At first the discussions are likely to be brief, simple, and monopolized by a few children. The teacher can prevent this, however, by insisting that everyone have the chance to say something or to "help solve our problem." New vocabulary, new concepts, and new ways of looking at old problems grow out of the process. The product (the solution) may be less than the best for a while, but with patience and continued encouragement, young children can become excellent evaluators. They can also become a genuine help in keeping things running smoothly.

The ability to judge and reason wisely is a skill that can be developed very early. Consistent management by persons important to the children is basic. Teachers must recognize that problem solving in the best sense facilitates both cognitive learning and language development. Expecting young children to use good judgment, setting the stage for it in thoughtful planning, and then allowing them to experiment and evaluate what they do helps develop intelligent behavior.

WORKING WITH CHILDREN WHO ARE COGNITIVELY DIFFERENT

Two groups of children may be identified during the early childhood period who have special needs related to differences in cognitive abilities and characteristics. These are children with significant cognitive delay and children who are highly gifted.

CHILDREN WITH COGNITIVE DISABILITIES

Identifying and labeling infants and preschoolers as having mild to moderate cognitive delays or learning disabilities is difficult to do with accuracy prior to for-

mal schooling. However, some young children will clearly demonstrate significantly delayed or impaired cognitive functioning early in life. The primary identifying characteristic of these children is significantly slowed development of cognitive skills, hence the older term **mental retardation.** In the 1980s and 1990s the term **developmental delay** was commonly used to refer to this disability. (Note: Parents often find the term misleading because it implies that the child will eventually "catch up" and that development is just proceeding at a slower pace.) We will use the term **cognitive disability.** It should be noted that today there are differing views of "intelligence." The notion that intelligence—or even cognitive ability—is some single measurable ability is no longer widely accepted (Carey, 1990, Gardner, 1983). Rather, it is believed there are many types of ability or "intelligences," such as verbal, motor, social, musical, and so on.

For purposes of our discussion here, we are referring to those cognitive processes and skills described by Piaget, and, in this section, to children who, very early in life, demonstrate significant difficulty with the kinds of skills discussed in this chapter. These cognitive challenges can be caused by many factors, including genetic disorders (e.g., Down syndrome); prenatal insult to the fetus from toxic substances (e.g., alcohol) Jones and Smith (1975) or viral infections (e.g., rubella); perinatal complications (e.g., anoxia); and postnatal influences such as head injury, asphyxia (e.g., near-drowning), and poisoning (e.g., lead poisoning). While these factors do not always cause significant cognitive impairment, it is a possible outcome. We are referring to global developmental/cognitive deficits, not impairments of specific neurological processes.

Characteristics of Children with Significant Cognitive Disabilities. The following are characteristics commonly associated with children who have significant cognitive disabilities.

1. According to Peterson (1987), the most obvious characteristic of children with retardation is their slower rate of development. They learn

slowly and require repeated, systematic instruction (Ford & Mirenda, 1984).

2. They experience significant difficulties with the kinds of basic cognitive processes described earlier in the chapter. They experience short-term memory deficits and difficulty attending to relevant stimuli.

3. Children with significant mental retardation experience particular difficulty with language development. While for most developmental domains the child will be functioning at a level similar to his or her mental age (i.e., cognitive level), language development is often below the child's mental age.

4. Many children with retardation process information more slowly than their normally developing peers and require more time to produce a response.

5. They often do not demonstrate learned skills spontaneously, and they do not *initiate* easily. They have difficulty generalizing skills to new situations (Horner, Sprague, & Wilcox, 1982).

Adapting Instruction

In light of these learning characteristics, several strategies can be effective in assisting young children who have significant cognitive impairments. These are summarized in Exhibit 10–1. These adaptations

EXHIBIT 10–1

Special Considerations for Children Who Need Extra Time and Spaced Practice

1. *Provide concrete, multisensory tasks.* Preschool-age children naturally learn more easily when tasks are three-dimensional and concrete rather than abstract.

2. *Find the child's most efficient mode of learning.* Observe carefully to determine each child's strongest mode of learning. If it is visual, then use visual cues to assist auditory directions. If auditory, then accompany visual tasks with auditory assists. If motoric, then use movement as much as possible to teach language and cognitive skills.

3. *Monitor pacing.* Children who must work extra hard to concentrate or to process information usually tire easily. The amount of effort exerted should be varied to allow for occasional rest times, quiet activities, or soft music. Children who process information more slowly should receive less information or should receive it over a longer time.

4. *Provide repetition.* Some children need to try things again and again or need to have something repeated several times before it can be grasped. Intermittent practice helps children to remember skills they have learned.

5. *Plan for modeling and imitation.* Some children do not acquire information incidentally. If a specific response is desired, plan experiences in which the behavior is demonstrated and positively reinforced. Once the child imitates the desired behavior, be certain to give the expected reinforcement.

6. *Task analyze.* Tasks must be broken into simple, short steps that can be sequenced from the easiest to the most difficult.

7. *Give explicit directions.* For some children it is necessary to give nearly all directions slowly and in small steps. One step can be completed before the next direction is given.

are easily incorporated into any preschool program. Nondisabled peers can often benefit from them as well. For example, during activities designed to facilitate classification skills, familiar, functional materials can be used, such as forks, knives and spoons, or different-colored socks. Another simple adaptation is to remind all staff to speak more slowly and increase the length of pauses. This adaptation will make it easier for all children to understand, and it will provide ample time for children to organize their ideas and communications. Particularly important are the use of repetition, creating a predictable environment, and facilitating active learning by teaching the child to initiate.

CHILDREN WHO ARE GIFTED

Nearly every early education center has children who are gifted enrolled. However, giftedness is difficult to identify during the early years. Not only are official definitions somewhat unclear, but they vary from state to state. In addition, some children who are gifted have not yet participated in experiences that reveal their talents. Others may have such a discrepancy between their cognitive development and their social-emotional development that their giftedness is masked behind withdrawal, aggression, or other forms of inappropriate behavior. Some states do support formalized identification procedures through screening and in-depth testing. (Recall the cautions surrounding the use of standardized tests discussed in Chapter 4.)

Given the inadequacies involved in testing young children and the lack of financial support, most teachers must turn to informal checklists to identify children who are potentially gifted. However, professional literature does contain criteria to help teachers identify these young children. Merle Karnes and her associates (1978), from the University of Illinois, have developed a Preschool Talent Checklist designed to identify preschoolers with talents in specific academic areas.

Even though a series of so-called typical "gifted" behaviors may be described, remember that not every child who is potentially gifted will display all or even most of the behaviors. Children from different cultural backgrounds will also display their giftedness in different ways from that of the majority culture (Torrance, 1977). In general, children who are potentially gifted tend to have large vocabularies, a great ability to concentrate, a high level of curiosity, and a good memory. They learn rapidly, show a mature sense of humor, are alert, and enjoy the challenge of problem solving and abstract thinking.

Children who are gifted need the special encouragement described in Exhibit 10–2. Enrichment of the regular early education environment will meet the needs of most young children who are gifted. This chapter contains numerous suggestions for the development of cognitive skills through active learning and problem solving. Teachers can increase the depth, complexity, or abstractness of these activities when children who are gifted are involved. "Questions and activities designed to elicit fluent, flexible, original, and elaborated thinking can be readily incorporated into many regularly scheduled activities, such as sharing, art, weather, and story reading" (Kitano, 1982, p. 19). Indeed, all of the steps described in the development of problem-solving skills are perfectly suited to the needs of children who are gifted.

In summary, the following recommendations made by Kitano reaffirm the appropriateness of most of the curriculum suggestions in this chapter as an appropriate foundation for any program serving young children who are gifted. Kitano recommends providing activities that enhance creativity; higher cognitive processes; and forecasting, planning, and decision making, as well as activities that promote inquiry, problem solving, and affective development.

READINESS TO LEARN

The 1991 U.S. educational reform plan *America 2000* stresses that by the year 2000 all children will enter school ready to learn. For the preschool child, one of

EXHIBIT 10–2

Children Who Are Gifted Need Special Encouragement

Children who are gifted are usually curious about everything. They want to experiment all of the time. They are persistent in problem solving. They have a large fund of information, often more than the teacher does, about things that particularly interest them. They are not easily distracted, and they want to remain at a particular task until they have mastered it. Their ability to attend and concentrate is usually greater than that of others.

If their insatiable curiosity is not rewarded, their unique abilities may be limited. If the messes they create as they experiment are the occasion for punishment, they may stop experimenting.

Young children who are gifted need expanded opportunities. The materials they can enjoy, the books they like to have read to them, and the conversations they will seek should be appropriate to their level of development. Often these children are particularly sensitive to the feelings of adults. They can be skillful manipulators. Be alert to help them to use their special gifts, but not abuse them.

Almost any material can be adapted to meet the needs of children who are capable of creative or divergent thinking. Attribute blocks are an obvious example. Most children who are gifted will quickly learn to sort by color, shape, and size. Advanced children can learn to sort the differences among more than one attribute. Making an alternating chain of one and two differences does challenge the minds of most preschoolers.

the greatest concerns regarding the development of cognition has to do with the cognitive skills that will ultimately support the learning of academic skills of reading, writing and mathematics, and classroom language skills. Many of the mental operations and thinking skills that evolve throughout the preschool years will be critical to school performance and the development of academic skills. This section addresses the teaching of these cognitive subskills.

However, it is important to realize that the development of academic skills—and literacy skills in particular—does not depend on levels of cognitive development alone but also on the social and linguistic experiences of the child. Thus, to truly understand academic readiness and to develop strategies for facilitating academic skills in young children, it is also necessary to understand the early development of literacy (currently referred to as "emergent literacy" [van Kleeck, 1990] within the social context of the young child's family and culture.

The reader is reminded also that the early caregiver interactions described in Chapters 6 and 9 play a critical role in children's later development of cognitive and academic skills.

FACILITATING COGNITIVE AND INFORMATION-PROCESSING SUBSKILLS RELATED TO ACADEMIC ACHIEVEMENT

The preschool years can be viewed as a period of preparation for the formal academic achievement that must take place in the early elementary school years: reading, writing, and mathematics. In addition, there is a fourth area that we now realize to be crucial to children's academic success. It is referred to as *school language.*

Significant debate exists regarding to what extent academics should be stressed during the preschool years. Preschool programming approaches often reflect one of two polar views. One view suggests that academic skills should be directly taught in preschool programs emphasizing learning the alphasuch as seriation, categorization, one-to-one cor-spondence, and transformations, form the cognitive bases for academics. The following sections provide developmentally appropriate classroom strategies for facilitating these processes and concepts.

Facilitating Attention Skills

Assessing Problems of Attention. To help young children develop appropriate capacities for concentration, the teacher must identify the factors that may be contributing to lack of attention. First, the teacher must be certain that the child has no health problems and no interference with normal vision or hearing. Obviously, many young children with special needs do have physical problems that affect their concentration. The guidelines in Chapter 6 offer some assistance in developing an environment most responsive to particular special needs.

Assuming that their attention expectations take into consideration each child's special needs, teachers will want to assess whether tasks match the child's abilities and are broken into manageable steps, directions are clear, vocabulary is at an appropriate level, and amount of stimulation is reasonable.

Stimulus Selection. Teachers should analyze the amount and complexity of stimuli to which the child is being asked to respond. Some distractible children may not be able to attend to a very colorful puppet with a very high voice while seated on the floor in a large group far away from the teacher. The same puppet might get a totally different response in a small group with two or three children seated at a table with a volunteer aide who uses a soft voice. Decreasing the amount and complexity of impinging stimuli will make it easier for the child to separate relevant from irrelevant stimuli.

When children have difficulty figuring out what stimuli are relevant, using novelty in the form of concrete objects, touch, and movement can help focus and sustain attention. It is believed that children first learn to interpret stimuli received through the sense of touch (tactually). Then around the age of 3 or 4 months, they integrate information presented visually

bet, sound-letter relationships, counting, and reading and writing numbers and letters. At the other end of the continuum are programs that stress that neither academics nor academic readiness skills are appropriate for the preschool classroom. These programs emphasize self-directed play and exploration and exclusively child-centered activities.

In light of the growing concern regarding the lack of school preparedness of millions of young children from impoverished environments who are at risk for a variety of biological and social reasons, there is probably an important middle ground somewhere between the two views. There is much that can be done within a child-centered program to enhance the child's cognitive, social, and linguistic foundations for the later development of academic skills. It is our position that the early childhood special educator must understand the nature of these foundations and be able to design educational programs that facilitate them, yet stop short of emphasizing the formal teaching of academic skills.

Basic information-processing skills such as attention and memory, as well as certain mental operations

...vell (Rowbury, 1982). Even so, for ...ch continues to help isolate the ...of a stimulus and increase the ...cus on them. When trying to teach ...walk across a street safely, giving each child a teddy bear to "instruct" in role plays might be an effective means of focusing attention and recall.

Duration of Attention. Initally the amount of time required for a task should be in keeping with the child's natural ability to sustain attention. Then, using positive reinforcement and in some cases a timer, the *time on task* requirement can be increased. Remember that often children do not sustain attention because the task itself is inappropriate. For the very young child, learning tasks need to have visually concrete (obvious) beginnings and endings. Because some children just do not know how to start an activity and have poor visual organizing skills, they are easily distracted. Through careful structuring of environmental demands, teachers can help children to have productive contact with early learning materials.

When environmental demands do not exceed children's response capabilities, frustration can be avoided and involvement sustained. Puzzles exemplify a type of material that often places inappropriate demands on children. Teachers are surprised at the difficulty level of many puzzles supposedly designed for young children. Even though puzzles do have concrete beginnings and endings, their difficulty level may be conducive to only limited involvement. Perhaps an appropriate puzzle is just not available when the child decides to visit the puzzle corner. He or she may then wander around or try to take another child's puzzle. This child's so-called "attention deficit" may be more related to the characteristics of the activity than to those of the child.

Active Looking and Listening. One of the ways we have found to encourage active looking, listening, and thinking is through cooking activities. For example, children love to crack eggs. This is a learned skill; it is messy but worth the effort.

Properly attired with an apron, and after protecting the table and floor with paper, each child is allowed to go to the refrigerator (one at a time) to get an egg. First, the teacher shows how, and then each child is encouraged to describe what he or she will do, and later, what was done. "Tap the egg on the edge of the bowl. Put your thumbs in the broken place. Pull it apart." Demonstrated and talked about, egg breaking is a fine motor lesson, a language lesson, and a sequence lesson all rolled into one.

Other cooking lessons teach many things. One class has a yellow bowl, a purple spoon, a green measuring cup, a red-handled scraper, and a shiny beater. Before the cooking lesson, these implements are lined up about 10 feet away from the cooking table. Ten children at a time sit around the rectangular table. The teacher asks, "What do we need first?" and at least one child says "The bowl." That child is directed, "Get the yellow bowl." This process is continued until the needed items are on the table. Each child has a particular part to play in making the simplest food. Making muffins is a good place to begin.

All of the concept words on the bulletin board are included in some way in the cooking lesson (see Exhibit 10–3 later in this chapter). Each child does at least one thing, although all should have a turn at stirring and beating. Putting the mix into the oven is part of the project, and of course eating the finished product is the reward. Using the experience as the basis for an experience story chart also makes it possible to combine reading and mathematics readiness into the lesson.

Hearing. Hearing what happens is far more difficult for most children, even if they have perfectly normal hearing. The activity just described is also an excellent way to teach children to listen. If they fail to attend to the directions, they may lose their turn to do something they really wanted to do. Of course, it is important to be careful to avoid punishing children who truly cannot understand.

For a child with a hearing impairment or a child with limited language comprehension, this lesson offers the teacher the opportunity to give the directions first and then lead the child through the activity. As the child completes what he or she was told to do, the teacher should say, "Good work. You brought the green measuring cup," or "You broke the egg just the

EXHIBIT 10–3

Snack Time: A Perfect Time to Develop Concepts

Most early education centers focus on teaching children how to enjoy a wide variety of foods. They stress good nutrition and encourage social manners. In addition, snack time provides a unique opportunity for developing concepts. Although different foods are eaten, the routine remains essentially the same each day: arranging the table, deciding how much food is needed, and discussing the qualities of the food. Eating is a multisensory experience that should not be taken for granted.

Unlike nouns, concept words cannot be taught directly, as they are not objects with names. Instead, concepts must be experienced, and appropriate concept words applied to the experiences. Snack time provides an ideal opportunity for many children to become directly involved in concept-related experiences. For example, a child's glass may be *full* or *empty,* the grapefruit is *larger* than the apple, there are *not enough* straws, but there are *more* on the table. Through lively conversations, observations can be guided, comparisons made, and concept words practiced. Meaningful questions readily bring light to number, size, and placement concepts.

Of course, snack time is not the only time to focus on concept development. It is just one of the best and often overlooked times. The ability to attend is greatly enhanced when touchable favorite foods can be smelled, seen, and tasted. Even children who are very easily distracted become intently involved when they have good things to eat.

right way." The teacher should be alert to model and expand what the child says. But the teacher should not stop the activity to insist on "good speech." Rather, the activity should be used simultaneously to develop thinking skills and listening skills.

Critical Observation. This is an advanced observation skill that can be taught. Even very young children know when they have been fooled. Learning to listen, see, touch, taste, smell, and observe carefully is a prelude to thinking critically. Understanding that some things are safe and others dangerous involves observation and critical thinking. Conversation that nurtures this awareness is needed. Asking "Do you think we should_____?" and "Is everything ready?" helps children to begin to solve problems. The teacher should avoid doing things for them whenever the opportunity to think and make choices is a possibility.

Imaginative Observation. Imaginative observation is basic to nurturing creativity. Just lying on one's back seeing animals in the clouds is a good place to begin. Seeing funny things in the shape of puddles after the rain and noticing the way a crumpled piece of paper looks are not expensive activities. But doing this consistently teaches children to observe imaginatively.

Often, teachers are careful to show children pictures as they read to them. But sometimes it is fun to offer them crayons and paper and see whether they can draw something about what has just been read. Perhaps they can look at a squashed tennis ball and, with a little help, see a mountain or a spaceship. Then, as they show and talk about their creations with friends, they will develop additional observations. Observation through the senses of smell, touch, and taste also enlivens the products of children's imaginations.

Structuring Learning Experiences

Young children who have not yet developed adequate attention, concentration, perceptual, or memory skills may not be making effective contact with their learning environment. By structuring the curriculum, teachers can help these children to become active problem solvers and effective learners. O'Connell (1986) has advocated the scheduling of a structured, isolated, small-group instructional session by restructuring the periods of the day traditionally called "free play time" or "center time." In a typical mainstreamed early education class, there might be 4 or 5 children with disabilities in a group of 20. While there may be only two teachers, volunteers are usually available so that one adult can be involved in each of three small groups. Ideally, each group would contain a mix of children with and without disabilities. The nondisabled children would function as models and could assist the children with special needs.

The children with disabilities would then be assigned to whichever small-group activity promotes skill development in their personal areas of weakness. As discussed in Chapter 6, many activities such as puzzles, cutting, and color recognition already provide for individual differences through the process of task analysis. Children can work side by side with puzzles of differing difficulty level or can cut with scissors designed to accommodate different levels of skill. O'Connell (1986) has further suggested that children with special needs be seated closest to the adult at the table, so that sufficient opportunities for reinforcement and prompts are available.

Rowbury and Baer (1980) suggested as an alternative that half the class group come to the work area, while the other half continues in free play. The second group comes to the work area after the first group has completed a designated number of individually prescribed tasks. The resulting advantage of having peer models for both preacademic tasks and social free play deserves consideration.

Planning Instruction. Many young children with special needs have to be helped to begin a task, stay with it, and recognize when it is completed. They may see a task as endless and fail to recognize when they should take pleasure in a product or in the process of learning to learn. To promote successful contact with the task and recognition of accomplishment, it may be best to begin with learning tasks that have visually concrete starts and completions. Functional activities such as picking up all the blocks after play time,

putting them in their proper container, putting the top on, and returning them to the shelf can be broken down into small units that are gradually combined as children develop increasing attention and concentration skills. Research suggests that helping a child to recognize and feel responsible for his or her own successes stimulates motivation or the desire to learn (Cook, 1983; Weiner, Graham, Taylor, & Meyer, 1983).

Structuring the Environment. To structure the learning environment, the teacher must match its features with the learning characteristics of the children. Rowbury (1982) discussed the following factors as important elements in the organization of an optimal learning environment:

1. *Location for learning.* A constant assigned location will reduce distraction and help to cue attentiveness and task orientation.

2. *Selection of materials.* Materials most appropriate for learners with delays include those that
   a. are concrete representations of the concept being taught.
   b. provide a maximum of tactile and visual information with little verbal interpretation.
   c. incorporate frequent but easily performed manipulative responses from the child.
   d. easily isolate the concept being taught.
   e. can be arranged in steps and presented to the child as specific, visible products to be completed.

3. *Visual arrangement of materials.* The following suggestions will be helpful to the child who has difficulty organizing his or her own work area. Such a problem is common to children who have delays in perceptual development.
   a. Limit materials to only those needed to complete the task.
   b. Arrange initially needed materials before the child arrives or ask the child to bring the red tub (which contains necessary materials) to the center. This prevents distractible children from having to wait and possibly beginning to lose interest.

c. Be certain that all materials are within the child's reach and at eye level.

d. Put loose materials in a container to avoid spills and their resulting distraction.

e. Use visual supports and guidelines such as the placement card holders that come with some visual matching cards to help the child develop necessary organization skills such as left-right progression.

Teaching Classification, Seriation, and Concept Development

Whatever the theoretical orientation of and the skills expected by kindergarten teachers, nearly every preschool curriculum has similar preacademic (or cognitive) goals. In one way or another activities are included related to classification (grouping), including sorting and matching, categorization, and seriation (ordering), and the development of concepts related to color, shape, space, time, number, opposites, and letters. In general, expectations move from the concrete to the abstract, from the simple to the complex, and from the here and now to the remote in time and space (Hohmann & Weikart, 1995).

Matching (a form of discrimination) and then putting things together that are the same or alike is among the first of the expected skills. Identical things are matched, whereas things that are alike in some way are *grouped. Sorting* is also a form of discrimination followed by separating according to differences. Both matching and sorting activities are described within the broader context of *classification* (distinguishing characteristics of things, then sorting, matching, or otherwise grouping them). Note that the ability to understand the concepts of "same" and "different" is essential to performing on tests and following directions. Teachers should carefully teach the verbal labels of "same" and "alike" and "different," "not the same," and "not alike." Children cannot understand these concepts without using the verbal labels unless prompted to do so.

As children learn to classify, they are encouraged to begin with concrete, multisensory objects.

Attention must be called to the various *attributes* (features or characteristics) of the objects. It is a pleasure to watch children as they move from the concrete to the abstract or from the simple to the complex in their thinking. For example, very young children are dominated by what they see, hear, smell, or touch. This is known as being "perceptually dominated." They will describe an orange as something that is orange in color, round, or rough (depending on the words within their vocabulary). Later they will be interested in its function and will classify it as "something to eat." Finally, it will become part of a whole class labeled "fruit." This cognitive hierarchy is reflected on intelligence tests that award a greater number of points to the answer "It's a fruit" than are awarded to "It's orange."

Seriation (ordering according to relative differences) is thought to be preliminary to understanding number concepts. Practice in serialization helps children to coordinate relationships as they begin to understand size, position, and time comparisons. Teachers begin with highly dissimilar objects and move gradually toward the discrimination of finer and finer differences.

Making comparisons to see what goes together and what does not enhances thinking skills. *Grouping* and *regrouping* in many different ways require flexibility of thought. This flexibility is basic to successful reasoning, judging, and problem solving.

Once critical preacademic skills are identified as preschool objectives, the next step is to translate them into a workable curriculum. The following sections present pragmatic suggestions for teaching and developing necessary preacademic skills in young children. Exhibit 10–1, presented earlier in the chapter, can help teachers implement their curriculum with children who need extra time and spaced practice.

Facilitating Classification

Classification is basic to making analogies. Classification instruction should stress teaching children to organize (group or sort) the same information in different ways. Most preschool curricula emphasize teaching colors, shapes, and sizes. Initial classification of things by these attributes should include a wide range of items. As children become adept at sorting things by color, they should be introduced to colored shapes. As they learn to sort by shapes, they should be provided with shapes of different sizes and thicknesses.

Sorting activities should never be limited to one set or one kind of materials. Children with special needs will need extensive practice sorting and matching familiar objects such as shoes, cups, cars, etc. before they can sort more abstract features such as shapes, colors, and size. Matching socks of different colors and sizes is as useful as using more elaborate teaching materials. Sorting colored balls into two boxes can be both a learning experience and a useful clean-up activity. The teacher should encourage children to think of *their own* criteria for grouping. In this way the teacher can reward their tendencies toward divergent or creative thinking.

Attribute Blocks. A good set of attribute blocks includes red, yellow, and blue circles, squares, rectangles, and triangles. Each shape is provided in two sizes and two thicknesses. Children can sort them into several identical plastic boxes with low sides to make it easy to see them. At first the children are taught to put all the red shapes together, mixing all the shapes in the same container but keeping the color constant. The blocks are mixed together on the floor in a pile, in equal amounts of red, yellow, and blue. The teacher begins by saying, "Let's put all the red ones here," and then picks up three or four red blocks one at a time, saying, "This one is red," each time. Next a child is directed to "Find another red one" and place it into the correct box. The process is continued until all of the blocks have been sorted according to color.

After a few days of doing this, circles and squares are contrasted. Again, blocks of all three colors and both shapes are mixed in a pile on the floor. The teacher sets the stage in the manner just described, except that now *shape* is the criterion.

As soon as the children are secure in this classification, multiple criteria can be introduced. Using the identical materials and boxes, they sort the blocks according to color *and* shape.

Blue squares can be placed in one box and yellow circles in another. Later, big blue squares and little blue squares may be segregated. Yellow circles and yellow triangles should be sorted before thin yellow circles are segregated from thick yellow circles.

Adapting Instruction. Individualizing behavioral objectives is important, because as in all teaching activities, the teacher's skill in making the activity interesting and enjoyable is important. There should never be a sense of solemnity or serious importance with games. It is critical for the teacher to be alert to support each child at his or her success level. If the lesson includes children of more than one skill level (and it should), all of the suggestions made for individualizing within the group should be followed.

A well-organized set of performance objectives enables the teacher to move forward or backward in providing the appropriate challenge while avoiding the overwhelming obstacle of failure. For example, the teacher may hand a red circle to Willie and say, "Let's put this big red circle with the other big red circles here" as she points and guides Willie's hand to the right box.

But she may say to Susie, sitting next to Willie, "Susie, what should go into this box?" as she points to the box with big red circles. Susie likely will respond, "Big red circles." In this way, each child is challenged but no child fails. They also learn from each other. Groups of 4 or 5 are optimum, but as many as 10 can enjoy this kind of classification lesson. Table 10–1 suggests the sequencing of the development of shape concepts that makes individualization possible.

Attending to Relevant Features

The attribute blocks can be used to develop the understanding of *rules*. During the beginning sorting activities, the teacher can say, "My rule (criterion) in this box is everything yellow," or, "My rule in this box is only circles." After several sessions using the term *rule* the teacher may ask, "What is my rule in this box?" as she points to a box with blocks of one characteristic. If the children seem puzzled, the teacher can simply answer the question, "My rule in this box is _____,"

Table 10–1   Example of en-route objective leading to a terminal objective

Sequential Steps	Descriptions
Area: Cognitive	
Goal: To teach children to identify shapes in the environment	
Terminal objective: The child will name shapes (circle, square, triangle, and rectangle) in his or her environment with 100% accuracy, no matter what size or color the shapes take.	
1. Matches shapes	Given an assortment of 10 objects of 2 different shapes and the teacher's statements "This (object) is (shape name)" and "Put all of the (shape's name) in this box," the child will place all of the items of the designated shape together.
2. Sorts shapes with verbal directions	Given 10 items of each of 2 shapes and the same relative size, and the teacher's request "Give me a (shape name)," the child will choose an item of the shape named and give it to the teacher. The teacher will randomize his or her requests to reduce the chances of successful guessing.
3. Imitates shape name	Given the teacher's spoken word model, "This shape is (shape name)" and the request for the child to "Tell me about this shape," the child will imitate what has been said.
4. Recalls shape name	When asked "What shape is this?" as the teacher shows one of the shapes, the child will respond correctly, naming the shape.
5. Recognizes shapes of toys	When told to "Show me something that is (shape name)," the child will respond by pointing to a toy, furniture, or any other item he or she can see of the shapes named.
6. Recalls shape names	When asked, "What shape is the (any environmental item)?" the child will respond correctly by saying the appropriate shape name.

and then call one child to "follow the rule" and choose a block to add to the box.

The teacher should continue to use the term *rule* and to assist any child who does not grasp the idea. Usually several children will begin to understand and use the word correctly. They provide continued practice for the others. For those who grasp the idea quickly, a new dimension can be added. By providing them with an assortment of blocks and boxes, the teacher can encourage the children to make up a rule and make the teacher figure out their rule. But this is difficult for many children long after they can quickly identify the teacher's rules. The teacher should be patient. Continuing to play with the blocks in this manner leads to a firm grasp of an important principle: The same things can be sorted (categorized or classified) in different ways.

Grouping the Same Things Using Different Rules. Awareness of grouping the same things using different rules is necessary for reading. After all, the same letters can be grouped in many different ways. Children must recognize that they can group things according to one category such as animals, food, things that go (transportation), and toys, and then that these things can be grouped in other ways. As soon as children grasp the idea of primary categories, they should be introduced to sorting each category into subclassifications. Foods divide into fruit, meat, and vegetables. Animals can be classified as farm and zoo, tame and wild, or pets and nonpets. Clothing can be sorted into things for the head, things for the feet, things to wear outdoors, and things to wear inside. Each of these cognitive skills requires knowing the names of things, the uses of things, and the ways in which they can be sorted. Remember, these are readiness activities for true hierarchical grouping that occurs later.

Encouraging Flexibility in Thinking. Teachers should encourage flexibility in thinking. Sorting toys into different storage containers at different times is one useful way of doing this. For example, a class had been keeping toy animals in a box with pictures of animals on it and Lincoln Logs in their special box. One day, two boys insisted that Lincoln Logs belonged with the animals. Their reasoning: "We plan to use the logs to make a fence in our zoo tomorrow." Because teaching children to think in flexible, creative ways is a major goal, the logs stayed with the animals. That is, until someone else decided they were just right for the farm. Then they sorted the zoo animals and the farm animals separately with no direction from the teacher. The logs moved to the farm.

Children enjoy the challenge of sorting anything if the teacher is enthusiastic and excited when they grasp new ideas. For example, a teacher laminated a large piece of cardboard and divided it into four sections. Pictures were chosen from categories the chil-

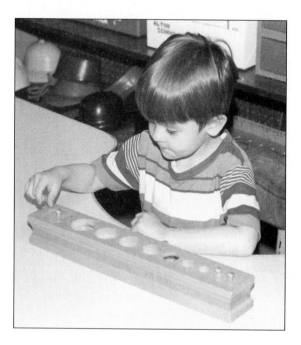

> ### Problem Solving in a Montessori Classroom
>
> A visit to a Montessori classroom would reveal an array of attractive materials. Each would emphasize teaching one dimension. Each would be "self-correcting" in that the material would reveal the error, allowing the child to correct himself or herself by further experimentation. For example, the knobbed cylinders shown in the picture fit snugly in only one corresponding hole. Focus between the ages of 3 and 6 would be on self-directed concentration.

dren had been studying. At first, the cardboard merely took the place of the boxes used in the first lessons. (For some children, it is useful to actually place the boxes on the cardboard at first.) Then, when they recognized that the task was the same (sorting according to categories), the boxes were removed. The teacher continued to refer to the divisions on the cardboard as boxes.

Later, the children will need to know that rectangles and squares in their kindergarten workbooks are called boxes. These earlier experiences help them to bridge the gap between real boxes and boxes on paper. Children who learn less quickly than some of their peers will benefit from a larger variety of materials. Not only does this help them to see more relationships, but it also lessens the likelihood of boredom in doing the same thing in the same way over a longer period.

Facilitating Seriation

Introducing children to serial ideas such as first and last should be done in the context of everyday activities, especially those that involve whole body movement. *First* and *last* may refer to place in line or when one does something. These concepts are critical for young children entering kindergarten. Most of the problems involved in lining up or being allowed to do something are caused by children's lack of understanding and experience with these terms. Understanding the concept (cognition) and using the correct label (language) cannot be separated. Without the concept words, one cannot talk about the concept. Without the idea, the word is useless.

Montessori cylinders and "nesting" toys are typical seriation materials. Hardware stores often provide sample paint cards that can be used to seriate from dark to light. The teacher should not overlook using household measuring cups or variously sized nails.

Facilitating Concept Development

Learning abstract concepts such as "many," "different," "whole," "taller," "tallest," "in front of," etc. is often a special challenge for children with disabilities. Providing children sufficient experiences with the many concepts they must learn and the association with the words is a challenge. Merely keeping track of the concepts requires a system. A system for teaching concepts includes the following features:

1. Identify the concepts to be taught.

2. Plan a large number of activities and experiences that make explicit the idea of each concept.

3. Use the associated concept word throughout many class sessions as the need for the word occurs. That is, grasp the moment most likely to demonstrate the concept meaning to the child and use the word at that moment.

4. Provide many experiences involving a particular concept close together, but in natural, spontaneous ways. For example, if grasping the idea of "first" is the target, play many different games requiring lining up in serial order. Focus on "first" in moving from one activity to another in the room. Lining toy animals in a row, identifying the animal that is "first," and then turning all the animals around to discover that the one that was first is last helps to make the concept clear.

5. Provide for contrived uses of the concept word by the children. That is, create the occasions when spontaneously using the target word throughout the day is appropriate.

6. When most of the children use the word some of the time and most of them appear to understand it, establish a system for regular review. Of course, if the concept words are used frequently because they are needed and useful, the review is spontaneous and effortless.

Each playgroup or classroom will want to focus on many of the same concept words. Needs are quite universal. An examination of teachers' manuals for kindergarten and first-grade reading and arithmetic yields a large number of necessary concept words. These should be introduced through real-life and play activities at least 2 years before the children encounter them in school. "Put your finger at the top of the page" is a much harder direction to understand if children have not learned about "the top shelf" or "the top of the page" in a book as someone reads a story. A review of the Boehm Test of Basic Concepts (Boehm, 1986) or the work of Bangs (1968) will be helpful in selecting target concepts.

Avoid Stereotyped, Labored Teaching of Concepts. Teachers should provide opportunities for children to learn the concepts through experiences appropriate to a particular setting. (See Exhibit 10-3 for an example.) They should not leave the learning of important concepts to chance. The basic procedure that should be followed is to

- Identify the concepts.
- Use them.
- Make meanings clear.
- Monitor use over time.

DEVELOPMENT OF LITERACY

The previous section considered certain cognitive subskills related to academic readiness. In this section, we consider social and linguistic factors related to literacy.

Morrison (1991) has suggested that literacy has become the current "hot topic" among early educators (p. 91). According to him, this is at least partly in response to the fact that 50 million Americans are functionally illiterate. It is also related to the growing numbers of children who enter school without the necessary prerequisite communication skills and early experiences that prepare children to participate in formal literacy education.

A term that reflects the increasing emphasis on the relationship of early experience to literacy is **"emergent literacy"** (van Kleeck, 1990). Literacy is not simply an accumulation of the specific skills related to reading and writing, but rather evolves through both social and cognitive processes that begin at birth. Literacy evolves gradually as a function of exposure to and interaction with print materials and exposure to other children and adults who are *using* print, that is, "literacy events."

Anderson and Stokes (1984) have described the types of early literacy materials and experiences to which young children may be exposed, including the following categories:

1. Daily living activities, such as making lists for grocery shopping; reading labels and recipes; going to various public services offices such as the departments of welfare, employment, and motor vehicles; and paying bills.

2. Entertainment, such as reading newspaper movie listings, television guides, and books; doing crossword puzzles; and reading subtitles or credits on films or videos.

3. Religious activities, such as attending Bible study groups, singing hymns, and reading daily devotions books.

4. Work-related activities, such as writing checks, reading instructions, following delivery instructions, and stocking shelves.

5. School-related activities, such as doing homework or playing "school."

6. Interpersonal communications, such as writing and reading notes, letters, and birthday cards.

7. Storybook time, in which children are read to, primarily for their entertainment.

8. Literacy techniques and skills, which include activities in which reading or writing is the specific focus of the interaction. Such activities are often initiated by the child (e.g., the child asks "What is this word?" or "How do you make a 'T'?").

Van Kleeck (1990) has pointed out that mere exposure to literacy materials and experiences is not sufficient for the development of literacy. Rather, it is the adult-child interaction around such events that is important.

The Precursors of Reading and Writing

Increasingly researchers in the area of literacy development acknowledge the relationship between certain early skills and experiences and the development of reading and writing (Katims, 1991; Sulzby, 1985; Teale & Sulzby, 1989).

Writing. Several developmental domains relate significantly to the development of children's writing skills. The development of fine motor and visual motor skills is obviously critical to the child's ability to eventually use pencils and markers to draw the abstract forms that make up letters of the alphabet. Specifically the following are important:

• Children's early experiences with art materials such as paints, crayons, and markers.

• Adult encouragement and assistance in controlling print tools to make lines and circles.

• Noticing similarities and differences in shapes and configurations.

Also important is the cognitive skill of representation:

• Recognizing that pictures represent real things.

• Attempts to use drawings as representation.

• Adult assistance in learning to draw faces, body parts, and houses, flowers, grass, sky, etc.

EXHIBIT 10–4

Sample of Emergent Literacy

Sequence of Emergence of Reading and Writing for One Child

Writing

1. Scribbles with marker and crayon
2. Makes lines and circles
3. Draws a face
4. Adds arms and legs to face
5. Draws a house
6. Pretends to write letters to friends using wavy lines
7. Practices making letter-like forms
8. Includes some real letters
9. Writes own name and the word "MOM"

Reading

1. Enjoys looking at books
2. Listens carefully to story while looking at pictures
3. Holds book right side up; turns pages from front to back
4. Talks about picture
5. Retells favorite stories by looking at pictures
6. Recognizes environmental print (*McDonalds* and *Coke* logos)
7. Tries to rhyme words; likes books with rhyming words
8. Pretends to "read" storybooks
9. Recognizes key words in familiar book
10. Associates "ss" and "puh" sound to initial letters S and P

Early social experiences are also critical in the emergence of writing. Particularly important is the opportunity for involvement in adults' functional uses of writing, such as making a grocery list, or writing a letter.

Reading. Certain achievements and experiences are also critical to the eventual development of reading.

In the area of language development, the following are important:

- The development of oral language, particularly the development of narrative (e.g., storytelling) skills.

- The development of a rich vocabulary.

- Auditory processing and phonological awareness skills such as sound discrimination and rhyming.

Early exposure to literate events in the home is also critical to learning to read, for example:

- Exposure and access to children's books.

- Being read to on a regular basis.

- Observation and participation in adults' functional uses of reading, e.g., reading recipes, correspondence from friends and relatives, reading menus in restaurants, etc.

There is little dispute that children's very early experiences with reading and writing set the stage for the development of literacy. Exhibit 10–4 presents an example of the sequence of development of emergent literacy skills for one child.

Watson, Layton, Pierce, and Abraham (1994) discuss the importance of including activities and materials that can facilitate the development of emergent literacy for all children, including those with speech and language impairments. They describe a preschool classroom which is designed to incorporate the following literacy activities throughout the day:

Print Awareness

- Recognizing environmental print (e.g., fast food logos on napkins, empty food containers and wrappers, stop signs, bathroom signs, etc.)

- Functional uses of print (e.g., daily attendance, lunch menus, job assignments, treasure hunts, letter writing center, pretend mailbox, etc.)

Concepts of Book Print

- Parts of a book (cover, pages, back)

- Book orientation (turning pages from back to front, top and bottom of page, reading left to right)

- Understands labels related to book print (e.g., word, letter)

Story Sense

- Recalls main story elements (e.g., characters, main event, ending [resolution])

- Can retell well-structured story (e.g., maintains main story elements in sequence)

Phonologic Awareness

- Can separate spoken words (e.g., knows that "I love you" contains three separate words)

- Can segment spoken words into syllables (e.g., can break up word "elephant" into "el-e-phant")

- Can break syllables into phonemes (sounds) (e.g., "pup" has three sounds: "p-uh-p")

- Can rhyme words

Speech/Print Match

- Can follow print while listening to familiar story

- Has some sight vocabulary

- Initial sound-letter association (e.g., knows that printed word "door" starts with "duh" sound, though child does not recognize entire word)

Control of Reading/Writing

- Tries to read and write

- Identifies letter names

- Can write some letters given the sound

- Uses invented spelling (i.e., makes up spelling; writes words like they sound)

Watson et al. (1994) make several specific suggestions for including literacy-rich activities and materials into each component of the preschool classroom. The following are just a few of these suggestions:

1. *Opening Circle Time*
   - Have children find their own mats for circle time by identifying their name on the mat, or their own picture symbol.
   - Assign children to daily jobs by hanging name tag next to duty assigned (e.g., "Jon—Pass out Cups").

2. *Storytime*
   - Repeat stories frequently.

- Select stories with concepts which are developmentally appropriate to child's cognitive level and interest.
- Select books with rhymes and predictable phrases.
- Provide extra copies of the book in the reading corner for individual use.
- Include *active* participation in storytime, both motorically and cognitively (e.g., invite children to act out parts of the story; ask children what they think will happen next).

3. *Literacy-rich Centers*
   - Art and writing center: drawing and writing tools, stationery, envelopes, blank pages and albums for making books, etc.
   - Role-playing center: In addition to usual dress-up materials and housekeeping toys, also include pads and pencils for shopping lists, a mailbox and envelopes, TV guide, cookbooks, checkbook, etc.
   - Book and library center: Include books with cassette tapes, copies of books read in circle time, predictable books, newspapers, and magazines. Make sure seating is comfortable and inviting for both adults and children.

4. *Snack Time*
   - Make alphabet soup.
   - Read labels on food containers.
   - Follow recipes.

5. *Outdoor Activities*
   - Play "Simon Says" using large word card or pictures. Combine name card with action card to encourage reading two words at a time (e.g., "Sandra—Jump" or "Everyone—Run").
   - Label storage areas (e.g., "BIKES," "BALLS")

6. *Closing Circle/Music Time*
   - Have a picture representing favorite songs on a large poster. Children choose closing songs by pointing to appropriate picture.
   - Send notes home with children for parents to read.
   - Children find own art project to take home by looking for name.

Early exposure to literacy activities is equally important to children with and without disabilities. A study by Katims (1991) found that preschool children with mild to moderate disabilities benefited very significantly from the addition of three types of literacy activities to the classroom: (a) classroom library with familiar and predictable books; (b) frequent group storybook reading; and (c) a classroom writing center.

Relationship Between Oral Language and Literacy

Much has been written about the relationship between oral language skills and literacy, (e.g., Cook-Gumperz, Gumperz, & Simons, 1981; Tannen, 1982) as well as the nature of the school discourse style, or "school language," that is required for successful performance in schools. Young children need to be familiar with certain types of language, sometimes referred to as **literate style language** or *autonomous language,* in order to learn to read and write. This type of language is more decontextualized than language that is used in the home. Language used in the home often has a great deal of shared understanding among speakers. Such language does not depend solely on the *words* used in the communication but also on gestures, facial expression, and intonation, as well as the shared knowledge and experience of the speakers. The examples in Exhibit 10-5 demonstrate two types of communication style: *interpersonal language style* typical of that used in the home or with close friends and *literate style,* which is the type required in the classroom and serves as the basis for the development of reading and writing. In addition, school classrooms require certain kinds of communication skills. These include answering questions, using language to "show and tell," raising hands before speaking, using language to talk about language and thinking, and so on.

The Nature of School Language

To be successful in school, children must be able to demonstrate certain kinds of communication skills.

◆ ◆ ◆

EXHIBIT 10–5

Demonstration of Literate and Interpersonal Language Styles in a 4-Year-Old

Interpersonal Style

Kisha: (Spilling chocolate milk on her dress) "Oh darn!"
Mother: "Oh oh. Take it off."

Kisha: "Should I put some of that stuff on it?"

Mother: "Good idea."

Kisha: "Hope it's not ruined."

Literate Style

Kisha: (Returning from a visit to her grandmother's) "Hi mom!"
Mother: "Did you have a good time? Tell me all about it."

Kisha: "Well, Grandma took me shopping at the mall. We went to the new Disney store there. They have the same stuff as in Disneyland. I saw a really cute Minnie Mouse doll, but it was awful expensive, so Grandma couldn't buy it for me. I did get a silver necklace, though. It has lots of things on it, like Mickey and Minnie and Pluto and even Goofy. After the mall we had supper at McDonald's."

In the first example, language is characterized by short utterances and frequent use of pronouns. There is little specificity or explicitness, because it is not necessary. Mother and child both share the same reference—the spilled milk and the stain on the dress.

In the second example, Kisha is engaging in a narrative; she is describing past events, much as she would tell a story. Her narrative has a beginning, a middle, and an end, and it represents the sequence in which events actually occurred. She is using explicit and specific language, which is necessary because her mother has not shared her experience. This type of language use is said to be more *decontextualized* because there are fewer contextual cues. It is also referred to as *autonomous* language because the words and sentences must stand alone without the assistance of shared context or visual props.

It is also important to note that in the second example there is clearly an expectation on mother's part that Kisha will "perform" the narrative account of her experiences. This helps prepare Kisha for the kinds of academic performances that will be required of her in school.

Some of these skills are linguistic and some are social or pragmatic.

Certain kinds of interactions required in classrooms may be unfamiliar to some children. The following are examples:

- Children are required to raise their hands before speaking.

- Children are expected to answer questions individually, addressing the group at large. (Many children may be more accustomed to demonstrating their understanding through action rather than words.)

- Children are expected to respond very quickly.

- Teachers ask questions that are "test questions"; that is, the teacher already knows the answer and is using the question to evaluate the child's knowledge. Such a format is unfamiliar to many children.

The linguistic skills required are those that have been alluded to earlier in the chapter, including the following:

- The child must use and understand language in the classroom that is often decontextualized (i.e., not embedded in the immediate context). For example, the teacher often gives instructions using only words, or the child is asked to describe a past event.

- Vocabulary is expected to be specific and precise.

- Syntax and grammar are used to carefully mark the relationships among sentences (e.g., "if," "but," "because," etc.).

- Narratives are expected to reflect sequence accurately and be coherent.

These literate language skills are built on the symbolic, referential language concepts that emerged during the preschool years. In turn, reading and writing skills, which must be learned in the primary grades, will be based on literate-style language. Many children do not have the kinds of early language experiences that prepare them for success in the early grades. In part this may be due to cultural differences. The following section addresses some of the ways in which children's early experiences with language and literacy may be different from what is expected in the classroom.

CULTURAL DIFFERENCES IN EARLY LANGUAGE AND LITERACY EXPERIENCES

Infants and young children are exposed to a wide variety of early experiences related to language use and reading and writing. Some of the most important research related to cultural differences in these early experiences was reported by Heath in her book *Ways with Words* (1983). Using the classic ethnographic research method of participant observation, Heath carefully observed families in two communities in the Piedmont area of Appalachia. Heath provided detailed descriptions of the interactions between adults and young children in a working class white community and in a rural African-American community. She compared these interactions with the types of interactions that are typical of what she referred to as white middle class "mainstream" families.

Differences in Children's Early Use of Narrative

Of particular importance, according to Heath, are differences found in the types of narratives that young children are encouraged to use. Narratives are important both because they are believed to form the foundation for learning to read and write and because children are expected to be able to perform certain types of narratives when they enter school.

Heath (1986) summarized the kinds of narratives most common among different cultures as follows.

1. *Recounts.* A **recount** is a report of an experience from the past. It is commonly parent initiated (e.g., "Jenny, tell Daddy about your field trip"). Recounts are the most common form of narrative required in the public school. Unfortunately, they are the least common form of narrative in nonmainstream cultures. In middle-class mainstream families, however, children are not only encouraged to produce recounts frequently but also encouraged to use literate-style language, that is, language that is precise, highly referential, and in proper sequence.

2. *Eventcasts.* An **eventcast** is a description of a current activity. It describes situations or activities that are immediate or obvious, for example, "I'm building a tower," or "Mommy's making pudding now." This type of communication is also common in mainstream families and in public schools (e.g., "John, tell us what the boy in the picture is doing"). It is very *un*common in many non-mainstream cultures, in which it is often considered ridiculous to talk about the obvious. Consider the effect of the following classroom scenario on a child who is not accustomed to the use of eventcasts. Paul is making a ball out of a piece of clay. The teacher notices and says to Paul, "Oh

Paul, tell us what you're making!" While a middle-class child might easily launch into a detailed description of what he was doing, Paul is somewhat bewildered and probably not sure he understood the teacher's question. He might even be concerned that describing such an obvious thing would be insulting to her.

As children get older, they learn to use eventcasts in **metalinguistic** and **metacognitive** ways. That is, they use language to reflect upon language or thinking (e.g., "Let me think about how to do that," or "Oops! I said that wrong"). This is an important school language behavior, and it is useful in learning how to learn.

Somewhat related to eventcasts is the kind of response required by the typical classroom test question format—the familiar teacher-student interaction consisting of a question-reply-evaluate sequence that predominates in school classrooms. The following is an example:

Teacher: "Sean, what is the first word?"

Sean: "Trucks."

Teacher: "No, that's wrong."

In this format, the child is being asked to answer a question that the adult already knows the answer to. For many children this is bizarre.

3. *Accounts.* **Accounts** are similar to recounts in that they tell about a past event. However, accounts are initiated by the child, rather than by an adult. Accounts are often accompanied by communication strategies designed to get and hold the listener's attention (e.g., "Hey, ya know what?!"). While these types of narratives are much more common in non-mainstream families than are recounts and eventcasts, they are discouraged in many public school classrooms and are often punished as interruptions or off-task behavior.

4. *Stories.* According to Heath (1986), the most common type of narrative among non-mainstream families is the story. **Stories** are often handed down from generation to generation, or they may evolve over a period of time within the child's early experience. Stories may begin with an adult teasing a child about a particular event. Stories evolve and change over time, and eventually some parts may be fictionalized. Stories contain strong elements of performance; the narrator's style is important, and listener participation in the story is often expected. Needless to say, such language activities do not follow the rules of school language, and they may be viewed as lying or attention-getting behavior.

Cultural Differences in Early Caregiver-Infant Interaction

Long before children learn to use narratives, important cultural differences can be observed in how parents interact with their infants and young children (e.g., Westby, 1985). These differences can determine whether or not young children have opportunities to learn literate-style language prior to school entry.

Middle-class caregivers are typically verbally responsive to their infants and young children. This may not be the case in certain other cultures. While caregivers from other cultures may be responsive physically through touch or through facial expression, they may not respond verbally. Westby (1985) pointed out many such differences among non-middle-class cultures.

Middle-class caregivers are also more likely to use highly referential language than are caregivers who are members of some nonmainstream cultures. **Referential language** is characterized by use of frequent labels and precise vocabulary with clear referents. Thus, typical middle-class communication practices expose children to both a large quantity of language and the quality of language that facilitates eventual development of literate school language skills. Examples of these different kinds of caregiver-child interaction are presented in the following dialogues:

Sample 1

Jason, 12 months old, sitting in his high chair, starts to whine.

Mother: "Jason, what's wrong?"

Jason: Looks down at the floor.

Mother: "Oops! Your cookie, huh? You dropped your cookie." (Mother picks up the cookie.) "Yuk. This cookie's all dirty. See, it's dirty 'cause it was on the floor."

Sample 2

Alice, 12 months old, sitting in her high chair, starts to whine.

Mother: Looks up at Alice.

Alice: Looks and reaches toward the floor.

Mother: Picks up the cookie and hands it to Alice, saying, "Here it is."

In both these examples, the caregiver is responsive to her infant's cues. However, in the first example the mother is both *verbally* responsive and *referential.* She uses the word *cookie* several times and uses other key words that specifically refer to the key features of the experience—*dropped, dirty,* and *floor.* In the second example, although the mother is responsive, her language is limited. When she does verbalize,

it is non-referential in that she does not explicitly name the object (cookie) or the location (floor). Instead, she uses the words *here* and *it.*

Cultural Differences in Uses of Print

Cultural differences can also be observed in children's early experience with reading and writing. While reading books for pleasure or information and using writing for communication are common in middle class homes, they may not be common in some non-mainstream homes. Anderson and Stokes (1984) described the kinds of reading and writing experiences that occurred among three different cultural groups. In this study, Anglo families engaged in twice as many literacy activities as did the other two cultural groups. More specifically, Anglo adults initiated significantly more interactions directly related to teaching literacy skills such as helping the child read food labels or words in books. They were also more

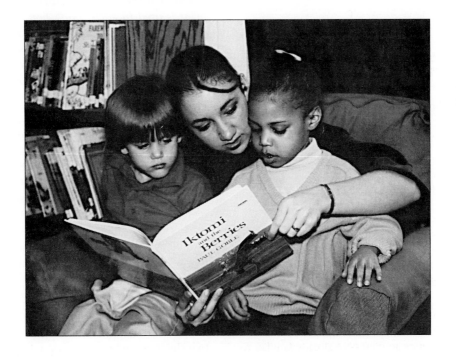

likely to use print for purposes of personal communication (i.e., writing notes and letters). Other cultural groups were more likely to engage in literacy events in religious contexts such as Bible reading.

In the 1990s, teachers commonly encounter children whose native language is not English. It is important to realize that the native language of the child is often not the only difference. The kinds of cultural differences just described can create a serious mismatch between teacher and child, and they may be even more problematic in the child's attempts to achieve school success (Iglesias, 1985). Saville-Troike (1979) suggested that American schools are designed primarily to prepare middle-class children to participate in their own culture.

The ways in which non-mainstream families provide early language and literacy experiences for their children are not wrong; they are simply different from those expected in our school systems. It is particularly important that teachers of young children with special needs understand these differences and be aware of educational strategies that can help children make a successful transition to public school settings.

STRATEGIES FOR FACILITATING EMERGENT LITERACY

In early childhood programs, the major goals related to the development of literacy are *not* learning to recognize letters and learning sight vocabulary. Rather, the more important goals, particularly for children with special needs, are to develop an awareness and understanding of the functions of reading and writing and to develop literate-style oral language skills. These skills will provide the foundation for reading and writing, as well as the skills necessary for successful teacher-student interaction in the classroom. (See Watson, et al. [1994] for ways of including activities throughout each component of the preschool classroom.)

In order to help children achieve these goals, teachers must begin by determining which kinds of language and literacy activities are already familiar to the children in their classes and then building on these experiences. As Heath (1986) stated, educators must find ways "to use what children do with language in their homes and communities to extend and enrich the school's repertoire of narrative genres" (p. 93). In addition, teachers must help young children understand the *value* of reading and writing. The following are examples of such strategies.

• *Demonstrate the functional uses of print.* This is one of the most powerful strategies teachers can use in the classroom. It includes such activities as reading the daily menu to see what will be served for lunch, listing on the board the names of children who are present or absent, writing notes to themselves as reminders to do something later, writing notes to other teachers, and so on. In these activities, children are *not* expected to read; more important, they are developing an understanding of the *functions* of reading and writing. As they observe the power of the printed word, children develop a fascination with decoding the mysterious symbols.

• *Work with parents to identify the ways in which print is used in each child's home.* This might include such activities as reading the television guide, reading recipes, reading food labels at the grocery store, reading comic books, and so on. Similar activities and materials can easily be incorporated into the classroom.

• *Incorporate literacy events into children's play.* Treasure hunts are exciting ways to demonstrate the use of print. Again, children are not expected to actually read the clues, but to experience their effectiveness in leading to the treasure. Other examples of play activities include playing postal service (letters are "written," placed in the mailbox, and delivered), going to the grocery store with a shopping list, and pretending to read a bedtime story to a doll. Reading recipes during cooking activities and writing notes that have been dictated by children to take home to parents are other good activities.

• *Play games that require referential language to facilitate literate-style oral language.* For example, two children can be separated by a screen. The child who is "It" draws a picture and instructs the other child to draw the same thing (e.g., "Make a big circle and color it blue. Now put two black eyes on it," etc.). The object of the game is to see how closely the pictures match. The same format can be used in playing with different shapes and colors of blocks or setting up a doll house. For children with severe disabilities, the game can be made simpler by using familiar objects and performing very simple tasks, for example, selecting objects such as a cup and a shoe to be placed in a box, then comparing to see whether both children end up with the same objects in the box.

• *Structure other activities that facilitate literate language style.* These might include helping children explain the rules of a game to someone else, go to the school office and deliver a verbal message, describe an exciting event to a student who was absent, and play the "telephone" game. Simpler versions might include having children feel objects in a sack and guess what they are or playing "Simon Says." These activities facilitate the use of specific autonomous language. For children who are less verbal, they demonstrate the functional uses of language for the purpose of sharing information and regulating others' behavior.

• *Read stories to both large and small groups and to individual children.* The importance of doing this cannot be overestimated. The stories selected must be meaningful to the children. They should be short, and they should be repeated often. Stories should also include props, such as a flannelgraph board, or actual objects to highlight important story points. Involving children's actions at key story points is also important. Including props and actions will make storytime more interesting for all children. As stories are repeated, pause at key points to allow the children to fill in the familiar phrases. Familiar storybooks should also be available to children during free-play time so they can "read" the stories to themselves or to a friend or doll. (This will necessitate having several copies of favorite books available.)

Exhibit 10–6 provides examples of activities that can be used during "Calendar Time" to facilitate learning.

Whole-Language Approaches to the Development of Literacy

Early childhood special educators must be aware of changes in trends in teaching reading and writing in the primary grades. An understanding of emergent literacy lead naturally to a view of reading and writing as a complex natural process related to social and communication processes and experiences. Goodman and Goodman (1986) described a **whole-language approach** in which reading, writing, speaking, and listening are viewed as interactive and interdependent. Reading and writing are not taught separately, nor are they broken mechanically into subskills. (See Moran, 1990, for a discussion of recoding versus interactive approaches.) Bunce (1990) suggested the following examples of whole-language activities that were common in early primary grades in the 90s.

- Language experience stories that children dictate to the teacher based on shared experiences. Stories are written by the teacher on flipcharts so they can be read again and again by the class. Students may copy the stories for their own reading later on.

- Choral reading of familiar stories or poems. Choral reading can play the same positive role that singing favorite songs plays for younger children. Choral reading combines this pleasurable repetition and predictability with written words.

- Use of predictable storybooks that include repetitions of sentences and key words.

- Journal writing and writing picture captions on students' own pictures.

Teaching Phonological and Phonemic Awareness

While the whole language approach clearly dominated the early reading methods philosophy for many years there is a current belief that the pendulum may have swung too far. While it is certainly the case that social/linguistic skills and experiences

EXHIBIT 10–6

Making Calendar Time Meaningful for All Children

Calendar time is an almost universal activity in preschool programs. Because of the abstractness of concepts of time, children with special needs often have difficulty relating to this activity. The following is an example of how calendar time might be made more meaningful for children with cognitive disabilities.

1. Rather than presenting the entire calendar month, highlight only the current week. Each day should be a different color, with Saturday and Sunday easily distinguishable from the days of the school week (e.g., they might be pastel, while the week days are primary colors).

SUNDAY	MONDAY	TUESDAY	WEDNESDAY	THURSDAY	FRIDAY	SATURDAY

2. Identify one activity for each school day that is only done on that day. For example, Monday is "Pudding" day; Tuesday is "Walk-to-the-Park" day; Wednesday is "Popcorn" day; Thursday is "Hat" day; and Friday is "Clean-Up" day.

3. Each of these days has a special symbol or picture representing that activity. The symbol is placed on a cardboard square of the same color as the corresponding day on the calendar and with the name of the day printed on the bottom.

ETC.
ETC.

4. Introduce the calendar activity by saying,"Who knows what day it is today? Right! It's Monday. What do we do on Monday? We make pudding. It's Monday and we're going to make pudding. Who can find the Monday card?"

5. Teach the children to learn to recognize the appropriate day-of-the-week card by relating the activity symbol to its matching color and word.

(For children with severe disabilities, show a duplicate of the activity card during the actual activity. This will help with symbolic representation and memory.)

380

EXHIBIT 10–6

6. At the end of the day, again say, "What day is it today? It's Monday and we made pudding." Then foreshadow a *future* event by saying, "Who knows what day it will be tomorrow? It's Tuesday. And what do we do on Tuesday?" Encourage the children to find the Tuesday card, but do not hang it on the calendar until the next day.

7. At the beginning of the next day, begin by asking, "Who knows what day it was *yesterday?* What did we do?" Point to the Monday activity card already placed on the calendar the previous day, and review the Monday activity. This facilitates children's learning of past tense.

8. Repeat steps 4, 5, and 6 for Tuesday, and so on.

9. As the week progresses, have the children mark the sequence of days and the passage of time as the activity cards fill up the calendar. As the week comes to a close, briefly review the week's events and talk about weekend plans.

   With this activity, a child who has severe cognitive disabilities can work on matching and eventually associate the activity symbol card with the activity and a particular day of the week. Non-disabled children can learn the days of the week; use language to describe past, current, and future events; and learn to read the names of the days of the week.

identified in whole language and emergent literacy approaches are very important, the child's ability to discriminate and recognize the *sound segments* of words is also a very necessary subskill in learning to read.

Phonological awareness is the term used to refer the ability to recognize and discriminate certain sound segments of language including phonemes, syllables and words, and the realization that these segments can be separated, linked, and moved around. **Phonemic awareness** refers more specifically to the ability to perceive and manipulate phonemes (i.e., the smallest linguistic units, such as the three phonemes in the word "pin": {pIn}). Children must ultimately learn the relationships between phonemes and letters of the alphabet in order to learn to read

(i.e., sound-letter association). Learning to read by focusing on these sound-letter associations is referred to as "**phonics.**"

Many children have not developed this kind of sound awareness by the time they enter school. Adams (1990) reported that 25% of middle-class children—and a much higher proportion of children from less "literacy-rich" environments—have not developed these skills by first grade. Needless to say, children with auditory-based learning disabilities also have difficulty with sound awareness.

Early childhood programs can make a significant contribution to the development of these skills. The following are examples of activities (adapted from Adams, Foorman, Lundberg & Beeler (1998) that can support the development of phonemic awareness.

- **Develop listening skills.** Children must first learn to *listen,* i.e., to concentrate and actively process auditory information. A wide variety of simple sound awareness games can be very helpful in developing children's ability to listen.
  1. With eyes closed ask children to identify different *environmental* sounds (e.g. running water, guitar, bell, drum, scrunching paper). Increase the difficulty of the game by asking children to identify the *location* of the sound, and then to identify the *sequence* of two or three sounds.
  2. Ask children to imitate or identify "soft" or "quiet" sounds versus "loud" sounds.
  3. Select a child to be "it." While he closes his eyes, an item with a subtle noise, such as a ticking clock or a timer, is hidden somewhere in the room. The child then has to listen carefully and try to find the item.
  4. Ask children to listen carefully and try to identify softly whispered words.

- **Develop rhyming skills.** Learning to produce and recognize words that rhyme is a first step in phonological awareness.
  1. Use ample nursery rhymes, poetry, and rhyming books in group activities. Allow children to fill in the rhyming words and to make up new rhymes.
  2. See how many words or nonsense syllables children can generate to rhyme with a certain word, e.g., "What rhymes with bike?"
  3. Complete rhyming pairs, e.g., *pie - sky; pin - fin; wig - ?; fire - ?,* etc.

- **Develop concept of a "word."** Children do not automatically know what a word is.
  1. Ask children to list different words, e.g. "How many color words can you think of?"
  2. Say a short sentence, e.g., "John ate pizza". Ask children to listen carefully and count the words. Explain that there are three different words.
  3. Help children identify "long" versus "short" words, e.g., *cat* vs. *refrigerator.*

- **Teach recognition of syllables.** Children must be taught to recognize that words are made up of syllables.
  1. Ask children to count say/count syllables in a word, e.g., re-frig-er-a-tor.
  2. Clap hands to each syllable in a word.

- **Synthesize words by combining syllables.** Help children listen to individual syllables in a word and synthesize them into the correct word.
  1. Say "Who can figure out what word I'm saying?" *tel- e- vi- sion*

- **Listen for initial sounds in single syllable words.**
  1. Listen to the word "PIN." What is the first *sound* in the word. What other word starts with the "puh" sound?
  2. Which word starts with "puh": cow, hat, or pig?

Note that many of the activities listed above can be easily adapted for children with disabilities. Use of repeated rhymes that include movement, and identifying the sources of environmental sounds, can be highly motivating activities even for children with severe disabilities.

TRANSITION TO KINDERGARTEN

Much has been written regarding the importance of collaborative planning and parent support for transition from preschool to kindergarten (e.g., Spiegel-McGill, Reed, Konig, & McGowan, 1990). Salisbury and Vincent (1990) have stressed the importance of teaching for the next environment, and many studies have described the survival skills necessary for kindergarten adjustment (e.g., Noonan & McCormick, 1993; Rule, Fiechtl, & Innocenti, 1990). While such skills are not the only goals important for preschool programming for children with special needs, they should be included to increase the likelihood of successful adjustment in kindergarten classrooms.

Establishing and maintaining contact with the staffs of the new environments can help children adjust to their new classrooms. When special consider-

EXHIBIT 10-7

Behaviors Needed for School Achievement*

1. Follows directions.
2. Concentrates long enough to complete a task.
3. Observes and remembers.
4. Answers questions about a simple story.
5. Contributes to conversations.
6. Directs and pays attention.
7. Solves simple problems.
8. Tolerates failure sufficiently to persist with a task.
9. Makes transitions easily.
10. Works on a task over a reasonable period.
11. Accepts adult direction without objection or resentment.
12. Works without constant supervision.
13. Accepts classroom routine.
14. Suppresses tendencies to interrupt others.

*Adapted from Adelman and Taylor (1986), p. 173.

Early education teachers can plan activities designed to prepare children for more structured environments. This preparation is not intended to be academic or like an early kindergarten; it is designed to acquaint children with new expectations, routines, schedules, and patterns of reinforcement. They will require increased independence and self-sufficiency as the ratio of children to teacher increases.

Such preparation could include gradually decreasing teacher attention, praise, instruction, and prompts. Children can learn to raise their hands when they wish to respond, if that is the expectation in the new environment. Practice in following such behavioral directions as standing in line or asking to be excused to the restroom can save children from some embarrassing moments later on. Attention spans will need to be lengthened gradually by increasing expectations for on-task behavior or requiring more self-sufficiency at free-play time.

It is the preschool teacher's responsibility to determine what skills children will need to develop before they move on. Exhibit 10–7 lists some representative skills. After these are determined, the teacher should try to incorporate practice in "kindergarten skill" development in ways that are as natural as possible. Ideally, continued contacts between kindergarten and preschool teachers will ensure a smooth transition. While we have addressed the importance of collaboration among professionals and between professionals and family members, it is necessary to consider the collaborative relationship that must be built between early intervention professionals and the paraprofessionals so crucial to effective service delivery. The final chapter offers practical techniques designed to ensure effective utilization of aides, students, and volunteers in early intervention programs.

ations are necessary, it is helpful to have a preliminary meeting that includes the child's present and future teachers and the parents. Receiving teachers can be informed of each child's current social and academic skills, while present teachers learn what remains to be done to prepare the child for transition.

Summary

All preschool and child care teachers share the responsibility of developing cognitive, active learning, and problem-solving skills together with academic readiness in young children. This task is especially important for teachers of children with developmental delays or disabilities. This chapter focused on practical ways to identify and teach these skills.

Piaget's stages of cognitive development were reviewed, as well as ways of observing cognitive development through children's play. Strategies for facilitating early cognitive skills were described, as were later skills related to problem solving and academic readiness.

Cognitive skills in preschoolers can be enhanced readily within a seemingly natural environment of play and curiosity. Elements from the major theories of child development help in devising strategies to stimulate problem-solving skills and academic readiness.

By giving children the freedom to explore and opportunities to learn from failure while remaining free from anxiety, early educators can easily incorporate problem-solving skill development into the curriculum. Examples and rationales are provided to illustrate how children can develop the skill to identify and define problems, consider alternative solutions, choose among alternatives, and evaluate results with flexible judgment. The relationship between problem solving and academic readiness becomes apparent as concepts and abstract images are translated into words that facilitate movement through the stages of problem solving.

The section on emergent literacy describes the importance of encouraging children's appreciation of the purposes of reading and writing, as well as the importance of developing phonologic and phonemic awareness. Also important is the development of literate-style language skills, which are necessary for school success. Teachers must be aware of the many cultural differences in children's early language and literacy experiences. These differences will significantly influence children's social adjustment and academic success in school.

If a preschool is to be successful in preparing children for the transition to kindergarten and beyond, it must identify the preacademic skills relevant to any local school district. In addition to "pays attention" and "follows directions," the curricula of most early childhood classrooms provide readiness activities involving classification (including sorting, matching, categorization, and seriation), colors, shapes, space, time, numbers, opposites, and letters. Suggestions for promoting a child's awareness of various attributes or relevant features necessary for generating and following rules used to manipulate concepts are included. Finally, special consideration is given to the needs of those who have cognitive skill deficits or potential for giftedness, or who will be making a transition to a new environment.

Discussion Topics and Activities

1. Think of several ways to create the need to solve a problem. Design situations appropriate for a 2-year-old and a 4-year-old.
2. Observe a preschool classroom and identify ways in which functional uses of print can be incorporated into the existing schedule and activities.
3. Think of ways to involve a child with severe cognitive impairments with nondisabled peers in a pretend block play activity in which children are building streets and houses.
4. Design some preschool lessons that will encourage children to experience cause-and-effect relationships. If possible, carry these out with children. What improvement could be made in your lesson design? Did you get the results you desired? Discuss the children's involvement with classmates. Perhaps a recording of the children's responses will help you to analyze the children's reactions in greater detail.
5. Why is it important to maintain a balance between social-emotional and intellectual activities in the preschool? This is a critical issue that is receiving attention nationally and should be thought through periodically. Recognize your own philosophy and investigate its implications for young children.
6. Role play your answer to a parent who insists that reading per se should be taught in preschool. Ask colleagues for constructive criticism.

7. Visit and observe a local kindergarten class. Be alert to the behavioral and academic expectations. Compare these expectations with the "exit" goals of preschool classrooms you have observed. Discuss what you learned with classmates.

8. Collect samples of environmental print, e.g. McDonald's cups, Coke cans, pizza boxes, airline ticket envelopes, etc.

Annotated Bibliography

Views of Human Learning

Ashton-Warner, S. (1986). *Teacher.* New York: Touchstone Publications.

Readers who can find a copy will delight in this old classic. Sylvia Ashton-Warner captures the imagination with her exciting description of the way she helped young Maori children bring meaning into the process of learning. Her approach illuminates the motivation readiness so important to the relationship between learning and life.

Glazer, S. M., & Burke, E. M. (1994). *An integrated approach to early literacy: Literature to language.* Needham Heights, MA: Allyn & Bacon.

This text is unique in that it details the development of two children who begin life as illiterates and emerge, as each of their first 8 years progress, into functional readers and writers. It covers the characteristics of human development, theories that guide caregivers to create appropriate environments for learning and practical strategies that emphasize children's literature.

Hohmann, M., & Weikart, D. P. (1995). *Educating young children: Active learning practices.* Ypsilanti, MI: High/Scope.

This comprehensive volume is an update of the High Scope Curriculum which is organized around a set of key experiences. These key experiences are derived from Piaget's theory and are thought to be the primary cognitive characteristics of children in the preoperational stage of development. They are the guidelines for the development and evaluation of the Cognitively Oriented Preschool Curriculum. All related classroom activities are built on concrete, active experience.

McGee, L. M., & Richgels, D. J. (1995). *Literacy's beginnings: Supporting young readers and writers.* Boston: Allyn & Bacon.

This text offers an integrated approach to early literacy keyed to the typical developmental stages through which most children pass. Of definite interest is the thorough description of ways to organize an environment to stimulate the growth of language, both written and oral, of children from birth to age 8.

Wadsworth, B. J. (1996). *Piaget's theory of cognitive and affective development.* New York: Longman.

Here is one of the more popular introductions to Piaget's theories, including affective as well as cognitive development. The four central concepts—schema, assimilation, accommodation, and equilibrium—are described. Piaget's four stages are explained in detail and with much appeal. The relationship between cognitive development and such factors as heredity, action, motivation, and developmental stages are considered. Finally, some of the implications of Piaget's work for child care and education are presented.

Facilitating Cognitive Skill Development, Problem Solving, and Literacy

Adams, M. J., Foorman, B. R., Lundberg, I., & Beeler, T. (1998). *Phonemic awareness in young children: A classroom curriculum.* Baltimore, MD: Paul H. Brookes.

This is a very useable curriculum for the development of phonemic awareness in young children. It provides a brief overview of the topic of phonemic awareness. It presents a detailed description of various games and activities to develop listening, rhyming, syllable awareness, initial and final sounds, and so on. The developmental level of the activities range from simple listening and rhyming skills appropriate for preschool children, through phonemic identification skills necessary for beginning reading.

Berk, L. E. (1985). Why children talk to themselves. *Young Children, 40,* 46–52.

This article presents an excellent overview of the research into what psychologists call *private speech.* It gives clear illustrations and helpful implications for practice. Besides being fascinating to the observer, private speech is an important way in which children organize, understand, and gain control over their environment. This article helps caregivers set the stage for constructive use of private speech as an effective learning tool.

Copple, C., Sigel, I. E., & Saunders, R. (1984). *Educating the young thinker: Classroom strategies for cognitive growth.* Mawah, NJ: L. Earlbaum.

This supplementary text combines a theoretical perspective with a practical approach. It demonstrates strategies to foster thinking and problem-solving skills. With a Piagetian orientation, it integrates problem-solving skills into daily activities including art, music, imaginative play, and science.

Gibson, L. (1989). *Literacy learning in the early years.* New York: Teachers College Press.

Connections and continuity within the total process of learning to read and write, from birth to age 8, are stressed. The book is organized into age-level performance components with each phase examined in relation to its unique contributions to and constraints on the potential growth of literacy in young children. Teaching strategies and programs appropriate for literacy acquisition are emphasized.

Goffin, S. G., & Tull, C. Q. (1985). Problem solving: Encouraging active learning. *Young Children, 40,* 28–32.

This timely article regards problem solving as distinctly different from academic learning. It clearly discusses helpful topics such as the importance of problem-solving possibilities, characteristics of good problems, the creation of problem-solving situations, and teacher strategies to challenge children to think.

Heath, S. B. (1983). *Ways with words: Language, life and work in communities and classrooms.* Cambridge, England: Cambridge University Press.

This book provides rich detail in describing the author's qualitative observations of culturally different communities in the Piedmont mountain area of Appalachia. Heath carefully describes the early communicative interactions between families and young children in the two communities of Roadville and Tracton. She also discusses the mismatch between these family and community experiences and early school experiences.

Kail, R. (1996). *The development of memory in children* (3rd ed.). New York: W. H. Freeman.

This unique book details the relationship between changes in memory development and cognition. Advanced students will appreciate the chapters on the development of mnemonic strategies, metamemory, early memory, mechanisms of memory development, and memory in children with mental retardation.

Rosenkoetter, S. E., Hains, A. H., & Fowler, S. A. (1994). *Bridging early services for children with special needs: A practical guide for transition planning.* Baltimore: Paul H. Brookes.

This practical guide leads service providers through the planning process to promote coordinated, uninterrupted services for children and their families. Its practical strategies are based on empirical research and meet federal requirements. Models of effective early childhood transitions for young children with differing abilities are described.

Sparling, J., & Lewis, I. (1979). *Learning games for the first three years.* New York: Berkeley.

This is a handy paperback with illustrated ideas and activities for parents and teachers to enhance infant-toddler development. The games include 100 experiences a child can enjoy from birth to 36 months of age. Child-caregiver interaction is encouraged. Most activities are adaptable for young children with special needs.

van Kleeck, A. (1990). Emergent literacy: Learning about print before learning to read. *Topics in Early Childhood Special Education, 10*(2), 25–45.

This article clearly describes ways in which young children are exposed to early literacy experiences and the role of caregiver-child interaction in learning to read and write. The author discusses the role of the preschool in the development of literacy and describes strategies for encouraging children's understanding of literacy.

Watson, L. R., Layton, T. L., Pierce, P. L., & Abraham, M. A. (1994). Enhancing emerging literacy in a language preschool. *Language, Speech and Hearing Services in Schools, 25*(3), 136–145.

This is an excellent article that emphasizes the importance of including activities and approaches that support emergent literacy for all preschool children, including children with language disabilities. The authors present a clear summary of the philosophical and research foundations supporting this approach. Most of the article is devoted to specifically delineating how to include emergent literacy activities in opening circle, storytime, small group activities, centers, snack time, outdoor play, and closing circle. The article has many practical suggestions.

Encouraging Active Involvement of the Young Child Who is Gifted

Clark, B. (1997). *Growing up gifted: Developing the potential of children at home and at school.* Columbus, OH: Merrill/Prentice.

This extremely thorough text is a classic. Especially appreciated is the in-depth discussion of the importance of early learning to the development of giftedness. Early environmental influences, understanding of early sensitive periods, specific suggestions for nurturing very young children who are gifted, and the problems their unique characteristics create receive much-needed attention. Guidelines to help parents select an appropriate early education program are included. Most impressive is the author's ability to consider giftedness within an overall understanding of child development.

Kitano, M. (1982). Young gifted children: Strategies for preschool teachers. *Young Children, 37,* 14–24.

This article briefly reviews the literature on education for young children who are gifted and offers specific methods for working with these children in regular early education

settings. Since children who are gifted are found in nearly every early education program, all teachers should read an article such as this. Its specific suggestions will help both beginners working with young children who are gifted and more experienced teachers who realize how much of any good program is already appropriate for the special needs of children who are gifted. (Inquiry, problem solving, affective development, and the incorporation of process objectives into the curriculum are worthwhile goals for any new or existing program.)

References

Adams, M., Foorman, B., Lundberg, I., & Beeler, T. (1998). *Phonemic awareness in young children.* Baltimore, MD: Paul H. Brookes.

Adams, M. (1990). *Learning to read: Thinking and learning about print.* Cambridge, MA: MIT Press.

Adelman, H. W., & Taylor, L. (1986). *An introduction to learning disabilities.* Glenview, IL: Scott, Foresman.

America 2000: An education strategy. (1991). Washington, DC: U.S. Department of Education.

American Psychiatric Association. (1980). *Diagnostic and statistical manual of mental disorders* (3rd ed., rev.). Washington, DC: APA.

Anderson, A., & Stokes, S. (1984). Social and institutional influences on the development and practice of literacy. In H. Goelman, A. Oberg, & F. Smith (Eds.), *Awakening to literacy.* Exeter, NH: Heinemann.

Anisfeld, M. (1984). *Language development from birth to three.* Hillsdale, NJ: Erlbaum.

Atkinson, P. C., & Shiffrin, P. M. (1968). Human memory: A proposed system and its control processes. In K. W. Spence & J. T. Spence (Eds.), *The psychology of learning and motivation: Advances in research and theory* (Vol. 2). New York: Academic Press.

Bangs, T. (1968). *Language and learning disorders of the pre-academic child.* Upper Saddle River, NJ: Prentice-Hall.

Bell-Gredler, M. E. (1986). *Learning and instruction: Theory into practice.* Upper Saddle River, NJ: Merrill/Prentice Hall.

Boehm, A. E. (1986). *Boehm test of basic concepts.* New York: Psychological Corporation.

Bunce, B. H. (1990). Bilingual/bicultural children and education. In L. McCormick and R. L. Schiefelbusch, (Eds.), *Early language intervention* (2nd ed.). Upper Saddle River, NJ: Merrill/Prentice Hall.

Carey, S. (1990). Cognitive development. In D. N. Osherson and E. E. Smith (Eds.). *An invitation to cognitive science. Vol. 3: Thinking.* Cambridge, MA: MIT Press.

Case, R. (1985). *Intellectual development: A systematic reinterpretation.* New York: Academic Press.

Cole, M., & Cole, S. (1989). *The development of children.* New York: American Scientific Books.

Cook, R. E. (1983). Why Jimmy doesn't try. *Academic Therapy, 19,* 155–163.

Cook, R. E., & Slife, B. D. (1985). Developing problem solving skills, *Academic Therapy, 21,* 5–13.

Cook-Gumperz, J., Gumperz, J., & Simons, H. (1981). *School-home ethnography project.* (Final Report to the National Institute of Education). Washington, DC: U.S. Department of Education.

DeVries, R., & Kohlberg L. (1987). *Programs of early education: The constructivist view.* New York: Longman.

Fewell, R. R. (1984). *Play assessment scale* (4th ed.). Unpublished document. Seattle: University of Washington.

Fodor, J. (1983). *The modularity of mind.* Cambridge, MA: MIT Press.

Ford, A., & Mirenda, P. (1984). Community instruction: A natural cues and correction decision model. *Journal of the Association for Persons with Severe Handicaps, 9,* 79–88.

Gallagher, J. M., & Reid, D. K. (1981). *The learning theory of Piaget and Inhelder.* Monterey, CA: Brooks/Cole.

Gardner, H. (1983). *Frames of mind: The theory of multiple intelligences.* New York: Basic Books.

Ginsburg, H., & Opper, S. (1969). *Piaget's theory of intellectual development.* Upper Saddle River, NJ: Prentice-Hall.

Goffin, S. G., & Tull, C. Q. (1985). Problem solving: Encouraging active learning. *Young Children, 40,* 28–32.

Goodman, K., & Goodman, Y. (1986). *What is whole about whole language.* Portsmouth, NH: Heinemann.

Guilford, J. P. (1967). *The nature of intelligence.* New York: McGraw-Hill.

Heath, S. B. (1983). *Ways with words: Language, life and work in communities and classrooms.* Cambridge, England: Cambridge University Press.

Heath, S. B. (1986). Taking a cross-cultural look at narratives. *Topics in Language Disorders, 7*(1), 84-96.

Hohmann, M., & Weikart, D.P. (1995). *Young children in action.* Ypsilanti, MI: High/Scope.

Horner, R. H., Sprague, J., & Wilcox, B. (1982). General case programming for community activity. In B. Wilcox & G. T. Bellamy (Eds.), *Design of high school programs for severely handicapped students* (pp. 61-98). Baltimore: Paul H. Brookes.

Iglesias, A. (1985). Cultural conflict in the classroom: The communicatively different child. In D. Ripich & F. Spinelli (Eds.), *School discourse problems* (pp.79-87). San Diego: College-Hill.

Jones, K. L., & Smith, D. W. (1975). The fetal alcohol syndrome. *Teratology, 12,* 1-10.

Karnes, M. B., & associates. (1978). *Preschool talent checklists manual.* Urbana, IL: Publications Office, Institute for Child Behavior and Development, University of Illinois.

Katims, D. S. (1991). Emergent literacy in early childhood special education: Curriculum and instruction. *Topics in Early Childhood Special Education, 11*(1), 69-84.

Kirk, S. A., & Chalfant, J. C. (1984). *Academic and developmental learning disabilities.* Denver: Love.

Kitano, M. (1982). Young gifted children: Strategies for preschool teachers. *Young Children, 37,* 14-24.

Klahr, D., & Wallace, J. G. (1976). *Cognitive development: An information processing view.* Hillsdale, NJ: Erlbaum.

Kodera, T. L., & Garwood, S. G. (1979). The acquisition of cognitive competence. In S.G. Garwood & colleagues (Eds.), *Educating young handicapped children.* Rockville, MD: Aspen.

Linder, T. (1990). *Transdisciplinary play-based assessment.* Baltimore: Paul H. Brookes.

Moran, M. R. (1990). Facilitating literacy in the primary grades. In L. McCormick & R. L. Schiefelbusch (Eds.), *Early language intervention* (2nd ed.). Upper Saddle River, NJ: Merrill/Prentice Hall.

Morrison, G. S. (1991). *Early childhood education today.* (5th ed.). Upper Saddle River, NJ: Merrill/Prentice Hall.

Nelson, K. (1986). *Event knowledge: Structure and function in development.* Hillsdale, NJ: Erlbaum.

Noonan, M. J., & McCormick, L. (1993). *Early intervention in natural environments.* Pacific Grove, CA: Brooks/Cole.

O'Connell, J. C. (1986). Managing small group instruction in an integrated preschool setting. *Teaching Exceptional Children, 18,* 166-171.

Peterson, N. L. (1987). *Early intervention for handicapped and at-risk children.* Denver: Love.

Piaget, J. (1954). *The construction of reality in the child.* New York: Basic.

Piaget, J. (1977). *The development of thought: Equilibration of cognitive structure.* New York: Viking.

Piaget, J., & Inhelder, B. (1969). *The psychology of the child.* New York: Basic.

Raudsepp, E. (1980, July). Creativity games: A little imagination goes a long way. *Machine Design,* 73-77.

Rowbury, T. G. (1982). Preacademic skills for the reluctant learner. In K. E. Allen & E. M. Goetz (Eds.), *Early childhood education: Special problems, special solutions* (pp. 201-228). Rockville, MD: Aspen.

Rowbury, T. G., & Baer, D. M. (1980). The applied analysis of young children's behavior. In D. S. Glenwick & L. A. Jason (Eds.), *Behavioral community psychology: Progress and prospects.* New York: Praeger.

Rule, S., Fiechtl, B. J., & Innocenti, M. S. (1990). Preparation for transition to mainstreamed post-preschool environments: Development of a survival skills curriculum. *Topics in Early Childhood Special Education, 9*(4), 78-90.

Salisbury, C. L., & Vincent, L. J. (1990). Criterion of the next environment and best practices: Mainstreaming and integration 10 years later. *Topics in Early Childhood Special Education, 10*(2), 78-89.

Saville-Troike, M. (1979). Culture language and education. In H. T. Trueba & C. Barnett-Mizrahi (Eds.), *Bilingual multicultural education and the professional: From theory to practice* (pp.139-148). Rowley, MA: Newberry House.

Silverman, R. E. (1975). *Psychology* (3rd ed.). Upper Saddle River, NJ: Prentice-Hall.

Speigel-McGill, P., Reed, D. J., Konig, C. S., & McGowan, P. A. (1990). Parent education: Easing the transition to preschool. *Topics in Early Childhood Special Education, 9*(4), 66-77.

Sulzby, E. (1985). Children's emergent reading of favorite story books: A developmental study. *Reading Research Quarterly, 20*(4), 458-480.

Swanson, H. L., & Reinert, H. R. (1984). *Teaching strategies for children in conflict.* Upper Saddle River, NJ: Merrill/Prentice Hall.

Tannen, D. (1982). The oral/literate continuum in discourse. In D. Tannen (Ed.), *Spoken and written language: Exploring orality and literacy.* Norwood, NJ: Ablex.

Teale, W. H., & Sulzby, E. (1989). Emergent literacy: New perspectives. In D. Strickland & L. Morrow (Eds.), *Emergent literacy: Young children learn to read and write* (pp.1-15). Newark, DE: International Reading Association.

Thurman, S., & Widerstrom, A. (1990). *Infants and young children with special needs: A developmental and ecological approach* (2nd ed.). Baltimore: Paul H. Brookes.

Torrance, E. P. (1977). *Discovery and nurturance of giftedness in the culturally different.* Reston, VA: The Council for Exceptional Children.

van Kleeck, A. (1990). Emergent literacy: Learning about print before learning to read. *Topics in Language Disorders, 10*(2), 25-45.

Watson, L. R., Layton, T. L., Pierce, P. L., & Abraham, M. A. (1994). Enhancing emerging literacy in a language preschool. *Language, Speech and Hearing Services in Schools, 25*(3), 136-145.

Weiner, B., Graham, S., Taylor, S., & Meyer, W. (1983). Social cognition in the classroom. *Educational Psychologist, 18,* 109-124.

Westby, C. (1980). Assessment of cognitive and language abilities through play. *Language, Speech and Hearing Services in Schools 11,* 154-168.

Westby, C. (1985, August). *Cultural differences in caregiver-child interaction.* Paper presented at the annual meeting of the American Speech-Language-Hearing Association, Albuquerque, NM.

Zimmerman, B. J., & Pike, E. C. (1972). Effects of modeling and reinforcement on the acquisition and generalization of question-asking behavior. *Child Development, 45,* 892-907.

Chapter 11

Effective Use of Paraprofessionals and Volunteers in Early Intervention Programs

Key Concepts

- Both paid and unpaid paraprofessionals can make significant contributions to the effectiveness of early intervention programs.

- The effectiveness of the paraprofessional's contribution depends primarily on how well the teacher or director prepares for and develops a working relationship with the paraprofessional.

- Clear, well-thought-out job descriptions that consider the strengths and desires of the paraprofessionals can serve to motivate and guide volunteers and aides.

- One-on-one assistants should provide only as much assistance as is necessary to meet the needs identified for the child.

- Early interventionists serve as role models for paraprofessionals.

- The creation of an optimal working relationship is highly dependent on effective communication of expectations, desires, and needs between the early interventionist and the paraprofessional.

- Feedback and evaluation can strengthen team relationships.

- Aides and volunteers deserve to be recognized for their contributions to early intervention services.

With the passage of the Individuals with Disabilities Education Act (IDEA) and its amendments, states are scrambling to find sufficient numbers of personnel who are qualified to provide early intervention services. IDEA recognizes an important role for paraprofessionals, in addressing the shortage of personnel to deliver services, by requiring that states develop training for paraprofessionals. This shortage of service providers is being complicated by the recognition that cultural competence is essential to the provision of family-centered practices. "Often a paraprofessional can best understand a family's culture and can combine this expertise with knowledge of the specialized needs of young children with disabilities and their families" (Striffler, 1993, p. 2). Realizing this, a number of states have integrated paraprofessionals into their service delivery system and have estab-

lished new occupational categories for paraprofessionals. This chapter provides guidelines for effectively developing and using paraprofessionals and volunteers in the center or classroom.

Paraprofessionals are individuals who by their assistance extend the capacity and effectiveness of teachers and other interventionists. By definition, paraprofessionals do not have the training and expertise of professional teachers, and they receive less in monetary compensation. Another category of auxiliary personnel is the volunteers who also assist or aid in classrooms and centers. Volunteers may be parents, students in training, or interested community members. They usually serve on a part-time or sporadic basis, while paid assistants or aides work according to a consistent schedule. Most of these people delight in caring for children, are patient with their fumbles, and understand their special needs. These basic qualities of respect, caring, and desire to serve are essential to effective involvement in early childhood education.

The motivation to serve in and of itself is not enough. Paraprofessionals and volunteers need guidance in effectively using their talents and may need to be willing to learn new skills. Some will need a willingness to change attitudes and philosophies about how to manage child behavior. Simply responding to special problems according to one's parental experience or values about "good" and "bad" behaviors may run contrary to the professional aims of the program and the teacher. For example, paraprofessionals and volunteers frequently have strong ideas about matters such as discipline and issues related to sex that may need tempering to be consistent with the goals and philosophy of the teacher.

The teacher or director has the responsibility to explain special needs, to provide specific guidelines, and to demonstrate desired techniques of behavior management. In effect, when working with parapro-

fessionals and volunteers, the teacher is a leader and a manager. For this adult-to-adult role relationship to work effectively, mutual respect among the participants is needed. Each will bring specific skills, interests, and talents to the tasks to be performed. Each will have a unique role to play in making children's and families' experiences pleasant and educationally appropriate. But it remains the teacher's responsibility to guide, develop, and use the interests, talents, and motivation of any and all paraprofessionals and volunteers who seek to contribute.

WHO ARE THE PARAPROFESSIONALS?

Various terms have been used to refer to those who participate in early intervention programs but lack the full training and certification necessary to function as fully as teachers or clinicians. Terms such as *teacher aide, early intervention assistant, paraedu-*

cator, special education program aide, and *instructional* or *therapist assistant* are common. Within the literature, a distinction among these terms or the roles they represent is usually not made (Jones & Bender, 1993). Therefore, throughout this chapter, the term *paraprofessional* or *teacher assistant* will generally refer to all those who provide assistance within early education programs, but who are not fully certified or credentialed. It is important to note, however, that there is a degree of dissatisfaction with the use of the term *paraprofessional,* as it is felt by some that the term does not encourage respectful rapport among all members of the early intervention team.

However, where the handling of paraprofessionals (assistants) and volunteers differs, the distinctions will be clearly stated. For example, schools typically do not have to recruit *paid* teacher aides and teacher assistants. Volunteer recruitment may be a critical element, however, in having sufficient adult resources to carry out needed instructional and support activities within budget limitations. Usually, the performance effectiveness of volunteers is not evaluated formally. Volunteers are most often thanked and praised for their help. With paraprofessionals who may aspire to become teachers, however, specifying tasks and formalizing the evaluation of their performance are fundamental parts of the learning-development process.

PREPARING TO WORK WITH PARAPROFESSIONALS

Recruiting, developing, and effectively involving paraprofessionals often places the teacher of young children in a role for which he or she may be ill-prepared. The prevailing emphasis in the education of teachers is toward theories of learning and child development, instructional methods, curricula, and behavior management. When paraprofessionals are used in any capacity to supplement and extend pupil-teacher contact, however, the teacher is thrust into the role of leader and manager of adults. In this leadership role, the responsibilities of the teacher differ only in de-

gree from many of the functions required of a manager in a business, a hospital, or a government agency.

The remainder of this chapter explores avenues for successfully working with paraprofessionals through the planning, organization, and leadership skills of the supervising professional. Before the teacher assistant or volunteer can begin to offer a major contribution to the classroom or center, several essential steps should be taken by the supervisor. These include the following:

1. Developing clear and appropriate job descriptions.

2. Recruiting selectively to find people with needed job qualities.

3. Becoming involved in a thorough orientation program and clearly defining the teacher's responsibilities to teacher aides and volunteers.

4. Attempting continually to discover and match classroom responsibilities with the special skills, work styles, and interests of paraprofessionals and to provide evaluative feedback (Pickett & Gerlach, 1997).

Designing and Defining Jobs

Designing and defining jobs is the starting point for effectively using paraprofessionals (Blalock, 1991). There are two primary reasons why **job design** is the appropriate point of departure. First, careful consideration of job design elements provides the criteria for recruiting and selecting paraprofessionals, especially paid teacher aides. Second, people work more effectively when they know what they are supposed to do and how and when they are supposed to do it. Job design thus frames the expectations that are so important to job functioning and role relationships. Because this responsibility falls on teachers, it clarifies in their minds the purposes, tasks, and conditions in which paraprofessionals are to be part of the classroom team. Similarly, a clearly defined set of tasks, responsibilities, and relationships establishes for paraprofessionals the framework within which they are expected to work.

Job design refers to specifying the content and relationships of any job, be it the job of teacher assistant, volunteer, teacher, principal, or director. Properly conceived, job design considers both the job holder as a person and the performance contributions expected on behalf of the organization (or classroom). A simple way of thinking about job design characteristics is to borrow concepts from a classical study of group dynamics in which Homans (1950) conceived of any work group (e.g., teacher, paraprofessionals, or pupils) as a social system. Homans identified three features common to any small work group: activities, interactions, and sentiments. With slight modification, the following are the basics for defining essential job design elements in centers and schools:

1. *Activities or tasks.* This feature defines the content of what a job holder is to do. What is the scope or breadth of tasks? To what degree are they to be standardized and routinized instead of creative? How often are they to be performed? What results are expected? How are they to be recognized (by both the paraprofessional and the teacher)?

2. *Interactions or role relationships.* This defines with whom the job holder is expected to interact, how often (or under what conditions) this is to happen, and the quality of that relationship. What relationship is the paraprofessional to have with the children? With other adults—staff members and parents? What are the paraprofessional's responsibilities and limits of authority relative to the teacher? How much autonomy or freedom (self-initiative) is given the paraprofessional for certain types of tasks? To what extent is teamwork instead of individual action expected?

3. *Sentiments or values and attitudes.* This defines the conditions under which work is to be performed and sources of satisfaction available to the job holder. By calling attention to sentiments, the teacher is forced to anticipate and build on essential questions that affect the quality of the paraprofessional's involvement in the classroom such as the following: What personal rewards are meaningful to the paraprofessional? How is the paraprofessional expected to view sensitive issues such as discipline methods and toilet habits? What values and attitudes held by the paraprofessional will contribute best to the program's objectives and be compatible with those of the teacher?

Developing Job Task Descriptions. According to McKenzie and Houk (1986):

Since each paraprofessional brings different skills and expectations to the job and each teacher's needs are different, the paraprofessional's job description must be tailored to reflect their unique interaction. An important part of the paraprofessional's job description is a statement permitting the cooperating teacher and/or coordinator to specify which skills the paraprofessional must acquire, the methods or opportunities available, and the timeline for acquiring this additional training. (pp. 249–250)

The job task descriptions should be expressed in writing, with each participant keeping a copy for reference. These should be rewritten at least once each year following performance evaluation and at any time there is a significant change in assignment. This

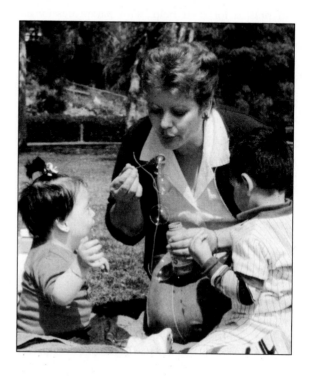

job description typically conveys more than a trite list of "responsible for" statements. As previously suggested, a written job description provides both the criteria for screening candidates (in the case of teacher assistants) and a picture of the job for the candidate. For a starting point in creating a useful statement of job task design, the supervisor should think about the ways in which a teacher assistant or a volunteer can be useful. One of the easiest ways to develop such a list of task possibilities is to jot down ideas as they occur during the day. Some of the ways paraprofessionals could be useful might include the following:

1. Preparing the room, including setting up centers, organizing materials needed for special projects, and locating daily supplies.

2. Greeting the children and assisting with all routines.

3. Supervising activities in the classroom and on the playground.

4. Nurturing appropriate behavior, including dealing with misbehaviors acceptably and effectively.

5. Directing specific activities planned by the teacher.

6. Assisting children with eating and toileting programs.

7. Helping children with assistive technology.

8. Charting behaviors during the implementation of behavior management programs.

9. Helping to order or build adaptive equipment.

10. Following specialists' instructions in helping to position or transport children.

11. Providing appropriate prompts to help ensure positive social integration.

12. Preparing, cataloging, and filing intervention games and materials.

13. Setting up media equipment.

14. Showing videotapes, slides, and special materials.

15. Contacting parents to set up conferences.

16. Helping with end-of-the-day routines, including clean-up.

Once the teacher has identified desirable tasks, he or she should record them to clarify (a) who is to conduct the activity, (b) how often it is to be performed, (c) the manner in which it is to be performed (if standardization or consistency is desired), and (d) how all concerned can recognize successful performance.

Visualizing Role Relationships. After the teacher has defined activity areas, he or she should think carefully about the role visualized for the paraprofessional. Will the paraprofessional be a creative, warm contributor to the children's learning, or merely the person behind the scenes who prepares materials? Will he or she be encouraged to suggest activities, or be relegated to doing only what the teacher has planned?

The answers to such role relationship questions reflect the philosophy and style of the teacher. Figure 11-1 depicts the extreme views of interaction that teachers have of themselves in relation to support personnel. A teacher who wants to be the boss and run a tight classroom or center ought to be aware of this philosophy. Such a situation will definitely restrict the range of freedom and autonomy given to paraprofessionals.

It is helpful if the teacher thinks carefully about his or her role-relationship philosophy before completing job descriptions and procedures for paraprofessionals. Whether or not it is recognized and clearly defined, the basic feeling (or sentiment) for what is appropriate and right will determine what the teacher will do in working with support personnel.

If the teacher discovers that the role assigned to and accepted by the teacher assistant reflects a subtle feeling that the teacher assistant cannot actually implement carefully planned and supervised activities, the teacher should experiment. He or she can provide explicit directions, demonstrate what is to be done, and then discuss ways to improve the activity the next time. This may convince the teacher that, given

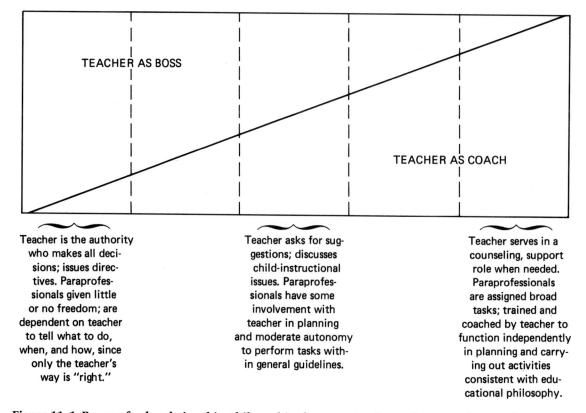

TEACHER AS BOSS

TEACHER AS COACH

Teacher is the authority who makes all decisions; issues directives. Paraprofessionals given little or no freedom; are dependent on teacher to tell what to do, when, and how, since only the teacher's way is "right."

Teacher asks for suggestions; discusses child-instructional issues. Paraprofessionals have some involvement with teacher in planning and moderate autonomy to perform tasks within general guidelines.

Teacher serves in a counseling, support role when needed. Paraprofessionals are assigned broad tasks; trained and coached by teacher to function independently in planning and carrying out activities consistent with educational philosophy.

Figure 11–1 Range of role relationship philosophies between teacher and paraprofessionals.

helpful supervision, the teacher assistant can be an effective assistant teacher. Of course, it is always the teacher's responsibility to determine what the activity should include and what the objectives must be. Techniques of behavior management cannot be left to chance or allowed to be inconsistent. These must be the teacher's responsibility. But with planning, guidance, and supervision, paraprofessionals can provide excellent instruction.

Translating Sentiments (Values and Attitudes) into Policy Guidelines. Few dedicated teachers would work without some form of lesson plan or curriculum guide. Similarly, the teacher plans in advance the essential performance tasks expected of paraprofessionals and clarifies intended relationships. This enables planned rather than reactive use of these po-

tentially valuable people. For optimum effectiveness, however, the teacher should also plan for and codify the *affective* behavior expected of paraprofessionals. This means in part explaining (in writing when possible) the ways in which teacher assistants and volunteers are to behave to be consistent with the philosophy and educational aims of the teacher and the school or center.

The most useful way of expressing such sentiments is to provide guidelines for behavior. Exhibit 11-1 illustrates several specific guidelines that were developed by one preschool director to emphasize the desired behaviors for volunteers to use when interacting with the children. A handout of these and other guidelines was given to each volunteer and explained as part of the orientation process. They subsequently served as criteria the teachers could use to

EXHIBIT 11–1

Child Interaction Guidelines for Paraprofessionals

1. *Create a pleasant atmosphere.* Tense children cannot become effectively involved. Help them feel comfortable by being warm and enthusiastic. If you relax and enjoy yourself, the children will feel this and follow your example.

2. *Your voice is your asset.* A soft, confident voice elicits a child's attention more quickly than a high or loud one. First gaining eye contact with a child and then speaking directly and softly to him or her will be more effective than shouting across the room.

3. *Be positive.* Instead of saying, "Don't spill your milk," it is better to say, "Hold your glass with two hands." "Good builders put their tools away carefully" is a better statement than "Don't throw your tools."

4. *Labels are for jelly jars, not for children.* Labels and phrases such as "naughty boy" or "bad girl" make children feel ashamed and unworthy. Children with these feelings cannot learn.

5. *Keep competition out of the classroom.* Nothing is to be gained from fostering competition among young children. Discourage children when they say, "I can draw better than Susie," by saying, "Each can draw in his or her own special way."

6. *Choices are for choosing.* When it is time to clean up, do not ask the children whether they want to clean up. Instead say, "It is time to clean up now." If you do not intend to accept no for an answer, do not give them a choice. Give them a choice only when you really want them to choose.

7. *Sharing is not simple.* Preschool-age children are just learning to share. If they are playing with something, in their minds the toy belongs to them at that moment. Children should be encouraged to ask whether they can have a turn and to tell others when they are through playing with something.

8. *Keep your eyes on the children.* Children must be within the visual range of supervising adults at all times. They need and deserve alert supervision, which is not possible when the responsible adult is engaged in adult conversation. If too many children are entering any one play area, redirect some to other areas.

9. *Do not dominate children's activities.* Children should be allowed to use their active imaginations as they experiment with ideas and materials. Unless you are teaching a specific lesson, stay in the background with supportive but not suppressive comments.

10. *Prevention is perfect.* Be alert so you can redirect behavior that can become a problem. Remember that children should not be allowed to hurt themselves or others.

---

discuss successes and problems with the volunteers. By periodically calling attention to specific guidelines, the teachers were able to guide most volunteers to adopt behaviors that were fairly consistent with the expected patterns.

As suggested by the guidelines in Exhibit 11-1, properly codified policies of role behavior state the way or tone of doing the job and *what* is to be done. They can also indicate *when* a particular behavior is considered appropriate. Thus the volunteer who is

supervising outdoor play in the vicinity of the sandbox, is not caught in the dilemma of wondering, "What do I do now?" when he or she sees Tony throwing sand.

Because they serve as a frame of reference for feedback, policy guidelines not only help in redirecting a paraprofessional's behavior when necessary but also stimulate job satisfaction. The paraprofessional knows when he or she has done a good job or has handled a difficult situation successfully and consistently with the program's standards. Guidelines also permit teachers to reinforce appropriate behavior. To the extent they allow the paraprofessional to make discretionary choices, the guidelines can help him or her feel more "professional" about being involved in the learning process.

RECRUITING PARAPROFESSIONAL SERVICES

When recruiting paraprofessional services, the teacher or director should keep in mind the necessary qualities of a successful paraprofessional. Agencies that use volunteers regularly are finding that an increasing number of them are generally mature and highly trained. Most volunteers today are middle aged, although retirees increasingly are being recognized as valuable assets to the classroom or center. They are usually devoted to their work and enjoy sharing their vast knowledge and skills gained from years of experience. Volunteer expenses are even tax deductible for some senior citizens. At the other end of the age-experience spectrum are students from elementary school through college who continue to offer their enthusiasm and desire to learn while working with young children. Many programs are hiring parents of children who have special needs to serve as parent paraprofessionals. Such parents provide invaluable support to parents who are new to the experience of having a child with disabilities (Hanson & Lynch, 1995).

Coordinating Recruitment Efforts

The first step in recruiting and organizing paraprofessional services might be to select a volunteer coordinator. Often a mother will eagerly take such a responsibility. It is helpful to have a coordinator who has previously been an enthusiastic volunteer. The enthusiasm will be most useful in the coordinator's recruiting efforts. The coordinator will also need to have organizational skills and a positive way of working with others.

This person, if not the teacher, works with the teacher in making a list of classroom jobs to be done and in determining the time of day service is needed. The coordinator is, then, in a position to search for individuals who can fill the needs outlined in the job task description. Exhibit 11–2 lists classroom jobs typically found in preschool or early intervention programs.

Recruitment Techniques

The volunteer coordinator might begin by telephoning parents of children in the program, members of local Parent-Teacher Organizations, and college instructors in the area. Inviting interested individuals to a coffee hour when program needs are presented and sign-up contracts are available may speed up the recruitment process. Holding the meeting in the center will make job explanations simple and will help generate necessary enthusiasm. If the teacher is not the coordinator, he or she is spared the uncomfortable feelings of asking for help.

Personal appearances at gatherings of interested service clubs, senior citizen groups, Parent-Teacher Organizations, new members of the community, college and high school classes, and youth organizations can be an effective recruitment technique. The volunteer coordinator should be able to explain clearly what is needed and to answer questions. A coordinator who has been volunteering for some time is often more able to answer questions and to generate enthusiasm. It also helps to have available brochures or flyers with illustrated samples of job responsibilities, places and times of volunteering, and the name and telephone number of the contact person. The same flyers can be distributed in the local library, medical offices, and churches. At all times, volunteer coordinators should be prepared to sign up individuals who indicate interest. Figure 11–2 offers a sample of one type of recruitment contract.

One effective means of reaching a number of individuals who might be interested in volunteering is to include an eye-catching recruitment letter in the report cards of elementary school children and possibly in report cards of older children. The letter

EXHIBIT 11–2

Some Services Commonly Provided by Volunteer Workers

Services Requiring Minimal Skills or Training

1. Assisting in decorating rooms.
2. Distributing supplies and snacks.
3. Helping with clothing and toileting.
4. Preparing materials for activity units.
5. Supervising outdoor play.
6. Arranging and helping with field trips.

Services Requiring Some Skills or Training

1. Typing newsletters, forms, and parent notices.
2. Instructing in special arts or crafts units.
3. Organizing and supervising a toy and therapeutic equipment loan program.
4. Assisting in health, vision, and hearing screening programs.
5. Interpreting and conducting classes for non-English-speaking families.
6. Teaching parents to make educational materials for home use.
7. Assisting parents in fundraising activities.
8. Making bibs, aprons, capes, or other sewn items.

---

should contain a checklist of skills, interests, and talents. The child can then return the completed form to the teacher. The same letter and checklist can be sent to college students, high school students, and community clubs. In some communities a newspaper advertisement is useful. Figure 11-3 is an example of a letter and checklist that have been used effectively.

Interviewing for a Good Match

McKenzie and Houk (1986) have outlined a four-step placement process that stresses the importance of achieving the best possible match between the supervising teacher and the paraprofessional. Effective involvement of a paraprofessional is based on the de-gree of correspondence between the paraprofessional's skills and the support needs of the teacher. The first two steps, which involve taking inventories of teachers' needs and paraprofessionals' skills, and the fourth step, developing individualized job descriptions, are discussed thoroughly in other sections of this chapter. The third step, "resolving differences," is often overlooked. The interview process allows the teacher or volunteer coordinator to review the job with the applicant and to discuss the appropriateness of the "match." This appropriateness may need to be reviewed occasionally to determine whether or not job descriptions still fit or whether special training should be provided for the paraprofessional.

The interview should be held in the classroom or center, if possible, and should be somewhat informal

VOLUNTEER CONTRACT

WHEREAS I believe in the value of nurturing and educating young children and care about their well-being, and

WHEREAS I seek to contribute my personal talents and energies on behalf of helping the teachers and children of the Early Childhood Center, in exchange for the joys of sharing a child's happiness,

THEREFORE, I willingly enter into this agreement to volunteer my personal services to the Early Childhood Center on the following days _____

_____ and times_____ ,

commencing on the _____ day of _____199 ___ , and

continuing until the _____ day of _____,199____.

THIS AGREEMENT entered into at_____ in the state

of _____ between

_____   _____
Volunteer   Date

Who resides at:

_____   _____
                                        Phone

_____

and

_____   _____
Volunteer Coordinator   Date

Figure 11–2 A volunteer recruitment contract.

Dear Friends:

This letter is sent to you because I believe that you join me in realizing that children are a most important resource. As a teacher of young children, I feel a special responsibility to recognize and provide for individual needs. The more I learn about child growth and development, the more convinced I become of the need to individualize intervention as much as possible as soon as possible.

Many of the young children in your child's program do need individualized attention. You have many and varied experiences that you could use to help our children here at school. We need volunteer teacher aides to help the children directly and/or to assist the teacher in providing more individual attention.

A list of possible volunteer responsibilities is attached. Please check those duties that you would be interested in doing or add any that have not been included. We invite you to a brief meeting on _____ or _____ to explain the volunteer program in detail. Please check the date that is most convenient for you and return the checklist to school by your child.

Yours truly,

Name _____   Address _____   Phone _____

I would like to:

[   ] Assist in the classroom
[   ] Help on the playground
[   ] Work with an individual child
[   ] Work with small groups of children
[   ] Help with clerical chores
[   ] Prepare instructional materials
[   ] Share my special talent
[   ] Assist with field trips
[   ] Substitute for a regular volunteer
[   ] Babysit for another volunteer

I prefer to help: [   ] At the center   [   ] At home
Day(s) I can help: [   ] M.   [   ] Tu.   [   ] W.   [   ] Th.   [   ] F.
Hours I can help: _____ _____ _____ _____ _____
Volunteer meeting I prefer to attend:
[   ]_____   [   ]_____
         (Day and time)   (Day and time)

Figure 11–3 Volunteer solicitation letter and checklist.

to ease tension. Interviewers should have a planned procedure and definite questions to ask. Typical situations ("What would you do if . . . ?") should be presented. The response gives the interviewer a feeling for the applicant's natural reactions and provides glimpses for the applicant of future day-to-day job situations. The teacher should invite the applicant to spend a morning with the children. This is an excellent way to observe not only the adult's behavior but also children's reactions to the adult. Those who automatically seek to communicate with young children at their eye level show by example that they know how to begin successful involvement with children. Those who resist spending a morning becoming acquainted with the children and the job demands suggest a lack of motivation.

MUTUAL LEARNING THROUGH ORIENTATION

Any new teacher assistant or volunteer must be socialized into the norms and practices of the teacher and the school or center. Similarly, the expectations and talents of paraprofessionals can never be comprehensively defined during the recruiting or screening stages. These emerge out of discussion and behavior in the classroom or center. What inevitably happens in the early days of the working relationship is the creation of a **psychological contract** (Coffey, Cook, & Hunsaker, 1994). In framing the psychological contract the paraprofessional typically considers the following: "What am I going to get out of my work in this classroom? How can I make use of my talents and interests so that I am doing something worthwhile and will be reasonably satisfied? How can my involvement support the attainment of my personal goals and needs, including learning or growth aspirations?"

The classroom teacher's considerations are more along the following lines: "How can I effectively use this person to complement my own skills, talents, and interests? How can I get him or her to accept my philosophies, policies, and goals? What can I do to motivate and develop in this person the abilities and commitments that will help me and the program re-

alize our educational goals?" The terms and conditions of the contract must be favorable to both.

The socialization process of building an effective working relationship is genuinely a mutual responsibility. Both people have to learn about each other. In the process of communicating (verbally, in writing, and through behaviors), they begin to expand their clarification of mutual role relationships. At its very essence, *a role is a set of expectations about what is appropriately to be done and what is to be avoided.* For paraprofessionals, the role can either be reasonably well defined and stimulating or ambiguous, conflicting, and stifling with unpleasant jobs and oppressive supervision.

Communication of Expectations

Both the teacher and the paraprofessional must communicate their expectations. It is an unusual paraprofessional who does not approach the first day of his or her assignment with some feelings of apprehension. For the teacher assistant or volunteer, the relationship with the teacher can make the experience rich and fulfilling or miserable and tedious. To help launch the relationship, a planned orientation meeting reaps greater rewards than the cost of the time invested.

If only one teacher and one teacher assistant are involved, the orientation may take place in a pleasant corner of the classroom, or it can take place at a restaurant during a planned lunch hour. The number of people involved will influence where the meeting takes place and how it is conducted, but it should not influence what is discussed.

It is a good idea for the teacher to begin with an overview explanation of his or her philosophy and that of the program. The teacher can then lead into a description of the purposes of the program and the plans to be followed in achieving these purposes. Finally, the teacher must describe procedures and role expectations. (Here films or videotapes can be useful). Later the teacher should provide time for discussion and questions.

Stressing the importance of communicating common goals, Boomer (1981) discussed specific key items to be considered in the orientation of paraprofessionals. These include design of classroom space, operation of instructional and office equipment, emergency procedures, and the schedule of activities, including the paraprofessionals' hourly responsibilities. One could add to this list the importance of professional conduct. The paraprofessionals who are expected to behave as professionals will usually do so. This includes being prompt, appropriately dressed, and respectful of all aspects of confidentiality regarding children's characteristics and behaviors.

Discovery and Use of Special Skills and Talents

To make the orientation truly an opportunity for two-way communication, the resourceful teacher should encourage new paraprofessionals to reveal their special interests, skills, and talents. Asking about previous work experience is important. Parenting and home-making skills, however, are equally important in preschools and child care centers. Very few skills cannot be adapted to useful and interesting classroom ac-

---

Working as a Paraprofessional in an Early Childhood Special Education Classroom

At least one of the paraprofessionals in this classroom would be paid and expected to conform to professional standards. Most paraprofessionals would be extensions of the teacher helping to provide additional individualized intervention. Many would be invited to participate in conferences, would learn to chart children's progress, and would be expected to model unique techniques of intervention. Some may be assigned to handle extra care needs of children with severe disabilities.

---

tivities. Everything from sports to needlework fits in somewhere. Hobbies can be the source of exciting lessons. Baking and gardening, as well as sewing and cleaning, can be the basis for preschool science and mathematics lessons.

One effective method of discovering the special skills and talents of paraprofessionals is to develop a simple questionnaire that can be filled out by

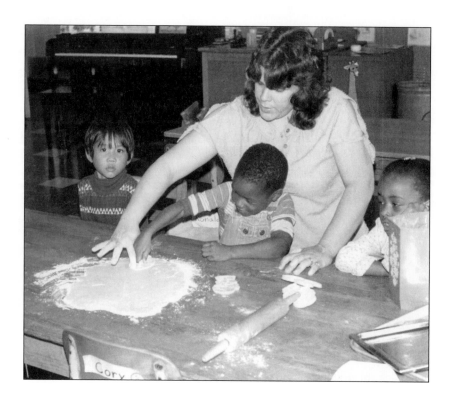

potential assistants. Many teachers ask parents to complete the questionnaire to encourage parent involvement. Others use the questionnaire with hired teacher assistants and with volunteers. The questionnaire in Figure 11–4 was designed to incorporate the needs of an early childhood center while allowing the respondents some latitude of choice.

Once the special interests, skills, and talents of the paraprofessional are known, the teacher may plan to adapt activities to them. A teacher assistant in one class loved to garden. An outdoor garden provided lessons in many concepts. Children learned about *straight, front,* and *back* rows. They learned about plants that grew *taller* and things that were *shorter.* They discovered the *shortest* stem and the *longest* vine. That garden was the basis of science lessons and nutrition themes, as well as a source of beauty and joy.

Another teacher assistant was particularly interested in puppets. She made sock puppets for each child and taught them basic skills. Puppet shows enlivened nutrition lessons and language lessons. Puppets sang the opening song and learned to say "please" and "thank you." Puppets helped with everything, and the teacher assistant felt proud of her accomplishment.

When the teacher gives special thought and care to matching classroom responsibilities with the paraprofessional's skills and talents, everyone benefits. Ideally a teacher assistant will be ready for anything, and many of them are. But even when paraprofessionals are willing to do "anything and everything," relationships and performances are better when interests are allowed to blossom and no one is pushed beyond his or her capacity to perform.

Most teacher assistants are expected to take care of many routine matters. Taking attendance, preparing snacks, and supervising the bathroom are often taken for granted. Getting materials ready and cleaning up

Name _____

	Mom	Dad	WOULD YOU LIKE TO:
1.	[ ]	[ ]	Read a story to some of the children?
2.	[ ]	[ ]	Lead a song or some other musical activity?
3.	[ ]	[ ]	Help children create something in art?
4.	[ ]	[ ]	Bring the family pet to visit the center?
5.	[ ]	[ ]	Help set up or supervise a field trip?
6.	[ ]	[ ]	Make a book of a child's story?
7.	[ ]	[ ]	Work puzzles or play games?
8.	[ ]	[ ]	Share your hobby with the class? Hobby:
9.	[ ]	[ ]	Show children how to use simple carpenter tools?
10.	[ ]	[ ]	Bring a guitar (or other instrument) and demonstrate?
11.	[ ]	[ ]	Help out and paste pictures?
12.	[ ]	[ ]	Teach the children something about your occupation?
13.	[ ]	[ ]	Conduct a simple science experiment?
14.	[ ]	[ ]	Wear clothing from another country and tell about it?
15.	[ ]	[ ]	Bring necessary materials and plant some seeds?
16.	[ ]	[ ]	Demonstrate rug weaving, leather tooling, or other crafts?
17.	[ ]	[ ]	Make jam or churn butter?
18.	[ ]	[ ]	Decorate a bulletin board?
19.	[ ]	[ ]	Sew dress-up and/or doll clothing?
20.	[ ]	[ ]	Construct special toys or equipment?

And if none of these appeals to you, what would you like to do?

Figure 11–4 Samples from a parent volunteer checklist.

are duties for many teacher assistants. But they can do much more, given encouragement and opportunity. A teacher assistant who plays the piano may also find pleasure in choosing songs and musical stories. One who sews will enjoy introducing simple sewing activities. Outdoor games may be the sports-minded paraprofessional's special delight. If the teacher tells the paraprofessional that his or her talents and interests are respected and used, the teacher can generate creative and resourceful suggestions.

DEFINING THE TEACHER'S RESPONSIBILITIES TO TEACHER ASSISTANTS OR VOLUNTEERS

So far, we have implied, if not stressed, thoughtful and kindly attitudes on the part of the teacher toward the teacher assistant or volunteer. A few of the com-

monly accepted responsibilities for leadership and guidance are summarized in Exhibit 11–3. However, this genuine caring must not interfere with the teacher's awareness of his or her role as the person on whom ultimate responsibility rests. What is done in and outside of the classroom or center and the way in which it is done are undeniably the teacher's responsibilities. Termination and replacement may be the best solution for the teacher assistant who does not share an understanding of this fact. A tug of war for the affections of the children or their parents is destructive and dysfunctional. Differing philosophies of what is best for children lead to subtle and disruptive experiences.

Just as the teacher avoids embarrassing or criticizing the teacher assistant or volunteer in front of parents and other adults, so must the paraprofessional avoid undermining the teacher. It is the teacher's responsibility to make this clear from the beginning.

EXHIBIT 11–3

Some Responsibilities of Teachers to Paraprofessionals

1. To exert active leadership and guidance to build a team of coordinated helpers.
2. To create an atmosphere in which paraprofessionals feel accepted and motivated to perform effectively.
3. To provide ample structure and direction so paraprofessionals know what is expected of them.
4. To hold an orientation session with new paraprofessionals to discuss program goals, procedures, policies, and what to expect of children with special needs.
5. To plan work in advance of the workday, and to build variety into the tasks paraprofessionals are assigned to perform.
6. To provide adequate information so that paraprofessionals can carry out their tasks, and to provide feedback so they know that you know how they are performing.
7. To have on hand the resources paraprofessionals will need to carry out assigned tasks; to show them where to find materials, how to set up an activity, and how to operate any special equipment. To make known any restrictions or special requirements to accommodate particular children.
8. To assign tasks within the range of competency of a paraprofessional while providing increased responsibility and autonomy as performance indicates increased competence.
9. To provide opportunities for regularly scheduled meetings between the teacher and the paraprofessional. Such meetings will allow for adequate planning and avoid waiting for a crisis to force communication. Impromptu meetings should not become substitutes for regularly scheduled meetings.

The teacher must be alert to recognize any overt or covert attempts to interfere with behavior management or teaching methods. Such interference should be dealt with immediately. If free and open discussion of the importance of consistent attitudes and management of children is established in the beginning, future problems will be minimized.

We have aimed most of the suggestions thus far at preparing for the entry of volunteers and teacher assistants into the early intervention program. These activities are of a managerial planning nature: defining essential tasks, developing policy guidelines for paraprofessional conduct, recruiting volunteers, and orienting teacher assistants and volunteers into the philosophy and ways of the program, while also learning of their special talents and interests. What follows is heavily focused on actions the teacher can take to motivate and stretch the abilities of teacher assistants and volunteers. These suggestions place the teacher of young children with disabilities in a leadership role, guiding, coaching, encouraging, and rewarding the efforts and developing skills of resourceful support personnel. As a starting point, it is useful to think of the teacher as a role model for paraprofessionals.

Being an Appropriate Role Model

Teachers must be appropriate role models. Saying one thing and behaving in a different way is inexcusable. What teachers *do* speaks louder than what they *say.* Advising someone to avoid spanking, yelling, and fault finding will not achieve the desired results unless the teacher also is consistent in avoiding these negative behaviors when interacting with children. What the teacher does will influence the teacher assistant's behavior. If a quiet manner is recommended by the teacher, then a quiet voice must be used by the teacher—at least most of the time.

Often it is useful for the teacher to tell the paraprofessional what will be demonstrated and to pinpoint what is to be observed. The teacher should explain what will be done and why it will be done. Sometimes a particular procedure should be written

and available for reference. This is important for new activities.

After the teacher completes a specific demonstration, the teacher assistant will want to practice. Usually (at least at first), the teacher should not observe this practice session. But it is helpful for the teacher to suggest that an observation will be made when the teacher assistant feels ready. Allow the assistant to take the initiative by extending an invitation such as, "Tomorrow when you feel ready for me to watch you, let me know."

Part of a teacher's responsibility as a role model is to build up, not undermine, the desire and productive energies of paraprofessionals. Just as the teacher's responsibility toward children is to help them to become more fully functioning independently rather than dependently, the same applies to paraprofessionals. But development of the independent skills and motivation of paraprofessionals does not occur through abandonment. A disorganized teacher whose actions reveal that he or she has given little thought to how paraprofessionals are to serve confuses and discourages those who seek to help. Perhaps the best way of looking at effective ways in which a teacher can help to develop and encourage a teacher assistant or a volunteer is through the eyes of those who work in paraprofessional roles. Exhibit 11–4 presents just such a perspective in a sensitive but strongly worded message from a practicing teacher assistant to teachers generally.

Making Sufficient Planning Time Available

The teacher assistant who provided the message for Exhibit 11–4 wrote about the implications of the teacher's planning (or failure to plan) on the motivation of assistants. Another facet of paraprofessional motivation and effectiveness comes from the teacher and the teacher assistant (or the volunteer) spending some time together to plan. Many federally funded programs in the 1960s and 1970s allowed for whole days for teachers and teacher assistants to plan together each week. Money was available for regular evaluation and planning sessions. Few programs

◆ ◆ ◆

EXHIBIT 11–4

Advice from a Paraprofessional to Teachers

Note: The comments that follow were written by an experienced teacher assistant. She has worked with a number of different teachers and has strong feelings about teacher actions that made her work effective and rewarding and those that interfered with her own effectiveness.

Treating your assistants as if they have no common sense will get you little help. Most aides are more intelligent than they are given credit for. Don't give them only menial chores, but also things that are more gratifying. Give them air to breathe and expand themselves and they will be more help to you as the teacher than you can imagine. One time I worked for a teacher just 1 day a week. Often when I came she said, "Oh! Are you here today? I didn't know you came this week." Really made me feel welcome and useful. Sometimes she just said, "I don't have anything for you to do today. Go see if any of the other teachers have something for you to do." So, planning ahead is important. Teachers complain of "having too much to do," and then they don't make good use of the assistant's time because they didn't plan.

Treat your assistant as an intelligent person. Aides can do much more than set up snacks and wash dirty faces. If you tell them what to do and why and then show them how, they can be really good teachers. Don't expect them to plan the lessons, but with a little help, they can teach little children very effectively. Answer all questions as soon as possible, and answer them as you would any other adult. Don't "talk down" to them. Your college degree doesn't give you the right to belittle their ability to understand. Tell why you do something, and if they don't understand the first time, tell them again in another way. Show them how to do something the right way yourself. Don't just tell them and leave.

Compliment your assistant sometimes, but not too much. Too much flattery is insulting. But a genuine "I like the way you showed Susie how to button her coat" helps to make it all worthwhile.

Let your assistants learn from their mistakes. Don't "catch them" every time. Just look the other way for a while. Give them a chance to change by themselves. But if they are really doing something wrong, or they are stuck in the same way, suggest, "Sometimes it helps to do it this way." And then show them or tell them again.

Never embarrass them in front of the children or parents, or anybody for that matter. If you must correct them, wait until you can do it when you are alone. Smart teachers know how to make suggestions look and sound like compliments. "You really are teaching Tommy how to wash his hands. Do you think he is ready to learn to use the brush?" is a lot better than "Don't you remember, I told you that you should teach the children to brush their fingernails when they wash their hands."

Listen to the assistants' comments. Let them have the satisfaction of suggesting things to you sometimes. An occasional "Oh, I'm so glad you suggested that" is better than a hundred insincere things. Ask your aides' opinions sometimes, and then listen.

Do remember, you are the teacher. You are responsible. You are in charge. Assistants need to know "their teacher" knows what to do. They need to respect all that education you've had. Give them a chance.

by Robbie Crane
Alton, Illinois

today include this necessity. Conversely, time for planning often seems a luxury.

As with everything else, teachers must do what they can. Day-to-day planning usually fits into very small time segments. The time after school, lunch periods, and so-called "breaks" become the scarce moments for planning. These daily time constraints make it necessary for the teacher to do overall planning before the school year begins. Necessary planning before the school year starts includes designing record-keeping systems, choosing basic activity plans, organizing the classroom, scheduling activities, preparing materials, and assigning responsibilities. The paraprofessional must learn how to use the instructional equipment and what to do in case of various emergencies. The paraprofessional's responsibilities within the daily schedule should be written out. There is rarely enough time before and after school for such comprehensive planning, no matter how dedicated the teacher and the teacher assistant may be.

Over time, however, teacher assistants and even volunteers should be encouraged to plan some of the specific activities. The teacher identifies the goals and objectives, but the "equivalent practice" (Chapter 6) can be suggested by paraprofessionals. For example, one teacher assistant raised tropical fish. With her help, the children planned an aquarium. They learned colors as they chose the stones for the bottom. They discovered water temperature as they planned for the fish. Feeding the fish developed measuring skills and a sense of responsibility.

During the months that the aquarium served as an excellent teaching tool, the teacher and the teacher assistant discussed many different ways in which it could be used. More than half of the excellent teaching ideas that evolved originated with the teacher assistant. The teacher continued to pinpoint specific objectives that could be achieved, but it was uniquely successful because of the teacher assistant's knowledge and enthusiasm to take charge of this project.

Planning sessions need not be overly drawn out. At times they focus on preparing for the next day's events for only one or two children. An example of an effective, brief planning session is presented in Exhibit 11–5. This scene also shows how a teacher can provide effective feedback in a helpful but non-threatening manner.

Providing Constructive Feedback

Just as routine planning time boosts effectiveness, so also does regular and constructive feedback from teacher to paraprofessional. The teacher must build in feedback about how the teacher assistant or volunteer is doing. Informal feedback should not be the occasion for a great deal of discussion. It should be specific, clearly stated, and timely. The teacher should identify strengths, behaviors, and attitudes to be changed or developed. The more straightforward the evaluation, the more effective it will be.

Avoid focusing on personalities. Focus on the task behaviors and the procedures that are changeable. For example, telling the teacher assistant that he or she is disorganized is not helpful. Explaining why the crayons and scissors should be placed within the reach of each child instead of at the end of the table, however, will help him or her to understand precisely how to become more organized and efficient. The teacher should discuss why specific things are important. If necessary, he or she should reteach and demonstrate again. It is especially important for the teacher to evaluate and provide suggestions to the teacher assistant with no other adults or children present or within hearing distance. The teacher's intent is to support and develop the teacher assistant's skills, not to undermine needed authority.

It is important not to exaggerate the negative effects of whatever the teacher assistant is doing wrong. Rather, state what is wanted, why it is desirable, and how it is to be achieved.

The teacher should not forget to reward effort and abilities as part of success. Things that are easy for the teacher may be difficult for an inexperienced teacher assistant. The teacher should not expect everything to be learned at once! Time is needed for practice. Recognition by way of "thank yous" for regular role-appropriate behaviors is as important as special rewards for exceptional success. But such spontaneous or informal feedback opportunities do not eliminate the need for periodic formal evaluation of paraprofessional behaviors, especially for teacher assistants.

Using a Paraprofessional as a One-to-one Assistant

Increasingly, and especially in inclusive settings, paraprofessionals are being used as one-to-one assistants. They are sometimes referred to as a "shadow side."

◆ ◆ ◆

EXHIBIT 11–5

A Teacher-Paraprofessional Planning Session

The Scene: It is after school. The children have gone home. Ms. McLynn and her teacher assistant, Ms. Robbie, are talking about an activity Ms. Robbie just completed.

Ms. Robbie: We were doing the activity from the kit that you had in the plan. The directions said that we should sit in a circle. Then, each child was supposed to roll the ball to a child of his or her choice and say "I'm rolling the ball to _____" and name the child. But Danny and Terry couldn't do it at all.

Ms. McLynn: Did the others understand?

Ms. Robbie: Most of them did. Some just said, "to Susie," but Danny just threw the ball and Terry wouldn't even do that.

Ms. McLynn: What do you think would have made the activity better?

Ms. Robbie: I'm not sure what the point of that activity is. It didn't give a reason for doing it, so I wasn't sure what to emphasize.

Ms. McLynn: Just enjoying an activity is important. Did they seem to like it?

Ms. Robbie: Terry and Danny just seemed confused by the whole thing. When I tried to make them say the whole sentence Danny just got mad and wouldn't do anything. Terry started to cry.

Ms. McLynn: That really wasn't much fun for you either. And activities are usually enjoyed by all when you teach the children. For now, let's just expect that Danny and Terry are learning by being there and watching the others and hearing them. Probably both of them will learn more than we think in that way. Tomorrow, try the activity again with that in mind. When it is Danny's turn, ask him "To whom will you roll the ball?" Do this just before you give him the ball. Gesture with a questioning look and a shrug of your shoulders. Talk to him, too, of course. Expect him to point to a child, and say something. Then you say, "to Jimmy" as a model for him, or name whomever he points to. Again, just before you give him the ball, look expectant, and model "to Jimmy" for him again if necessary. Accept any attempt to say anything now. Later, you can require a better approximation of the speech. Do the same thing for Terry.

Ms. Robbie: What if another child rolls the ball to one of them? Should I take it away from them, and make them listen to me first?

Ms. McLynn: No, but if you have one on each side of you, you could put your hand on the ball while you talk to them. Keep it just as spontaneous and natural as you can. But do contrive it so that they have to say some part of it. As soon as they can do that much, you can make what they say longer—perhaps "rolling to Susie." Part of what they must develop is auditory memory span. Right now, a few sounds are all they can remember. As you play in this way, that skill will grow rapidly.

Ms. Robbie: Okay. I'll try it that way tomorrow.

The assignment of a one-to-one assistant exclusively to a specific child can have definite drawbacks. The early childhood special educator often assumes that the assistant has been well-trained to work with the designated child, when usually this is not the case. Another disadvantage is that the child often becomes very attached to the assistant because of the intensity and exclusivity of the relationship, and may avoid interacting with the children and other adults.

In some situations, such as in the case of a child who is extremely aggressive, self-injurious, or medically fragile and technology dependent, it is necessary to assign a one-to-one assistant, or the child would have to be removed from the program. However, it is important to remember that the use of a one-to-one assistant may be just as restrictive as a segregated special education setting.

In fact, Giangreco, Edelman, Luiselli, and MacFarland, (1997), actually found that the unnecessary proximity of instructional assistants to children with special needs in general education can actually impede the progress of these children. They identified eight areas which of concern related to the "hovering" of instructional assistants. These are: (1) general educators' tendency to avoid assuming responsibility and ownership for the education of students who have one-to-one assistants; (2) the assistant's tendency to separate the child from the rest of the group; (3) prolonged close proximity where assistants prompt excessively fostered dependency of the child on the adult; (4) excessive proximity sometimes interfered with peer interactions; (5) unrealistic instructional expectations or lack of training of the assistants led to inadequate academic instruction of the children under their care; (6) students who had difficulty communicating often found their assistant speaking and making decisions for them; (7) The student's gender became secondary to that of the assistant in such matters as toileting; and (8) sometimes, the assistant's behavior was a distraction during large group discussions.

Even though this significant research involved older children, the results do present many cautions for early childhood special educators. The authors made several recommendations, including that the growing tendency to assign one-to-one assistants be reconsidered. Instead, assistants could be hired for whole groups of children. They urged the development of definite guidelines to ensure the fading of prompts, the use of natural supports such as peer support, awareness of the potential harmful effects of excessive proximity, clarification of role responsibilities, and additional training of both the paraprofessional and his or her supervisor.

Additional guidelines for effective use of one-to-one assistants include the following:

- Clearly define the purpose of the one-to-one assistant.
- Put the specific daily responsibilities and activities of the assistant in writing.
- In consultation with parents, gradually decrease the intensity and proximity of the assistant.
- Gradually have the assistant move further and further away from the child.
- Gradually include more and more children in the target child's space.
- Whenever possible, view the one-to-one assistant as a temporary assignment.
- DO NOT assume the child's needs are being met and, thus, reduce your own interaction with the child.
- Encourage the child's attachment to other staff.
- DO NOT allow the assistant to become a constant barrier/buffer between the child and his or her environment.

EVALUATING PARAPROFESSIONAL SERVICES

Evaluating paraprofessional services is a critical step in developing improved and successful programs for young children. Informal daily feedback helps create an atmosphere in which the paraprofessional feels secure, worthy, appreciated, and professional. But more formal periodic evaluations are helpful for persons whose service is expected to be ongoing. Formal evaluations not only help personnel development but also can strengthen program development.

Typically, the first evaluation is not too long after initial employment to focus on and correct misunderstandings and confused expectations. (It may be helpful to begin with a 1-month probationary period. This, of course, can be extended or dropped, depending on the results of this initial evaluation.) Such a clarification serves the interests of both parties because an effective evaluation acknowledges that the

---

Successful Use of a One-on-one Assistant

James was a 30-month-old child with Down Syndrome. Meal times were very challenging for James because of frequent choking. He was also occasionally aggressive toward other children. He was fully included in a large day-care setting, and both his mother and teacher were concerned that the staff ratio and skill level did not provide adequate support for him in this environment. The decision was made to employ a one-to-one assistant for James. Initially, there were problems because the one-to-one assistant hovered over him every moment, even though he only had choking episodes when eating, and his aggressive behavior was unpredictable.

In a team meeting including the mother and the assistant, it was decided that the only time close proximity of the assistant was necessary was at meal times. A careful functional behavioral analysis revealed that the aggressive behavior only occurred when other children were crowding James. Rather than shadowing the child all day, the assistant simply watched for and managed those situations that typically triggered the aggressive behaviors.

Within 6 months, James was no longer choking, and the staff had learned how to prevent aggressive behavior. At this time, the use of the assistant was terminated.

---

teacher, as well as the paraprofessional, can learn from the experience. The time between subsequent evaluations is lengthened to 3 or 4 months. For an experienced teacher assistant, once a year may be adequate.

Using Self-Evaluations

One formal technique is to allow paraprofessionals the opportunity to evaluate their own contributions and feelings. If the paraprofessional feels comfortable in sharing this self-evaluation with the supervising teacher, chances for growth and development can be enhanced. Perceptions of self-performance are tested against the teacher's observations and expectations. The teacher has the opportunity to provide constructive feedback, to offer encouragement, and to coach. The self-evaluation process may be open-ended, or it may be guided by a checklist such as the one illustrated in Figure 11–5.

As noted in the directions in Figure 11–5, using recent critical incidents is typically a practical technique for clarifying role behaviors and learning. By contrasting a successful event with a not-so-successful one, a problem-solving approach can emphasize conditions necessary for future success rather than belabor criticism of a past problem. When a teacher assistant or volunteer has not been doing something believed necessary (e.g., has failed to listen to children), the teacher can probe the consequences of such behav-

ior. The teacher should be prepared to provide an example of when such a failure or neglect led to an inappropriate consequence. Then both the teacher and the teacher assistant should work toward a plan of action for reducing the frequency of the undesirable behavior.

Teacher-Initiated Evaluations of Assistants

Teacher-initiated evaluations of assistants are necessary because some people see their own behaviors in a more positive light than do others. Thus the self-evaluation conference potentially must deal with distortions in perception between the teacher assistant and the teacher. As long as the primary reason for evaluation is personal and team improvement, however, the dangers of conflict due to differing perceptions are reduced. An evaluation initiated by the teacher overcomes the potential clash between views, especially when the teacher uses a form or checklist. However, teacher-initiated evaluation can generate anxiety and defensiveness on the part of the person being evaluated. Success in either case hinges on the manner in which the teacher handles the conference.

It is better for the teacher to focus on specific generalities such as dependability or interpersonal relations. To do this effectively, the teacher needs to take the time to describe specific behaviors of the

Check the appropriate box for each question as it applies to you. On the back of this page, note briefly two examples (contrasting if possible) of recent experiences for each question.

HOW OFTEN DO I . . .	Usually	Some-times	Seldom
1. Follow directions of the classroom teacher?	[ ]	[ ]	[ ]
2. Observe closely techniques used by the teacher and put them into pratice when working with children and groups?	[ ]	[ ]	[ ]
3. Offer my services to the teacher when there is an apparent need for help?	[ ]	[ ]	[ ]
4. Plan for assigned tasks with children rather than wing it on a hit-or-miss basis?	[ ]	[ ]	[ ]
5. Observe closely to realize individual children's likes, dislikes, interests, and limitations?	[ ]	[ ]	[ ]
6. Allow children time to think and act on their own before giving directive help?	[ ]	[ ]	[ ]
7. Find opportunities for giving children choices in daily activities?	[ ]	[ ]	[ ]
8. Really listen to what children have to say?	[ ]	[ ]	[ ]
9. Acknowledge children's successes and appropriate behaviors and minimize failures or inappropriate behaviors?	[ ]	[ ]	[ ]
10. Accept suggestions and criticisms without becoming emotionally upset?	[ ]	[ ]	[ ]

Figure 11–5 Self-evaluation worksheet for paraprofessionals.

teacher assistant that are helping and hindering performance effectiveness. An easy technique for organizing a face-to-face evaluation conference is for the teacher to list a select few behavioral descriptions under the following three focal areas (adapted from Harrison, 1978):

1. If you would increase or do more often the following things, they would help your performance.

2. If you would decrease or stop doing these things, your performance would be better.

3. To help maintain good performance, keep doing these things much the same as you have been doing.

The teacher and the teacher assistant then discuss each of the behaviors to be increased, decreased, or maintained. Specific incidents are used to interpret and demonstrate why the change (or maintenance) would be helpful. The lists for each category should not be too long. The objective is to identify a few important behaviors that conceivably could be changed with concentrated effort. The teacher encourages commitment to some plan of action for changing, but improvement of the assistant's performance may mean that the teacher has to change also if he or she is part of the cause of the problem.

The key to a meaningful evaluation is not what is written, but the discussion of the recorded comments between the teacher and the teacher assistant. The conference is the basis for developing objectives or intended targets of change (and behavior maintenance) in the future. In a "management by objectives" fashion, any objectives and action plans agreed on by the teacher and the teacher assistant can be briefly written, dated, and signed by both (Dyer, Daines, & Giauque, 1990). Each subsequent review considers progress toward attaining the previously formulated objectives. Collectively, these periodic evaluations are the basis for the year-end evaluation required for teacher assistants in most school districts. As a psychological benefit, however, the periodic conferences reduce the chances that the teacher will take the teacher assistant for granted, and they encourage professional-like involvement.

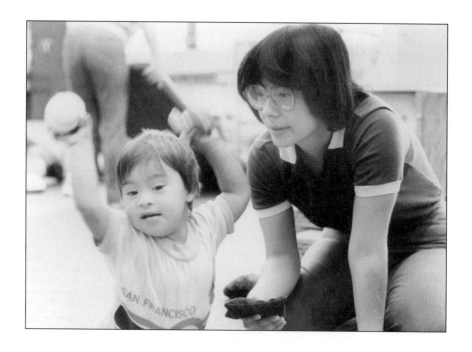

Evaluation of the Teacher by the Assistant

Teachers who are dedicated to developing an effective use of paraprofessional services find it valuable to evaluate themselves as responsible models of instructional excellence and supervisors of paraprofessionals. If teachers and the paraprofessionals have developed a relationship of trust and professionalism, teachers can gain much from the paraprofessionals' evaluative feedback. Teachers need to know when their directions are not clear, when they are expecting too much, and when they have been unappreciative or unresponsive. Most teachers do not wish to be negative or ineffective. They are human, however, and do err from time to time. Everyone will benefit if a two-way communication of constructive feedback and positive reinforcement is in effect.

Since the objective of an assistant's evaluation of the teacher is to improve their role relationship and team performance, the process needs to be kept simple. Teacher assistants need to be given an opportunity to capture their thoughts on paper, however, before any face-to-face meeting. This provides the teacher assistant the security of having reflected on and organized thoughts about the quality of the role relationship. A time should be scheduled and the teacher assistant should be requested to bring in some written comments or feedback. A most effective way of promoting such preparation is to use a simple three-part variation of the technique mentioned in the previous section. Such an evaluation form is presented in Figure 11-6.

If the teacher and the teacher assistant both use a variation of the same three "increase, decrease, or continue" role behavior issues, the process is enhanced. The simplicity of this single-page sheet enables the teacher and the teacher assistant to think in parallel terms, considering what each of them can do to help the other so they both benefit. The concept of increasing, decreasing, or maintaining certain behaviors is easily understood. Not using scales, scores, or rating points reduces the defensiveness or anxiety of either party. The conference focuses on the three levels, inviting objectives and strategies for dealing with the specific identified behaviors. With mutual evaluations, everyone can learn and grow.

RECOGNIZING AND REWARDING TIME AND SERVICE

The importance of daily recognition and praise for time and service cannot be overstressed. Teachers must be careful, however, to be sincere and specific in the comments they make. Each time a teacher assistant or a volunteer is told specifically what was helpful, he or she is able to clarify future behavior expectations. Consider the difference between the following two statements:

1. "Ms. Jones, I really appreciated your willingness to help today."
2. "Ms. Jones, I really appreciated your quick response and willingness to help the children clean up the spilled paint. If it had been left on the floor 1 minute longer, two or three children would have walked through it and we would really have had a mess."

Whereas the first comment was obviously positive, it did not tell the teacher assistant exactly what was particularly appreciated. The second comment was not only positive but it conveyed to the teacher assistant the importance of quick, preventive action. It also helped the teacher assistant to know that the teacher is actually observing and really does feel responsible.

Besides daily recognition, paraprofessionals need and deserve some form of more public, tangible recognition and reward. This is especially true of nonpaid volunteers. Many schools choose to publicly honor volunteers at school assemblies, at Parent-Teacher Organization meetings, and at specially planned dinners or coffees. A certificate of recognition is often awarded (Figure 11-7). It is not necessary for the teacher to purchase commercially made certificates. The certificates can be made on a computer by teachers or designed by art teachers, or the children themselves.

Names of volunteers and the nature of their service can be listed in the local newspaper or center

A TECHNIQUE FOR AN AIDE'S EVALUATION OF TEACHER

To (Teacher): _____

From (Aide): _____

Date: _____

1. You could help my performance and our team effort if you would increase or do more often the following things:

2. I could do a better job of helping you if you would decrease or stop doing these things:

3. To help maintain good performance, keep doing these things much the same as you have been doing:

Figure 11–6 Technique for an assistant's evaluation of the teacher.

Thank you for being a
LeClaire School Parent Volunteer
and serving the children........

......'N TRUE LOVE.*

Parent Volunteers are a very special breed,
They come forward when there's an urgent need.

No matter what the task or chore,
They're always there to do a little more.

Volunteers add that important extra touch,
That to us all means so very much.

No matter what or which endeavor,
LeClaire School Volunteers should
live on forever!

*(The title of this poem was made
from the letters of the word
"Volunteer")

Figure 11–7 Example of a parent volunteer "certificate." (Poem by Bettie Duncan, LeClaire School, Edwardsville, IL) newsletter. Personal letters from the teacher, director, or school superintendent are always welcome. One early childhood center hosts a special potluck dinner for the staff members and the volunteers once or twice a year. These are festive occasions in which everyone anticipates with pleasure. One elementary school features a "Volunteer of the Week" bulletin board to recognize the contribution of a particular volunteer. Of course, permission of the volunteer is obtained first. Another school provides tickets to special performances at the local theater in an effort to say "thank you." The possibilities for volunteer recognition are limited only by imagination and resources.

PREVENTING BURNOUT AMONG PARAPROFESSIONALS

The tendency toward extreme disillusionment with one's job—professional burnout—is common among paraprofessionals. Frith and Mims (1985) outline several reasons for disillusionment, including the following:

1. Stagnation due to lack of opportunity for professional advancement.

2. Inadequate training, which keeps some paraprofessionals from actively becoming involved in the professional team.

3. Poor organizational structure due to undefined role descriptions and unclear understanding of lines of authority.

4. Poor salaries for those who do not have the opportunity to climb a career ladder.

5. Lack of recognition when highly competent paraprofessionals are a threat to those in a position of supervisory responsibility. (pp. 225–227)

Even though teachers may not be in a position to implement a career ladder, they can provide opportunities for paraprofessionals to feel valued and needed. We have discussed the importance of clear job descriptions, the need to discover and incorporate special skills and talents to help the paraprofessional feel like a contributing member of the team, and some helpful ways to show appreciation. Even these basic strategies will go a long way toward preventing burnout for those paraprofessionals who have become creditable members of early education teams.

Summary

Paraprofessionals are potentially valuable resources for extending the teacher's care and development of young children. The extent to which this potential is realized depends primarily on how the teacher prepares for and develops a working relationship with paraprofessionals.

To initiate a planned program of using paraprofessionals, it is necessary to design the jobs that assistants and volunteers can do. But job design should not be aimed merely at enabling the teacher to eliminate routine or unpleasant tasks. The teacher should remember that effectiveness also involves motivation. Since paraprofessionals work more because of a desire to help young children than for tangible rewards, the jobs they are expected to do should allow for the growth of their abilities. Feelings of competency and learning reinforce paraprofessionals' motivational desires to work thoughtfully with children and to perform other tasks.

The jobs performed by paraprofessionals typically require relationships with either the children or the adult members of the educational team. The teacher should plan the nature of these role relationships so that all participants are behaving appropriately given a common philosophy and a common set of expectations. Guidelines for the ways volunteers and teacher assistants are to interact with children should even be formalized in writing.

The following are several advantages to having such job descriptions and policy guidelines in writing and available as handouts:

1. They help in recruiting and selecting paraprofessionals by giving a focused idea of the nature of the work and the working environment.

2. The orientation is focused on those attributes that are important to the teacher and the program.

3. Expectations are clarified and made public to minimize future misunderstandings.

4. They can be a basis for feedback and evaluation about how appropriately the teacher assistant or volunteer is acting in relation to the needs and standards of the teacher.

As a leader, the teacher is a role model for paraprofessionals, especially in helping them to understand how to work with the children. The degree and quality of preparation for using the time and talents of paraprofessionals set the stage for appropriate behaviors. If the teacher fails to plan how to use a teacher assistant's or volunteer's time, paraprofessionals can assume that planning is not a quality necessary for early intervention; that their job is basically babysitting; and that if learning should happen to occur, well, then that is also all right.

If the teacher has planned and organized the tasks of paraprofessionals and clarified the ways of working within the program, then feedback and evaluation can be a natural part of the experience. Rather than functioning as a punishment or as a "here is what you have been doing wrong" response, frequent feedback and periodic evaluations should be a time for personal development and for strengthening team relationships. Performance evaluation does not have to be a one-way street or something the teacher inflicts on the teacher assistant or the volunteer. Quite the contrary, effective teachers will invite teacher assistants to evaluate them. After all, the common goal is to discover ways of improving what happens in the classroom and on the playground. If this means the teacher makes some changes in his or her ways of working with paraprofessionals (e.g., being less critical or giving more autonomy), both the teacher and the paraprofessional are probably better off for the change.

Similarly, teacher assistants and volunteers need to be recognized for what they contribute. This extends to formal recognition at year's end and at well-spaced times throughout the year. Teacher recognition of paraprofessionals is a way of saying, "Thanks for making my job easier and more successful."

Discussion Topics and Activities

1. Role play an interview with a prospective assistant. Be alert to questions that help you get to know something about the individual's talents, skills, interests, motives, and biases. Think ahead and be prepared to be explicit about what you will want the teacher assistant to do or not do. Observers may give constructive feedback to the participants by sharing their reactions and what they learned from watching the interaction.

2. Gather or prepare useful techniques for evaluating the success of a paraprofessional program. Refer to Figure 11–5 for suggestions. Check to see that your evaluation elements match the jobs you have designed.

3. Prepare a recruitment letter and an accompanying interest inventory. Discuss with classmates how these can be used effectively. Try your ideas out on public school personnel who are familiar with or merely interested in paraprofessional services.

4. Prepare an agenda for a volunteer orientation meeting. Take turns role playing various stages of the meeting. Discuss how you would make individuals feel welcome, the "musts" you will cover, and techniques for developing commitments on the part of the participants. Be alert to a tendency to be too technical in your language.

5. Write a paraprofessional's job description. Give specific examples of tasks that are consistent with your philosophy and that of your program. Ask another classmate to check the job description for clarity and adherence to program guidelines.

Annotated Bibliography

Baird, S. (1994). *Preparing paraprofessional early interventionists.* San Antonio, TX: The Psychological Corporation.

This is a curriculum designed to train paraprofessionals to serve infants, toddlers and their families in home-based settings. Included are seven reproducible study modules, a trainer's manual, and a video with short vignettes. The modules focus on policies, social support, effective communication, principles of adult learning, infant-parent interaction, and the family adjustment process.

Blalock, G. (1991). Paraprofessionals: Critical team members in our special education programs. *Intervention in School and Clinic, 26,* 200-214.

This comprehensive article addresses the question, What should we be doing to ensure that the utilization of paraprofessionals is as fully effective as individuals with disabilities deserve? It outlines numerous steps that can be readily implemented to guarantee that learning takes place and paraprofessionals are effectively involved.

Courson, F. H., & Heward, W. L. (1989). Using senior citizen volunteers in special education classrooms. *Academic Therapy, 24,* 525-532.

This article provides suggestions for recruiting, training, using, scheduling, and retaining senior citizen volunteers in special education settings.

Doyle, M. B. (1997). *The paraprofessional's guide to the inclusive classroom.* Baltimore, MD: Paul H. Brookes.

This innovative handbook focuses on the many roles and increasing responsibilities of paraprofessionals in inclusive classrooms. It is jargon-free and offers basic, practical guidance on issues such as communicating with teachers and other team members, reading and using IEPs, maintaining confidentiality, and fostering student independence. Interactive follow-up activities enable administrators to easily introduce inclusion practices, orient new team members, and design appropriate instructional programs.

Frank, A. R., Keith, T. Z., & Steil, D. A. (1988). Training needs of special education paraprofessionals. *Exceptional Children, 55,* 253-258.

In surveying 245 special education teacher/paraprofessional pairs, these researchers found that teachers viewed clerical and supervision skills as more important than other paraprofessional skills. While teachers and paraprofessionals tended to agree in their ratings of the importance of various skills, it was evident that the skills needed depended on the type of educational setting.

Frith, G. H., & Mims, A. (1985). Burnout among special education paraprofessionals. Teaching *Exceptional Children, 17,* 225-227.

This brief article is a welcome addition to the sparse literature devoted to the needs of paraprofessionals. The problem of burnout occurs throughout the field of education and especially among those who work with children who have severe disabilities. Frith and Mims offer keen insight into the variables influencing burnout and offer useful ideas on its prevention.

Gartner, A., & Pickett, A. L. (1988). *A comprehensive program of technical assistance to prepare administrators and staff developers to improve the performance and training of paraprofessionals.* New York: City University of New York. Contact the National Resource Center for Professionals in Special Education, Center for Advanced Study in Education, New Careers Training Laboratory, 33 West 42nd Street, New York, NY 10032.

This project offers guidelines and materials to more fully integrate paraprofessional personnel into special education programs. Suggestions for structuring personnel practices and training programs to improve the performance and management of paraprofessionals are included along with five competence-based instructional training modules involving specific activities and handouts.

Jimenez, B. C., & Iseyama, D. A. (1987). A model for training and using communication assistants. *Language, Speech, and Hearing Services in Schools, 18,* 168-171.

A four-phase model for training communication assistants to provide speech and language services in a Head Start center is presented.

Jones, K. H., & Bender, W. N. (1993). Utilization of paraprofessionals in special education: A review of the literature. *Remedial and Special Education, 14(1),* 7-14.

This review attests to the phenomenal growth in utilization of paraprofessionals in special education and indicates a need for additional information on this use. Included is a review of the efficacy literature, professional educators' attitudes toward use of paraprofessionals, and information available on training models.

Krupicka, W. M., & Fimian, M. J. (1987). Using the microcomputer to match special education teacher needs with volunteer interests. *Journal of Special Education Technology, 9(1),* 30-37.

This article describes a user-friendly "index card" software resource that was developed to help local and district school personnel match identified special education classroom needs with volunteer resources.

McKenzie, R., & Houk, C. S. (1986). The paraprofessional in special education. *Teaching Exceptional Children, 18,* 246–252.

This article outlines a four-step placement process that allows the following three goals to be accomplished: (1) determination of suitable and unsuitable teacher-paraprofessional teams; (2) development of clearly stated job descriptions; and (3) identification of areas in which the paraprofessional may require further training.

Pickett, A. L. (1986). *A training program to prepare teachers to supervise and work more effectively with paraprofessional personnel.* New York: City University of New York. Contact the Center for Advanced Study in Education, 33 West 42nd Street, New York, NY 10036.

The eight training modules include management and supervision; the instructional team of teacher and paraprofessional; setting goals and objectives for integrating the paraprofessional into the classroom; directing and delegating; interpersonal problem solving; communication and team building; evaluating paraprofessional performance; and helping teacher participants develop a personalized plan for changing and improving their management skills.

Pickett, A. L. (1988). *Paraprofessional bibliography: Training materials and resources for paraprofessionals working in programs for people with disabilities.* New York: City University of New York. Contact The Center for Advanced Study in Education, 33 West 42nd Street, New York, NY 10036.

This annotated bibliography serves as a resource for strengthening and developing systematic training programs for paraprofessional staff. Included are entries on instructional materials, films, and videotapes, as well as items from professional journals, books, and doctoral dissertations on topics ranging from the impact of paraprofessionals on the quality of service delivery, to burnout, career development and advancement, and personnel practices.

Pickett, A. L., & Gerlach, K. (1997). *Supervising paraeducators in school settings.* Austin, TX: Pro-Ed.

The purpose of this manuscript is to prepare teachers, related services personnel, and administrators to work effectively with paraprofessionals. It provides guidelines and methods related to topics such as team building, team roles, management, professional and ethical responsibilities, and administrative issues. As the role of a paraeducator is ever expanding, this is a much needed resource.

Skelton, K. (1998). *Paraprofessionals in education.* Albany, NY: Delmar Publishers.

This book is written for the aspiring paraprofessional. It focuses on how to become an effective team member. Included are hints on job-seeking, daily routines, legal issues, general child development, classroom management and organization. Of significant value are ideas on how to get started, jobs descriptions, and specific suggestions for working and playing with infants, toddlers, and preschoolers.

References

Blalock, G. (1991). Paraprofessionals: Critical team members in our special education programs. *Intervention in School and Clinic, 26,* 200–214.

Boomer, L. W. (1981). Meeting common goals through effective teacher-paraprofessional communication. *Teaching Exceptional Children, 13,* 51–53.

Coffey, R. E., Cook, C. W., & Hunsaker, P. L. (1994). *Management and organizational behavior.* Burr Ridge, IL: Irwin.

Dyer, W., Daines, R., & Giauque, W. (1990). *The challenge of management.* San Diego, CA: Harcourt Brace Jovanovich.

Frith, G. H., & Mims, A. (1985). Burnout among special education paraprofessionals. *Teaching Exceptional Children, 17,* 225–227.

Giangreco, M. F., Edelman, S. W., Luiselli, T. E., & MacFarland, S. Z. (1997). Helping or hovering? Effects of instructional assistant proximity on students with disabilities. *Exceptional Children, 64*(1), 7–18.

Hanson, M. J., & Lynch, E. W. (1995). *Early intervention: Implementing child and family services for infants and toddlers who are at-risk or disabled.* Austin, TX: Pro-Ed.

Harrison, R. (1978). When power conflicts trigger team spirit. In W. L. French, C. H. Bell, Jr., & R. A. Zawacki (Eds.), *Organization development.* Dallas: Business Publications.

Homans, G. C. (1950, 1992). *The human group.* New York: Transaction Publishers.

Jones, K. H., & Bender, W. N. (1993). Utilization of paraprofessionals in special education: A review of the literature. *Remedial and Special Education, 14*(1), 7–14.

Karnes, M. B., & Lee, R. C. (1978). *Early childhood.* Reston, VA: The Council for Exceptional Children.

Kelly, C. M. (1983). Remedial MBO. *Business Horizons, 26,* 64–65.

Krupicka, W. M., & Fimian, M. J. (1987). Using the microcomputer to match special education teacher needs with volunteer interests. *Journal of Special Education Technology, 9(1),* 30–37.

Lindeman, D. P., & Beegle, G. P. (1988). Preservice teacher training and use of the classroom paraprofessional: A national survey. *Teacher Education and Special Education, 11*(4), 183–186.

McKenzie, R., & Houk, C. S. (1986). The paraprofessional in special education. *Teaching Exceptional Children, 18,* 246–252.

Pickett, A. L., & Gerlach, K. (Eds.). (1997). *Supervising paraeducators in school settings.* Austin, TX: Pro-Ed.

Striffler, N. (1993). Current trends in the use of paraprofessionals in early intervention and preschool services. *NEC*TAS Synthesis Report,* Chapel Hill, NC: National Early Childhood Technical Assistance System.

Appendix A

Chart of Typical Development*

	Gross Motor Skills	Fine Motor Skills	Language Comprehension	Expressive Communication
0–3 Months	Holds head up in prone position. Lifts head when held at shoulder. Kicks reciprocally. Rolls from side to supine position.	Moves arms symmetrically. Follows with eyes to midline. Brings hands to midline in supine position. Activates arms on sight of toy.	Responds to voice. Watches speaker's eyes and mouth. Searches with eyes for sound.	Cries when hungry or uncomfortable. Makes comfort sounds.
3–6 Months	Holds head in line with body when pulled to sitting. Bears weight on hands in prone position. Sits with light support. Holds head steady in supported sitting position. Rolls from supine position to side.	Follows with eyes without moving head. Keeps hands open most of time. Uses palmar grasp. Reaches and grasps objects.	Quiets to mother's voice. Distinguishes between friendly and angry voices. Responds to own name.	Coos variety of vowel sounds. Laughs. Takes turns. Responds to speech by vocalizing. Expresses displeasure and excitement.
6–9 Months	Exhibits body-righting reaction. Extends arms protectively.	Transfers object. Manipulates toy actively with wrist movement.	Looks at pictures briefly. Looks for family members or pets when named.	Babbles to people. Produces variety of consonants in babbling.

*Adapted from the following sources:

CRC Education and Human Development, Inc. for the Administration for Children, Youth and Families. (1978). Mainstreaming preschoolers. U.S. Government Printing Office, 1979620-182/5708

Furuno, S., O'Reilly, K. A., Hosaka, C. M., Inatsuka, T. T., Allman, T. L., & Zeisloft, B. (1985). *HELP Hawaii Early Learning Profile activity guide.* Palo Alto, CA: VORT.

Help for special preschoolers assessment checklist. (1987). Palo Alto, CA: VORT.

Cognitive Skills	Self-Help Skills	Social Skills
Inspects surroundings. Shows anticipation. Inspects own hands.	Opens mouth in response to food stimulus. Coordinates sucking, swallowing, and breathing.	Regards face. Enjoys physical contact; molds, relaxes body when held. Makes eye contact. Expresses distress.
Begins rattle play. Repeats/continues familiar activity. Uses hands and mouth for sensory exploration of objects. Plays with own hands, fingers, toes.	Brings hand to mouth holding toy or object. Swallows strained or pureed foods. Inhibits rooting reflex.	Smiles socially. Discriminates strangers. Demands attention. Vocalizes pleasure or displeasure. Enjoys social play, e.g., "This Little Piggy." Lifts arms to mother.
Works to obtain desired out-of-reach object. Finds object observed being hidden.	Uses tongue to move food in mouth (4–8 months).	Recognizes mother (4–8 months). Displays stranger anxiety.

Johnson-Martin, N., Attermeier, S. M., & Hacker, B. (1990). *The Carolina curriculum for preschoolers with special needs.* Baltimore, MD: Paul H. Brookes.

Johnson-Martin, N., Jens, K. G., & Attermeier, S. M. (1986). *The Carolina curriculum for handicapped infants and infants at risk.* Baltimore, MD: Paul H. Brookes.

Linder, T. W. (1990). *Transdisciplinary play-based assessment: A functional approach to working with young children.* Baltimore, MD: Paul H. Brookes.

	Gross Motor Skills	Fine Motor Skills	Language Comprehension	Expressive Communication
6–9 Months *(Continued)*	Sits independently, but may use hands. Stands holding on. Pulls to stand. Crawls backward. Gets into sitting position without assistance.	Reaches and grasps with extended elbow.	Responds to simple requests with gesture.	Babbles with adult inflection. Babbles reduplicated syllables, "mama," "baba," etc. Vocalizes loudly to get attention.
9–12 Months	Creeps on hands and knees. Moves from sitting to prone position. Stands momentarily. Walks holding on to furniture (cruises).	Takes objects out of container. Uses both hands freely. Tries to imitate scribble. Puts object into container. Releases object voluntarily. Pokes with index finger. Uses neat pincer grasp.	Understands "no no." Listens selectively to familiar words. Enjoys looking at books.	Babbles single consonant-vowel syllables, e.g., "ba." Responds to certain words (e.g., "wave bye bye") with appropriate gesture. Uses behaviors and vocalization to express needs.
12–18 Months	Stands from supine position. Walks without support. Throws ball. Creeps up stairs. Pulls toy while walking. Carries large toy while walking. Moves to music.	Uses two hands in midline, one holding, one manipulating. Scribbles spontaneously. Places pegs in pegboard. Builds two- to three-cube tower.	Responds to simple verbal requests; identifies one body part. Understands many nouns. Brings objects from another room on request.	Combines gestures and vocalizations to express a variety of communicative functions. Says "Dada" or "Mama" purposefully. Uses single words. Uses exclamations, e.g., "Oh, oh!" Says "no" meaningfully. Uses 10–15 words (by 18 months).

Cognitive Skills	Self-Help Skills	Social Skills
Touches adult's hand or toy to restart an activity. Plays 2 to 3 minutes with single toy. Follows trajectory of fast-moving object. Shows interest in sounds of object.	Holds own bottle. Mouths and gums solid foods. Bites voluntarily; inhibits bite reflex. Feeds self a cracker.	Smiles at mirror image. Shows anxiety to separation from mother.
Overcomes obstacle to obtain object. Retrieves object using other material. Imitates gestures. Unwraps a toy. Enjoys looking at books.	Finger feeds variety of foods. Holds spoon. Cooperates with dressing by extending arm or leg. Chews by munching.	Enjoys turn-taking game. Resists supine position. Shows like and dislike for certain people, objects, or situations. Shows toys to others; does not release. Tests parents' reactions at feeding and bedtime by new and mischievous behavior.
Understands adult's pointing. Hands toy back to adult. Matches objects. Places round and square pieces in form board. Nests two or three cans. Identifies self in mirror.	May refuse food; appetite decreases. Brings spoon to mouth. Drinks from cup with some spilling. Indicates discomfort over soiled pants. Removes socks.	Displays independent behavior; may be difficult to discipline. May display tantrum behavior. Demonstrates sense of humor. Is easily distractible; has difficulty sitting still.

	Gross Motor Skills	Fine Motor Skills	Language Comprehension	Expressive Communication
18–24 Months	Moves on "ride-on" toys without pedals. Walks upstairs holding railing, both feet on step. Picks up toy from floor without falling. Runs.	Imitates circular scribble. Imitates horizontal stroke. Holds crayon with fist.	Identifies three to six body parts. Matches sounds to animals. Understands personal pronouns, some action verbs, and some adjectives. Enjoys nursery rhymes.	Uses intelligible words about 65% of the time. May use jargon (syllable strings that sound like speech). Tells experience using jargon and words. Uses two-word sentences. Names two or three pictures. Attempts to sing songs with words. Imitates three- to four-word phrase.
24–36 Months	Runs forward well. Jumps in place, two feet together. Stands on one foot, with aid. Walks on tiptoe. Kicks ball forward.	Strings four large beads. Turns pages singly. Snips with scissors. Holds crayon with thumb and fingers, not fist. Uses one hand consistently in most activities. Paints with some wrist action; makes dots, lines, circular strokes. Rolls, pounds, squeezes, and pulls clay.	Points to pictures of common objects when they are named. Can identify objects when told their use. Understands question forms *what* and *where.* Understands negatives *no, not, can't,* and *don't.* Enjoys listening to simple storybooks and requests them again.	Joins vocabulary words together in two-word phrases. Gives first and last name. Asks *what* and *where* questions. Makes negative statements (e.g., "Can't open it"). Shows frustration at not being understood. Sustains conversation for two or three turns.

Cognitive Skills		Self-Help Skills	Social Skills
Finds object not observed being hidden. Activates mechanical toy. Matches objects to pictures. Sorts objects. Explores cabinets and drawers. Remembers where objects belong. Recognizes self in photo.		Scoops food, feeds self with spoon. Chews with rotary jaw movements. Plays with food. Removes shoe when laces undone. Zips/unzips large zipper. Shows awareness of need to eliminate.	Expresses affection. Expresses wide range of emotions including jealousy, fear, anger, sympathy, embarrassment, anxiety, and joy. Attempts to control others; resists control; peer interaction is somewhat aggressive. Engages in parallel play. Enjoys solitary play occasionally.
Selects and looks at picture books, names pictured objects, and identifies several objects within one picture. Matches and uses associated objects meaningfully (e.g., given cup, saucer, and bead, puts cup and saucer together). Stacks rings on peg in order of size. Uses self and objects in pretend play.	Can talk briefly about what he or she is doing. Imitates adult actions (e.g., housekeeping play). Has limited attention span; learning is through exploration and adult direction (as in reading of picture stories). Is beginning to understand functional concepts of familiar objects (e.g., that a spoon is used for eating) and part/whole concepts (e.g., parts of the body).	Gets drink from fountain or faucet unassisted. Opens door by turning handle. Takes off coat. Puts on coat with assistance. Washes and dries hands with assistance.	Watches other children; joins briefly in their play. Defends own possessions. Begins to play house. Participates in simple group activity (e.g., sings, claps, dances). Knows gender identity.

	Gross Motor Skills	Fine Motor Skills	Language Comprehension	Expressive Communication
36–48 Months	Runs around obstacles. Walks on a line. Balances on one foot for 5 to 10 seconds. Hops on one foot. Pushes, pulls, steers wheeled toys. Rides (i.e., steers and pedals) tricycle. Uses slide without assistance. Jumps over 15 cm. (6 in.) high object, landing on both feet together. Throws ball over head. Catches ball bounced to him or her.	Builds tower of nine small blocks. Drives nails and pegs. Copies circle. Imitates cross. Manipulates clay materials (e.g., rolls balls, snakes, cookies).	Begins to understand sentences involving time concepts (e.g., "We are going to the zoo tomorrow"). Understands size comparatives such as *big* and *bigger*. Understands relationships expressed by *if . . . then* or *because* sentences. Carries out a series of two to four related directions. Understands when told, "Let's pretend."	Talks in sentences of three or more words, which take the form agent-action-object ("I see the ball") or agent-action-location ("Daddy sit on chair"). Tells about past experiences. Uses *s* on nouns to indicate plurals. Uses *ed* on verbs to include past tense. Refers to self using pronouns *I* or *me*. Repeats at least one nursery rhyme and can sing a song. Speech is understandable to strangers, but there are still some sound errors.
48–60 Months	Walks backward toe-heel. Jumps forward 10 times without falling. Walks up and down stairs alone, alternating feet. Turns somersault.	Cuts on line continuously. Copies cross. Copies square. Prints a few capital letters.	Follows three unrelated commands in proper order. Understands comparatives such as *pretty*, *prettier*, and *prettiest*. Listens to long stories, but often misinterprets the facts. Incorporates verbal directions into play activities. *(Continued)*	Asks *when*, *how*, and *why* questions. Uses modals such as *can*, *will*, *shall*, *should*, and *might*. Joins sentences together (e.g., "I went to the store and I bought some ice cream"). Talks about causality by using *because* and *so*. Tells the content of a story but may confuse facts.

Cognitive Skills		Self-Help Skills	Social Skills
Recognizes and matches six colors. Intentionally stacks blocks or rings in order of size. Draws somewhat recognizable picture that is meaningful to child, if not to adult; names and briefly explains picture. Asks questions for information: *why* and *how* questions requiring simple answers. Knows own age. Knows own last name.	Has short attention span; learns through observing and imitating adults, and by adult instruction and explanation; is easily distracted. Has increased understanding of concepts of the functions and grouping of objects (e.g., can put doll house furniture in correct rooms); part/whole (e.g., can identify pictures of hand and foot as parts of body). Begins to be aware of past and present (e.g., "Yesterday we went to the park. Today we go to the library").	Pours well from small pitcher. Spreads soft butter with knife. Buttons and unbuttons large buttons. Washes hands unassisted. Blows nose when reminded. Uses toilet independently.	Joins in play with other children; begins to interact. Shares toys; takes turns with assistance. Begins dramatic play, acting out whole scenes (for example, traveling, playing house, pretending to be animals). Comforts peers in distress.
Points to and names four to six colors. Matches pictures of familiar objects (e.g., shoe, sock, foot, apple, orange, banana). Draws a person with two to six recognizable parts, such as head, arms, legs; can name or match drawn parts to own body. *(Continued)*	Knows own street and town. Has more extended attention span; learns through observing and listening to adults as well as through exploration; is easily distracted. Has increased understanding of concepts of function, time, part/whole relationships. *(Continued)*	Cuts easy foods with a knife (e.g., hamburger patty, tomato slice). Laces shoes.	Plays and interacts with other children. Plays dress-up. Shows interest in exploring sex differences.

	Gross Motor Skills	Fine Motor Skills	Language Comprehension	Expressive Communication
48–60 Months *(Continued)*			Understands sequencing of events when told them (e.g., "First we have to go to the store, then we can make the cake, and tomorrow we will eat it").	
60–72 Months	Runs lightly on toes. Walks on balance beam. Can cover 2 meters ($6\frac{1}{2}$ feet) hopping. Skips on alternate feet. Jumps rope. Skates.	Cuts out simple shapes. Copies triangle. Traces diamond. Copies first name. Prints numerals 1 to 5. Colors within lines. Has adult grasp of pencil. Has handedness well established (i.e., child is left- or right-handed). Pastes and glues appropriately. Uses classroom tools appropriately.	Demonstrates preacademic skills.	There are few obvious differences between child's grammar and adult's grammar. Still needs to learn such things as subject-verb agreement and some irregular past tense verbs. Can take appropriate turns in a conversation. Gives and receives information. Communicates well with family, friends, or strangers. Retells story from picture book with accuracy.

Cognitive Skills		Self-Help Skills	Social Skills
Draws, names, and describes recognizable picture. Rote counts to 5, imitating adults. Describes what will happen next. Dramatic play is closer to reality, with attention paid to detail, time, and space.	Function or use of objects may be stated in addition to names of objects. Time concepts are expanding. The child can talk about yesterday or last week (a long time ago), about today, and about what will happen tomorrow.		
Names some letters and numerals. Rote counts to 10. Sorts objects by single characteristics (e.g., by color, shape, or size—if the difference is obvious). Is beginning to use accurately time concepts of *tomorrow* and *yesterday*.	Begins to relate clock time to daily schedule. Attention span increases noticeably; learns through adult instruction; when interested, can ignore distractions. Concepts of function increase as well as understanding of why things happen; time concepts are expanding into an understanding of the future in terms of major events (e.g., "Christmas will come after two weekends").	Dresses self completely. Ties bow. Brushes teeth unassisted. Crosses street safely.	Chooses own friend(s). Plays simple table games. Plays competitive games. Engages in cooperative play with other children involving group decisions, role assignments, fair play.

Appendix B

◆ ◆ ◆

Find Your Child's Speech
and Hearing Age*

Instructions: Read each question through your child's age group and check yes or no. Add the total and score:

All yes = Good! Your child is developing hearing, speech, and language normally.
1–3 no = Caution! Your child may have delayed hearing, speech, and language development.
More than 3 no = Action! Take your child for professional help.

Check One		Hearing and Understanding	Child's Age	Talking	Check One	
Yes	No				Yes	No
☐	☐	Does your child hear and understand most speech in the home?	*5 years*	Does your child say all sounds correctly except perhaps s and th?	☐	☐
☐	☐	Does your child hear and answer when first called?		Does your child use the same sentence structure as the family?	☐	☐
☐	☐	Does your child hear quiet speech?		Does your child's voice sound clear, like other children's?	☐	☐
☐	☐	Does everyone who knows your child think he or she hears well (teacher, babysitter, grandparent, etc.)?				
☐	☐	Does your child understand conversation easily?	*2½–4 years*	Does your child say most sounds, except perhaps r, s, th, and l?	☐	☐
☐	☐	Does your child hear you when you call from another room?		Does your child sometimes repeat words in a sentence?	☐	☐
☐	☐	Does your child hear television or radio at the same loudness level as other members of the family?		Does your child use 200–300 words?	☐	☐
☐	☐	Does your child understand differences in meaning ("go—stop;" "the car pushed the truck—the truck pushed the car")?		Does your child use two- to three-word sentences?	☐	☐
				Does your child ask lots of "why" and "what" questions?	☐	☐
☐	☐	Can your child point to pictures in a book upon hearing them named?		Have your child's jargon and repeating disappeared?	☐	☐
☐	☐	Does your child notice sounds (dog barking, telephone ringing, television sound, knocking at door and so on)?		Does your child like to name things?	☐	☐

*Adapted from public information materials of the American Speech-Language-Hearing Association. Used with permission.

Check One		Hearing and Understanding	Child's Age	Talking	Check One	
Yes	No				Yes	No
☐	☐	Can your child follow two requests ("Get the ball and put it on the table")?	$1\frac{1}{2}$-2 years	Does your child have 10-15 words (by age 2)?	☐	☐
				Does your child sometimes repeat requests?	☐	☐
				Does your child ask one- to two-word questions ("Where kitty? Go bye-bye? More?")?	☐	☐
				Does your child put two words together ("more cookie")?	☐	☐
☐	☐	Has your child begun to respond to requests ("Come here"; "Do you want more")?	9 months-1 year	Does your child say words (8-10 words at age $1\frac{1}{2}$; 2-3 words at age 1. Words may not be clear).	☐	☐
☐	☐	Does your child turn or look up when you call?		Does your child enjoy imitating sounds?	☐	☐
☐	☐	Does your child search or look around when hearing new sounds?		Does your child use jargon (babbling that sounds like real speech)?	☐	☐
☐	☐	Does your child listen to people talking?		Does your child use voice to get attention?	☐	☐
☐	☐	Does your child respond to "no" and her or his name?	6 months	Does your child's babbling sound like the parent's speech, only not clear?	☐	☐
☐	☐	Does your child notice and look around for the source of new sounds?		Does your child make lots of different sounds?	☐	☐
☐	☐	Does your child turn her or his head toward the side where the sound is coming from?				
☐	☐	Does your child try to turn toward the speaker?	3 months	Does your child babble?	☐	☐
☐	☐	Does your child smile when spoken to?		Does your child cry differently for different needs?	☐	☐
☐	☐	Does your child stop playing and appear to listen to sounds or speech?		Does your child repeat the same sounds a lot?	☐	☐
☐	☐	Does your child seem to recognize mother's voice?				
☐	☐	Does your child listen to speech?	Birth	Does your child coo or gurgle?	☐	☐
☐	☐	Does your child startle or cry at noises?				
☐	☐	Does your child awaken at loud sounds?				

*Adapted from public information materials of the American Speech-Language-Hearing Association. Used with permission.

Appendix C

Reflexes, Reactions, and Implications*

Normal Age Range	Reflex	How to Elicit	Motor Response	Implications
Birth to 3–5 months	Biting	Rub index finger on child's upper lateral gum area. Both sides. (Do not attempt on child with teeth.)	Child will rhythmically open and close mouth.	If retained, it will inhibit lateral jaw movement necessary for chewing.
Birth to 3–4 months	Rooting	Stroke with finger from corner of child's mouth to across cheek to earlobe.	Turns head to stimulated side.	If retained, the reflex will interfere with development of natural feeding patterns.
	Grasping	Place object (pencil, rattle, index finger) on palm just below child's fourth and fifth fingers.	Grasps examiner's finger, rattle, pencil, etc.	If not present at birth, indicates abnormality in motor area. If retained, prevents normal grasp and release.
	Stepping	Hold child upright in standing position with weight on feet and lean baby's body slightly forward.	Child will take a few high steps (as if walking).	If not present at birth, indicates neurological problem. If retained, will interfere with gross motor skills.
Birth to 4–6 months	Asymmetrical tonic neck reflex (ATNR)	Child on back with head in midline, arms and legs relaxed.	Child will partially or totally straighten the arm and leg on side of body toward which the head is turned. The opposite arm and leg are partially or totally bent (fencer's position).	Hand use activities in midline, sitting, balance, and control of extremities will be impaired when the head is turned.

Age	Reflex	Stimulus	Response	Significance
Birth to 6 months	Moro	With child on back with head in midline, arms by side, Examiner places hand on the back of child's neck and raises head off surface. Release head support, letting the head drop back. *Catch child's head before it reaches the surface.*	Child's arms straighten out sideways and then move to midline.	If not present at birth, there are indications of neurological immaturity or abnormality. If retained, reflex interferes with general motor control.
Birth to 6 months	Neck righting (log rolling)	Child on back with head in midline, arms straight down by sides. Put your hands on each side of head and turn it to the side.	The body rotates as a unit in the same direction as head is turned.	If retained, reflex will interfere with sequential rolling.
6 months to 18 months	Segmental rolling (body righting on body)	Stimulate as for neck righting.	First head turns, then shoulders, then pelvis.	Becomes voluntary and provides trunk rotation for normal rolling patterns (i.e., leading from hip).
6 months to 24 months	Landau reaction	Hold the child horizontally in space with support under the trunk between the shoulders and pelvis. (Use two hands to support.)	Child fully straightens head, trunk, and hips ("swan dive" position).	If not present, development of extensor pattern necessary for standing and walking will be delayed or possibly prevented.
6 months and beyond	Protective extensor reaction (parachute)	1. Child is held in air, stomach toward ground with support under stomach. Rapidly lower child, head first toward testing table or floor.	Child moves arms forward and catches weight on open hands. Note if child does not use both arms for protection.	If not present, child cannot maintain sitting balance.
		2. Child is sitting independently. Gently push forward or backward or sideways.	Child extends arms and catches weight for support.	

Sources: Ulrey & Rogers (1982); Fiorentino, M. R., (1972); Adaptive Performance Scale (1980). (See Chapter 8 references.)

Appendix D

Referral Signals Checklist

AUDITORY SIGNALS			
Observable Signs, Symptoms, or Complaints	**Sometimes**	**Yes**	**No**
Has fluid running from ears.	[ ]	[ ]	[ ]
Has frequent earaches.	[ ]	[ ]	[ ]
Has frequent colds or sore throats.	[ ]	[ ]	[ ]
Has recurring tonsillitis.	[ ]	[ ]	[ ]
Breathes through mouth.	[ ]	[ ]	[ ]
Complains of noises in head.	[ ]	[ ]	[ ]
Voice is too loud or too soft.	[ ]	[ ]	[ ]
Has delayed or abnormal speech, excessive articulation errors.	[ ]	[ ]	[ ]
Seems to "hear what he or she wants to hear."	[ ]	[ ]	[ ]
Seems to be daydreaming.	[ ]	[ ]	[ ]
Often looks puzzled, frowns, or strains when addressed.	[ ]	[ ]	[ ]
Appears uninterested in things others find interesting.	[ ]	[ ]	[ ]
Observable Behaviors			
Turns or cocks head to hear speaker.	[ ]	[ ]	[ ]
Scans when called rather than turning to source.	[ ]	[ ]	[ ]
Does not pay attention.	[ ]	[ ]	[ ]
Is especially inattentive in large groups.	[ ]	[ ]	[ ]
Exhibits extreme shyness in speaking.	[ ]	[ ]	[ ]
Has difficulty in following oral directions (and records).	[ ]	[ ]	[ ]
Acts out; appears stubborn, shy, or withdrawn.	[ ]	[ ]	[ ]
Exhibits marked discrepancy between abilities in verbal and performance test items.	[ ]	[ ]	[ ]

NOTE: One or two symptoms do not a problem make. Tables of normal development found in Appendix A should be checked carefully because preschoolers naturally exhibit some degree of many of these behaviors. Patterns should be noted and observation continued when there is a question. Language signals can be found in Chapter 9. Adapted from Garwood et al. (1979); Gearhart and Weishahn. (1984).

	Sometimes	Yes	No
Watches classmates to see what they are doing before beginning to participate.	[ ]	[ ]	[ ]
Often does not finish work.	[ ]	[ ]	[ ]
Hears teacher only when he or she sees teacher.	[ ]	[ ]	[ ]
Hears some days but not others.	[ ]	[ ]	[ ]
Gives answers totally unrelated to question asked.	[ ]	[ ]	[ ]
Frequently, requests repetition or says "Huh?"	[ ]	[ ]	[ ]

VISUAL SIGNALS

Observable Signs, Symptoms, or Complaints

	Sometimes	Yes	No
Red eyelids.	[ ]	[ ]	[ ]
Pupils turned in, out, up, or down (perhaps independent of each other).	[ ]	[ ]	[ ]
Watery eyes or discharges.	[ ]	[ ]	[ ]
Crusts on lids or among the lashes.	[ ]	[ ]	[ ]
Recurring styes or swollen lids.	[ ]	[ ]	[ ]
Pupils of uneven size.	[ ]	[ ]	[ ]
Excessive movement of pupils.	[ ]	[ ]	[ ]
Drooping eyelids.	[ ]	[ ]	[ ]
Excessive rubbing of eyes (seems to brush away blurs.)	[ ]	[ ]	[ ]
Shutting or covering one eye.	[ ]	[ ]	[ ]
Tracking or focusing difficulties.	[ ]	[ ]	[ ]
Headaches or nausea after close work.	[ ]	[ ]	[ ]
Tensing up during visual tasks.	[ ]	[ ]	[ ]
Squinting, blinking, frowning, and distorting face while doing close work.	[ ]	[ ]	[ ]

Observable Behaviors

	Sometimes	Yes	No
Tilts head (possibly to use one eye) or thrusts forward.	[ ]	[ ]	[ ]
Tries to avoid or complains about light.	[ ]	[ ]	[ ]
Complains of pain or ache in eyes.	[ ]	[ ]	[ ]
Holds objects close to face.	[ ]	[ ]	[ ]

	Sometimes	Yes	No
Complains of itchy, scratchy, or stinging eyes.	[ ]	[ ]	[ ]
Avoids or is irritable when doing close work.	[ ]	[ ]	[ ]
Moves head rather than eyes to look at object.	[ ]	[ ]	[ ]
Tires easily after visual tasks.	[ ]	[ ]	[ ]
Frequently confuses similarly shaped letters, numbers, or designs.	[ ]	[ ]	[ ]
Is unusually clumsy or awkward; trips over small objects.	[ ]	[ ]	[ ]
Has poor eye-hand coordination.	[ ]	[ ]	[ ]
Cannot follow a moving target held 10 to 12 inches in front of him.	[ ]	[ ]	[ ]

HEALTH OR PHYSICAL SIGNALS

Observable Signs, Symptoms, or Complaints

	Sometimes	Yes	No
Flushes easily or has slightly bluish color to cheeks, lips, or fingertips.	[ ]	[ ]	[ ]
Has excessive low-grade fevers or colds.	[ ]	[ ]	[ ]
Has frequently dry coughs or complains of chest pains after physical exertion.	[ ]	[ ]	[ ]
Is unusually breathless after exercise.	[ ]	[ ]	[ ]
Is extremely slow or sluggish.	[ ]	[ ]	[ ]
Is abnormal in size.	[ ]	[ ]	[ ]
Is excessively hungry or thirsty.	[ ]	[ ]	[ ]
Complains of pains in arms, legs, or joints.	[ ]	[ ]	[ ]
Has poor motor control or coordination.	[ ]	[ ]	[ ]
Walks awkwardly or with a limp.	[ ]	[ ]	[ ]
Shows signs of pain during exercise.	[ ]	[ ]	[ ]
Moves in a jerky or shaky manner.	[ ]	[ ]	[ ]
Walks on tiptoe; feet turn in.	[ ]	[ ]	[ ]
Has hives or rashes.	[ ]	[ ]	[ ]
Loses weight without dieting.	[ ]	[ ]	[ ]
Appears to be easily fatigued.	[ ]	[ ]	[ ]
Has excessive or frequent bruises, welts, or swelling.	[ ]	[ ]	[ ]

Observable Behaviors	Sometimes	Yes	No
Moves extremely slowly or in a sluggish manner.	[ ]	[ ]	[ ]
Is excessively hungry or thirsty.	[ ]	[ ]	[ ]
Complains of pains in arms, legs, or joints.	[ ]	[ ]	[ ]
Is excessively restless or overactive.	[ ]	[ ]	[ ]
Is extremely inactive; avoids physical exercise.	[ ]	[ ]	[ ]
Faints easily.	[ ]	[ ]	[ ]
Is extremely inattentive.	[ ]	[ ]	[ ]
Is unable to chew and swallow well.	[ ]	[ ]	[ ]
Exhibits difficulty with motor tasks, including balance.	[ ]	[ ]	[ ]
Complains of pain or discomfort in the genital area.	[ ]	[ ]	[ ]

LEARNING SIGNALS

Observable Signs, Symptoms, or Complaints

	Sometimes	Yes	No
Cries easily; is easily frustrated.	[ ]	[ ]	[ ]
Is clumsy, awkward; has visual motor difficulties (for example, unusual difficulty with coloring, puzzles, or cutting).	[ ]	[ ]	[ ]
Exhibits visual or auditory perceptual difficulties.	[ ]	[ ]	[ ]
Appears easily disturbed by loud noises.	[ ]	[ ]	[ ]
Often seems confused or unsure of self.	[ ]	[ ]	[ ]

Observable Behaviors

	Sometimes	Yes	No
Works very slowly or rushes through everything.	[ ]	[ ]	[ ]
Has difficulty working independently.	[ ]	[ ]	[ ]
Is highly distractible, impulsive.	[ ]	[ ]	[ ]
Has extremely short attention span.	[ ]	[ ]	[ ]
Is unable to follow directions.	[ ]	[ ]	[ ]
Is excessively active or excessively inactive.	[ ]	[ ]	[ ]
Perseverates (repeats activity over and over)	[ ]	[ ]	[ ]
Seems to catch on quickly in some areas but not in others.	[ ]	[ ]	[ ]
Is extremely inconsistent in performance.	[ ]	[ ]	[ ]
Does not transfer what is learned in one area to another.	[ ]	[ ]	[ ]

	Sometimes	Yes	No
Actively resists change.	[ ]	[ ]	[ ]
Constantly disrupts class.	[ ]	[ ]	[ ]
Does not remember classroom routine; has other memory problems.	[ ]	[ ]	[ ]
Has difficulty making choices.	[ ]	[ ]	[ ]
Lacks inventiveness; has interests below age level.	[ ]	[ ]	[ ]
Learns so slowly that he or she cannot participate well with others.	[ ]	[ ]	[ ]

Appendix E

Competencies for Trainees in Early Childhood Special Eduction

	Nonexistent	Poor	Satisfactory	Good	Excellent
I. *Appropriately and competently assesses strengths and needs.*					
A. Selects appropriate formal instruments.	1	2	3	4	5
B. Selects appropriate informal strategies.	1	2	3	4	5
C. Monitors child's progress frequently and systematically.	1	2	3	4	5
D. Evaluates family involvement and satisfaction.	1	2	3	4	5
II. *Plans effective intervention programs.*					
A. Works collaboratively with parents in selecting goals and objectives and strategies.	1	2	3	4	5
B. Goals are related to assessment results.	1	2	3	4	5
C. Goals and objectives are clear and relevant to high-priority child and family needs.	1	2	3	4	5
D. Plan is communicated to parents clearly both verbally and in writing.	1	2	3	4	5
III. *Demonstrates understanding of how children learn and ability to utilize generic teaching strategies, including the following:*					
A. Role of social interaction.	1	2	3	4	5
B. Motivation (e.g., identifies high-preference objects, people, and events).	1	2	3	4	5
C. Arrangement of physical environment.	1	2	3	4	5
D. Use of play as both context and method.	1	2	3	4	5
E. Behavioral analysis (including task analysis and identification of antecedents and consequences).	1	2	3	4	5
F. Behavioral analysis (including use of positive reinforcement, use of cues and prompts, shaping, fading, chaining, and stimulus generalization).	1	2	3	4	5
G. Repetition and routines.	1	2	3	4	5
H. Appropriate caregiver-child interaction.	1	2	3	4	5
I. Critical role of family in child's development.	1	2	3	4	5

	Nonexistent	Poor	Satisfactory	Good	Excellent
IV. *Manages classroom environment to optimize learning.*					
A. Effectively arranges physical environment.	1	2	3	4	5
B. Creates appropriate classroom schedule.	1	2	3	4	5
C. Utilizes daily routines for training.	1	2	3	4	5
D. Creates effective play routines.	1	2	3	4	5
E. Provides opportunity for rest and quiet time.	1	2	3	4	5
F. Creates comfortable atmosphere for parent involvement.	1	2	3	4	5
G. Takes responsibility for children's safety.	1	2	3	4	5
H. Effectively manages, coordinates, and involves paraprofessionals, volunteers, and consultants.	1	2	3	4	5
I. Selects highly motivating activities.	1	2	3	4	5
J. Utilizes individual as well as small and total group formats appropriately.	1	2	3	4	5
K. Integrates all developmental domains (i.e., language, cognition, motor, social-emotional, and self-help) into each activity.	1	2	3	4	5
V. *Facilitates the development of communication skills.*					
A. Recognizes and correctly interprets communicative cues.	1	2	3	4	5
B. Understands the stages and characteristics of language and speech development.	1	2	3	4	5
C. Establishes turn taking.	1	2	3	4	5
D. Is responsive to child's communicative intents; follows child's lead.	1	2	3	4	5
E. Uses repetition and recasts.	1	2	3	4	5
F. Uses appropriate pacing and speech rate; waits for child's response.	1	2	3	4	5
G. Appropriately labels objects and key events.	1	2	3	4	5
H. Expands child's utterance.	1	2	3	4	5
I. Knows how to "up the ante" (i.e., prompt for better turn).	1	2	3	4	5
J. Utilizes play routines.	1	2	3	4	5
K. Selects relevant and functional communication goals.	1	2	3	4	5
L. Develops augmentative communication systems and skills as needed.	1	2	3	4	5
M. Provides opportunity for choices.	1	2	3	4	5
N. Facilitates literate, autonomous uses of language (e.g., narrative, explanation, story telling).	1	2	3	4	5
VI. *Facilitates the development of cognitive skills.*					
A. Understands the stages and characteristics of typical cognitive development.	1	2	3	4	5

	Nonexistent	Poor	Satisfactory	Good	Excellent
B. Creates opportunities for all children to experience "effectance" (i.e., to develop intentional behavior), and assists child to understand cause and effect.	1	2	3	4	5
C. Effectively encourages exploration and trial and error behavior through modeling, scaffolding, and use of cues and prompts.	1	2	3	4	5
D. Teaches object permanence.	1	2	3	4	5
E. Utilizes activities and materials that encourage mental representation and memory.	1	2	3	4	5
F. Develops symbolic behavior such as pretend play and recognition of graphic symbols.	1	2	3	4	5
G. Creates opportunities for problem solving and assists children in discovering solutions.	1	2	3	4	5
VII. *Facilitates emotional and social growth.*					
A. Understands stages of social and emotional development.	1	2	3	4	5
B. Engages in positive reciprocal interactions with child.	1	2	3	4	5
C. Models and labels a wide range of emotions.	1	2	3	4	5
D. Interprets and validates child's emotional reactions and states.	1	2	3	4	5
E. Uses symbolic play to enhance social and emotional development (at appropriate developmental stage).	1	2	3	4	5
F. Builds self-esteem through emotional nurturing, encouraging trust, and mastery and independence.	1	2	3	4	5
G. Sets appropriate limits and consistent, yet flexible, behavioral guidelines (i.e., "rules").	1	2	3	4	5
H. To the extent possible, assists in providing a stable caregiving environment for child.	1	2	3	4	5
I. Effectively fosters peer-peer interaction, with both peers with disabilities and nondisabled peers.	1	2	3	4	5
J. Encourages altruistic behavior and "manners" in developmentally and culturally appropriate ways.	1	2	3	4	5

	Nonexistent	Poor	Satisfactory	Good	Excellent
VIII. *Facilitates development of motor skills.*					
A. Understands stages and characteristics of typical motor development.	1	2	3	4	5
B. (In consultation with appropriate therapists if necessary), *positions* child appropriately for each activity in order to encourage optimal fine and gross movement and to maximize participation and independence.	1	2	3	4	5
C. Changes child's position frequently.	1	2	3	4	5
D. Effectively builds child's motor competence and self-confidence by gradually moving toward independent ambulations.	1	2	3	4	5
E. Utilizes appropriate assistive devices.	1	2	3	4	5
F. Utilizes effective teaching strategies to encourage functional fine motor skills and eye-hand coordination.	1	2	3	4	5
G. Utilizes outdoor activities for development of large muscle skills such as running, climbing, and throwing.	1	2	3	4	5
IX. *Facilitates learning of self-help skills.*					
A. Creates positive mealtime environment.	1	2	3	4	5
B. Assists child in development of chewing and swallowing a variety of foods and textures; finger feeding; use of utensils (adapted as necessary).	1	2	3	4	5
C. Establishes appropriate toileting schedule.	1	2	3	4	5
D. In cooperation with parent, develops consistent and appropriate toilet training procedures.	1	2	3	4	5
E. Provides frequent opportunities in natural contexts to learn dressing skills.	1	2	3	4	5
F. Adapts clothing as necessary to support independence.	1	2	3	4	5
G. When necessary, applies task analysis and behavioral techniques in teaching self-help skills.	1	2	3	4	5
X. *Facilitates academic readiness.*					
A. Uses developmentally appropriate techniques and materials and everyday contexts to teach cognitive operations such as classification, conservation, and seriation.	1	2	3	4	5
B. Demonstrates functional use of print (i.e., teacher models use of writing and reading in ways that are meaningful to children and displays print throughout classroom).	1	2	3	4	5

	Nonexistent	Poor	Satisfactory	Good	Excellent
C. Creates opportunity for children to experience function and relevance of literacy behavior (e.g., treasure hunt clues, playing mailman, etc.).	1	2	3	4	5
D. Teaches important preacademic concepts such as opposites ("same" and "different," "big" and "little"); comparative terms ("taller," "tallest"); spatial terms ("in front of," "beside," "behind"); and quantity ("many," "few," "more") in *natural* contexts.	1	2	3	4	5
E. Teaches number and quantity concepts in meaningful ways (i.e., teaches "twoness" and "threeness," not simply rote counting).	1	2	3	4	5
F. Teaches auditory recognition, discrimination, and rhyming of sounds and sound combinations.	1	2	3	4	5
XI. *Encourages "normalization."*					
A. Creates opportunity for involvement with nondisabled peers.	1	2	3	4	5
B. Creates opportunity for child and family to participate in and utilize community resources.	1	2	3	4	5
C. Develops child's ability to engage in age-appropriate and culturally appropriate activities through instruction and environmental adaptation.	1	2	3	4	5
XII. *Demonstrates collaborative and interpersonal skills.*					
A. Facilitates team approaches and works collaboratively with other disciplines.	1	2	3	4	5
B. Facilitates the development of children with low-incidence disabilities and medical risk conditions in consultation and close collaboration with disability specialists.	1	2	3	4	5
C. Understands roles of each discipline in providing early intervention services.	1	2	3	4	5
D. Effectively manages staff and develops competence and self-esteem of each staff member.	1	2	3	4	5
E. Develops positive work relations with both professional and nonprofessional staff.	1	2	3	4	5
F. Establishes appropriate partnerships with parents.	1	2	3	4	5
G. Communicates with parents in clear and culturally sensitive ways.	1	2	3	4	5
H. Demonstrates flexibility and approaches difficult situations with problem-solving strategies.	1	2	3	4	5

u u u

Individual Materials for Use with Young Children: A Sampling

Sensorimotor Development columns: Balance, Body Awareness, Coordination, Controlled Movement, Fine Motor Dexterity, Laterality, Sensory Awareness, Self-Help Skills, Visual-Motor Integration. Perceptual Efficiency columns: Attention and Concentration, Directionality, Visual Discrimination, Visual Memory, Visualization, Spatial Relationships.

Material	Balance	Body Awareness	Coordination	Controlled Movement	Fine Motor Dexterity	Laterality	Sensory Awareness	Self-Help Skills	Visual-Motor Integration	Attention and Concentration	Directionality	Visual Discrimination	Visual Memory	Visualization	Spatial Relationships
Abacus					X	X			X				X		X
Association picture cards															
Attribute blocks									X			X	X		X
Balls			X	X					X						
Beads			X	X	X	X			X			X	X		X
Bean bags		X	X	X		X			X	X	X		X		X
Blocks		X	X	X	X				X		X		X		X
Books		X			X	X	X			X		X	X	X	
Bowling set			X	X					X	X	X				X
Cars and trucks			X	X					X		X				X
Chalkboard			X	X	X	X			X	X	X		X	X	X
Clay (Playdoh)		X	X	X	X		X	X	X						X
Climbing equipment	X	X	X	X		X	X		X		X				X
Color cubes			X	X	X	X			X		X	X	X	X	X
Crayons			X	X	X	X			X		X				
Dolls		X			X		X	X	X					X	
Dominoes			X	X	X	X			X		X				X
Dressing frames		X	X	X	X	X		X	X	X	X				X
Dress-up clothes		X	X		X	X	X	X	X				X		
Easel and paints			X	X	X	X	X		X			X	X		X

Author's Note: This chart lists a sampling of individual instructional materials that are useful in early childhood classrooms. The methods of using these materials are dependent on the philosophy and goals of each program and on the individual characteristics of children who are enrolled. The skills listed represent target behaviors within many programs, although they may not merit universal agreement. We have made no attempt to provide an exhaustive list of either skills or materials; we simply list resource ideas. They are provided to stimulate imagination and further analysis of available materials.

	Communication					Cognition and Academic Readiness								Social and Emotional Development					
	Auditory Memory	Comprehension	Nonverbal Expression	Verbal Facility	Vocabulary	Academic Readiness	Association	Classification	Creativity	Part-to-Whole Relationships	Problem Solving	Serialization	Quantitative Skills	Cooperation	Imitation	Self-Control	Self-Expression	Self-Esteem	Understanding Feelings
		X			X		X	X		X			X						
		X			X	X	X	X			X		X	X	X	X			
	X					X		X			X	X	X	X		X			
		X	X		X	X		X	X	X	X	X	X	X	X	X	X	X	X
			X	X			X	X	X				X	X	X	X	X		
			X			X				X			X	X	X	X	X	X	
			X						X	X		X		X	X	X	X		X
	X		X			X			X				X	X	X	X	X		
			X	X		X		X				X	X	X	X				
			X	X					X				X			X	X	X	X
						X				X		X	X	X				X	
			X				X	X						X	X		X	X	X
			X				X	X								X	X	X	

	Sensorimotor Development									Perceptual Efficiency					
	Balance	Body Awareness	Coordination	Controlled Movement	Fine Motor Dexterity	Laterality	Sensory Awareness	Self-Help Skills	Visual-Motor Integration	Attention and Concentration	Directionality	Visual Discrimination	Visual Memory	Visualization	Spatial Relationships
Etch-a-Sketch			X	X	X	X			X	X	X			X	X
Farm animals												X			
Flannel and felt board					X	X			X	X	X	X	X	X	X
Form board						X			X		X		X		X
Geo boards			X	X	X	X			X		X		X		X
Housekeeping equipment		X			X		X	X	X					X	
Hula Hoops	X	X	X	X		X	X		X	X					X
Knob boards					X				X				X		
Lacing boards			X	X	X	X		X	X		X			X	X
Legos			X	X	X				X					X	X
Lotto					X				X	X		X	X		
Magic Markers			X	X	X	X			X		X			X	X
Magnetic board				X	X	X			X		X		X	X	X
Match-ups					X				X	X		X		X	
Mirrors		X				X	X	X			X	X	X		X
Musical instruments		X	X	X			X		X	X					
Nesting toys			X	X	X				X			X		X	
Parquetry			X	X	X				X			X	X	X	X
Peg boards			X	X	X	X			X		X		X	X	X
Photographs		X						X					X	X	
Pictures		X								X		X	X	X	
Play store					X			X	X			X	X		
Punching clown				X					X		X				X
Puppets															
Puzzles		X							X	X		X	X	X	X
Records		X		X			X			X					
Sandbox			X		X		X	X	X						
Science equipment					X		X		X	X		X	X	X	X
Scissors			X	X	X	X		X	X	X					
Sequence cards					X	X			X			X	X	X	
Shape sorting toys			X	X	X				X			X			X
Sound boxes							X								
Tactile surfaces							X					X	X		
Telephones		X					X	X		X					
Tunnel	X	X		X		X	X		X		X				X
Unifix cubes				X	X	X			X			X	X		X
Water play toys		X			X		X	X	X						
Wheeled toys	X	X	X	X					X						
Work bench		X	X	X	X	X			X	X				X	X
Zoo animals									X					X	

	Communication					Cognition and Academic Readiness								Social and Emotional Development					
	Auditory Memory	Comprehension	Nonverbal Expression	Verbal Facility	Vocabulary	Academic Readiness	Association	Classification	Creativity	Part-to-Whole Relationships	Problem Solving	Serialization	Quantitative Skills	Cooperation	Imitation	Self-Control	Self-Expression	Self-Esteem	Understanding Feelings
			X						X	X				X		X		X	
			X	X			X	X	X			X							
			X	X	X	X	X	X	X	X		X	X				X		
							X	X			X	X							
						X				X			X						
			X	X			X	X	X			X	X	X	X	X	X	X	
												X	X				X		
	X	X	X		X	X	X	X	X			X	X	X		X		X	
									X					X		X			
									X	X		X	X	X	X	X	X	X	
			X				X	X	X	X				X					
			X		X	X	X	X	X	X	X	X	X				X	X	X
							X		X						X		X	X	X
	X	X	X	X			X		X			X		X	X	X	X		
						X				X	X	X							
							X		X	X	X	X							
										X									
			X	X		X	X		X			X	X	X	X			X	X
		X		X	X		X	X	X	X		X		X	X	X	X		X
							X	X							X		X		X
			X	X					X					X	X	X	X		X
	X	X	X		X		X			X		X						X	
				X			X					X							
	X	X	X	X	X	X	X	X		X		X	X						
						X	X	X				X	X						
					X		X	X					X						
	X	X			X	X	X	X				X							
	X	X	X	X	X		X	X	X			X		X	X		X		X
					X									X		X			
						X	X	X					X						
				X					X					X		X		X	
														X		X	X		X
														X	X	X	X		
		X		X			X	X	X		X			X		X			
			X	X					X										

451

Appendix G

AAC (Augmentative and Alternative Communication) Resources

Augmentative and Alternative Communication
Decker Publishing, Inc.
One James T. South
P.O. Box 620
L.C.D. 1
Hamilton, Ontario L8N 3K7
Canada

USAAC Newsletter
1850 Sandhill Rd. Apt. 10
Palo Alto, CA 94304

Don Johnston Developmental Equipment, Inc.
P.O. Box 639, Wauconda, IL 60084
(800) 999-4660

Crestwood Company
6625 Sidney Pl
Milwaukee, WI 53209
(414) 352-5678

Prentke Romich
1022 Heyl Rd.
Wooster, OH 44691

Trace Research and Development Center
S-151 Waisman Center
1500 Highland Ave.
Madison, WI 53705

Zygo Industries
P.O. Box 1008
Portland, OR 97207
(800) 234-6006

Appendix H

Periodicals Relevant to Early Intervention

Beginnings
P.O. Box 2890
Redmond, WA 98073

Child Care Quarterly
Behavioral Publications
72 Fifth Avenue
New York, NY 10011

Child Development
Society for Research in Child Development
Univ of Chicago Press
Journals Division
5720 S. Woodlawn Ave.
Chicago, IL 60637

Child Welfare
Child Welfare League of America, Inc.
Dept. 3092
Rutgers University
New Brunswick, NJ 08903

Childhood Education
Association for Childhood Educational International
11561 Georgia Avenue, Suite 312
Wheaton, MD 20902

Children in Contemporary Society
Pittsburgh Association for the Education of Young
   Children
P.O. Box 11173
Pittsburgh, PA 15237
Children Today

U.S. Department of Health and Human Services
Administration for Children and Families
Office of Public Affairs
370 L'Enfant Promenade, S.W., 7th Floor
Washington, DC 20447

Cycles
TADS (Technical Assistance Development System)
625 West Cameron Avenue
Chapel Hill, NC 27514

Day Care and Early Education
Human Science Press, Inc.
233 Spring Street
New York, New York 10013-1578

Early Child Development and Care
Gordon and Breach Science Publishers, Inc.
820 Town Center Drive
Langhorre, PA 19047

Educating Children, Early and Middle Years
American Association of Elementary-Kindergarten-
   Nursery Educators
1201 16th Street, N.W.
Washington, DC 20036

ERIC-ECE Newsletter
ERIC Clearinghouse on Early Childhood Education
805 West Pennsylvania
Urbana, IL 61801

Exceptional Children
The Council for Exceptional Children
1920 Association Drive
Reston, VA 22091-1589

Focus on Autism and
    Other Developmental Disabilities
Pro-Ed
8700 Shoal Creek Boulevard
Austin, Texas 78757–6897

Infant Mental Health Journal
The Clinical Psychology Publishing Company
4 Conant Square
Brandon, VT 05733

Infants and Young Children
Aspen Publishers, Inc.
7201 McKinney Circle
Frederick, MD 21701

Journal of Child Language
Cambridge University Press
Journals Department
40 W. 20th Street
New York, NY 10011

Journal of Early Intervention
Division for Early Childhood
The Council for Exceptional Children
1920 Association Drive
Reston, VA 22091

Journal of Speech and Hearing Disorders
American Speech-Language, Hearing Association
10801 Rockville Pike
Rockville, MD 20852-6897

Journal of Speech and Hearing Research
American Speech-Language, Hearing Association
10801 Rockville Pike
Rockville, MD 20852-3279

Merrill-Palmer Quarterly
Wayne State University Press
5959 Woodward Avenue
Detroit, MI 48202

Report of Pre-school Education
Capitol Publications, Inc.
2430 Pennsylvania Avenue, N.W.
Washington, DC 20037

Teaching Exceptional Children
The Council for Exceptional Children
1920 Association Drive
Reston, VA 22091

The Exceptional Parent
Psy–Ed Corporation
209 Harvard Street, Suite 303
Brookline, MA 02146-5005

The Volta Review
The Alexander Graham Bell Association for the Deaf,
    Inc.
3417 Volta Place, N.W.
Washington, DC 20007

Topics in Early Childhood Special Education
Pro-Ed
8700 Shoal Creek Boulevard
Austin, TX 78757-6897

Topics in Language Disorders
Aspen Publishers, Inc.
200 Orchard Ridge Drive
Gaithersburg, MD 20878

Young Children
National Association for the Education of Young
    Children
1509 16th Street, N.W.
Washington, DC 20036-1426

Young Exceptional Children
Division for Early Childhood
The Council for Exceptional Children
1444 Wazee Street, Suite 230
Denver, CO 80202

Zero to Three
National Center for Clinical Infant Programs
2000 14th Street, N, Suite 380
Arlington, VA 22201-2500

Appendix I

Web Sites Related to Early Childhood Special Education

Assistive Technology

Assistive Technology Education Network (ATEN)
http://www.webable.com/

Closing the Gap
http:www.closingthegap.com

The Boulevard
http://www/blvd.com

Assistive Technology
http:/www.webable.com/

Disability Information

Autism
http://www.web.syr.edu/~jmwobus/autism/

Deaf Blind Link
http://www.tr.wosc.osshe.edu/dblink/index.htm

Epilepsy Foundation
http://www.epilepsy-socalif.org

National Association for Down Syndrome
http://www.nads.org

National Organization for Rare Diseases (NORD)
http://www.rarediseases.org

Special Education Resources on the Internet
http://www.hood.edu/seri/

United Cerebral Palsy
http://www.ucpa.org

ERIC

Eric Digests
http://wwwericeece.org/pubs/digests.html

Eric Clearinghouse on Elementary and Early Childhood
   Education
http://ericeece.org/

Families

National Center for Fathering
http://www.fathers.com

National Parent to Parent Support & Information
   System, Inc. (NPPSIS)
http://www.NPPSIS.org

Parents Helping Parents
http://www.php.com

The Family Education Network
(Exceptional Parent)
http://familyeducation.com/home/

The National Parent Network on Disabilities (NPND)
http://www.npnd.org

455

The Pacer Center
http://www.pacer.org

Positive Parenting
http://www.positiveparenting.com

Organizations

The Council for Exeptional Children (CEC)
http://www.cec.sped.org

CEC—The Division for Early Childrhood (DEC)
http://www.dec-sped.org

Federation for Children with Special Needs
http://www.fcsn.org/

National Association for the Education of Young
Children (NAEYC)
http://www.naeyc.org

National Early Childhood Technical Assistance System
(NEC*TAS)
http://www.nectas.unc.edu

National Information Center for Children and Youth
with Diabilities (NICHCY)
http://www.nichcy.org/

Zero to Three: National Center for Infants,Toddlers and
Families
http://www.zerotothree.org

Glossary

abduction: Movement of a limb outward (away) from the body.

acquired: Referring to a feature, state, or disease that happened after birth (acquired conditions are not inherited, but rather a response to the environment).

acquired immune deficiency syndrome (AIDS): A communicable disease that reduces the body's ability to fight some types of infection.

acuity: Degree to which one is able to hear sounds and see visual images.

adapt: To change or modify while retaining the basic model.

adaptive behavior: The ability to adjust to new situations and to apply familiar or new skills to those situations.

adaptive equipment: Any device that is modified to enhance the independence of the user.

adduction: Movement of a limb inward (toward) the body.

advocate: One who acts on behalf of another.

affective: Pertaining to emotion, feeling, or attitude.

anecdotal record: A factual account of a child's behavior.

anomaly: Abnormality.

anoxia: The lack of oxygen.

apnea: A pause in breathing that lasts 20 seconds or longer.

apnea monitor: A monitor that sounds an alarm when an infant has a period of apnea.

apraxia: A loss of the ability to perform voluntary, purposeful movements due to damage to the brain, e.g., inability to perform movements of a command such as "Clap your hands."

arena assessment: The process of one professional conducting assessment while other team members, including the family, observe and contribute.

arthritis: Inflammation of a joint or joints.

articulation: The manner in which speech sounds are produced.

assessment: Either a test or an observation that determines a child's strengths or weaknesses in a particular area of development.

association: The process of relating one concept to another.

asthma: A complicated pulmonary symptom characterized by obstruction, labored breathing, and wheezing.

asymmetrical: Unequal; lack of similarity in form between two sides of the body.

ataxia: Characterized by disturbance of balance and awkward movements caused by damage to brain or spinal cord.

ataxic: Unbalanced and jerky.

athetoid: Moving uncontrollably and continuously.

atrophy: Wasting away or diminution in size.

atypical: Not typical. Different from the norm or average.

audiologist: A trained professional who measures hearing acuity, diagnoses hearing impairments, and assists in planning for remediation, including hearing aids and educational adaptations.

auditory discrimination: The ability to distinguish one sound from another.

auditory memory: The ability to retain and recall what has been heard.

augmentative communication: Any method of communicating without speech, such as using signs, gestures, picture boards, and electronic or non-electronic devices.

backward chaining: Teaching the steps of a skill backward, beginning with the last step.

behavior modification: Systematic, consistent efforts to change an individual's behavior. Carefully planned consequences for specific behaviors are designed to help a learner develop new and more appropriate responses to situations and experiences.

behavioral objective (also referred to as performance objective): Identifies exactly what the teacher will do, provide, or restrict; describes the learner's observable behavior; and defines how well the learner must perform.

bilateral: Both sides.

biological risk: Insult to bodily systems that makes normal development problematic.

body awareness (image): Awareness of one's own body and its position in time and space.

bolster or therapy roll: A cylindrical piece of equipment (often made of foam) on which infant is placed to help develop muscle strength, balance, and protective reactions.

case management: Responsible for coordinating services for a family and ensuring that individual family service plans are written and carried out. Currently referred to as service coordination.

categorical placement: Placement of children according to classification of their suspected disabilities. Classrooms that are categorical usually group children according to disability labels, for example, classes for children who have learning disabilities or emotional disturbance.

catheter: Small, flexible tube inserted into a body channel to distend or maintain an opening to an internal cavity.

cerebral palsy: Disorder of posture, muscle tone, and movement resulting from brain damage.

child-find: The process of finding and identifying children with special needs.

choreoathetosis: Type of cerebral palsy in which there are uncontrolled muscle movements in all four limbs of the body and sometimes in the face.

chromosomal abnormality: A genetic disorder caused by too few or too many chromosomes, or by chromosomes with extra or missing pieces. Down Syndrome is caused by a chromosomal abnormality (an extra chromosome 21).

chronological age (CA): A child's actual age in years and months.

classification: Distinguishing characteristics of things, then sorting, matching, or otherwise grouping them.

cognition: Analytical, logical acts of mental behavior that result in the act of knowing.

collaboration: Laboring together. Working side by side with mutual respect and cooperation to complete a task.

concepts: Mental images or ideas.

confidentiality: Records and other information about children must not be shown to anyone other than those who have been approved to have the information. Parental consent in writing must be obtained before information can be released to other individuals or facilities.

congenital: Presumed to be present at birth.

contracture: Permanently tight muscles and joints.

coordination: Harmonious functioning of muscles or groups of muscles in movement.

corrected age (of infants): Calculated by subtracting the number of weeks of prematurity from the chronological age.

correlation: The relationship between factors.

The Council for Exceptional Children (CEC): A national professional organization for anyone working for and with gifted children and children with disabilities.

criterion: A norm or standard for a behavior or item.

criterion-referenced tests: Tests or observations that compare a child's performance on a particular task to a standard established for that specific task. Such tests identify what a child can and cannot do.

cross-categorical program: A program designed to serve children who have differing disabling conditions.

curriculum: All of the specific features of a master teaching plan that have been chosen by a particular teacher for his or her classroom. Curricula may vary widely from school to school, but each curriculum reflects the skills, tasks, and behaviors that a school has decided are important for children to acquire.

custodial care: Usually refers to the constant supervision and care of bodily needs provided in institutional settings.

cystic fibrosis: A chronic disorder often causing respiratory and digestive problems.

decibel: Unit used to measure hearing intensity or loudness.

decoding: The act of deciphering or obtaining meaning from what is seen or heard.

developmental age: The age at which a child is functioning (demonstrating specific abilities), based on assessment of the child's skills and comparison of those skills to the age at which they are considered typical.

developmental curriculum checklist: A checklist of behavior often prepared by choosing items from standardized tests or scales. Duplicate items are deleted and those remaining are arranged in a developmental sequence. The checklist is then used as a guide in designing curriculum and in providing a record of individual children's progress through the curriculum.

developmental delay: Classification for children with or without established diagnosis who perform significantly behind developmental norms.

developmentally disabled (delayed): Persons who have an identifiable delay in mental or physical development compared with established norms are referred to in this way, rather than as "impaired" or "retarded."

developmental quotient (DQ): A score similar to an IQ that describes an infant's developmental level.

diabetes mellitus: A metabolic disorder related to insufficient insulin.

diagnosis: A diagnosis is an effort to find the cause of a problem by observing the child and considering the results of tests.

diplegia: Condition of cerebral palsy with major involvement of the legs and minor involvement of the arms.

directionality: The ability to know right from left, up from down, forward from backward, and other directional orientation.

discrimination: The ability to differentiate among similar stimuli.

distal: Further from the point of origin. For example, the fingers are distal to the shoulder, while the elbow is proximal to the shoulder.

divergent thinking: Thinking that is unusual, different, and searching.

dyskinesia: Difficulty in performing voluntary movement, usually due to damage to basal ganglia of the brain. Examples are *chorea* and *athetosis.*

dystonia: 1. Abnormal muscle tone, either increased or decreased. 2. A genetic disorder in which child experiences severe muscle spasms and exhibits abnormal movements and postures, especially when walking.

dystrophy: Weakness and degeneration of muscle.

early intervention: Services for children (and families) from birth to school age.

echolalia: A habit of repeating (without meaning), or "echoing," what is said by others.

eclecticism: Method or practice of selecting what seems best from various systems or programs.

efficacy: Positive effects or impact of a program, strategy, or procedure.

emerging skills: As children learn, they may use a new skill some, but not all of the time. A skill observed at least some of the time is said to be emerging.

encoding: The act of expressing oneself in words or gestures.

en-route behaviors: Tasks to be mastered or behaviors to be demonstrated as the child moves from one level of functioning (entry behavior) to a designated goal or objective (terminal behavior).

entry behavior: The level of functioning or behavior already acquired before beginning a series of tasks.

environment: Everything the child encounters. The rooms, furniture, toys, the opportunity to experience new and different places, and the behaviors of those around the child constitute the environment.

environmental risk conditions: The presence of factors in the family or community that lead to experiences that may result in developmental delay.

epilepsy: A brain disorder frequently resulting in seizure activity that may be very mild or severe enough to cause loss of consciousness.

equivalent practice: To prevent boredom in repetition, the teacher provides equivalent practice by offering a variety of materials and activities that are designed to develop the same skill. The task must also be at the same level of difficulty and provide the same kind of practice to be equivalent.

established risk condition: The presence of a diagnosed physical or medical condition that is likely to lead to developmental delay.

etiology: The study of the causes of diseases or disabilities.

evaluation: 1. The process of making value judgments based on behavioral information about the effectiveness of a program in meeting the needs of children enrolled. 2. Under Part H, the term evaluation refers to the assessment procedures used to determine a child's eligibility for services.

eversion: Turning out.

expansion: Adults expand a child's utterance by stating the child's idea in a longer phrase or sentence.

expressive language: What is said or written to communicate an idea or a question.

extension: Straightening of trunk and limbs of body.

extensor pattern: A pattern of muscle movement that causes a straightening out of a limb.

family-focused early intervention: Concentrating intervention equally on the child's family and on the child.

family systems perspective: The family is viewed as an interactive unit; what affects one member affects all.

feedback: The receipt of knowledge of results (the effect) of one's own behavior.

figure-ground discrimination: The ability to attend to one aspect of a visual or auditory field while relegating other aspects of the environment to the background.

fine motor skills: Activities with the fingers and hands.

First Chance programs: Preschool programs for children with disabilities funded by the Bureau of Education for the Handicapped.

flexion: Bending of elbows, hips, knees, etc.

floppy: Loose or weak posture and movements.

forward chaining: A method of teaching a skill in which it is broken down into steps, beginning with the least difficult step.

fragile X syndrome: An X-linked disorder that often, but not always, causes mild to severe mental retardation. Some children with fragile X have average intelligence, with or without a learning disability.

Free appropriate public education (FAPE): Designed by Public Law 94-142 to mean special education and related services provided at public expense. Such services are to be described in the individualized education program, appropriate to the child's individual needs, and meet requirements of the state agency.

functional skills: Skills that will be immediately useful to the child and that will be used relatively frequently in the child's typical environment.

genetic: Having to do with the principles of heredity.

gestational age: The age of a fetus or infant stated in weeks from first day of the mother's last menstrual period before conception until the baby reaches term (40 weeks).

goals: The general statement on the individualized education program that states what teaching is expected to accomplish, for example, "To improve Johnny's fine motor skills."

grammar: The linguistic rules of language.

gross motor skills: Activities such as running, climbing, throwing, and jumping that use large muscles.

hand-over-hand guidance: Physically guiding a child through movements involved in a fine motor task, e.g., helping the child to grasp a spoon and bring it to his or her mouth.

hemiplegia: Condition of cerebral palsy with major involvement of one side of the body.

hereditary: Referring to a trait (such as eye color) or defect or disease (such as cystic fibrosis). Not all hereditary disorders are apparent at birth and not all birth defects are hereditary.

high-risk signals: Those signs that when observed in very young children have been known to be predictive of more than normal likelihood of future disabilities or developmental delays.

hydrocephalus: Congenital condition in which the accumulation of the fluid in the brain causes enlargement of the skull.

hyperactivity: Exceedingly active behavior not typical of most children.

hypertonicity: Condition in which muscles are stretched and constantly excited.

hypoactivity: Opposite of hyperactivity; lethargy.

hypotonicity: Condition in which muscles are limp and do not exhibit resistance to stretching.

IDEA: Individuals with Disabilities Education Act (PL 101-476) Part H of the law focuses on services to infants and toddlers who are at-risk or have developmental disabilities.

identification: The process of finding and screening individuals to determine whether they might benefit from specialized services.

inclusion: Another term used for integration of children with disabilities with non-disabled peers.

inclusive settings: Sites, classrooms, programs where inclusion takes place.

individualize: Match a teaching task to the capacity of the particular individual being taught.

Individualized education program (IEP): A written plan that states a child's present level of functioning; specific areas that need special services; annual goals; short-term objectives; services to be provided; and the method of evaluation to be implemented. An individualized education program is required for every child receiving services while Public Law 101-476 is in effect.

innate: Inherent within an individual.

inner language: The language in which thinking occurs. The process of internalizing and organizing experiences that can be expressed by symbols.

instructional objectives: These define specific accomplishments to be achieved. See "Behavioral objectives."

integration: Education of children with disabilities together with their non-disabled classmates to the maximum extent appropriate.

interdisciplinary approach: Professionals from different disciplines work together to assess and provide intervention based on mutual decision making.

interindividual differences: Differences between individuals.

intraindividual differences: Differences in performance within one child on different factors or on the same factor at different times.

inversion: Turning in.

involuntary movements: Unintended movements.

kinesthesia: The muscle sense by which the child is aware of his or her body position and his or her movements in relation to the environment.

labeling: Giving a categorical term (label) to a disabling condition and to those who exhibit such a condition; for example, "emotionally disturbed" or "mentally retarded."

laterality: Awareness of sidedness; left and right of the body.

least restrictive environment (LRE): This is a concept inherent in Public Law 94-142 that requires children with disabilities to be educated with non-disabled peers in regular educational settings to the maximum extent appropriate.

litigation: The act or process of contesting by law through lawsuits.

locomotor: Pertaining to movement from one location to another.

low tone/low muscle tone: Hypotonia.

mainstreaming: The practice of placing children with special needs in regular classrooms whenever appropriate.

medically fragile: Referring to an infant or child whose health status either is unstable or renders him or her at risk for developmental delay (often due to poor health or limitations on the infant's ability to participate in normal activities).

mental age: Level of mental functioning. A child with a mental age (MA) of 4-0 is thought to be mentally functioning like a 4 year old.

microcephaly: An abnormally small head size, resulting in poor brain growth and mental retardation.

mixed-type cerebral palsy: A form of cerebral palsy in which both spasticity and choreoathetoid movements are present.

modality: The pathways through which an individual receives information and thereby learns. Some individuals are thought to learn more quickly through one modality than another; for example, some process auditory information more efficiently than visual information and would thus be classified as auditory learners.

modeling: Providing a demonstration of an expected behavior.

motor planning: The ability to organize sensory information in order to plan and carry out the appropriate sequence of movements required to complete a task.

multidisciplinary approach: Individuals from different disciplines carry out evaluations, and intervention may be offered with little opportunity for professional interaction or integrated planning.

multiple sclerosis: A progressive central nervous system disease affecting motor control.

multisensory learning: A technique to facilitate learning that employs a combination of sense modalities at the same time.

muscular dystrophy: A central nervous system disease that affects skeletal and respiratory functions.

neonatal intensive care unit (NICU): The hospital unit staffed with specially trained medical practitioners who care for critically ill newborns, both premature babies and sick full-term babies.

neurological examination: An examination of sensory or motor responses to determine whether there are impairments of the nervous system.

noncategorical: Grouping children together without labeling or categorizing according to suspected disabilities.

nonlocomotor: Lack of movement from one place to another.

nonverbal ability: Having skill to perform a task that does not involve using words.

norm-referenced tests: These are tests that report a particular child's performance in relation to other children of the same chronological age. Such tests are highly standardized and usually do not include individuals with disabling conditions in the normative sample against which behavior is being compared.

norms: A sample of a large number of people's behavior against which a particular behavior can be compared.

observable behavior: Behavior that can be seen, heard, or felt.

occupational therapy: Treatment given to improve movement for daily living.

ocular pursuit: Following an object with the eye.

olfactory: Pertaining to the sense of smell.

ophthalmologist: A physician trained in the diagnosis and treatment of diseases of the eyes.

optometrist: A vision specialist trained to measure refraction and prescribe glasses but not licensed to treat eye diseases.

oral stimulation: Referring to the natural mouthing of toys that emerges in the infant between 3 and 6 months of age, or to the specific activities (such as massaging the gums or lips) designed to help the child with *oral tactile defensiveness* tolerate having things placed in his or her mouth.

orthotic: A custom-made orthopedic appliance (such as a brace, splint, or cast) used to promote proper body alignment, to stabilize joints, or to passively stretch muscle or other soft tissue.

otitis media: Inflammation of the middle ear; a common infection.

otolaryngologist: A medical doctor who specializes in the diagnosis and treatment of disorders of the ear, nose, and throat.

otologist: A physician trained to treat problems of the ear.

parallel talk: Parents of young children often talk about what their children are doing as it is happening. Their "talk" occurs parallel to what the child is doing. This practice appears to help young children learn language.

paraplegia: Paralysis of both legs.

paraprofessional: A trained assistant to a professional teacher, often referred to as a teacher aide.

patterning: Guiding the child's arms or legs through a series of passive movements in order to stimulate normal movement patterns.

pediatrician: A physician whose specialty is working with and treating infants and young children.

percentile rank: The percentage of persons in a normal distribution who score below a particular point.

perception: The process of interpreting what is received by the five senses.

perceptual-motor: The interaction of various channels of perception with motor activity, for example, the act of kicking is a perceptual-motor interaction between sight and gross motor responses.

performance objectives: See "Behavioral objectives."

perinatal: Around the time of birth.

perseveration: Continuous repetition of the same action characterized by the inability to shift readily from one activity to another.

physiotherapy: Treatment of disorders of movement.

pincer grasp: Coordination of index finger and thumb.

positioning: Placing a child in certain postures in order to promote symmetrical body alignment, normalize muscle tone, and promote functional skills.

post-ictal sleep: The sleep that occurs naturally after seizures.

pragmatics: The use of language in social contexts, including how language is used for communication.

premature infant: A baby born before 37 weeks gestation.

prenatally exposed to drugs (PED): Referring to an infant who was exposed to drugs as a fetus due to maternal substance abuse.

primitive reflex: A reflex response to a stimulus such as touch or movement that is normal in infants. The word "primitive" refers to the fact that these are involuntary survival responses with which infants are born.

prognosis: A forecast of the probable course of disease or illness.

prompting: Using cues and partial cues to build desired behavior. Verbal prompting often involves saying a single sound or word to help a child remember what to say or do. Physical prompting that involves physical assistance or touch can be helpful to initiate a motor or self-help skill. Prompts should be reduced gradually (faded) until they can be eliminated.

pronation: Turning of the palm downward or backward.

prone: Lying on the stomach.

prosthesis: Artificial device used to replace a missing body part.

psycholinguistics: The field of study that combines psychology and linguistics to create an understanding of the total language process.

quadraplegia: Condition of cerebral palsy with major involvement of arms and legs.

range of motion: The total distance through which a joint can be moved in natural directions.

rapport: A harmonious relationship. When working with a child, establishing rapport involves developing a climate or atmosphere in which the child feels comfortable enough to perform as well as possible.

receptive language: The ability to understand the intent and meaning of someone's effort to communicate.

reciprocal movement: Alternating movements of arms and legs, such as movement involved in walking or in creeping on hands and knees.

reflexes: Postures and movements completely out of the child's control.

reinforcer: An event or consequence (reward) that increases the likelihood of a behavior being repeated. May be concrete or social.

reliability: Extent to which a test measures a given performance consistently. The degree to which it is dependable, stable, and relatively free from errors of measurement.

remission: Period during which the symptoms of a condition disappear for an unpredictable period of time.

residual hearing: Auditory acuity of an individual after an impairment without amplification.

respite care: Skilled child care service that can be provided in place of the parent of a child who is seriously ill or disabled.

retarded: Traditionally this term was used to describe any individual who was slow to learn or difficult to teach. The term is not precise and is less often used today. Laws specify that one must correlate test scores, adaptive behavior, and other factors before this term can be used appropriately.

retinopathy of prematurity (ROP): An eye disorder that can develop in premature infants. There is an increased incidence in infants who are given high levels of oxygen for long periods.

reversal: A transposition of letters.

reverse chaining: Top down; begin teaching with the last step of a task and work backward. Particularly useful with self-help skills.

reverse mainstreaming: Non–disabled children are integrated into classes composed primarily of children with identifiable special needs.

righting: Ability to put in or restore the head and body to a proper position when in an abnormal or uncomfortable position.

rigidity: A type of cerebral palsy characterized by widespread continuous muscle tension. Muscles of the body become very stiff.

role release: The systematic training of other professionals in one's own discipline-specific skills.

schemata: Patterns.

scissor pattern: Body movement in which one leg crosses over the other.

screening: The process of sorting out from a total group children who may have problems. It is often a part of a total program called Child-Find, or Child-Check. The intent is to test all children with specially designed screening instruments to determine those who need further diagnostic testing and to determine if a problem really does exist.

self-fulfilling prophecy: The tendency for individuals to behave in accordance with views they perceive others to have of them.

sensorimotor: The combination of input of sense organs and output of motor activity.

sensory integration: The ability of the central nervous system to receive, process, and learn from sensation (such as touch, movement, sight, sound, smell, and the pull of gravity) in order to develop skills.

sensory overload: The condition that occurs when one or more senses have been overstimulated beyond the child's level of tolerance. It may occur as a result of too much noise, light or movement.

seriation: Ordering according to relative differences.

service coordination: Professional assistance designed to help families procure, coordinate, and manage the diverse services needed by a child and family. (See case management.)

sexually transmitted disease (STD): A contagious disease transmitted through sexual contact. STD can also be transmitted in other ways, such as through blood contact (as with drug users who share needles).

shaping: A technique of behavior modification in which behaviors that are successive approximations of the target behavior are reinforced until target behavior is acquired.

sickle cell anemia: A hereditary condition in which misshapen blood cells clump together in the blood vessels causing varied symptoms: painful joints, chronic ulcers of the ankles, episodes of abdominal pain, and neurological disturbances.

small for gestational age (SGA): A newborn whose weight is low (below the 10th percentile) for his gestational age.

soft sign: Any of several neurological indicators that collectively suggest the presence of damage to the central nervous system. They include disturbance of balance, visual motor difficulties, a lack of motor coordination, etc.

sorting: Discrimination and separation according to differences.

spasm: Sudden tightening of the muscles.

spasticity: Muscular incoordination resulting from sudden, involuntary contractions of the muscles; a type of cerebral palsy.

spatial relationships: The ability to perceive the position of two or more objects in relation to oneself and in relation to each other.

spina bifida: A disorder of the spinal column that may affect motor coordination and body functions.

standardization: The procedure of having standard directions and scoring so that normative data about others who have taken the test can be used.

standardized tests: Tests that are administered in a specifically described standard way, scored in a particular way, and then compared with the performance of a standard group.

stanine: A single digit derived score based on the normal curve. It ranges in value from 1 to 9 with a mean of 5.

status epilepticus: Refers to a situation in which a person has two major seizures, one right after the other; signals that an ambulance should be called immediately.

stimuli: Information that can be received by the senses.

stoma: Opening in the abdominal wall, created through surgery, to allow the urine from the kidneys to drain into a collecting bag.

strabismus: A condition in which the eyes do not work together, in that *one* eye deviates (wanders) from its position, relative to the other eye. It may go inward (cross-eye) or outward (wall-eye).

stuttering: A speech impairment evidenced by hesitations, repetitions, or spasms of breathing.

successive approximation: The process of gradually increasing expectations for a child to display behaviors that are more like the desired target behavior; used in shaping behaviors not previously a part of the child's behavior pattern.

sudden infant death syndrome (SIDS): The unexpected and sudden death of an infant who has appeared to be healthy. SIDS occurs during sleep and is the most common cause of death in infants 1 month to 1 year. Cause is still unknown.

supine: Lying on back.

symmetrical: Similarity in form between two sides of the body.

syndactyly: A congenital anomaly in which there is partial or complete webbing or fusion of fingers or toes.

systematic fading: The gradual removal of any support that assists a child's learning.

systemic: Refers to a disease that can exist throughout the body, e.g., arthritis.

tactile: Refers to the sense of touch.

tactile defensiveness: An abnormal sensitivity to touch, indicated by infant's avoidance or rejection of touching and handling.

target behavior: The terminal objective or final desired behavior that is the goal of shaping when using behavioral (performance) objectives. This same term, when used in relation to behavior modification, refers to the negative behavior to be changed.

task analysis: Breaking down a difficult task into small steps that lead to doing the difficult task. En-route behaviors are behavioral objectives that state the individual subskills leading toward the terminal objective or the difficult task.

terminal objective: The behavioral objective that a particular teacher has chosen as the highest level of skill he or she intends to strive toward to help a child or children achieve.

tone: Firmness of muscles.

tonic neck reflex: Uncontrollable movement in which turning of the head causes one arm to straighten and stiffen and the other to bend.

tongue thrust: The strong involuntary (reflexive) protrusion of the tongue. It may be seen in some forms of cerebral palsy.

total communication: A philosophy involved in teaching individuals with hearing impairments that includes using aural, manual, and oral methods to ensure effective communication.

tracking: Following an object with one's eyes.

transdisciplinary approach: The use of a team approach to services in which team members work across disciplinary boundaries to plan and provide integrated services.

transition: The purposeful, organized process of helping children who are at risk or have developmental disabilities move from one program to the next, such as from an infant development program to an inclusive preschool program.

trauma: The condition, physical or mental, that results from shock or a violently produced wound or injury.

tremor: Involuntary vibration in large muscles.

utterance: Something that is said or produced orally. It is not necessary that an utterance be spoken correctly to be counted in the child's mean length of utterance (MLU).

validity: The extent to which an instrument measures what it is supposed to measure or what the test giver needs it to measure.

verbal expression: The ability to express one's ideas verbally.

vestibular stimulation: An activity that stimulates the vestibular apparatus (the structures contained in the inner ear that provide the sense of balance) and helps the child to develop awareness of body position in space, as well as balance reactions.

visual association: The process of relating concepts that have been presented visually.

visual discrimination: The ability to differentiate between and among various shapes, sizes, colors, numbers, and/or letters.

visualization: Imagery; the ability to retrieve a mental image or to produce a mental image.

voluntary muscles: The muscles in the body over which there is conscious control of contraction.

women, infants, and children program (WIC): A federally funded program that provides pregnant women, new mothers, infants, and young children with food vouchers, nutrition counseling, and referrals to health care.

"w" sitting position: Sitting on the buttocks between the heels of the feet (the knees are bent, forming a "W").

zero project: The principle that no child should be refused a free, appropriate education if other children the same age are being served.

Many definitions came from: Coleman, J. G. (1999). *The early intervention dictionary.* Rockville, MD: Woodbine House.

Name Index

Subject Index

About the Authors

Ruth E. Cook is a professor of special education and director of the early intervention specialist personnel preparation program at Santa Clara University, California. Dr. Cook received her Ph.D. with an emphasis in developmental psychology and two related M.A. degrees from the University of California at Los Angeles. Her interest in inclusion of young children with special needs focused while serving as director of the Early Childhood Center at Southern Illinois University at Edwardsville and the Child Development Center at Mount Saint Mary's College in Los Angeles. Currently, she consults widely in the areas of family-professional relationships and strategies for effective inclusion.

Annette Tessier is a professor emeritus of special education and former director of Centro de Niñnos y Padres, a model early intervention program on the campus of California State University, Los Angeles. Dr. Tessier received her graduate degrees from the University of California at Los Angeles and has a background in physical therapy and early childhood education.

M. Diane Klein is currently a professor and Chair of the Division of special education at California State University, Los Angeles, and coordinator of training programs in early childhood special education. Dr. Klein received her M.A. in speech-language pathology and audiology from Western Michigan University and her Ph.D. in developmental psychology from Michigan State University. She has worked with young children who have severe disabilities as well as high-risk infants and their families. She has directed projects involving caregiver-child interaction, working with infants with severe and multiple disabilities, and training of inclusion support personnel.